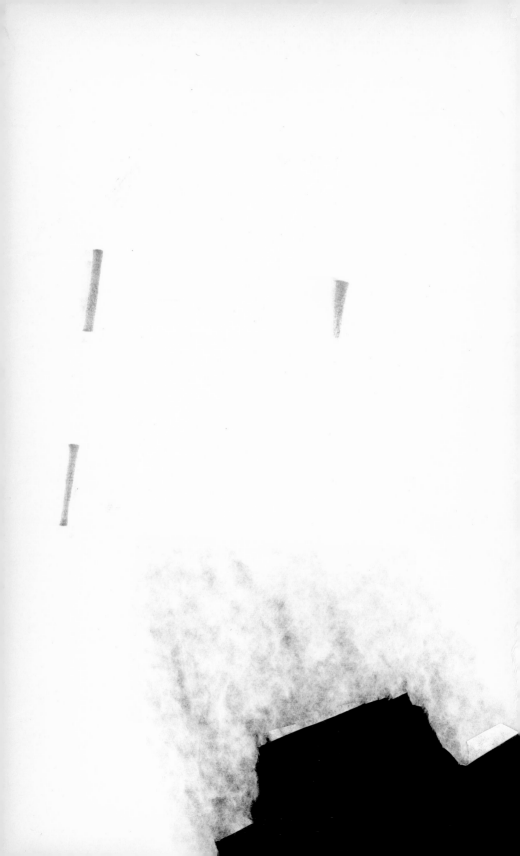

Physics of III-V Compounds

WILEY SERIES ON THE SCIENCE AND TECHNOLOGY OF MATERIALS
Advisory Editors: J. H. Hollomon, J. E. Burke, B. Chalmers, R. L. Sproull, A. V. Tobolsky

Physics of III-V Compounds
Otfried Madelung (translation by D. Meyerhofer)

Physics of Magnetism
Sōshin Chikazumi

Principles of Solidification
Bruce Chalmers

Applied Superconductivity
Vernon L. Newhouse

The Mechanical Properties of Matter
A. H. Cottrell

The Art and Science of Growing Crystals
J. J. Gilman, editor

Columbium and Tantalum
Frank T. Sisco and Edward Epremian, editors

Mechanical Properties of Metals
D. McLean

The Metallurgy of Welding
D. Séférian—Translated by E. Bishop

Thermodynamics of Solids
Richard A. Swalin

Transmission Electron Microscopy of Metals
Gareth Thomas

Plasticity and Creep of Metals
J. D. Lubahn and R. P. Felgar

Introduction to Ceramics
W. D. Kingery

Properties and Structure of Polymers
Arthur V. Tobolsky

Magnesium and Its Alloys
C. Sheldon Roberts

Physical Metallurgy
Bruce Chalmers

Ferrites
J. Smit and H. P. J. Wijn

Zone Melting
William G. Pfann

The Metallurgy of Vanadium
William Rostoker

Introduction to Solid State Physics, Second Edition
Charles Kittel

Physics of III-V Compounds

by Prof. Dr. Otfried Madelung

INSTITUTE FOR THEORETICAL PHYSICS

UNIVERSITY OF MARBURG/LAHN, GERMANY

translated by Dr. Dietrich Meyerhofer

RCA LABORATORIES

John Wiley & Sons, Inc., New York · London · Sydney

Library of Congress Catalog Card Number: 64-23849
Printed in the United States of America

Preface

Twelve years ago H. Welker's first paper on the semiconducting properties of the III-V compounds appeared. At that time it could not be predicted what a fruitful field of semiconductor physics would be opened up by that paper. Welker's experimental results, combined with his theoretical predictions, did suggest that the III-V compounds are semiconductors with properties similar to those of germanium and silicon. But it was impossible to imagine that InSb would have an electron mobility an order of magnitude higher than the largest previously known value. It would have been equally difficult to predict the almost universal self-adjusting stoichiometry of the III-V compounds, the isotropy of the conduction band of InSb, or other typical properties of this group of semiconducting compounds.

It was precisely these latter properties, and the possibility of their technical application, that caused interest in the III-V compounds to grow rapidly. A decade of intensive research followed, at the end of which the quantitative model of the physical properties of the III-V compounds had been developed to such an extent that it was complete in its main features. Since then the major emphasis of the investigations has shifted to the technology and the applications of these semiconductors. This development is reflected in the number of papers on the physics of the III-V compounds published per year (N), which can quite accurately be represented as follows:

$$\begin{aligned} N &= 125[e^{0.1(t-1952)} - 1] \quad & t \leqslant 1961 \\ &= \text{const.} & t \geqslant 1961 \end{aligned}$$

A large number of summarizing reviews of the III-V compounds have appeared, from the first report of H. Weiss and H. Welker in Vol. 3 of *Solid State Physics* to the book by C. Hilsum and A. C. Rose-Innes. All these reports appeared during the time of the rapid growth in knowledge about the III-V compounds. Now that the subject has matured it seems justified to present a book on the physical properties of the III-V compounds only, without including the technology or the applications of these semiconductors. For one thing, continued rapid advances in technology and applications may be expected in the years to come, which would cause such material to become outdated rapidly. For another, the huge flow of publications would seem to make it impossible to combine all possible aspects of a group of semiconductors in one monograph. Also, an excellent volume on the technology of the III-V compounds (R.K. Willardson and H. L. Goering, *Preparation of III-V Compounds*, Reinhold Publishing Corp., 1962) already exists, and a book on applications is in preparation.

The present book is intended not as an introduction into semiconductor physics, but rather as a monograph on a particularly interesting group of semiconductors. Consequently, the reader is expected to be acquainted with the foundations of semiconductor theory and to be familiar with the most important properties of the elemental semiconductors germanium and silicon. In the text, the theoretical foundations required for understanding the experimental data, as well as the necessary facts for comparison with other semiconductors, are always clearly presented, but no literature references are attached to them. Doing so would have increased the number of references unduly without adding significantly to the value of the text. In any case, the reader can find the necessary background in the cited papers on the III-V compounds.

I have attempted to quote the literature on the physics of III-V compounds as completely as possible. However, it was neither feasible nor desirable to reproduce in the text the contents of the more than 1000 papers. In choosing the ones to be discussed more thoroughly, I was not able to acknowledge all equivalent studies equally. The reader will therefore frequently encounter references to "further literature" on a given subject, which does not mean that these works are necessarily of lesser interest. Similarly, when the value of a certain parameter is given, it does not mean that that value is the only measured one or that the author cited is the only one to have measured this parameter. The selection from among a flood of equally valuable papers always introduces a subjective factor into a monograph, and no author of such a monograph can evaluate with complete justice in these circumstances.

I wish to express my deepest appreciation to H. Welker. For almost a decade I was able to participate in the research on III-V compounds taking place in his laboratory.

Many colleagues helped in the preparation of this book by making unpublished work available to me. I wish to thank them at this time. I should also like to acknowledge the help of my co-workers who read the manuscript and pointed out inaccuracies and parts that needed clarification. The major credit for the book's appearing in its present form is D. Meyerhofer's. He has not only translated the German manuscript into English in exemplary fashion, but also made many suggestions for improving the arrangement of the text. I owe him a large measure of gratitude. The editor, Professor R. Sproull, and the technical staff of John Wiley & Sons have supported me in every respect and have deferred to all my wishes.

OTFRIED MADELUNG

Marburg/Lahn, Germany
July, 1964

Contents

List of Symbols

Only those symbols that are used throughout the book are included in this list. Other, less frequently used symbols are defined as they appear.

$\mathbf{B}$	magnetic induction
b	mobility ratio
c	speed of light
D	diffusion coefficient
E	energy
E_c	lower edge of the conduction band
E_{F}	Fermi level
E_G	width of the forbidden gap
$E_{L,X}$	energy difference between the conduction and the valence band at points L and X of the Brillouin zone
E_v	upper edge of the valence band
$\Delta E_{\Gamma\Delta}$, $\Delta E_{\Gamma\Lambda}$, ΔE_{12}	energy differences between subbands of the conduction band
ΔE_D, ΔE_A	ionization energies of the donors and acceptors
$\boldsymbol{\mathcal{E}}$	electric field
e	electronic charge (absolute value)
e^*	effective ion charge
I	current
i	current density
K	absorption constant
k	Boltzmann constant, absorption coefficient
$\mathbf{k}$	wave vector
L	diffusion length
m	electron mass
m^*	effective mass (general)
m_c	effective mass determined by cyclotron resonance
m_n, m_p, m_{p1}, . . .	effective masses of the electrons, of the holes, of the holes in the V_1 valence band, . . .
m_{opt}	effective mass determined by optical experiments
n	electron concentration

n_A, n_D	acceptor and donor concentration, respectively
n_i	intrinsic carrier concentration
n_r	index of refraction
p	hole concentration
Q	Nernst coefficient
R	reflection coefficient
$R(B)$, $R(0)$	resistance in a magnetic field and without field
R_{H}	Hall coefficient
r	exponent of the energy dependence of the relaxation time
T	transmission coefficient
$V_{1,2,3}$	subbands of the valence band
$\mathbf{w}$	thermal current density
z	thermoelectric figure of merit
Δ	spin-orbit splitting of valence band at point Γ
Δ_L	spin-orbit splitting of valence band at point L
ϵ_0	permittivity of free space
κ	dielectric constant
κ'	thermal conductivity
μ	mobility
μ_{H}	Hall mobility
μ_{B}	Bohr magneton
Π	Peltier coefficient
ρ	resistivity
σ	conductivity
τ	lifetime of electron-hole pairs
τ_0	collision time, relaxation time
ω	frequency
ω_c	cyclotron resonance frequency
ω_p	plasma frequency
ω_0	scattering frequency ($= 1/\tau_0$)
ω_t, ω_l	frequencies of transverse and longitudinal optical phonons

Physics of III-V Compounds

1

Introduction

1.0 Historical Note

Semiconductor physics in the period between 1940 and 1950 was characterized by a strong emphasis on the semiconducting elements germanium and silicon. The technology of germanium, especially, was solved early, and this material became the prime substance for a systematic investigation of the semiconductor mechanism. It was possible to derive a self-consistent model of the semiconductor properties of germanium, which had not proved feasible in the case of the earlier known semiconductors. This model could be extended to silicon. The climax of this development was the invention of the transistor.

In contrast, the study of semiconducting compounds was neglected for a long time. The compounds then known were technologically much more difficult to prepare, and their physical properties could not be studied in a similarly systematic fashion. The theoretical model that had been developed for the covalently bonded elements germanium and silicon could generally not be extended to the more ionic compounds.

Some of the semiconducting compounds were known to crystallize in the zinc-blende and wurtzite structures and consequently to have a binding mechanism similar to that of germanium and silicon. Examples are binary compounds between elements of groups II and VI of the periodic table, such as ZnS and CdSe, and of groups I and VII, such as CuBr and AgI. In contrast, compounds between elements of groups III and V were generally neglected. It was known that most of them crystallize in the zinc-blende structure (25F1), (26G1), (41I1). Only rough estimates had been made about their physical properties; for example, AlN was found to be an "insulator" rather than a "metal" (25F1). Quantitative results existed only about the magnetic susceptibility of the system aluminum-antimony (13H1) and about the melting properties of InSb (51B1), (51G1).

It was Welker who demonstrated, in 1952, that the III-V compounds have particularly interesting properties, that they are all semiconductors, and that they have a close relationship to the semiconducting elements of the fourth column of the periodic table (52W1), (53W2). In addition he was able to predict the important new characteristics of these semiconductors and to prove them experimentally. Thus, the connection was formed between germanium and silicon, on one hand, and the II-VI and I-VII compounds, on the other hand.

Most of these semiconductors form lattices which are dominated by the coordination number 4; that is, every atom is surrounded by four nearest neighbors. Before we can consider the properties of such semiconductors we must first discuss their crystal structure more thoroughly.

11 Crystal Structure of the Tetrahedral Phases

Elements and binary compounds, which average four valence electrons per atom, preferentially form a tetrahedral phase. Each atom

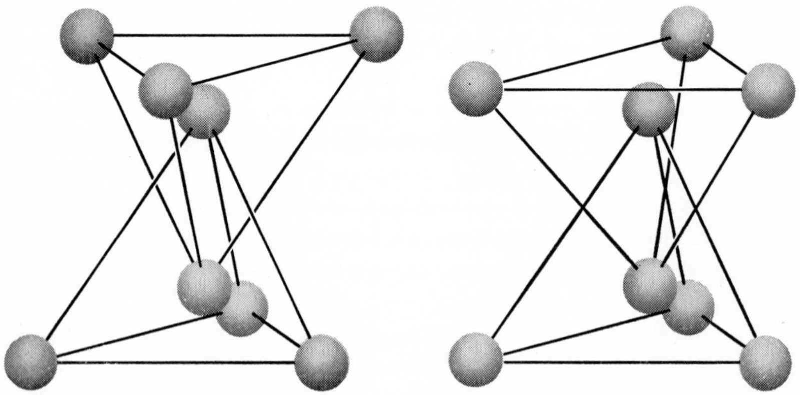

(a) (b)

Fig. 1.1 Two possible relative orientations of nearest-neighbor tetrahedrons surrounding one of the atoms in the tetrahedral phase: (a) base triangles are rotated 60° with respect to each other; (b) all base triangles are oriented parallel to each other.

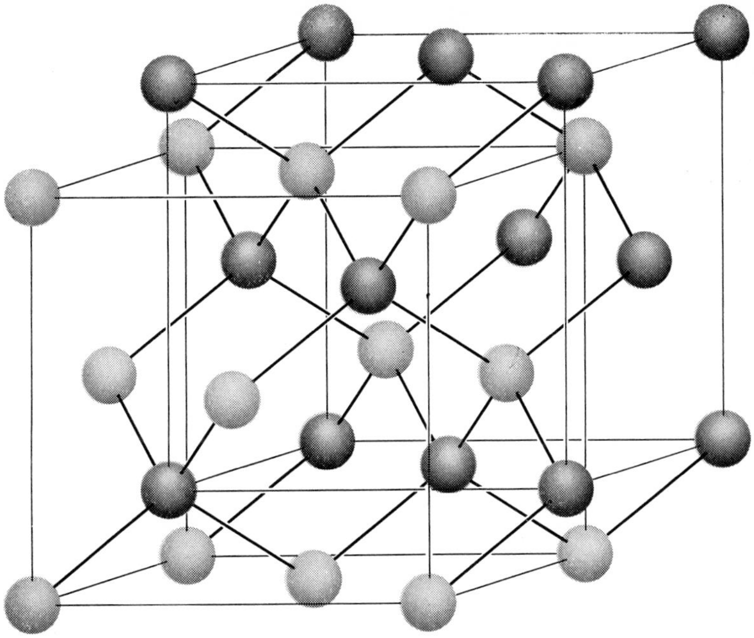

Fig. 1.2 Zinc-blende lattice. The elementary cubes of the two interpenetrating face-centered cubic lattices are shown.

is then surrounded by four nearest neighbors which lie with equal distance at the corners of a tetrahedron. The bond between two nearest neighbors is formed by two electrons with opposite spins (see Section 20).

The most important lattices with a tetrahedral arrangement are the *diamond* lattice, the *zinc-blende* lattice, and the *wurtzite* lattice.

The *diamond* lattice is constructed as follows. Each atom lies in the center of a tetrahedron formed by the four nearest neighbors. Two neighboring tetrahedrons are oriented in such a way that the base triangles are rotated by 60° from one another (Fig. 1.1a).

The *zinc-blende* structure is formed in the same way except that the two nearest-neighbor points are occupied by different elements. The diamond lattice is consequently restricted to elements, the zinc-blende structure, to binary compounds. Ternary compounds can also form tetrahedral phases; we will discuss them separately in Chapter 6.

The structure shown in Fig. 1.1a is not the only one possible. One of the four nearest-neighbor tetrahedrons can be oriented in such a way that the two bases lie exactly over each other (Fig. 1.1b); this results, for binary compounds, in the *wurtzite* structure. Elements are not arranged in such a fashion.

The three tetrahedral lattices can also be understood in a different way. The *diamond* and *zinc-blende* lattices can be described as two intertwined face-centered cubic lattices. This is demonstrated in Fig. 1.2; in the diamond lattice all atoms are identical, whereas in the zinc-blende structure the two sublattices contain different atoms. The two sublattices are oriented parallel to each other and are displaced from one another by the vector $\boldsymbol{\tau} = (a/4, a/4, a/4)$, where a is the edge-length of the elementary cube of the face-centered lattice. The length of the vector $\boldsymbol{\tau}$ is $\sqrt{3}\, a/4 \approx 0.433a$; τ is also the distance

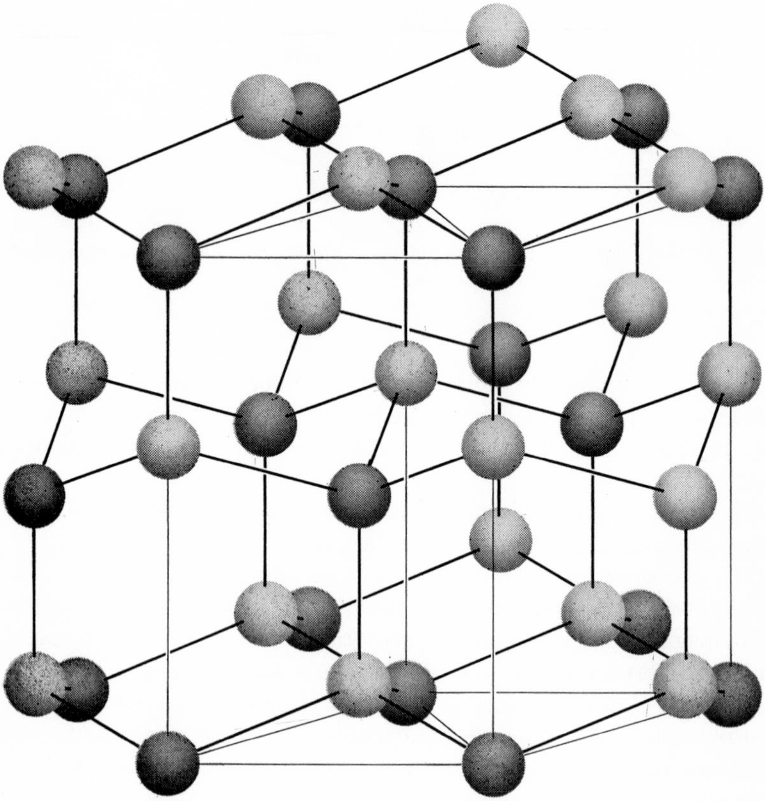

Fig. 1.3 Wurtzite lattice. The "black" atoms form a close-packed cubic lattice; the "white" atoms another one, displaced from the "black" one along the vertical axis. The unit cell of the hexagonal lattice is also shown.

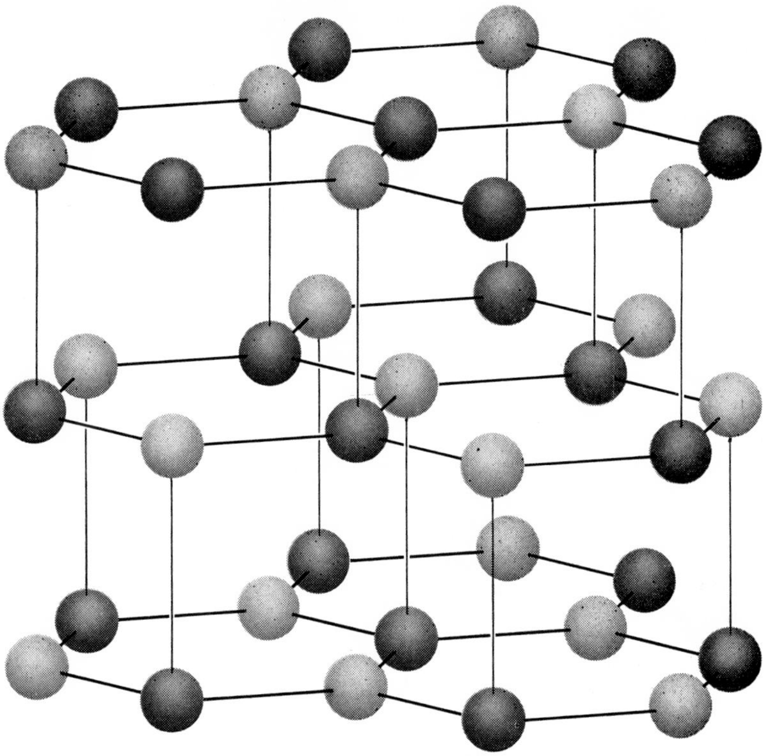

Fig. 1.4 Lattice of BN.

between nearest-neighbor atoms. These lattices are not Bravais lattices, as the unit cell contains two atoms.

The *wurtzite* lattice is not cubic but can be considered as two interpenetrating, close-packed hexagonal lattices. This is shown in Fig. 1.3.

In the class of solids under consideration, namely, the elements of the fourth column and the III-V, II-VI, and I-VII compounds, there are also found a few lattices which can be considered as distorted forms of the ones described, and others which have no relation to the tetrahedral phases. The *boron nitride* lattice is formed by distorting the wurtzite lattice in such a fashion that three of the four nearest neighbors lie in the same plane with the atom, while the fourth neighbor is oriented at right angles to this plane (Fig. 1.4). This creates a layer structure with the layers consisting of rings of six atoms and with identical orientation of the layers above each other. *Graphite* crystallizes in a

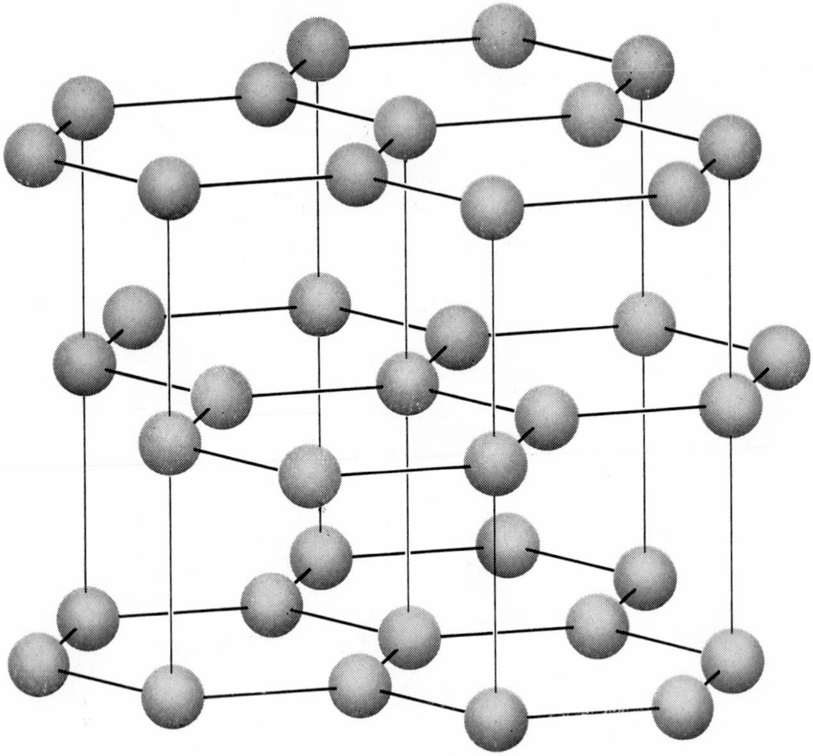

Fig. 1.5 Graphite lattice.

similar lattice, with a different orientation of the layers with respect to each other (Fig. 1.5).

Other lattices which are similar to the tetrahedral phases are those of *white tin* and *indium bismuth.* The white tin lattice still has four nearest neighbors for each atom, and its unit cell is body-centered tetragonal (Fig. 1.6). It is a distortion of the zinc-blende lattice by a contraction in the vertical direction of Fig. 1.6. While each indium atom in InBi (Fig. 1.7) is surrounded tetrahedrally by four bismuth atoms, the nearest neighbors of each bismuth atom are four indium atoms, forming a square below it. The lattice separates into layers.

The remaining lattices found in this group have no similarities with the ones described so far. They are the face-centered cubic lattice of lead and the NaCl and CsCl structures, which are to be considered as interpenetrating cubic lattices with coordination numbers 6 and 8, respectively.

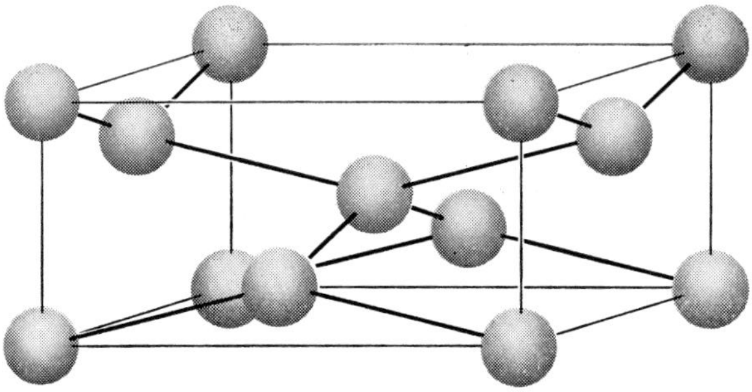

Fig. 1.6 Unit cell of the white tin lattice.

The diamond structure dominates in the *elements of group IV* of the periodic table. Carbon crystallizes in two modifications, diamond and graphite; silicon and germanium occur only in the diamond structure; while tin again has two modifications, gray tin (α-tin) with diamond

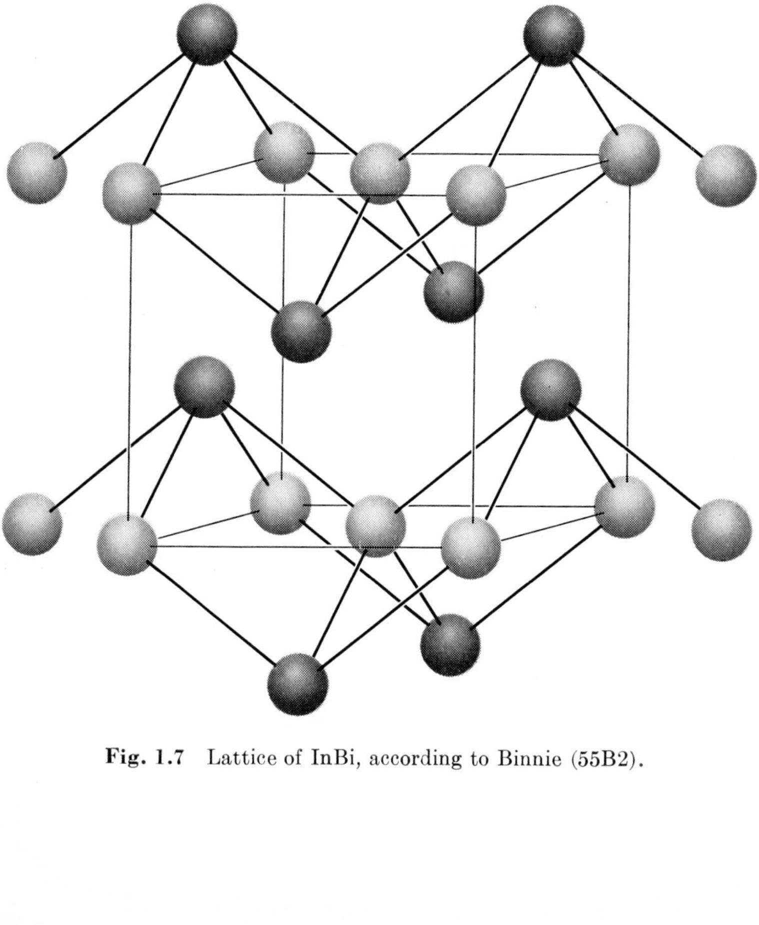

Fig. 1.7 Lattice of InBi, according to Binnie (55B2).

structure (stable only below room temperature) and white tin (β-tin). All elements of this group are semiconductors with the exception of white tin and the face-centered cubic lead. Carbon and silicon form a compound, silicon carbide, with zinc-blende structure.

Among the *III-V compounds* we consider only compounds between the elements of groups IIIb (B, Al, Ga, In, Tl) and Vb (N, P, As, Sb, Bi). Only very few compounds of the types IIIa-Va, IIIa-Vb, and IIIb-Va exist, and these are found to have NaCl structure. So far they have been studied only superficially. Twelve of the remaining 25 compounds have zinc-blende structure, namely, the phosphides, arsenides, and antimonides of boron, aluminum, gallium, and indium. Boron nitride has two modifications; the BN lattice predominates, but it can be prepared with zinc-blende structure (Borazon). The nitrides of aluminum, gallium, and indium have the wurtzite lattice. Among the remaining compounds only InBi, TlSb, and TlBi are known; the InBi lattice has been discussed above, and the two thallium compounds have CsCl structure. All three compounds are metallic.

As the difference between the column numbers of the two elements increases, the NaCl and CsCl structures become more and more dominating. Among the *II-VI compounds* the oxides of beryllium and zinc, and the sulphides, selenides, and tellurides of beryllium, zinc, cadmium, and mercury, as well as MgTe, have zinc-blende or wurtzite structure, but among the *I-VII compounds* only the four copper compounds, CuF, CuCl, CuBr, CuI, and AgI (56W4) have these structures.

No structure corresponding to β-tin has been found in these compounds under normal conditions. The III-V compounds which crystallize in the zinc-blende structure do, however, make a transition to a metallic state under very high pressures (60G6), (61J1), (62M9), (62S9), (63J2). Even though the possibility exists that this transition is to a liquid state, there are many indications that it is a phase change. The transition pressures increase from 23 kbar for InSb to more than 550 kbar for GaP (62M9), (62M10). In the case of InSb, Smith and Martin (62S9) and Banus *et al.* (63B2), (64H4) believe that the high-pressure phase does have a structure corresponding to β-tin, whereas Rooymans (63R3) finds indications for a lattice with NaCl structure.

We will now look at the symmetry properties of the two most important lattices, that of diamond and that of zinc-blende, in more detail.

A crystal lattice is invariant under a number of symmetry operations. These symmetry operations are primitive translations, rotations, reflections, and inversions, both alone and combined with nonprimitive translations (screw-axis and glide-plane operations). All these operations form the *space group* of the crystal. The primitive translations alone form an invariant subgroup of the space group. They are given by

$$\mathbf{x}' = \mathbf{x} + \mathbf{R}_q; \qquad \mathbf{R}_q = q_1\mathbf{t}_1 + q_2\mathbf{t}_2 + q_3\mathbf{t}_3 \tag{1.1}$$

where q_i are integers, and the $\mathbf{t}_i$ are basis vectors. In the case of the diamond and the zinc-blende structure the latter go from one of the corners of the cube shown in Fig. 1.2 to the centers of the three adjacent faces. All primitive translations $\mathbf{R}_q$, given in (1.1), define a *point lattice* which, for the diamond and the zinc-blende structure, is the face-centered cubic lattice.

All rotations and reflections, whether combined in the space group with nonprimitive translations or not, form the *point group* of the crystal. The point group of the zinc-blende structure does not contain all the symmetry elements of the point group of the face-centered cubic lattice. The latter point group (designated as cubic group O_h or $m3m$) contains all the operations which leave a cube invariant, namely, besides the identity element E, three rotations by 180° about the cubic axes (C_4^2), six rotations by $\pm 90°$ about the same axes (C_4), six more rotations by 180° about the six face diagonals of the cube (C_2), eight rotations by 120° about the four body diagonals (C_3), as well as the inversion (I) and all the rotations combined with the inversion ($IC_4^2 \cdot \cdot \cdot IC_3$). Only half of these 48 elements of the cubic group O_h are contained in the point group of the zinc-blende structure. An inspection of Fig. 1.2 shows that both the indicated cubes contain four atoms of the other element which are arranged tetrahedrally to one another. Consequently, the only applicable symmetry elements of O_h are those which leave a tetrahedron invariant. They are the 24 elements $E, C_4^2(3), C_3(8), IC_2(6)$, and $IC_4(6)$ (tetrahedral group T_d or $\bar{4}3m$). T_d does not contain an inversion center; that is, no two elements can be brought into coincidence by an inversion of the coordinates.

There are no nonprimitive translations connected with the rotations and reflection-rotations in the space group of the *zinc-blende* lattice (T_d^2 or $F\bar{4}3m$). Consequently the space group is a direct product of the point group T_d and the translation group given by (1.1). Every symmetry operation of the zinc-blende lattice can be described by

$$\mathbf{x}' = R_{T_d}\mathbf{x} + \mathbf{R}_q \tag{1.2}$$

where R_{T_d} is a point group operator.

The *diamond* lattice differs from the zinc-blende lattice in that all the atoms are identical. The point lattice given by the primitive translation (1.1) is therefore the same as that of the zinc-blende structure. The point group contains all the symmetry operations which leave a cube invariant, i.e., it is O_h. In the space group (O_h^7 or $Fd3m$) the operations IC_4^2, IC_3, C_2, and C_4, which are the ones not contained in T_d, are, however, combined with the nonprimitive translation $\boldsymbol{\tau} = (a/4, a/4, a/4)$. The symmetry operations of the diamond lattice are consequently given by (1.2) plus the additional operations

$$\mathbf{x}' = R_{O_h \neq T_d}\mathbf{x} + \boldsymbol{\tau} + \mathbf{R}_q \tag{1.3}$$

where $R_{O_h \neq T_d}$ is one of the additional symmetry operations.

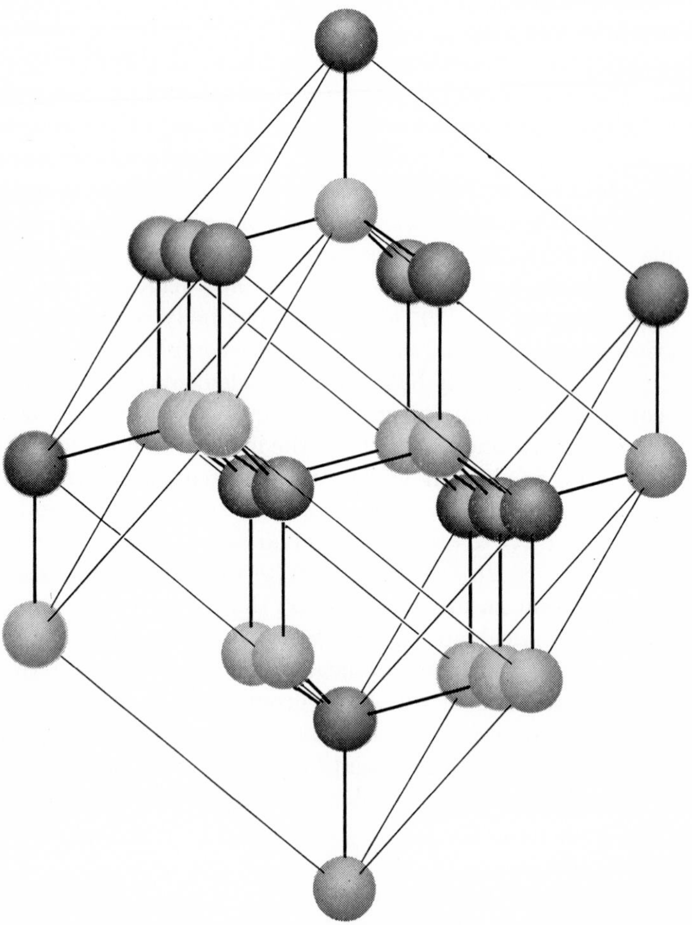

Fig. 1.8 Zinc-blende lattice, observed perpendicular to a [111]-axis, and along a [110]-axis (cf. Fig. 1.2).

Table 1.1 Lattice Constants of the III-V Compounds with Zinc-Blende Structure (values in parentheses are calculated from the covalent radii)

Compound	Lattice Constant (Å)	Reference
BN (Borazon)	3.615	(57W3)
BP	4.538	(58G3)
BAs	4.777	"
BSb	(5.17)	
AlP	(5.45)	
AlAs	(5.61)	
AlSb	6.1356	(58G3)
GaP	5.4506	"
GaAs	5.6535	"
GaSb	6.0955	"
InP	5.8688	"
InAs	6.0585	"
InSb	6.4789	"

The symmetry operations of the *wurtzite* lattice will not be considered in detail. The point group (C_{6v} or $6mm$) contains twelve elements, the identity, five rotations about the sixfold c-axis, and six reflections at the symmetry planes containing the c-axis. The space group (C_{6v}^4 or $P6_3mc$) is identical with that of hexagonal close-packing except that it lacks a mirror plane perpendicular to the c-axis.

The *zinc-blende* lattice of Fig. 1.2 is redrawn from a different viewpoint in Fig. 1.8. In the former case the direction of observation is along the [100]-axis; in the latter it is along the [110]-axis, i.e., the face diagonal of the basic cube. The [111]-axis (body diagonal) is at right angles to the observation. It is apparent from Fig. 1.8 that identical hexagonal rings are stacked upon each other in the [110]-direction. In the [111]-direction, planes containing only one kind of atoms follow each other, the spacing between two successive planes alternating between two different values. If we call the layers A and B, the succession of the layers in the [111]-direction can be described by A-B—A-B—A-B—, whereas in the $[\bar{1}\bar{1}\bar{1}]$-direction it is B-A—B-A—B-A—. The two directions can consequently be distinguished from one another, which means that the [111]-axis is a *polar axis* in the zinc-blende structure. This is a consequence of the absence of the inversion center. The special properties of the III-V compounds which are due to the presence of the polar axis will be considered in more detail later.

The measured lattice constants of the III-V compounds with zincblende structure are tabulated in Table 1.1. As mentioned earlier, the nearest-neighbor distance is calculated by multiplying the lattice constant by $\sqrt{3}/4 \approx 0.433$.

12 Characterization of the Important III-V Compounds

Only some of the III-V compounds listed in Section 11 will be considered in detail. The boron compounds, BN, BP, BAs, and BSb, are technologically very difficult to handle. Boron nitride is the best-known one of the group, but only very small crystals of the cubic modifications have been produced. Boron phosphide is unstable above 1250°C, and BAs transforms to an orthorhombic structure above 920°C (58P2). Hardly anything is known about BSb.

The aluminum compounds also have properties which make them difficult to work with. They are all unstable in air. Only AlSb has been studied in some detail and has created interest of technical applications because of its peculiar properties.

Among the gallium and indium compounds the physical properties of the nitrides are not yet well known. There is also some thermal instability, in the case of GaN above 600°C (62L6). Indium bismuth is metallic (54B7).

The remaining compounds, GaP, GaAs, GaSb, InP, InAs, and InSb, together with AlSb, are of great physical and technical importance. Although the technology of some of these semiconductors is more difficult than that of the semiconducting elements of group IV, there is no inherent reason why they cannot be purified and prepared in single-crystal form. Technological questions are not included in this book, but there will be occasion in Chapter 5 to list the most important methods of preparation.

The device applications of the III-V compounds will be considered only when the physical properties lead to new uses. For further information we refer to the many summarizing articles.

The III-V compounds form a link between the semiconducting elements of the fourth column of the periodic table and the II-VI and I-VII compounds (with tetrahedral structure). Consequently, it is possible to deduce the main properties of the III-V compounds from those of the neighboring substances.

The *width of the forbidden gap* E_G is one of the most important semiconductor parameters. It is known from semiconducting diamond, silicon, germanium, and α-tin that E_G decreases with increasing atomic weight. The forbidden gap in diamond is 5.3 eV, in Si 1.12 eV, in Ge 0.72 eV, and in α-Sn 0.08 eV. This means that these compounds range from the almost pure insulator of defect-free diamond to the metallic conductor of strongly doped gray tin. The width of the energy gap is considerably larger in the II-VI compounds and increases further in the I-VII compounds. The II-VI compounds also show E_G decreasing with increasing atomic weight. In the sequence ZnS, ZnSe, and ZnTe, E_G decreases from 3.5 to 2.8 to 0.85 eV.

Among the III-V compounds we can therefore expect the lightest compound, BN, to have the largest forbidden gap (>5.3 eV), and the heaviest compound, InSb, to have the smallest one (>0.08 eV). As we shall see later, the measured values are approximately 10 eV for BN and 0.25 eV for InSb. The E_G values of the other III-V compounds will lie in between. Their order can be estimated if we consider the III-V compounds as "derivatives" of the fourth-column elements, as was done by Welker (52W1). This means that we consider a III-V compound to be formed out of the corresponding "isoelectronic" element by replacing one half of the tetra-valent atoms by tri-valent atoms, the other half by penta-valent ones. In this picture BN is derived from diamond, while BP and AlN are derived from SiC. Boron arsenide, AlP, and GaN correspond to silicon; InN, GaP, and BSb to a mixed crystal of $Ge_{0.5}Si_{0.5}$; AlSb, GaAs, and InP to germanium; InAs and GaSb to a hypothetical GeSn compound; and finally InSb to α-Sn.

This concept of deriving the compounds from the elements is partially justified by the fact that the corresponding compounds and elements have almost identical lattice constants. This can be seen by comparing the lattice constants of Table 1.1 with the values for diamond (3.56 Å), Si (5.40 Å), Ge (5.65 Å), and α-Sn (6.48 Å). Even the corresponding II-VI and I-VII compounds have only slightly larger lattice constants. In particular the lattice constants within the isoelectronic row, germanium, GaAs, ZnSe, CuBr, vary by less than 1%.

The *mobility* of electrons and holes is another important property of semiconductors. It is determined by two factors, the effective mass of the charge carriers and their interaction with the lattice. The influence of these factors is very difficult to estimate. Welker has pointed out that the lattice of the III-V compounds is more tightly bound because of a small amount of ionic character in the binding. This could result in a weaker interaction between charge carriers and the lattice and in a larger mobility in the III-V compounds as compared to the elements. Still larger increasing ionicity could be predicted to lead to decreasing mobility, as the values for purely ionic crystals are generally very small. We will see later that the mobility does indeed go through a maximum in the III-V compounds, but that this is primarily due to the small values of the effective electron mass.

Among the elements the electron mobility increases from diamond to silicon to germanium, but decreases somewhat for gray tin. Consequently, the electron mobility can be predicted roughly to increase with increasing atomic weight. This has also been found in the II-VI compounds. Among the III-V compounds the largest value will be expected in the case of InSb, the smallest one for BN.

The nature of the dominant *lattice defects* differs considerably between the group IV elements and the II-VI compounds. Generally, departures from stoichiometry are expected in semiconducting compounds. The excess of one of the two components forms lattice defects which influence the conduction properties. Such nonstoichiometric behavior does not exist in the case of the elements. This is one of the reasons why germanium has formed such an ideal model for the study of semiconduction. In addition, the foreign atoms are generally built into germanium substitutionally and are therefore tightly bound. Consequently the physical properties of germanium do not change irreversibly during measurements over a wide temperature range, in contrast to many of the semiconducting compounds.

It has been found unexpectedly that the III-V compounds show almost no deviations from stoichiometry. Even when a melt contains a large excess of one of the components, the solidified compound will be completely stoichiometric. The most important impurities are also built into the lattice substitutionally, and the III-V compounds consequently combine the advantages of the semiconductors germanium and silicon with a much broader variety of interesting semiconductor properties. This is the reason for their particular physical and technical importance.

Actually only those III-V compounds whose forbidden gap is not too large can be considered as "similar to germanium." Otherwise their properties resemble those of insulators and photoconductors. Properties similar to those of germanium are also found in some of the II-VI compounds: the ones with large atomic weights, according to our previous discussion. Indeed, HgSe and HgTe have properties which are closely related to those of germanium, silicon, GaAs, InSb, and similar semiconductors. It would therefore be meaningful to consider all these semiconductors together. Despite the unity of this group with respect to some of the important properties, there are other properties which call for other groupings, and this book is therefore restricted, somewhat arbitrarily, to the III-V compounds.

In this section we have not yet considered some of the fundamental questions, namely, the connections between crystal structure, chemical binding, and the band model of the III-V compounds. These topics will be discussed in Chapter 2, as far as it is possible to do so without reference to the experimental results. It will be shown that important deductions about the chemical binding and the band structure can be made from the crystal structure of the III-V compounds. Knowledge of the physical properties of germanium and silicon will help us to lay a theoretical foundation for the collection and interpretation of the experimental measurements on III-V compounds, which will be presented in later chapters.

2

Theoretical Foundations

20 Chemical Binding in the Tetrahedral Phases

In the diamond, zinc-blende, and wurtzite lattices every atom is surrounded by four nearest neighbors. The elements which crystallize in the *diamond* lattice belong to the fourth column of the periodic table and consequently have four valence electrons. The chemical binding between nearest-neighbor atoms can be visualized as "electron bridges," each formed by two valence electrons with opposite spins (paired electrons). This *homopolar* bonding is well known from the hydrogen molecule. It is described quantum mechanically by sp^3-hybrid wave functions. These are the four independent linear combinations of the wave functions of the free tetravalent atom (s,p_xp_y,p_z), namely

$$\tfrac{1}{2}(s + p_x + p_y + p_z)$$
$$\tfrac{1}{2}(s + p_x - p_y - p_z)$$
$$\tfrac{1}{2}(s - p_x + p_y - p_z)$$

and

$$\tfrac{1}{2}(s - p_x - p_y + p_z)$$

so all the valence electrons are identical as far as binding is concerned. The four wave functions are each almost completely concentrated in one direction, and point to the four corners of a tetrahedron surrounding the atom.

The same arrangement of nearest neighbors is found in the *zinc-blende* and *wurtzite* lattices, but the neighbors have unequal numbers of valence electrons. In the III-V, II-VI, and I-VII compounds with these structures the sum of valence electrons of two nearest neighbors is always eight. Each atom, *on the average*, still has four valence electrons available for formation of the bonds. Consequently homopolar bonding may also take place in this case, even though it is not expected to be completely identical with the binding of the diamond lattice because of the unequal charges on the atomic cores. For example, the atomic cores of germanium are Ge^{4+} ions, while in GaAs they are Ga^{3+} and As^{5+} ions.

There are other possible binding mechanisms for the same lattices. Instead of binding by paired-spin electrons there may be a *heteropolar* bonding. In this case one component loses all valence electrons to the other one, so that both kinds of atoms have closed electron shells. The binding is formed by the electrostatic attraction of the ions. The best-known example is NaCl. In the case of the III-V compounds this would imply that the trivalent component would be threefold positively charged, and the pentavalent one threefold negatively; for example, for GaAs the ions would be Ga^{3+} and As^{3-}.

The two kinds of binding exist not only by themselves, but also in combinations. Welker assumed in his first publications that the III-V compounds are primarily homopolar bound, with only a small heteropolar contribution. The latter is due to the fact that in the lattice of the III-V compounds the atomic cores have charges which differ from those of the diamond lattice by $\pm e$.

Such an ionic contribution to the binding causes a resonance strengthening of the lattice and a consequent increase of the melting point and widening of the forbidden gap. We will not discuss the connection between band model and chemical binding until Chapter 9 after consideration of the band theory and the experimental results. Only two facts will be mentioned here which tend to support Welker's thesis. There is no question that the elements with diamond lattice are essentially purely homopolar. Now we have seen in Section 12 that the lattice constants vary only slightly within an isoelectronic row as long as the materials crystallize in one of the mentioned lattice structures. In particular, the lattice constant of an element with diamond structure is practically identical with that of the isoelectronic III-V compound. The heteropolar contribution to the III-V compound should therefore not be very large. In addition it is possible to assign a "covalent radius" (Pauling) to each atom, such that the sum of the covalent radii of two nearest neighbors in IV-IV, III-V, etc., compounds agrees well with the distance between the two neighbors. This seems to be additional evidence that the chemical binding is identical in these materials. The covalent radii are listed in Table 2.1.

Folberth (60F5) has critically discussed these and other arguments in

Table 2.1 Covalent Radii of the Atoms of Groups III, IV, and V of the Periodic System (according to Pauling)

Element	Covalent Radius (Å)
B	0.88
C	0.77
N	0.70
Al	1.26
Si	1.17
P	1.10
Ga	1.26
Ge	1.22
As	1.18
In	1.44
Sn	1.40
Sb	1.36
Tl	1.47
Pb	1.46
Bi	1.46

favor of a primarily homopolar character of III-V compounds. He has been able to show that it is also possible to assume a larger ionic contribution to the binding. For example, fictitious "covalent" radii for the ionically bound lattices of the NaCl structure can be calculated which fit well into the system of true covalent radii. This implies that covalent radii are parameters which are not restricted to homopolar binding, and furthermore that the transition from one type of binding to the other only slightly influences the lattice constant. This has been supported by Heywang and Seraphin's calculation (56H4) of the binding energy of a hypothetical molecule with core charges of $(1 + \lambda^*)e$ and $(1 - \lambda^*)e$ for the two atoms. In that case the binding energy of the lowest state grows with increasing λ^*, or ionicity, accompanied by only a small change of the distance between the two atoms.

It will be seen later that the physical properties of the III-V compounds are similar to those of the group IV semiconductors. This similarity has been used as another argument for the primarily homopolar nature of the III-V binding.

In this connection it must be noted that there is another kind of binding which has not yet been discussed, namely, *neutral bonding* (54S3), (55G1), (58F4). Consider an electron bridge of an $A^{III}B^{V}$ compound. We have called the case, where the center of gravity of the "electron bridge" is halfway between the A^{3+} and B^{5+} ions, homopolar. The ionic charges are screened by the valence electrons in the bonds, so that the lattice atoms have the *effective* charge $\pm e$. The homopolar binding is then characterized by the formula $A^{1-}B^{1+}$. In the opposite case of pure ionic binding the formula, as we have seen, is $A^{3+}B^{3-}$. Continuous transitions are possible between these two extremes, and they can be described in two ways. Either one starts from the symmetrical bond and describes the ionic contribution as a displacement of the center of gravity of the bond (polarization of the "bridge"), or one starts from pure ionic bonding and considers the appearance of electron bridges as a polarization of the ions towards the nearest neighbors. Both descriptions are equivalent, and the use of one or the other is merely a matter of practicality. There is, however, one important intermediate case where the center of gravity of the electron bridges is moved to such an extent toward the B atoms that the effective charge of the lattice atoms is zero. This case, which is described by the formula A^0B^0, represents neutral bonding.

If we now compare these possibilities with the binding of the diamond lattice, we see that the last-mentioned bonding is both homopolar and neutral. Properties of III-V compounds similar to those of the column IV semiconductors can therefore also be explained by assuming the binding in the III-V compounds to be approximately neutral.

We have so far not defined a quantitative measure for the heteropolar and homopolar contributions to a given binding. Various such definitions have been suggested which depend on the electronegativity of the components of a compound, on their radii, or on their "effective charges" determined according to various procedures. We shall mention only one of these quantitative methods, which is based on the work of Coulson, Redei, and Stocker (62C8). The homopolar binding of two nearest neighbors A and B can be described by a combination of the sp^3-hybrid wavefunctions $\phi_{A,B}$ of the two atoms

$$\psi = \phi_A + \phi_B \tag{2.1}$$

This description will be extended to the case of binding with heteropolar contribution as follows:

$$\psi = \lambda\phi_A + \phi_B \tag{2.2}$$

Here λ is a parameter which must be determined by a variational pro-

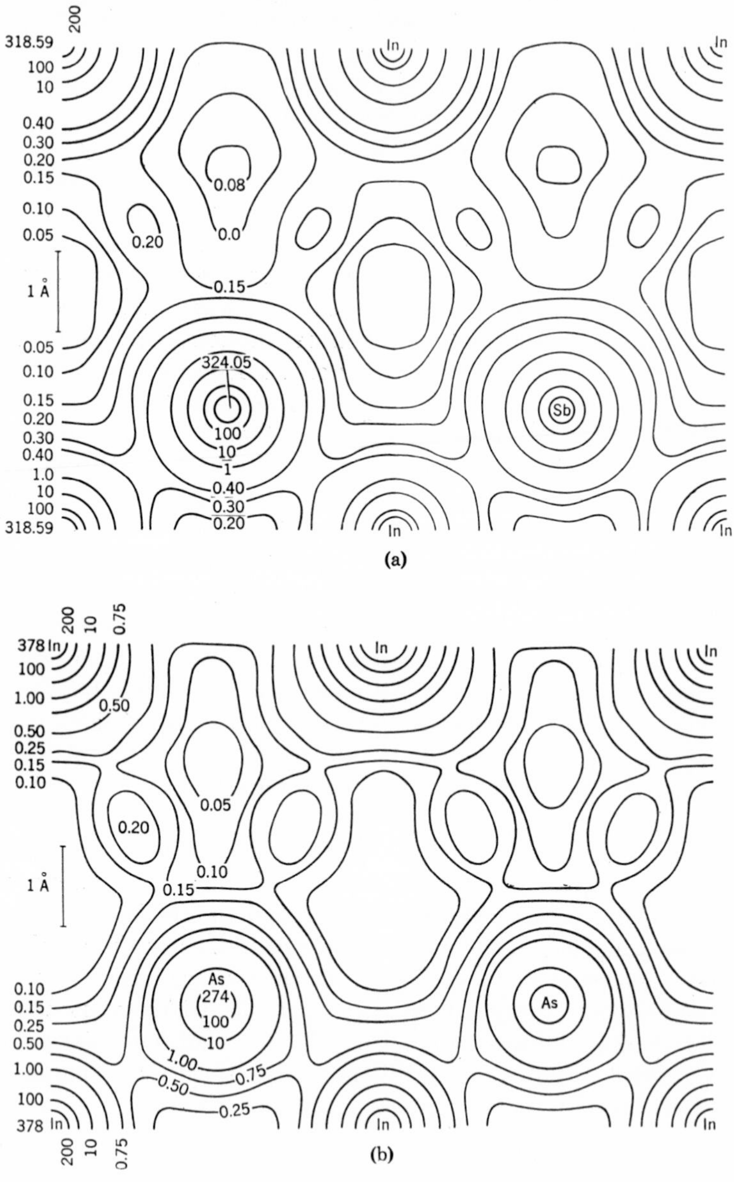

Fig. 2.1 Electron-density distribution in the (100)-plane, according to Sirota

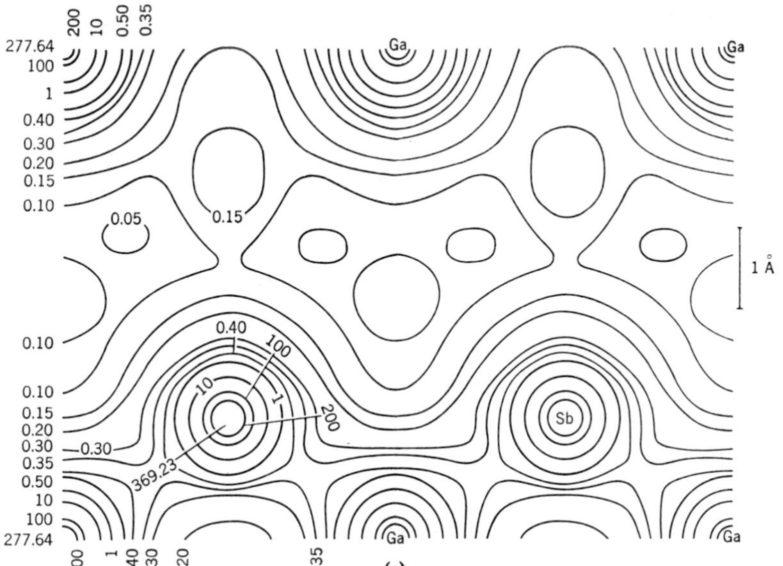

(c)

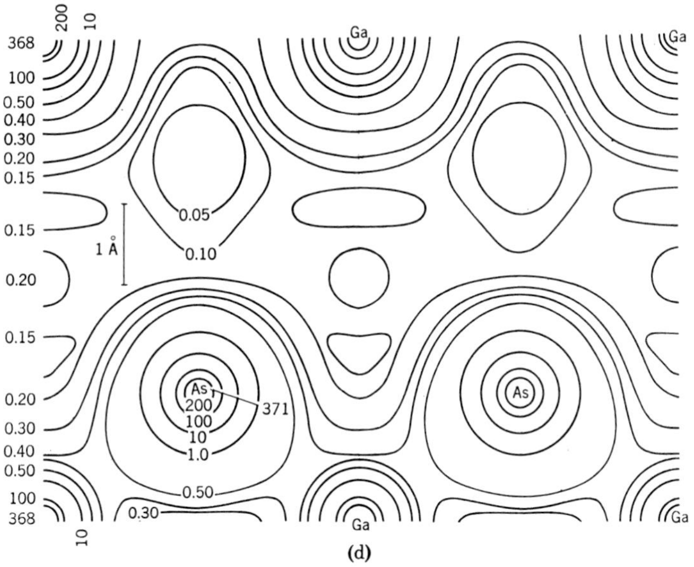

(d)

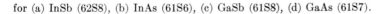

for (a) InSb (62S8), (b) InAs (61S6), (c) GaSb (61S8), (d) GaAs (61S7).

cedure. The effective ionic charge of the two atoms can be calculated if λ is known. The fraction of time an electron spends at atom A is given by (2.2) as $\lambda^2/(1 + \lambda^2)$, that at atom B as $1/(1 + \lambda^2)$. The average number of electrons at an A atom, from which four electron bonds extend, is then $-[8e\lambda^2/(1 + \lambda^2)]$, and the effective charge of the atom is

$$e_A^* = \left(3 - \frac{8\lambda^2}{1 + \lambda^2}\right) e = \frac{3 - 5\lambda^2}{1 + \lambda^2} e$$

The effective charge of the B atom is then $e_B^* = -e_A^*$. The parameter λ varies from 1 in the case of pure homopolar binding ($e_A^* = -e$) to 0 for pure ionic binding ($e_A^* = +3e$). Neutral binding occurs at $\lambda = \sqrt{3/5} = 0.774$.

Coulson and co-workers have calculated values of the parameter λ and of the effective charge for BN and other III-V compounds by the LCAO method. For BN the effective charge $0.26e < e^* < 0.50e$ results. A similar value ($0.3e$) was found by Kleinman and Phillips (60K4). This means that the binding is slightly on the ionic side of the neutral point. Values for some of the other III-V compounds are listed in Table 2.2. The values all lie beyond the neutral point. They can

Table 2.2 Effective Charges of the A Atoms of the $A^{III}B^V$ Compounds with Zinc-Blende Structure [after Coulson, Redei, and Stocker (62C8)]

Compound	e^*/e
BN	0.43
AlN	0.56
GaN	0.55
InN	0.58
BP	0.32
AlP	0.46
GaP	0.45
InP	0.49
AlAs	0.47
GaAs	0.46
InAs	0.49
AlSb	0.44
GaSb	0.43
InSb	0.46

be ordered according to increasing ionicity: (BP), (BN, GaSb), (AlSb), (GaP), (GaAs, AlP, InSb), (AlAs), (InP, InAs). One must not conclude herefrom that this series is continued in increasing order by the II-VI and I-VII compounds. Rather, according to Coulson's results, the II-VI and I-VII compounds which crystallize in the zinc-blende structure have values of e^* which lie between those of the III-V compounds listed in Table 2.2.

The distributions of the electrons in the (110)-plane of InSb, InAs, GaSb, and GaAs have been obtained by Sirota and co-workers (61S6), (61S7), (61S8), (62S8) from x-ray structure analysis. His results have been reproduced in Fig. 2.1. A small polarization of the "electron bridges" can be noticed, but it is not possible to determine the effective ionic charge quantitatively. For InSb similar results have been obtained by Attard and Azároff (63A8).

The discussion of the chemical binding of the III-V compounds will be interrupted at this point and continued in Chapter 9. This topic is less important for the quantitative understanding of the experimental results than the band theory, which will be discussed in the following sections.

21 Theory of the Band Model of the III-V Compounds

210 Introduction. The theoretical foundations for the band model of III-V compounds will be considered in this section. This discussion will form the basis for the treatment of the experimental results in the following chapters.

In principle the band structure of a solid, i.e., the functional dependence of energy on wave-number vector for the various bands, $E_n(\mathbf{k})$, is defined by the Schrödinger equation of the corresponding one-electron problem. In practice difficulties are encountered in such a calculation, which go beyond the problems of choosing a suitable approximation procedure and performing the very considerable numerical calculations required. The periodic crystal potential is generally only approximately known, and the consequent uncertainties in the results of the band structure calculation cannot be estimated easily. Not many quantitative results have therefore been obtained. Such procedures, however, do lead to a qualitatively correct picture of the band structure which provides information about the general shape of the bands, the location of the band extrema within the Brillouin zone, and the degeneracies and anisotropies of the bands.

It is often possible to derive such qualitative statements from considerations of the symmetry properties of the wave functions at characteristic symmetry points and lines of the Brillouin zone and to extend these statements to the surrounding regions through perturbation theory. One can thereby determine all possible locations and shapes of the band extrema of a given solid. The ones actually occurring are identified by comparison with experiment.

Simple theoretical arguments, then, lead to a picture of the band structure near the extrema containing a number of parameters. These can be calculated only from a more exact theory which requires a knowledge of the actual crystal potential. If, however, the parameters are determined from the experiment, this model results in a quantitative picture for those regions of the bands which are important for semiconductors.

The band model of the III-V compounds in its basic outline is similar to that of germanium and silicon. We will therefore survey the most important properties of the energy bands of semiconductors with diamond structures first and then discuss the differences between diamond and zinc-blende structures caused by their different symmetry properties. The derived results form the foundation for the semiempirical theory of Kane. This quantitative model, the only one available so far, will here be presented for the III-V compounds in general. Other, more comprehensive, theoretical considerations will be treated subsequently.

211 The band model of semiconductors with diamond structure. The Brillouin zone of the diamond and zinc-blende lattices is given by their crystal structure, which was discussed in Section 11. Both lattices can be considered as two interpenetrating face-centered cubic lattices. The unit cell is that of the face-centered lattice containing two atoms (two equal ones in diamond, two unequal ones in zinc blende). The associated Brillouin zone is consequently also identical for the two lattice types and is a truncated octahedron (Fig. 2.2). The most important symmetry points and lines are shown in Fig. 2.2. We will consider particularly the center of the zone (Γ), the [111]-axes (Λ) and their intersections with the zone edge (L), and the [100]-axes (Δ) and their intersections (X). Group-theoretical methods determine the symmetry properties of the wave functions for various values of the wave vector, i.e., points in the zone, and a perturbation calculation gives the qualitative behavior of the bands in the regions surrounding these points. Beyond such statements of the symmetry properties extensive theoretical band structure calculations have been performed for germanium and silicon. These result in the picture shown in Fig. 2.3.

As long as the spin is neglected in the Schrödinger equation, the *valence band* is composed of four subbands. Three of the four bands are degenerate at $\mathbf{k} = 0$ (symmetry type $\Gamma_{25'}$) and form the upper edge of the band. The fourth one forms the bottom (Γ_1). For $\mathbf{k} \neq 0$ the threefold degeneracy at the top of the band is split into a twofold degenerate and a nondegenerate band. If spin is taken into account, each band is doubled. Furthermore the spin-orbit interaction causes a splitting of the bands at $\mathbf{k} = 0$; the $\Gamma_{25'}$-term separates into a fourfold degenerate term (Γ_8-symmetry) and a twofold degenerate term (Γ_7-symmetry) which lies lower by the "spin-orbit energy." The Γ_8-term splits into two bands away from $\mathbf{k} = 0$. The two approximately parabolic bands have very different curvatures: V_1-band (*heavy holes*) and V_2-band (*light holes*). The Γ_7-term forms the top of the V_3-band. All these bands are doubly (spin) degenerate along the symmetry lines shown in Fig. 2.3.

The *conduction band* is composed of a number of subbands. Minima can appear at $\mathbf{k} = 0$ ($\Gamma_{2'}$ and Γ_{15}), along the [111]-axes (Λ_1 or L_1), and along the [100]-axes (Δ_1). Symmetry considerations alone do not determine which of these minima is the lowest one and forms the bottom of the conduction band. Experiment shows that in silicon the Δ-minimum is the lowest, in germanium it is the L-minimum, and in gray tin the Γ- and the L-minima are probably very close together.

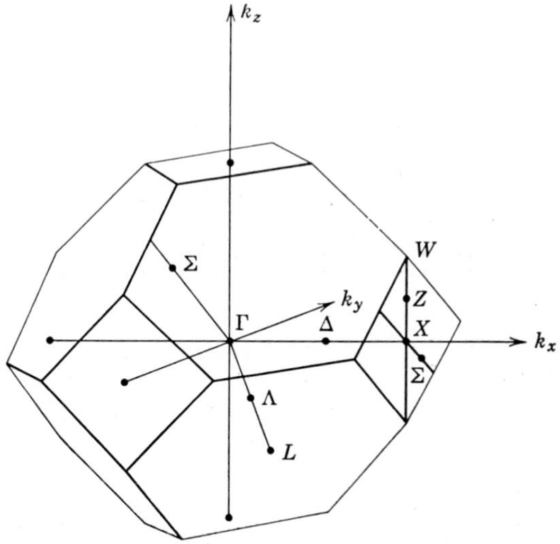

Fig. 2.2 Brillouin zone of the diamond and zinc-blende lattices.

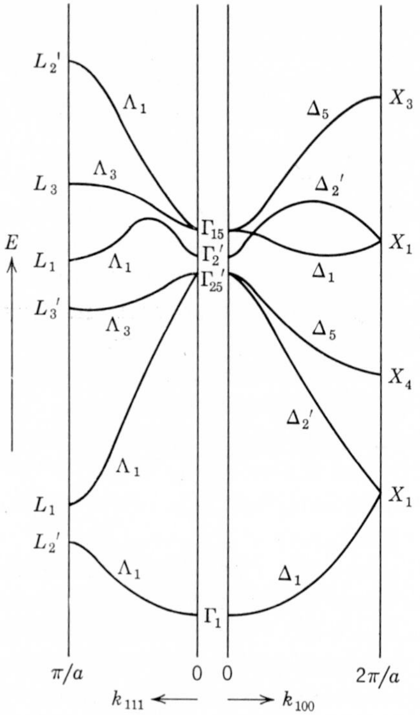

Fig. 2.3 Band structure of germanium calculated by Herman (58H1). Spin is not taken into account.

The shapes of the energy surfaces near the Γ-extrema are spheres if there is no degeneracy, or warped spheres for the degenerate case, such as in the valence band. Near the L- and Δ-extrema these shapes are ellipsoids of revolution with symmetry axes in the Λ- and Δ-directions, respectively. Including the spin does not change these considerations.

212 Symmetries in the band structure of the III-V compounds. All the characteristics of the diamond structure obtained from symmetry considerations remain for the zinc-blende structure as long as the spin is neglected. Only at point X_1 is the degeneracy split. This can cause the appearance of forbidden gaps within the conduction or valence bands of the III-V compounds. Figure 2.4 shows the shape of the energy bands of crystals with diamond and zinc-blende structure between the symmetry points Γ, X, and L along the Δ- and Λ-axes of the Brillouin zone. The *qualitative* picture of the energy bands in the diamond structure, which was discussed in Section 211, is redrawn in Figs. 2.4a and b. The energy differences and relative orders of the subbands do not correspond to any real band structure of diamond-type semiconductors. Symmetry considerations do not furnish such quantitative information; they only provide statements about the connection of subbands and their degeneracy. Figures 2.4c and d represent the band structure of the zinc-blende crystals in the same approximations as Figs. 2.4a and b, respectively.

The various features that distinguish the band structure of the zinc-blende lattice including spin (Fig. 2.4d) from the other cases are, according to Dresselhaus (55D4) and Parmenter (55P1), as follows. The spin degeneracy is lifted at all nonspecific points of the Brillouin zone. Along the symmetry lines shown in Fig. 2.4 the spin degeneracy of the Λ_3-subband of Fig. 2.4c, as well as that of the $\Lambda_4+\Lambda_5$-subband of Fig. 2.4b, is removed. The degeneracy of the Δ_6- and Δ_7-subbands is also removed at point X_5 (Fig. 2.4b). The symmetry point Γ_8 (top of the valence band in the diamond structure) is no longer an extremum. The **k**-dependence of the energy contains terms linear in **k** at Γ. If Γ_8 remains the highest subband of the valence band at Γ in the III-V compounds, then the maxima of the valence band are along the [111]- axes, i.e., along Λ_5. The energy surfaces near these (nondegenerate) maxima are ellipsoids of revolution about the [111]-direction, according to Dresselhaus (55D4). The other two possible extrema at Γ (bottom of the conduction band and top of the V_3-band in the diamond lattices) remain extrema of the subbands in the zinc-blende structure. Similarly, conduction-band extrema may still appear along the [111]- and [100]-axes.

We have considered only the symmetry points and lines shown in Fig. 2.4. These are the ones of importance in diamond-like semiconductors, and it is suggested (without proof) that the interesting band extrema in the III-V compounds also fall on these points and lines. In principle, band extrema may also appear at other places in the Brillouin zone. Point W is certainly an extremum, and the energy surfaces around it are ellipsoids with the same orientation as that around the extrema along the Δ-axes. Consequently it is often not possible to determine the location of extrema experimentally. The assumption of band extrema lying at Γ and along Δ and Λ will be sufficient for our purposes in the following chapters, but we will not be able to prove that they really exist. At present they can be identified only by symmetry considerations or from analogy with the situation in diamond-like semiconductors.

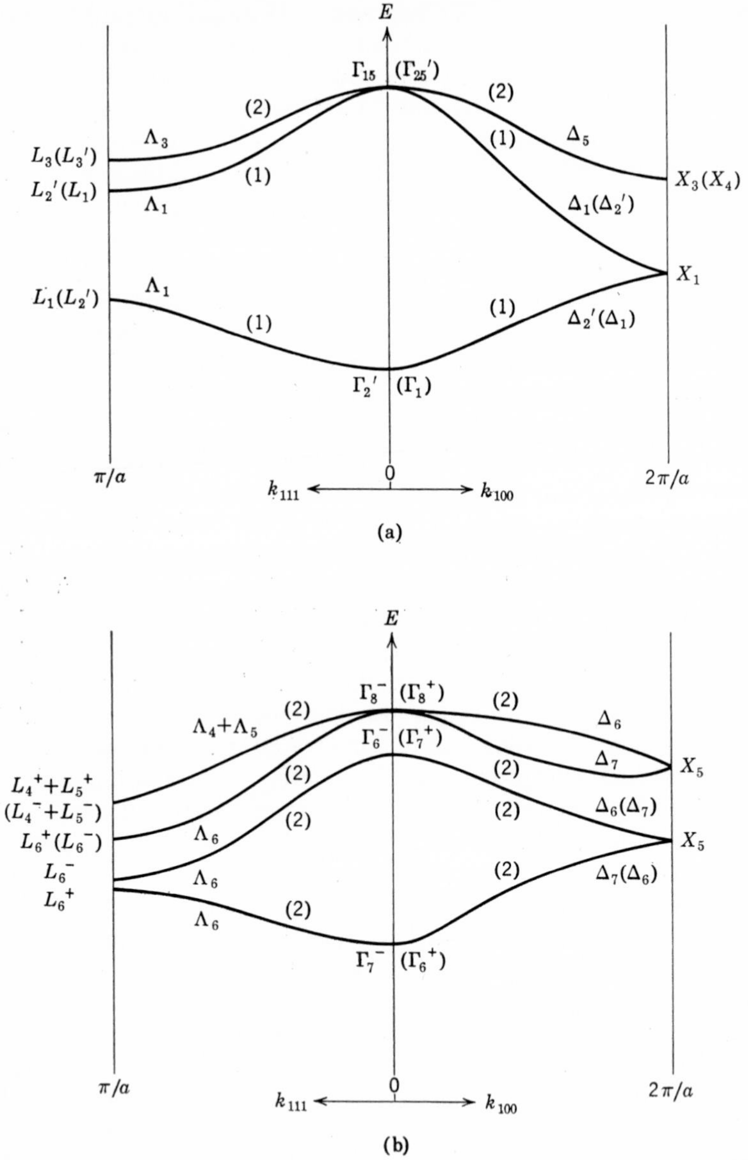

Fig. 2.4 Qualitative picture of the band structures of the diamond and zinc-blende lattices: (a) diamond lattice without inclusion of spin; (b) diamond lattice when spin is taken into account; (c) zinc-blende lattice without spin; (d) zinc-blende lattice with spin. In all cases the qualitative shape of the bands shown applies both to the valence and to the conduction band. The symmetry symbols

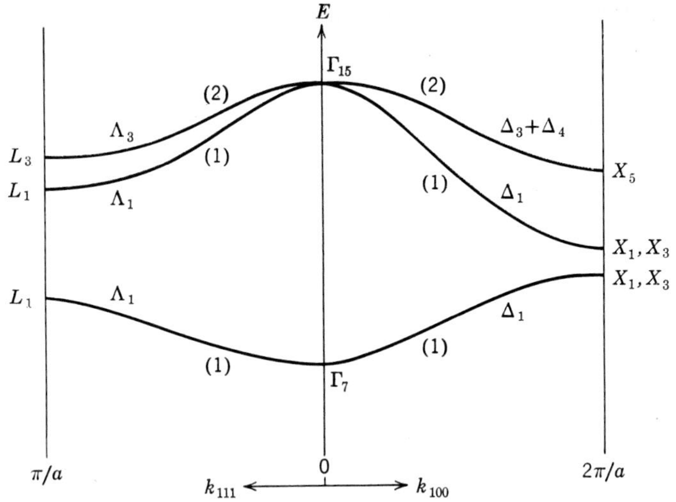

(c)

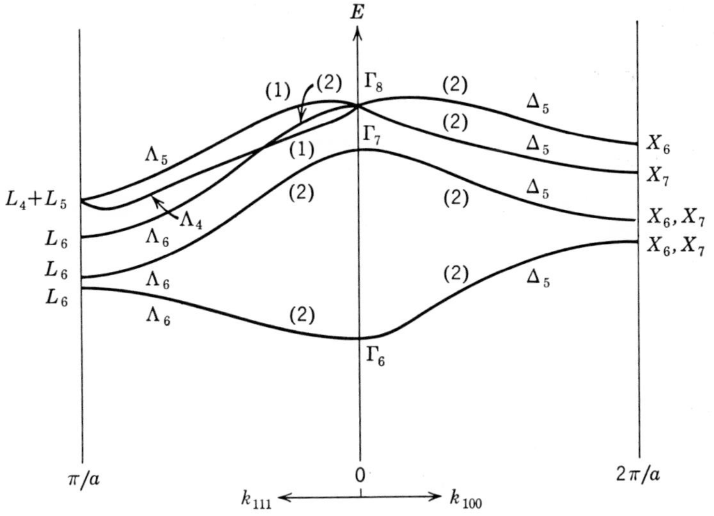

(d)

are the same for the two cases except where valence-band symbols differing from those of the conduction band are shown in brackets. When a point or line is labeled with two symbols without brackets, it means that symmetry arguments alone cannot distinguish between the two possibilities.

The symmetry properties of the wurtzite structure will not be considered. The III-V compounds crystallizing in this structure have not yet been investigated sufficiently to draw any conclusions about their band structures. Investigations of the symmetry, as was done by Parmenter and Dresselhaus for the zinc-blende lattice, do exist (59G3), (59R2), (60B1), but comparison with the band model of the diamond structure is more difficult, since wurtzite and diamond belong to different crystal classes.

213 Kane's theory. With the symmetry considerations of Section 212 as foundation one can construct a semiquantitative theory of the band structure in the vicinity of a symmetry point. Such a theory was developed quantitatively by Kane (57K2) for the region surrounding Γ. Previously Dresselhaus (55D4) had also calculated the shape of the bands in the vicinity of the most important symmetry points. Both authors made use of the so-called $k \cdot p$ perturbation calculation. We will now describe Kane's theory in detail, because it forms the foundation for the discussion of the experimental results of the following chapters.

The Schrödinger equation for an electron in the periodic potential $V(\mathbf{r})$, with inclusion of the spin-orbit coupling, is

$$\left[\frac{\mathbf{p}^2}{2m} + V + \frac{\hbar}{4m^2c^2}(\text{grad } V \times \mathbf{p}) \cdot \boldsymbol{\sigma}\right]\Psi_k = E_k\Psi_k \tag{2.3}$$

Here $\mathbf{p}$ is the momentum operator, and $\boldsymbol{\sigma}$ the spin operator. Using the Bloch functions $\Psi_k = u_k(\mathbf{r})e^{i\mathbf{k}\cdot\mathbf{r}}$, the equation for the lattice periodic function $u_k(\mathbf{r})$ follows:

$$(H_0 + H_1 + H_2 + H_3)u_k = E_k' u_k \tag{2.4}$$

with

$$H_0 = \frac{\mathbf{p}^2}{2m} + V(\mathbf{r}), \quad H_1 = \frac{\hbar}{m}\mathbf{k} \cdot \mathbf{p}, \quad H_2 = \frac{\hbar}{4m^2c^2}(\text{grad } V \times \mathbf{p}) \cdot \boldsymbol{\sigma}$$

$$H_3 = \frac{\hbar^2}{4m^2c^2}(\text{grad } V \times \mathbf{k}) \cdot \boldsymbol{\sigma}, \quad \text{and} \quad E_k' = E_k - \frac{\hbar^2k^2}{2m}$$

In eq. (2.4) H_0 is now considered to be the Hamiltonian of the unperturbed problem. Then H_1 (for small $\mathbf{k}$) is a spin-independent perturbation, while $H_2 + H_3$ is a spin-dependent perturbation. The wave functions of the perturbed problem are expanded in terms of the wave functions of the unperturbed problem. This leads, in the first order of perturbation theory, to a system of linear equations for the expansion coefficients whose secular determinant must vanish. The solution of this secular determinant fixes the energies to first order. Higher orders can be obtained subsequently in the usual fashion.

The zero-order base functions that Kane uses for the expansion of the wave function of eq. (2.4) are two s-functions, with opposite spins, S_+ and S_-, and six p-functions, $X_\pm$, $Y_\pm$, and $Z_\pm$. These functions are derived from the assumption that the unperturbed problem (point Γ without spin) results in a lower conduction band edge with Γ_1-symmetry and an upper valence band edge with Γ_{15}-symmetry. Restricting oneself to these eight wave functions means that the influence of higher- and lower-lying bands is considered to be small in this approximation. The assumption appears to be justified for InSb, where experiments have determined that the two band edges lie at $\mathbf{k} = 0$ and that E_G is small compared to all other energy separations at Γ. Kane therefore restricts his model to InSb. We will see later, however, that the results of theory are also suited for the interpretation of the experimental results on other III-V compounds.

An 8×8 secular determinant is then obtained. Most of the matrix elements vanish because of the special symmetry properties of the base functions. The only remaining parameters of the theory are a parameter E_G of the unperturbed problem, and the matrix elements

$$P = -i\frac{\hbar}{m}\langle S|p_z|Z\rangle \tag{2.5}$$

and

$$\Delta = \frac{3\hbar i}{4m^2c^2}\langle X|(\operatorname{grad} V \times \mathbf{p})_z|Y\rangle \tag{2.6}$$

The solution of the secular determinant then results in the equation

$$E'\{E'(E' - E_G)(E' + \Delta) - k^2P^2(E' + \tfrac{2}{3}\Delta)\} = 0 \tag{2.7}$$

to first order in H_1 and H_2.

It follows from (2.7) that the four eigenvalues for $\mathbf{k} = 0$ are $E_1 = E_G$, $E_2 = E_3 = 0$, $E_4 = -\Delta$. We can identify E_1 as the bottom of the conduction band (E_c), E_2 and E_3 (in analogy to germanium) as the top of the valence bands of the heavy (E_{v1}) and light (E_{v2}) holes, and E_4 as the third valence band (E_{v3}), split off by the spin-orbit interaction. E_G is then the width of the forbidden zone, and Δ the spin-orbit splitting at $\mathbf{k} = 0$.

The influence of the higher- and lower-lying bands is included by a second-order perturbation calculation in H_1 and H_2. The solutions of (2.7) are then supplemented by the perturbation terms, and the following band structure results:

$$
\begin{aligned}
&(1)\ k \approx 0: \quad E_c = E_G + \frac{\hbar^2 k^2}{2m} + \frac{k^2 P^2}{3}\left(\frac{2}{E_G} + \frac{1}{E_G + \Delta}\right) + ak^2 \\
&E_{v1} = \frac{\hbar^2 k^2}{2m} + (a_1 + b_1 s)k^2 \pm 3\sqrt{3}\,K(s - t)^{1/2}k \\
&E_{v2} = \frac{\hbar^2 k^2}{2m} - \frac{2k^2P^2}{3E_G} + (a_2 + b_1 s)k^2 \pm \sqrt{3}\,K(s - 9t)^{1/2}k \\
&E_{v3} = -\Delta + \frac{\hbar^2 k^2}{2m} - \frac{k^2P^2}{3(E_G + \Delta)} + a_3 k^2
\end{aligned}
\tag{2.8}
$$

$$
\begin{aligned}
&(2)\ kP, E_G \ll \Delta: \quad E_c = E_G + \frac{\hbar^2 k^2}{2m} + \frac{E_G}{2}\left[\left(1 + \frac{8k^2P^2}{3E_G{}^2}\right)^{1/2} - 1\right] + \delta E_c \\
&E_{v1} = \frac{\hbar^2 k^2}{2m} + \delta E_{v1} \\
&E_{v2} = \frac{\hbar^2 k^2}{2m} - \frac{E_G}{2}\left[\left(1 + \frac{8k^2P^2}{3E_G{}^2}\right)^{1/2} - 1\right] + \delta E_{v2} \\
&E_{v3} = -\Delta + \frac{\hbar^2 k^2}{2m} - \frac{k^2P^2}{3(E_G + \Delta)} + \delta E_{v3}
\end{aligned}
\tag{2.9}
$$

$$
\begin{aligned}
&(3)\ \Delta \ll E_G: \quad E_c = E_G + \frac{\hbar^2 k^2}{2m} + \frac{E_G}{2}\left[\left(1 + \frac{4k^2P^2}{E_G{}^2}\right)^{1/2} - 1\right] + \delta E_c \\
&E_{v1} = \frac{\hbar^2 k^2}{2m} + \delta E_{v1} \\
&\left.\begin{aligned}
E_{v2} &= \frac{\hbar^2 k^2}{2m} - \frac{2k^2P^2}{3E_G} + \delta E_{v2} \\
E_{v3} &= -\Delta + \frac{\hbar^2 k^2}{2m} - \frac{k^2P^2}{3E_G} + \delta E_{v3}
\end{aligned}\right\} kP \ll \Delta
\end{aligned}
\tag{2.10}
$$

The δE_i's in (2.9) and (2.10) are given by

$$
\begin{aligned}
\delta E_c &= [a + bs \pm c(s - 9t)^{1/2}]k^2 \\
\delta E_{v1} &= (a_1 + b_1 s)k^2 \pm 3\sqrt{3}\,K(s - t)^{1/2}k \\
\delta E_{v2} &= [a_2 + b_2 s \pm c_2(s - 9t)^{1/2}]k^2 \pm \sqrt{3}\,K(s - 9t)^{1/2}k \\
\delta E_{v3} &= [a_3 + b_3 s \pm c_3(s - 9t)^{1/2}]k^2
\end{aligned}
\tag{2.11}
$$

The coefficients a_i, b_i, c_i, and K contain seven more matrix elements.

The two coefficients s and t are anisotropy coefficients of the following form:

$$s = \frac{k_x^2 k_y^2 + k_y^2 k_z^2 + k_z^2 k_x^2}{k^4}$$
$$t = \frac{k_x^2 k_y^2 k_z^2}{k^6} \qquad (2.12)$$

From eqs. (2.8)–(2.12) the following picture of the band structure is obtained (Fig. 2.5). The *conduction band* is parabolic near its minimum. With increasing $\mathbf{k}$ the curvature decreases, and the effective mass of the electrons therefore increases. The influence of the higher- and lower-lying bands causes a shift of the band at $\mathbf{k} \neq 0$ to higher energies and a lifting of the spin degeneracy except in the [100]- and [111]-directions.

The *topmost valence band* (V_1-band) is not influenced at all by the conduction band but is affected strongly by all the other bands. The spin degeneracy is lifted even at $\mathbf{k} \approx 0$ (except in the [100]-direction)

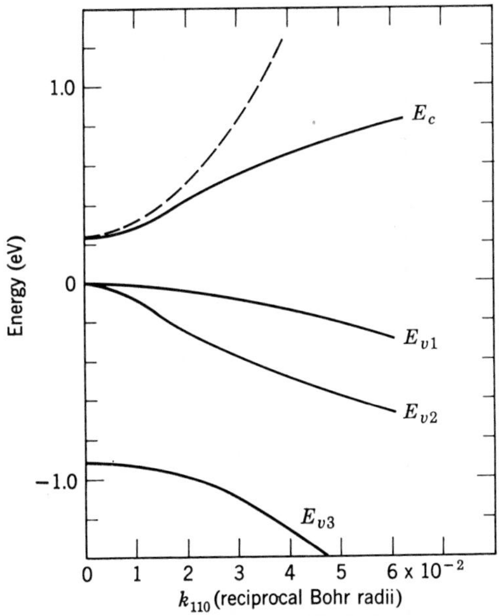

Fig. 2.5 Energy vs. wave number in [110]-direction for InSb according to Kane (57K2). Splitting of the two-fold degeneracy has not been included. The dashed curve represents the parabolic approximation for the conduction band.

by terms linear in **k**. The maxima of the band lie on the [111]-axes outside of $\mathbf{k} = 0$.

The *next-highest valence band* (V_2-band) is degenerate with the V_1-band at $\mathbf{k} = 0$. It is nonparabolic, similar to the conduction band, and it contains terms linear in **k** which lift the spin degeneracy except in the [100]- and [111]-directions.

The V_3-*band* is similar to the V_2-band except for the absence of linear **k**-terms.

An estimate of the magnitude of the coefficients shows that *in first approximation* the conduction band and the two lower-lying bands are not influenced by other bands. Only the effective mass of the heavy holes m_{p1} is entirely determined by this influence. If m_{p1} is determined from experiment, then, in this approximation, the only unknown parameters remaining in (2.8)–(2.10) are E_G and Δ, which can be determined from optical measurements, and P. The latter can then be derived from the effective mass of the electrons m_n at the band edge, namely, according to (2.8) by the relation:

$$P^2 = \frac{3\hbar^2}{2}\left(\frac{1}{m_n} - \frac{1}{m}\right)\frac{E_G(E_G + \Delta)}{3E_G + 2\Delta} \tag{2.13}$$

In this approximation the bands are isotropic and spin-degenerate. In the subsequent discussion we will generally find this description to be sufficient.

If H_3 in the Hamiltonian of eq. (2.4) is included, then a first-order perturbation calculation will introduce more linear **k**-terms into the $E(\mathbf{k})$-dependence of the valence band; they are, however, smaller than the ones discussed above.

Kane's theory has been extended by Braunstein and Kane (62B12) and by Cardona (63C3). Both authors aim to theoretically calculate the effective masses m_n, m_{p1}, m_{p2}, and m_{p3} from other experimentally determined quantities.

Braunstein and Kane attempt primarily to estimate the spin-orbit splitting Δ more accurately from theory than is possible from the somewhat uncertain experiments. Cardona calculates the influence of the interaction among Γ_1- and Γ_{15}-subbands of the conduction band on the effective masses. In this way he obtains improvements of the first-order effective mass values m_n, m_{p2}, and m_{p3} of Kane's theory as well as theoretical values for m_{p1}.

The numerical values will be presented in Chapter 9 (Table 9.2), where they will be compared with experimental results.

Kane's theory applies rigorously only at $T = 0°\mathrm{K}$. Ehrenreich

(57E2) has shown that for $T \neq 0°K$ the quantity E_G in eqs. (2.7) ff. is not identical with the experimentally determined $E_{G,\,\mathrm{exp}}(T)$. Rather, according to eq. (2.13), E_G is coupled with the temperature dependence of the curvature of the conduction band at $\mathbf{k} = 0$, $m_n(T)$. Since we will not take these small differences into consideration in the following chapters, we refer to Ehrenreich's paper for a more detailed discussion of this "density of states" band gap, as well as for the calculation of the equilibrium concentrations of the electrons and holes in Kane's model.

In the theory discussed, the concept of an effective mass is not clearly defined, because of the nonparabolicity of the conduction band and of the V_2-band. Just as we have to distinguish between a transverse and a longitudinal mass in the case of an anisotropic band, so three different effective masses must be introduced for an isotropic but non-parabolic band. These three ("differential") effective masses may be defined, according to Kopeć (60K9), by the equations

$$E = \frac{\hbar^2 k^2}{2m^*} \tag{2.14}$$

$$\frac{1}{M_{ij}} F_j = \frac{dv_i}{dt} \tag{2.15}$$

$$N(E)\, dE = \frac{4\pi}{h^3} (2m_{ds})^{3/2} E^{1/2}\, dE \tag{2.16}$$

Equation (2.14) is the fundamental definition; m^* is the proportionality factor in the energy-momentum relation of the quasi-free charge carriers. Equation (2.15) is the relationship between the acceleration, $d\mathbf{v}/dt$, and the applied force, $\mathbf{F}$. Generally $1/M$ is a tensor quantity. Finally (2.16) is the well-known density-of-states equation.

According to Stern (57S5), three other definitions are also suitable, namely,

$$E = \frac{\hbar^2 k^2}{2m_1} \tag{2.17}$$

$$\frac{dE}{dk} = \frac{\hbar^2 k}{m_2} \tag{2.18}$$

$$\frac{d^2E}{dk^2} = \frac{\hbar^2}{m_3} \qquad 2.19)$$

Here $m^* = m_1$, $m_{ds} = (m_1 m_2^2)^{1/3}$, and $1/M$ is given by

$$\frac{1}{M_{ij}} = \frac{1}{m_2}\,\delta_{ij} + \left(\frac{1}{m_3} - \frac{1}{m_2}\right)\frac{k_i k_j}{k^2} \tag{2.20}$$

Calculated values of m_1, m_2, m_3 at the Fermi level for InSb and InAs (57S5) are shown in Table 2.3 as functions of electron concentration (complete degeneracy).

Only for an isotropic parabolic band are all the effective masses defined by (2.14)–(2.19) identical. It should also be noted that even for an isotropic band structure the acceleration of the charge carriers is not necessarily parallel to the direction of the applied force. This is the case only if $m_2 = m_3$, namely, when the band is parabolic.

The three effective mass parameters are energy dependent. This means that m_{ds} is not the conventionally defined density-of-states mass, which determines the number of electrons and holes that fill up a band to a certain energy. The latter quantity is an average value, obtained by integrating m_{ds} over all the carriers.

At the edge of a band all the effective masses become identical. Consequently our goal in the following chapters will always be to determine this limiting value. We will discuss only as far as necessary the question of which of the effective masses, or which combination thereof,

Table 2.3 Effective Masses $m_1 = \hbar^2k^2/2E$, $m_2 = \hbar^2k/(dE/dk)$, $m_3 = \hbar^2/(d^2E/dk^2)$ at $E = E_F$ for InSb and InAs [according to Kane's theory, Stern (57S5)]

The values are in units of one electron mass. The electron concentration n is related to the Fermi level E_F by the equation $E_F = \dfrac{\hbar_2}{2m_1}\left(\dfrac{3n}{8\pi}\right)^{2/3}$ (degenerate case).

Electron Concentration (cm^{-3})	InSb			InAs		
	m_1	m_2	m_3	m_1	m_2	m_3
3×10^{16}	0.015	0.016	0.023	0.024	0.025	0.028
1×10^{17}	0.016	0.019	0.038	0.025	0.026	0.034
3×10^{17}	0.019	0.024	0.075	0.026	0.029	0.048
1×10^{18}	0.023	0.032	0.20	0.029	0.036	0.086
3×10^{18}	0.029	0.045	1.0	0.034	0.045	0.18
1×10^{19}	0.039	0.067	−1.0	0.043	0.064	0.58
3×10^{19}	0.054	0.102	−0.5	0.056	0.090	5.3

plays a role in any given process. For a more extensive discussion we refer to Kopeć (60K9) and to a number of papers by Kołodziejczak (61K6), (62K4), (62K5), (62K6).

214 Perturbational methods. It was first pointed out by Herman (55H1) that the similarity of the zinc-blende and diamond lattices suggests that the band model of the III-V compounds can be derived from that of the semiconductors of Group IV.

Every III-V compound can be imagined to be formed out of the isoelectronic IV-IV compound (or the corresponding element) by substitution of two atoms of the fourth column by the adjacent atoms of the third and fifth columns in the periodic system (cf. Section 12). This means that cubic BN corresponds to diamond, AlP to silicon, GaAs to germanium, and InSb to gray tin. Boron phosphide and AlN can be assigned to SiC, but the remaining III-V compounds have to be related to hypothetical IV-IV compounds, such as SiGe and GeSn.

If the band model of the IV-IV compound or element is known, the band model of the corresponding III-V compound can be derived by a quantum-mechanical perturbation calculation. Herman restricted himself to the most important aspects of this method and drew a few conclusions as to the relative positions of the Γ-, Λ-, and Δ-minima of the conduction bands of some of the III-V compounds, using experimental E_G values. We will not consider this in detail, since the experimental material to be presented in Chapter 3 allows much more detailed conclusions about the band structure of the III-V compounds than was possible at the time of Herman's work.

The perturbation methods suggested by Herman have been used by Kleinman and Phillips (60K4) for the determination of the band model of cubic BN (Borazon) from that of diamond, and by Callaway (57C1) for the determination of the band model of GaAs from that of germanium. The main findings of Kleinman and Phillips are as follows (see Fig. 2.6).

1. The degeneracy of the symmetry point X_1 of the diamond lattice is removed for BN. At the same time the minimum of the conduction band is shifted from a general point on the Δ-axis in the case of diamond to the intersection point X.

2. The top of the valence band remains at $\Gamma_{25'}$ but is lowered considerably by interaction with the conduction band. This leads to a broadening of E_G from 5 eV for diamond to 10 eV for BN.

3. The lifting of the X_1-degeneracy in the valence band leads to a splitting of the valence band into an upper subband with a width of

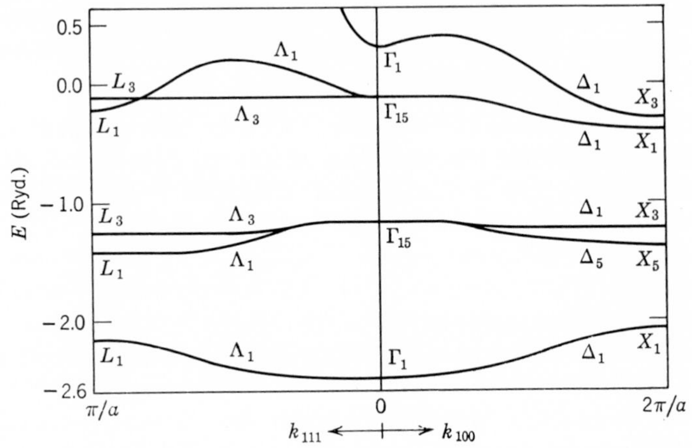

Fig. 2.6 Energy bands of cubic BN after Kleinman and Phillips (60K4).

4 eV and a lower subband with a width of 5 eV. The separation of the two subbands is given as about 10 eV. The spin-orbit splitting was not considered.

Callaway (57C1) finds that in going from germanium to GaAs the forbidden gap is widened, the conduction-band minimum moves from L to Γ, the valence band splits at X_1 by about 2 eV, and the valence-band extrema move slightly towards each other. Spin-orbit interaction influences the GaAs band model similarly to that of germanium, according to Callaway.

There have been a number of attempts to calculate the energy parameters of the valence bands of some of the III-V compounds by approximate methods. The results differ considerably, so that the quantitative values are of only slight importance. Generally, energy gaps are found in the valence band (and in the conduction band) at X. Coulson, Redei, and Stocker (62C8), who used a calculation of hybrid wave functions by the LCBO method (linear combination of bond orbitals), as was mentioned in Section 20, found the width of the valence band to be 12.7 eV for BN, 7.2 eV for AlP, 6.6 eV for GaAs, and 6.4 eV for InSb. The band structure of the valence band (without spin) for all these compounds is of the type shown in Fig. 2.4c.

Bassani and Celli (61B2) use an approximate OPW method (orthogonalized plane waves) for the calculation of the germanium and GaAs band structures. They calculate that the valence band of GaAs is considerably wider, namely 12 eV, with an energy gap of 6 eV at X_1. The lowest conduction band, which is separated from the others by an energy gap, is very narrow and has a minimum at Γ. Bassani and Yoshimine (63B3) have extended the calculations to the groups Si-BN and SiC-AlP. Rather than trying to determine exact values for the band-structure parameters, these authors examine the reliability of the OPW method and the approximations used in their work by comparing their results with the experimental values.

With a similar method Gashimzade and Khartsiev (61G2) find a still larger width of the valence band of GaAs (17.5 eV) with an energy gap of 10.4 eV. Gubanov and Nran'yan (59G14) have developed an "equivalent orbital method" which results in 20 eV for the same energy difference and in a gap of 3.5 eV (60N7).

This example shows the poor quantitative agreement between different perturbation calculations, and we will not consider other numerical values presented in the works mentioned. In particular, the last-cited article contains energy parameters and effective masses for the valence band of many III-V compounds.

Instead we consider the collective results of all the workers as a confirmation of the qualitative band model of the III-V compounds as presented in Figs. 2.4c and 2.4d, and we will attempt to determine the energy parameters from the experimental results of the later chapters.

215 One-dimensional models. There were early attempts by Seraphin (54S2) and Adawi (57A1) to study the main differences between the band structure of the III-V compounds and that of the fourth-column semiconductors according to one-dimensional models. These authors extended the well-known Kronig-Penney model to the case of a two-atomic chain with δ-function potentials of different strengths ($S \pm \Delta S$) and spacings ($a/2 \pm \alpha a$):

$$V(x) = \sum_{q=-\infty}^{+\infty} \left\{ (S - \Delta S)\,\delta(x - qa) + (S + \Delta S)\,\delta\left[x + \frac{a}{2} - (q - \alpha)a\right]\right\} \qquad (2.21)$$

Seraphin sets the ratio of the separations of an atom from its two nearest neighbors as 3:1, i.e., $\alpha = 1/4$. This is the same ratio as that of the spacings between planes of similar atoms along the [111]-direction in the diamond and zinc-blende lattices. Adawi drops this restriction.

The main result is that the distance between the two lowest bands (assumed to be the valence and conduction bands) and the effective masses of the electrons and holes at the band edges (given by the second derivative of the energy with respect to the wave number) both increase with increasing ΔS and increasing α. This would mean that the III-V compounds would have a wider forbidden zone and their charge carriers heavier effective masses than the corresponding isoelectronic semiconductors of the fourth column.

It is doubtful, however, whether these results have any physical meaning. For one thing, the polarization of the electron bridges, discussed in Section 20, predicts an approximately neutral bonding in the III-V compounds. In such a case, the δ-functions must be taken of equal strength, since they are to represent alternately deep narrow and shallow wide potential wells. Also, as has been emphasized by Gubanov (56G6), the choice of the [111]-direction as the representative direction in the diamond and zinc-blende lattices is not justified, since the nearest-neighbor distances within a given (111)-plane are larger than those between planes. Finally, according to Gubanov, an equidistant chain is more strongly justified as a one-dimensional analog of the zinc-blende structure, because the results of a Wigner-Seitz calculation for diamond are equivalent to the band structure of such an equidistant chain. Gubanov extends these results by three-dimensional considerations and finds a widening of the forbidden zone during the transition from the diamond to the zinc-blende structure. No statement about the effective masses, i.e., the curvature of the bands at the extrema, was possible in this case.

Raychaudhuri (59R3) also finds, for a three-dimensional model similar to that of Seraphin, a widening of E_G when passing through an isoelectronic row with a simultaneous decrease of the effective mass of the holes.

216 Summary. With the results of the theoretical endeavors discussed in the previous sections we can design the following qualitative model of the band structure of the III-V compounds.

The *conduction band* consists of a number of subbands which have minima at $\mathbf{k} = 0$, and on the [111]- and [100]-axes. It can generally not be predicted theoretically which of these minima is the lowest. The spin degeneracy of the individual subbands is lifted. If the minimum of the lowest subband is at $\mathbf{k} = 0$ and as long as the other subbands lie enough higher so that they are not occupied by electrons, it follows from Kane's theory that the band is nonparabolic, but isotropic, except for small anisotropy caused by the lifting of the spin degeneracy. The electrons in this band therefore possess a varying scalar effective mass. The energy gap which appears at higher energies in the conduction band is unimportant for the semiconducting properties of the III-V compounds.

The *valence band* consists of two subbands which are degenerate at $\mathbf{k} = 0$ and another spin-orbit-split lower-lying band. We therefore expect two kinds of holes with different effective masses, as in germanium. The spin degeneracy is also lifted here. This leads to the fact that the band maximum is not exactly at $\mathbf{k} = 0$, but nearby along the [111]-axes.

Except for this peculiarity, the valence-band structure of the III-V compounds corresponds to that of germanium and silicon. The fourth subband, which is separated from the others by an energy gap, is uninteresting for the semiconductor properties.

This model can be developed into a quantitative description of the band structure by an experimental determination of the energy differences between the individual extremal values of the subbands, of their position in the Brillouin zone, and of the $E(\mathbf{k})$-dependence in the vicinity of the extrema (effective masses). The determination of these parameters will therefore be our special concern in the following chapters.

3

Optical Properties of the III-V Compounds

30 Introduction

The theoretical foundations for the interpretation of the experimental results on III-V compounds were given in Chapter 2. We have seen that it is possible to predict the general structure of the energy bands but that the theoretical determination of quantitative values is limited. On the other hand, Kane's theory allows a quantitative band-structure picture to be derived from the experimental determination of a small number of parameters. The characteristic distances between band extrema and the effective masses of the charge carriers are such parameters. Optical measurements are particularly suited for the determination of these quantities. Electrical measurements, such as the determination of conductivity, Hall coefficient, and magnetoresistance, are less valuable despite the fact that a particularly large number of such measurements is available for the semiconductors of group IV of the periodic table and for the III-V compounds. The reason is that, in transport phenomena, energy separations in the band model can be determined only indirectly, e.g., from the measurement of the temperature dependence of electrical quantities. Also, the effective masses influence the electrical properties through the mobility of the charge carriers, where the quantity m^* is always coupled with other, relatively unknown, parameters.

The optical phenomena are less ambiguous. Here the most important observable quantities are the transmission coefficient T and the reflection coefficient R. Both are interrelated with the optical index of refraction n_r, the absorption coefficient k, and the absorption constant $K = (2\omega/c)k$ by the following expressions:

$$T = \frac{(1 - R^2)e^{-Kx}}{1 - R^2e^{-2Kx}} \tag{3.1}$$

$$R = \frac{(n_r - 1)^2 + k^2}{(n_r + 1)^2 + k^2} \tag{3.2}$$

Here x is the thickness of the transmitting sample.

Consider absorption first. Light quanta are absorbed in a solid by two processes. On one hand, their energy can be used to lift an electron to a point in the band model which lies at an energy $\hbar\omega$ higher; on the other hand, lattice vibrations can be excited. The latter process gives information about the bonding properties of the lattice, the effective charges of the lattice atoms, and the characteristic frequencies of the lattice vibrations. In contrast, the interaction of the photons with the electrons is determined by the structure of the energy bands and consequently gives information about the parameters of the band model.

The light-induced transitions can occur between different bands or within a single band. The first possibility leads to the appearance of absorption edges in the absorption spectrum at the minimum transition energy, or to the appearance of absorption peaks if the transitions are confined to narrow energy regions. Consequently, the characteristic energy differences in the band model can be determined from such phenomena. The transitions within a single band (free-carrier absorption) are determined by the nature of the charge carrier. The measurements can therefore lead to the effective masses. The absorption is also characteristically changed by external influences, such as an applied magnetic field or applied pressure.

All phenomena which determine the absorption are also found in the reflection spectrum.

Luminescence, or emission of radiation, is the inverse process to absorption. It occurs mainly in connection with electron transitions from the conduction band into the valence band. Its spectrum consists of one or more peaks centered at the band gap and can provide additional information about the parameters of the band model. The excess electrons are introduced into the conduction band either by high-energy radiation (photoluminescence) or by electrical injection (electroluminescence).

In this chapter we will consider first the transitions between different bands and then the interaction of the light with the free carriers and finally with the lattice vibrations. The results will be used in Chapter

9 to sketch a quantitative picture of the band structure of the most important III-V compounds.

31 Band-to-Band Transitions

310 The absorption edge. The most important semiconductor parameter which can be determined from optical measurements is the "width of the forbidden energy gap E_G," namely, the energy difference between the top of the valence band and the bottom of the conduction band. Since E_G is the *minimum* energy for the transition of an electron from the valence band into the conduction band, the absorption spectrum is characterized by a strong increase of the absorption coefficient at $\hbar\omega = E_G$. Details of the band structure near the band extrema are determined from the position and shape of this "absorption edge" and from its dependence on temperature, magnetic field, pressure, impurity concentration, and other parameters. Table 3.1 is a survey of the position of the absorption edge of the most important III-V compounds. The values are those at which, arbitrarily, the absorption constant is 10 cm^{-1}. The values at $T = 0°K$ are extrapolated from measurements at two different temperatures with the assumption of a constant temperature coefficient dE_G/dT.

For a more exact analysis of the absorption edge it must first be

Table 3.1 Typical Values of the Width of the Forbidden Gap and Its Temperature Dependence for the Most Important III-V Compounds

The values are determined from the position of the absorption edge. The experimental values of the temperature dependence apply only to the region between 80 and 300°K. For a more detailed discussion and for literature references, see Section 313.

Compound	$E_G(T)$ (eV)	$E_G(300°K)$ (eV)
InSb	$0.25 - 2.8 \times 10^{-4}T$	0.167
InAs	$0.44 - 2.8 \times 10^{-4}T$	0.35
InP	$1.41 - 4.6 \times 10^{-4}T$	1.26
GaSb	$0.78 - 3.5 \times 10^{-4}T$	0.67
GaAs	$1.53 - 5.0 \times 10^{-4}T$	1.35
GaP	$2.40 - 5.5 \times 10^{-4}T$	2.24
AlSb	$1.7 - 3.5 \times 10^{-4}T$	1.6

determined whether the transitions are direct or indirect, that is it is necessary to know the location of the band extrema in the Brillouin zone. Information about the extrema can be deduced from the pressure dependence of the absorption edge, which will therefore be discussed first. Furthermore, it must be ascertained whether the transitions at energy E_G are at all possible, that is, whether there are states occupied with electrons at the top of the valence band and empty states at the bottom of the conduction band, and whether the selection rules permit these transitions. We will consider this topic in a subsequent section and only after that analyze the shape of the absorption edge in III-V compounds more exactly.

311 Pressure dependence of the absorption edge. When hydrostatic pressure is applied to a solid its electrical and optical properties change. The pressure decreases the lattice constant and thus changes the band structure. We will distinguish two effects, energy changes of the bands relative to each other and distortions of the individual bands. Changing the relative positions of the bands will influence all the properties which are determined by transitions between bands, such as the location of the absorption edges and the distribution of the electrons among the bands and the impurity states (position of the Fermi level, intrinsic carrier concentration). The deformation of individual bands changes the density of states and thereby the effective mass of the charge carriers.

In this section we will consider only the pressure dependence of the optical properties of the III-V compounds, primarily the shift of the absorption edge with pressure. The change of electrical properties with pressure will be discussed in Section 414.

There is one problem where a study of the pressure dependence of the absorption edge can make a particularly important contribution. This is the question of how the conduction band of the III-V compounds is divided into subbands of different symmetry. We know from Chapter 2 that the conduction band of the group IV elements is composed of three subbands with possible minima in the Brillouin zone at $\mathbf{k} = 0$ (Γ), along the [111]-axes (Λ or L), and along the [100]-axes (Δ or X). For germanium and silicon the energy difference between subbands is so large that only one of them is occupied with electrons under equilibrium conditions, namely, in silicon the (100)-subband and in germanium the (111)-subband. The existence of the higher-lying subbands is known (aside from their appearance in the theoretical calculations of the band structure) from magneto-optical studies, from the optical absorption, and, primarily, from the study of the mixed crystals Si_xGe_{1-x}. In the last study it is found that the separation of the (111)-subband from the valence band increases faster with increasing x than the separation of the (100)-subband from the valence band. Consequently, the two subband edges coincide at 15 atomic % Si; at lower silicon concentrations the (111)-minimum lies lower, at higher silicon concentration the (100)-minimum. Pressure studies have shown that the change of position of the subband edges with respect to the valence band with increasing pressure is characteristically different for the three subbands. In germanium the pressure coefficient $(dE_G/dP)_T$ is found to be 12×10^{-6} eV/kg cm^{-2} for the (000)-minimum, 5×10^{-6} eV/kg cm^{-2} for the (111)-minimum, and -2×10^{-6} eV/kg cm^{-2} for the (100)-minimum. The coefficients are of the same order of magnitude for silicon.

Now it appears, according to the theoretical considerations of Chapter 2, that the general outline of the band structure is the same in the III-V compounds as in the group IV elements. The valence bands are the same except for small differences, and the conduction bands can differ only in a different relative position of the subbands. We will see, furthermore, that the measured pressure coefficients in the III-V compounds fall into three groups whose values are identical with the ones given above for germanium. We can suspect that the three subbands have characteristic pressure coefficients independent of the compound, and use this hypothesis to identify the subbands (61P6).

We will now list the experimental results on the III-V compounds and discuss them according to this hypothesis.

Aluminum Antimonide. Edwards and Drickamer (61E1) measured the shift of the absorption edge with pressures up to 50,000 kg/cm^2 and found a pressure coefficient of -1.6×10^{-6} eV/kg cm^{-2}. Since there are at present no other guide points to the nature of the conduction band of AlSb, this measurement can be taken as a first indication that the lowest minimum of the conduction band lies along the [100]-axis.

Gallium Phosphide. Edwards, Slykhouse, and Drickamer (59E3) measured a pressure coefficient of -1.7×10^{-6} eV/kg cm^{-2} for the lowest-lying band [(100)?] and found indications of another slightly higher-lying subband. Measurements of Zallen (61P6) confirmed the value of the pressure coefficient.

Zallen and Paul (64Z1) deduced the following energy differences from the pressure dependence of several absorption peaks and edges in GaP:

$$\Gamma_{15} \text{ (valence band)} \rightarrow X_1 \text{ (conduction band): } 2.2 \text{ eV}$$
$$\rightarrow \Gamma_1 \text{ (conduction band): } 2.8 \text{ eV}$$
$$\rightarrow \Gamma_{15} \text{ (conduction band): } 3.7 \text{ eV}$$

and a gap in the conduction band at X, of $X_3 - X_1 = 0.3$ eV.

Gallium Arsenide. Two separate regions must be distinguished in the pressure dependence. Figure 3.1 shows the measurements of Edwards, Slykhouse, and Drickamer (59E3). Below 60,000 kg/cm^2, $dE_G/dP = 9.4 \times 10^{-6}$ eV/kg cm^{-2}; above that value it is -8.7×10^{-6} eV/kg cm^{-2}. According to Paul and Warschauer, the pressure coefficient at small pressures is 12×10^{-6} eV/kg cm^{-2} (61P6). In emission measurements from p-n junctions (cf. Section 74) Feinleib, Groves, Paul, and Zallen (63F2) observed a pressure coefficient of 11×10^{-6} eV/kg cm^{-2}, and Fenner (63F3) a value of 10.9×10^{-6} eV/kg cm^{-2}.

We must consequently assume the appearance of two subbands, one with a (000-) minimum which at ordinary pressures lies lower, and a higher-lying (100)-band.

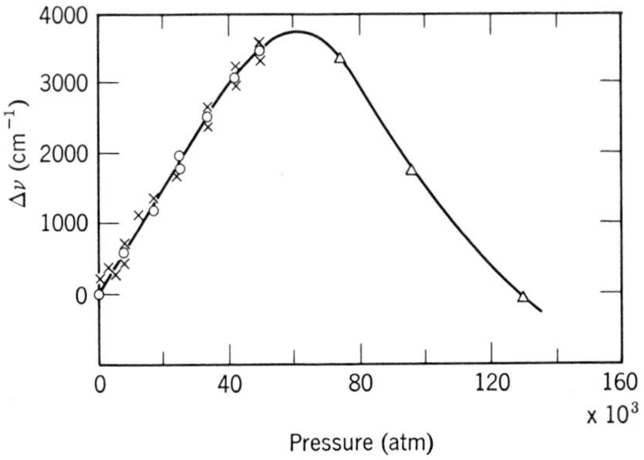

Fig. 3.1 Shift of the absorption edge in GaAs with hydrostatic pressure [after Edwards, Slykhouse, and Drickamer (59E3)].

Gallium Antimonide. The following values of pressure coefficients are given by Edwards and Drickamer (61E1):

$$
\begin{aligned}
dE_G/dP &= 12 \times 10^{-6}\ \text{eV/kg cm}^{-2} \text{ for } P < 18{,}000\ \text{kg/cm}^2 \\
&= 7.3 \times 10^{-6}\ \text{eV/kg cm}^{-2} \text{ for } 18{,}000\ \text{kg/cm}^2 < P < 45{,}000\ \text{kg/cm}^2 \\
&= \text{negative} \quad \text{for } P > 45{,}000\ \text{kg/cm}^2
\end{aligned}
$$

Taylor (58T1) finds a similar value in the low-pressure range (15.7×10^{-6} eV/kg cm^{-2}).

It appears that in GaSb all three subbands must be considered. At normal pressures the (000)-band lies lowest, followed by a (111)-band and finally by a (100)-band.

Indium Antimonide. There are no measurements of the pressure dependence of the absorption edge for InSb. However, the pressure dependence of E_G was determined from measurements of the conductivity of intrinsic InSb by Keyes (55K3) and Long (55L2). We will not consider the pressure dependence of the electrical properties until Chapter 4, but we include the results for InSb at this point for comparison. Keyes and Long found pressure coefficients of 15.5 and 14.2×10^{-6} eV/kg cm^{-2}, respectively, and no indications of more than one subband. Paul (61P6) has confirmed this result for pressures up to 30,000 kg/cm^2. This means that InSb has only one important subband with minimum at $\mathbf{k} = 0$.

Indium Arsenide. Taylor (58T1) found a pressure coefficient of 8.5×10^{-6} eV/kg cm^{-2} from optical measurements, while Edwards and Drickamer (61E1) obtained a value of 4.8×10^{-6} eV/kg cm^{-2} below 20,000 kg/cm^2 and 3.2×10^{-6} eV/kg cm^{-2} between 20,000 and 50,000 kg/cm^2. These values at first glance predict a (111)-minimum. This is contradicted by the decrease of the pressure coefficient at 20,000 kg/cm^2, which rather points to a transition from an originally lower-lying (000)-minimum to a subsequently dominating (111)-minimum. We will see later that the properties of InAs are the same as those of InSb over a wide range, and consequently a (000)-minimum is indicated. The electrons in both InSb and InAs have very small effective masses. Thus even relatively pure samples are degenerate, and therefore the absorption edge lies at an energy larger than E_G (cf. Section 312). This means that, aside from the pressure dependence of E_G, that of the effective mass must also be considered, and the pressure dependence of E_G can differ from that of the absorption edge.

Indium Phosphide. The pressure-coefficient value of 4.6×10^{-6} eV/kg cm^{-2} given by Edwards and Drickamer (61E1) points to a (111)-minimum. However, we will see later that here also a (000)-minimum of the conduction band is more likely.

The pressure coefficient reverses sign above 40,000 kg/cm^2 and takes on the unusually high value of -10×10^{-6} eV/kg cm^{-2} (61E1). This means that at 0.7 eV above the lowest conduction band there is a further (100)-band.

The pressure coefficients are summarized in Table 3.2. The hypothesis of constant values of the three pressure coefficients through-

Table 3.2 Pressure Coefficients of the Three Conduction-Band Minima of Germanium (Relative to the Top of the Valence Band) and Pressure Coefficients of the Absorption Edge of the Main III-V Compounds

Material	$(dE_G/dP)_T$ (10^{-6} eV/kg cm^{-2})	Pressure Range (kg/cm^2)	Minimum Assigned to That Pressure Range
Ge	5		(111)
	12		(000)
	~ −2		(100)
InSb	{15.5, 14.2}	<30,000	(000) (obtained from conductivity measurements)
InAs	{8.5, 4.8}	<20,000	(000) (assignment is not clearcut)
	3.2	>20,000	(111)
InP	4.6	<40,000	(111) or (000) (assignment is not clearcut)
	−10	>40,000	(100)
GaSb	12	<18,000	(000)
	7.3	18,000–45,000	(111)
	Negative	>45,000	(100)
GaAs	{9.4, 12}	<60,000	(000)
	−8.7	>60,000	(100)
GaP	−1.7	<50,000	(100)
AlSb	−1.6	<50,000	(100)

out the semiconductors of group IV and the III-V compounds has already given us significant indications of the conduction-band structure of the most important III-V compounds. The appearance of a number of subbands in some of the III-V compounds supports this hypothesis. Further evidence is the fact that, analogously to the sequence silicon, germanium, α-tin, the (000)-minima increase in importance in the compounds with high atomic mass, while in those with low-mass components the (100)-minima determine the semiconductor properties. We see also that, in the transition from a semiconducting element of group IV of the periodic system to its isoelectronic compound (α-Sn $\rightarrow$ InSb, Ge $\rightarrow$ GaAs, etc.), the position of the (000)-minimum relative to the valence band increases more slowly than that of the (111)- and (100)-minima. We will test these results in the following sections and be able to confirm them in most cases. For a more detailed discussion of the results presented in this section we refer to the work of Paul (61P6).

312 Effect of the free-charge carriers on the absorption edge. We have assumed, up to now, that the position of the absorption edge is determined by the separation of the highest state of the valence band from the lowest state of the conduction band. This is true only if transitions between these states are possible, that is, if there are electrons at the upper edge of the valence band and unoccupied states at the bottom of the conduction band.

Consider a degenerate n-type semiconductor. Here the Fermi level E_F lies within the conduction band and unoccupied states exist only above an energy about $(E_F - 4kT)$. Optical transitions are then possible only above the energy $\hbar\omega = E_F - 4kT - E_v$. A more exact estimate of the lower limit for direct transitions is obtained if one notices that the transition must take place under conservation of the electron wave vector:

$$\hbar\omega \geqslant E_{G,\mathrm{opt}} = E_c + \frac{\hbar^2k^2}{2m_n} - E_v - \frac{\hbar^2k^2}{2m_p}$$

$$= E_G + (E_F - 4kT - E_c)\left(1 + \frac{m_n}{m_p}\right) \quad (3.3)$$

Similar considerations can be made for degenerate p-semiconductors.

This effect will be important for semiconductors with small effective mass of the charge carriers, since then the density of states is small, and degeneracy appears already at small doping. In such cases we can expect a displacement of the absorption edge to shorter wavelengths with increasing doping.

A dependence of $E_{G,\text{opt}}$ on doping was first found by Tanenbaum and Briggs (53T2) in n-InSb, and interpreted by Burstein (54B8). Quantitative measurements of Hrostowski, Wheatley, and Flood (54H4) showed an increase of $E_{G,\text{opt}}$ with increasing doping from a starting value of 0.18 eV up to 0.5 eV at $n = 10^{19}$ cm^{-3}. A similar, somewhat smaller, "Burstein shift" has been found for InAs (54H4), (54B5), (55K1) (cf. Fig. 3.4), GaAs (63K4), and other III-V-compounds.

A strong doping can also lead to a *decrease* of the width of the optical energy gap. The impurity energy levels, which are discrete at small concentration, coalesce with increasing doping to an impurity band which finally, above a certain limiting value, overlaps the free-carrier band. According to Stern and Dixon (59S12), this takes place at

$$n_{\text{imp}} \geqslant 3 \times 10^{23} \left(\frac{m^*}{m\kappa}\right)^3 \text{cm}^{-3} \tag{3.4}$$

where m^* is the effective mass, and κ the dielectric constant. Under this condition $E_{G,\text{opt}}$ is decreased by the width of the impurity band. One easily calculates an impurity-band width of 0.047 eV for InSb and one of 0.062 eV for InAs, at $n_{\text{imp}} = 10^{19}$ cm^{-3}.

This effect can be observed only if the donors and acceptors exactly compensate each other. Only then is the concentration of free-charge carriers in the bands not changed by the doping, and no Burstein shift appears.

Figure 3.2 shows the measurements of Stern and Dixon on InAs.

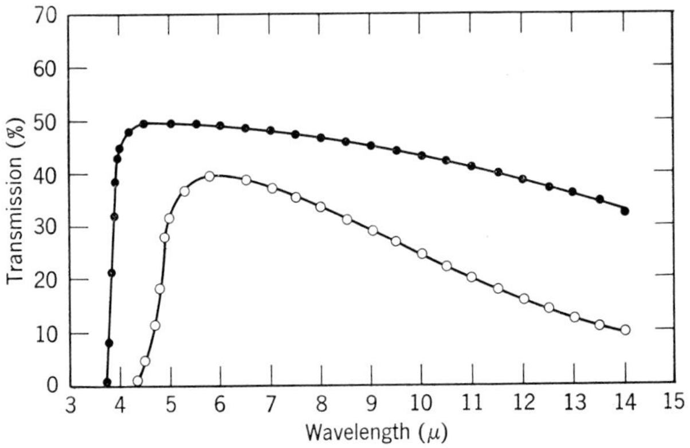

Fig. 3.2 Optical transmission of two samples of InAs. Solid points: relatively pure sample with $n = n_D = 4 \times 10^{16}$ cm^{-3}; open circles: strongly compensated sample with $n = 9 \times 10^{15}$ cm^{-3} and $n_D = 5 \times 10^{18}$ cm^{-3} [after Stern and Dixon (59S12)].

The shift of the absorption edge with increasing doping can be seen clearly. The value of $\Delta E_{G,\mathrm{opt}} = 0.07$ eV, determined from this shift, agrees well with the model developed above.

Similar observations have been made on other III-V compounds, e.g., on InAs [Talley and Enright (54T1), Stern and Talley (55S2), Dixon and Ellis (61D3)], InSb [Roberts and Quarrington (55R2)], InP [Newman (58N3)], and GaAs [absorption: Braunstein *et al.* (63B14), Turner and Reese (64T4), and Hill (64H5); photoluminescence: Nathan *et al.* (62N10),(63N6)].

313 Transitions from the valence band to the conduction band. The shape of the absorption edge is determined by the nature of the optical transitions between the upper edge of the valence band and the lower edge of the conduction band. If both band extrema lie at the same point in the Brillouin zone, *direct* transitions (with approximate conservation of the electron wave vector) are possible. These can be separated into "allowed" and "forbidden" transitions, depending on whether the dipole matrix element which determines the transition probability exists or vanishes in first approximation. The absorption constant is proportional to

$$K \sim (\hbar\omega - \Delta E)^{\gamma} \tag{3.5}$$

where ΔE is the smallest energy difference between the initial and final states, and γ takes on the value of $\frac{1}{2}$ for allowed transitions and $\frac{3}{2}$ for forbidden transitions.

When the band extrema lie at different $\mathbf{k}$ values, only *indirect* transitions with phonon participation are possible between them. The absorption constant is composed of two terms which describe the two possible processes, "direct transition of the electron + absorption or emission of a phonon." Equation (3.5) is replaced by

$$K = K_+ + K_-, \quad K_\pm \sim (\hbar\omega - \Delta E \pm k\theta)^2 \tag{3.6}$$

where $k\theta$ is the phonon energy.

Dumke (58D2) has shown that indirect transitions are also possible between band extrema with the same wave-number vector. In that case the electron first makes a virtual transition to an intermediate state in the conduction band and then transfers to the final state by absorption of a low-wave-number phonon. The process is important when the absorbed phonon is an optical one, since these transitions are then separated in energy from the simultaneously allowed direct transitions.

The shape of the absorption edge can also be changed, particularly in its long-wavelength tail by other, independent processes, such as absorption by free-charge carriers, transitions within the valence or conduction bands, and exciton formation.

The absorption edge of **InSb** is characterized by a very steep behavior at high energies and a shallower extension at lower energies. The steep absorption dependence for $K > 100\ \text{cm}^{-1}$ can be interpreted as due to direct transitions. Deductions of the width of the forbidden gap after eq. (3.5) fluctuate between 0.167 and 0.185 eV (53T2), (54O2), (55K1), (56F1). The temperature coefficient is about -2.8×10^{-4} eV/°K (54A2), (55O1), (55K1). Kane (57K2) analyzed the absorption curves of Fan and Gobeli with his $(\mathbf{k} \cdot \mathbf{p})$ theory and found quantitative agreement if he assumed the effective mass of the electrons at the bottom of the nonparabolic conduction band to have the value 0.013 m. Other careful measurements of the absorption edge in InSb have been made by Roberts and Quarrington (55R2) and Moss (56M4).

The dependence in the region of weak absorption suggests the appearance of indirect transitions. Blount, Callaway, Cohen, Dumke, and Philipps (56B1) were able to quantitatively interpret room-temperature absorption measurements, assuming two indirect transitions with optical phonon participation. Potter (56P3) showed later, however, that this analysis is not unambiguous and that the curves can also be interpreted as due to a transition with participation of two optical and two acoustical phonons. Both possibilities require a minimum of the conduction band at $\mathbf{k} = 0$ and valence-band maxima along the [111]-axes, as is to be expected from symmetry considerations of the band model of InSb. A quantitative agreement can be obtained, however, only if the minima of the valence band are assumed to lie far away from the center of the Brillouin zone. This is contrary to other experimental results. We will see later that it is much more likely that the maxima of the valence band lie close to $\mathbf{k} = 0$ in InSb. The problem was resolved by Dumke (58D2), who was able to show that the absorption edge could be explained quantitatively by his previously mentioned theory of indirect transitions between two band extrema which lie at the same point $(\mathbf{k} = 0)$. The comparison of his theory with the experimental curves is shown in Fig. 3.3.

Consequently, the shape of the absorption edge in InSb does not explain the location of the band extrema in InSb unambiguously, but neither does it contradict other experimental facts. Later measurements of Kurnick and Powell (59K5) confirmed Dumke's interpretation in its main points but also showed that the theory is not able to

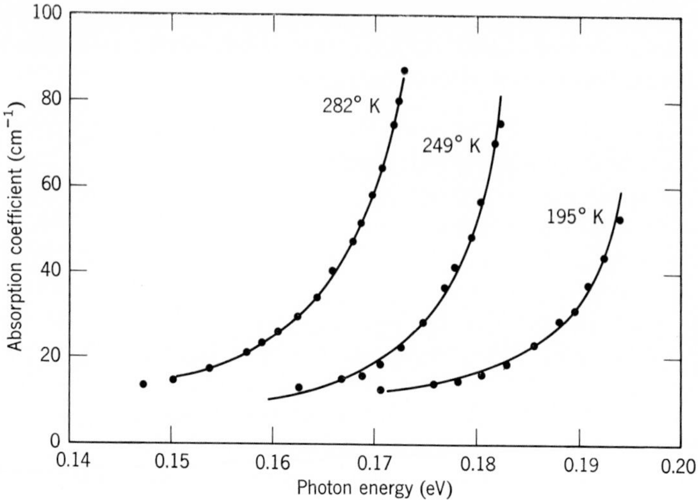

Fig. 3.3 Comparison of the experimental results on the shape of the absorption edge in InSb [Roberts and Quarrington (55R2)] with Dumke's theory (58D2). The theoretical curves have been calulated assuming $m_p/m_n = 5$ and a Debye temperature of 290°K.

explain all the details, particularly the dependence of the absorption edge on temperature and acceptor concentration. The strong dependence of the absorption edge on donor density (Burstein shift) was discussed in Section 312.

The most detailed discussion of the shape of the absorption edge in **InAs** was given by Dixon and Ellis (61D3). Figure 3.4 shows the measurements on three n-type samples of different doping. Whereas the absorption constant of the purest sample falls off sharply, the corresponding fall-off in the other two cases is much more gradual and is displaced to higher energies (Burstein shift).

This dependence is easily interpreted qualitatively. In the purest sample the Fermi level lies below the conduction band. The density of the unoccupied states, into which transitions from the valence band can take place, increases sharply with increasing energy. In the two other samples the Fermi level lies in the conduction band, and the density of unoccupied states grows only slowly with increasing energy, starting at about $(E_F - 4kT)$.

Since the extrema of the valence and conduction bands lie at $\mathbf{k} = 0$ in InAs (except for the small spin splitting of the V_1-band), direct transitions are possible. Equation (3.5) cannot be used for the interpretation, since it applies only for parabolic bands. The expected absorption dependence according to Kane's theory was calculated by Stern (61S12). His results are compared with experiment in Fig. 3.5. The excellent agreement confirms the applicability of Kane's theory to InAs with resulting values of the energy gap at room temperature, $E_G = 0.35$ eV, and of the effective mass at the edge of the conduction band, $m_n = (0.024 \pm 0.003)\ m$.

At low absorption values the absorption edge shows a distinct departure from the expected dependence. The data can be described by an exponential law. Similar observations have also been made on InSb (59K5). This behavior has not yet been satisfactorily

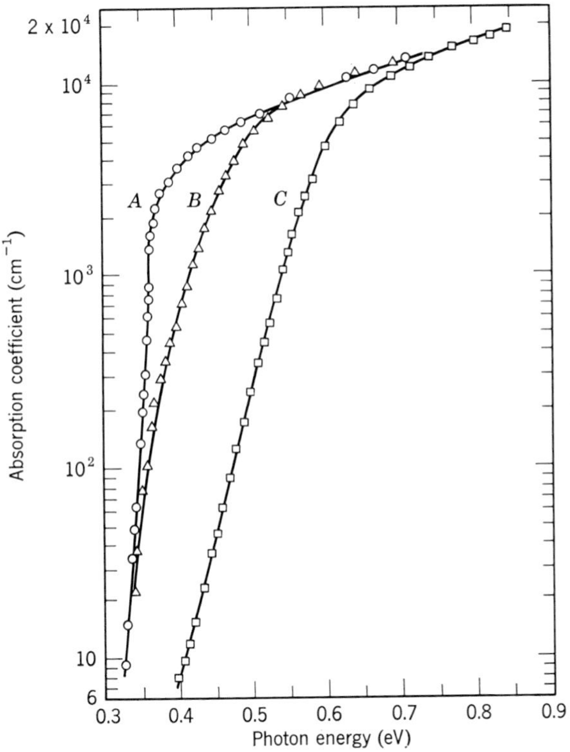

Fig. 3.4 Absorption edge for three samples of n-InAs with different electron concentrations: $A: n = 3.6 \times 10^{16}$ cm^{-3}; $B: n = 6.0 \times 10^{17}$ cm^{-3}; $C: n = 3.8 \times 10^{18}$ cm^{-3} [after Dixon and Ellis (61D3)].

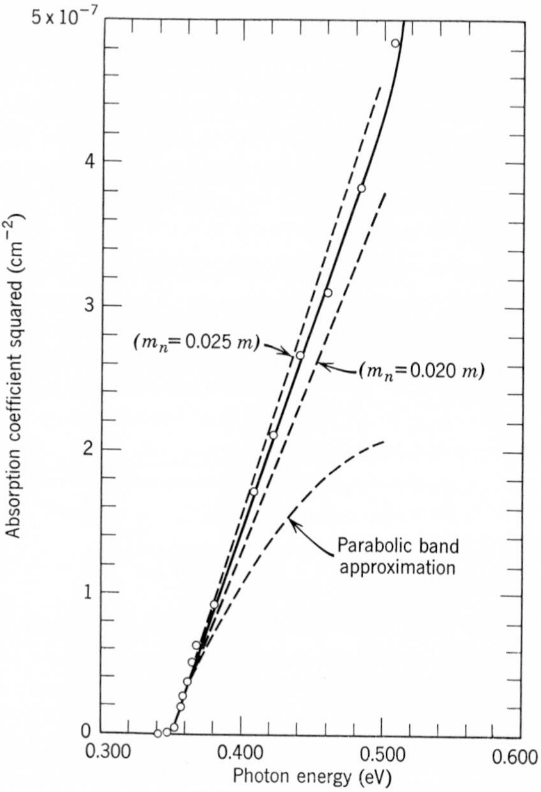

Fig. 3.5 Comparison of the high-absorption part of the absorption edge in InAs with Kane's theory: experimental values (full line and circles) by Dixon and Ellis (61D3), theoretical values (broken lines) calculated by Stern (61S12).

explained. It may be due to transitions into an impurity band which overlaps with the conduction band (cf. 58M3).

The temperature coefficient of the absorption edge is constant between room temperature and 80°K, $(-2.8 \pm 0.1) \times 10^{-4}$ eV/°K. It decreases below 80°K and leads to a 0°K value of E_G of about 0.425 eV, while a linear extrapolation gives 0.44 eV. Other measurements of the InAs absorption edge have been given by Hrostowski and Tanenbaum (54H5), Oswald (55O1), Stern and Talley (55S2), Spitzer and Fan (57S3), and Matossi (58M3). The values for E_G vary from 0.31 to 0.36 eV; those for the temperature coefficient, from -2.5×10^{-4} to -4.5×10^{-4} eV/°K.

Mooradian and Fan (64M2) found in the photoluminescence of n-InAs several emission lines which they ascribe to the recombination of electrons and holes at different impurities.

Fewer measurements are available for **InP** (54O1), (54O2), (55O1), (58N3). The absorption edge is very steep and suggests direct transitions. Quantitative agreement cannot be obtained with eq. (3.5). Oswald (55O1) gives a room-temperature value of the forbidden zone, $E_G = 1.26$ eV, and a temperature coefficient of -4.6×10^{-4} eV/°K.

Accurate measurements of photoluminescence have been made on n- and p-InP. Turner and Pettit (63T4) observed a number of different emission lines at 6°K. Four lines can be ascribed to the recombination of electron-hole pairs at a shallow impurity level with the simultaneous emission of zero, one, two, or three optical phonons, two bands are caused by recombination at unknown impurity states, and one line, at 1.416 eV, must be caused by exciton recombination. It follows that E_G at 6°K is larger than or equal to 1.416 eV. Similar results were found at 77°K, where $E_G \geqslant 1.409$ eV.

The absorption edge of **GaSb** is very steep at high values of the absorption constant and again shows a shallower fall-off at low values. Measurements of Oswald and Schade (54O2), Blunt, Hosler, and Frederikse (54B2), and Roberts and Quarrington (55R2) give values of E_G between 0.67 and 0.70 eV at room temperature and temperature coefficients between -2.9×10^{-4} and -3.5×10^{-4} eV/°K. Roberts and Quarrington conclude from their measurements that the transitions are indirect, while Ramdas and Fan (58R1) ascribe the absorption dependence for $K > 100$ cm^{-1} to direct transitions. We have seen in Section 312 that the pressure measurements on GaSb suggest that, slightly above a conduction band with minimum at $\mathbf{k} = 0$, there is another subband with extrema along the [111]-axes. Using this model, Becker, Ramdas, and Fan (61B7) interpret measurements of the absorption edge which are reproduced in Fig. 3.6. Curve 1 represents measurements on a p-type sample at room temperature, while curves 2,3, and 4 come from p-type samples at 80°K. Curves 5 and 6 are the absorption of two degenerate n-doped crystals of different donor concentrations at 4.2°K. They show a clearly noticeable Burstein effect. The magnitude of the shift of the purer sample determines an effective mass, m_n, of 0.052 m. The shift of the absorption edge of the more impure samples is considerably less than theoretically predicted. Quantitative agreement can be obtained if one assumes that the bottom of the (111)-subband lies 0.08 eV above the

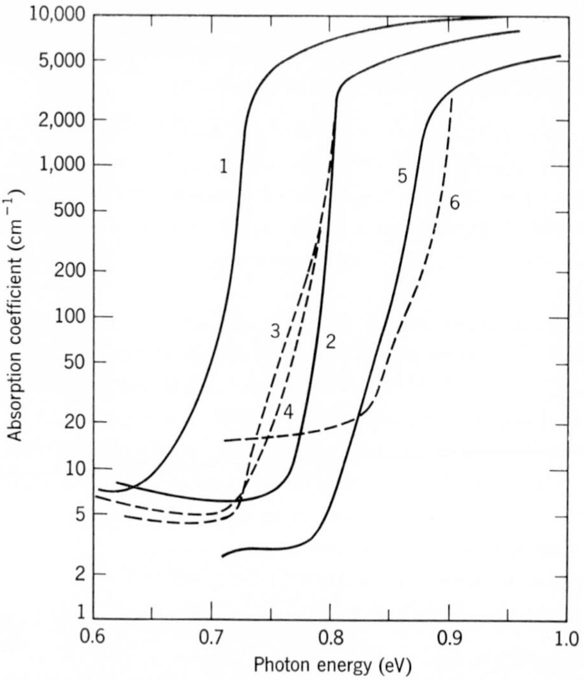

Fig. 3.6 Absorption edge of four *p*-type (1–4) and two *n*-type (5,6) samples of GaSb at different temperatures [after Becker, Ramdas, and Fan (61B7)].

bottom of the (000)-subband (this follows from galvanomagnetic measurements of Becker and co-workers which will be considered in Chapter 4). Thus the Fermi level in the impure samples lies in the (111)-subband and moves only slowly to higher energies with increasing doping.

The *p*-type samples show a steeply increasing absorption edge which indicates direct transitions at $\mathbf{k} = 0$ and gives the following values for the energy gap:

$$E_G = 0.725 \text{ eV at } T = 300°\text{K}$$
$$0.80 \text{ eV at } T = 80°\text{K}$$
$$0.81 \text{ eV at } T = 4.2°\text{K}$$

The shallow tail at low absorption suggests indirect transitions at an energy 0.08 eV less than that of the direct transitions. This can be explained either by valence-band maxima which lie 0.08 eV higher than the $\mathbf{k} = 0$ energy value, or by transitions to impurity states which lie above the valence band by this energy. Since the first possibility is in disagreement with the theoretical considerations of Chapter 2, the second interpretation is more likely.

Exciton lines have been observed in GaSb by Johnson and Fan (62J1). At 1.7°K these lines lie at 0.8100, 0.8049, and 0.7960 eV.

A few measurements of the absorption edge of **GaAs** are available. Barrie, Cunnell, Edmond, and Ross (54B1) report a room-temperature value of 1.35 eV for E_G; the temperature dependence of the absorption edge is, according to Oswald (55O1), $E_G = (1.53 - 5.0 \times 10^{-4}T)$ eV. The absorption increases very strongly above $K = 1000\ \text{cm}^{-1}$. Quantitative agreement with Kane's theory exists in this region, according to Moss (61M15), (62M12). For $K < 1000\ \text{cm}^{-1}$ the drop-off is shallower and not yet explained.

In degenerate p-type GaAs Kudman and Seidel (61K8), (62K9) observe a weak Burstein shift and an absorption dependence which corresponds to direct transitions. They obtain $E_G = (1.39 \pm 0.02)$ eV at room temperature.

The absorption edge of high-resistivity GaAs (cf. Section 532) shows a low-temperature structure which, according to Hobden and Sturge (61H13), (62S13), is to be ascribed to transitions from the valence band into free and bound exciton states. If this interpretation is accepted, the following values of the width of the forbidden zone (larger than the ones given above) are obtained:

$$E_G = (1.430 \pm 0.002)\ \text{eV at } 290°\text{K}$$

$$(1.510 \pm 0.001)\ \text{eV at } 77°\text{K}$$

$$(1.517 \pm 0.001)\ \text{eV at } 20°\text{K}$$

The corresponding exciton binding energies are 0.0025, 0.0027, and 0.0033 eV, respectively.

The spectral distribution of fluorescence in the band-gap region of GaAs was investigated carefully by Nathan and Burns (63N5). At 4.2°K they found sharp emission lines at (1.5154 ± 0.0005) eV, at (1.4919 ± 0.0005) eV, and at 0.037 and 0.074 eV below the latter value. Nathan and Burns assign the 1.5154-line to the recombination of a free exciton, the 1.4919-line to that of a bound exciton. The two remaining lines are then assigned to the same bound exciton, the separations of 0.037 and 0.074 eV corresponding to the energies of one and two longitudinal optical phonons taking part in the recombination. This interpretation is consistent with the results of the absorption measurement of Hobden and Sturge.

In the compounds discussed so far, InSb, InAs, InP, GaSb, and GaAs, we have found indications for direct transitions; hence the lowest conduction-band minimum must be assigned to the point $\mathbf{k} = 0$. In contrast, the absorption in GaP and AlSb has a much shallower dependence. According to the pressure investigations discussed in Section 311, we expect for these III-V compounds an anisotropic conduction band with minima along the (100)-axes. The absorption edge must therefore be similar to that of silicon. This is confirmed by experiment.

For **GaP** Spitzer, Gershenzon, Frosch, and Gibbs (59S7) find that eq. (3.6) applies with a slightly different value of the exponent, namely, 2.2. A very steep increase at high absorptions, which indicates transitions into the higher-lying (000)-band, will be considered in Section 314. The temperature dependence of the absorption edge is $E_G = (2.4 - 5.5 \times 10^{-4}T)$ eV, according to Folberth and Oswald (54F1), (55O1).

At low absorption the absorption edge of GaP shows a very distinct structure (Fig. 3.7). The flat shape of the edge in this region shows, first of all, that it is due to indirect transitions. The knees in the curve are, according to Gershenzon, Thomas, and Dietz (62G5), threshold energies for the formation of a free exciton with simultaneous emission of a characteristic phonon. The phonons [longi-

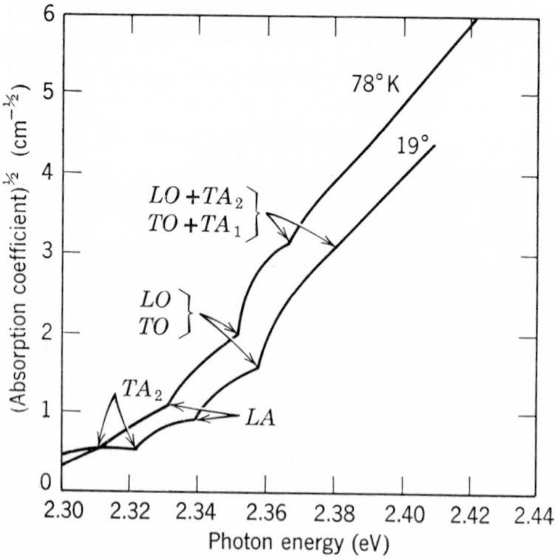

Fig. 3.7 Threshold energies for the formation of excitons with phonon emission in the absorption edge of GaP [after Gershenzon, Thomas, and Dietz (62G5)].

tudinal (L) and transverse (T), optical (O) and acoustical (A)] assigned to the various knees are indicated in Fig. 3.7. The energies assigned to these phonons are identical with those of the phonons making up the combination bands of the lattice vibrations (cf. Section 33).

Numerous, much sharper absorption lines have been observed in GaP just below the band edge. Some of these have also been found in fluorescent recombination radiation. Gershenzon, Thomas, Hopfield, and co-workers assign them to the formation of bound excitons with simultaneous phonon emission (61G21), (62G5), (63T1), (63Y1), (64N1) [cf. also (63G11)] and to donor-acceptor transitions (63H6), (64T1).

If the above interpretation of the low-temperature structure of the absorption edge is correct, the actual absorption edge is determined after subtraction of the exciton absorption. Gershenzon and co-workers find the result $E_G = (2.325 \pm 0.003 - 1.17 \times 10^{-6}T^2)$ eV. Near room temperature this law can be approximated by a linear dependence which has the same value as that given by Folberth and Oswald.

The absorption edge of **AlSb** lies at about 1.6 eV. Blunt, Frederikse, Becker, and Hosler (54B3) give a value $E_G = (1.7 - 3.5 \times 10^{-4}T)$ eV. Measurements of Turner and Reese (60T4) will be discussed in Section 314.

Measurement on thin films of **BP** by Stone and Hill (60S8) indicate a width of the forbidden zone of about 6 eV, but unambiguous results are not available.

For **GaN** and **AlN** Kauer and Rabenau (57K3) find $E_G = 3.25$ eV and $E_G > 5$ eV, respectively.

So far we have considered only that absorption edge which is due to transitions between extrema of the valence and conduction bands. We have drawn conclusions about the nature of the transitions and the location of the band extrema. However, measurements of the absorption due to transitions between valence and conduction band can also allow the determination of the structure of the bands at other points in the Brillouin zone and the relative position of the subbands within one of the bands.

Information about the *shape of the valence band* may be obtained from the band-to-band absorption of degenerate samples, where the Fermi level lies within one of the bands. Consider a semiconductor with isotropic conduction band and two valence bands which are degenerate at $\mathbf{k} = 0$ (Fig. 3.8). If the sample is n-type, the Fermi level lies in the conduction band (left half of Fig. 3.8). Direct band-to-band transitions take place only above an energy $\Delta E_1 > E_G$. The absorption edge is displaced to higher energies. Additional transitions from the V_2-band above ΔE_2 lead to an increased absorption. The measurement of the absorption coefficient consequently makes it possible to determine the energy difference, $\Delta E_1 - \Delta E_2$, and, if the bands are parabolic, the ratio of effective masses, m_{p2}/m_{p1}. When the Fermi level lies in the valence band (right half of Fig. 3.8), the absorption starts at ΔE_2 and increases once more discontinuously at ΔE_1. If the V_2-band has a large curvature, ΔE_2 is almost equal to E_G. The absorption edge is then not shifted by degeneracy.

Using such considerations, Gobeli and Fan (60G7) interpret the absorption measurements on **InSb**. Figure 3.9 shows measurements on degenerate p-InSb at 5°K. The absorption dependence confirms the foregoing considerations qualitatively. The increase of the absorption coefficient at the lower energies is due to the inter-valence-band transitions, which will be discussed in Section 314. The absorption edge is essentially independent of the hole concentration. However, the appearance of the ΔE_1-transitions takes place gradually. Gobeli and Fan interpret this deviation from the expected behavior by the anisotropic structure of the V_1-band. According to Kane's theory [eqs. (2.8)–(2.11)], the V_1-band (when splitting is neglected) is

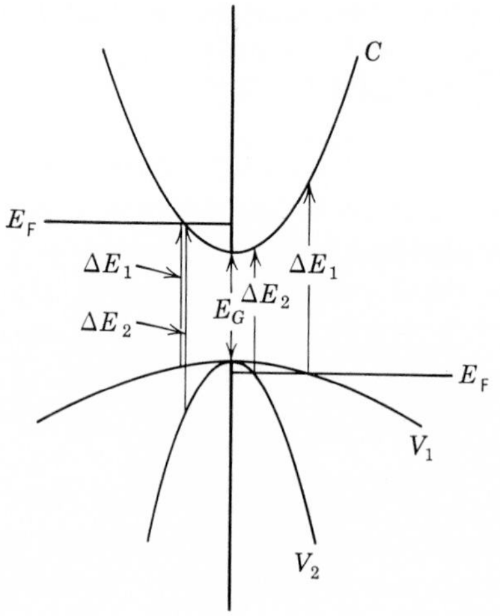

Fig. 3.8 Band model for an isotropic semiconductor with a single parabolic conduction band (C) and two at $\mathbf{k} = 0$ degenerate valence bands (V_1 and V_2). Fermi levels and optical transition thresholds are indicated for both degenerate n-type samples (left side) and degenerate p-type samples (right side).

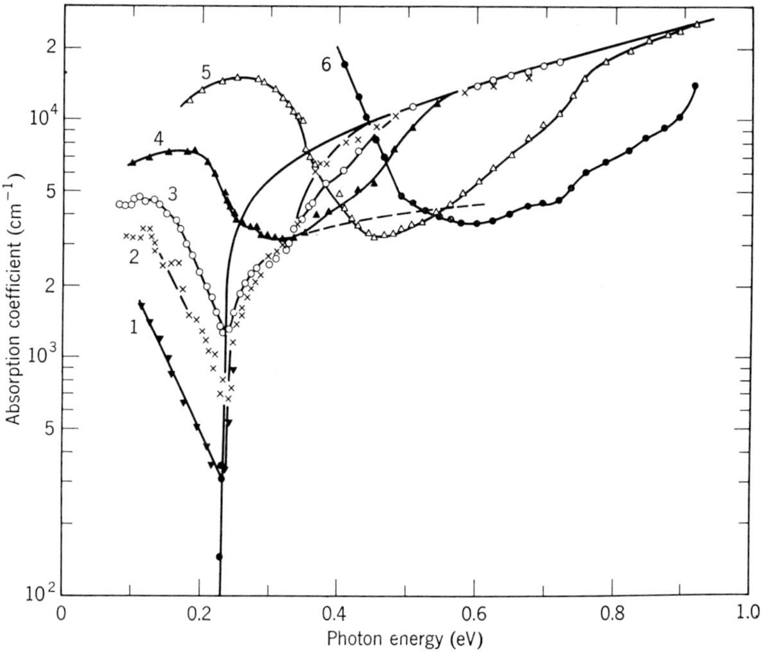

Fig. 3.9 Optical absorption in degenerate p-InSb at 5°K for six samples (1–6) with hole concentrations of 5.5×10^{17}, 9.0×10^{17}, 1.56×10^{18}, 2.6×10^{18}, 9.4×10^{18}, and 2.0×10^{19} cm^{-3} [after Gobeli and Fan (60G7)].

given by

$$E_{v1} = \frac{\hbar^2 k^2}{2m_{p1}} + b_1 s k^2 = \frac{\hbar^2 k^2}{2m_{p1}} [1 - \gamma(k_x{}^2 k_y{}^2 + k_y{}^2 k_z{}^2 + k_z{}^2 k_x{}^2)] \quad (3.7)$$

Here m_{p1} is the effective mass along the [100]-axes in the Brillouin zone, while the curvature along the [111]-axes is given by the effective mass $m'_{p1} = m_{p1}(1 - \gamma/3)^{-1}$. The transitions from the V_1-band to the conduction band therefore take place at different **k**-values, and the required energy lies between $\Delta E_1(111)$ and $\Delta E_1(100)$. The difference between these two energy values is $\Delta E = (E_v - E_F)(m'_{p1} - m_{p1})/m_n$. A quantitative fitting to the measured curves of Fig. 3.9 results in the values $m'_{p1}/m_{p1} = 3$, i.e., $\gamma = 2$.

For degenerate n-type samples Gobeli and Fan found the expected increase at the threshold of the ΔE_2-transitions of Fig. 3.8. They evaluated the effective masses of the holes in the V_2-band as $m_{p2} =$ 0.012 m.

All these measurements could be interpreted without including the spin splitting of the valence bands, indicating that its value is small for InSb.

Besides the transitions between the highest occupied state of the valence band and the lowest unoccupied state of the conduction band which determine the absorption edge, other characteristic transitions are possible. Such transitions appear at those points **k** in the Brillouin zone where $\text{grad}_k\,[E_c(\mathbf{k}) - E_v(\mathbf{k})] = 0$. The indices c and v refer to the conduction and valence bands. In germanium and silicon transitions at points L and X of the Brillouin zone are known. Reflection peaks in the range between 1 and 20 eV have been identified in these semiconductors as L-transitions between the highest state of the valence band (L_3', cf. Fig. 2.3) and the two lowest subbands of the conduction band (L_1 and L_3). Other transitions have been demonstrated to take place at point X between the valence and conduction bands (X_4 to X_1) and at point Γ from the upper edge of the valence band into a higher-lying subband of the conduction band ($\Gamma_{25'}$ to Γ_{15}). Considering the spin-orbit splittings of point L_3 and L_3', the L_3'-L_1-transitions are doublets and the L_3'-L_3-transitions quartets. Phillips and Liu (62P6) have shown, however, that in germanium, silicon, and the III-V compounds the L_3-splitting must be small compared to the L_3'-splitting. In that case again only two lines are expected at the L_3'-L_3-transition. None of the other transitions are split up.

According to the theoretical considerations of Chapter 2 (especially Fig. 2.4), we expect the same transitions in the III-V compounds, except that the X-transition is also split because of lower symmetry of the zinc-blende lattice.

Figure 3.10 shows measurements of Ehrenreich, Philipp, and Phillips (62E4) which confirm these expectations. Several transitions have also been identified by Tauc and Abrahám (61T1), Tauc and Antončik (60T1), Cardona (61C4), (61C5), Stern (61S13), Zallen, Paul, and Tauc (62Z1), Tauc (62T1), Phillips (62P7), and Greenaway (62G10) [for reflection measurements between 0 and 6 eV see also Morrison (61M13)].

The energies of the transitions identified for germanium and some of the III-V compounds are listed in Table 3.3. In the literature these transitions are labeled the same way in the III-V compounds as in germanium; for example, a L_3-L_1-transition (cf. Fig. 2.4) is labeled L_3'-L_1. The notation is still used when spin-orbit splitting is included, even though the two components should then be labeled the L_6-L_6- and the $(L_4 + L_5)$-L_6-transition according to Fig. 2.4d.

The table shows strong similarities of the III-V compounds among each other and to germanium, which were already noticed in Fig. 3.10. The values in the table were deduced from reflection measurements. Cardona and Harbeke (62C2), (63C4) have confirmed some of the values in transmission measurements.

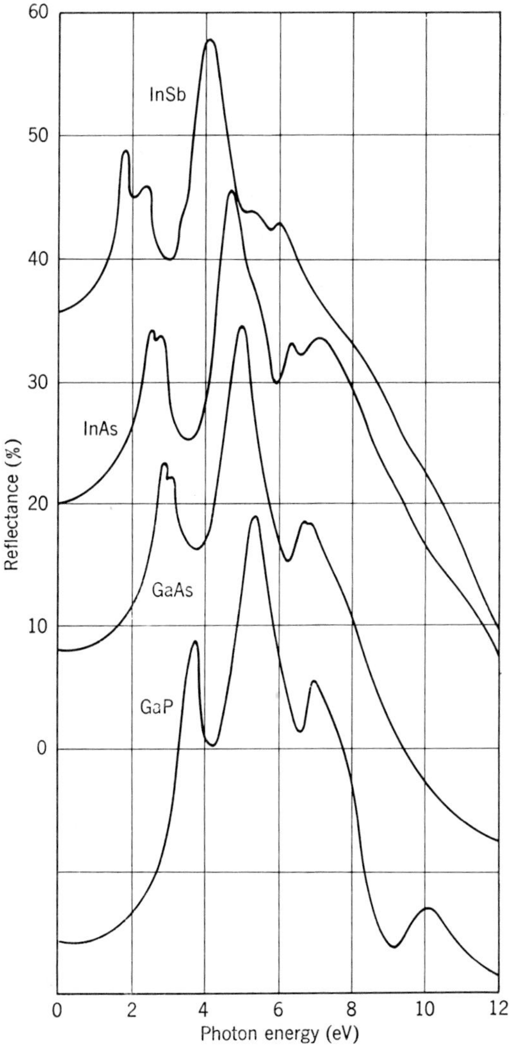

Fig. 3.10 Reflectance of several III-V compounds at room temperature [after Ehrenreich, Philipp, and Phillips (62E4)].

Table 3.3 Characteristic Energies of Transitions from the Valence Band into the Conduction Band of Germanium and of III-V Compounds

The first two groups of transitions take place from the spin-orbit-split highest valence band at L (L_3') to the lowest and next-highest conduction bands at L (cf. Fig. 2.4). They therefore each have two maxima which differ by the spin-orbit splitting. The third group corresponds to transitions from the highest valence band at X into the lowest states in the conduction band (which are degenerate for germanium). The last column gives the transition energy from the top of the V_1-band to a higher subband of the conduction band at Γ. The values in brackets are uncertain. For the temperature dependence of some of these transitions see Lukeš and Schmidt (62L8) and Cardona and Harbeke (63C4).

Material	L_3'-L_1	L_3'-L_3	X_4-X_1	Γ_{25}'-Γ_{15}
Ge	2.1[a] 2.3[a]	5.9[g] 6.1[g]	4.4[a]	3.1[g]
InSb	1.8[e] 2.3[e] 1.82[f] 2.38[f] 1.87[h] 2.45[h] 1.835[i] 2.35[i]	5.3[g] 6.0[g]	4.13[f] 4.20[h] 4.70[h] 4.095[l]	3.4[g] (2.8[h]) 3.45[h]
InAs	2.5[e] 2.85[e,h] 2.53[f] 2.82[f] 2.48[l] 2.745[l]	6.4[g] 7.0[g]	(4.4)[i] 4.72[f] 4.83[h] 5.30[h]	5.2[g] 4.63[h] 3.9[m]
InP	3.15[d] 3.29[d] 3.2[c] 3.36[c]	6.9[m]	5.0[d,c]	4.1[m]
GaSb	2.00[f] 2.48[f,k] 2.08[h] 2.55[h] 1.95[b] 2.47[b] 2.015[l] 2.46[l]	5.7[m]	4.22[f] 4.33[h] 4.70[h] 4.3[b] 4.25[l]	3.74[h]
GaAs	2.94[f] 3.20[f,e] 2.99[h] 3.23[h] 3.0[e] 2.875[i] 3.13[l]	6.6[g] 6.9[g]	5.1[f,e] 5.0[g] 5.9[g] 5.12[h] 5.55[h]	(4.2[h]) 4.52[h]
GaP	3.71[d]	7.0[m]	5.3[g] (5.7[g])	3.76[m]
AlSb	2.78[d] 3.18[d]	6.5[m]	4.5[m]	4.3[m]

[a] (60T1). [b] (60C2). [c] (61C4). [d] (61C5). [e] (61S13). [f] (61T1). [g] (62E4). [h] (62G10). [i] (62P7). [k] (62Z1). [l] (62L8). [m] (63C3).

A fine structure in the X_4-X_1-transitions of GaSb, InSb, and InAs was discovered by Lukeš and Schmidt (62L7), (62L8) but has not yet been analyzed in detail. References (62L8) and (63C4) also contain some results about the temperature dependence of these transitions.

The temperature dependence of the L-transition in InP was found by Cardona (61C4) to be identical with that of the forbidden zone at Γ. There are also some measurements of the pressure dependence of the L-transitions in GaSb (62Z1). Finally, Cardona and Harbeke (62C2) have found direct exciton transitions at L in some of the III-V compounds.

Optical transitions have also been demonstrated at higher energies. Philipp and Ehrenreich (62P5), (63P6) have observed transitions above 16 eV from indium d-bands in the case of InSb and InAs and from gallium d-bands in GaAs and GaP. The real and imaginary parts of the dielectric constants were obtained in the range from 0 to 25 eV with the help of the Kramers-Kronig relations. The transitions have also been discussed by Deslattes (63D1).

314 Transitions within the valence and conduction bands. Absorption maxima due to transitions within the *valence band* were demonstrated by Braunstein (58B3), (59B14) in p-GaAs. Figure 3.11 shows a typical experimental result on a sample with 9.7×10^{16} holes/cm^3. At 295°K one recognizes an absorption maximum at 0.42 eV, another weaker one at 0.31 eV, and the beginning of a third one at 0.25 eV. Whereas their position is only weakly temperature dependent, their form changes drastically with temperature. Similar absorption peaks appear in all p-type samples, but never in n-type samples, thus demonstrating that they are due to transitions between the three subbands of the valence band. Braunstein assigns the maxima to the following direct transitions: $V_3 \rightarrow V_1$ (0.42 eV), $V_3 \rightarrow V_2$ (0.31 eV), and $V_2 \rightarrow V_1$ (0.25 eV). By the use of Kane's theory the spin-orbit splitting and the effective mass of the V_3-band can be determined: $\Delta \cong 0.33$ eV, $m_{p1}/m_{p3} = 3.38$, $m_{p3}/m_{p2} = 1.70$.

Similar observations on p-InAs by Stern and Talley (57S4) and Dixon (61D2) showed a maximum at 0.17 eV, which is ascribed to $V_2 \rightarrow V_1$-transitions. The other transitions could not be observed, as their energy is larger than E_G, and the peaks therefore lie above the absorption edge. An analysis with Kane's theory gives here $\Delta = 0.43$ eV and $m_{p1} = 0.4\ m$. According to Matossi and Stern (58M2) the location of this maximum is temperature independent above 420°K and shifts to lower energies with decreasing temperature. Furthermore, the maximum becomes shallower as the temperature decreases

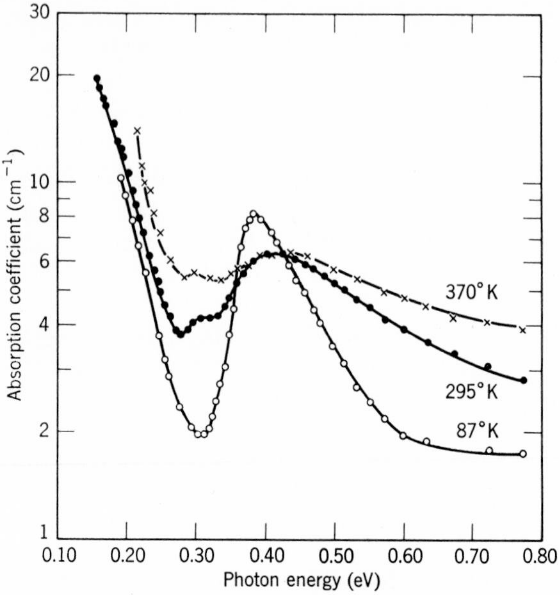

Fig. 3.11 Absorption spectrum of p-GaAs for a sample with $p = 9.7 \times 10^{16}$ cm^{-3} at three different temperatures [after Braunstein (59B14)].

down to room temperature and then grows again at lower temperatures. These observations are easily interpreted within the framework of Kane's theory and furnish further support for the assumption of inter-valence-band transitions: within the band into which the transitions take place, the density of states grows with increasing **k**. Since, on the other hand, the occupation probability for holes decreases with increasing **k**, there is a maximum in the hole concentration at a fixed **k** value. Most of the transitions from the lower-lying subband take place at this **k** value, and the absorption maximum lies at the corresponding energy difference. At high temperatures the occupation maximum of the V_1-band in p-InAs lies at **k** values where the V_1- and V_2-bands are approximately parallel (cf. Fig. 3.12). The absorption maximum is temperature-independent. At lower temperatures the occupation maximum moves to smaller **k** values, at which the separation between V_2 and V_1 is smaller. Simultaneously, the total hole density decreases, as long as the sample is intrinsic, and the absorption peak decreases. Only when the hole density has fallen to the density of the ionized acceptors does the hole concentration become constant, and the holes concentrate themselves into narrower band regions with decreasing temperature. The absorption maximum then shifts to lower energies and becomes sharper again.

If both subbands coincide at $\mathbf{k} = 0$, the absorption maximum will continuously shift to smaller energies with falling temperature. If, however, the band structure contains terms linear in $\mathbf{k}$ (cf. Section 213), the shift will end at a definite limiting energy which corresponds to the separation of the V_2-band from the V_1-band at the maximum of the latter. Here there is then a possibility to test the structure of the valence band of the III-V compounds predicted by Kane. Matossi and Stern compared the measured absorption curves with Kane's theory and obtained optimum agreement under the assumption that the maxima of the V_1-band lie on the [111]-axes of the Brillouin zone, separated from $\mathbf{k} = 0$ by a distance equal to 3% of the separation of the points Γ and L. The energy separation of the maxima relative to the energy at $\mathbf{k} = 0$ could not be determined exactly but must be less than 0.006 eV. The other parameter values of InAs used by Matossi and Stern are as follows: $E_G = 0.41$ eV, $\Delta = 0.43$ eV, $m_n = 0.021\ m$, $m_{p1} = 0.41\ m$ at a sufficient distance from the band edge, $m_{p2} = 0.025\ m$, and $m_{p3} = 0.083m$ for $\mathbf{k} \approx 0$. The corresponding band structure is reproduced in Fig. 3.12.

The results we have described constitute the only experimental proof

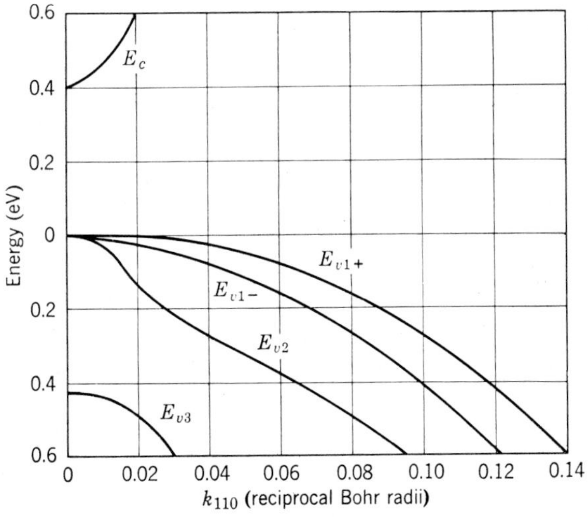

Fig. 3.12 Band model of InAs according to Kane's theory with parameter values experimentally determined by Matossi and Stern (58M2). The splitting of the light-hole band has been neglected.

so far for the linear terms in the $E(\mathbf{k})$-dependence of the valence band of the III-V compounds predicted by Kane's theory. Stern (59S11) has discussed the question of under what condition these terms could also influence the electrical properties.

In *p*-AlSb Braunstein and Kane (62B12) identified V_3-V_1-transitions at 0.75 eV and V_2-V_1-transitions at 0.15 eV.

Transitions between the subbands of the *conduction band* have been reported in GaP, GaAs, GaSb, and AlSb. In transmission measurements on *n*-GaP in the wavelength range of 1–10 μ Spitzer, Gershenzon, Frosch, and Gibbs (59S7) found an absorption band at 4 μ (0.31 eV), above the continuous free-carrier absorption. They assign it to transitions between two subbands of the conduction band. This assumption is supported by the fact that this band appears only in *n*-type GaP, and by the shape of the absorption edge. In its long-wavelength tail the absorption constant is proportional to $(\hbar\omega - E_G)^{2.2}$. This corresponds to indirect transitions [theoretical exponent 2.0, cf. (3.6)]. At higher values of K there is, however, a rapid increase, which leads one to suspect the beginning of transitions to an energetically higher-lying maximum. The exact theoretical interpretation gives a separation of the subbands of 0.35 eV in agreement with the value determined from the absorption band.

This means that GaP has a lowest minimum at $\mathbf{k} \neq 0$, and a slightly higher-lying one at $\mathbf{k} = 0$, in agreement with the results of Section 311.

Spitzer and Whelan (59S6) found a similar absorption band in *n*-GaAs. It has the long-wavelength edge at (0.25 ± 0.03) eV, and its intensity depends strongly on doping. Transitions from the lowest (000)-minimum into a higher-lying subband seem to be responsible for it. The data are shown in Fig. 3.13.

An absorption band in *n*-AlSb in the same wavelength region, measured by Blunt, Frederikse, Becker, and Hosler (54B3), was assigned to transitions from the lowest-lying minimum outside of $\mathbf{k} = 0$ to a (000)-subband lying 0.29 eV higher, by Turner and Reese (60T4). This is supported by the shape and temperature dependence of this band, its linear dependence on electron concentration, and its independence of donor type. The assignment of the minima is again derived from the shape of the absorption edge. Turner and Reese could also determine the spin-orbit splitting of the valence band as $\Delta = 0.75$ eV, from these measurements.

According to Becker, Ramdas, and Fan (61B7), transitions with $\Delta E = 0.25$ eV have been observed in *n*-GaSb, which probably lead from the (000)-conduction band into a higher (100)-band.

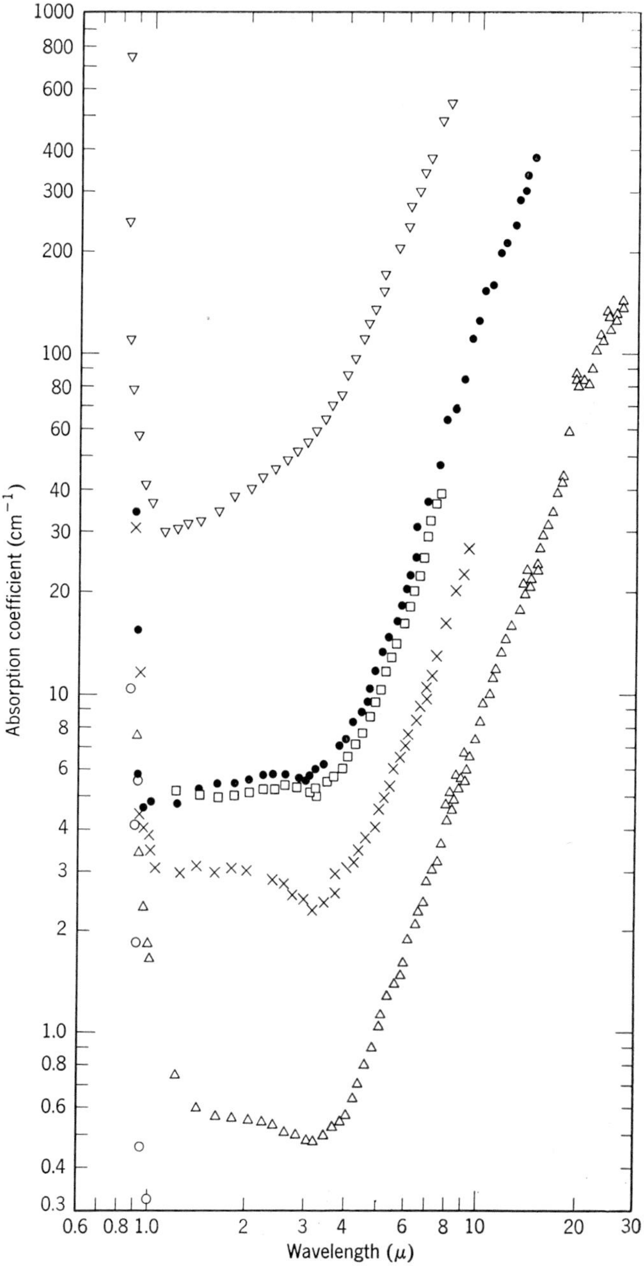

Fig. 3.13 Absorption coefficient of n-GaAs at room temperature for six samples of different purity [after Spitzer and Whelan (59S6)].

315 Absorption and reflection in magnetic fields. The band structure of a semiconductor is strongly influenced by an external magnetic field. Consider an electron of thermal velocity v. Under the influence of the magnetic field it describes circular tracks in a plane perpendicular to the magnetic field with angular frequency $\omega_c = eB/m^*$ and radius $r = v/\omega_c$. This periodic movement is quantized, and in place of the simple relation

$$E = E_c + \frac{\hbar^2 k^2}{2m^*} \tag{3.8}$$

there appears for the parabolic conduction band of an isotropic semiconductor in a magnetic field the expression

$$E = E_c + (n + \tfrac{1}{2})\hbar\omega_c + \frac{\hbar^2 k_B{}^2}{2m^*} \tag{3.9}$$

Here k_B is the component of the wave vector in the direction of the magnetic field, and n takes on all positive integer values, 0, 1, 2, ... In place of a three-dimensional conduction band in **k**-space there accordingly appears a succession of one-dimensional subbands. The separations between the band edges of these subbands ($k_B = 0$) are all equal to $\hbar\omega_c$, i.e., inversely proportional to the effective mass m^*. The bottom of the lowest subband lies higher than in the field-free case by $\hbar\omega_c/2$. These relationships are shown in the left half of Fig. 3.14, together with the corresponding splitting of a valence band consisting of two isotropic subbands. In addition any spin degeneracy existing in the field-free case is removed, so that every subband separates into two subbands displaced by $\pm\frac{1}{2}g\mu_B B$, where g is the g-factor of the band and μ_B the Bohr magneton (right half of Fig. 3.14).

These considerations apply strictly only if the scattering of the charge carriers is neglected, because the periodic motion is interrupted by scattering processes. Quantum effects take place only if the mean free path of the charge carriers, $l = v\tau_0$ (τ_0 = collision time), is large compared to the radius of the circular track. Thus one criterion for the applicability of eq. (3.9) is that $\omega_c\tau_0$ is much larger than 1.

So far we have not considered the departures from the simple parabolic isotropic band model which occur in the III-V compounds. According to Kane's theory, the deviations from parabolicity in the conduction band and V_2-band cause a dependence of the effective mass and of the g-factor on the magnetic field and on the quantum number n. The complicated structure of the valence band near $\mathbf{k} = 0$ causes a displacement of the subbands of low quantum number. The model of Fig. 3.14 therefore applies only for high quantum numbers.

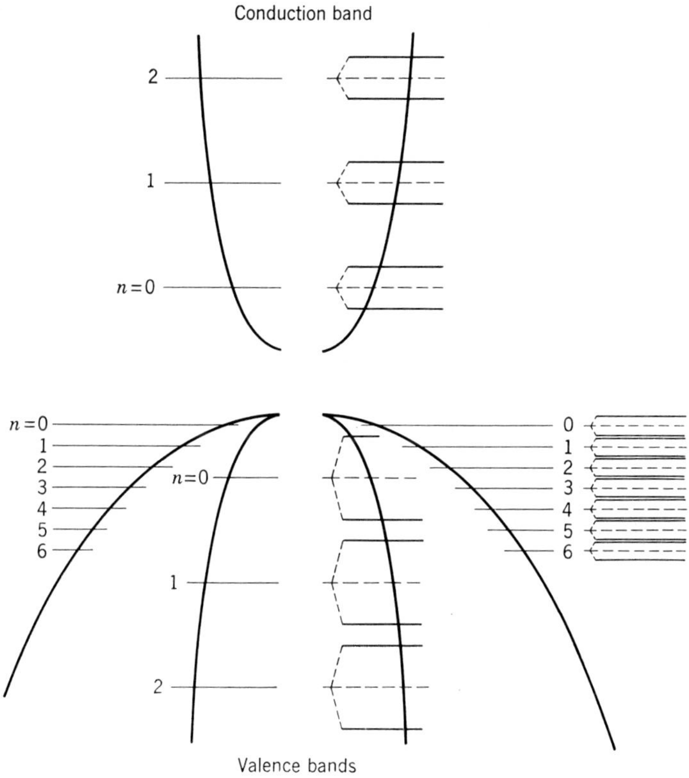

Fig. 3.14 Magnetic splitting of the **k** = 0 terms in the band model of an isotropic semiconductor with one conduction band and two valence bands. When the nonparabolicity, the valence-band degeneracy and anisotropy, and the linear **k** terms of Kane's theory are taken into account, the magnetic sublevels become considerably more complicated at low quantum numbers. Spin splitting of the sublevels is shown at the right side of the figure [after (61Z2)].

The modification of the band structure by the magnetic field changes the absorption spectrum decisively. In place of one characteristic transition of energy E_G there now appears a multitude of transitions between the various magnetic subbands of the valence and conduction bands. Instead of eq. (3.5), the frequency dependence of the absorption constant for *direct* allowed transitions becomes

$$K(\omega,B) \sim \hbar\omega_{c,r} \sum_n [\hbar\omega - E_G + (n + \tfrac{1}{2})\hbar\omega_{c,r}]^{-\frac{1}{2}} \qquad (3.10)$$

where $\omega_{c,r} = \omega_{cn} + \omega_{cp} = eB/m_r$, $m_r = m_n m_p/(m_n + m_p)$. The summation runs over all n for which the root is real; n is the quantum number of the initial and the final state. This is a consequence of the selection rule that transitions can take place only between magnetic subbands of equal quantum number. When spin splitting is considered, additional terms $\pm\frac{1}{2}g\mu_B B$ appear in the roots of eq. (3.10).

The degeneracy of the valence band in the III-V compounds furthermore modifies the selection rules for the possible transitions. Additional terms must be included in eq. (3.10) for comparison with experiment.

The following structure of the absorption spectrum results from all these considerations. The absorption edge is shifted by $\frac{1}{2}\hbar\omega_c$ in the magnetic field. Because of the difference terms in the denominators of eq. (3.10) the absorption becomes infinite whenever the photon energy becomes equal to the minimum energy for one of the transitions in the sum. When scattering is taken into account in the exact theory, damping terms appear in the resonance denominators, so that the absorption spectrum consists of a sequence of absorption peaks and consequently has an oscillatory character.

In the case of *indirect* transitions the oscillatory spectrum is replaced by a staircase-like spectrum. We will not consider the latter at this time, since so far only oscillatory spectra have been observed in III-V compounds.

Studies of the magnetic field dependence of the optical absorption give a great deal of information about the parameters of the semiconductor band models; the separations between the absorption peaks allow the determination of the splitting between the various magnetic subbands and thereby of the effective mass and of the g-factor; the positions of the absorption peaks can be extrapolated to $B = 0$, where the splitting into the magnetic subbands disappears. This allows a very accurate determination of the width of the forbidden gap.

For the more exact theory of the magnetoabsorption we refer to the work of Roth, Lax, and Zwerdling (59R9) and of Burstein, Picus, Wallis, and Blatt (59B17), and also to (60L2). Here we will only mention a formula for the g-factor of electrons in the conduction band which we will need later, and which was derived by Roth (59R9) and Zawadzki (63Z1) from Kane's theory:

$$g_n(k) = 2\left\{1 - \left[\frac{m}{m_n(k)} - 1\right]\frac{\Delta}{[E_c'(k) - E_v]}\right\} \qquad (3.11)$$

Here $m_n(k)$ is m_3 of eq. (2.19), and Δ is again the energy difference between the upper edge of the valence band and the V_3-subband.

$E_c'(k) = E_c(k) - \hbar^2k^2/2m$ as in eq. (2.7); for $k = 0$, $[E_c'(k) - E_v]$ becomes E_G. If the spin-orbit interaction is neglected, $\Delta = 0$, and the g-factor takes on the normal value of 2. Because of the spin-orbit coupling this factor can take on abnormally large (negative) values in semiconductors with a small effective electron mass. If $\Delta \gg E_c' - E_v$ and $m \gg m_n$, then (3.11) becomes $g_n = -m/m_n$.

In InSb, for example, $g_n = -50.7$ for 2×10^{14} electrons/cm^3, according to spin-resonance measurements of Bemski (60B6). Equation (3.11) predicts that $-g_n$ should decrease with increasing k. Indeed, for 3×10^{15} electrons/cm^3 Bemski found $g_n = -48.8$, and at still higher concentrations g decreases even more rapidly (63Z1). One more spin-resonance measurement that must be mentioned at this point was performed by Duncan and Schneider (63D3) on n-GaAs and gave $g_n = 0.5228 \pm 0.0001$.

The first *measurements* of magnetoabsorption in III-V compounds were made by Burstein and co-workers (56B3), (57B6), (59B17) on InSb. Later results on InSb, InAs, and GaSb have been reported by Lax *et al.* (56Z1), (57Z1), (59L2), (59R9), (59Z3), (61W10), (61Z2).

Figure 3.15 shows the first measurement of Burstein, Picus, Gebbie, and Blatt (56B3), which clearly indicates the shift of the absorption edge with increasing magnetic field. Measurements at larger photon energies are shown in Fig. 3.16. Here the absorption maxima (trans-

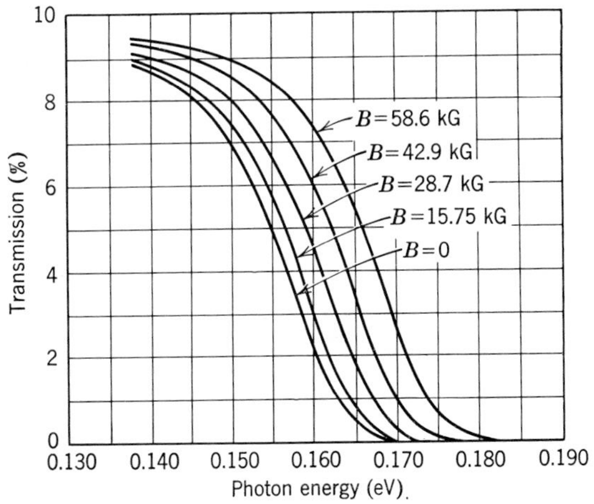

Fig. 3.15 Shift of the absorption edge of InSb with magnetic field at room temperature [after Burstein, Picus, Gebbie, and Blatt (56B3)].

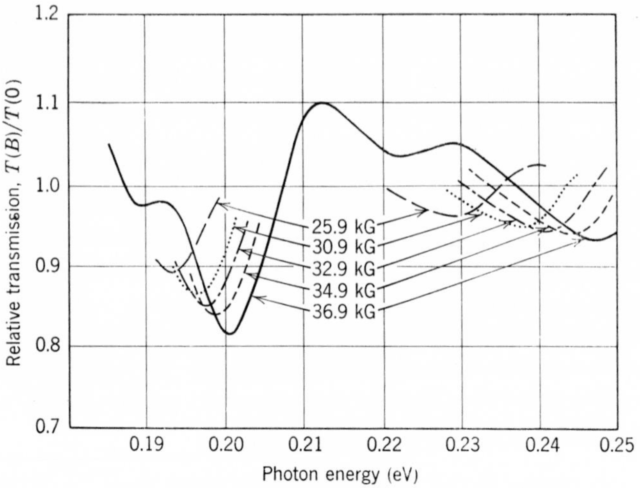

Fig. 3.16 Relative transmission of InSb as a function of photon energy at room temperature for various magnetic fields [after Zwerdling, Lax, and Roth (57Z1)].

mission minima in the figure) and their magnetic-field dependence (57Z1) are observed. Extrapolation to $B = 0$ results in a room-temperature value of the energy gap, E_G, of (0.180 ± 0.002) eV. When the absorption peaks are assigned to transitions between magnetic subbands their separations result in electron effective-mass values of $m_n = 0.014\ m$ for InSb. Similar measurements on InAs at room temperature gave these values: $E_G = (0.360 \pm 0.002)$ eV and $m_n = 0.03\ m$.

At lower temperatures the oscillatory spectrum is more clearly resolved. Figure 3.17 shows the spectrum of InSb at helium temperature for two different values of magnetic induction (61Z2). The measurements were performed on a 5-μ-thick sample with 2×10^{14} electrons/cm^3. The resolution allowed the absorption peaks to be localized with an accuracy of 5×10^{-5} eV. Sixteen peaks were observed. Almost all experimentally observed lines can be identified as to both position and intensity with the theoretically calculated spectrum if the anomalies of the band structure of InSb are taken into account. This identification is possible only if one assumes that not only the conduction band but also the V_2-band is nonparabolic. This result of Kane's theory is thereby experimentally verified for the first time. At small quantum numbers the measured transition energies are systematically displaced relative to the theoretically calculated ones. This can be interpreted by the hypothesis that in the final state the electron is still bound to its hole by Coulomb attraction (formation of an exciton). The energy difference between the experimentally determined and the theoretically calculated positions is then the binding energy of the excitons.

The following parameter values are thereby determined: $E_G = (0.2357 \pm 0.0005)$ eV at helium temperature, $m_n = (0.0145 \pm 0.0003)\,m$, $m_{p2} = 0.0149\,m$. The g-factor of the electrons at the band edge is given as -48, which, according to (3.11), gives a band-splitting Δ of 0.98 eV.

More detailed measurements, particularly of the anisotropy of the magnetoabsorption at helium temperature, permitted Zwerdling,

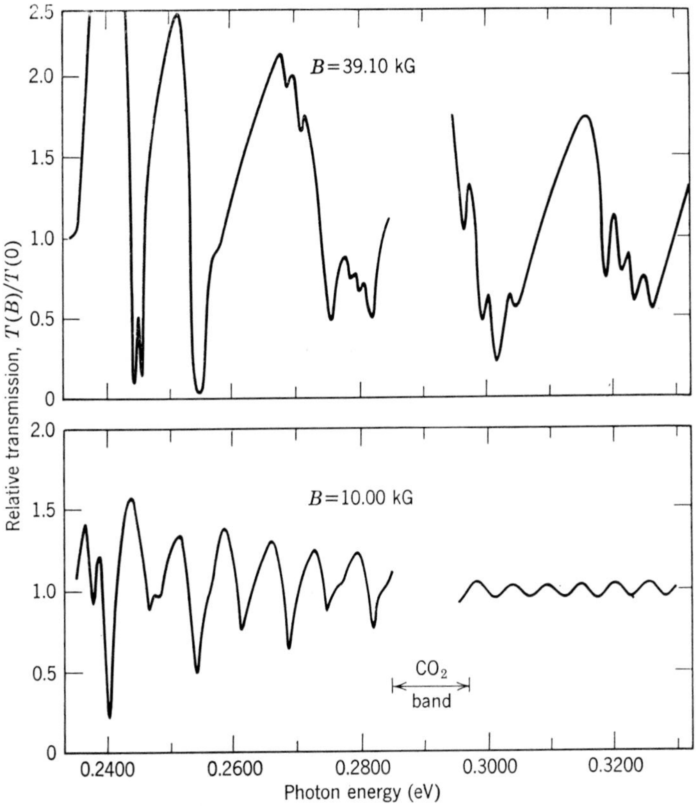

Fig. 3.17 Oscillatory magnetoabsorption in InSb at 4°K for two different magnetic fields (polarization **E** ⊥ **B**) [after Zwerdling, Kleiner and Theriault (61Z2)].

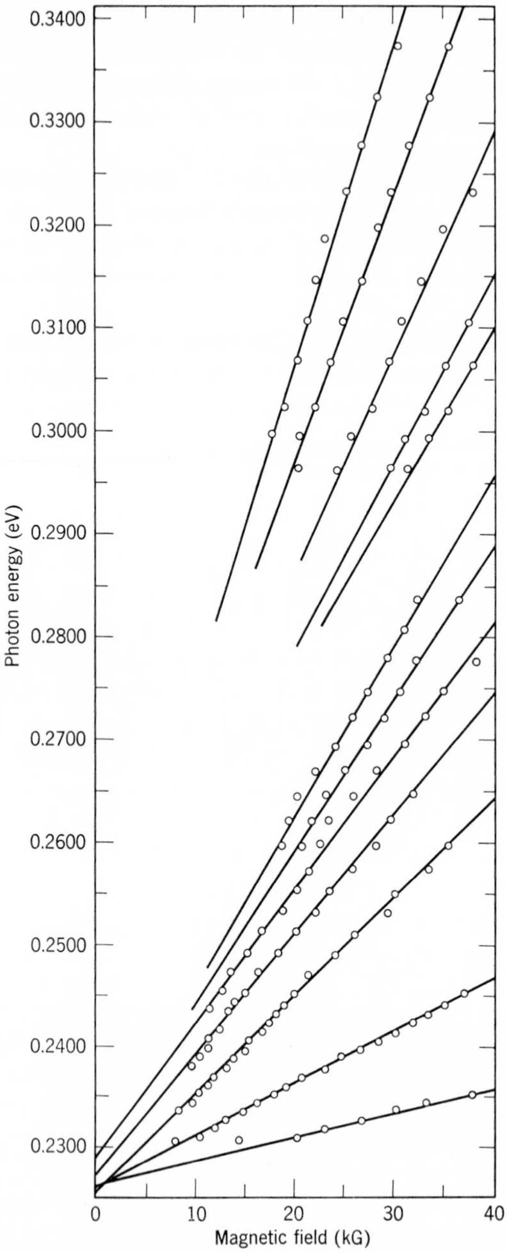

Fig. 3.18 Energy differences between magnetic subbands of the valence and conduction bands of InSb at 85°K determined from the magnetoreflection spectrum [after Wright and Lax (61W10)].

Kleiner, and Theriault (62Z7) to also determine the parameters of the V_2-band. An effective mass of $(0.18 \pm 0.03)\ m$ resulted for the heavy holes, and for the anisotropy coefficient of eq. (3.7) a value of 1.4.

For GaSb Zwerdling, Lax, Button, and Roth (59Z3) found an oscillatory absorption spectrum at 1.5°K, from which the values $E_G = (0.813 \pm 0.001)$ eV and $m_n = (0.047 \pm 0.003)\ m$ were determined.

The indicated value for the effective mass of the electrons does not follow directly from the measurements, since eq. (3.10) gives only an average value, $m_r = m_n m_p/(m_n + m_p)$. The strong similarity of the oscillatory absorption spectrum of GaSb to that of germanium does suggest, however, that the hole effective masses are of the same order of magnitude for the two semiconductors. In that case $m_p \gg m_n$, and m_n can be determined with good accuracy from m_r and from an approximate value of m_p.

The transitions between magnetic subbands cause not only the absorption spectrum but also the reflection spectrum to be oscillatory. Interband magnetoreflection was observed by Wright and Lax (61W10) in InSb at 78°K. In the same way as in absorption, the shape of the reflection spectrum permitted extrapolation to $B = 0$ and thereby determination of the width of the forbidden zone. This is shown in Fig. 3.18, from which a value of E_G (85°K) $= 0.228$ eV follows. The theory of magnetoreflection is discussed in (61W10).

Boyle and Brailsford (57B4) report measurements of the absorption of an n-InSb sample of $n = 2 \times 10^{14}\ \text{cm}^{-3}$ in the range between 70 and 120 μ. Here transmission minima appear in the magnetic field; these are assigned to transitions of bound electrons between donor states, which are split in a fashion similar to that in the conduction band.

32 Free Charge Carriers

320 Theory. The behavior of free charge carriers under the influence of the periodic electric field of a light wave can be described in first approximation by a model where the charge carriers move in a viscous medium of friction coefficient $\omega_0 = 1/\tau_0$ (τ_0 = collision time) (Drude's theory). The equation of motion is then

$$m^*(\dot{\mathbf{v}} + \omega_0 \mathbf{v}) = e\boldsymbol{\mathcal{E}}_0 e^{i\omega t} \tag{3.12}$$

The solution of (3.12) leads to the complex conductivity

$$\sigma = \sigma_0 \omega_0 \frac{\omega_0 - i\omega}{{\omega_0}^2 + \omega^2} \tag{3.13}$$

and from there to the optical constants: index of refraction n_r, absorption coefficient k, absorption-constant K, and dielectric constant κ:

$$2n_r k = \frac{\mathrm{Re}\,(\sigma)}{\epsilon_0 \omega} = \kappa_l \frac{\omega_0}{\omega} \cdot \frac{\omega_p{}^2}{\omega^2 + \omega_0{}^2} \tag{3.14a}$$

$$\kappa = n_r{}^2 - k^2 = \kappa_l + \frac{\mathrm{Im}\,(\sigma)}{\epsilon_0 \omega} = \kappa_l \left(1 - \frac{\omega_p{}^2}{\omega^2 + \omega_0{}^2}\right) \tag{3.14b}$$

$$K = \frac{2\omega}{c} k \tag{3.14c}$$

Here we have also introduced the "plasma frequency,"

$$\omega_p = \left(\frac{ne^2}{m^* \epsilon_0 \kappa_l}\right)^{1/2}$$

where ϵ_0 is the permittivity of free space and κ_l the lattice dielectric constant without the free-carrier contribution.

The contribution of the free charge carriers to the dielectric constant (electric susceptibility) becomes, for $\omega \gg \omega_0$,

$$\chi_c = \kappa - \kappa_l = -\kappa_l \frac{\omega_p{}^2}{\omega^2} = -\frac{e^2 n}{m^* \epsilon_0 \omega^2} \tag{3.15}$$

The measurement of the reflection coefficient

$$R = \left| \frac{\kappa^{1/2} - 1}{\kappa^{1/2} + 1} \right|^2 \tag{3.16}$$

then gives the possibility of determining the effective mass m^* if the carrier concentration n is known.

The electric susceptibility of the free carriers (3.15) is calculated more accurately from the Boltzmann equation (57S3):

$$\chi_c = \frac{e^2}{3\omega^2 \hbar^2 \epsilon_0} \frac{2}{(2\pi)^3} \int \Delta_k E \, f_0 \, d\mathbf{k} \tag{3.17}$$

where f_0 is the Fermi distribution.

Since $n = \dfrac{2}{(2\pi)^3} \displaystyle\int f_0 \, d\mathbf{k}$, the optically determined effective mass m_{opt} is:

$$m_{\mathrm{opt}} = 3\hbar^2 \frac{\int f_0 \, d\mathbf{k}}{\int \Delta_k E \, f_0 \, d\mathbf{k}} \tag{3.18}$$

For an isotropic parabolic band, where $E = \hbar^2 k^2 / 2m^*$, $m_{\mathrm{opt}} = m^*$. Furthermore, we obtain:

(*a*) For bands with ellipsoidal energy surfaces, $E = \frac{\hbar^2}{2}\left(\frac{k_1^2}{m_1} + \frac{k_2^2}{m_2} + \frac{k_3^2}{m_3}\right)$:

$$\frac{1}{m_{\text{opt}}} = \frac{1}{3}\left(\frac{1}{m_1} + \frac{1}{m_2} + \frac{1}{m_3}\right) \tag{3.19}$$

(*b*) For two bands with effective masses m_1 and m_2, which are degenerate at $\mathbf{k} = 0$:

$$\frac{1}{m_{\text{opt}}} = \frac{m_1^{1/2} + m_2^{1/2}}{m_1^{3/2} + m_2^{3/2}} \tag{3.20}$$

(*c*) For one isotropic nonparabolic band $E = Ak^2 + Bk^4 + \cdots$ (61C1):

$$\frac{1}{m_{\text{opt}}} = \frac{2A}{\hbar^2}\left[1 + \frac{10}{3}\frac{B}{A^2}kT\frac{\int_0^\infty x^{3/2}f_0(x-\eta)\,dx}{\int_0^\infty x^{1/2}f_0(x-\eta)\,dx}\right]; \eta = \frac{E_{\text{F}}}{kT} \tag{3.21}$$

(*d*) For complete degeneracy $(E_{\text{F}} - E_c) \gg kT$:

$$\frac{1}{m_{\text{opt}}} = \frac{1}{\hbar^2}\left(\frac{1}{k}\frac{dE}{dk}\right)_{E_{\text{F}}} \tag{3.22}$$

This means that in the last case one measures the slope of the $E(k)$ curve at the Fermi energy, and not its curvature [m_2 of eq. (2.19)]. Neglecting these differences can lead to serious errors, particularly in semiconductors with nonparabolic conduction band (cf. Table 2.3).

Absorption measurements are mainly performed in the frequency region $\omega \gg \omega_p, \omega_0$. There K has the form

$$K = \sqrt{\kappa_l}\,\frac{\omega_p^2\omega_0}{c\omega^2} \tag{3.23}$$

according to (3.14). The absorption increases with the square of the wavelength.

In contrast, *reflection* measurements are of particular interest in the frequency region $\omega \approx \omega_p$, if simultaneously the condition $\kappa \approx n_r^2$ (weak absorption) is satisfied. Then (3.14) and (3.16) give

$$\kappa = 1, \text{ i.e., } R = 0, \text{ for } \omega = \omega_p\sqrt{\frac{\kappa_l}{\kappa_l - 1}} \tag{3.24}$$

$$\kappa = 0, \text{ i.e., } R = 1, \text{ for } \omega = \omega_p \tag{3.25}$$

Since the dielectric constant is very large in semiconductors (κ = 10–15), a sharp reflection edge at ω_p (*plasma reflection*) is obtained. Its measurement gives another value for ω_p and so for m_{opt}.

The effective masses of the free carriers can also be determined from *magneto-optical* effects. If one adds the term $e\mathbf{v} \times \mathbf{B}$ ($\mathbf{B}$ = static magnetic field) to the right-hand side of eq. (3.12), one obtains, in place of (3.14):

(*a*) For the magnetic field parallel to the propagation direction of the light:

$$\kappa = n_r^2 - k^2 = \kappa_l \left[1 - \frac{\omega_p^2}{\omega} \frac{\omega \pm \omega_c}{(\omega \pm \omega_c)^2 + \omega_0^2}\right] \tag{3.26a}$$

$$2n_r k = \kappa_l \frac{\omega_0 \omega_p^2}{\omega} \frac{1}{(\omega \pm \omega_c)^2 + \omega_0^2} \tag{3.26b}$$

for circularly polarized light. The two signs refer to the two possible directions of polarization.

(*b*) For the magnetic field perpendicular to the propagation direction of the light and linear polarization:

$$\kappa = n_r^2 - k^2 = \kappa_l \left(1 - \frac{\omega_p^2 \beta}{\omega^2 \beta^2 + \omega_0^2 \alpha^2}\right) \tag{3.27a}$$

$$2n_r k = \kappa_l \frac{\omega_0 \omega_p^2}{\omega} \frac{\alpha}{\omega^2 \beta^2 + \omega_0^2 \alpha^2} \tag{3.27b}$$

where for $\mathbf{B} \parallel \mathcal{E}$

$$\alpha = \beta = 1 \tag{3.28}$$

and for $\mathbf{B} \perp \mathcal{E}$

$$\alpha = 1 + \frac{\omega^2 \omega_c^2}{\omega^2 \omega_0^2 + (\omega^2 - \omega_p^2)^2} \tag{3.29a}$$

$$\beta = 1 - \frac{\omega_c^2 (\omega^2 - \omega_p^2)}{\omega^2 \omega_0^2 + (\omega^2 - \omega_p^2)^2} \tag{3.29b}$$

In these equations $\omega_c = eB/m^*$ is the so-called *cyclotron-resonance frequency*, which was introduced in Section 315. Equations (3.26)–(3.29) contain four characteristic frequencies, ω, ω_c, ω_p, and ω_0, representing the influence of the light, of the magnetic field, of the charge-carrier concentration, and of the lattice vibrations. Depending on the relative orders of magnitude of the four parameters, we obtain various interesting effects, which we will now discuss.

(1) $\omega \approx \omega_c \gg \omega_0 \gg \omega_p$

From (3.26b) an absorption constant for linearly polarized light proportional to

$$\frac{\omega_0^2 + \omega_c^2 + \omega^2}{(\omega_0^2 + \omega_c^2 - \omega^2)^2 + 4\omega_0^2\omega^2} \tag{3.30}$$

follows, which has a maximum at $\omega \approx \omega_c$ (*cyclotron resonance*).

(2) $\omega \approx \omega_p \gg \omega_c \gg \omega_0$

The plasma-reflection edge is shifted by the magnetic field from the ($\omega_c = 0$) value by an amount which can be calculated from (3.26a). The reflection maximum ($R = 1$) is given, in place of (3.25), by the equation

$$R = 1 \text{ for } \omega = \omega_p \pm \frac{\omega_c}{2} + \frac{1}{8}\frac{\omega_c^2}{\omega_p} + \cdots \tag{3.31}$$

The two signs apply to the two circular-polarization directions of the light (case a).

The two shifts are superimposed for unpolarized light. The reflection edge is then split into two parts, and the difference between the two reflection maxima is equal to ω_c for small fields (*magnetoplasma reflection*). Here is another independent possibility for the determination of ω_c and thereby m^*.

In case *b* (magnetic field perpendicular to the propagation direction of the light) there is also a splitting of the reflection edge according to (3.27)–(3.29) if $\mathbf{B} \perp \boldsymbol{\varepsilon}$. Here two reflection minima are obtained, one of which goes over into the minimum (3.24) for $\mathbf{B} \to 0$, while the other approaches ω_p and then disappears for $\mathbf{B} = 0$.

(3) $\omega \gg \omega_c, \omega_p, \omega_0$.

The polarization of a light beam passing through a semiconductor changes because of the different indices of refraction for right- and left-circularly polarized light in case *a* and for $\boldsymbol{\varepsilon} \perp$ or $\parallel$ $\mathbf{B}$ in case *b*. The resulting phase difference for a sample of thickness d is

$$\delta = \frac{\omega}{c}(n_{r1} - n_{r2})d \tag{3.32}$$

If n_1 and n_2 differ only slightly, this can be approximated as

$$\delta = \frac{\omega}{2n_r c}(n_{r1}^2 - n_{r2}^2)d \tag{3.33}$$

In case *a* linearly polarized light is rotated by an angle ϑ which is equal to half the phase difference (3.33) of its two circularly polarized components:

$$\vartheta = \frac{\omega}{4n_r c}(n_{r1}^2 - n_{r2}^2)d \tag{3.34}$$

(*Faraday effect*).

In case *b* linearly polarized light with the electric vector at 45° to the direction of the magnetic field is transformed into elliptically polarized light (*Voigt effect*). Here the phase difference δ (3.32) is itself defined as the characteristic angle. Inserting (3.26)–(3.29) into (3.32)–(3.34) gives, for $\omega \gg \omega_0, \omega_c, \omega_p$:

$$\vartheta = \frac{\kappa_l d}{2n_r c}\frac{\omega_p{}^2\omega_c}{\omega^2} \sim \frac{B}{\omega^2 m^{*2}} \tag{3.35}$$

$$\delta = \vartheta\frac{\omega_c}{\omega} \sim \frac{B^2}{\omega^3 m^{*3}} \tag{3.36}$$

The ratio of Voigt angle δ to Faraday angle ϑ is consequently directly proportional to the cyclotron-resonance frequency.

The simple theory which has been discussed in this section will have to be extended for quantitative comparison with experiment. This will be considered in the following sections.

321 Absorption. The absorption by free charge carriers increases with the square of the wavelength according to eq. (3.23). This statement is valid only for the simple Drude theory used in Section 320 (assumption of an energy-independent relaxation time). The quantum-mechanical treatment assumes that the electron is excited into an intermediate virtual state by the photon and then is scattered. The calculation confirms the quadratic result for large wavelengths and for interaction of the excited electron with acoustical phonons. For polar scattering of the electron (interaction with optical phonons) Visvanathan (60V1) calculated a wavelength dependence of the absorption proportional to 2.5. The exponent can take on values as high as 3.5 for scattering at ionized impurities.

In *n*-type III-V compounds the measured free-carrier absorption can always be expressed by a power law. The data for the various III-V compounds are collected in Table 3.4. The values of the exponents lie between 2 and 3.5 with the exception of those for GaP. The electron effective masses can in principle be determined from these measurements. Kurnick and Powell (59K5) found for InSb $m_n = 0.025\,m$; Perlmutter (57P1) for GaAs, $m_n = 0.075\,m$; and Turner and

Table 3.4 Absorption Cross Section $\sigma_n = K/n$ for the Absorption by Free Carriers in n-Type III-V Compounds

The values were measured at 9 μ, and the wavelength dependence is represented by the exponent α of the power law $\sigma_n \sim \lambda^\alpha$. After Stern (61S13).

Compound	n (10^{17} cm^{-3})	σ_n (10^{-17} cm^2)	α	References
InSb	1–3	2.3	2	(59K5)
InAs	0.3–8	3.6	3.0	(58D1)
InP	0.4–4	4.5	2.6	(58N3)
GaAs	1–10	4.7	3.1	(59S6)
GaP	1	12	1.4	(60K5)
	10	31	1.7	(59S7)
AlSb	0.4–4	15	2	(60T4)

Reese (60T4) for AlSb, $m_n = 0.3\ m$. These values must be considered only rough estimates.

The absorption by free-charge carriers in p-type material is independent of wavelength in most cases. This can be understood if one considers that the valence band of a III-V compound contains a number of subbands. Whereas in the free-electron absorption, scattering *within* one of the subbands takes place, the holes are primarily scattered between the V_2- and V_1-bands. The absorption cross section $\sigma_p = K/p$ is then considerably larger than $\sigma_n = K/n$ of n-type material. Kurnick and Powell (59K5) found, for example, in InSb at $\lambda = 9\ \mu$ ratios of $\sigma_p/\sigma_n = 37.5$ at room temperature and $\sigma_p/\sigma_n = 215$ at 78°K, from measurements of the doping dependence of the absorption. At room temperature the cross section per hole is $\sigma_p = 8.65 \times 10^{-16}$ cm^2 in approximate agreement with a theoretical estimate of the V_2-V_1-scattering (3×10^{-16} cm^2). Similar results were obtained by Kaiser and Fan (55K1), (56F1).

The absorption by free carriers in degenerate n-InSb was investigated by Kessler and Sutter (61K1). According to (3.23), K is proportional to the electron concentration and inversely proportional to the effective electron mass at any given wavelength. Because of the nonparabolicity of the conduction band m^* depends on the electron concentration [m_2 of eq. (2.19)]. The absorption coefficient is no longer a linear function of the electron concentration. Kessler and Sutter used this fact to determine the effective mass of the electrons as a function of the occupation of the conduction band from the concentration dependence of the absorption coefficient. From the resulting dependence of the effective mass m^* on the magnitude of the wave vector **k**, one obtains the $E(k)$-dependence after double integration of $1/m^* \sim \partial^2 E/\partial k^2$. Figure 3.19 shows the results. For comparison an $E(k)$ curve of Spitzer and Fan (57S3) is also shown, which was obtained from reflection measurements on *n*-InSb by a similar procedure. The agreement between the two procedures is good, but they both lead to an effective mass at the band edge of 0.016 *m*, which is larger than other values that have been presented in this chapter.

Further optical absorption investigations on InSb have been made (54A3), (54M2), (57M2), (57M4).

In degenerate semiconductors the application of an external magnetic field is expected to produce oscillations in the free-carrier absorption, just as is the case for band-to-band transitions (Section 315). The density of states at the Fermi level changes in a periodic fashion with increasing magnetic field. This produces variations in the transition probability of an electron from a lower-lying magnetic subband of the conduction band into an unoccupied level at the Fermi energy. Such oscillations were observed in InSb by Palik and Wallis (63P1).

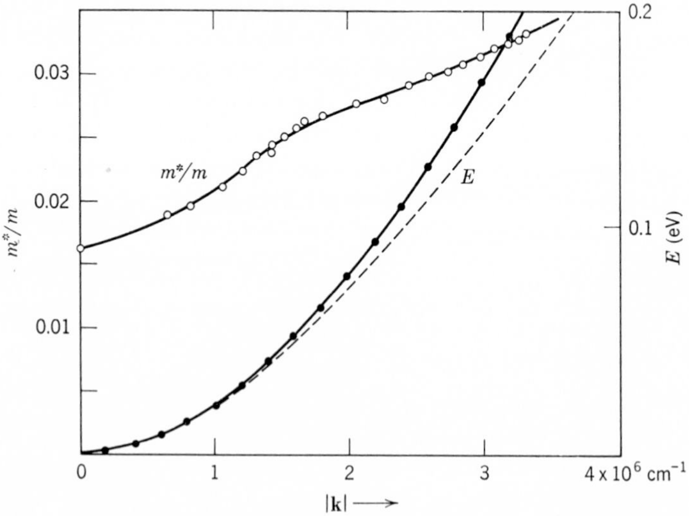

Fig. 3.19 Energy and effective mass of electrons in InSb as a function of wave number k according to measurements of free-carrier absorption by Kessler and Sutter (61K1). Broken curve: $E(k)$ after Spitzer and Fan (57S3).

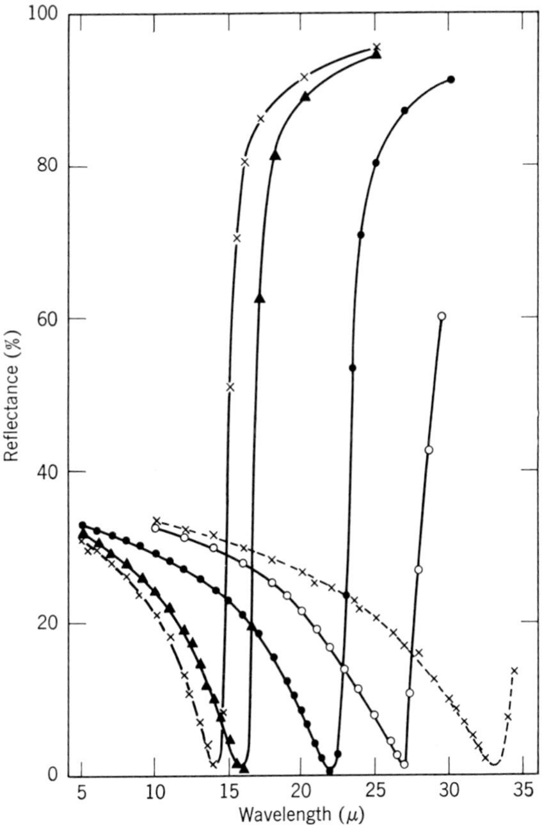

Fig. 3.20 Reflectivity of five n-InSb samples (from left to right: 3.5×10^{17} to 4.0×10^{18} electrons/cm^3) at room temperature [after Spitzer and Fan (57S3)].

322 Reflection. The measurement of the reflection minimum (eq. 3.24) allows the determination of the plasma frequency ω_p and thereby the effective mass m_{opt}, as we have seen in Section 320. The first evaluations of reflection measurements for determination of effective masses were made on n-type **InSb** by Yoshinaga and Oetjen (56Y2) and by Spitzer and Fan (57S3). Reflection curves of five Te-doped samples are shown in Fig. 3.20 (57S3). The absorption is very weak in that region of wavelength, and the reflection coefficient sinks almost to zero. For the five samples the following effective masses are obtained: $m_{n,\text{opt}} = 0.023\ m$ ($n = 3.5 \times 10^{17}$ cm^{-3}), $= 0.029$ (4.2×10^{17}), $= 0.032$ (1.2×10^{18}), $= 0.040$ (2.8×10^{18}),

$= 0.041$ (4.0×10^{18}). In comparing these values with Kane's theory (Table 2.3), it must be remembered that m_{opt} is given by (3.22) for the degenerate case, and therefore must be identified with the effective mass m_2 in the table. The agreement is satisfactory and again confirms the applicability of Kane's theory to InSb.

The values given by Spitzer and Fan (57S3) and Cardona (61C3) for ***n*-InAs** are plotted in Fig. 3.21. The theoretical curve shown was calculated under the assumption that for these samples eq. (2.7) can be simplified by $E' \ll E_G + \frac{2}{3}\Delta$. Then it follows from (2.7) that

$$E - E_c = \frac{E_G}{2}\left[\left(1 + \frac{4k^2\gamma^2}{E_G{}^2}\right)^{\frac{1}{2}} - 1\right]; \quad \gamma^2 = P^2\frac{E_G + \frac{2}{3}\Delta}{E_G + \Delta} \tag{3.37}$$

The square root can be expended in terms of $\mathbf{k}^2$, and the effective mass determined from eq. (3.21).

In **InP** samples of 5×10^{18} electrons/cm^3, Newman (58N3) and Cardona (61C1) found, respectively, $m_n = 0.2\ m$ and $0.26\ m$.

Measurements of Spitzer and Whelan (59S6) on n-type **GaAs** gave values of $m_{n,\text{opt}}$ varying from $0.079\ m$ at $n = 5 \times 10^{17}$ cm^{-3} to $0.086\ m$ at $n = 5.4 \times 10^{18}$ cm^{-3}. Cardona (61C1) compared these measurements and his own results (0.067–$0.096\ m$ for the same doping range) with Kane's theory and obtained satisfactory agreement. The same procedure as in the case of InAs was used for the evaluation, except that eq. (2.7) was further simplified by the approximation (valid for GaAs) $\Delta \ll E_G$ (i.e., $\gamma = P$).

Barcus, Perlmutter, and Callaway (58B1) calculated the wave-

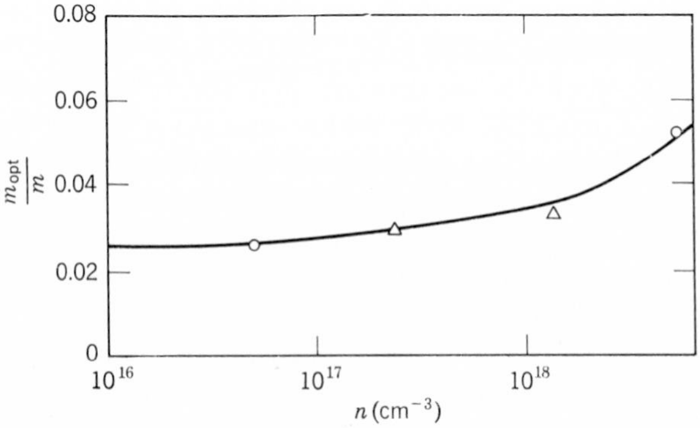

Fig. 3.21 Optical effective mass of electrons in InAs as a function of carrier concentration. Circles after Cardona (61C3); triangles after Spitzer and Fan (57S3); curve: Kane's theory.

length dependence of the index of refraction of a GaAs sample with $n = 6.9 \times 10^{17}$ cm^{-3} from reflection measurements between 2 and 22 μ. The results could be described quantitatively by the relationship $n_r^2 = \kappa_l - A\lambda^2$, where $\kappa_l = 11.06 \pm 0.14$ and $A = (0.0143 \pm 0.0005)$ cm^{-2}. From this relation the effective electron mass is determined by eq. (3.14): $m_n = (0.043 \pm 0.005)\ m$.

Reflection measurements on ***n*-GaSb** are more difficult to interpret because of the complicated structure of the conduction band. Becker, Ramdas, and Fan (61B7) and Cardona (61C2) conducted a thorough analysis of such reflection measurements in conjunction with measurements of electric and galvanomagnetic properties of this semiconductor. The results are based on the model of a (000)-band with a slightly higher-lying (111)-band, which was postulated in Section 311. This will be considered further in Chapter 4. At this point we mention only the effective mass of holes, $m_{p1} = 0.23\ m$, obtained from reflection measurements (58R1).

The strong dependence of the reflection coefficient near the plasma-reflection edge on the density of the charge carriers makes it possible to determine concentration fluctuations in inhomogeneous semiconductors with great accuracy. Edwards and Maker (62E3) were able to observe density variations of 0.5% in InSb by this procedure.

323 Cyclotron resonance. We saw in Section 320 that the optical absorption by free-charge carriers in a magnetic field shows a maximum when the circular frequency of the light is equal to the characteristic frequency ω_c [eq. (3.30)]. This *cyclotron-resonance* effect can be understood classically as a resonance absorption by the charge carriers rotating about the magnetic field with frequency ω_c in a plane perpendicular to the field. Quantum-mechanically it follows from the theory of the coalescence of a band into one-dimensional subbands in a magnetic field, which was sketched in Section 315. At that point we were considering only transitions from the magnetic subbands of the valence band into those of the conduction band. In addition, transitions are possible between the subbands of one of the bands, which, according to eq. (3.9), require an energy $\hbar\omega_c$. These are the transitions causing the cyclotron resonance. The simple theory which led to (3.30) needs to be improved in a number of points. For one thing the condition $\omega \gg \omega_p, \omega_0$ is often not fulfilled. The influence of the plasma frequency ω_p can be taken into account theoretically and leads to a displacement of the maximum absorption to the point $\omega = \omega_c[1 - (\omega_p/\omega)^2]^{1/2}$. Depolarization effects are possible; they can, however, be eliminated by suitable choice of the geometry of the sample (55D3). In the determination of the cyclotron-resonance frequency one must also consider the displacement of the plasma-reflection edge by the magnetic field [eq. (3.31)], which in transmission measurements leads to a too large value of ω_c. These plasma corrections can be eliminated by the use of sufficiently high magnetic fields.

In addition, for III-V compounds with the lowest conduction-band edge at $\mathbf{k} = 0$, Kane's theory must be used for the analysis of the results. The theory was extended to include the effect of a static magnetic field by Lax, Mavroides, Zeiger, and Keyes (61L4) for $k_B = 0$. According to this work the equation $E = (\hbar eB/m^*)(n + \frac{1}{2}) \pm \frac{1}{2} g \mu_B B$ [eqs. (3.9ff.)] for the magnetic subbands of the conduction band is also valid in the framework of Kane's theory if the effective mass

$$\frac{1}{m^*} = \frac{1}{m_0^*} \frac{E_G(E_G + \Delta)}{3E_G + 2\Delta} \left(\frac{2}{E + E_G} + \frac{1}{E + E_G + \Delta} \right) \tag{3.38}$$

(m_0^* is the effective mass at the bottom edge of the conduction band) is used and if the value of the g-factor is taken as

$$g^* = g_0^* \frac{E_G(E_G + \Delta)}{\Delta} \left(\frac{1}{E + E_G} - \frac{1}{E + E_G + \Delta} \right) \tag{3.39}$$

where g_0^* is given by (3.11) for $\mathbf{k} = 0$. Both values are therefore energy dependent. The results have been extended to the case $k_z \neq 0$ by Palik, Picus, Teitler, and Wallis (61P3). It follows that ω_c does not increase linearly with magnetic field B, as for an isotropic parabolic band, but has a more complicated field dependence. This also causes the experimentally determined cyclotron-resonance mass $m_c = eB/\omega_c$ to be field dependent. Only its extrapolation to $B = 0$ gives the effective mass at the band edge.

The first measurements of cyclotron resonance in III-V compounds were made at microwave frequencies and at low temperatures. Dresselhaus, Kip, Kittel, and Wagoner (55D3) observed a resonance line in InSb at 24 kMc and 2.2°K which led to an effective mass of the electrons of $(0.013 \pm 0.001)\ m$. These measurements were strongly influenced by magnetoplasma effects. The electron concentration in InSb does not go to zero at low temperatures because of the overlap of the conduction band and an impurity band. Furthermore, the available samples were not sufficiently pure, and impurity scattering caused a short relaxation time at low temperatures. The cyclotron-resonance frequency was therefore smaller than ω_0 and ω_p. Considerable improvement was made by infrared room-temperature

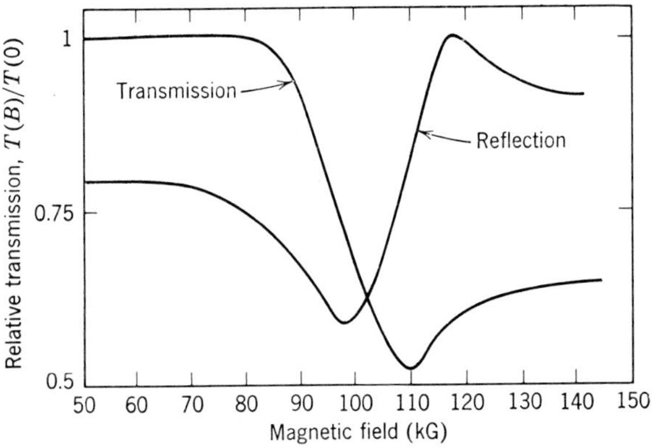

Fig. 3.22 Transmission and reflection of an InSb sample at 19.4 μ in the cyclotron-resonance region [after Lax, Mavroides, Zeiger, and Keyes (61L4)].

investigations of Burstein, Picus, and Gebbie (56B4) and of Keyes, Zwerdling, Foner, Kolm, and Lax (56K3). Static magnetic fields up to 6×10^4 gauss and pulsed fields up to 3.2×10^5 gauss were used. These investigations were later continued by Palik, Wallis, and co-workers (58W1), (61P1)–(61P5), (63P1), by Lax, Mavroides, Zeiger, and Keyes (61L4), and extended to InAs, InP, and GaAs.

The magnetic-field dependence of the transmission and reflection of an InSb sample at 19.4 μ and room temperature is shown in Fig. 3.22 (61L4). The transmission minimum and the inflection point of the reflection curve (which indicate the resonance point) both lie at the same magnetic field. Figure 3.23 shows the effective masses m_c determined from such measurements and their dependence on magnetic field. The solid line was determined by the theoretical considerations discussed. The extrapolation to $B = 0$ results in an effective mass of the electrons at the band edge of $m_n = (0.0116 \pm 0.0005)\ m$ at room temperature. With Kane's theory, m_n can be calculated at other temperatures. According to (2.13), m_n is determined by P, E_G, and Δ. If one assumes that E_G is the only one of these parameters that is temperature dependent, and if one uses its temperature dependence known from other measurements, it follows that $m_n = (0.0155 \pm 0.0005)\ m$ at 4°K. This is consistent with a measurement of Palik, Pikus, Teitler, and Wallis (61P3), which gave an intermediate value of $(0.0145 \pm 0.001)\ m$ at 80°K. These same authors, however, give a room-temperature value of $0.0135\ m$. For further analysis of the cyclotron resonance in InSb we refer to the articles mentioned, in

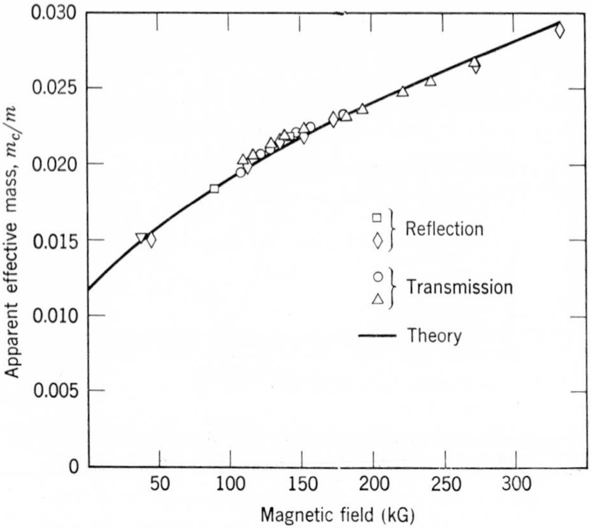

Fig. 3.23 Dependence of the cyclotron-resonance electron mass m_c of InSb on the magnetic field. Experimental points after Burstein, Picus, and Gebbie (56B4) and Lax, Mavroides, Zeiger, and Keyes (61L4).

particular to (61P3) and (61L4). A general discussion is also contained in (60L2).

Results for *p*-InSb are given below.

For InAs (56K3), (61P2), (63P1), InP (61P2), and GaAs (61P5) no such accurate results have yet been obtained. In all cases the effective cyclotron-resonance mass m_c was field dependent. All three semiconductors can consequently be assumed to have a nonparabolic conduction band similar to that of InSb. Measurements between 100 and 200 kG gave effective masses of 0.025 and 0.030 m for two samples of InAs of different purity. The magnetic field dependence of the effective mass of one of these samples allowed the extrapolation to the ($B = 0$) value of 0.015 m at room temperature (56K3). However, Palik and Wallis (61P2) obtained the rather different value of m_n (78°K) $= (0.023 \pm 0.002)$ m from an extrapolation of measurements made between 10 and 60 kG.

The best value given so far for InP is $m_n = (0.077 \pm 0.005)$ m, and for GaAs $m_n = (0.071 \pm 0.005)$ m. Both values are for 78°K.

In InSb (61P3) and InAs (63P1) additional structure in the form of satellite lines has been observed. This may be explained by the unequal spin splitting of the magnetic sublevels caused by the **k**-dependence of the g-factor of the electrons.

Cyclotron resonance in p-type material has so far been observed only in InSb. Bagguley, Robinson, and Stradling (63B1) found resonances at low temperatures in the millimeter wave region. From these they obtained the following hole values:

$$\begin{aligned} m_{p1} &= 0.45 \quad \pm 0.03\ m \quad \text{in the [111]-direction} \\ &\ 0.42 \quad \pm 0.03\ m \quad \text{in the [110]-direction} \\ &\ 0.34 \quad \pm 0.03\ m \quad \text{in the [100]-direction} \\ m_{p2} &= 0.021 \pm 0.005\ m \end{aligned}$$

The anisotropy of the heavy hole mass is similar to that found in germanium and silicon.

Earlier measurements of cyclotron resonance in p-InSb were made by Dresselhaus, Kip, Kittel, and Wagoner (55D3), who observed a very much lower effective mass value of $m_{p1} = 0.18\ m$. Plasma effects somewhat obscured this resonance, however. Magnetoabsorption measurements (cf. Section 315) have resulted in a similar low value. Consequently 0.18 m had long been assumed to be the true value of the heavy hole mass in InSb. A number of analyses of the properties of InSb are based on this value. We will see later that in contrast to this the electrical properties generally suggest the larger effective mass value. Indeed, the first-mentioned cyclotron resonance values must be considered to be the more reliable ones, since they were confirmed at a number of different temperatures.

324 Magnetoplasma reflection. The splitting of the plasma-reflection edge into two parts separated by ω_c [eq. (3.31)] has been observed in InSb and InAs by Wright and Lax (60L1), (61W10), and by Palik, Teitler, Henvis, and Wallis (62P1), and in InAs and GaAs by Maker, Baker, and Edwards (61M1). Figure 3.24 shows the transverse magnetoplasma reflection in InAs as an example. The evaluation gives effective-mass values which are consistent with those from other determinations. If the limiting condition $\omega_c \ll \omega_p$, which leads to (3.31), is lifted, then two reflection minima are obtained at $\omega \approx \omega_c + (\omega_p{}^2/\omega_c)$ and $\omega \approx \omega_p{}^2/\omega_c$ from (3.26a), (3.27a) and (3.29). The first one of these gives the plasma correction of the cyclotron resonance mentioned in Section 323, and the second leads to the appearance of a *magnetoplasma resonance.* The latter was observed in InSb by Dresselhaus, Kip, and Kittel (55D2).

A shift of the magnetoplasma resonance in InSb by heating of the

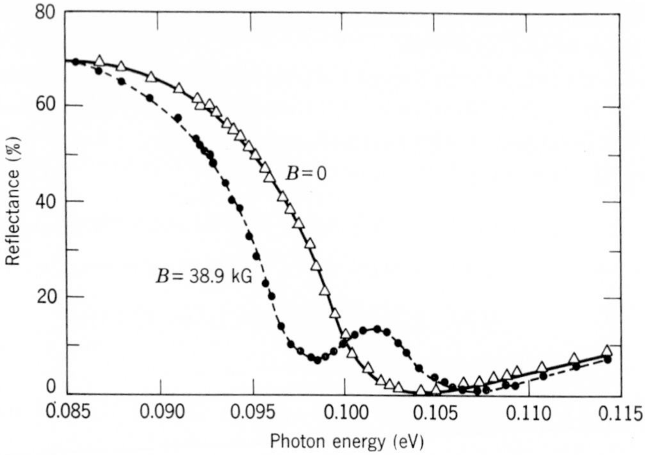

Fig. 3.24 Transverse magnetoplasma reflection in a sample of n-InAs at room temperature ($n = 5.3 \times 10^{18}$ cm^{-3}) [after Wright and Lax (61W10)].

electrons in an electric field was observed by Bemski (62B6). It was explained by the larger average effective mass of the hot electrons in the nonparabolic conduction band of InSb.

325 Faraday and Voigt effects. The Faraday angle ϑ is proportional to the square of the wavelength, inversely proportional to the square of the effective mass, and a linear function of the magnetic field, according to (3.35). It is particularly advantageous to determine the effective mass from the Faraday effect if the necessary condition for cyclotron resonance, $\omega_c \gg \omega_0$, cannot be fulfilled.

Cardona (61C1) has shown that, for nonparabolic bands, the effective mass determined from the Faraday effect with (3.35) is identical with the value m_{opt} determined from reflection measurements [Eq. (3.31)]. For degenerate semiconductors the Faraday effect gives the effective mass of eq. (3.22); it is determined by the slope (and not the curvature) of the band at the Fermi energy. The theory of the Faraday effect, taking Kane's band structure into account, was also discussed by Kołodziejczak (62K6).

Kimmel (57K4) made the first measurements of the Faraday effect in III-V compounds (InP, GaAs, GaP). He did not analyze the results and only pointed out the large value of the Faraday angle in these compounds.

Moss, Smith, and Taylor (59M6), (59S5), (60S6), (61M14) report measurements on InSb which lead to effective masses in good agreement with values determined in other ways. The effective mass determined by (3.22) increases with increasing doping. The dependence of the energy in the InSb conduction band is given by the first eq. (2.9) in Kane's theory. If this equation is inserted in (3.22), the dependence of the effective electron mass on the wave number $|\mathbf{k}|$ is obtained. The value of the electron concentration in a degenerate semiconductor is given by the product of the density of states in **k**-space and the volume surrounded by the surface $E = E_F$:

$$\frac{2}{(2\pi)^3}\frac{4\pi}{3}|\mathbf{k}|^3$$

Thus from Kane's theory a dependence of m_n on the electron concentration follows:

$$m_n{}^2/(m - m_n)^2 = 32.5 \times 10^{-32}\frac{E_G{}^2}{P^4} + 8.27 \times 10^{-30}\frac{n^{2/3}}{P^2} \qquad (3.40)$$

(P in eV cm, E_G in eV, n in cm^{-3}). If we substitute $P = 8.7 \times 10^{-8}$ eV cm, and for E_G the value of Table 3.1, the curve of Fig. 3.25 follows (cf. Table 2.3). The corresponding experimental points were obtained from measurements of the Faraday effect (59S5), of the plasma reflection (57S3), and of the magnetoplasma reflection (61W10).

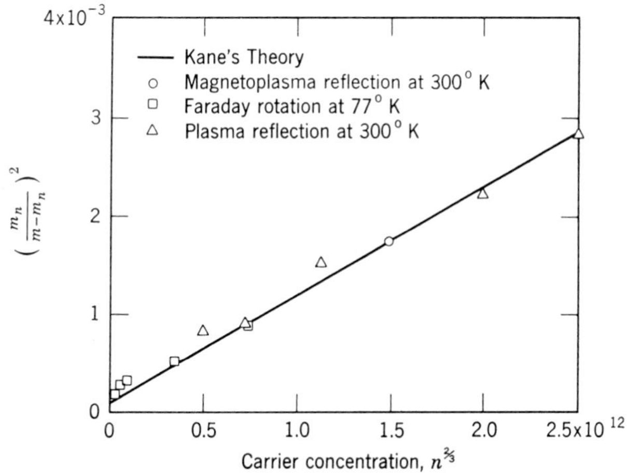

Fig. 3.25 Variation of the effective electron mass [m_2 of eq. (2.19)] in InSb with electron concentration [after Wright and Lax (61W10)].

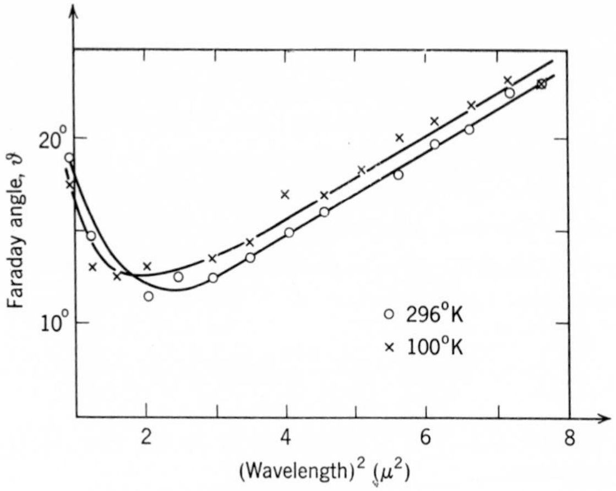

Fig. 3.26 Faraday rotation in n-GaAs ($n = 2.36 \times 10^{18}$ cm^{-3}) as a function of the square of the wavelength (magnetic field 8330 gauss) [after Cardona (61C3)].

It is obvious that the various optical determinations of the effective mass supplement each other and that all are consistent with Kane's theory for InSb.

Smith, Pidgeon, and Prosser (62S10) also give an extensive discussion of their Faraday-effect measurements in InSb and of the possibility of calculating the effective masses therefrom. Here again the electron mass determined from Kane's theory agrees very well with the experimental results, both in value and in temperature dependence.

To determine m^* from (3.35) it is necessary to measure the electron density independently. In most cases the Hall effect is used for this purpose. In InSb (and InAs) another method is possible. If the magnetic field is increased to the case $(\omega_c - \omega) \gg \omega_0$, while $\omega \gg \omega_p$ still applies, the Faraday angle becomes a linear function of n/B, independent of the effective mass and wavelength. An independent measurement of n is therefore possible in this range. Thus Palik, Teitler, and Wallis (61P4) determined an effective electron mass of 0.015 m for an InSb sample of $n = 1.5 \times 10^{15}$ cm^{-3}.

For other measurements on InSb see, e.g., (62U1), (63U2).

Faraday-effect measurements on InAs (60A16), (61C3), (61P2), (63U2), InP (59M7), (60A16), (64K2), GaAs (59M8), (61C3), (63U1), GaP (63U2), and AlSb (62M13), (64M3) gave the following effective masses for the purest samples measured in the various cases:

$$\text{InAs:}\ m_n = 0.027\ m\ (+8\%;\ -3\%)\ \text{for}\ n = 4.9 \times 10^{16}\ \text{cm}^{-3}$$
$$= 0.043\ m \qquad n = 1.04 \times 10^{18}\ \text{cm}^{-3}$$
$$\text{InP:}\ m_n = 0.075 \pm 0.008\ m \qquad \text{for}\ n = 1.07 \times 10^{16}\ \text{cm}^{-3}$$
$$= 0.1\ m \qquad n = 1.1 \times 10^{17}\ \text{cm}^{-3}$$
$$\text{GaAs:}\ m_n = 0.067 \pm 0.002\ m \qquad \text{for}\ n = 1.48 \times 10^{17}\ \text{cm}^{-3}$$
$$\text{GaP:}\ m_n = 0.34 \pm 0.02\ m \qquad \text{for}\ n = 2.48 \times 10^{18}\ \text{cm}^{-3}$$
$$\text{AlSb:}\ m_n = 0.39 \pm 0.06\ m \qquad \text{for}\ n = 2 \times 10^{18}\ \text{cm}^{-3}$$

In all cases a growing effective mass with increasing doping and temperature was noted.

For GaSb, Piller (63P8), (63P10) obtained the following values from Faraday-effect measurements: $m_n(000) = 0.049\ (+0.005,\ -0.003)\ m$ for a sample with 3.77×10^{17} electrons/cm^3. The ratio of the electron mobilities in the two conduction bands was measured to be $\mu_{111}/\mu_{000} = \frac{1}{6}$, and that of the density of state masses to be $m_{111}/m_{000} = 14.3$.

Figures 3.26 and 3.27 show the dependence of the Faraday angle on the square of the wavelength in InAs and GaAs as measured by Cardona (61C3). The linear dependence expected from (3.35) is apparent at large λ. There are strong deviations, however, at wavelengths corresponding to energies near E_G; they consist of an additional negative contribution for InAs and an additional positive contribution

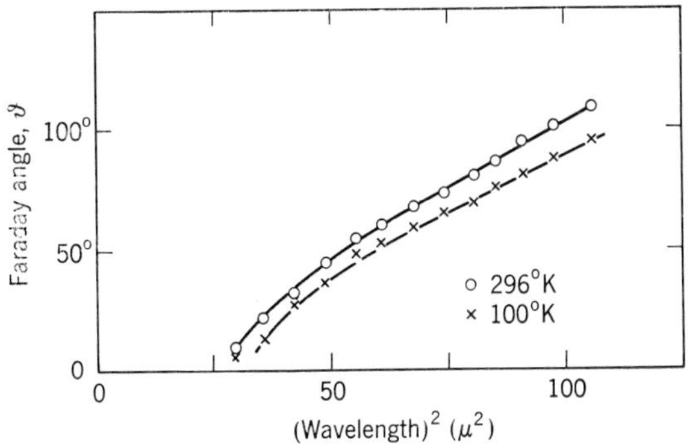

Fig. 3.27 Faraday rotation in n-InAs ($n = 4.9 \times 10^{16}$ cm^{-3}) as a function of the square of the wavelength (magnetic field 8330 gauss) [after Cardona (61C3)].

for GaAs. In InSb the deviation is similar to InAs. These contributions must be assigned to transitions from valence to conduction band. It can be shown that a dispersion is associated with absorption due to direct transitions [eq. (3.5)]. This dispersion is different for right- and left-polarized light. The contribution of the interband transitions to the Faraday rotation, according to Cardona, is positive if the sum of the g-factors of the magnetic subbands, between which the transition takes place, is positive, and negative if this sum is negative. The g-factor of the conduction band is considerably larger than that of the valence band in the III-V compounds under consideration, so that only the former must be taken into account. We will see in Chapter 9 that g is negative in InSb and InAs, and probably slightly positive in GaAs.

Lax (61L3) obtains a similar result but emphasizes that this interpretation oversimplifies the problem. For a more exact theory of the interband-Faraday effect see (61L5), (62L1), (64R1); for further experiments, (62U1), (63P11).

Measurements of the Voigt effect on InSb, InAs, and GaAs by Palik, Teitler, and Wallis (60T3), (61P4), (61T2) result in values of the effective masses which agree well with those determined from the Faraday effect.

33 Lattice Vibrations

Because of the polar contribution to the binding in the zinc-blende lattice there is a strong absorption in the long-wavelength region of the spectrum due to excitation of vibration modes of the lattice. The theory of the lattice absorption gives for the dielectric constant the dispersion relation (54B4):

$$\kappa(\omega) = \kappa(\infty) + [\kappa(0) - \kappa(\infty)] \frac{\omega_t^2}{\omega_t^2 - \omega^2 + i\gamma\omega} \tag{3.41}$$

where ω_t is the frequency of the transverse optical lattice vibrations, $\kappa(0)$ and $\kappa(\infty)$ are the dielectric constants in the limit of very small and very large frequencies ω, and γ is a damping constant. The difference between these two limiting values of the dielectric constant is given by

$$\kappa(0) - \kappa(\infty) = \frac{e_s^{*2}}{\epsilon_0 M v_a \omega_t^2} \left[\frac{\kappa(\infty) + 2}{3}\right]^2 = \frac{e_c^{*2}\kappa^2(\infty)}{\epsilon_0 M v_a \omega_t^2} \tag{3.42}$$

where M is the reduced mass of the lattice atoms, and v_a is the volume of the unit cell of the lattice. The terms e_s^* and e_c^* are two effective ion charges, which were introduced by Szigeti and by Callen, and which can be considered to be a measure of the heteropolar contribution to the lattice binding. The relation between them, according to (3.42), is

$$e_s^* = e_c^* \frac{3\kappa(\infty)}{\kappa(\infty) + 2} \tag{3.43}$$

Using eqs. (3.41) and (3.42), one can calculate the optical frequencies of the transverse lattice vibrations and of the longitudinal lattice vibrations, $\omega_l = \left(\frac{\kappa(0)}{\kappa(\infty)}\right)^{1/2} \omega_t$, from reflection measurements, and thereby determine the effective ion charges. The reflection coefficient is

$$R = \left| \frac{\kappa^{1/2} - 1}{\kappa^{1/2} + 1} \right|^2 \tag{3.44}$$

according to (3.2). Consider first the case $\gamma = 0$. Then R increases with increasing frequency from the value $R = \left[\frac{\sqrt{\kappa(0)} - 1}{\sqrt{\kappa(0)} + 1}\right]^2$ to 1 at $\omega = \omega_t$. In the region $\omega_t < \omega < \omega_l$, κ is negative, $\sqrt{\kappa}$ therefore

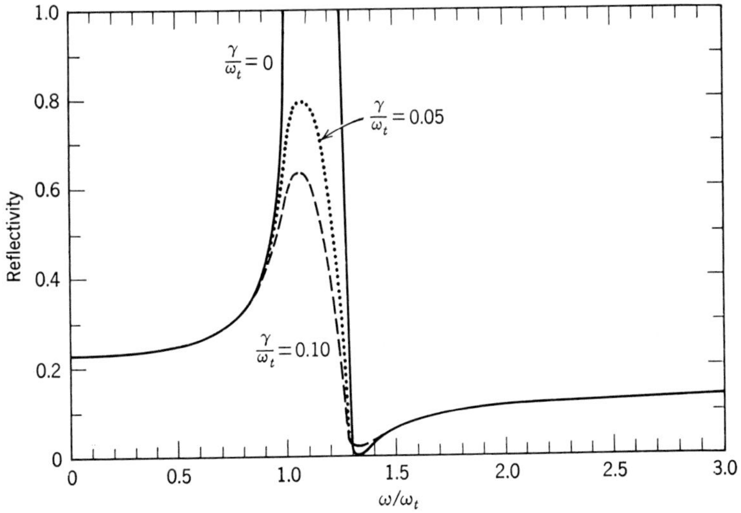

Fig. 3.28 Theoretical reflectivity curves for various values of the damping constant γ and $\kappa(0) = 8$, $\kappa(\infty) = 5$ [after Picus, Burstein, Henvis, and Hass (59P3)].

imaginary, and $R = 1$ (region of the Reststrahlen reflection). For $\omega > \omega_l$, R decreases rapidly to zero at $\omega = \omega_t \left[1 + \frac{\kappa(0) - \kappa(\infty)}{\kappa(\infty) - 1}\right]^{1/2}$ and then increases again slowly to the limiting value at $\omega = \infty$. This behavior is shown in Fig. 3.28 (59P3). Other reflection curves for various finite values of the damping constant are also shown. In those cases the reflection coefficient does not attain the value 1, and the optical vibration frequencies can only be estimated from the experiment.

Extensive measurements of the reflection in the Reststrahlen region were undertaken by Picus, Burstein, Henvis, and Hass (59P3). Figure 3.29 shows one of their experimental curves for GaAs, together with theoretical curves.

Corresponding measurements were made by Kleinman and Spitzer (60K5) on GaP. The following values were determined: $\kappa(0) = 10.182 \pm 0.2$, $\kappa(\infty) = 8.457 \pm 0.2$, $e_s{}^* = 0.58e$, $\nu_t = (1.098 \pm 0.002) \times 10^{13}$ sec^{-1}, $\gamma = (0.003 \pm 0.0005)$ sec^{-1}. Table 3.5 shows a number of experimental values of $\bar{\nu}_l = \nu_l/c$ and $\bar{\nu}_t = \nu_t/c$, and of effective ion charges calculated from these.

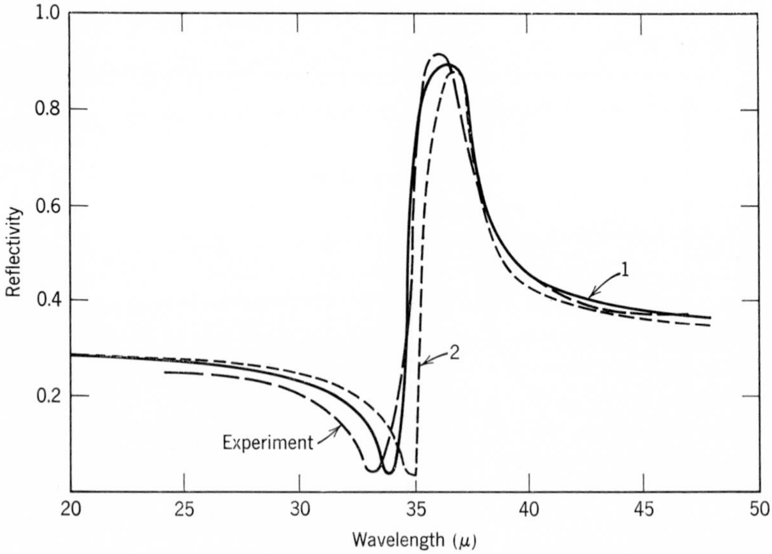

Fig. 3.29 Reflectivity of GaAs. Experimental curve after Picus, Burstein, Henvis, and Hass (59P3); theoretical curves (1 and 2) for two different sets of parameters after Ehrenreich (60E3).

Table 3.5 Transverse and Longitudinal Lattice Vibrations and Effective Ionic Charges of Some III-V Compounds [after Hass and Henvis (62H9)]

e_c^* is calculated from e_s^*, using the optical data given by Oswald and Schade (5402).

Compound	$\bar{\nu}_t$ (cm^{-1})	$\bar{\nu}_l$ (cm^{-1})	e_s^*/e	e_c^*/e	$\kappa(\infty)$
AlSb	318 ± 8	345 ± 5	0.53	0.21	11.6
GaAs	373.3 ± 3	297.3 ± 2	0.51	0.20	11.6
GaSb	230.5 ± 3	240.3 ± 2	0.33	0.125	15.2
InP	307 ± 8	351 ± 5	0.68	0.27	10.9
InAs	218.9 ± 3	243.3 ± 2	0.56	0.23	11.6
InSb	184.7 ± 3	197.2 ± 2	0.42	0.16	16.8

Hambleton, Hilsum, and Holeman (61H6) determined the static and optical dielectric constants for GaAs by direct measurement and therefrom calculated the effective ion charges. Their numerical values are $\kappa(0) = 12.53 \pm 0.26$, $\kappa(\infty) = 10.90 \pm 0.04$, $e_s^* = 0.46e$.

Further experimental measurements were made by Spitzer and Fan (55S1) on InSb, Newman (58N3) on InP, and Turner and Reese (60T4) on AlSb.

Besides the Reststrahlen absorption there are other bands in the lattice-absorption spectrum, due to interaction of the photon with more than one phonon. Two mechanisms are responsible for the "combination bands," the anharmonicity of the lattice forces (60K6) and higher-order electrical moments (55L1). The spectral position of the bands is given by the sum of the energies of the phonons involved. The individual combination bands can be identified by trial and error, using the temperature dependence to distinguish between two- and three-phonon processes. It is possible to interpret all measurements by the combinations of a few characteristic phonon energies. The results for InSb [Fray, Johnson, and Jones (60F9), (61J2)], AlSb [Turner and Reese (62T4)], GaAs [Cochran, Fray, Johnson, Quarrington, and Williams (61C9), (61F2), and Spitzer (63S4)], GaP [Kleinman and Spitzer (60K5)], and InP [Hilsum and Rose-Innes (61H12)], are listed in Table 3.6. Empirical correlations between the phonon energies and other parameters were given by Keyes (62K1) and Mitra (63M10).

The dispersion relations for the lattice vibrations in GaAs have been

Table 3.6 Energies of the Phonons which Make Up the Measured Combination Bands

Values are in reciprocal wave numbers $\bar{\nu}$ (cm^{-1}); O—optical branch, A—acoustical branch, L—longitudinal, T—transverse. For GaAs two possible sets of values are given.

Phonon	InSb	AlSb	GaAs		GaP	InP
TO	180	297	{275, 254}	247	361	316
LO	156	316	233	262	378	316
LA	117	132	189	207	197	126
TA	43	65	72	{181, 127}	{115, 66}	63

investigated by neutron spectroscopy by Waugh and Dolling (63W2). For results we refer to this work.

34 Index of Refraction

Values of the index of refraction for various III-V compounds have been given in the previous sections. Thus only some remarks are added here. Table 3.5 contains values of $\kappa(\infty)$, which is equal to the square of the index of refraction for high frequencies. The corresponding values of n_r were first reported by Oswald and Schade (54O2) and Folberth and Oswald (54F1).

Since the index of refraction depends on ω_p according to (3.14), n_r is not only frequency dependent but also, through n and m^*, doping and temperature dependent. Cardona (61C1) found from interferometric measurements on thin layers between 5 and 20 μ the following values of the temperature dependence:

Compound	n or p (cm^{-3})	n_r(297°K)	$\frac{1}{n_r}\frac{dn_r}{dT}$ (°C^{-1})
n-InSb	10^{17}	3.3 ± 0.15	$(2.7 \pm 0.3) \times 10^{-5}$
n-GaAs	10^{16}	3.4 ± 0.15	$(4.5 \pm 0.2) \times 10^{-5}$
p-GaAs	10^{17}	3.7 ± 0.15	$(8.2 \pm 0.2) \times 10^{-5}$

Edwards and Hayne (59E2) compared two techniques for determining the index of refraction in GaSb, prism and reflection measurements. In the region between 1.8 and 2.5 μ the first method gave values between 3.820 and 3.749 with an uncertainty of ± 0.013; the second method, values between 3.61 and 3.49 with an accuracy of 2%. The difference between the results appears to lie in the method of measurement: prism measurements give results depending on the properties of the bulk material; reflection measurements are influenced by the properties of a surface layer only.

4

Transport Properties

40 Introduction

The transport properties of the III-V compounds, which will be discussed in this chapter, include all those processes in which the movement of the charge carriers causes a transport of charge or energy through the semiconductor. Under the influence of an *electric field* the electrons and holes move in opposite directions along the field lines. The quantity which is characteristic for the current transport is the mobility of the charge carriers; it is defined as the proportionality factor between the average velocity of the carriers and the electric-field strength. Under the additional influence of a *magnetic field* the charge carriers are deflected in a direction perpendicular to the magnetic field and perpendicular to their propagation direction.

All transport properties originating in electric and magnetic fields (electric and galvanomagnetic effects) will be considered in Section 41.

A *temperature gradient* may cause diffusion currents which transport charge and energy through the solid. When only one kind of charge carriers diffuses, there frequently appear space charge regions and internal fields, which prevent the charge transport. Energy transport is still possible, because the diffusion current and the charge-compensating field current can carry different amounts of energy. The transport processes in the III-V compounds which are connected with a temperature gradient will be discussed in Section 42.

Application of *light* creates additional free-charge carriers because of electron transitions from impurity levels or from the valence band into the conduction band. The influence of such additional charge carriers on the transport processes and the recombination of these charge carriers will be discussed in Section 43.

All these transport processes will confirm and supplement the statements about the band structure of the III-V compounds that were deduced in Chapter 3. In addition, they will give information about the interaction of the charge carriers with the lattice (scattering mechanisms) and about their behavior under the influence of external fields.

41 Electric and Galvanomagnetic Properties

410 Mobility. In the corpuscular model of the mobility the motion of the electrons and holes in semiconductors under the influence of an electric field is described as a sequence of unimpeded accelerations of the charge carrier by the electric field $\mathbf{\mathcal{E}}$ and subsequent collisions with the lattice accompanied by energy and momentum transfer. This process of alternating acceleration and collision causes the charge carrier to move with an average velocity $\mathbf{v} = \mu\mathbf{\mathcal{E}}$, superimposed on the random thermal velocity. An average mean free path l and a time of flight τ_0 between two collisions (collision time) can be defined for each charge carrier; they will depend on its energy. The term τ_0 can also be considered as the relaxation time, in which a disturbance of the equilibrium distribution of the electrons decays to $1/e$ of its value.

This picture gives only a qualitative description of the transport phenomena. The quantitative theory takes into account that the interaction of the charge carriers with lattice atoms takes place through the lattice vibrations. It depicts this interaction as scattering processes in which phonons, the vibration quanta of the lattice, are emitted or absorbed.

The frequency spectrum of the lattice vibrations in crystals with more than one atom in the unit cell consists of two branches. The acoustic branch describes an energy-momentum relation for the phonons, for which, at $\hbar\mathbf{k} = 0$, also $\hbar\omega = 0$. In the optical branch the phonons with zero momentum have the energy $\hbar\omega_l$ or $\hbar\omega_t$, where the ω's are the limiting frequencies of the longitudinal and transverse optical lattice vibrations which were mentioned in Section 33.

In the interaction of the charge carriers with the lattice we must consider various *scattering mechanisms.* In addition to the scattering by optical and acoustic phonons there may be scattering of charge carriers by one another and by lattice imperfections. One of these mechanisms may predominate under any given experimental condition (temperature, doping, etc.) and limit the mobility of the carriers.

In germanium and silicon the interaction of the charge carriers with the *acoustic* vibrations is the most important scattering mechanism. It also limits the mobility in the III-V compounds as long as the average thermal energy kT is small compared to the energy of the optical phonons and provided that any additional impurity scattering is small. For pure acoustic scattering the mobility is given by Bardeen and Shockley as

$$\mu = \frac{\sqrt{8\pi}\, e\hbar^4 C_{ll}}{3E_1{}^2 m^{*5/2}(kT)^{3/2}} \tag{4.1}$$

Here C_{ll} is the average longitudinal elastic constant of the semiconductor, and E_1 is the displacement of the edge of the conduction band (for holes, the edge of the valence band) per unit dilatation of the lattice ("deformation potential"). The mobility is proportional to $m^{*-5/2}$ and $T^{-3/2}$. A relaxation time can be defined, and its dependence on the energy of the charge carriers is $\tau_0 \sim E^{-1/2}$.

For the theoretical description of the transport processes it is advantageous if the scattering mechanism can be characterized by a relaxation time. If the transport processes are described by the Boltzmann equation, all transport coefficients (conductivity, Hall coefficient, thermal conductivity, etc.) are given by integrals, which in addition to the distribution function and a power of the velocity, contain the relaxation time. These transport coefficients can therefore be determined immediately if the energy dependence of the relaxation time is known. Also, if more than one scattering mechanism influences the mobility, the individual relaxation times are added reciprocally.

The most important scattering mechanism in the III-V compounds is the *polar* interaction of the charge carriers with the *optical* lattice vibrations. This interaction plays a special role because a strong polarization is connected with the relative motion of the two (for III-V compounds *unequal*) atoms within the unit cell of the lattice (polar optical interaction). On the other hand, the two atoms in the unit cell are the same in the semiconducting elements with diamond structure and the associated nonpolar optical interaction is of only minor importance.

In contrast to the acoustic scattering, no relaxation time can be defined for the polar scattering. This fact complicates considerably the theoretical analysis of the experimental results. The transport coefficients can no longer be written as integrals over various powers of the relaxation time and energy, but must be calculated in each case by a separate variational procedure. Also, the combination of different scattering mechanisms can no longer be performed by addition of the reciprocal relaxation times in the integrand of the transport integral, but must be considered in the variational procedure. For the case of combined polar scattering and scattering by ionized impurities, Ehrenreich [compare (60E3)] finds for the mobility:

$$\mu = \frac{\sqrt{2}\,\hbar(kT)^{1/2}Mv_a\omega_l}{3\pi e e_c{}^* m^{*3/2}} (e^{\hbar\omega_l/kT} - 1)F_{1/2}^{-1}\left(\frac{\zeta}{kT}\right)G_1\left(\frac{\zeta}{kT}, \frac{\hbar\omega_l}{kT}\right) \quad (4.2)$$

Here $e_c{}^*$, M, v_a, and ω_l are the parameters of the polar lattice vibrations which were introduced in Section 33, ζ is the energy of the Fermi level with respect to the band edge, $F_{1/2}$ is a Fermi integral, and G_1 is a function which cannot generally be given in analytical form. For the simplest case (Boltzmann statistics, parabolic band, low density of carriers), $G_1 = f\,(\hbar\omega_l/kT)e^{\zeta/kT}$, where f takes on the value 1 for high temperatures and sinks to about 0.6 at lower temperatures and then increases again slightly. For larger concentrations of the charge carriers the polar interaction of one carrier with the lattice is screened by the other carriers. This leads, according to Ehrenreich (59E4), to a dependence of the function f on the plasma frequency ω_p (see Section 320). Except at high temperature (where f is always 1) f increases strongly with increasing ratio of ω_p/ω_l. For quantitative information we refer to (59E4).

In the general case G_1 is dependent on the amount of degeneracy, on the departure of the band structure from isotropic parabolic behavior, and on the correct combination of the scattering mechanisms. The electron-hole scattering, which becomes important above 100°K for the III-V compounds, can also be taken into account. We will not go into further details here, but rather we will discuss them in the following sections on experimental results.

We do want to mention at this point a discussion of Ehrenreich's (59E4), wherein he investigated how far the theoretical formulas for the mobility, Hall coefficient, and thermoelectric power, which were calculated by the variational procedure, could be formally reproduced by a solution of the Boltzmann equation, with the assumption of a relaxation time $\tau_0 \sim E^r$. Ehrenreich found that at high temperature r is equal to $\frac{1}{2}$ for all three coefficients. It falls with decreasing temperature to zero at $\hbar\omega_l = kT$. Below that the assumption fails completely, and at very low temperatures r takes on different values for the three coefficients. The complete curves are shown in Fig. 4.1.

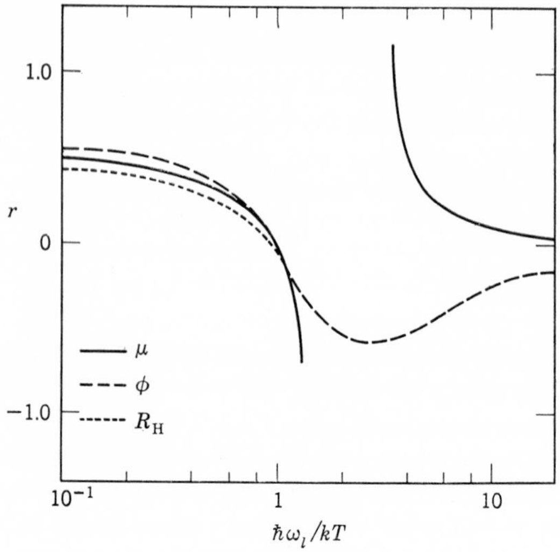

Fig. 4.1 Exponent r of the energy dependence of the effective relaxation time $\tau_0 \sim E^r$ for polar scattering. Since no true relaxation time can be defined, different effective relaxation times apply for the mobility μ, the thermoelectric power ϕ, and the Hall coefficient R_H [after Ehrenreich (61E4)].

Table 4.1 contains the characteristic temperatures, $T_l = \hbar\omega_l/k$, of the most important III-V compounds, calculated from the values of Table 3.6.

Table 4.1 Temperature Equivalents of the Longitudinal Optical Lattice Vibrations $T_l = \hbar\omega_l/k$ of the Most Important III-V Compounds

InSb	264°K	GaSb	336°K	AlSb	482°K
InAs	334°K	GaAs	408°K		
InP	487°K	GaP	578°K		

Electrons scatter at all kinds of lattice imperfections but only *ionized-impurity* scattering is of importance. The scattering event is described by a modified Rutherford scattering formula. A relaxation time can be defined ($\tau_0 \sim E^{3/2}$). The mobility, for nondegenerate semiconductors, according to Brooks, Herring, and Dingle, is

$$\mu = \frac{2^{7/2}\kappa^2\epsilon_0{}^2(kT)^{3/2}}{n_{\text{ion}}\pi^{3/2}e^3m^{*1/2}\ln y} \tag{4.3}$$

$$\ln y = \ln(1+b) - \frac{b}{1+b}; \quad b = \frac{6\kappa\epsilon_0 m^*(kT)^2}{\pi n\hbar^2 e^2} \tag{4.4}$$

n_{ion} is the concentration of ionized impurities, and n is the concentration of the free-charge carriers. For degenerate semiconductors b becomes $(2\kappa\epsilon_0 kT/e^2)(\pi/3n)^{1/3}$.

Aside from these three major scattering mechanisms the *electron-hole* scattering has some importance. It can be described analogously to the ionized-impurity scattering. *Electron-electron* scattering and scattering at *neutral impurities* need generally not be taken into account but may have an influence on the mobility under certain special conditions. In semiconductors, where the band structure has a number of extrema, or subbands, the charge carriers can be scattered from one of these into another (*intervalley* scattering). Furthermore, since the III-V compounds are piezoelectric, the electrical polarization connected with the lattice vibrations can influence the scattering [*piezoelectric* scattering, Harrison (56H3)]. In the later sections, all these scattering mechanisms will be considered only as far as it is necessary for comparison of experimental results with theory.

There is the interesting special case where the relaxation time is independent of energy. This situation obtains under certain conditions for polar scattering, according to Fig. 4.1, and its importance lies in the formal simplification of the theory of the transport properties. It means that the energy spectrum of the charge carriers has no influence on the scattering processes. All charge carriers behave in the same way. The statistical factors disappear from the transport coefficients, and the pictorial interpretation of the events taking place is much easier. The mobility then becomes $\mu = e\tau_0/m^*$. This approximation was used in Section 320 for the theory of the optical properties of free-charge carriers.

411 Conductivity and Hall coefficient. The *conductivity* is defined as the proportionality factor between the current density and the electric field. For a mixed semiconductor we write

$$\mathbf{i} = \sigma\mathbf{\mathcal{E}}; \quad \sigma = e(\mu_n n + \mu_p p) \tag{4.5}$$

The mobilities μ_n and μ_p are given by the equations of Section 410.

The concentrations of the charge carriers n and p in case of parabolic bands are given by

$$n = n_0 \frac{2}{\sqrt{\pi}} F_{1/2}\left(\frac{E_F - E_c}{kT}\right), \quad p = p_0 \frac{2}{\sqrt{\pi}} F_{1/2}\left(\frac{E_v - E_F}{kT}\right)$$
$$n_0 = 2\left(\frac{2\pi m_n kT}{h^2}\right)^{3/2}, \qquad p_0 = 2\left(\frac{2\pi m_p kT}{h^2}\right)^{3/2} \tag{4.6}$$

where $F_{1/2}(x)$ is the Fermi integral which goes over into $(\sqrt{\pi}/2)e^x$ for the case of Boltzmann statistics (nondegenerate semiconductor); n and p are interrelated by the mass-action law ($np = n_i^2$) and the neutrality condition ($n + n_{A^-} = p + n_{D^+}$). Finally, the concentration of electrons and holes for the intrinsic conduction (nondegenerate) is given by

$$n_i = \sqrt{n_0 p_0}\, e^{-(E_G/2kT)} = 4.9 \times 10^{15} \left(\frac{m_n m_p}{m^2}\right)^{3/4} T^{3/2} e^{-(E_G/2kT)} (\text{cm}^{-3}) \tag{4.7}$$

The *Hall coefficient* R_H is defined as the ratio of the Hall field $\mathcal{E}_y$ to the product of the current density i_x and the magnetic induction B_z. For nondegenerate semiconductors and small magnetic fields it is given by

$$R_H = r_R \frac{1}{e} \frac{p - b^2 n}{(p + bn)^2}; \quad b = \frac{\mu_n}{\mu_p} \tag{4.8}$$

The factor r_R is determined by the scattering mechanism and is of the order of 1.

If the relaxation time varies as $\tau_0 \sim E^r$, then $r_R = \Gamma_2 \Gamma_0 / \Gamma_1^2$, where Γ_a are gamma functions of argument $(ar + \frac{5}{2})$. For an energy-independent relaxation time, r is zero; for acoustic scattering, $-\frac{1}{2}$; and for ionized-impurity scattering, $+\frac{3}{2}$.

In the following discussion we will assume r_R to be equal to 1, unless an alternate value is specifically indicated.

Equations (4.5)–(4.8) become more complicated if more than one subband must be considered in the valence or conduction band. The appropriate equations will be discussed later in connection with the experimental results.

Both the mobilities and the width of the forbidden gap can be determined from the conductivity and the Hall coefficient. For extrinsic conduction ($n \gg p$ or $p \gg n$) and nondegeneracy the product $|R_H|\sigma$ is equal to the mobility except for the factor r_R, according to

(4.5) and (4.8). The quantity $|R_H|\sigma$ is defined as the *Hall mobility*, μ_H. It is to be distinguished from the *drift mobility*, μ, which enters into the conductivity and does not contain the factor r_R.

To obtain the band gap the intrinsic concentration n_i is determined from σ or R_H. If one then plots ln (n_i^2/T^3) vs. $1/T$, one obtains, according to (4.7), for nondegenerate samples a straight line, whose slope is equal to $-E_G/k$. This value of the width of the forbidden gap must not be compared directly with the values that were given in Chapter 3 because of its variation with temperature. If one assumes a linear temperature dependence for E_G and sets $E_G = E_G(0) - aT$ in (4.7), then only $E(0)$ appears in the exponent, while n_i contains a factor $e^{-a/2k}$. Consequently the quantity E_G, determined from the slope of the ln (n_i^2/T^3) vs. $1/T$ curve, is "the linearly to zero-temperature extrapolated value of the forbidden gap." We have indicated values of $E_G(0)$ extrapolated from optical measurements in Table 3.1.

Let us now consider the experimental results obtained on the most important III-V compounds.

Indium Antimonide. The III-V compound whose electrical properties have been investigated most thoroughly is InSb. This is partly due to the fact that this compound can be prepared rather easily, and partly due to its extremely high electron mobility, which leads to a number of phenomena that do not appear in other semiconductors (or are present in only a moderate amount).

In his first paper Welker (52W1) pointed to the high value of the electron mobility as a particularly important characteristic of n-InSb. Figure 4.2 shows the first extensive measurements of the conductivity and the Hall coefficient by Weiss (53W1), (53M1). In addition to the curves of the two n-type samples (A and B) with impurity concentrations of 1.3×10^{16} cm^{-3} and 1.0×10^{17} cm^{-3} and the four p-type samples (1–4, n_A between 4.0×10^{15} cm^{-3} and 2.0×10^{17} cm^{-3}), we have also plotted the conductivity and the Hall coefficient of the purest InSb sample obtained so far, which had $n_D - n_A \approx 10^{13}$ cm^{-3} [Volokobinskaya, Galavanov, and Nasledov (59V4)].

A characteristic feature of the data in Fig. 4.2 is the curvature of the intrinsic-conductivity curve at high temperature. It is caused by the degeneracy of the electron gas. Furthermore, the intrinsic-conductivity curve does not have the lowest conductivity of all samples, as in germanium and silicon; the p-type samples lie even lower. The minimum of the conductivity lies in the region of mixed conduction where $p > n$. This points out that the electron mobility is

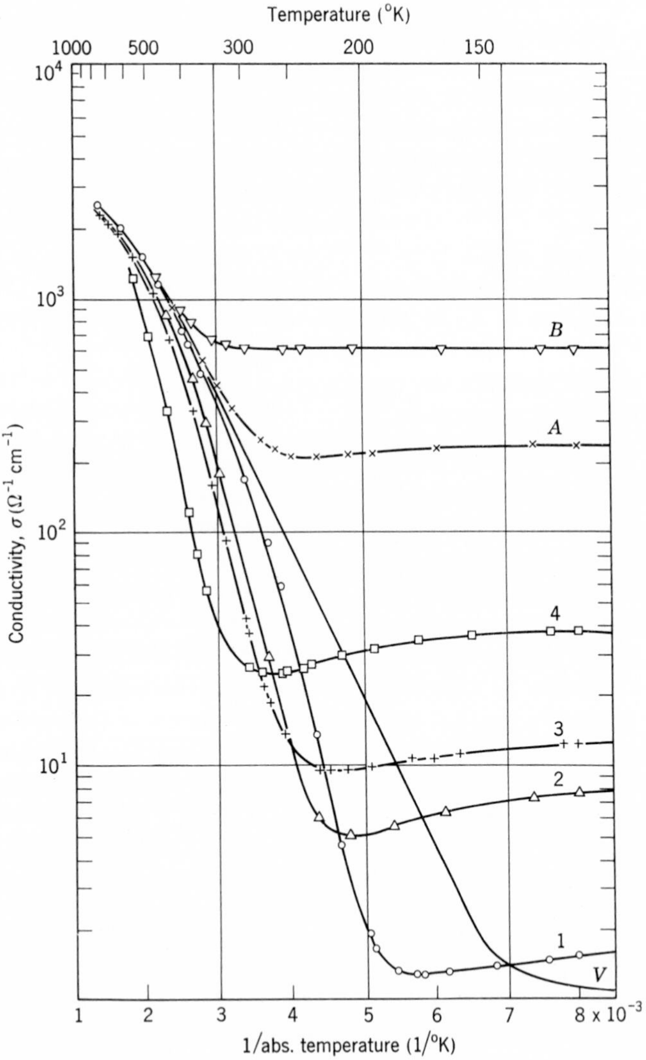

(a)

Fig. 4.2 Temperature dependence of the conductivity and the Hall coefficient of InSb for two n-type (A,B) and four p-type (1–4) samples [after Madelung and

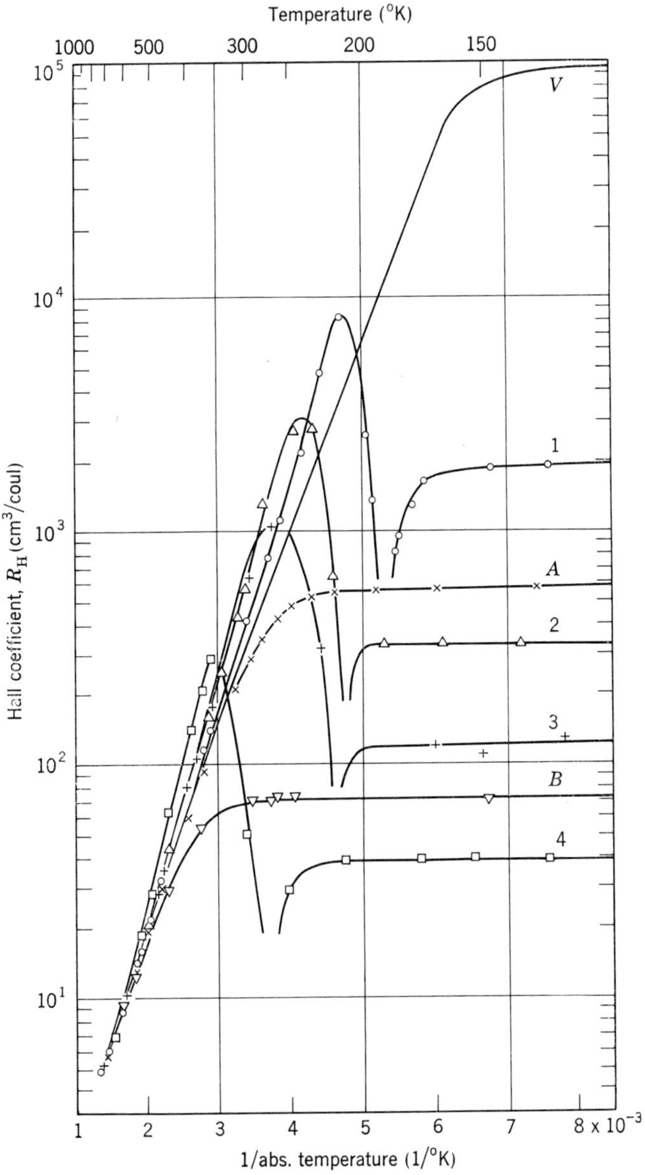

(b)

Weiss (54M1)] and for one *n*-type sample of high purity (*V*) [after Volokobinskaya, Galavanov, and Nasledov (59V4)].

considerably larger than the hole mobility (53F2). From the equation $\sigma = e(\mu_n n + \mu_p p)$ it follows that the minimum of σ is at $p = (\mu_n/\mu_p)n$. Furthermore, according to (4.8), the maximum of the Hall coefficient lies in the region of mixed conductivity at $p = (b/3)n$, for large values of $b = \mu_n/\mu_p$. This causes the curves in Fig. 4.2b also to cross. The crossing of the $\sigma(T)$-curves and the consequent steeper increase of the conductivity with increasing temperature for p-type samples than for intrinsic ones led to deductions of excessively large values of the band gap in InSb in the early studies.

Before we consider the extensive literature on the conductivity and the galvanomagnetic effects in InSb, we will derive a preliminary survey of the most important transport parameters from the results shown in Fig. 4.2. The purest samples show intrinsic conductivity over a wide temperature range, so that it is easily possible to determine n_i and therefrom $E_G(0)$. In the extrinsic region the product of conductivity and Hall coefficient gives the Hall mobility of the charge carriers. The analysis of the curves according to Madelung and Weiss (54M1) gives the following values: width of the forbidden gap $E_G = (0.27 - 3 \times 10^{-4}T)$ eV. This value was obtained from the slope of the ln (n_i^2/T^3) vs. $1/T$ curve [eq. (4.7)] under consideration of the degeneracy. The Hall mobility for the electrons is 77,000 cm^2/V sec for the purest samples at room temperature. Its temperature dependence follows a $T^{-1.66}$ law, as long as ionized-impurity scattering does not limit the mobility. The hole mobility is about two orders of magnitude smaller and is proportional to $T^{-\alpha}$ with $\alpha > 1.66$.

Because of the small effective mass of the electrons, which is related to the high electron mobility, the degeneracy concentration n_0 is very small. In n-type samples, degeneracy must be taken into account at all temperatures, in intrinsic samples above 200°K. The determination of the intrinsic concentration in InSb is made considerably easier by the high mobility ratio. The holes contribute only a few per cent to the intrinsic conductivity. For the discussion of the Hall coefficient in the intrinsic case the influence of the holes can be neglected completely, since, according to (4.8), the mobility ratio enters as the square into R_H. However, the amount of degeneracy must be taken into account.

Hrostowski and co-workers (55H4) find for the intrinsic concentration between 200 and 600°K a value of

$$n_i = 6.0 \times 10^{14} T^{3/2} e^{-0.26/2kT} \text{ cm}^{-3}$$

Because of degeneracy the value 0.26 in the exponent is not exactly equal to the width of the forbidden gap $E_G(0)$, but is somewhat smaller.

From a more careful analysis Hrostowski finds $E_G(0) = 0.29$ eV. The value was obtained by using the optically measured room-temperature E_G value and extrapolating it to zero by the temperature dependence of the forbidden gap obtained from the measured n_i. Within the accuracy of the measurements Putley (59P7) arrives at the same result.

We will now consider the various mobility measurements. Numerous workers have confirmed the value of the maximum *electron mobility* given above: $\mu_n = 77{,}000(T/300)^{-1.66}$ cm^2/V sec.

Ehrenreich (57E2), (59E5) has made a comparison with the theory. The extremely high values of electron mobility are to be expected from the very small effective mass of the electrons in InSb, according to the simple formula $\mu \approx e\tau_0/m^*$. For acoustic scattering μ also depends on the constant E_1 of the deformation potential (4.1), which is known only inaccurately. An estimate from the pressure dependence of the conductivity (see Section 414) gives $E_1 \approx -7$ eV. The remaining parameters in (4.1) are known. The room-temperature value of $\mu_n = 10^7$ cm^2/V sec is then obtained for intrinsic InSb from eq. (4.1). This value is much too high, and the electron mobility cannot be limited by acoustic scattering. In contrast, polar interaction combined with electron-hole scattering gives reasonable mobility values for $T > 200$°K according to (4.2). Figure 4.3 shows a comparison of the measured Hall mobility [Hrostowski *et al.* (55H4), Busch and Steigmeier (61B22)] with the theoretically calculated curves, for screened polar scattering combined with electron-hole scattering. The experimental curve was transformed from the measured Hall mobility $|R_{\mathrm{H}}|\sigma$ to the drift mobility σ/en with the theoretically obtained temperature dependence of the factor μ_{H}/μ. This factor lies between 1.0 and 1.1 in this temperature range. The theoretical curve calculated for combined scattering and $e_c^* = 0.13e$ agrees satisfactorily with experiment if one considers that the experimental mobility is reduced at low temperatures by impurity scattering, and at high temperatures by electron-electron scattering. Also the energy states $[(E - E_c) > E_G]$ which become occupied at high temperatures are not accurately described in Kane's theory.

We can consequently assume that polar scattering is the limiting scattering mechanism in n-InSb above 200°K. Below this temperature Putley (59P6) finds good agreement between theory and experiment if he assumes combined ionized-impurity scattering and acoustic scattering. That here the acoustic scattering actually becomes dominating seems rather doubtful, both because ion scattering is important in the samples under consideration, and because polar scattering has a temperature dependence very similar to that of acoustic scattering in this special case. It is just this similar temperature dependence which leads to the fact that in a large number of papers the assumption of acoustic scattering leads to reasonable agreement between theory and experiment even at higher temperatures.

In a number of papers (60K7), (60K8), (61K7), Kopeć has shown that, if the nonparabolicity of the conduction band of InSb is taken into consideration, acoustic scattering alone is sufficient to explain the temperature and doping dependence of the electron mobility. However, he does not explain the low absolute value of the mobility.

The question of which scattering mechanism dominates at low temperatures in InSb can be decided only by study of very pure samples. There do exist measurements on such samples with excess donor concentration of about 10^{13} cm^{-3} (57V1), (59H6), (59V4).

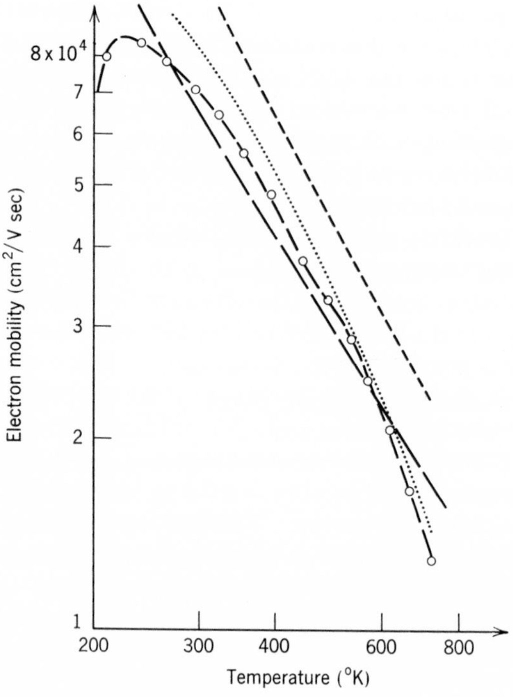

Fig. 4.3 Hall mobility of electrons in InSb as a function of the temperature. Experimental curves: —○—○—, Busch and Steigmeier (61B22); ·······, Hrostowski, Morin, Geballe, and Wheatley (55H4); theoretical curves after Ehrenreich's theory (——— for $e_c^* = 0.20\ e$, - - - for $e_c^* = 0.13\ e$).

We have shown the conductivity and the Hall coefficient of such a sample, which was intrinsic above 140°K, in Fig. 4.2. However, the measurements have not yet been made in sufficient detail, and the degree of compensation is not known accurately. In addition, measurements on such samples can be influenced by external conditions. For example, the conductivity depends strongly on the surface treatment, according to Lyan Chzhi-chao and Nasledov (59L5).

We also mention here an extensive discussion of σ and R_{H} measurements below $T = 100$°K, using the Kane model and the assumption of pure ion scattering, by Kołodziejczak (61K5), (61K6).

Below 40°K the measurements can no longer be interpreted quantitatively with any usual scattering mechanisms, according to Putley (56P7). The expected effect due to a donor activation energy does not appear, and the conductivity and the Hall coefficient become temperature independent. We will discuss the very-low-temperature measurements in more detail in Section 413. Here we will only mention that McLean and Paige (61M9) found theoretically that at low temperatures electron-hole scattering and electron-electron scattering should become important. In pure uncompensated material the electron mobility can be reduced 20% or more, below 30°K, by electron-electron scattering. Through electron-hole interaction the hole mobility could then even become negative. These anomalies have not yet been observed experimentally.

The maximum room-temperature value, $\mu_n = 77{,}000$ cm^2/V sec, persists in uncompensated material up to donor concentrations of 10^{16} cm^{-3}. At higher doping, μ_n decreases rapidly and falls below the value of 10,000 cm^2/V sec at 5×10^{18} impurities/cm^3. Figure 4.4 shows the dependence of the electron mobility on doping, from measurements of Rupprecht, Weber, and Weiss (60R6) on Te-doped material [see also (62V4)].

At 77°K an electron mobility of 620,000 cm^2/V sec was measured on an uncompensated sample of $n_D = 1.7 \times 10^{14}$ cm^{-3} (59B1). The values measured on "ultra-pure" material are usually lower, since such material still contains mutually compensating defects, which reduce the mobility by ionized-impurity scattering. The electron mobility also decreases rapidly with increasing impurity concentration and differs only insignificantly from the room-temperature values at high doping.

The maximum value of the *hole mobility*, μ_p, can be determined only indirectly at room temperature. Samples with sufficiently small acceptor concentration already show mixed conduction at room temperature, and the product of Hall coefficient and conductivity, accord-

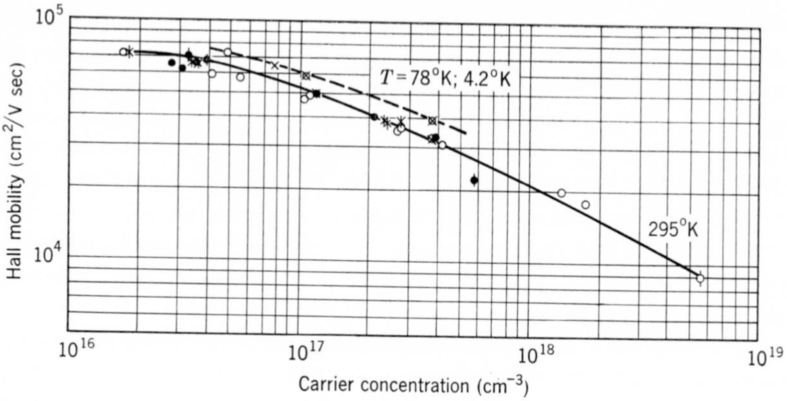

Fig. 4.4 Dependence of the Hall mobility of electrons in InSb on the carrier concentration at various temperatures. The different experimental points correspond to different orientations of the current direction relative to the crystal axes [after Rupprecht, Weber, and Weiss (60R6)].

ing to (4.5) and (4.8), is no longer a measure of the hole mobility. Higher-doped samples, where the influence of the electrons can still be neglected at room temperature, contain so many defects that the mobility is limited by ionized-impurity scattering. Putley (59P5) found in the temperature region of 30–100°K a hole mobility of $\mu_p = 5.40 \times 10^6 T^{-1.45}$ cm^2/V sec, while for above 100°K Cunningham, Harp, and Bullis (62C9) give $\mu_p = 2.55 \times 10^7 T^{-1.81}$ cm^2/V sec. The highest room-temperature value, indirectly determined, is $\mu_p \approx 700$ cm^2/V sec (58H3). This behavior suggests that, as in n-type material, the hole conductivity in p-type InSb is limited by polar scattering above 100°K.

Hilsum (60H9) estimated the expected mobility for pure polar scattering according to Ehrenreich's theory. Using the older cyclotron-resonance value of $m_{p1} = 0.18\ m$, he obtains $\mu_p = 3600$ cm^2/V sec. To obtain the experimental value of the hole mobility mentioned above, he requires an effective hole mass of 0.5 m. This result supports the newer cyclotron-resonance measurements mentioned in Section 323, which determined an m_{p1} value of about 0.4–0.5 m.

The latter deduction may still not be entirely conclusive. Kołodziejczak and Kowalczyk (62K5) showed that even if $m_{p1} = 0.18\ m$ the electric measurements would predict higher values. A single hole mass is not sufficient to characterize the valence band, according to Kane's model. However, one may define an "apparent density-of-states mass," $m_p{}^*$, for the holes of the valence band from (4.6).

In other words, one inserts all the deviations of the valence-band structure from a simple isotropic parabolic model into m_p^* and accepts the fact that m_p^* is therefore dependent on external parameters. Kołodziejczak and Kowalczyk evaluate this apparent density-of-states mass from the measurements of the intrinsic carrier concentration [Hrostowski (55H4), Putley (59P7)] and find an increase of m_p^* from 0.18 m at 0°K to 0.43 m at 300°K and 0.65 m at 700°K. Inserting this effective density-of-states mass into (4.2), one obtains good agreement between the theory for polar scattering and the mobility measurements of Hrostowski and of Putley. The curves are included in Fig. 4.31 in Section 412 on magnetoresistance, where the hole mobility in InSb will be discussed in more detail.

The doping dependence of the hole mobility is similar to that of the electron mobility. We refer to (55H4), (58H3), and (59S13) for the experimental results.

In contrast to the donors, the acceptors in InSb have a measurable ionization energy. Putley (59P5) finds $\Delta E_A = 0.0075$ eV for crystals containing zinc or cadmium. This value is confirmed by other authors. Crystals which have been rendered p-type by heat-treatment have an ionization energy of 0.018 eV. We will return to these measurements in Chapter 5. For the impurity, which causes the p-conductivity in undoped p-InSb, Broom and Rose-Innes (56B2) find the following dependence of the ionization energy: $\Delta E_A = (0.010 - 2 \times 10^{-8} n_A^{1/3})$ eV. This empirical law, which was also found in silicon, makes it possible to compare the limiting value 0.010 eV with the hydrogen-like model of impurities. For a dielectric constant of 16 a hole effective mass of $m_p = 0.19\ m$ is obtained.

Determining effective masses from electrical and galvanomagnetic data alone is relatively inaccurate and has therefore been tried in only a few cases. Hrostowski, Morin, Geballe, and Wheatley (55H4) analyze the mobility in the region of mixed lattice and ionized-impurity scattering and find the best values to be $0.01\ m < m_n < 0.02\ m$ and $m_p \approx 0.17\ m$. Sladek (57S2) investigated n-InSb at low temperatures and determined the position of the Fermi level from the behavior of σ and R_H. In the degenerate case this position depends only on the electron concentration and the effective mass, so that this procedure allows the determination of the effective electron mass. Sladek finds $m_n = (0.016 \pm 0.007)\ m$. None of these procedures takes polar scattering or the nonparabolic band curvature into account, and the results can be only approximate. The determination of the hole effective mass by Kołodziejczak and Kowalczyk has been discussed above.

In this section we have discussed only those results for the transport parameters in InSb which can be derived from the conductivity and the Hall coefficient at small magnetic fields, where only the linear term of the expansion of the galvanomagnetic transport coefficients in powers of the magnetic field needs to be taken into account. The measurement of the magnetic-field dependence of conductivity and Hall coefficient leads to new possibilities for the study of the conduction process in InSb. This topic will be considered in Section 412.

The few characteristic results which were presented in this section are confirmed by other measurements [compare (53W2), (53T1), (53C1), (53B1), (54A2), (54H1), (54H5), (54B6), (55T2), (57A3), and the references cited in the following sections].

The extremely high electron mobility in InSb permits the use of

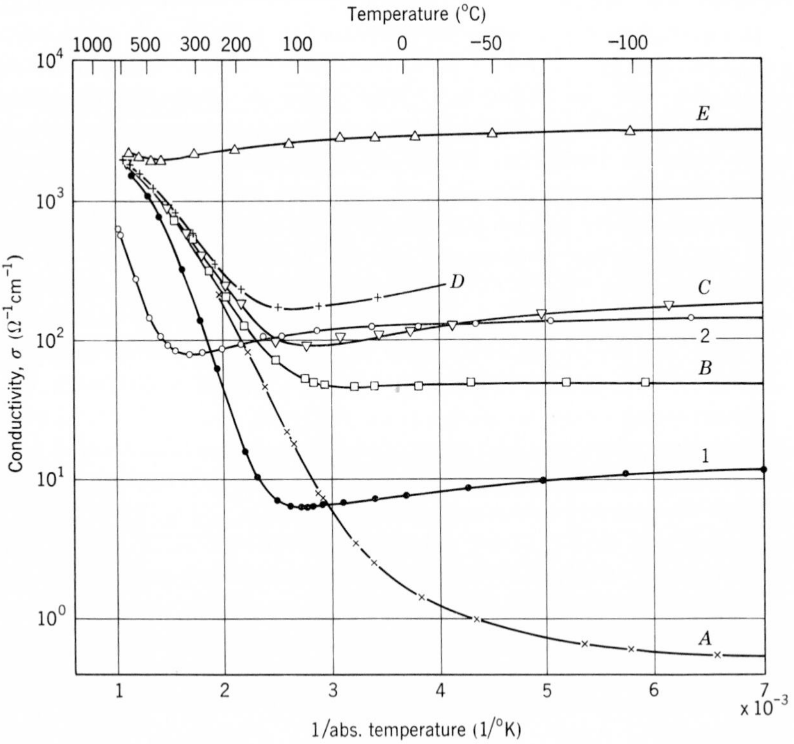

(a)

Fig. 4.5 Temperature dependence of the conductivity and the Hall coefficient of InAs for five n-type (A–E) and two p-type (1,2) samples [after Folberth, this semiconductor as a *Hall generator* for measurement of magnetic fields and for many other technical applications. We do not consider these questions in this book; the reader is referred to the specialized literature on Hall generators, for example, (54H2), (54K1), (54K2), (55R4), (57B1), (57R2), (58A4), (58E1), (59G13), (59K4), (59R6), (59Z2), (60H5), (60H8), (60S9), and (61K2).

Indium Arsenide. The electrical properties of InAs are similar to those of InSb. Figure 4.5 shows the conductivity and the Hall coefficient of five *n*-type and two *p*-type samples as functions of tem-

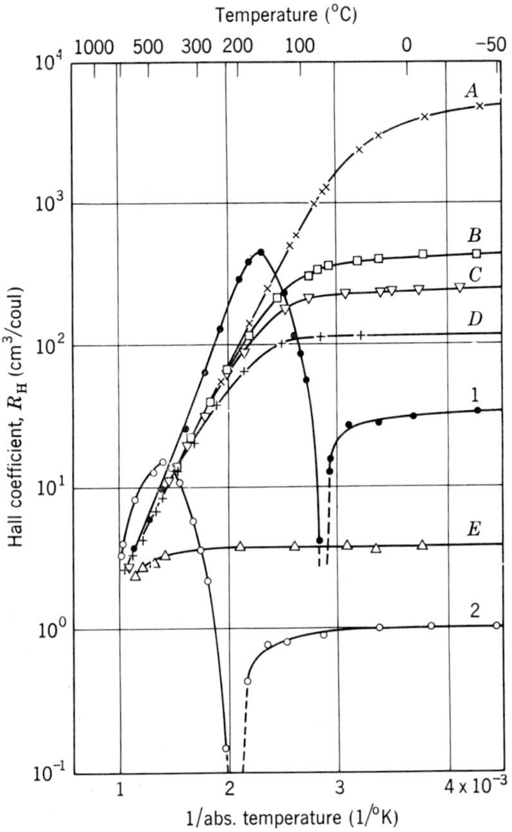

(b)

Madelung, and Weiss (54F2)].

perature (54F2). An analysis of these measurements gives $E_G(0) = (0.47 \pm 0.02)$ eV, $dE_G/dT = -4.5 \times 10^{-4}$ eV/°K, $\mu_n \approx 23{,}000\ \text{cm}^2/V$ sec, $\mu_p \approx 200\ \text{cm}^2/V$ sec at room temperature, with temperature dependence of the electron mobility $T^{-1.5}$, of the hole mobility $T^{-\alpha}$ with $\alpha > 2$. These results are generally confirmed by other workers: (52W1), (53W2), (53F1), (54W2), (57A3), (56N2), and (56H2).

The effective mass of the electrons in a pure sample was determined by Sladek (57S2), from the position of the Fermi level, as $m_n = (0.02 \pm 0.005)\ m$. The effective electron mass determined from electrical measurements is doping dependent, a sign of the nonparabolicity of the conduction band. There are no indications of impurity ionization energies in n-type material (56H2), (56N2), just as in InSb. Also the doping dependence of the mobilities is similar. For experimental values we refer to the papers mentioned above.

The mobility of the electrons in InAs is, as in InSb, determined over a wide temperature range by polar scattering. Figure 4.6 shows a comparison between the measurements of Antell, Chasmar, Champion, and Cohen (57A3) and theory (59E6). Degeneracy was neglected in calculating the theoretical curve. The impurity scattering was taken into account approximately by adding the reciprocal mobilities of polar scattering and ionized-impurity scattering (Brooks-Herring formula). Agreement between experiment and theory is not as good as in the case of InSb, but is in the right order of magnitude. Chasmar (61C7) has confirmed that polar scattering is the limiting mechanism in pure InAs. The theoretical mobility value due to polar scattering alone is $\mu_n = 21{,}000\ \text{cm}^2/\text{V}$ sec at room temperature (59E6), (60H9), (61C7). A different choice of ion charge and effective electron masses, neither of which is known sufficiently accurately from experiment, raises the theoretical mobility value to 40,000 cm^2/V sec, so that the experimental peak value of 30,000 cm^2/V sec does not contradict the theoretical expectation.

The hole mobility also appears to be limited by polar scattering. The highest experimental values are 450 cm^2/V sec. The theory gives $\mu_p = 500\ \text{cm}^2/\text{V}$ sec for pure polar scattering (60H9).

The analysis of measurements on lightly doped material is complicated, however, by a number of anomalies. Although strongly doped p-type samples show a normal behavior of the temperature dependence of the Hall coefficient, there appears a second sign reversal in weakly doped material ($n_A < 2 \times 10^{17}\ \text{cm}^{-3}$), according to Folberth and Weiss (56F2). This is in addition to the usual sign reversal just below the intrinsic conduction (change from positive to negative values with increasing temperature). The Hall coefficient is negative

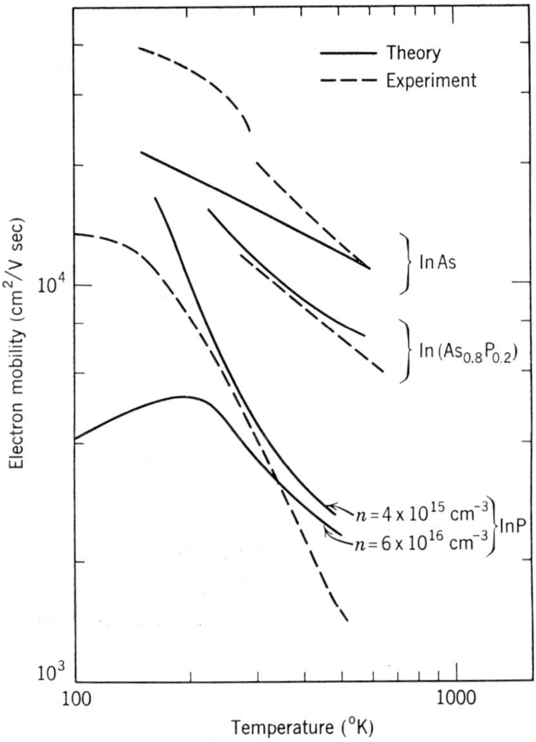

Fig. 4.6 Electron mobility of InAs, InP, and $InAs_{0.8}P_{0.2}$. The theoretical curves have been calculated by Ehrenreich (59E6) for combined polar and ionized-impurity scattering. Experimental curves for InAs after Antell, Chasmar, Champion, and Cohen (57A3), for InP after Reid and Willardson (58R2), and for $InAs_{0.8}P_{0.2}$ after Weiss (56W2).

at low temperatures and takes on positive values in only a very limited temperature region. Rupprecht (58R5) showed that this anomalous behavior can be introduced and eliminated reversibly by grinding and etching of the surface. Potential measurements along the width of the semiconductor between the potential probes [Rupprecht and Weiss (59R10)] gave further indications that this is a surface effect. They showed that the potential drop in the interior of the crystal always has the direction prescribed for p-type conductors. For ground surfaces there is, however, an additional opposite potential drop near the surfaces, which can overcompensate for the potential drop in the interior.

This behavior has two possible interpretations. If one assumes that grinding introduces impurities and defects into the crystal which make the surface layer n-type, then the Hall voltages in the interior and in the two surface layers add up. The Hall field of the n-type region is much larger than that of the p-type region because of the large ratio of electron to hole mobility, and so the surface regions may determine the sign of the entire Hall voltage. In contradiction to this, it appears unlikely that n-type layers produced by polishing would cover the whole surface uniformly so that they could be considered as homogeneous n-type material. The effect can, however, also be explained by the appearance of p-n junctions at the potential probes between which the Hall voltage is measured (59M1). At these p-n junctions a "floating potential" appears in a magnetic field, which must be added to the Hall voltage in the interior and which has the opposite sign. Which interpretation is correct has not yet been decided.

The introduction of an n-type layer by grinding can, according to Dixon (59D3), be explained by the formation of dislocations which act as donors. This model is used by others to explain the electrical properties of InAs under heat treatment. This problem and other questions concerning the nature of impurities in InAs will be considered in Chapter 5.

Indium Phosphide. The first detailed measurements of the electrical properties of InP were made by Folberth and Weiss (55F1). Figure 4.7 shows the temperature dependence of the conductivity and the Hall coefficient of two n-type and one p-type samples. The purest (n-type) sample had a room-temperature electron concentration of 4×10^{15} cm^{-3}. The measured mobilities were $\mu_n = 4000$ cm^2/V sec and $\mu_p = 60$ cm^2/V sec. The mobility ratio is consequently very large. The intrinsic concentration n_i was calculated from the Hall coefficient of the purest sample, and from the linear dependence of $\ln (n_i^2/T^3)$ vs. $1/T$ the energy gap was determined as $E_G(0) = 1.34$ eV. Finally, from the absolute value of n_i the geometric average of the two effective masses $(m_n m_p)^{1/2} = 0.23\, m$ follows.

Extensive measurements of Glicksman and Weiser (58G4), (60W2) on n-InP gave, for a sample of $n = 6.3 \times 10^{15}$ cm^{-3}, an electron mobility of 4500 cm^2/V sec at room temperature and 23,400 cm^2/V sec at 77°K. This is a sample of similar doping to the purest one investigated by Folberth and Weiss. The lattice mobility was determined from measurements on samples of varying purity. Figure 4.8 shows the measured mobilities. At high temperatures the lattice mobility appears to have a temperature dependence of T^{-2}. The

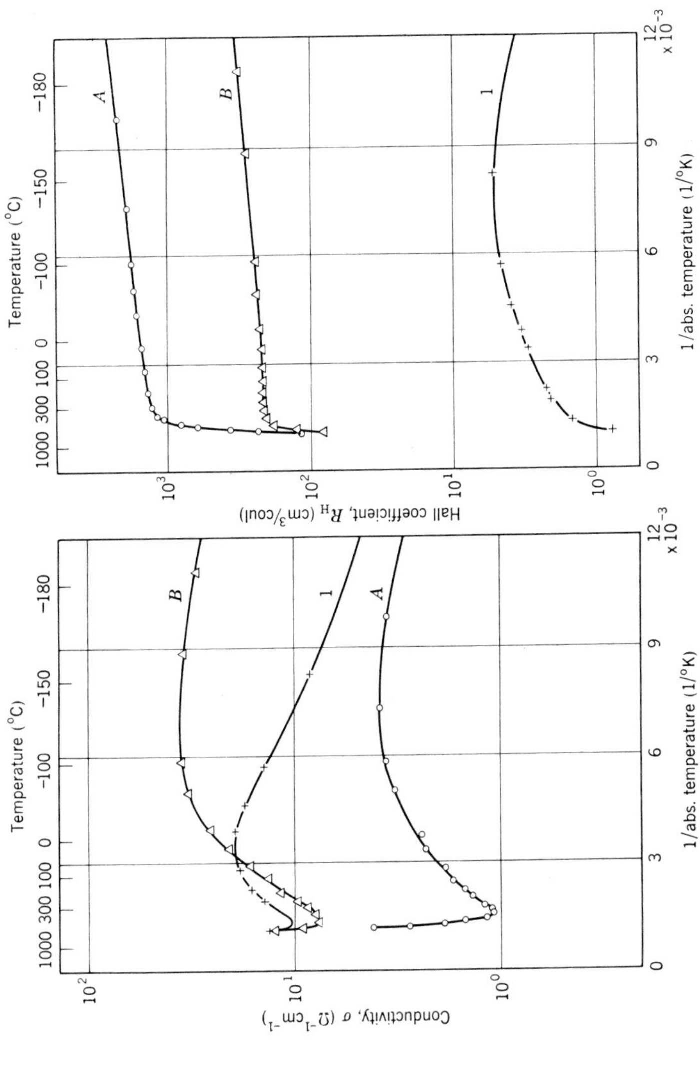

Fig. 4.7 Temperature dependence of the conductivity and the Hall coefficient of two n-type and one p-type sample of InP [after Folberth and Weiss (55F1)].

extrapolated room-temperature value is $\mu_n = 5000$ cm^2/V sec. Using this value and the assumed temperature dependence, the ion-scattering part of the experimental results was determined and compared with the Brooks-Herring formula (4.3). The only unknown quantity in this formula is m_n, and an effective electron mass can be determined in this fashion. The procedure leads to different values at different temperatures, an indication that an incorrect lattice mobility was assumed. It was possible to determine an upper limit, $m_n < 0.05\ m$. Similar estimates by Reid and Willardson (58R2) under the assumption of a $T^{-3/2}$ law for lattice mobility led to the values $\mu_n = 6600$ cm^2/V sec and $m_n = 0.06\ m$.

The same analysis was made by Glicksman and Weiser (59G4) on two p-type samples. The purer sample had a hole mobility of 150 cm^2/V sec at 290°K and 1200 cm^2/V sec at 77°K. From this the

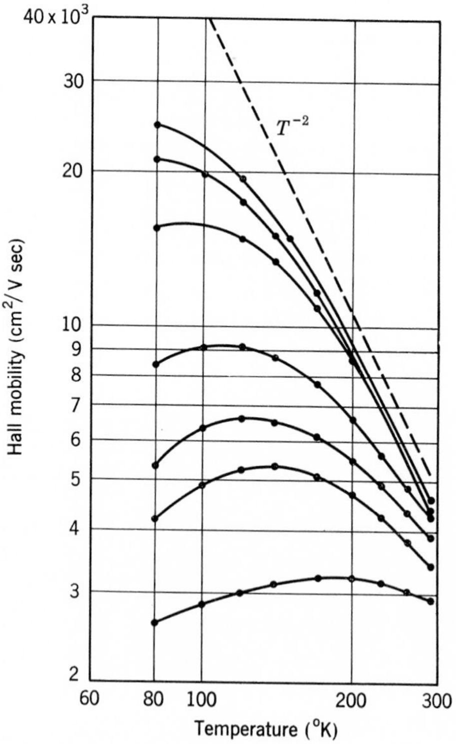

Fig. 4.8 Hall mobilities of electrons in InP as a function of temperature [after Glicksman and Weiser (58G4)].

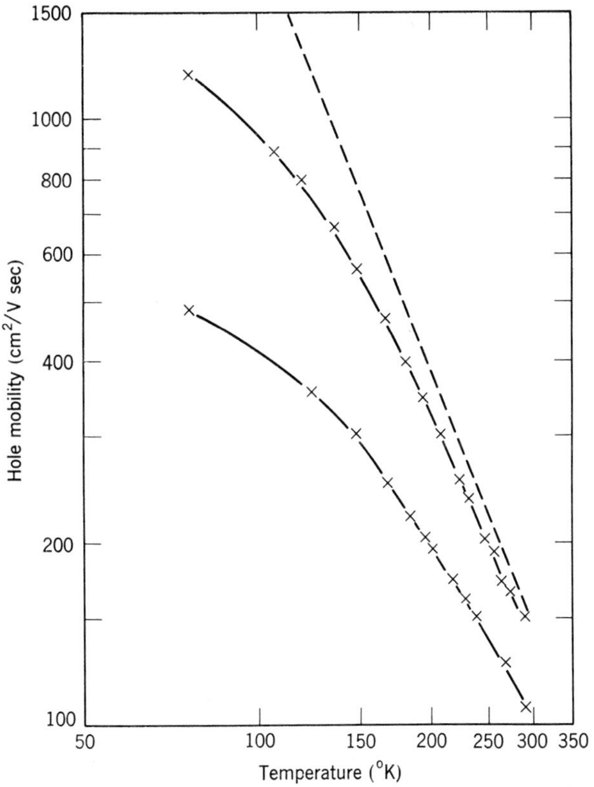

Fig. 4.9 Hall mobilities of holes in InP as a function of temperature [after Glicksman and Weiser (59G4)].

lattice mobility was estimated as $\mu_p = 160 \text{ cm}^2/\text{V sec}$, and the effective mass of the holes as $m_p = 0.2\ m$. The temperature dependence of the lattice mobility approximately follows a $T^{-2.4}$ law (Fig. 4.9).

In these analyses of the experimental data the lattice mobility was always assumed to follow an exponential law T^{-x}. Such laws do apply for a number of scattering mechanisms, but not for polar scattering, which certainly must play a role in *n*-InP at room temperature. For this reason Ehrenreich compared the experimental results with the theory of combined polar and ionized-impurity scattering (59E6). Figure 4.6 shows the comparison between measurements of Reid and Willardson (58R2) and two theoretical curves which were calculated for different concentrations of impurity centers. The upper curve applies for the case that the impurity concentration is equal to the (experimentally determined) electron concentration; the lower, for a strongly compensated sample. The agreement is satisfactory and shows that in n-InP polar scattering can be the limiting scattering mechanism. Ehrenreich finds for the maximum value of the mobility under polar scattering, at 300°K, $\mu_n = 4700$ cm^2/V sec. This value lies lower than the extrapolations mentioned above. However, we emphasize again that the methods used in the latter cases have not been justified with certainty. Furthermore, the theoretical values of μ_{polar} are uncertain, since some of the parameters in (4.2) are not well known. Hilsum (60H9) finds a value of 6800 cm^2/V sec for $\mu_{n,\text{polar}}$, but the smaller value appears to be more reliable.

Gallium Antimonide. The preparation of highly purified samples of the indium compounds which have been discussed above did not encounter any basic difficulties. In contrast, all methods of preparation used so far for GaSb result in material with a residual acceptor concentration of 10^{17} cm^{-3}. Undoped material is therefore generally p-type. Since n-type material is produced by counterdoping with donors, such as selenium and tellurium, it is always strongly compensated.

The first investigations on GaSb were made on undoped p-type material. They were limited to an analysis of the conductivity and Hall coefficient for determining the width of the forbidden gap, the ionization energy of the impurities, and the mobilities of the charge carriers (54B2), (53W2), (54H5), (54L1), (54W2), (55D1), (59E2). The E_G values, determined from the slope of the ln (n_i^2/T^3)-$1/T$ curve, vary between 0.77 and 0.82 eV. The largest measured mobilities were $\mu_n = 2500$ cm^2/V sec (55D1) and $\mu_p = 1420$ cm^2/V sec (59E2). The temperature dependence of the conductivity and the Hall coefficient of four p-type samples is shown in Fig. 4.10. Leifer and Dunlap (54L1) [see also (62I2)] give a detailed analysis of measurements on p-type GaSb and find a mobility ratio of 5 and effective masses $m_n = 0.20\ m$ and $m_p = 0.39\ m$.

The results of optical measurements, reported in Chapter 3, showed that in InSb, InAs, and InP the influence of the higher-lying subbands on the transport properties can be neglected. Either no higher subbands have been found in these compounds, or they lie so high that they contain practically no electrons in thermal equilibrium, even though electrons can be excited optically into these bands. In the remaining III-V compounds, GaSb, GaAs, GaP, and AlSb, higher subbands can play a role, however. This is particularly true for GaSb,

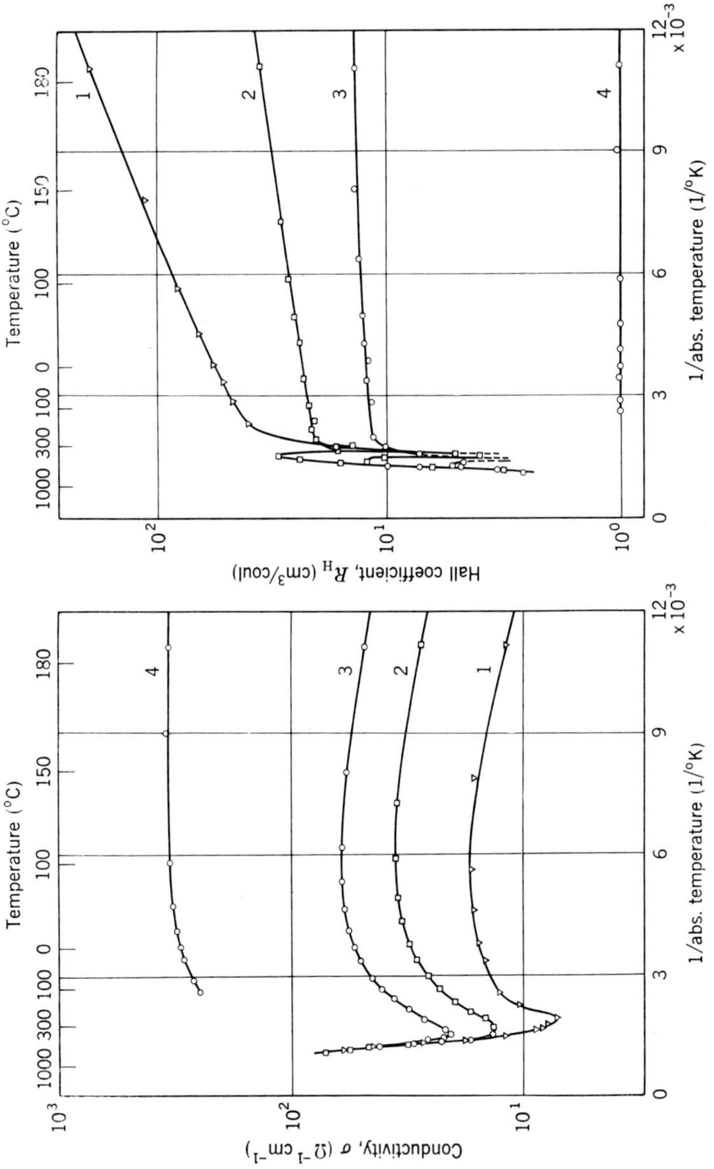

Fig. 4.10 Temperature dependence of the conductivity and the Hall coefficient of four *p*-type samples of GaSb [after Welker (54W2)].

where about 0.08 eV above the (000)-minimum a subband with minima on the [111]-axes begins, and above that a third, (100)-band, has been observed.

Measurements on n-GaSb therefore can not be analyzed with the equations of this section. Conductivity and Hall coefficient are given by a two-band model with charge carriers of the *same* sign (if the hole contribution is neglected):

$$\sigma = e(\mu_1 n_1 + \mu_2 n_2) = (\gamma_1 + \gamma_2)\sigma \tag{4.9}$$

$$R_{\mathrm{H}} = -\frac{1}{e}\frac{\mu_{\mathrm{H}1}^2 n_1 + \mu_{\mathrm{H}2}^2 n_2}{(\mu_1 n_1 + \mu_2 n_2)^2} = \gamma_1^2 R_{\mathrm{H}1} + \gamma_2^2 R_{\mathrm{H}2} \tag{4.10}$$

The indices 1 and 2 refer to the two bands, and γ_i is the ratio of conductivity of the electrons in band i to the total conductivity. The Hall mobility, finally, is given by

$$\mu_{\mathrm{H}} = |R_{\mathrm{H}}|\sigma = \frac{\mu_{\mathrm{H}1}^2 n_1 + \mu_{\mathrm{H}2}^2 n_2}{\mu_1 n_1 + \mu_2 n_2} = \gamma_1 \mu_{\mathrm{H}1} + \gamma_2 \mu_{\mathrm{H}2} \tag{4.11}$$

Sagar (60S1) has made measurements of the Hall coefficient on n-type material and discussed them on the basis of the two-band model. Figure 4.11 shows the temperature dependence of the Hall coefficient in a region where the contribution of the holes to the conductivity can be neglected. The various curves refer to samples of different purity, the purer samples having the larger Hall coefficient at any

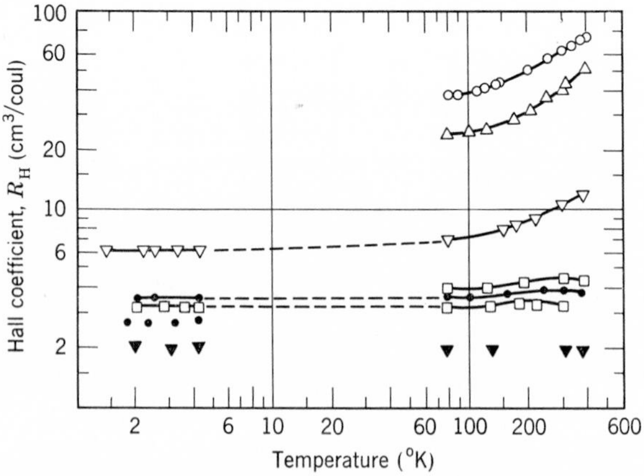

Fig. 4.11 Hall coefficient of n-GaSb in the extrinsic region for eight samples with different carrier concentrations [after Sagar 60S1)].

given temperature. The special feature is the increasing Hall coefficient with increasing temperature for the pure samples and the appearance of a maximum for the heavier-doped crystals. This can be explained by the two-band model. It is reasonable to assume that the electrons in the higher band have the smaller mobility, since generally the mass at the (000)-minima is smaller than that at the (111)-minima. Then (4.10) predicts for a constant total number of electrons an increasing Hall coefficient with increasing occupation ratio n_2/n_1, i.e., with increasing temperature. A maximum is reached when the total number of electrons starts to increase at the onset of the intrinsic region, since then R_H drops rapidly.

The best agreement between these measurements and the theory was obtained when the distance between the (000)- and (111)-minima was assumed to be $\Delta E_{12} = 0.074$ eV, independent of temperature, with a mobility ratio of $\mu_1/\mu_2 = 6$. Then a typical result for a sample with a room-temperature effective electron mobility of $\mu_H = 2240$ cm^2/V sec is as follows: $\mu_1 = 3870$ cm^2/V sec, $\mu_2 = 645$ cm^2/V sec, $\gamma_2 = 0.478$, $n_2/n = 0.847$. Sagar supports these results by simultaneous measurements of the piezoresistance and of the pressure dependence of the galvanomagnetic effects, which will be discussed in Section 414.

Although this model must be correct in its basic outline, there remain some questions to be clarified. Using the same method of evaluation, Cardona (61C2) found for a sample at room temperature $n_2/n = 0.772$, and for the same sample at 89°K $n_2/n = 0.626$. The temperature dependence of all the quantities in the theory except ΔE_{12} is known, so that this measurement allows the determination of the temperature coefficient of ΔE_{12}. A value of $d\,\Delta E_{12}/dT \approx 1 \times 10^{-4}$ eV/°K is obtained in contrast to the value of -3×10^{-4} eV/°K calculated by Sagar from the piezoresistance.

Measurements by Strauss (61S16) show a characteristic difference in the doping dependence of the Hall coefficient for Se- and Te-doped samples. The difference is most pronounced at heavy doping and disappears for very pure samples. One possible interpretation is that impurity-band conduction is dominating in this region, and that this depends on the nature of the donor, similarly to what has been observed in germanium. We will learn of another possible explanation in Section 510. Further experimental results will be considered in Section 412 on magnetoresistance.

Consider now the (000)-band. The room-temperature mobility was found to be about 4000 cm^2/V sec. In contrast, the limiting value due to polar scattering is calculated to be 44,000 cm^2/V sec (60H9), (61E4). If intervalley scattering and the nonparabolicity of the (000)-band are included, a theoretical electron mobility of 14,000 cm^2/V sec results, according to Ehrenreich (61E4). The remaining discrepancy of a factor of 3 between theory and experiment cannot be explained by any scattering mechanisms encountered so far.

Gallium Arsenide. Measurements of conductivity and Hall coefficient on three *n*-type and two *p*-type samples (55F1) are shown in Fig. 4.12. Since intrinsic conductivity is reached only at high tem-

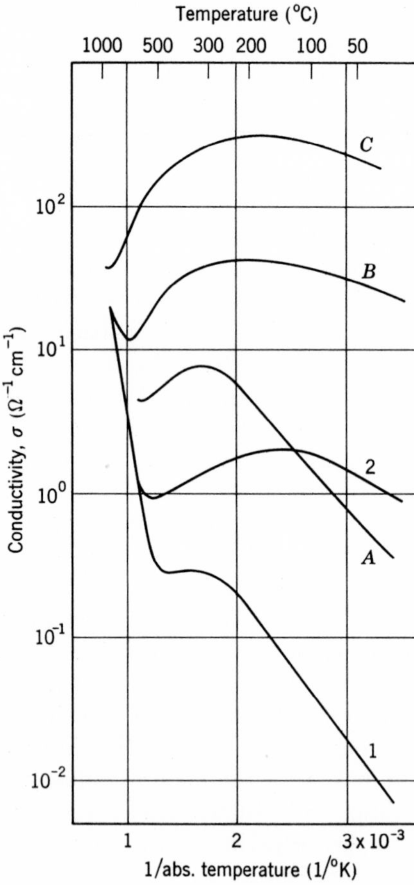

(a)

Fig. 4.12 Temperature dependence of the conductivity (*a*) and Hall coefficient (*b*) of three *n*-type (*A–C*) and two *p*-type (1,2) samples of GaAs [after Folberth peratures, the energy gap can be determined only approximately. Folberth and Weiss find $E_G \approx 1.4$ eV. These early measurements also give an electron mobility of 3400 cm^2/V sec and a hole mobility of 200 cm^2/V sec at room temperature.

Figure 4.13 shows later measurements of Whelan and Wheatley (58W6). Sample 4 is intrinsic over a larger temperature region and allows a more accurate deduction of $E_G(0)$. Whelan and Wheatley find $E_G(0) = (1.58 \pm 0.05)$ eV.

Later measurements of the Hall mobility of electrons have given larger values (58R2), (58W3), (60W2), (62O1). The highest values reported are $\mu_n = 8500$ cm^2/V sec at room temperature (60E3) and 22,000 cm^2/V sec at 72°K (62O1).

The measurements of Hall coefficient as a function of temperature show a maximum before the onset of the intrinsic region. This fact suggests—just as in GaSb—that we have to assume a contribution from a higher subband of the conduction band, as was to be expected accord-

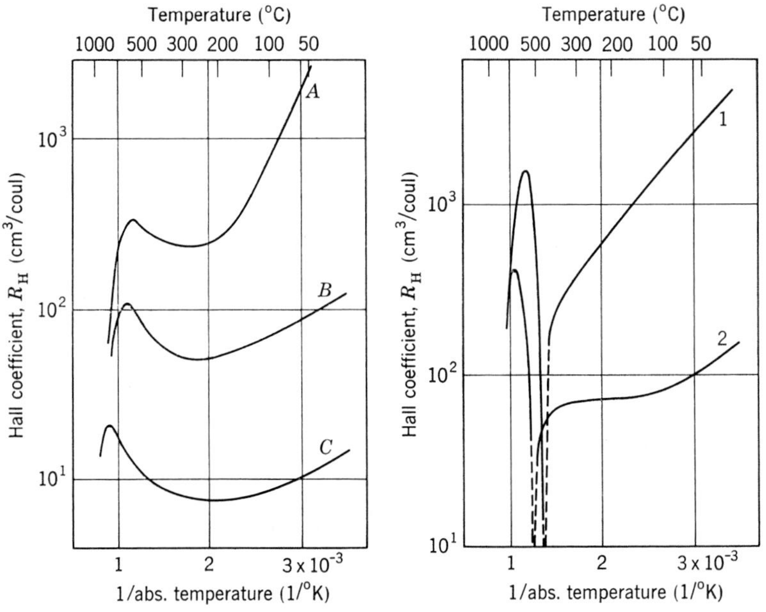

(b)

and Weiss (55F1)].

ing to the optical measurements reported in Chapter 3. Compared to GaSb, this subband lies considerably higher. The most important parameter values of this subband can be determined directly from the value and temperature of the Hall coefficient maximum [Aukerman and Willardson (60A15)]. If we again assign the index 1 to the parameters of the lower band, and the index 2 to those of the higher band, and call the distance separating the minima ΔE_{12}, then, for nondegenerate semiconductors, it follows from (4.10) that

$$\frac{R_{\mathrm{H}} - R_{\mathrm{H1}}}{R_{\mathrm{H1}}} = \frac{(b-1)^2 \beta^{3/2} e^{\Delta E_{12}/kT}}{(1 + b\beta^{3/2} e^{\Delta E_{12}/kT})^2} \approx (b-1)^2 b^{-2} \beta^{-3/2} e^{\Delta E_{12}/kT} \qquad (4.12)$$

The second expression is valid for small deviations of the Hall coefficient from its value R_{H1} for $n_2 = 0$. The parameter b is the ratio of the mobilities, μ_1/μ_2, and β is the corresponding ratio of the effective masses, m_1/m_2. This equation does not contain the electron densities in the subbands and is therefore independent of the doping of the

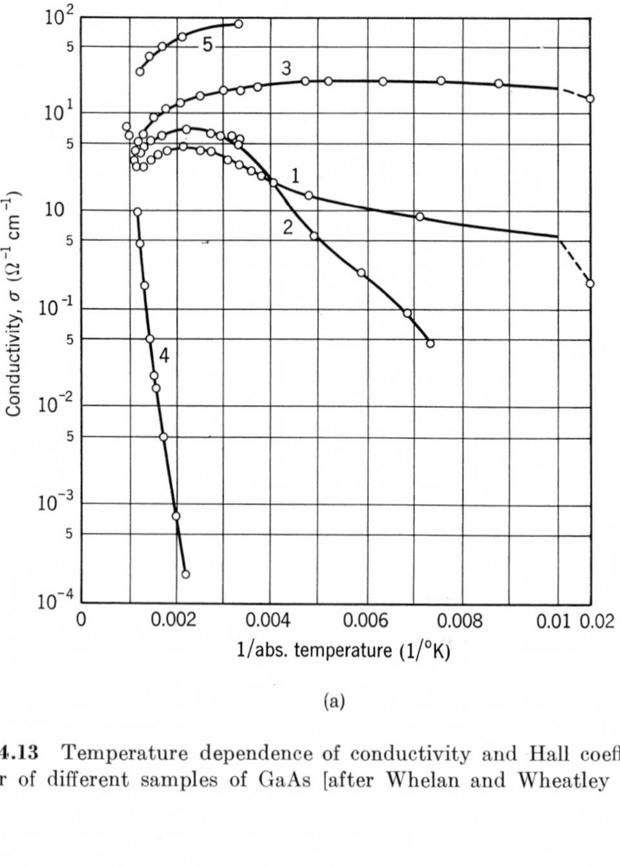

(a)

Fig. 4.13 Temperature dependence of conductivity and Hall coefficient of a number of different samples of GaAs [after Whelan and Wheatley (58W6)].

sample. Figure 4.14 shows that this conclusion is verified by three samples of different purity (and consequently of different Hall coefficients). The value of R_{H1} was determined from an extrapolation of the Hall coefficient in the region below the maximum. From the slope of the curve it follows that $\Delta E_{12} = 0.38$ eV. This value actually applies only for 0°K, since a linear temperature dependence of ΔE_{12} would not appear in the exponent of (4.12), but only in the constant in front. As long as this temperature dependence is not known, the effective-mass ratio m_1/m_2 cannot be calculated from (4.12). Aukerman and Willardson give a value of $\beta = 0.04$ for the case that ΔE_{12} is temperature independent. For a temperature coefficient of -10^{-4} eV/°K it follows that $\beta = 0.07$. The mobility ratio b appears to be at least 10.

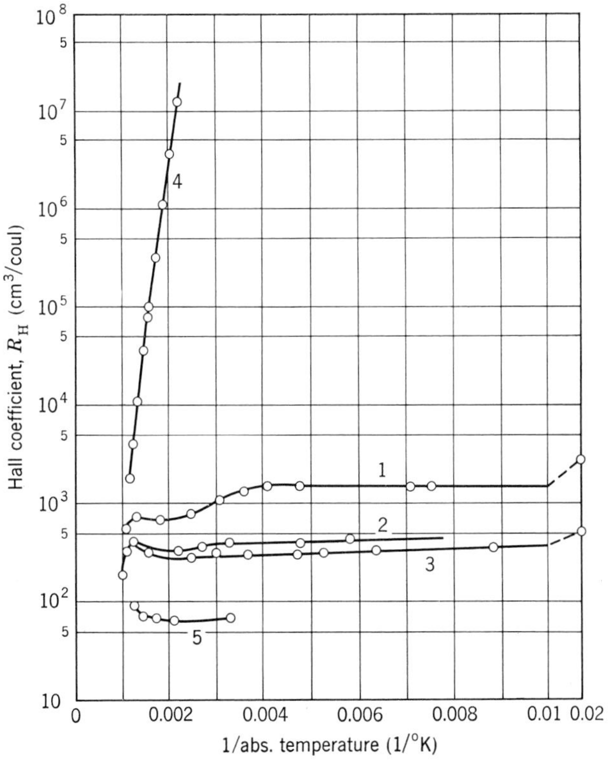

(b)

Sample 4 is "high-resistivity GaAs" (see the discussion on p. 140 and in Section 531).

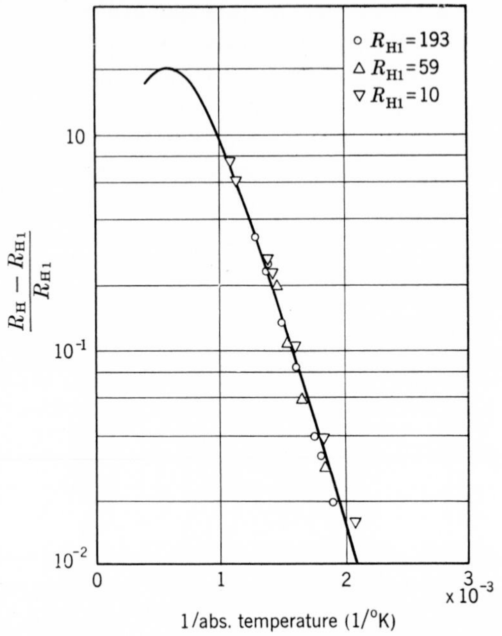

Fig. 4.14 Comparison of eq. (4.12) with experimental results for three *n*-GaAs samples of different purity (different Hall coefficient) [after Aukerman and Willardson (60A15)].

Ehrenreich (60E3) repeated this analysis under somewhat different assumptions and found $\Delta E_{12} = 0.36$ eV and $\beta = 0.06$. If one takes the cyclotron-resonance value for m_1 (0.071 m), the effective mass of the upper band becomes $m_2 = 1.2\ m$. This value is almost identical with the electron mass of the (100)-minimum in silicon. This would appear to be a further confirmation that the higher subband in GaAs has minima on the [100]-axes.

We come now to the question of the dominant scattering mechanism in GaAs. The most extensive theoretical analysis of the electron mobility was made by Ehrenreich (60E3), (61E3). Figure 4.15 shows the results and compares them with the measurements of Miller and Reid and of Whelan and Wheatley (58W6). Curve 1 is the theoretical electron mobility for pure acoustic scattering. The room-temperature value of this quantity is over 100,000 cm^2/V sec, and this mechanism does not dominate in any region. Pure polar scattering (curve 2) gives the right order of magnitude at high temperature. The theoretical room-temperature value is 9300 cm^2/V sec according to Ehrenreich, and 11,000 cm^2/V sec according to Hilsum (60H9). At low temperatures the mobility grows exponentially and surpasses the experimental values. Curve 3 was calculated for a combination of polar and ionized-impurity scattering, and gives good agreement with experiment. Finally, curve 4 is a composite of curves 1 and 3 and furthermore takes account of the nonparabolicity of the lower conduction band. The latter causes an increase in the average effective

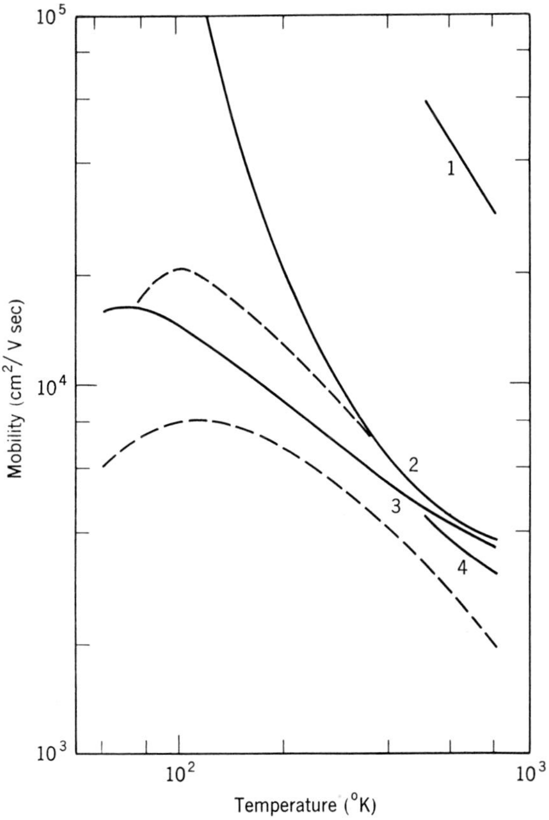

Fig. 4.15 Comparison of the experimental Hall mobility of *n*-GaAs (upper broken curve after Miller and Reid, lower broken curve after Whelan and Wheatley) with theory: curve 1: deformation potential scattering; curve 2: screened polar scattering; curve 3: polar plus ionized-impurity scattering; curve 4: a combination of curves 1 and 3 with the effect of the nonparabolicity of the conduction band included [after Ehrenreich (60E3)].

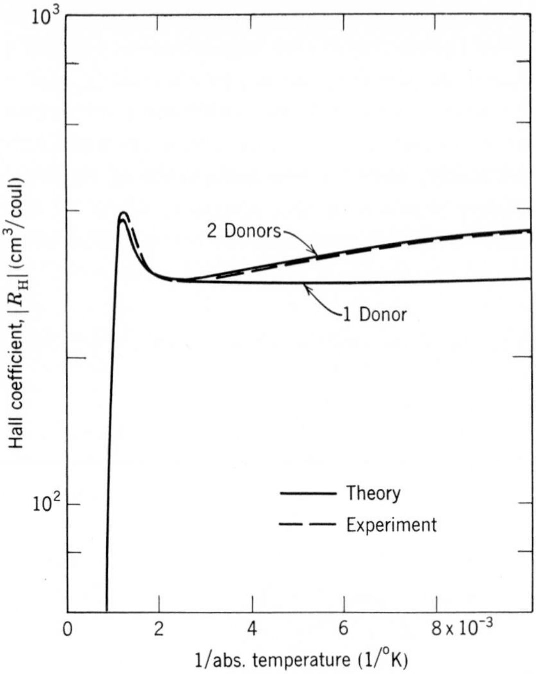

Fig. 4.16 Temperature dependence of the Hall coefficient of an n-GaAs sample of Whelan and Wheatley (58W6) and theoretical curves of Ehrenreich (60E3).

mass of the electrons with growing occupation of the band and thereby a mobility reduction. The theoretical curves do not take into account any contribution from electrons in the higher subband. Such a contribution can only be estimated crudely, as long as the mobility ratio, μ_1/μ_2, is not known any better. Certainly it must reduce the mobility at high temperatures, an effect which can only improve the fit of the theory to the experiment.

Ehrenreich calculated the Hall coefficient in the temperature region above 100°K, using these results and the energy separation of the subbands of the conduction band calculated from the Hall coefficient maximum. This theoretical curve is shown in Fig. 4.16 together with an experimental curve of Whelan and Wheatley (58W6). In the region above room temperature the contribution of the holes was taken into account through a combination of eqs. (4.8) and (4.10). Below room temperature agreement between theory and experiment could be obtained only if two types of donors were assumed with ionization energies of 0 and 0.04 eV and concentration ratio of 10:1. The existence of these two donors is also expected from other experiences (see Chapter 5).

According to Oliver (62O1), (62O2), the temperature dependence of the electron mobility down to 30°K can be explained by polar scattering. Below this temperature piezoelectric scattering must be assumed to be the dominant mechanism.

The maximum value of the mobility at a given temperature has frequently been determined by comparing the measured mobilities on samples of various doping with the expected mobility for pure ionized-impurity scattering according to the Brooks-Herring formula (4.3). This can only be done in simple form if the scattering mechanism competing with the impurity scattering is acoustic scattering, or at least a scattering mechanism with a well-defined relaxation time. Such analyses have been made by Weisberg and co-workers (58W3), (60W2) and Reid and Willardson (58R2) under the assumption that the competing scattering is acoustic. The resulting extrapolated room-temperature mobilities (μ_n = 12,500 and 11,500 cm^2/V sec, respectively) lie above the maximum value to be expected for polar

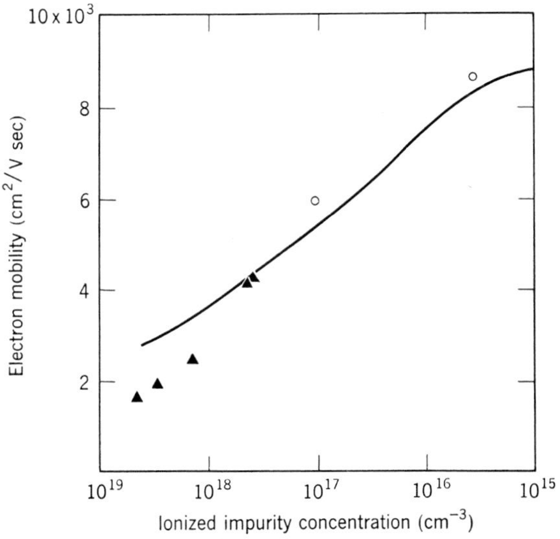

Fig. 4.17 Electron mobility in GaAs vs. impurity concentration at 300°K. Curve: theory with combined polar and ionized-impurity scattering after Ehrenreich (61E4), exprimental points: ∘, Reid and Willardson (58R2); ▲, Weisberg, Rosi, and Herkart (60W2).

scattering according to Ehrenreich. The comparison between the theoretical dependence of the electron mobility (combined polar and ionized-impurity scattering) on the impurity concentration and the experimental results of the authors we have mentioned is shown in Fig. 4.17. The experimental points refer to the maximum measured mobility among a number of samples with the same electron concentration; that is, they represent the least-compensated samples. The deviation at high impurity concentration may be due to neglect of the electron-electron scattering or to a failure of the Brooks-Herring formula at these high dopings.

Gallium arsenide prepared without intentional doping usually is found to be of low-resistivity n-type. Sometimes very-high-resistivity crystals (1 MΩ or more) are obtained. Such material contains traps which have been ascribed to oxygen impurities (possibly also to iron, cobalt, or nickel). We will discuss this "high-resistivity GaAs" in detail in Section 531. Measurement of conductivity and Hall coefficient on this kind of material (Fig. 4.13, curve 4) leads to very small values of electron concentration (down to $n = 10^8$ cm^{-3}) and simultaneously to small values of electron mobility ($\leqslant 4000$ cm^2/V sec). This is related to the screening of ionized impurities by free-charge

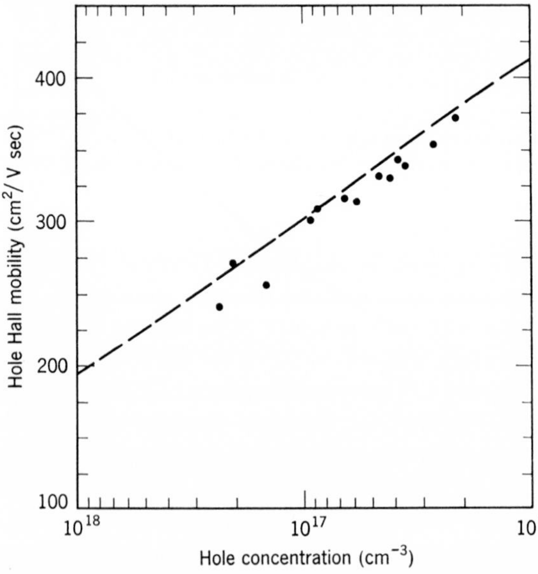

Fig. 4.18 Dependence of hole Hall mobility of GaAs on the hole concentration at room temperature [after Weisberg, Rosi, and Herkart (60W2)].

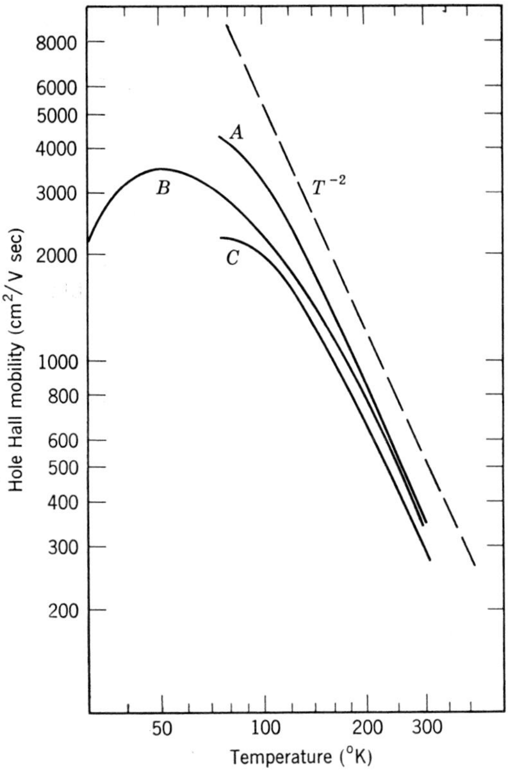

Fig. 4.19 Temperature dependence of the hole Hall mobility for three *p*-GaAs samples of different purity [after Weisberg, Rosi, and Herkart (60W2)].

carriers and can be seen in the Brooks-Herring relation (4.3) by the dependence on both n_{ion} and the electron density n. For constant n_{ion}, μ_n decreases with decreasing n. The highest resistivity measured at room temperature was $6.2 \times 10^8\ \Omega$ cm (60W2).

The hole mobility in GaAs was measured by Rosi, Meyerhofer, and Jensen (60R5), (60W2) on samples obtained from high-resistivity GaAs by doping with copper and zinc. Figures 4.18 and 4.19 show the dependence of the hole mobility on the hole concentration at room temperature and its temperature dependence. The theoretical curve in Fig. 4.18 was calculated from the Brooks-Herring formula (4.3) with values of m_p of 0.5 m and of the lattice mobility μ_p of 435 $(T/295°\text{K})^{-2}$ cm²/V sec. This lattice mobility is the dashed line in Fig. 4.19. Different authors give values of the temperature exponent between 2.0 and 2.3. The limiting scattering mechanism at room temperature appears to be polar scattering. According to Hilsum (60H9), $\mu_{p,\mathrm{polar}} = 600\ \mathrm{cm}^2/\mathrm{V\ sec}$. A theoretical analysis of the temperature dependence of the hole mobility has not yet been attempted.

Gallium Phosphide. Information about the electrical properties of GaP is quite limited so far. We know from optical measurements (Chapter 3) that the conduction band minima lie on the [100]-axes. The properties of n-GaP must therefore resemble those of silicon.

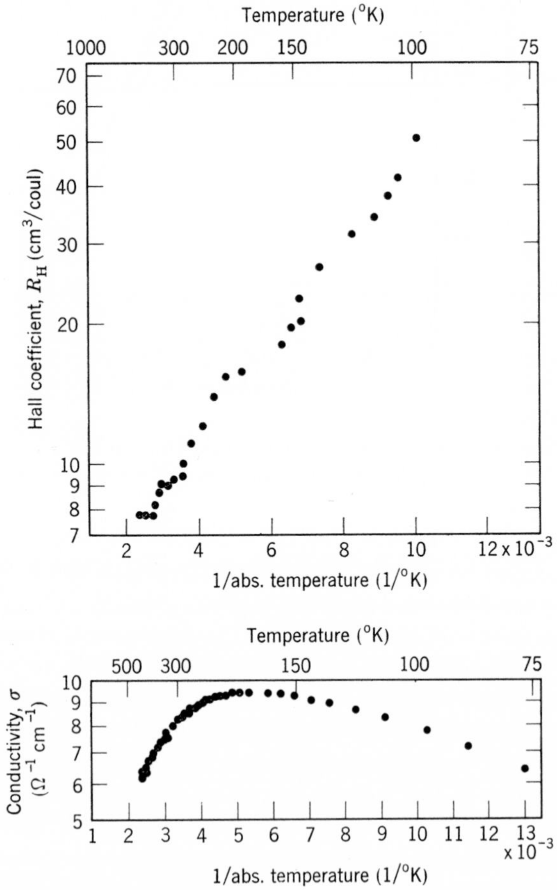

Fig. 4.20 Hall coefficient and conductivity as functions of temperature for GaP [after Alfrey and Wiggins (60A6)].

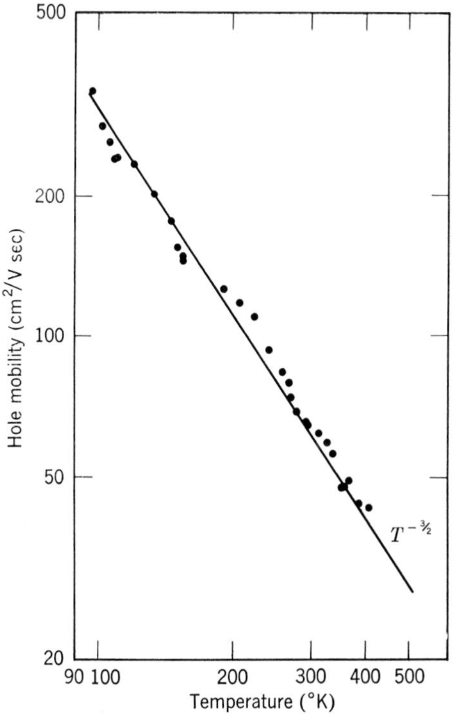

Fig. 4.21 Hole mobility in GaP as a function of temperature [after Alfrey and Wiggins (60A6)].

Electron mobilities of 130 cm^2/V sec have been measured (60D1), (62N2), but the maximum value undoubtedly lies much higher. Estimates of the latter have been made by comparing the properties of the III-V compounds among each other, using the theory of chemical binding, by Goodman (55G1) and Folberth and Welker (59F3). These estimates lead to values of $\mu_n = 1000$ cm^2/V sec and higher. Such values must, however, be too high, since an important point was neglected, namely, that the bottom of the conduction band is formed by a different subband in GaP than in the compounds used for the comparison, such as GaSb and GaAs.

For *p*-type material investigations have been made by Alfrey and Wiggins (60A6) and Cherry and Allen (62C6). Figures 4.20 and 4.21 illustrate typical results. The hole mobility obeys a temperature dependence of $T^{-3/2}$ over a wide temperature range. The highest room-temperature value measured so far is $\mu_p = 150$ cm^2/V sec

(62C6). These data give some idea about the type of hole scattering in GaP. Inserting the GaP parameter values into eqs. (4.1) and (4.2) results, for $m_p < 0.7\ m$, in $\mu_{\text{polar}} < \mu_{\text{acoust}}$. Since low-temperature mobility measurements of Cherry and Allen give $m_p \approx 0.5\ m$, the conclusion follows that here also polar scattering limits the mobility. An upper limit of $\mu_p \approx 250\ \text{cm}^2/\text{V sec}$ is therefore expected for the mobility.

No further parameters of GaP can be deduced from the available measurements. Intrinsic conduction is expected only for very pure samples or at very high temperatures because of the band gap of 2.4 eV. From the temperature dependence of the Hall coefficient in Fig. 4.20 at low temperatures, an acceptor ionization energy of 0.04 eV can be estimated.

Aluminum Antimonide. Despite a number of measurements of the electrical properties of AlSb, values of the mobilities and effective masses have not yet been determined with the same accuracy as for other important III-V compounds. A typical example of the tem-

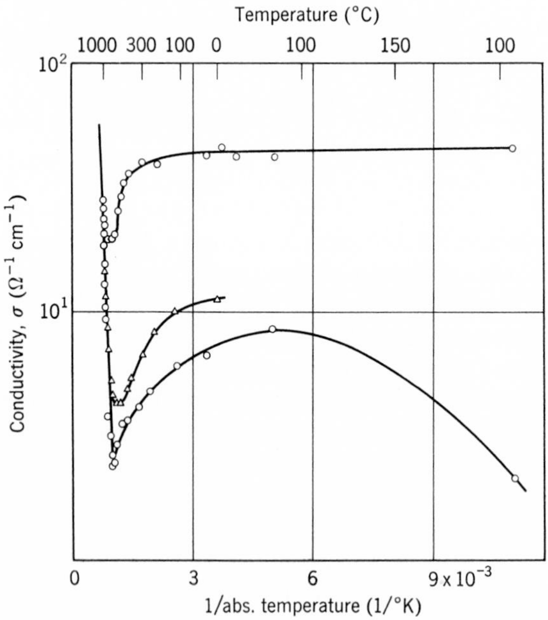

Fig. 4.22 Temperature dependence of conductivity in *p*-AlSb [after Welker (53W2)].

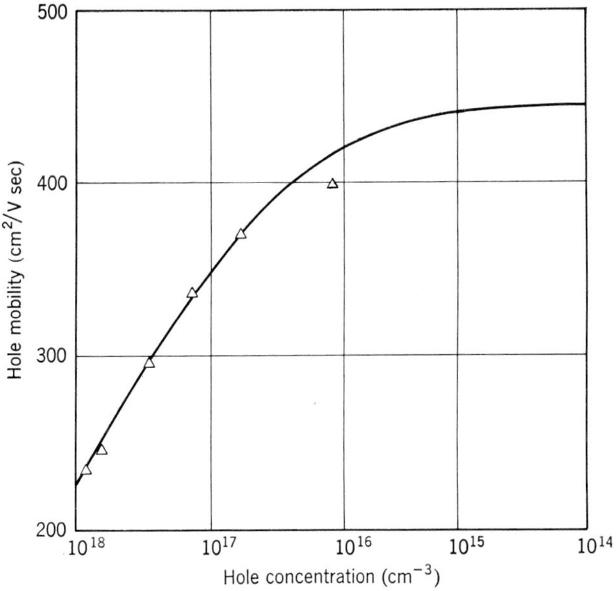

Fig. 4.23 Hole mobility vs. hole concentration in AlSb [after Reid and Willardson (58R2)]. Theoretical curve: combination of ionized-impurity scattering and acoustic scattering with the following parameters: $\kappa = 10$, $m_p = 0.41$, $\mu_{\text{lattice}} = 450\ \text{cm}^2/\text{V sec}$, $T = 300°\text{K}$.

perature dependence of the conductivity of p-type samples is shown in Fig. 4.22 (53W2). The straight line in the intrinsic region suggests a small mobility ratio. From its slope a band gap of 1.65 eV is obtained. Measurements of conductivity and Hall coefficient by other authors give values of E_G between 1.55 and 1.70 eV (54B3), (54B6), (54W3), (58N2), (59N3).

Nasledov and Slobotchikov (59N3), Blunt, Frederikse, Becker, and Hosler (54B3), and Sasaki, Sakamoto, and Kuno (54S1) have studied n-AlSb in more detail. In Se- and Te-doped samples Nasledov and Slobotchikov find an electron mobility of about 60 cm^2/V sec at room temperature and a temperature dependence proportional to $T^{-\alpha}$, with $1.4 < \alpha < 1.6$ at high temperatures. This value is measured in the region of mixed scattering and does not represent the maximum possible mobility. Other data on electron mobility and its temperature dependence vary so strongly that we refrain from a discussion of the dominant scattering mechanism.

An exact analysis of hole mobility from conductivity and Hall-effect measurements was performed by Reid and Willardson (58R2) [compare also (60A9)]. In their samples the hole mobility increased with increasing purity up to a room-temperature value of 400 cm^2/V sec at a hole concentration of 10^{16} cm^{-3} (Fig. 4.23). From these measured values the hole mobility for pure lattice scattering is calculated with the Brooks-Herring formula (4.3). The hole effective mass is an adjustable parameter. For a value of $m_p = 0.4\ m$, Reid and Willardson find $\mu_{p,\max} = 450$ cm^2/V sec (theoretical curve in Fig. 4.23). In contrast Nasledov and Slobotchikov (58N2) find $m_p = (0.9 \pm 0.1)\ m$. We have shown during the discussion of the electron mobility in GaAs that this sort of analysis can lead to the wrong results if polar scattering is the limiting lattice-scattering mechanism. Hilsum (60H9) finds from (4.2) that $\mu_{p,\text{polar}} = 800$ cm^2/V sec. It appears somewhat premature to conclude from these values that in AlSb at room temperature acoustic scattering dominates, in contrast to the situation in all the other III-V compounds discussed. More detailed measurements of the parameters in (4.2) are required. The temperature dependence is observed to obey a law of $T^{-\alpha}$ with $\alpha \leqslant 2$. For other experimental measurements see (53J1), (54B3), (54H5), (56K4), (58A4), (58H2), (58N2), (60K10).

Boron Phosphide. Because of the difficulty of preparing cubic BP only one measurement of the Hall coefficient and conductivity on single crystals is available [Stone and Hill (60S8)]. On some p-type crystals the Hall coefficient was temperature independent between 160 and 900°K. An acceptor concentration of about 10^{18} cm^{-3} was deduced. The room-temperature hole mobility varied between 30 and 70 cm^2/V sec. The temperature dependence suggested maximum mobilities of 300–500 cm^2/V sec. On needle-shaped n-type crystals only the conductivity was measured, and impurity concentrations of 10^{17} cm^{-3} were estimated.

Only a few measurements have been made of the change of conductivity and Hall coefficient at the *melting point* (54B9), (61G11), (62G7). The conductivity increases discontinuously by a factor of 2 or 3 and drops slowly at higher temperatures. The Hall coefficient drops at the same time by a somewhat larger amount. This means that the carrier concentrations increase abruptly upon melting, which can be explained by the breakup of a large number of electron bonds. Nevertheless, semiconductor properties are still observed in the melt, a sign that the tetrahedral orientation of nearest neighbors does not disappear.

412 Dependence of the conductivity and Hall coefficient on magnetic field. In Section 411 the Hall effect was considered in the limit of small magnetic fields only, and the influence of the magnetic field on the conductivity was neglected.

In the region of extrinsic conductivity the *Hall coefficient* is only weakly field dependent. The factor r_R of eq. (4.8) approaches 1 with increasing magnetic field. This statement applies for an isotropic semiconductor in the framework of classical theory. It neglects the effect of the magnetic field on the band model, i.e., the quantization of the electron orbits (cf. Section 315). We will restrict the discussion to the classical region in this section and will consider the limit of high magnetic fields in Section 413.

The *conductivity* σ decreases with increasing magnetic field. It is more convenient to discuss the resistivity ρ, since that is usually the measured quantity (*magnetoresistance*). For small magnetic fields, isotropic bands, and mixed conductivity its change is given by

$$\frac{\rho(B) - \rho(0)}{\rho(B)} = \frac{\Delta\rho}{\rho(B)} = \left[A_1 \frac{\mu_n{}^3 n + \mu_p{}^3 p}{\mu_n n + \mu_p p} - A_2 \left(\frac{\mu_n{}^2 n - \mu_p{}^2 p}{\mu_n n + \mu_p p}\right)^2\right] B_z{}^2 \tag{4.13}$$

It is proportional to the square of the magnetic-field component perpendicular to the direction of current flow. For scattering mechanisms with a relaxation time, the factors A_1 and A_2 are given by $A_1 = \Gamma_0{}^2\Gamma_3/\Gamma_1{}^3$, and $A_2 = (\Gamma_0\Gamma_2/\Gamma_1{}^2)^2$ [see the discussion accompanying eq. (4.8)]. For pure extrinsic conduction $\Delta\rho/\rho(B) = (A_1 - A_2)(\mu B_z)^2$. With increasing magnetic field $\Delta\rho/\rho(B)$ saturates, according to the classical theory.

The expression for the change of the resistance of a semiconductor by a magnetic field (4.13) consists of two terms. The first describes the deflection of the charge carriers by the Lorentz force of the electric and magnetic fields; the second describes the opposite deflection by the Hall field. The two contributions almost compensate as long as there is only one kind of charge carrier. The resistivity is changed because the Lorentz force is different for carriers of different velocities, while the Hall field can only compensate the average deflection. This fact means that the current paths of the individual carriers have a component perpendicular to the sample axis. Only the sum of all these components is zero.

This picture [eq. (4.13)] applies only in the case of an infinitely thin rod, where the total transverse component of current is really zero. For an infinitely wide sample, current compensation is not required

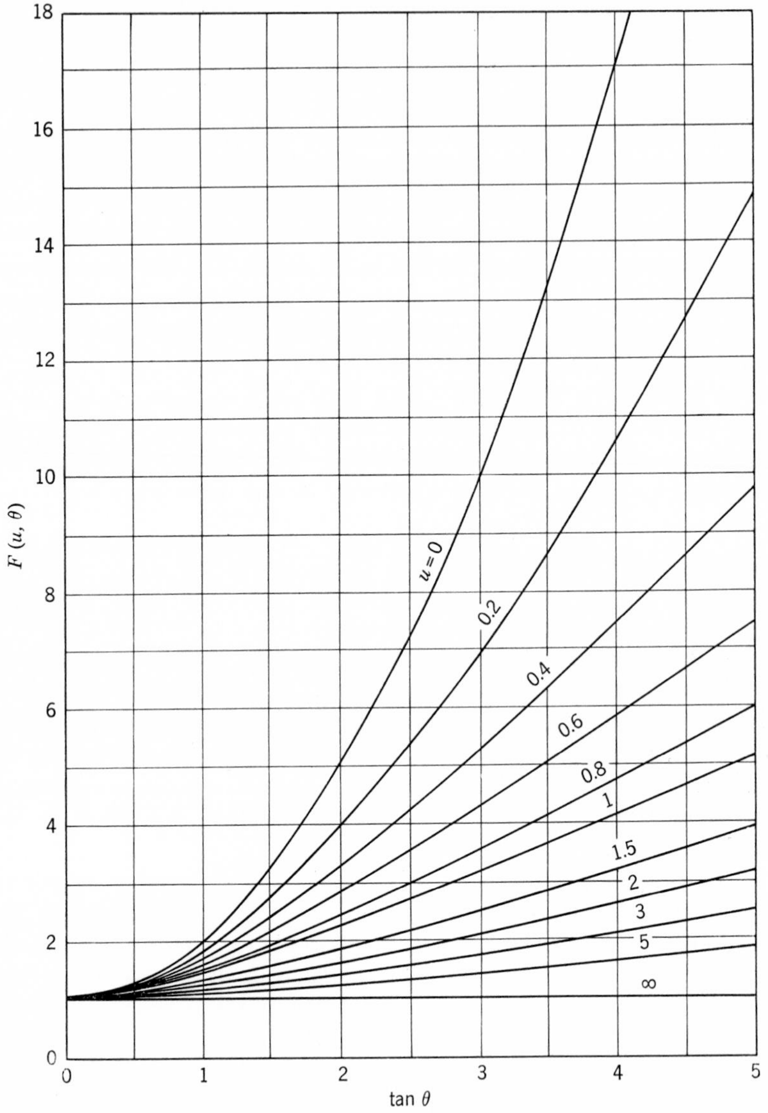

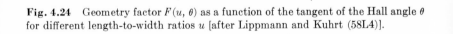

Fig. 4.24 Geometry factor $F(u, \theta)$ as a function of the tangent of the Hall angle θ for different length-to-width ratios u [after Lippmann and Kuhrt (58L4)].

and the resistivity change is given by the first term of eq. (4.13) alone. This means that the magnetoresistance depends on the geometry of the sample. The magnetoresistance increases with decreasing ratio of sample length to sample width (u), while the Hall voltage sinks and disappears for $u = 0$. The theory of the general case was developed by Lippmann and Kuhrt (58L3), (58L4), (58L5) and Drabble and Wolfe (57D2).

For certain cases the expressions can be given explicitly [$R(B)$ is the sample resistance in the field B]:

$$
\begin{aligned}
R(u, B) &= R(\infty, B)F(u, \tan\theta) & & \\
F(u, \tan\theta) &= 1 & &\text{for } u = \infty \\
&= \sqrt{1 + \tan^2\theta} & &\text{for } u = 1 \\
&= 1 + \tan^2\theta & &\text{for } u = 0
\end{aligned}
\tag{4.14}
$$

where θ is the Hall angle ($\tan\theta = \mathcal{E}_y/\mathcal{E}_x = \sigma R_{\mathrm{H}} B_z$).

No explicit expressions can be given for other values of u. The geometry function F is plotted vs. Hall angle in Fig. 4.24 for various u values.

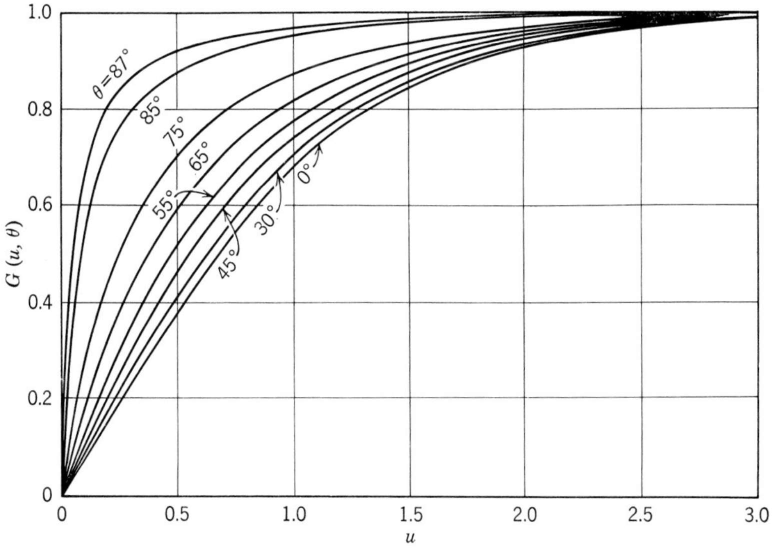

Fig. 4.25 Geometry factor $G(u, \theta)$ as a function of the length-to-width ratio u for different Hall angles θ [after Lippmann and Kuhrt (58L5)].

The corresponding expression for the Hall voltage is

$$V_H(u) = V_H(\infty)G(u, \tan\theta) \tag{4.15}$$

The geometry function G is shown in Fig. 4.25.

The geometry dependence of the galvanomagnetic effects for mixed conductivity has not yet been investigated theoretically.

The limit $u = 0$ (infinitely wide sample) can be realized experimentally by using a circular disk with one electrode in the center and the other along the periphery (Corbino disk). The electric field has then only a radial component, and the current paths are logarithmic spirals which make an angle equal to the Hall angle with the radial direction (Fig. 4.26). It is easy to show that in this case the magnetoresistance is identical to that of an infinite plate.

According to eq. (4.14), the influence of the sample shape is larger, the larger the Hall angle is, i.e., the larger the product of mobility and magnetic field is. It is therefore of particular importance for semiconductors of high mobility, such as n-InSb and n-InAs.

Indium Antimonide. In n-InSb deviations from the approximations used in Section 411 appear already at very small magnetic fields. The range of applicability of this approximation can easily be estimated. In the theory of the galvanomagnetic effects the magnetic field always appears as the product μB. An expansion in increasing powers of B therefore means an expansion based on the parameter μB. The

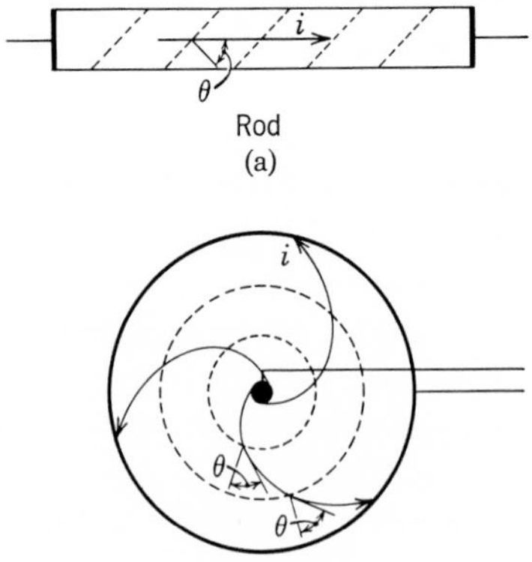

Fig. 4.26 Equipotential lines and field lines for a long thin rod and for the Corbino disk in a magnetic field [after Welker and Weiss (54W1)].

termination of this expansion after the first nonvanishing term is justified only if $\mu B \ll 1$. In this condition μB must be chosen dimensionless so that, when μ is given in cm^2/V sec, B is given in V sec/cm^2 or 10^8 gauss. In pure n-type material $\mu_n = 77{,}000$ cm^2/V sec at room temperature and $>620{,}000$ cm^2/V sec at 77°K. The magnetic-field dependence of the galvanomagnetic effects will therefore already be substantial at $B = 1300$ gauss and 160 gauss, respectively.

On the other hand, we have seen in Section 315 that the band model is modified by the magnetic field as soon as $\omega_c\tau_0 \gg 1$, where ω_c is the cyclotron-resonance frequency and equals eB/m^*, and τ_0 is the relaxation time. If the simplest relation between relaxation time and mobility, $\mu = e\tau_0/m^*$, is assumed, this condition becomes $\mu B \gg 1$. This does not mean, however, that quantum effects are necessarily expected to be observed in this range, since a second criterion must also be fulfilled. The magnetic subbands which appear for $\mu B \gg 1$ are filled at high temperatures up to high quantum numbers, and the correspondence principle prescribes that the conditions can then be described classically. For the observation of quantum effects we must therefore also require that the separation between two magnetic subbands is comparable to or greater than the thermal energy kT ($\hbar\omega_c \gtrsim kT$). When the n-InSb parameters are inserted, this becomes B (gauss) $\gtrsim 100 \times T$(°K).

Even within the range of validity of the classical theory of the field dependence of the galvanomagnetic effects there are other anomalies, related to the large electron mobility, which impede the comparison of the experimental results with this theory.

We have already pointed out the dependence of the galvanomagnetic effects on the *geometric shape* of the sample. This relation is more important the larger the Hall angle is. Figure 4.27 shows this influence clearly. The relative resistance $R(B)/R(0)$ is shown for four differently shaped InSb samples of equal purity. The figure is taken from the work of Weiss and Welker (54W1), who were the first to point to the importance of the geometry effect in semiconductors of high mobility. Even for long thin rods the resistance change is due mainly to geometry effects at the rod ends. The separation of the resistance change into a "geometric" and a "physical" part was thoroughly discussed by Simmons (61S5) and experimentally investigated by potential measurements along a rod for different ratios of length to width. Other geometric shapes have been investigated by Green (63G10).

It is possible to create an artificial "geometric" increase in the resistance by introducing oriented highly conducting inclusions into

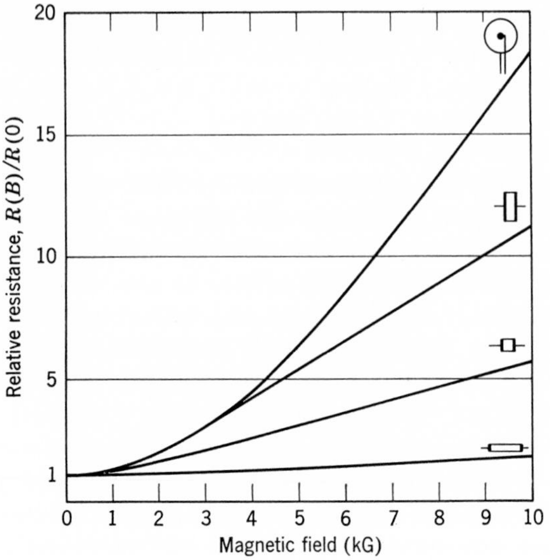

Fig. 4.27 Relative resistance of four samples of InSb of equal purity but different shape [after Welker and Weiss (54W1)].

the lattice. To demonstrate this, Weiss and Wilhelm (63W8) produced InSb with needle-shaped NiSb inclusions by directional freezing of the InSb-NiSb eutectic. This material exhibited very large magnetoresistance under suitable orientation.

The magnetoresistance is also strongly affected by *inhomogeneities* in the impurity distribution. Such inhomogeneities appear, for example, during the pulling of single crystals from the melt. The incorporation of impurities does not take place continuously but rather occurs in a periodical fashion. The resulting crystal contains fluctuations in the impurity distribution in the pulling direction. Let us consider a simplified model of a semiconductor which consists of alternating layers of different conductivity in the x-direction. Within each layer the distribution is uniform, and the electric current flows in the x-direction in the absence of a magnetic field. In a magnetic field the Hall field must be continuous across the boundary between two layers because of the condition $\nabla \times \mathcal{E} = 0$. This is possible only if the current density has a component perpendicular to the x-direction which changes sign in passing through the boundary. We obtain a distortion of the current flow, similar to the geometry effect, which increases the resistance change considerably. Herring (60H7) finds in this case

$$\frac{\Delta\rho}{\rho(0)} = \left(\frac{\Delta\rho}{\rho(0)}\right)_{\max} \frac{\sin^2\vartheta}{1 + (\mu B)^2 \cos^2\vartheta} \tag{4.16}$$

where the "physical" resistance change caused by statistics is neglected [$A_1 = A_2$ in eq. (4.13)]. Here ϑ is the angle between the primary current direction and the magnetic field. The factor $(\Delta\rho/\rho(0))_{\max}$ is given by the thickness and the conductivity of the layers. Only in the limit of small fields is this magnetoresistance proportional to $\sin^2\vartheta$, as eq. (4.13) prescribes for the homogeneous case. In the limit of very high fields the magnetoresistance goes as $\tan^2\vartheta$ [eq. (4.16)].

The situation becomes more complicated when the sample is not cut parallel to the crystal-growth axis. If we call the angle between this axis and the sample axis δ, then ϑ in eq. (4.16) is replaced by $\vartheta + \delta$, as long as the two axes are in the same plane with the magnetic field. The angle dependence of the abnormal magnetoresistance then has the same form as the normal one, but the curve is displaced by the angle $-\delta$. For other possible orientations between the two axes

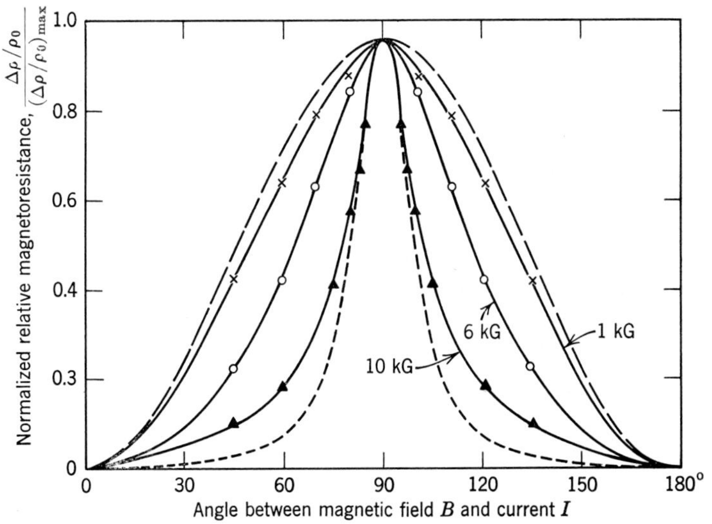

Fig. 4.28 Normalized magnetoresistance of n-InSb ($n = 5.4 \times 10^{16}$ cm^{-3}) as a function of the angle between the magnetic field and the current; measured curves for various magnetic fields (——), calculated curves for 10 kG (-----) and in the low-field approximation (– – –) [after Weiss (61W2)].

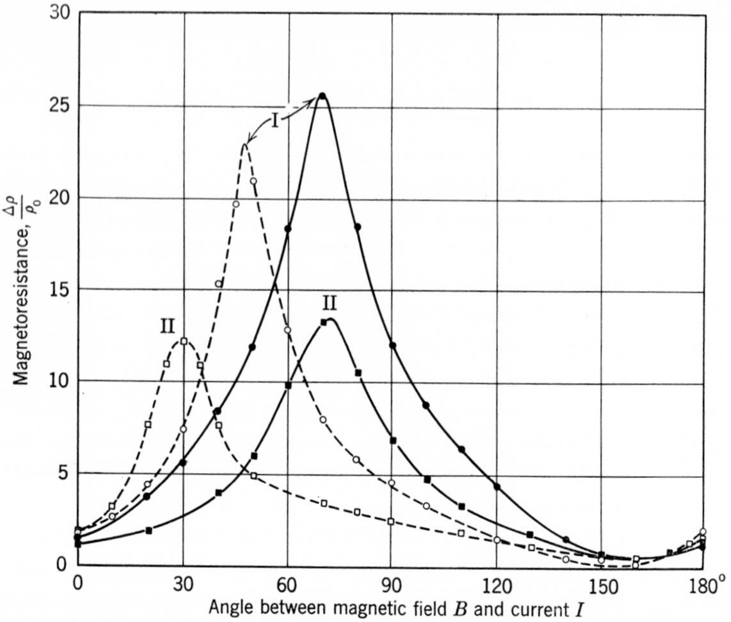

Fig. 4.29 Magnetoresistance of two specimens of n-InSb cut from the same single crystal at 20° resp. 45° to the pulling direction as a function of the angle between the magnetic field and the current. For curves --- the samples have been rotated by 90° around their axes compared with curves —— [after Weiss (61W2)].

and the field we refer to the literature cited in the discussion which follows. In all cases the maximum resistance change occurs when B lies in the plane of the layers.

These theoretical statements are completely confirmed by experiment. The deviations from the $\sin^2 \vartheta$ law and the appearance of a maximum at $\vartheta \neq (\pi/2)$ were first observed during investigations of galvanomagnetic effects in Te-doped InSb by Rupprecht, Weber and Weiss, (60R6). They were analyzed by these authors in later works (61R4), (61W2), (61B17). Figures 4.28 and 4.29 show the magnetoresistance for the case where sample and crystal growth axes coincide, according to eq. (4.16), and the displacement of the maxima as δ is varied. The excellent agreement between theory and experiment supports the hypothesis of a layer structure. Furthermore, it is found that the anomalies disappear when the crystal-pulling speed is increased. Such an increase must lead to a more homogeneous impurity distribution, because the distribution coefficient approaches

1 with increasing pulling speed. Indeed Rupprecht (61R4) found a well-developed anisotropy, as given by (4.16), for a pulling speed of 0.25 mm/min; for a speed of 4.2 mm/min, however, the magnetoresistance was independent of the orientation between the crystal-growth axis and the sample axis. In addition $(\Delta\rho/\rho)_{max}$ decreased from 70 to 2%. This justifies the neglect of the "physical"-resistance change in (4.16) in the comparison of theory and experiment in n-type InSb.

Bate and Beer have studied the influence of inhomogeneities on the galvanomagnetic effects in InSb theoretically and experimentally in a number of papers (61B3), (61B4), (61B5), (61B8). As examples, they chose a model of a single step-shaped discontinuity in the conductivity and another where the conductivity decreased exponentially along the sample axis. They found again that the contribution of the inhomogeneities to the magnetoresistance and Hall coefficient can outweigh the "normal" contribution.

It is for this reason that the available measurements of magnetoresistance at small fields and of the field dependence of Hall coefficient and magnetoresistance itself [(53P1), (54B5), (54H3), (55M2), (55R3), (56N1), (57F1), (58C1), (59V1), (61C6), (63C5), and other material which will be mentioned] generally cannot be compared with theory. The small field magnetoresistance does agree with a simple isotropic conduction band. However, the theoretically predicted saturation at high fields was not found. This can be explained by geometrical effects. As Weiss (61W2) has emphasized, the existence of any "physical" magnetoresistance in n-InSb has not been proved. All measured values can be explained by geometry effects, by inhomogeneities in the impurity distribution, or by mixed conduction.

No theory is yet available for the magnetoresistance under polar scattering. The fact that only a small "physical" magnetoresistance exists in InSb, can, however, be made plausible. According to (4.13), this quantity is proportional to $(A_1 - A_2)$ in n-InSb, and this factor is determined by the exponent r of the energy dependence of the relaxation time $\tau_0 \sim E^r$. For $r = -\frac{1}{2}$ (acoustic scattering), $(A_1 - A_2)$ is 0.378; for $r = 0$ (energy-independent relaxation time), it is zero; and it increases to 0.106 for $r = +\frac{1}{2}$ and to 2.15 for $r = +\frac{3}{2}$ (ionized-impurity scattering). At room temperature, $\hbar\omega_l/kT = 0.88$ for InSb, according to Table 4.1, and Fig. 4.1 shows that polar scattering can then adequately be described by a relaxation time with r near zero for the calculation of μ, R_H and ϕ. It is reasonable to assume that this result is also valid for calculating the magnetoresistance, which then takes on a negligible value for InSb at room temperature.

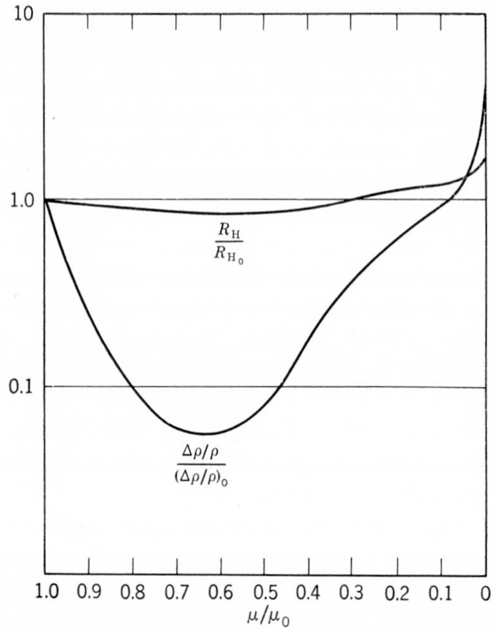

Fig. 4.30 Hall coefficient and magnetoresistance of an isotropic nondegenerate semiconductor for combined acoustic (index 0) and ionized-impurity scattering [according to Willardson and Duga (60W6)].

Another mechanism which reduces the magnetoresistance is the combined lattice and ionized-impurity scattering. Although the above values indicate that $\Delta\rho/\rho$ is larger for ionized-impurity scattering than for acoustic scattering by the factor $2.15/0.378 = 5.68$, $\Delta\rho/\rho$ can take on very small values if the two mechanisms are combined. Figure 4.30 shows the change in the Hall coefficient and magnetoresistance when ion scattering is added, according to (60W6). The index 0 denotes the parameter values for pure acoustic scattering. One can see from the figure that, for example, when ion scattering reduces the mobility by only 35%, the magnetoresistance drops to about 6% of the original value. The Hall coefficient is hardly influenced.

The nonexistence of a "physical" magnetoresistance requires a compensation of the two terms of eq. (4.13) for extrinsic conduction $(A_1 - A_2)$. The two terms can, however, be measured separately. The second term is the square of the Hall angle, and the first one the magnetoresistance for zero Hall voltage (infinitely wide sample, Corbino disk). Among the large number of measurements on Corbino disks we select the ones of Weiss (61W2), Beer (61B8), and Green (61G18). Weiss investigated the doping dependence of the relative resistance $R(B)/R(0)$ at 6 and 10 kG. The theory postulates a rapid increase with increasing σ and after a maximum at a few hundred $(\text{ohm cm})^{-1}$ a slow decrease. This was confirmed experimentally. At 10 kG the calculated maximum lies at approximately 300 $(\text{ohm cm})^{-1}$. At this conductivity the theoretical value is $R(B)/R(0) = 42$, with the experimental one somewhat lower: $R(B)/R(0) = 38$. Beer and Green investigated the magnetic-field dependence of the Corbino effect and found good agreement with theoretical expectations.

The measurements on p-type material can be analyzed more easily, since the hole mobility is two orders of magnitude smaller than the electron mobility. The product μB is therefore smaller than 1 up to very high fields. Since the valence band has a structure similar to that of germanium, we can expect a behavior of the galvanomagnetic effects similar to the well-known one of germanium. Investigations of Frederikse and Hosler (57F4), Champness (58C1), Fischer (60F3), and Hrostowski, Morin, Geballe, and Wheatley (55H4) show a magnetic-field dependence of the galvanomagnetic effects in p-InSb which indicates the existence of both "light" and "heavy" holes in the valence band. At low fields $\Delta\rho/\rho$ is proportional to B^2, but if one calculates the mobility from the coefficient of B^2, assuming only one kind of holes, one obtains a value which is 10 times as large as the product of Hall coefficient and conductivity. With increasing magnetic field, $\Delta\rho/\rho$ departs from the B^2 law, long before the simple theory would predict a saturation. The Hall coefficient depends strongly on magnetic field and is reduced to less than half its value at 10 kG.

This behavior was analyzed by Champness (58C2) on the basis of a two-band model. For simplifications he neglected the "physical" magnetoresistance, set the statistical factor r_R equal to 1, and set $A_1 = A_2$. Furthermore, the two valence bands were assumed to be isotropic and parabolic. Formulas similar to (4.8) and (4.9) apply to that case. The analysis on three samples gave for the purest sample at 77°K the following values: heavy holes—$p_1 = 3.6 \times 10^{14}$ cm^{-3}, $\mu_1 = 8400$ cm^2/V sec; light holes—$p_2 = 4.6 \times 10^{12}$ cm^{-3}, $\mu_2 = 62{,}000$ cm^2/V sec. In this case 1.3% of the charge carriers are light holes with a mobility 7.4 times larger. This light-hole mobility still appears to be limited by ionized-impurity scattering.

The same analysis was performed by Schönwald (64S1) for the region between 300 and 700°K. Figure 4.31 shows the values of μ_{p1}, μ_{p2}, and μ_n for InSb calculated from $\Delta\rho/\rho$ on the basis of the three-carrier model. Also shown is other, independent information about the temperature dependence of μ_{p1}. These results are contrasted with an evaluation of the magnetoresistance on a two-carrier model (curve 1). It was observed that the latter method results both in erroneous absolute values and in a magnetic-field dependence of the so-evaluated "apparent" hole mobility. The contribution of the light holes in these measurements was determined to be 1% at room temperature and 3% at 492°C.

At room temperature most *p*-type samples are already in the region of *mixed conduction.* Among the experimental investigations two papers by Howarth, Jones, and Putley (57H4) and by Hilsum and Barrie (58H3) must be mentioned. Howarth, Jones, and Putley measured the field dependence of the Hall coefficient between 170 and 260°K. In this region the Hall coefficient is determined by four parameters, the electron and hole concentrations and the two mobilities. The hole concentration can be determined from the Hall coefficient in the extrinsic region. By the use of σ and the Hall coefficient at low

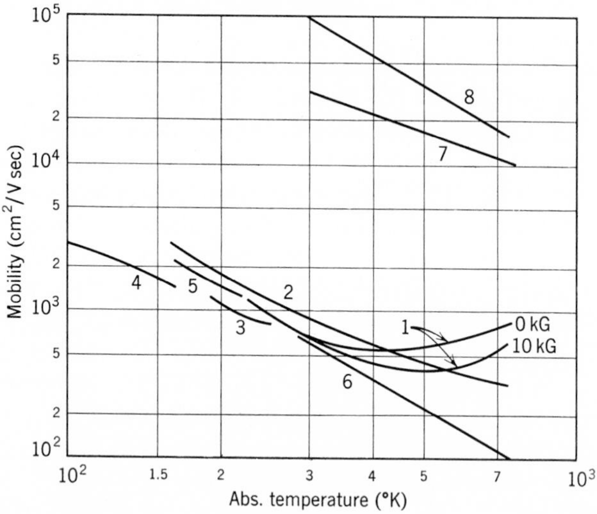

Fig. 4.31 Mobility of charge carriers in InSb. Curves 1 and 8: μ_p and μ_n calculated from the magnetoresistance at small magnetic fields and at 10 kG with a two-carrier model. Curves 6, 7, and 8: mobilities of light holes, heavy holes, and electrons calculated from the magnitoresistances on the basis of a three-carrier model [after Schönwald (64S1)]. For comparison, measurements of the hole mobility by Howarth *et al.* (57H4) (curves 3 and 5) and by Tannenbaum (53T1) (curve 4) are also shown. Curve 2 is calculated by Kołodziejczak and Kowalczyk (62K5).

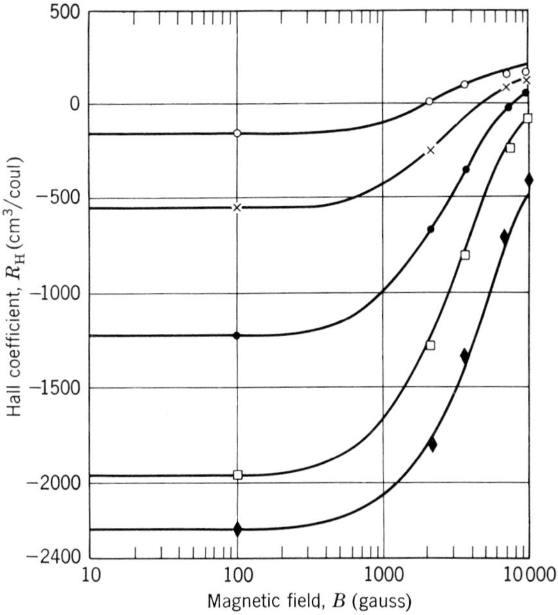

Fig. 4.32 Variation of the Hall coefficient with magnetic field at various temperatures between 208°K (highest curve) and 250°K (lowest curve). The points represent experimental data; the curves are theoretical results [after Howarth, Jones, and Putley (57H4)].

fields, two more unknowns are eliminated, so that the remaining unknown can be deduced from the magnetic-field dependence of the Hall coefficient. To simplify the analysis acoustic scattering was generally assumed, and deviations from isotropy and parabolicity of the bands, and also degeneracy effects, were neglected. Such an analysis of measurements on two samples of different purity gave almost quantitative agreement of the data with the simple theory. An example is shown in Fig. 4.32 for the field dependence of the Hall coefficient in the region where it passes through zero and R_H depends particularly strongly on B.

Hilsum and Barrie (58H3) interpreted their measurements of magnetoresistance and Hall coefficient of p-type InSb at room temperature with the same model, under the assumption of an energy-independent relaxation time (no "physical" magnetoresistance). The field dependence of R_H and $\Delta\rho/\rho$ was quantitatively described by the theory on eight samples of different purity. Hilsum and Barrie could show furthermore that the agreement was not as good if acoustic scattering was assumed to dominate. These results show that for p-type InSb also an energy-independent collision time can be used to describe the transport processes at room temperature, a fact which is in agreement with a predominantly polar scattering mechanism, according to Fig. 4.1. It must, however, be remarked that this conclusion is not entirely certain, since besides polar scattering ionized-impurity scattering must have influenced the mobilities in the samples of Hilsum and Barrie to a considerable extent. The question cannot be finally decided without the availability of an exact theory of combined polar and ion scattering.

Except in the region of the sign reversal the *Hall coefficient* in InSb is constant up to high magnetic fields (62H11), (63G1). In intrinsic and strongly n-type InSb Hieronymus and Weiss (62H11) found no field dependence of the Hall coefficient up to 150 kG; in weakly doped n-type material R_{H} increased slightly, while in weakly p-doped material it decreased slightly. This behavior makes InSb Hall generators usable up to extremely high magnetic fields.

The magnetoresistance of InSb has been measured by Sun (64S6) up to microwave frequencies (10 Gc/sec).

Indium Arsenide. Because of the high electron mobility in InAs the results found for InSb apply also to InAs. The magnetoresistance is strongly influenced by geometric effects. Figure 4.33 shows the resistance change of an InAs rod with a length-to-width ratio of 25:2 (57W1). The upper curve gives the resistance change of the rod measured between the rod ends; the lower curve, the same quantity measured between two probes away from the ends. The "physical" magneto-resistance here can be seen to be at most 20% of the total magneto-resistance of the rod. The magnetic-field dependence was $B^{1.65}$ in both cases. This deviation from the theoretically required B^2-dependence of the "physical" part has not yet been explained. Champness and Chasmar (57C2) arrived at the same results.

The smallness of the "physical" magnetoresistance in n-InAs can again be interpreted by polar scattering of the electrons.

Further results on InAs are similar to those on InSb, so that we need not consider them in detail. The Hall coefficient of n-InAs remains constant at room temperature up to 180 kG (60B15).

As we have mentioned, the classical theory of the galvanomagnetic effects applies even at high fields if the condition $\hbar\omega_c \ll kT$ is fulfilled. Under these conditions the limiting value of the Hall coefficient for n-type conduction is given by $R_{\mathrm{H}}(B \rightarrow \infty) = 1/en$. Then R_{H} does

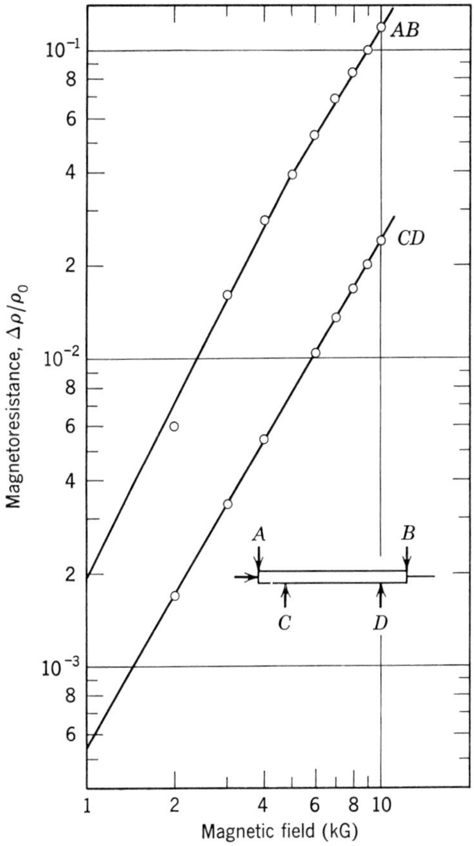

Fig. 4.33 Magnetoresistance of n-InAs for two different locations of the voltage probes [after Weiss (57W2)].

not contain the statistical factor r_R, as it appears in (4.8), and is consequently independent of the scattering mechanism. This allows one to determine the effective mass of the carriers more accurately, since it enters R_H only through the electron concentration. In this manner Shalyt (61S3) finds, for n-InAs, $m_n = 0.025\ m$ for $n = 3 \times 10^{16}\ cm^{-3}$. This value is in good agreement with the ones obtained from optical measurements (cf. Fig. 3.21).

Indium Phosphide. The magnetoresistance of n-type InP was measured by Glicksman (59G6) on samples of varying purity. For the purest sample ($n \lesssim 10^{16}\ cm^{-3}$) the angular dependence of the resistance change follows the $\sin^2 \vartheta$ law expected for isotropic semiconductors. All measurements are consistent with an isotropic (000)-band. The less pure samples show a weak but unambiguous anisotropy of the same kind as is found in silicon. This suggests the existence of a higher-lying (100)-subband, as is required by the pressure measurements of the absorption edge. We have seen, however, in Section 311 that the latter measurements are consistent with a separation of 0.3 eV between the (000)-minimum and the (100)-minimum. With such a separation no contribution of the upper band to the galvanomagnetic effects can be expected in the samples investigated by Glicksman. This contradiction has not yet been explained. Furthermore, we will see in Section 414 that the pressure dependence of the galvanomagnetic effects gives no indication of the existence of a second subband in the conduction band of InSb.

The absolute value of the transverse magnetoresistance was in all cases considerably smaller than is expected from acoustic scattering. This again points to the dominating influence of polar scattering in InP at room temperature.

Gallium Antimonide. The two subbands of the conduction band of GaSb both contribute strongly to the magnetoresistance. Figure 4.34

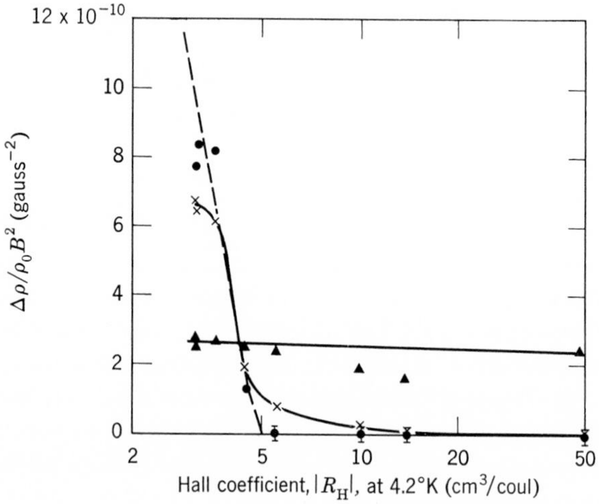

Fig. 4.34 Transverse magnetoresistance of six n-GaSb samples with different purity (different Hall coefficient) for three temperatures (triangles: 300°K; crosses: 77°K; solid points: 4.2°K). The broken line has been calculated with the parameter values given in the text [after Becker, Ramdas and Fan (61B7)].

shows measurements of the resistance change for six n-type samples at 300, 77, and 4.2°K, after Becker, Ramdas, and Fan (61B7). The Hall coefficient of the six samples at 4.2°K is indicated on the abscissa. Larger absolute value of the Hall coefficient means smaller electron concentration, i.e., purer samples. The magnetoresistance of the purer samples ($|R_{\rm H}| > 5$ cm^3/coul) decreases to very small values with decreasing temperature. This is in agreement with the classical theory of the magnetoresistance in an isotropic band, if one considers that the degeneracy increases with decreasing temperature. In a completely degenerate electron gas only electrons near the Fermi level take part in the electrical conductivity. All these have the same energy, and the statistical factors A_1 and A_2 in (4.13) are equal. Then the magnetoresistance disappears. In samples with smaller $|R_{\rm H}|$, i.e., larger electron concentration, we find the opposite behavior. The magnetoresistance increases with decreasing temperature.

This reversal of the temperature dependence can be explained on the basis of a two-band model. The influence of the second band becomes noticeable as soon as the Hall coefficient becomes smaller than 5 cm^3/coul, i.e., as soon as the electron concentration surpasses the value of 1.25×10^{18} cm^{-3}. From the known density of states we deduce that the influence of the second band appears when $E_{\rm F}$ lies more than 0.09 eV above the minimum of the conduction band. This agrees well with the value of the separation of the subbands obtained from optical measurements, as well as from the Hall measurements.

We will not go into the very detailed analyses that were made of these data in combination with the previously mentioned measurements of Hall coefficient, absorption edge, and free-carrier absorption and reflection. The results lead to a consistent picture of the conduction band of GaSb. The lower subband is isotropic; the higher one shows a definite (111)-anisotropy that can be seen in the behavior of the magnetoresistance in heavily doped samples. One sample with a Hall coefficient of $R_{\rm H} = -3.19$ cm^3/coul gave the following parameter values for the upper subband (index 1—lower subband, index 2—upper subband): $\Delta E_{12} = 0.08$ eV, $n_1 = 1.48 \times 10^{18}$ cm^{-3}, $n_2/n_1 = 2.67$, $\mu_2/\mu_1 = 0.06$, $m_1 = 0.052\ m$, $m_2/m_1 = 17.3$. The dashed curve in Fig. 4.34 shows the dependence of the magnetoresistance on the Hall coefficient, or doping, at $T = 4.2$°K, calculated from the two-band model with these parameter values. The good agreement again confirms the validity of this model.

The foregoing values of the effective masses are "density-of-states masses" m_d, which are obtained from the formula for the electron concentration. We saw in Section 320 that the "optical mass" $m_{\rm opt}$

obtained from optical measurements can have a different value. This latter mass was determined from reflection measurements and gave a value of 0.04 m for three samples of similar doping. If one assumes an isotropic parabolic lower subband ($m_{\text{opt},1}$ is equal to $m_{d,1}$), the entire difference between the two measured values must lie in the anisotropy of the upper subband, according to eq. (3.19). The ratio of longitudinal mass to transverse mass of one of the (111)-minima can consequently be determined from these results. Preliminary values of m_l/m_t lie between 6.75 and 11.4 for three samples if $m_1 = 0.052\,m$ and between 4.1 and 5.84 if $m_1 = 0.047\,m$ (the value given by magneto-absorption, cf. Section 315).

The magnetoresistance in p-GaSb shows a strong similarity to that of p-Ge and p-Si (61B7), (61H9), (61T4). Using the method of Champness, which was described in the discussion of the magnetoresistance of InSb, Harper, Roth and Teutsch (61H9) determined the parameters of the light and heavy holes. Becker, Ramdas, and Fan (61B7) were able to find a definite anisotropy in the transverse magnetoresistance, which can be explained by "warped" energy surfaces in the subband of the heavy holes.

Gallium Arsenide. The magnetoresistance in n-GaAs is dependent on the orientation of the crystal axes relative to the magnetic field, according to measurements of Glicksman (59G6) and Kravchenko and Fan (62K8), (63K2). Glicksman interpreted this dependence as due to poor contacts and concluded from his measurements that the conduction band in GaAs is isotropic. Kravchenko and Fan, however, found a real anisotropy with (100)-character. An analysis of these measurements, together with a new determination of the effective mass by thermoelectric and optical methods, led these authors to the conclusion that the lowest conduction band in GaAs is a (000)-band, but that the (100)-minima lie only 0.05 eV higher. This result is in disagreement with all the other measurements on n-GaAs. In particular, the pressure measurements show the (100)-minima to lie 0.4 eV above the (000)-minimum. Other measurements support this model. A possible explanation of the disagreement may lie in the fact that Kravchenko and Fan used relatively impure, compensated samples in their measurements.

Willardson and Duga (60W6) analyzed extensive measurements of magnetoresistance in n-GaAs at small magnetic fields with a theory of mixed ion and lattice scattering. They showed a complete agreement between theory and experiment even though polar scattering was not taken into account. Instead they used acoustic lattice scattering with a temperature dependence of $T^{-3/2}$ and a room-temperature value of 11,500 cm^2/V sec. The strong decrease of the magnetoresistance for mixed scattering as compared to pure (ion or lattice) scattering, which was shown in Fig. 4.30, was confirmed experimentally.

Aluminum Antimonide. According to Beer (59B6), the magnetic-field dependence of the Hall coefficient of p-type AlSb shows a fine structure similar to that observed in silicon. It can be explained by the warped nature of the V_1-band. This indicates a similarity between the valence bands of AlSb and of silicon, such as we have observed for all the other III-V compounds in comparison with germanium and silicon.

Measurements of the magnetic-field dependence of the galvanomagnetic effects sufficiently accurate for an analysis of the conduction band of AlSb are not yet available.

413 Anomalies of the galvanomagnetic effects at low temperatures and under high magnetic fields. We have seen in Section 412 that, aside from the anomalies in the galvanomagnetic effects of InSb and InAs due to geometry effects and inhomogeneities, there are other deviations from the classical theory of the galvanomagnetic effects at low temperatures and high magnetic fields.

At *low temperatures* the appearance of impurity-band conduction is known from germanium and silicon. At sufficiently high doping the wave functions of the electrons localized at the impurities overlap. It is no longer possible to treat the impurity states as discrete levels in the band model. Rather we must assume the existence of an *impurity band.*

In n-type **InSb** the effective mass of the electrons is so small that we must take an impurity band into account even at low doping. If a hydrogen-like model is used for the impurity states, the "Bohr radius" of a localized electron contains a factor $1/m^*$, and the "effective volume" of the impurity state is therefore very large. Simultaneously the ionization energy on an impurity becomes very small. In the hydrogen model this quantity is given by $\Delta E_D = m^*/m\kappa^{-2}\, Ry$ with the Rydberg energy $Ry = 13.6$ eV. For InSb this gives $\Delta E_D = 7 \times 10^{-4}$ eV. An ionization energy of this order of magnitude was found by Nasledov (60N4) on ultra-pure InSb. This small value and the large "effective volume" of the donors in InSb cause an impurity band at already very small doping. Even at $n_D = 10^{14}$ cm^{-3} the average distance between two donors is only three times the effective Bohr radius of the impurity state. In addition the impurity band overlaps with the conduction band because of its finite width. In that case no ionization energy can be observed experimentally [compare, e.g., (58S4) and (60P2)]. Even at the lowest temperatures free carriers are present. The properties of such an impurity band have been thoroughly discussed by Stern and Talley (55S2).

The overlap of the two bands can, however, be lifted by a magnetic field. Yafet, Keyes, and Adams (56Y1) have discussed the influence of a magnetic field on the ionization energy of impurity states with the hydrogen-like model in the limit of high magnetic fields. In that case the effect of the magnetic field in the Schrödinger equation can no longer be treated by perturbation theory. The magnetic forces, which act on the electron cloud in the plane perpendicular to B, surpass the Coulomb forces and deform the spherical cloud to an ellipsoid. Simultaneously they reduce the dimensions of the atom in all directions, resulting in an increase of the ionization energy. The detailed calculations show that the condition for the appearance of this effect is that the quantum energy $\hbar\omega_c$ is large compared to the Rydberg energy. This leads to the condition:

$$B \gg 2 \times 10^9/(m^*\kappa/m)^2 \text{ (gauss)}$$

Then one obtains for the ionization energy in the first approximation

$$\Delta E_D = \frac{8}{\pi}\left[\left(\ln\frac{\alpha}{2}\right)^2 - 1\right] \text{eV} \tag{4.17}$$

where

$$\left(\ln\frac{2}{\alpha} - 1\right)\alpha^{-1} = \frac{1}{8}\left(\frac{\hbar\omega_c}{Ry}\right)^{1/2}$$

A direct test of these theoretical predictions is difficult, since every experimentally measured quantity contains additional parameters which can be influenced by the magnetic field. Also the extension of the classical theory developed for small magnetic fields to large fields is not justified. The Hall coefficient is probably least dependent on these limitations. For n-InSb there are measurements by Keyes and Sladek (56K2) and by Frederikse and Hosler (57F3), (60F10), at 4.2°K, which show a very steep increase of the Hall coefficient at about 20,000 gauss in pure samples ($n_D = 10^{14} - 10^{15}$ cm^{-3}) that is not observed for impure samples. The explanation of this behavior is as follows. Because of the contraction of the electron cloud of the donors in the magnetic field the impurity band moves away from the conduction band, and some of the conduction electrons fall in the donor states as a result of the increased ionization energy (freeze-out effect). The assumption that this is the effect discussed by Yafet, Keyes, and

Adams, and not some other magnetic-field dependence of the electron concentration is supported by the fact that the Hall coefficient of impure samples is not affected by B (the impurity band is too wide) and by the observation that in the freeze-out effect the application of a strong electric field re-emits the charge carriers into the conduction band (reduction of the Hall coefficient).

Figures 4.35 and 4.36 show some representative examples. The Hall coefficient in a strongly compensated sample of n-InSb is plotted in Fig. 4.35 as a function of the reciprocal temperature for different magnetic fields. The rapid growth of the Hall coefficient with increasing magnetic field is caused by the conduction electrons dropping into the impurity band. The re-emission of the impurity-band electrons due to impact ionization by conduction electrons is demonstrated in Fig. 4.36 by the sudden increase in the conductivity and the decrease of the Hall coefficient with growing electric field at constant B and T.

Sladek (58S4), (59S3) analyzed these results on a two-band model of impurity band and conduction band to obtain information about the impurity band. For the conduction band a one-dimensional subband was assumed, since the experimental data excluded any occupation of higher subbands (quantum limit). The ionization energy and the mobility of the electrons in the impurity band were determined

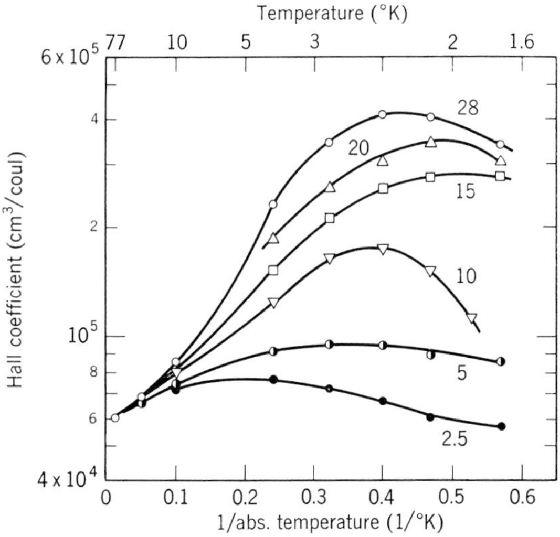

Fig. 4.35 Hall coefficient of an n-type InSb sample as a function of $1/T$ for various magnetic fields (parameter values in kilogauss) [after Sladek (58S4)].

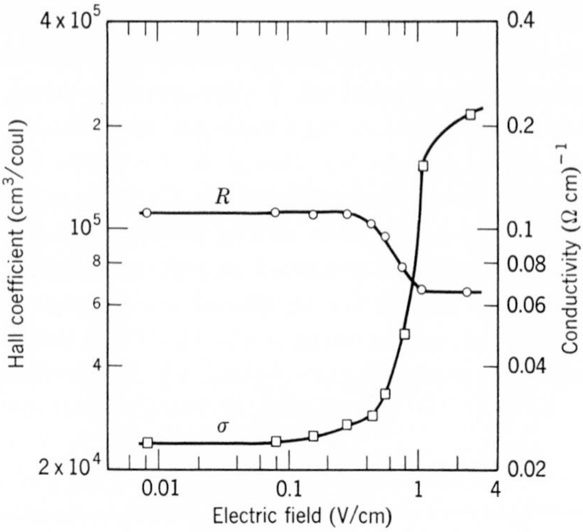

Fig. 4.36 Hall coefficient and conductivity of n-InSb at 10^4 gauss and 1.89°K as a function of the electric field [after Sladek (58S4)].

from this model. For the former, Sladek found good agreement with (4.17), at least for the magnetic-field dependence. The electron mobility decreases with increasing field because of the growing contraction of the electron orbits around the impurity atoms. The measured dependence of μ on B can be explained quantitatively by the reduced transition probability between donors (magnetic-field dependence of the exchange integrals according to the Yafet-Keyes-Adams theory).

At high impurity concentrations the Yafet-Keyes-Adams theory fails. The impurities cannot be treated as separated atoms. A better approximation has been given by Miller (64M1), who treats neighboring impurities as H_2 molecules. In this model a decrease of E_D with increasing magnetic field is found. This explains observations by Phelan and Love (64P1) on n-InSb at low temperature.

Impurity conduction is also found in p-type InSb at low temperature. Since the acceptors have a large ionization energy the impurity band usually does not overlap with the valence band. The behavior of conductivity and Hall coefficient at low temperature is identical with the known behavior in germanium. The Hall coefficient increases with decreasing temperature, reaches a maximum, and falls to small values in the impurity-band conduction region. The conductivity increases with decreasing temperature, rapidly above the maximum of R_H, slowly below it. The temperature dependence of the two transport coefficients is strongly dependent on doping, since the mobility in the impurity band is determined by the average distance between acceptors. Figure 4.37 shows this behavior according to measurements of Fritzsche and Lark-Horovitz (55F4). Other authors arrive at similar results [see, e.g., the work of Lyan Chzhi-chao and Nasledov (59L5), (60L6), (61L8), (61L9) on *n*- and *p*-type InSb]. Figure 4.37 also shows the temperature dependence of the magnetoresistance, $\Delta\rho/\rho$. This becomes negative with decreasing temperature; that is, the resistance *decreases* in the magnetic field. This behavior has not yet been observed in germanium.

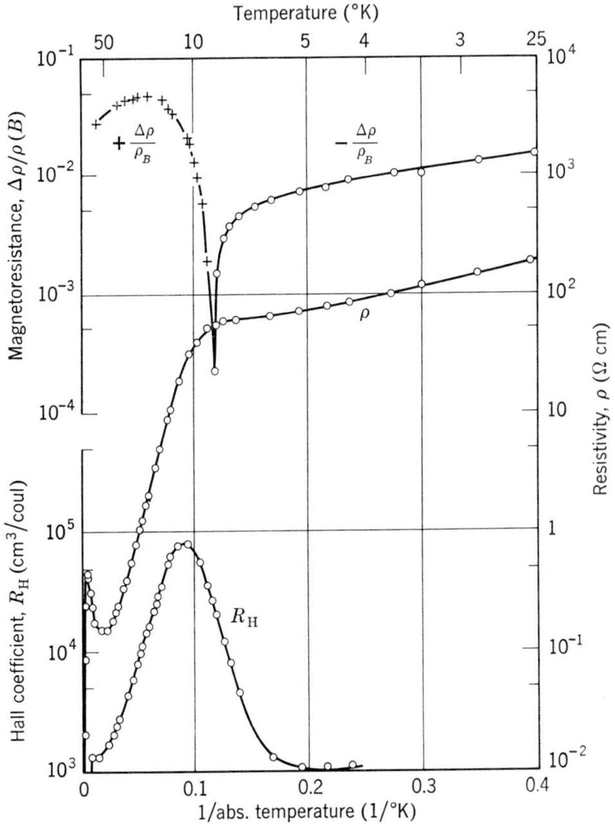

Fig. 4.37 Low-temperature Hall coefficient, resistivity, and magnetoresistance of *p*-InSb as a function of $1/T$ [after Fritzsche and Lark-Horovitz (55F4)].

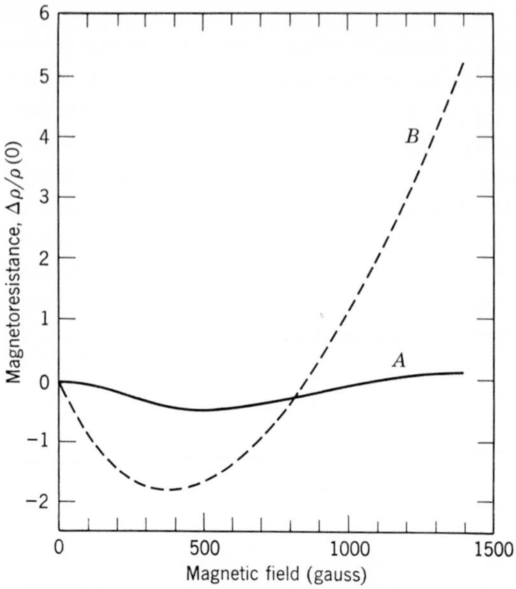

Fig. 4.38 Magnetic field dependence of the magnetoresistance of n-InSb for two samples with different dislocation density [after Broom (58B4)].

In InSb negative magnetoresistance has been observed in both n-type and p-type material. The cause appears to be different in the two cases, however. Broom (58B4) was able to change the sign of the magnetoresistance in n-InSb at low temperatures and weak magnetic fields by varying the surface treatments and by plastic deformation. The magnetic-field dependence of the longitudinal resistance change in n-InSb at 4.2°K is shown in Fig. 4.38. Curve A was taken on a pure sample; curve B, however, on a sample that had a large dislocation density introduced by plastic deformation. Samples cut by sand-blasting always show positive $\Delta\rho/\rho$. Subsequent polishing of the surface leads to a change of sign of the magnetoresistance, which is no longer affected by etching of the surfaces. A volume effect caused by polishing must therefore be involved, such as creation of "dislocation cracks." That negative magnetoresistance in n- and p-type InSb has different origins was also shown by Frederikse and Hosler (57F3), (57F4), (60F10). In n-type samples they observed a positive longitudinal magnetoresistance, which sometimes became negative with increasing magnetic field, but in p-type samples a negative (transverse and longitudinal) magnetoresistance which became positive with increasing field (independent of the surface treatment). Putley (59P6) found a double (structure-dependent) sign reversal of the magnetoresistance at low temperatures. Other experimental investigations show that the appearance of a negative magnetoresistance in p-InSb is always connected with impurity-band conduction, whereas in n-InSb this is only occasionally the case (59S1), (59S2). Theoretical suggestions for the explanation of these effects have been made. Interpretations in terms of a paramagnetic splitting of impurity states in the magnetic field were attempted by Mackintosh (56M2), Rigeaux and Thullier (56R1), and other authors, in terms of quantum effects by Barrie (59B2), and in terms of impurity-band conduction by Toyozawa (61T3). Final clarification of the question is still lacking.

Even the questions of impurity-band conduction are only partially explained theoretically. An observation by Putley (59P5) must be mentioned here. In a pure p-InSb sample ($p = 5 \times 10^{13}$ cm^{-3}) a maximum of the Hall coefficient appeared at 6°K, as is characteristic for impurity-band conduction. It could, however, be removed by etching the surfaces, and the Hall coefficient then showed no more indications of impurity-band conduction at any temperature.

Other deviations from the classical theory of the galvanomagnetic effects that have been found in **InSb** and **InAs** are as follows:

1. Appearance of a longitudinal magnetoresistance.
2. Absence of saturation of the transverse magnetoresistance at high fields.
3. Oscillations in the magnetoresistance and the Hall effect in degenerate material (de Haas-Shubnikov effect).

The second and third anomalies can be ascribed to quantum effects which are related to the changes of band structure in the magnetic field. A longitudinal magnetoresistance in semiconductors with isotropic conduction and valence band can also be attributed to this cause, but inhomogeneities in the impurity distribution may be responsible, as well. We will not discuss longitudinal magnetoresistance in any more detail; the reader is referred to the work of Frederikse and Hosler (57F4) for the experimental data.

In Section 412 we gave two conditions for the appearance of quantum effects. The band structure is affected by the magnetic field as soon as $\mu B \gg 1$. The band coalesces into a number of one-dimensional magnetic subbands whose extrema are displaced by $\hbar\omega_c$ from one another. A discrete structure in the distribution of the carriers among the subbands can be observed only if the separation of two subbands is large compared to the thermal energy kT. This leads to the additional condition $\hbar\omega_c \gg kT$.

For the discussion of the quantum effects we can distinguish two cases which are characterized by the location of the Fermi level. In nondegenerate material and in degenerate material at extremely high fields the Fermi level lies well below the second subband, so that only the lowest subband is occupied with carriers ("quantum limit"). This very high magnetic field limit is responsible for the failure of the magnetoresistance to saturate.

At not-too-high fields the Fermi level in degenerate material is located so far in the band that subbands of high quantum numbers are still occupied. The magnetic-field dependence of the galvanomagnetic effects then shows oscillations, which can be explained qualitatively as follows. In the theory of the band model in a magnetic field we have to take the exact form of the density of states in one of the magnetic subbands into account. This density of states drops rapidly with increasing energy and is larger, the larger the magnetic field is. Consider now a degenerate semiconductor in a magnetic field. Let the subbands be occupied up to quantum number n'. Then the Fermi level lies just above the band edge $E_{n'} = (n' + \frac{1}{2})\hbar\omega_c$ of that subband. The conductivity and galvanomagnetic effects are then entirely determined by the carriers in the n'-band, since all the lower subbands have a negligible density of states in the vicinity of E_F under the condition $\hbar\omega_c \gg kT$. If we now increase the magnetic field, the distance between the subbands becomes larger, and, because of the increasing density of states, the electrons drop into lower subbands. All subbands move to higher energies relative to E_F, and in regular intervals E_F falls on one subband edge after another. This leads to periodic fluctuations of the galvanomagnetic effects, since they depend on the position of the Fermi level relative to the band edge. Finally, when the field has increased so far that E_F lies below the $(n' = 2)$-subband, the "quantum limit" is reached.

To observe the oscillation, the following condition is therefore required, in addition to the two mentioned above: $E_F - E_c \gg \hbar\omega_c$. This requires degenerate semiconductors with large mobilities and small effective masses, such as is the case for InSb and InAs at low temperatures.

Oscillations in InSb have been observed by Frederikse and Hosler (57F3), (56F3), (60F10), Busch, Kern, and Lüthi (57B7), Kanai and Sasaki (55K2), (56K1), (57K1), (59S1), Broom (58B4), and Putley (59P6), in InAs by Frederikse and Hosler (58F5), (60F10), Sladek (58S3), Amirkhanov *et al.* (63A5), (63A6), and Bemski and Szymanski

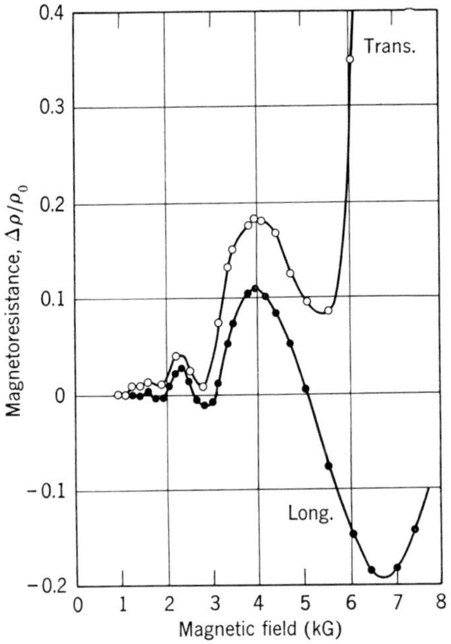

Fig. 4.39 Longitudinal and transverse magnetoresistance of n-InSb as a function of the magnetic field at 1.7°K [after Frederikse and Hosler (57F3)].

(61B10), and in GaAs by Becker and Fan (63B6), (64B1). Typical results are shown in Figs. 4.39 and 4.40. In Fig. 4.39 the longitudinal and transverse magnetoresistance of InSb ($n = 2.3 \times 10^{15}$ cm^{-3}) at 1.7°K is shown as a function of B; in Fig. 4.40 the same quantities in InAs ($n = 2.8 \times 10^{16}$ cm^{-3}) are shown at various temperatures as a function of $1/B$.

The second representation has the following advantage. The theory of the de Haas-Shubnikov effect predicts oscillations consisting of sine and cosine terms of the argument $(2\pi E_F q/\hbar\omega_c - \phi)$ with $q = 1, 2, \ldots$. In a $(1/B)$-representation these terms then have the period $\hbar e/E_F m^* q$. This period becomes field dependent when only a few subbands lie below E_F ($E_F - E_c \approx \hbar\omega_c$), and also when the band splitting is not uniform with separation $\hbar\omega_c$ (deviation from the simple parabolic band structure).

The data shown in Figs. 4.39 and 4.40 exhibit a single period, which in the case of Fig. 4.40 takes on the value 3.5×10^{-5} gauss^{-1}. If it is identified with the term $q = 1$, then $n = 2.74 \times 10^{16}$ cm^{-3} follows in good agreement with the above value, calculated from the Hall effect.

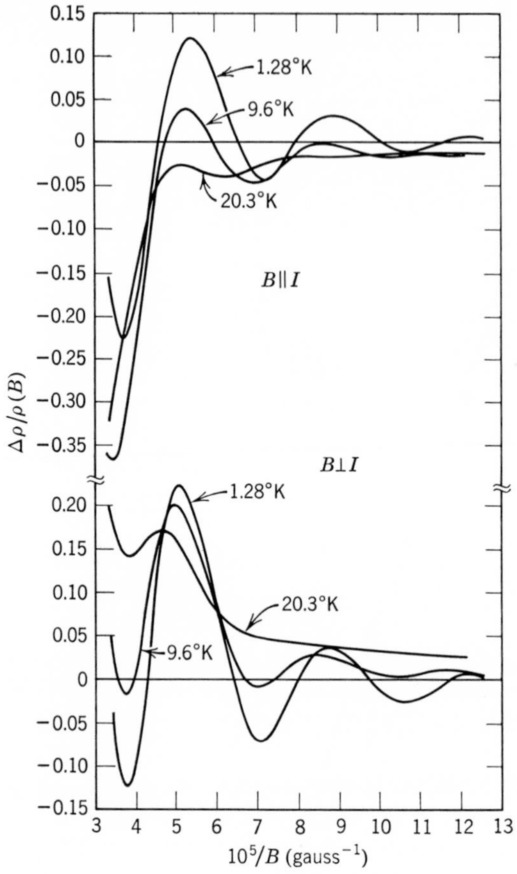

Fig. 4.40 Longitudinal and transverse magnetoresistance of n-InAs as a function of the reciprocal magnetic field for various temperatures [after Sladek (58S3)].

Note that the period is independent of the effective mass and depends only weakly on temperature through E_F. For a discussion of the amplitude and of the more complete theory we refer to the papers mentioned above and to a theoretical treatment by Shalyt and Éfros (62S2).

In transverse magnetoresistance of n-InSb at helium temperature Putley (59P6) found oscillations which cannot be ascribed to the de Haas-Shubnikov effect. They are characterized by multiple change of sign of the magnetoresistance with increasing field (Fig. 4.41). The origin of this effect has not yet been explained.

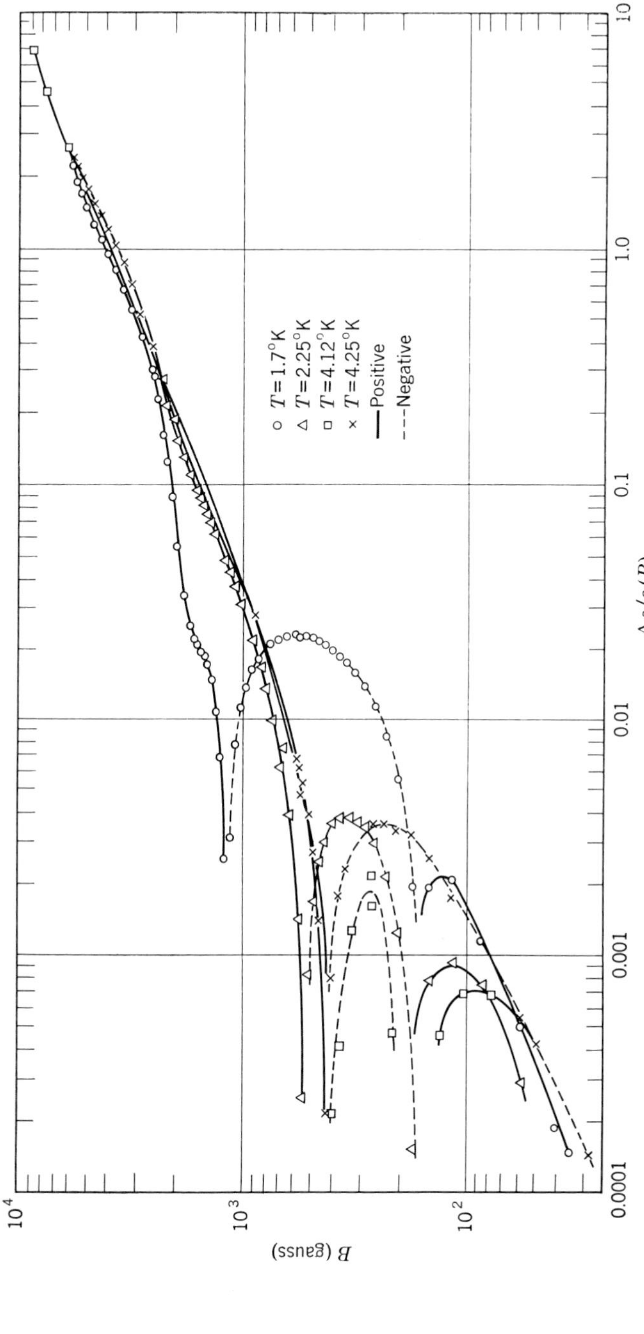

Fig. 4.41 Anomalies in the magnetoresistance of an InSb sample at low temperatures [after Putley (59P6)].

Among the investigations of the galvanomagnetic effects in n-InSb in the "quantum limit" [(59B1), (59H1), (60A10), (61L6) and other works cited in this section] we will consider only the one of Sladek (60S4). He measured the magnetoresistance in very pure InSb ($n = 2.85 \times 10^{14}$ cm^{-3} at 77°K) over the temperature range from 50 to 111°K and for fields up to 28 kG. The absence of saturation in $\Delta\rho/\rho$ was confirmed. At all temperatures the field dependence of the transverse magnetoresistance was $(\Delta\rho/\rho)_{\text{tr}} \sim B^{0.9}$. In addition to the transverse resistance change a longitudinal one was also observed. Above 10 kG $(\Delta\rho/\rho)_{\text{long}}$ was independent of the magnetic field.

Similar results on n-InSb were obtained by Haslett and Love (59H1) with fields up to 180 kG and by Amirkhanov, Bashirov, and Zakiev (60A10), (63A4) up to 800 kG, and on n-InAs by Amirkhanov, Bashirov, and Zakiev (61A5).

The most extensive theoretical study of the galvanomagnetic effects in the "quantum limit" was made by Adams and Holstein (59A2). The theory predicts power laws for the magnetic-field dependence and the temperature dependence of transverse and longitudinal resistance change, where the exponents depend on the scattering mechanisms and are different for degeneracy and nondegeneracy. When theory and experiment are compared for InSb, the best agreement is obtained under the assumption of piezoelectric scattering. However, this result for the "quantum limit" in InSb must be considered tentative, since the experimental and theoretical results are still very incomplete. For further details we refer to the papers cited.

Oscillations in the magnetoresistance of n-InSb in the quantum limit were ascribed by Puri and Geballe (63P15) to the scattering of the electrons by optical phonons into the second and third magnetic subbands.

Measurements of the conductivity and Hall coefficient of GaAs down to 1.5°K were performed by Emel'yanenko and co-workers (58E2), (61E6), (62G7). For heavily doped n-type samples ($n = 10^{17} - 10^{18}$ cm^{-3} at room temperature) conductivity and Hall coefficient remain approximately constant between 300 and 1.5°K. This absence of any ionization energy indicates, as in InSb, that an impurity band is formed which overlaps with the band edge. Because of the small effective electron mass GaAs is degenerate in this temperature range. In less heavily doped samples the behavior at low temperatures is similar to that of germanium, silicon, and InSb for impurity-band conduction. The appearance of a maximum in the temperature dependence of the Hall coefficient and a strong decrease

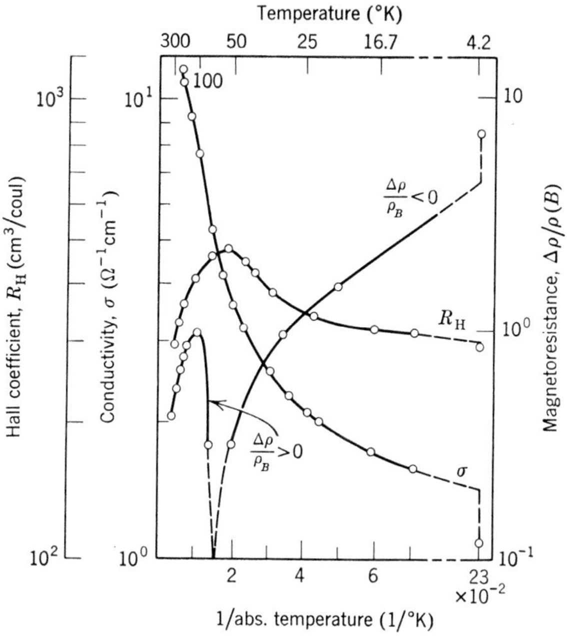

Fig. 4.42 Hall coefficient, conductivity, and magnetoresistance of n-GaAs as a function of $1/T$ for low temperatures [after Emel'yanenko, Lagunova, and Nasledov (61E6)].

of the conductivity are observed in this range, combined with a negative magnetoresistance (Fig. 4.42).

Typical impurity-band effects were also observed at low temperatures in p-type samples with hole concentrations between 10^{17} and 10^{18} cm^{-3} (61E3), (61M10), as well as in n-InP (64K3) and n-InAs (63Z3).

414 Pressure dependence of the electrical properties. In Section 311 we discussed the dependence of the width of the forbidden gap on the hydrostatic pressure, as far as optical measurements can give this information. We will now supplement this discussion by considering the pressure dependence of the conductivity and of the galvanomagnetic effects. In addition we will go into the dependence of the resistance on uniaxial stress (piezoresistance). All these measurements give information about the position of the band extrema in the Brillouin zone. We will see that the results confirm the assignment of conduction-band extrema to different points in the Brillouin zone that was made in Table 3.2.

Dependence on Hydrostatic Pressure. We have already discussed the measurements of Keyes (55K3) and Long (55L2) on **InSb** in Section 311, as far as they concerned the change of E_G by hydrostatic pressure. We must now consider the pressure dependence of the mobility. The Hall coefficient and the electric resistance increase exponentially with increasing pressure, according to Long. If one ascribes this dependence solely to the change of the effective mass and of the energy gap, one can determine the effective mass contribution from the pressure dependence of the Hall mobility. Since conductivity and Hall coefficient also determine the intrinsic concentration n_i, which depends on m^* and E_G, the measurement of the pressure dependence of this parameter gives dE_G/dP. In this fashion the values given in Section 311 were determined.

A decrease of 14% was measured in the electron mobility at 2000 kg/cm^2. These results were confirmed by Gielessen and v. Klitzing (56G1) and were also found at pressures up to 30,000 kg/cm^2 by Gebbie, Smith, Austin, and King (60G6) and Paul (61P6). They are consistent with the pressure dependence of the magnetoresistance (56L4).

The hole mobility is pressure independent. From these results Keyes derived a valence-band structure with maxima along the [111]-axes or along the [100]-axes, far from the center of the Brillouin zone. This conclusion does not seem to be justified when the many indications of a Ge-like structure of the InSb valence band are considered.

Similar results were found by Taylor (55T3) for **InAs**. The measured pressure coefficient of the energy gap agrees with the value given in Table 3.2. These measurements were confirmed by de Meis (61P6) up to 30,000 kg/cm^2. No indications of a higher-lying subband of the conduction band were found in InSb or InAs. The same statement applies to **InP** (61P6), (61S1).

Extensive measurements of the pressure dependence of the resistance, the Hall coefficient, and the thermoelectric power of **GaSb** were made by Sagar and Miller (61S1) and by Howard (61P6). Figure 4.43 shows measurements of Howard. The two changes of the slope of $\rho(P)$ suggest the presence of three subbands in the conduction band. These results are consistent with the optical and electrical measurements discussed in earlier sections. The third subband appears only at 25,000 kg/cm^2, according to Fig. 4.43. Therefore Sagar and Miller were able to interpret their results below this pressure by a two-band model with a separation of the band edges of 0.075 eV

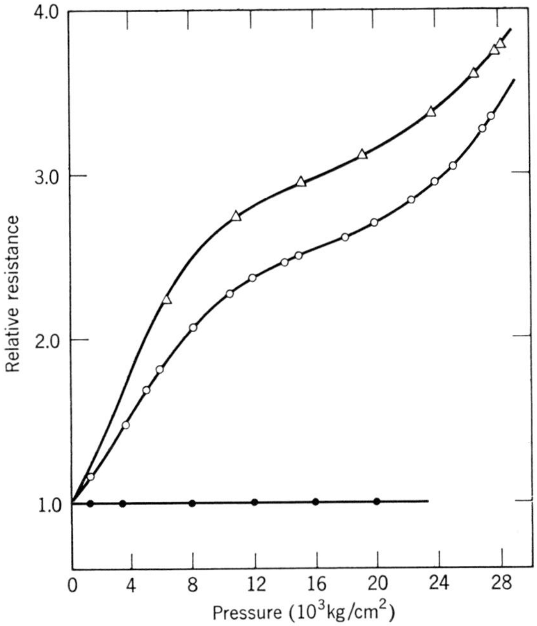

Fig. 4.43 Pressure dependence of the resistivity of GaSb at room temperature (triangles: n-type sample with $n = 10^{18}$ cm^{-3}; open circles: n-type sample with $n = 3 \times 10^{18}$ cm^{-3}; solid circles: p-type sample) [after Paul (61P6)].

at normal pressure. This value agrees with ΔE_{12} obtained from optical measurements.

On **GaAs** the pressure investigation of the electrical resistance also confirmed the existence of a second subband. Ehrenreich (60E3) analyzed measurements of Sagar and Howard on a two-band model and was able to determine the separation between the band edges of the two subbands as

$$\Delta E_{12} = [0.36 - 1.08 \times 10^{-5} P \text{ (kg/cm}^2)] \text{ (eV)}$$

If one adds to this result the optically determined pressure coefficient of the lowest conduction-band minimum (9.4×10^{-6} eV/kg cm^{-2}), the pressure coefficient of the second subband (relative to the valence band) follows as -1.4×10^{-6} eV/kg cm^{-2}. The value is of the same order of magnitude as the pressure coefficient of the (100)-minimum in silicon, so that this is another indication that the second subband in n-GaAs has Δ-symmetry.

Finally, in **GaP** Sagar and Miller (61S1) found a dependence of the resistance on pressure similar to that in silicon, as is expected from Table 3.2.

Piezoresistance. If uniaxial stress is applied to a semiconductor, the bands are changed in such a way that points lying symmetrically in the Brillouin zone are displaced by different amounts of energy. This will, of course, change the electrical properties.

In an isotropic conduction band this change is only small. The energy surfaces are deformed, but only a shift of one band edge relative to another will have a noticeable effect. In an anisotropic band, however, with minima along preferred axes in **k**-space, there will be an important rearrangement of the charge carriers within the band. Depending on the direction of the applied stress, the band edges of the individual minima will be moved by different amounts of energy and will therefore be occupied by different numbers of charge carriers. In a cubic crystal with minima lying at the same energy, all minima contribute anisotropic parts to the conductivity, which for no pressure add up to an isotropic conductivity. This means that there will now be a pressure- and orientation-dependent anisotropy of the conductivity (piezoresistance). We will first consider the phenomenological theory of the effect.

The general relationship between current and field in an electric anisotropic crystal can be expressed by the resistance tensor ρ_{ik}:

$$\mathcal{E}_i = \sum_k \rho_{ik} i_k \tag{4.18}$$

According to the Onsager relations, this tensor is symmetric and contains only six different components: $\rho_{11}, \rho_{22}, \rho_{33}, \rho_{23}, \rho_{13}, \rho_{12}$. These components can be combined into a six-component vector, ρ_i ($i = 1 \ldots 6$). The stress tensor T_{ik} and the deformation tensor e_{ik} are also symmetric tensors which can be expressed as six-component vectors T_i and e_i. Thus the relation between them may be expressed as $T_i = \sum_k C_{ik}e_k$, where C_{ik} are the elastic constants of the crystal.

The relative change of the electrical resistance in a deformed crystal can then be related to T_i and e_i:

$$\left.\frac{\delta\rho}{\rho}\right|_i = \sum_{j=1}^{6} \pi_{ij}T_j = \sum_{j=1}^{6} m_{ij}e_j; \quad m_{ij} = \sum_l \pi_{il}C_{lj} \tag{4.19}$$

where the π_{ij} and m_{ij} form six-matrices. They are called the piezoresistance coefficients and elastoresistance coefficients, respectively. The six-component vectors ρ_i, T_i, and e_i transform as follows under rotation of the axes:

$$\rho_i' = \sum_{k=1}^{6} \alpha_{ik}\rho_k \tag{4.20}$$

α_{ik} is a six-matrix whose elements are products of the direction cosines l_i, m_i, and n_i between the axes of the original and the rotated coordinate systems.

The π_{ik} then transform according to

$$\pi_{ik}' = \sum_{l,m} \alpha_{il}\pi_{lm}\alpha_{mk}^{-1} \tag{4.21}$$

and the e_{ik} transform in the same way.

These relations are used to reduce the number of independent π_{ik}- and m_{ik}-terms for a crystal of given symmetry; for every symmetry operation of the crystal lattice the tensor components must remain unchanged. For the diamond structure (crystal class O_h) and the zinc-blende structure (T_d) one obtains for the π_{ik}

$$\pi_{ik} = \left\| \begin{matrix} \pi_{11} & \pi_{12} & \pi_{12} & 0 & 0 & 0 \\ \pi_{12} & \pi_{11} & \pi_{12} & 0 & 0 & 0 \\ \pi_{12} & \pi_{12} & \pi_{11} & 0 & 0 & 0 \\ 0 & 0 & 0 & \pi_{44} & 0 & 0 \\ 0 & 0 & 0 & 0 & \pi_{44} & 0 \\ 0 & 0 & 0 & 0 & 0 & \pi_{44} \end{matrix} \right\| \tag{4.22}$$

if one chooses a right-angle coordinate system as reference system with axes along the cubic [100]-, [010]-, and [001]-axes. The corresponding matrix is obtained for the m_{ik} and elastic constants C_{ik}. The resistance tensor ρ_{ik} reduces to a scalar, i.e., $\rho_{11} = \rho_{22} = \rho_{33} = \rho_0$, $\rho_{12} = \rho_{23} = \rho_{31} = 0$.

One determines π_{ik} and m_{ik} experimentally by measuring the electric-field strength in a crystal under stress with a given current flowing. From the relationship $\mathcal{E}_i = \rho_0 i_i$ and $\delta\mathcal{E}_i = \sum_k \delta\rho_{ik} i_k$ the $\left.\frac{\delta\rho}{\rho}\right|_i$ follow, and if T_i and C_{ik} are given, the desired coefficients can be calculated. For this, three independent measurements are necessary. One generally chooses "longitudinal" measurements (stress parallel to the current direction) or "transverse" measurements (stress perpendicular to the current direction). In longitudinal measurements π_{ik}' is determined in a coordinate system in which the x-axis is the current direction. From the inverse transformation of (4.21) the π_{ik} is obtained. Thus a measurement in the [100]-direction immediately gives π_{11}; a measurement in the [110]-direction, the combination $\frac{1}{2}(\pi_{11} + \pi_{12} + \pi_{44})$, and one in the [111]-direction, $\frac{1}{3}(\pi_{11} + 2\pi_{12} + 2\pi_{44})$. A hydrostatic compression gives the combination $\pi_{11} + 2\pi_{12}$.

The theory of the piezoresistance in the conduction band of a cubic semiconductor was developed by Herring (55H2). The important results for the following discussion are these:

1. For a band with minimum at $\mathbf{k} = 0$, $m_{11} - m_{12} = m_{44} = 0$.
2. If the minima lie on the [100]-axes, $m_{44} = 0$ and $m_{11} - m_{12} \neq 0$.
3. Minima on the [111]-axes give $m_{44} \neq 0$ and $m_{11} - m_{12} = 0$.

This means that the coefficients which most clearly characterize the band structure are the anisotropy coefficients m_{44} and $(m_{11} - m_{12})/2$, and the hydrostatic-pressure coefficient $(m_{11} + 2m_{12})/3$. These combinations are related to the piezoresistance coefficients through (4.19):

$$\begin{aligned}(m_{11} + 2m_{12}) &= (\pi_{11} + 2\pi_{12})(C_{11} + 2C_{12}) \\ m_{44} &= \pi_{44}C_{44} \\ (m_{11} - m_{12}) &= (\pi_{11} - \pi_{12})(C_{11} - C_{12})\end{aligned} \tag{4.23}$$

The main result of the corresponding theory for a valence band with warped energy surfaces, by Adams (54A1), is that m_{44} should be large compared with the pressure coefficient $(m_{11} + 2m_{12})/3$.

A stress also lifts the degeneracy of the V_1- and V_2-bands at $\mathbf{k} = 0$. This leads to a strong deformation of the V_2-band near $\mathbf{k} = 0$. Through the interaction between V_2-band and conduction band, the effective mass of the electrons is also changed. The theory of the effect and other consequences of the lifting of the V_1-V_2-degeneracy are discussed by Bir and Picus (61B13).

According to the considerations we have mentioned, the elastoresistance coefficients of a semiconductor will depend strongly on the occupation of the bands, and consequently on temperature and impurity concentration. We will therefore have to restrict ourselves to a qualitative discussion of the data, as far as they can be used in the determination of the band structure of a semiconductor.

Measurements of the piezoresistance of **InSb** have been performed by Potter (57P4), Tuzzolino (57T1), (58T3), Burns and Fleischer (57B5), and Keyes and Pollak (60K2). For intrinsic InSb Burns and Fleischer find at room temperature the values $m_{11} = -138.6$, $m_{12} = -148.7$, $m_{44} = 10$. This means that $(m_{11} - m_{12})/2 = -5$

and $(m_{11} + 2m_{12})/3 = -145$. The anisotropy coefficients are therefore small; the pressure coefficient, large. Because of the larger mobility of the electrons, the conductivity in the intrinsic range is determined by the electrons, and these results force the conclusion that the conduction band is isotropic with minimum at $\mathbf{k} = 0$. This is also seen from the fact that the three m_{ik}-combinations for the longitudinal effects in the [100]-, [110]-, and [111]-directions give the same value, -139.

These results were supported by measurements of Potter, who found on a strongly n-type sample at 77°K anisotropy coefficients of -1.1 and -1.3 and a pressure coefficient of -16.

In p-type InSb Tuzzolino found on one sample at 77°K the values $(m_{11} + 2m_{12})/3 = 1.7$, $(m_{11} - m_{12})/2 = 23.5$, $m_{44} = 133$. Both he and Potter found qualitatively similar results on other samples. These values are of the same order of magnitude as those measured on germanium and silicon and support the assumption that the valence band of InSb coincides in its main outline with the valence bands in these elements.

Schönwald (64S1) was able to quantitatively describe changes in conductivity and Hall coefficient of p-InSb with uniaxial stress under the assumption that the V_2-band is displaced relative to the V_1-band and that μ_{p1} is pressure dependent.

The m_{ik} do change with added hydrostatic pressure, according to Keyes and Pollak.

For an n-type **InAs** sample of 1.1×10^{17} electrons/cm^3 Tuzzolino (58T2) found $\pi_{11} = \pi_{12} = (-5 \pm 3) \times 10^{-12}$ cm^2/dyn and $\pi_{44} = 3 \times 10^{-12}$ cm^2/dyn at 300°K, and similar values at 77°K. These values result in an anisotropy coefficient of $(0 \pm 3) \times 10^{-12}$ cm^2/dyn and in an equally small pressure coefficient. The conduction band of InAs is therefore isotropic with a minimum at $\mathbf{k} = 0$.

On **InP** only one set of incomplete measurements by Sagar (60S2) on a sample of $n = 2.5 \times 10^{16}$ cm^{-3} is available: $(\pi_{11} + 2\pi_{12})/3 = -2.7 \times 10^{-12}$ cm^2/dyn and $(\pi_{11} + \pi_{12} + \pi_{44})/2 = 1.3 \times 10^{-12}$ cm^2/dyn. This is not enough to calculate the anisotropy parameters separately. A combination of these parameters, in the form $(\pi_{11} - \pi_{12}) + 3\pi_{44}$, can be calculated to be 8.6×10^{-12} cm^2/dyn. This excludes the possibility that one of the coefficients is very large, the other small, as would be required for (100)- or (111)-minima. We can therefore expect that in n-InP the conduction band minimum is also at $\mathbf{k} = 0$.

Sagar (60S1) found at room temperature for two n-type samples of **GaSb** the values $\pi_{44} = -78$ and -89×10^{-12} cm^2/dyn, respec-

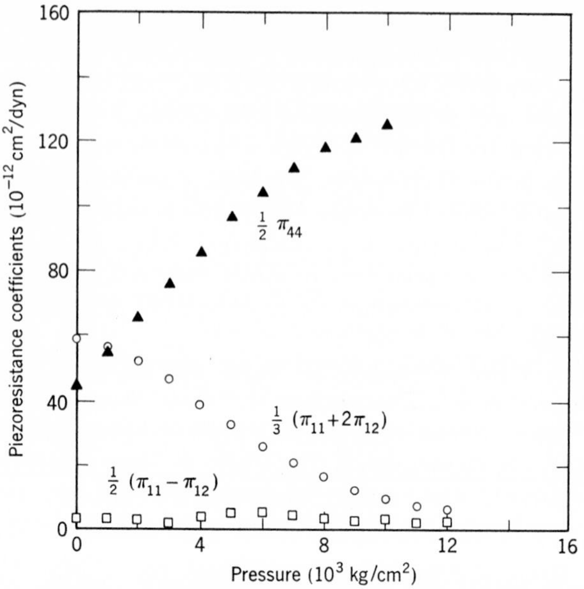

Fig. 4.44 Piezoresistance coefficients of n-GaSb vs. pressure at room temperature [after Keyes and Pollak (60K2)].

tively, $(\pi_{11} - \pi_{12})/2 = -1.4$ and -2.1×10^{-2} cm^2/dyn, and $(\pi_{11} + 2\pi_{12})/3 = -57$ and -36×10^{-12} cm^2/dyn. Here, then, $\pi_{44} \gg (\pi_{11} - \pi_{12})/2$, pointing to the existence of a (111)-minimum.

Now we know that this is not the lowest minimum, but lies just above a (000)-minimum. However, the latter contributes almost nothing to the anisotropy coefficients. In fact, Sagar found theoretically that the existence of a (000)-subband lowers the coefficient π_{44} by the factor σ_{111}/σ, where σ_{111} is the contribution of the electrons in the (111)-subband to the total conductivity, $\sigma = \sigma_{111} + \sigma_{000}$.

Keyes and Pollak (60K2) tested these assumptions by measuring the π-coefficients under additional hydrostatic pressure. According to Section 311, the (000)-subband is displaced upward relative to the (111)-subband with increasing pressure. Its contribution to the conductivity therefore decreases. The results for one of the two samples of Sagar mentioned above are plotted in Fig. 4.44. As expected, π_{44} increases with increasing pressure and reaches a saturation value at pressures at which the contribution of the (000)-subband disappears. The value $(\pi_{11} - \pi_{12})/2$ remains small and pressure independent. Thus, even at higher pressures there is no contribution of a (100)-band.

Eventually the pressure coefficient decreases and reaches the small value also observed in the other III-V compounds. In further support of Sagar's assumption Keyes and Pollak find that the product $\pi_{44}\sigma = \pi_{44}^{111}\sigma_{111}$ is constant in the measured pressure range. This is explained by the fact that the density of states in the (000)-band is considerably smaller than in the (111)-band. First there are only few electrons in the (000)-band, which, however, contribute considerably to the conductivity because of their high mobility. When these electrons are brought into the (111)-band by pressure, their small number does not add much to the contribution of this subband to the conductivity and piezoresistance.

In p-type GaSb, according to Tufte and Stelzer (64T3), $\pi_{11} = 5 \times 10^{-12}$ cm²/dyn, $\pi_{12} = -2.4 \times 10^{-12}$ cm²/dyn, and $\pi_{44} = 87 \times 10^{-2}$ cm²/dyn. These values again point to the similarity of the valence bands in GaSb and Ge.

Sagar (58S1) [cf. also (63S3)] measured the following values in an n-type sample of **GaAs** with $n = 8 \times 10^{16}$ cm^{-3} at 300 °K: $(m_{11} - m_{12})/2 = 0.5$, $m_{44} = -1.4$, and $(m_{11} + 2m_{12})/3 = -7.4$. These coefficients are all small and indicate that the lowest conduction band in GaAs is isotropic. This result was also obtained by Zerbst (62Z2).

Measurements on p-type samples do not agree well with one another. Zerbst (62Z2) found the following values for the three coefficients π_{11}, π_{12}, and π_{44} (in 10^{-12} cm²/dyn): -12, -0.6, and $+46$; whereas Hollander and Castro (62H12) give these values: $+40$, -25, and $+74$. The measurements of Zerbst were made on samples with impurity concentrations of about 10^{19} cm^{-3}, those of Hollander and Castro on samples with $p = 10^{17}$ cm^{-3}.

415 High electric fields; impact ionization. Current density and electric field are proportional to each other only at small electric fields (Ohm's law). With increasing $\mathcal{E}$ deviations appear, since the carriers can no longer transfer the energy obtained from the field instantaneously to the lattice. The average temperature of the carriers increases over that of the lattice ("warm" and "hot" electrons). If the formal relationship (4.5) between current density and electric field is still applied, one has to assume a dependence of the mobility on the electric field. The theory for "warm" electrons (small deviations of the electron temperature from the lattice temperature) gives

$$\mu = \mu_0(1 + \beta\mathcal{E}^2) \qquad (4.24)$$

Here β is a factor which is determined by the electron-lattice interaction. For a scattering mechanism with a relaxation time the sign of β is equal to the sign of the exponent of the energy dependence of the relaxation time.

Deviations from Ohm's law in InSb have been observed by many authors [(58K1), (58K2), (59P7), (60K1), (60S5), and others]. The most extensive measurements of the properties of warm electrons were performed by Sladek (60S5). They were used to determine the scattering mechanism at temperatures below 77°K. A continuous transition from positive to negative values with increasing purity of the sample was observed at 77°K. This is explained by the increasing contribution of lattice scattering (negative β) with increasing purity, compared to ionized-impurity scattering (positive β). The theory of the galvanomagnetic effects in the "quantum limit" (see Section 413) postulates another sign reversal of β at high longitudinal magnetic fields for some of the lattice-scattering mechanisms. This effect was also found experimentally. For further measurements on hot electrons in InSb we refer to (63G7).

At higher electric fields the quadratic $\mathcal{E}$-dependence of the mobility (eq. 4.24) no longer applies. The charge carriers take up so much energy from the field that they can lose this energy not only by the excitation of lattice vibrations but also by the creation of secondary electrons by *impact ionization.* Therefore not only the mobility but also the carrier concentration is field dependent. When impact ionization starts above a critical field strength, the current density increases very strongly because of the increase in the number of carriers.

The first observations of impact ionization in *n*-**InSb** were made by Prior (58P4), Glicksman and Steele (58G5), (59S8), and Kanai (59K2). Figure 4.45 shows the current density and the Hall coefficient at liquid-nitrogen temperature as functions of the electric field. Below 10^2 V/cm there are only small deviations from Ohm's law. The Hall coefficient, i.e., the number of carriers, is constant. Above 150–200 V/cm current density and carrier concentration increase steeply. In a transverse magnetic field the dependence of current on electric field is practically unchanged, but there is an increase in the resistance.

This rapid increase must definitely be ascribed to the creation of electron-hole pairs by impact ionization. Any ionization of impurity levels or a strong injection of additional carriers from the contacts can be excluded. If one compares the curves of Fig. 4.45 with the theory of impact ionization, one finds that the steep increase takes place at the expected critical field strength, but that the theory predicts a much steeper increase.

This discrepancy is explained by the appearance of a *pinch effect.*

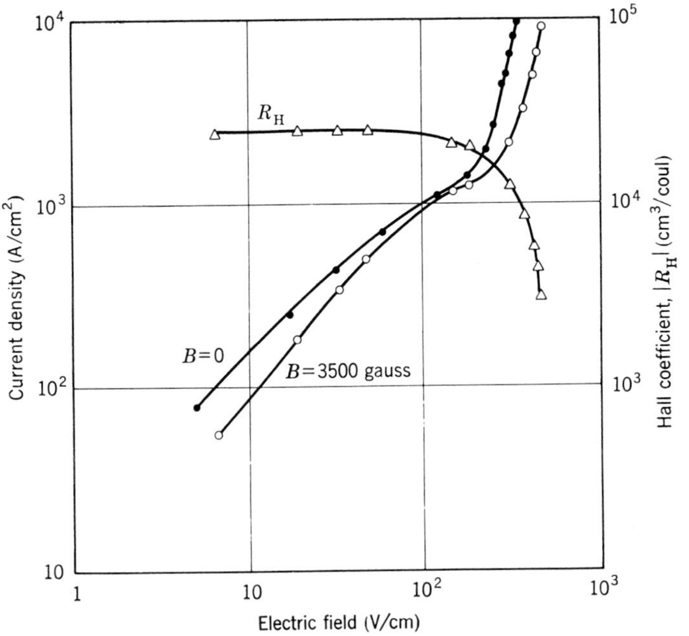

Fig. 4.45 Current density and Hall coefficient of n-InSb as a function of the electric field at 77°K [after Steele and Glicksman (59S8)].

The strong azimuthal magnetic field of the current confines the current flow to a region which is considerably smaller than the cross section of the sample. The measured quantity, the electric current, is no longer proportional to the current density, since the cross section of the pinch is field dependent. With increasing field the current density increases faster than the current.

The appearance of the pinch effect can be expected when the energy density of the azimuthal magnetic field, $B_\theta^2/2\mu_0$, is equal to the energy density of the current, $k(nT_n + pT_p)$, where T_n and T_p are the average temperatures of electrons and holes. If one sets $B_\theta = I/\mu_0 2\pi d$, $n = p$ (the number of electron-hole pairs created by impact ionization is much larger than the primary electron concentration), and $I/\pi d^2 = nev$, where d is the radius of the pinch and v the sum of the drift velocities of electrons and holes, the critical field strength for the start of the pinch effect becomes

$$I_{\text{crit}} = \frac{8\pi kT}{\mu_0 ev} \tag{4.25}$$

A more exact calculation leads to a proportionality factor of the same order of magnitude.

In a longitudinal magnetic field B_z the energy density of this field must be added to the energy density of the charge carriers. In place of (4.25) the following relation appears (61C8):

$$I_{\text{crit}} = I_{\text{crit}}(B_z = 0) + \left(\frac{4\pi B_z}{\mu_0}\right)^2 \left(\frac{d_R}{2}\right)^2 I_{\text{crit}}^{-1} \tag{4.26}$$

where d_R is the radius of the sample. The longitudinal field can be seen to delay the start of the pinch effect. In addition such a field increases the cross section of a pinch or completely prevents the pinch. The experimental confirmation of these statements is the strongest evidence for the appearance of a pinch effect in n-InSb. Figure 4.46 depicts the current-voltage characteristics in n-InSb for various longitudinal magnetic fields, in the region where the pinch sets in.

The explanation of this effect was first given by Glicksman and Steele (59G5). Additional papers by Glicksman and Powlus (61G12) and Chynoweth and Murray (61C8) gave more details about the critical field strength at which impact ionization takes place in n-InSb (180 ± 25 V/cm), about the progress of the pinch formation with time, and about instabilities and oscillations, which appear particularly in the region between the two extreme curves of Fig. 4.46. The formation of the pinch takes place faster, the larger the carrier mobility is. Since at high current densities only pulse measurements are possible, the pinch effect cannot be observed in most semiconductors, as the maximum pulse length will be small compared to the formation time of the pinch. It appears that InSb is one of the few semiconductors in which the pinch effect can be observed at all.

In addition to measuring the impact ionization in n-InSb Steele and Glicksman (60S7) have also investigated p-InSb. After impact ionization sets in, the properties of the electron-hole plasma in p-type material do not differ from those in n-type material. However, the question of whether the impact ionization is started by a hole or by an electron has not been completely answered. Steele and Glicksman found the critical field strength to be about 700 V/cm in p-InSb, but ionization has also been observed at smaller fields, possibly because of injected electrons or "light" holes (58K1), (58S5), (61B18). Even at 700 V/cm it is not clear whether the impact ionization setting in at that point is caused by electrons or holes, as was emphasized by Glicksman and Steele in an extensive discussion of the origin of impact ionization in p-InSb (60S7).

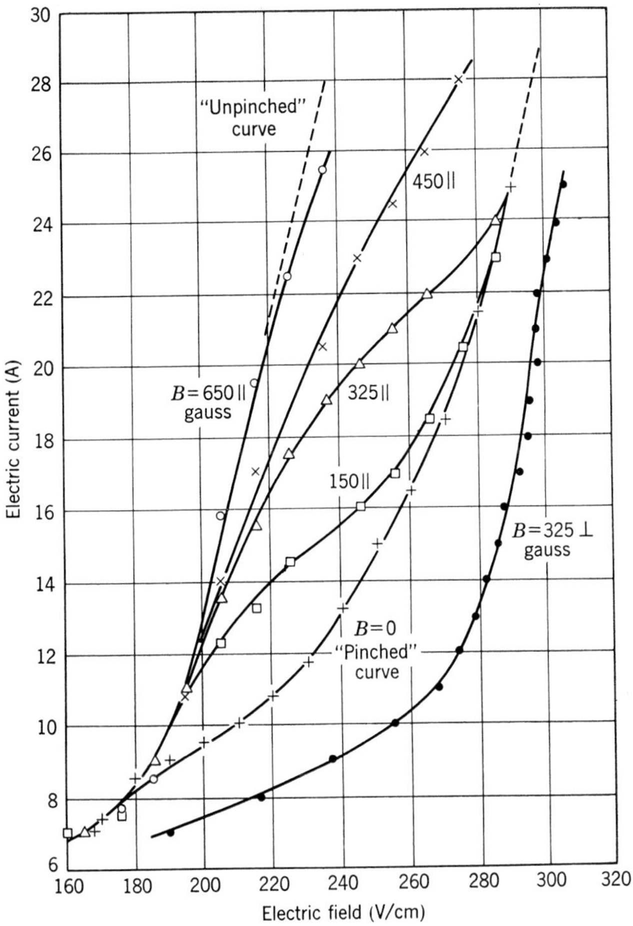

Fig. 4.46 Current vs. electric field in n-InSb for various longitudinal and transverse magnetic fields [after Chynoweth and Murray (61C8)].

Data on p-InSb analogous to that of Fig. 4.45 shows a sign reversal of the Hall coefficient at the onset of impact ionization. This behavior is expected, since sign reversal takes place at $p/n = b^2$, according to (4.8), and the ratio of hole concentration to electron concentration decreases from a very large value toward 1 as the formation of electron-hole pairs proceeds.

The properties of a plasma in p-InSb formed by injected electrons (pinch effect, instabilities, behavior in longitudinal and transverse magnetic field) were investigated by Ancker-Johnson, Cohen, and Glicksman (61A7), (63A7). There are no significant differences compared to n-InSb. Oscillations which appear in the region of impact ionization were studied by Bok and Veilex (61B18) and Ancker-Johnson (62A2), (62A3). Among other works on InSb we point out the observation of recombination radiation of recombining electron-hole pairs at 78°K and a current density of 100 A/mm^2 [Basov, Osipov, and Khvoshchev (61B1), (62O4)] and the increase of microwave reflection at 80°K caused by the increase of carrier concentration in InSb due to impact ionization [Rose (62R3)].

The acceleration of a primary particle by an electric field is only one of the possible causes for the formation of an avalanche of electron-hole pairs by impact ionization. The primary energy can also be supplied by a light quantum (photoeffect). Although we will not consider photoelectric processes until Section 43, we want to mention the studies of Tauc and Abraham (59T1), (59T2) at this point, as far as they concern the impact ionization of InSb. Figure 4.47 shows the result of a measurement of the quantum yield (number of electron-hole pairs formed per impinging photon) in InSb as a function of photon energy. For small energies the quantum yield is equal to 1; that is, each absorbed photon creates one electron-hole pair. Above 0.47 eV the quantum yield increases above 1, however. The primary electron-hole pair creates further carriers by impact ionization. The curve shows an anomaly between 0.47 and 0.6 eV, in contrast to measurements on germanium.

One possible explanation is as follows (59T2). For energies just above 0.47 eV the excess energy of the photon, above the pair-for-

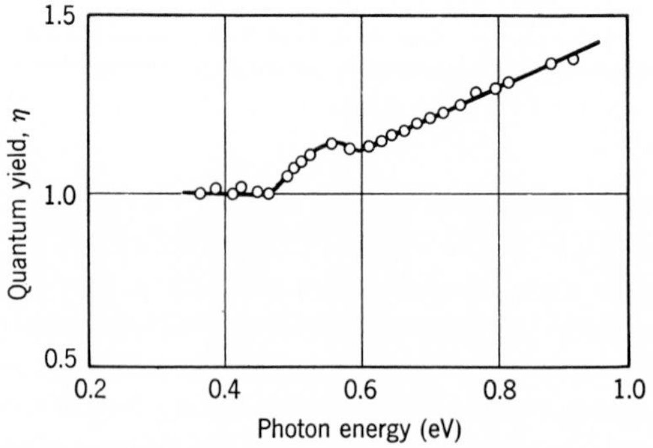

Fig. 4.47 Quantum yield in InSb [after Tauc (59T1)].

mation energy E_G, is given to the electron as kinetic energy, since $m_n \ll m_p$. Only the electron can therefore create further electron-hole pairs by impact ionization. With increasing photon energy the electron is raised to higher and higher parts of the conduction band. Because of the nonparabolicity of the conduction band of InSb the electron mass increases, and the hole of the primary electron-hole pair receives a larger and larger fraction of the energy. The quantum yield ceases to increase as long as the energy given to the hole is not sufficient for secondary ionization processes. Only when the holes can ionize does the yield increase again.

A different interpretation is proposed by Beattie (62B4). The formation of the primary electron-hole pair can be a transition from the V_1-band or from the V_2-band. The second electron-hole pair can be formed by the primary electron, which thereby loses kinetic energy, but it can also be created by the primary (light or heavy) hole. In this case the required energy can be supplied by transitions of the hole within the V_1- or the V_2-band or by a V_1-V_2-transition. In all, ten competing processes are possible with different threshold energies. Beattie shows that the first increase, at 0.44 eV, in Fig. 4.47 can be ascribed to the impact ionization by an electron under formation of an electron-heavy-hole pair (theoretical threshold, 0.47 eV) and the second increase, at 0.60 eV, to impact ionization by the light holes, creation of electron-heavy-hole pairs, and transition of the light holes to the V_1-band (theoretical threshold 0.62 eV).

Investigations of impact ionization in III-V compounds have so far mainly concerned InSb. In addition, impact ionization has been observed in InAs (59S9) and InP (59S10).

42 Thermoelectric Properties

420 Thermoelectric power. When a temperature gradient is applied to a semiconductor in addition to an electric field, the resulting current density is

$$\mathbf{i} = \sigma\left(\frac{1}{e}\,\nabla E_{\mathrm{F}} - \phi\,\nabla T\right) \tag{4.27}$$

Here E_{F} is the electrochemical potential (equal to the Fermi energy), σ the conductivity, and ϕ the differential *thermoelectric power*. In the absence of current the two terms on the right-hand side of (4.27) must be equal. The diffusion current caused by the temperature gradient is compensated by the opposing field current. In a homogeneous semiconductor it follows from (4.27) that the electric field is $\mathcal{E} = -\phi \nabla T$. If this is integrated over a closed loop consisting of the two different conductors a and b, whose contacts are at the temperatures T and $(T + \Delta T)$, then the emf

$$\oint \mathcal{E} \cdot ds = (\phi_a - \phi_b)\, \Delta T \tag{4.28}$$

follows. For a scattering mechanism with relaxation time $\tau_0 \sim E^r$, the thermoelectric power is given by

$$\phi = -\frac{k}{\sigma}\left[\left(A_n + \frac{\zeta_n}{kT}\right)\mu_n n - \left(A_p + \frac{\zeta_p}{kT}\right)\mu_p p\right] \tag{4.29}$$

where

$$A_{n,p} = \frac{r + \frac{5}{2}\, F_{r+3/2}(\zeta_{n,p}/kT)}{r + \frac{3}{2}\, F_{r+5/2}(\zeta_{n,p}/kT)}$$

$$\zeta_n = E_{\mathrm{F}} - E_c,\ \zeta_p = E_v - E_{\mathrm{F}},\ F_\alpha(y) = \int_0^\infty \frac{x^\alpha}{1 + e^{x-y}}\, dx$$

For a nondegenerate semiconductor (4.29) is simplified to

$$\phi = -\frac{k}{\sigma}\left[\left(\frac{5}{2} + r + \ln\frac{n}{n_0}\right) n\mu_n - \left(\frac{5}{2} + r + \ln\frac{p}{p_0}\right) p\mu_p\right] \tag{4.30}$$

where n_0 and p_0 are given by eq. (4.6).

This means that ϕ is negative for an n-type conductor, and positive for a pure p-type conductor. This fact is often used to determine the conduction type of a sample. The measurement of the thermoelectric power also makes it possible to determine the position of the Fermi level relative to the band edges and, using n_0 or p_0, the effective masses of the charge carriers. This method is not as accurate as the direct determinations of m^* in Chapter 3 but was often used in the first superficial investigations of the III-V compounds.

Among the numerous measurements of the thermoelectric power in **InSb** we will consider only a few. The first measurements (55B1), (55F3), (55T2), (56C1) showed that the electron mass is strongly doping dependent. A more accurate measurement of the doping dependence was made by Emel'yanenko, Kesamanly, and Nasledov (61E7), (63G2) and compared with the expectations of Kane's theory.

The temperature dependence of the thermoelectric power and therefore of the effective masses was studied thoroughly by Weiss (56W1) and Busch and Steigmeier (61B22). Figure 4.48 shows the tem-

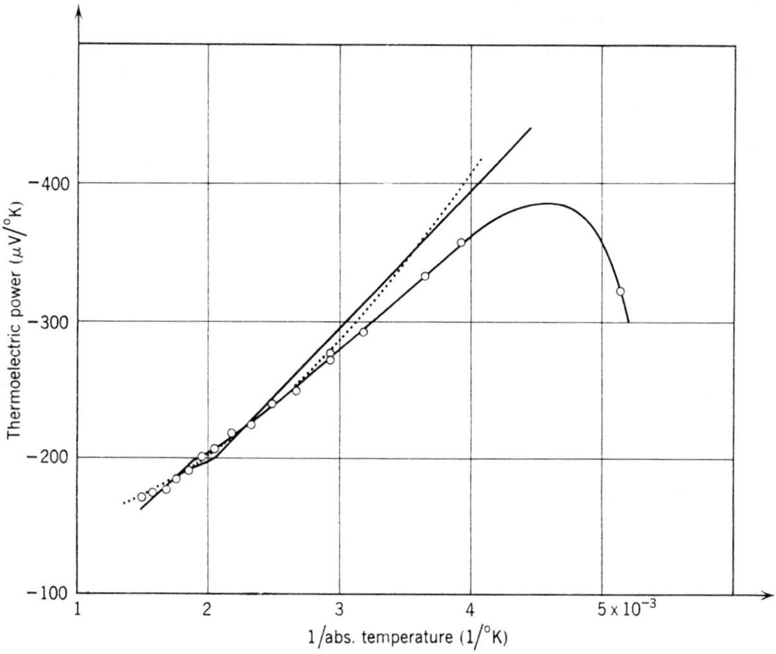

Fig. 4.48 Thermoelectric power of n-InSb as a function of $1/T$: ——, after Weiss (56W1); ∘—∘—, after Busch and Steigmeier (61B22); ...., theory for combined polar and electron-hole scattering after Ehrenreich (59E5).

perature dependence of the thermoelectric power of some relatively pure n-type samples of InSb above 200°K and a theoretical curve, which was calculated by Ehrenreich (59E5), for combined polar and electron-hole scattering. The same parameters were used here as in the calculation of the theoretical curve of the electron mobility in Fig. 4.3. The agreement is excellent and shows again how correct Ehrenreich's picture of the scattering mechanism in InSb is. At 500°K the measurement of Weiss shows a step in the otherwise smooth behavior of the thermoelectric curve. A similar step is seen in the mobility measurements of Busch and Steigmeier in Fig. 4.3. This anomaly must be contained in the effective mass which is common to both parameters. It cannot be explained by Kane's theory. Mobility and thermoelectric-power measurements of other authors have so far not been able to confirm this step. The effective electron mass is 0.037 m at 333°K, according to Weiss, and increases further up to 0.05 m at the melting point; the effective hole mass at 333°K is 0.18 m.

The determination of the effective mass from measurements of the thermoelectric power requires a knowledge of the scattering mechanism, because of the strong dependence on the parameter r [eq. (4.29)] (61E7). Therefore Mochan, Obrastsov, and Smirnova (62M11) evaluate measurements at high magnetic fields, where the dependence on the scattering mechanism disappears. They find $m_n = (0.0143 \pm 0.007)\ m$, in good agreement with the cyclotron-resonance value.

Kołodziejczak and Sosnowski (62K4) applied Kane's band model and a combination of polar and ionized-impurity scattering to the calculation of the thermoelectric power under heavy doping. They obtained excellent agreement with measurements on samples of $10^{16}\ \text{cm}^{-3} < n < 10^{19}\ \text{cm}^{-3}$. The pressure dependence of the thermoelectric power can also be described quantitatively by this theory.

When InSb melts, the thermoelectric power increases abruptly, indicating a sudden increase in the electron density. This behavior was investigated by Blum and Ryabtsova (59B7).

At low temperatures (4.29) becomes invalid. The thermoelectric power is strongly increased by directional phonon scattering (phonon drag), as is known from germanium and silicon. The effect has been observed in InSb (57G1). In addition a quantum effect in the behavior of the thermoelectric power in a magnetic field was found by Puri (63P14) and ascribed to the increasing influence of the phonon drag with increasing magnetic field.

In n-type **InAs** Weiss (56W1) found an electron mass of 0.064 m in the range of 500 to 800°K, and a hole mass of 0.33 m in the same temperature region. The dependence of thermoelectric power on doping was measured by Gashimzade and Kasamanly (61G3). The electron mass thereby deduced increased with increasing doping. Two different, approximately parallel $m_n(n)$-curves were obtained, depending on whether acoustic or ionized-impurity scattering was assumed to be dominant. Gashimzade and Kasamanly compared these two results with the expected n-dependence of the effective mass in Kane's theory and found the latter to lie between the two experimental values. This result agrees again with the assumption that polar scattering can be described by a relaxation time proportional to E^r, where r varies between the limits of acoustic and ion scattering. Figure 4.49 gives a comparison of the theory of eq. (4.29) with experiment on three n-type and three p-type samples [Weiss (56W1)]. The onset of degeneracy at higher temperatures and mixed lattice and ion scattering were taken into account. Agreement is good even though acoustic scattering rather than polar scattering was assumed.

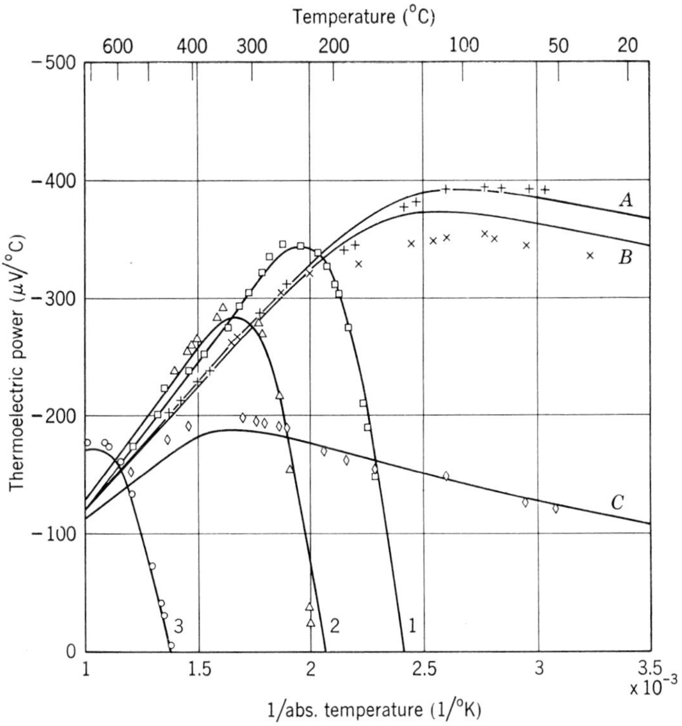

Fig. 4.49 Temperature dependence of the thermoelectric power of InAs. Experimental points for three n-type (A–C) and three p-type (1–3) samples; curves calculated with eq. (4.29) [after Weiss (56W1)].

Korenblit, Mashovets, and Shalyt (64K4) found good agreement between measurements of the Hall coefficient and of the thermoelectric power of n-InAs at 77°K with Kane's theory for electron concentrations up to 10^{18} cm^{-3}.

Blum (59B8), (61N2) reported measurements of the thermoelectric power of p-type **GaSb** in the temperature region from 280°K to above the melting point and found an effective mass of the holes which is strongly temperature and doping dependent, in contrast to other data on the effective mass of holes. As in InSb, an abrupt change of the thermoelectric power is observed at the melting point.

For measurements of the thermoelectric power in **InP** we refer to Kudman and Steigmeier (64K5).

Values of the effective electron mass in **GaAs** determined from the thermoelectric power vary between 0.03 m (54B1) and 0.06 m (57E1). The hole mass is equal to 0.5 m, according to (57E1).

The reported hole effective mass values in **AlSb** also vary strongly. Nasledov and Slobotchikov (58N2) find $m_p = (0.9 \pm 0.1)\ m$; Sasaki, Sakamoto, and Kuno (54S1), $(1.8 \pm 0.8)\ m$.

421 Thermal conductivity. The thermal current flowing in a semiconductor under the influence of an electric field and a temperature gradient is given by

$$\mathbf{w} = \Pi \mathbf{i} - \kappa' \nabla T \tag{4.31}$$

Here $\mathbf{w}$ is the thermal current density (entropy current density times absolute temperature) and $\mathbf{i}$ is obtained from (4.27). The terms Π and κ' are the Peltier coefficient and the coefficient of thermal conductivity, respectively. For $\mathbf{i} = 0$ the thermal current density is proportional to the temperature gradient. The theory of thermal conductivity gives, for a scattering mechanism with relaxation time $\tau_0 \sim E^r$,

$$\kappa' = \kappa_l' + \left(\frac{k}{e}\right)^2 T \left\{ (B_n - A_n^2)\,\sigma_n + (B_p - A_p^2)\sigma_p + \frac{\sigma_n\sigma_p}{\sigma}\left[\frac{E_G}{kT} + A_n + A_p\right]^2 \right\} \tag{4.32}$$

$$B_{n,p} = \frac{r + \frac{7}{2}}{r + \frac{3}{2}} \frac{F_{r+5/2}(\zeta_{n,p}/kT)}{F_{r+1/2}(\zeta_{n,p}/kT)}$$

κ_l' is the lattice thermal conductivity. The meaning of the other terms is given in the discussion of (4.29).

It is seen that the charge-carrier contribution consists of two terms according to the two different mechanisms of thermal conduction by charge carriers. The diffusion and field currents, which mutually compensate each other in the current-free case, carry different amounts of heat. The first and second terms in the curved brackets of (4.32) represent this difference. The third term describes the heat transport by charge-free electron-hole current (ambipolar diffusion) and consists of the formation energy of an electron-hole pair E_G and of the kinetic energies of the two carriers.

Figure 4.50 contains measurements of the specific thermal conductivity of **InSb** by different authors. The most reliable measurement [Busch and Steigmeier (61B22)] is given by the solid line. Also shown are the results on two samples of different purity by

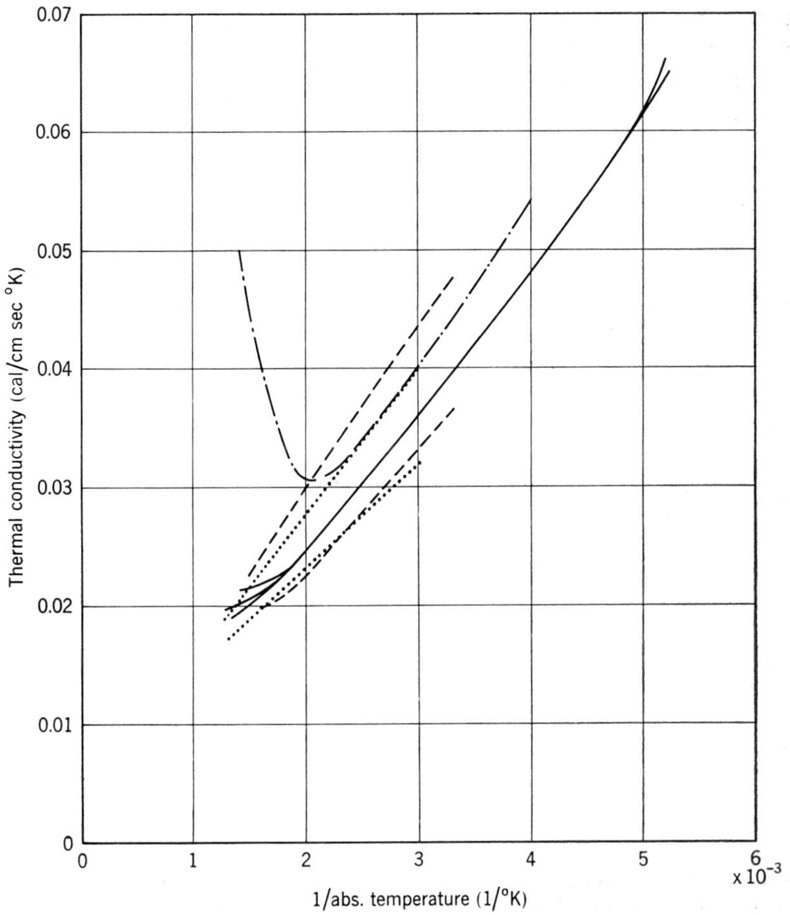

Fig. 4.50 Thermal conductivity of *n*-InSb as a function of the reciprocal temperature: —·—·—, early measurements (see the text); ———, after Busch and Steigmeier (61B22); – – –, after Stuckes (57S6) (two different samples); . . . . , after Bowers, Ure, Bauerle, and Cornish (59B13).

Stuckes (57S6), (57S7), and the upper and lower limits of accuracy of measurements by Bowers, Ure, Bauerle, and Cornish (59B13). All these measurements agree well. Another curve shown in the figure increases steeply at high temperatures. This dependence was found in early measurements by Busch and Schneider (54B10), (54B11) and by Weiss (58W5) and was first explained by a contribution of ambipolar diffusion to the thermal conductivity (55T4), (55P3), (56P4). However, it was later found to be due to a neglect of radiation losses. The room-temperature value of 0.04 cal/cm sec deg shown in the figure is also supported by data of Zhuse (54Z1), Goldsmid (54G1), and Kanai and Nii (59K1).

The temperature dependence of the thermal conductivity according to Fig. 4.50 is in general agreement with the theory. A quantitative comparison cannot be made because (4.32) does not contain the non-parabolicity of the conduction band and because polar scattering can be included only qualitatively by a temperature-dependent "effective relaxation time." Busch and Steigmeier have therefore done the reverse and first determined r as a function of T from mobility measurements. This r is then put into (4.32) and the charge-carrier contribution to κ' calculated. For the "Lorenz factor" of the electrons $(B_n - A_n^2)$, a value between 2 and 2.6 follows. For acoustic scattering without degeneracy the expected value is 2; for complete degeneracy, $\pi^2/3$. However, the resulting $r(T)$ does not agree with the value used in Fig. 4.1 for other transport parameters (decrease from $r = 0$ to $r = -0.75$ for temperature increase from 300 to 700°K).

The lattice contribution to the thermal conductivity, which is obtained after subtracting the charge-carrier contribution, agrees qualititatively with the theory. For a more detailed discussion we refer to the paper of Busch and Steigmeier (61B22) and to one of Steigmeier and Kudman (63S6), and for low temperatures to the works of Geballe (57G1) and Mielczarek and Frederikse (59M5).

Similar measurements of thermal conductivity have been made on **InAs.** The results of Bowers, Ure, Bauerle, and Cornish (59B13), Stuckes (60S10), and Steigmeier and Kudman (63S6) agree qualitatively with theoretical expectation. A quantitative comparison shows a number of difficulties, which, according to Sheard (60S3), are caused by incorrect assumptions in (4.32). Measurements at low temperatures have been discussed by Shalyt (62S3).

For measurements on other III-V compounds we refer to (63S6), (64K5), and (64V1).

Knowing the coefficient of thermal conductivity, the thermoelectric power, and the specific conductivity, one can evaluate the possibility of using a semiconductor for a *thermoelectric generator*. A simple theory [see, e.g., (59B13)] evaluates the efficiency of a thermoelectric generator as

$$\eta = \frac{T_h - T_c}{T_h} \frac{\left[1 + \frac{z}{2}(T_h + T_c)\right]^{1/2} - 1}{\left[1 + \frac{z}{2}(T_h + T_c)\right]^{1/2} + \frac{T_c}{T_h}} \tag{4.33}$$

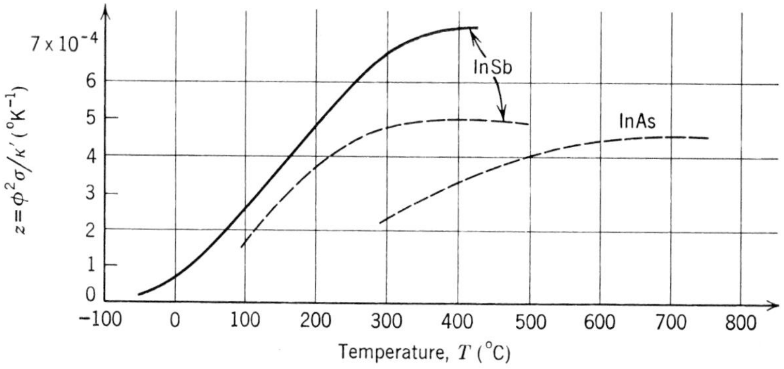

Fig. 4.51 Thermoelectric figure of merit z for InSb and InAs as a function of temperature; ———, after Busch and Steigmeier (61B22); – – –, after Bowers, Ure, Bauerle, and Cornish (59B13).

where T_h and T_c are the temperatures of the hot and cold junctions, respectively, and z is given by $\phi^2\sigma/\kappa'$ (thermoelectric figure of merit). Figure 4.51 shows z as a function of T for InSb and InAs according to the measurements of Busch and Steigmeier (61B22) and Bowers and co-workers (59B13).

422 Thermomagnetic effects. When current flows in a material under a transverse magnetic field, we expect a perpendicular field and a resistance change to be established (galvanomagnetic effects). Similarly, when the primary current is a thermal current caused by a temperature gradient, we expect a transverse and longitudinal emf. These two thermomagnetic effects are called *Nernst effect* (transverse Nernst-Ettingshausen effect) and *change of thermoelectric power in the magnetic field* (longitudinal Nernst-Ettingshausen effect, magneto-thermoelectric effect). Two other thermomagnetic effects are the *Righi-Leduc effect* (transverse temperature gradient caused by a primary temperature gradient) and the *change of thermal conductivity in the magnetic field* (Maggi-Righi-Leduc effect).

The theory for the Nernst effect, for a relaxation time $\tau_0 \sim E^r$ and nondegenerate conditions in an isotropic semiconductor with two parabolic bands, gives for the Nernst coefficient Q:

$$Q = \frac{E_y}{B_z(\partial T/\partial x)} = \frac{k}{e}\frac{\Gamma(\frac{5}{2}+2r)\Gamma(\frac{5}{2})}{\Gamma^2(\frac{5}{2}+r)}\left[\frac{{\sigma_n}^2}{\sigma^2}\mu_n r + \frac{{\sigma_p}^2}{\sigma^2}\mu_p r + \frac{\sigma_n\sigma_p}{\sigma^2}(\mu_n+\mu_p)\left(\frac{E_G}{kT}+5+3r\right)\right] \tag{4.34}$$

(In the Russian literature the Nernst coefficient has the opposite sign.)

When the ambipolar term dominates in (4.34) (mixed conduction), the Nernst coefficient Q is positive. For extrinsic conduction, however, the sign of Q is determined by the scattering mechanism: Q is positive for ionized-impurity scattering and polar scattering, and negative for acoustic scattering.

The change of thermoelectric power in the transverse magnetic field is also proportional to r, for extrinsic conduction, so that the sign is determined by the scattering mechanism. For the theory of this effect, the work of Rodot (56R2), (59R7), (60R3), for example, may be consulted.

Experimental investigations of the Nernst effect have been made on InSb by Zhuse and Tsidil'kovskii (58Z1), Rodot (59R7), (60R3), Amirkhanov *et al.* (61A5), (61A6), Emel'yanenko and Nasledov (61N2), (62E6), and Wagini (64W1); on InAs by Emel'yanenko, Zotova, and Nasledov (59E9), (62Z6) and Amirkhanov, Bashirov, and Gadzhialiev (61A6); on InP by Kesamanly *et al.* (64K2); on GaSb by Amirkhanova (60A11) and Silverman, Carlson, and Ehrenreich (63S2); and on GaAs by Emel'yanenko and Nasledov (59E10), (60E4), (61N2) and Carlson, Silverman, and Ehrenreich (61E4), (62C3). In some of these papers, (56A1), (57R1), (58Z1), (59E10), (59E9), (60R3), (61A13), and in (64W1) measurements on the change of thermoelectric power in a magnetic field have also been reported. Finally, Amirkhanova and Bashirov (60A12) and Wagini (64W1) measured the change of thermal conductivity of InSb in a magnetic field, and Wagini and Mette (63M7) the Righi-Leduc effect.

The most complete measurements on four InSb samples by Wagini (64W1) are shown in Fig. 4.52. These curves demonstrate the behavior of the four thermomagnetic coefficients listed in the introduction of this section.

We will now discuss the measurements of the *Nernst effect* in more detail. For weak magnetic fields such measurements give information about the dominant scattering mechanism, according to (4.34). Particularly the Russian papers cited contain numerous measurements of the temperature dependence of Q for n- and p-type material. A sign change from positive to negative with increasing temperature was observed in many samples of InSb, InAs, and GaAs. In some cases this was followed by a second sign reversal. Measurements of Emel'yanenko (60E4) (61N2) on p-GaAs are shown in Fig. 4.53 as an example. These curves were interpreted by a change from ionized-impurity scattering (r positive) at low temperature to acoustic scattering (r negative) at higher temperature, and then to the case of mixed conduction, in which the ambipolar (positive) term in (4.34) dominates.

In contrast, however, all other experimental facts can be made consistent only by assuming polar scattering above room temperature in InSb, InAs, and GaAs. Also the magnetic-field dependence of the Nernst coefficient in n- and p-InSb at room temperature, measured by Rodot (57R1), (60R3), (61R2), can be explained satisfactorily only by polar scattering.

A repeat of the measurements of Nasledov on n-GaAs by Carlson,

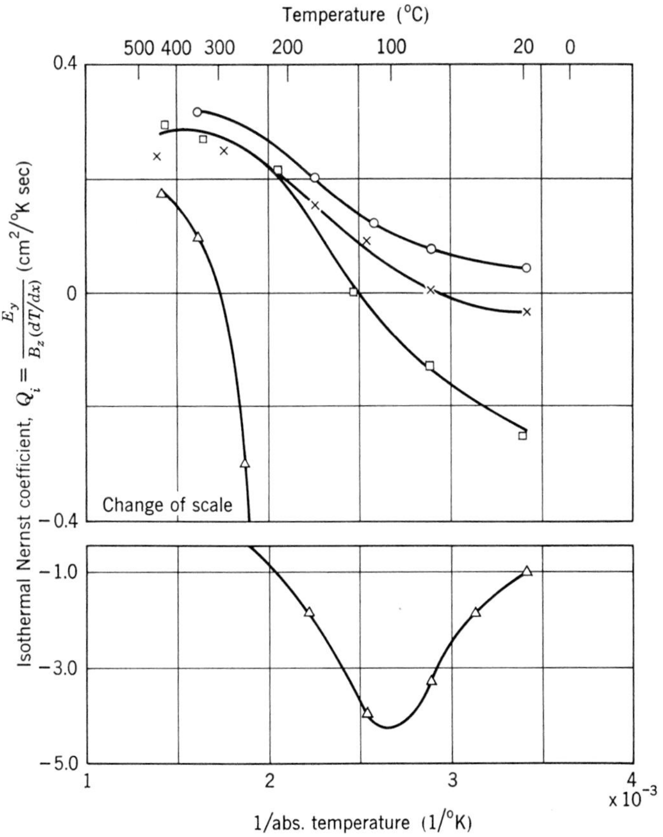

(a)

Fig. 4.52 Temperature dependence of the thermomagnetic effects in InSb at low magnetic fields [after Wagini (64W1)]. (a) Nernst effect; (b) Righi-Leduc effect; (c) isothermal change of thermoelectric power in a magnetic field; (d) isothermal change of thermal conductivity in a magnetic field. □ $n = 3.5 \times 10^{15}$ cm^{-3}; × $n = 2.4 \times 10^{16}$ cm^{-3}; ○ $n = 8 \times 10^{17}$ cm^{-3}; △ $p = 5 \times 10^{17}$ cm^{-3}.

Silverman, and Ehrenreich (62C3) on purer samples could not confirm the measured sign reversal. Over the entire temperature range Q remained positive. For this special case there is a possibility of explaining the negative value of Q by considering the two subbands in n-GaAs. Carlson, Silverman, and Ehrenreich make the assumption of $\tau_0 \sim E^r$ for energies below the upper subband and $\tau_0 = 0$ for higher energies. This is justified by the strong intervalley scattering in the upper subband. Under this assumption Q can also be negative for polar scattering, and the results of Nasledov can thereby be interpreted qualitatively.

We mention here also that the measurements of Carlson, Silverman,

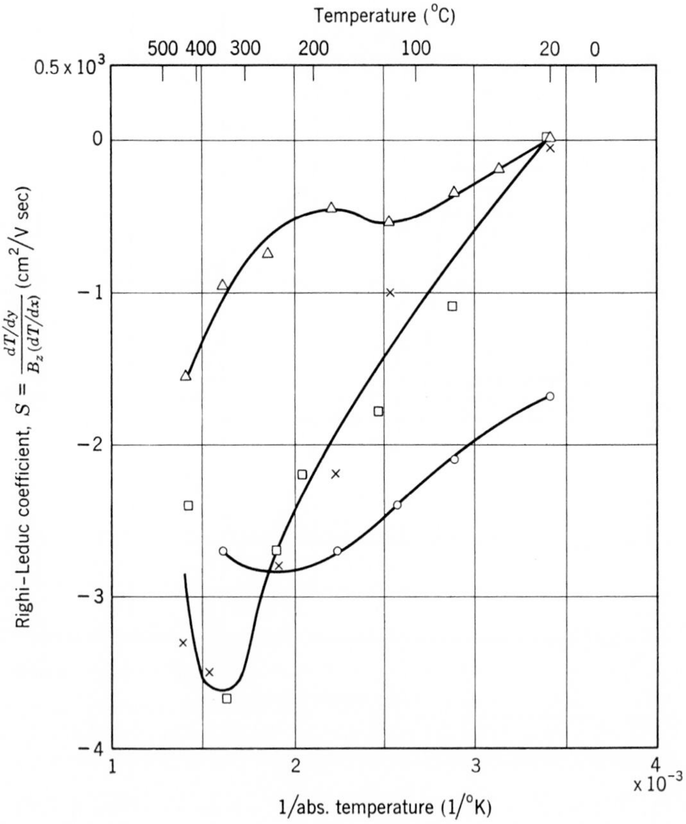

(b)

Fig. 4.52 (*Continued*)

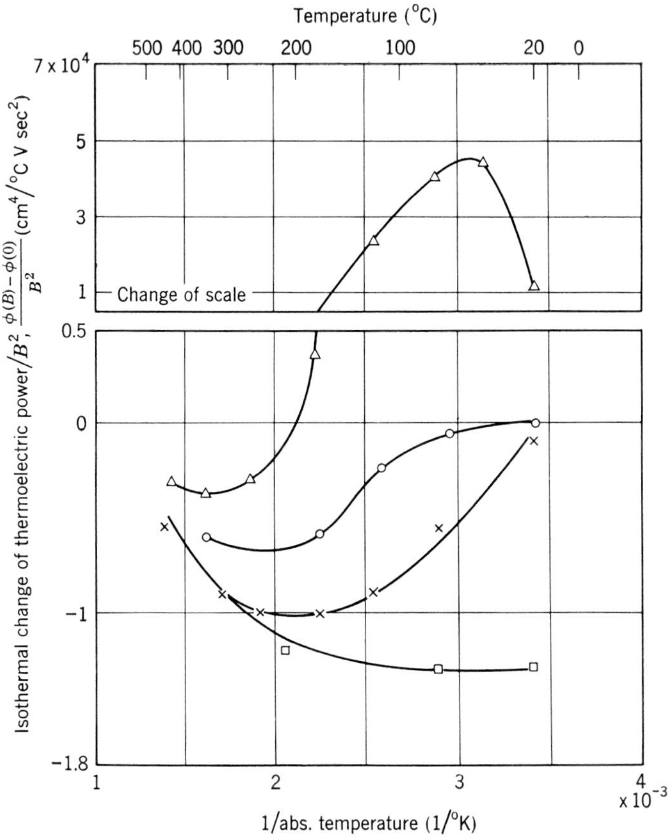

(c)

Fig. 4.52 (*Continued*)

and Ehrenreich give a weakly temperature-dependent r with values between 0.34 and 0.76, as seems reasonable for polar scattering with ion- and electron-hole-scattering contribution.

Even if the two-band hypothesis is correct for n-GaAs, the discrepancy between the measurements on p-GaAs and on InSb and InAs, and the theory, remains. The explanation for InSb and InAs lies in the nonparabolicity of the conduction band. According to Kołodziejczak, Sosnowski, and Zawadzki (62K6), (62K7), the Nernst coefficient is proportional to $r - (1 - m_2/m_3)$ for strong degeneracy, where m_2 and m_3 are the effective masses defined in Table 2.3. For a parabolic band, $m_2 = m_3$, the Nernst coefficient is proportional to r, and the scattering mechanism alone determines the sign of Q. For a nonparabolic band, however, the Nernst coefficient can become negative even for positive r. This conclusion has been reached also by Tsidil'kovskii and Guseva (62G13) (62T2) [cf. (64G1) and (64T2)], (62T3), (63G10).

More extensive studies of the transport processes in a conduction band of the Kane type have been made by Wagini (64W1) and by Harman, Honig, and Tarmy (63H2). The results of these papers fully confirm the previous conclusions. In particular, Wagini compared his measurements of the thermomagnetic effects on an intrinsic sample (shown in Fig. 4.52) as well as measurements of the thermo-

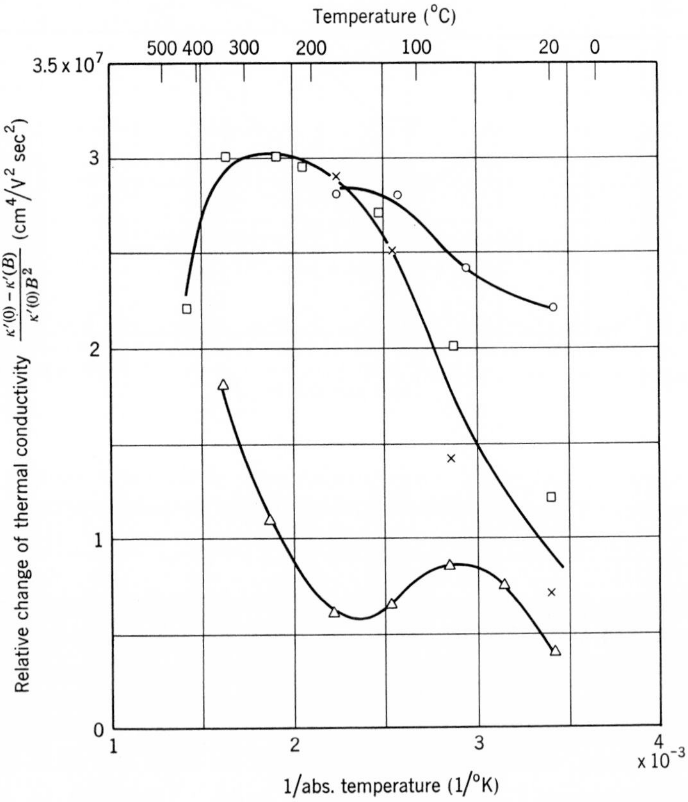

(d)

Fig. 4.52 *(Continued)*

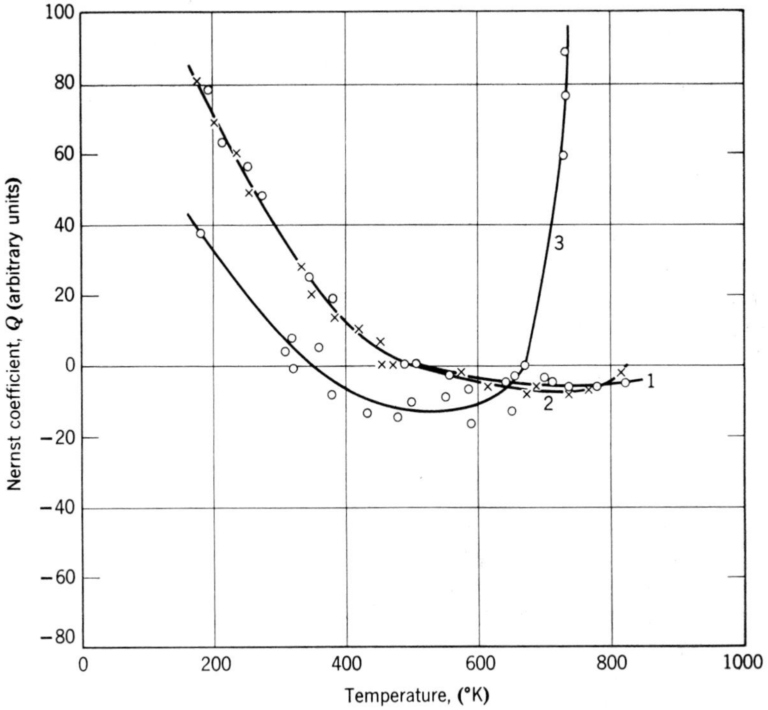

Fig. 4.53 Nernst coefficient of p-GaAs for three samples, with $p = 4.5 \times 10^{18}$ cm^{-3} (1), $p = 1.0 \times 10^{18}$ cm^{-3} (2), and $p = 1.0 \times 10^{17}$ cm^{-3} (3) [after Nasledov (61N2)].

electric power and of the magnetoresistance of the same sample with the theory. Agreement could be reached only for polar scattering and with a nonparabolic conduction band according to Kane's theory [cf. also (63B16)].

Amirkhanov and co-workers (61A4), (61A6) report measurements of the magnetic-field dependence of Q in n-InSb and n-InAs at high magnetic fields, at which the quantization becomes noticeable ($\hbar\omega_c \gg kT$). Measurements in this region are interpreted satisfactorily by a theory of Ansel'm and Askerov (61A9).

43 Nonequilibrium Processes

The galvanomagnetic, thermoelectric, and thermomagnetic phenomena treated in the previous sections of this chapter are equilibrium processes. The concentration of electrons and holes in the interior of a homogeneous semiconductor is changed by only a negligible amount. There do exist local density deviations at all boundaries that prevent a current flow of charge carriers, but these deviations form space charges and are thus restricted to regions of a few Debye lengths.

The opposite situation obtains in the photoelectric processes, where the main interest concerns the change of the transport properties caused by external disturbances of the charge-carrier concentration. The absorption of light of suitable wavelength in a semiconductor is connected with the creation of free electrons or holes (photoionization of an impurity state) or of free electron-hole pairs (electron transitions from the valence band into the conduction band). These additional charge carriers influence the transport properties in a characteristic way.

The *creation* of additional free carriers by light falls into the field of optics and was therefore discussed in Chapter 3. From the photoelectric effect we can obtain information about the *recombination* of carriers. We will restrict ourselves in this section mostly to small deviations from the equilibrium. In this case the recombination may be characterized by the so-called *lifetime* τ of a charge carrier. For steady-state conditions (sustaining of a certain density deviation δn by constant radiation, and consequent creation of G carriers per second per cubic centimeter) τ is defined as the average time a charge carrier remains in the band: $\delta n = G\tau$. For decay processes, after removal of the radiation, τ is defined as the time in which the number of additional carriers decreases to $1/e$ of the original value: $\delta n(t) \sim e^{-t/\tau}$. The two definitions are identical for only the simplest recombination mechanisms.

Recombination mechanisms are the following ones:

1. *Radiative band-to-band transitions.* The recombinations of an electron-hole pair, i.e., the transitions of electrons from the conduction band to the valence band, are possible by the emission of a photon under conservation of the electron wave vector. This is the inverse process of the direct optical transitions. The lifetime of this process is inversely proportional to the sum of the equilibrium concentrations of electrons and holes (for small deviations from equilibrium). The proportionality factor can be calculated from the theory of van Roosbroeck and Shockley (54R2).

Recombination via indirect transition is of course also possible.

Radiative recombination is generally considered to be the process which forms the upper limit for the lifetime of electron-hole pairs in a semiconductor. This statement is, however, only partially correct. Dumke (57D3) has pointed out that a photon given off in a recombination process can be reabsorbed in the crystal under formation of a new electron-hole pair. In this case the lifetime of a single electron-hole pair is determined by the radiative recombination, while the physically measurable lifetime (defined as the time constant for the exponential decrease of the excited electron-hole pairs) is much longer. Only when the emitted photons leave the crystal does the radiative recombination determine the lifetime. This is the case in germanium and silicon. In these semiconductors the absorption constant is small in the region of the maximum of the recombination radiation (about 10 cm^{-1}), since only indirect transitions take place near the absorption edge. In most III-V compounds these transitions are direct. Then the absorption constant is large (in InSb about 10^3 cm^{-1}), and there is a strong internal reabsorption of the recombination radiation.

2. *Auger recombination.* The energy which is released by the recombination of an electron-hole pair can be transferred by the Auger effect to another free electron or hole. This is the inverse process of the impact ionization. For the theory of this mechanism the work of Beattie and Landsberg (59B5), (59L1), (60B5) may be consulted.

3. *Recombination via recombination centers (traps).* When the transition of an electron from the conduction band to the valence band does not take place directly, but as a multistep process via impurity states in the forbidden gap, the selection rule for the wave vector of the electron need not be satisfied. This is the lifetime-limiting mechanism in most semiconductors over a wide temperature range. For small concentrations of "recombination centers" the two steps of the recombination process, which can be described as the transitions of an electron and of a hole into the center, are coupled to one another. For large concentrations the two processes are decoupled, since sufficient recombination centers exist in both kinds of charge states necessary for the two processes. Lifetimes will then be different for electrons and holes and also for steady-state measurements and decay measurements. The theory of this recombination mechanism was given by Shockley and Read and by Hall.

These three mechanisms are the main processes which limit the lifetime of electron-hole pairs in the interior of the III-V compounds. The process of recombination in impurity photoconduction, namely, a carrier dropping into an impurity state, is identical with one of the two processes involved in the recombination of an electron-hole pair via recombination centers.

At the surface a strong distortion of the uniform lattice structure leads to a concentration of recombination centers there, and thus to different recombination in the volume and in regions near the surface. The latter is generally described by a surface-recombination velocity s, where s is the velocity of a current of excess electron-hole pairs directed toward the surface, which can just be absorbed at the surface by recombination. To compare the recombination ability of the volume and of the surface the lifetime τ must be compared with D/s^2, where D is the (ambipolar) diffusion coefficient. Alternatively, one can compare the diffusion length associated with τ, $L = \sqrt{D\tau}$, with the "surface-diffusion length," $L_s = D/s$.

Measurements of lifetimes in III-V compounds have generally been made by photoconduction (PC effect) or by the photoelectromagnetic effect (PEM effect).

The elementary theory for the photocurrent, i.e., the additional electric current caused by irradiation of a bar-shaped semiconductor, is given by

$$I_{\text{PC}} = \int_0^a \int_0^b e(\mu_n + \mu_p)\, \delta n\, \mathcal{E}_x\, dy\, dz = e\,(\mu_n + \mu_p)\, \Delta n\, \mathcal{E}_x \quad (4.35)$$

where $\mathcal{E}_x$ is the applied electric field, δn the local density increase of electron-hole pairs, and Δn the number of electron-hole pairs continuously created per centimeter length of the bar. The quantities a and b are the dimensions of the rod perpendicular to the axis.

In the PEM effect the short-circuit current is measured, which appears when a constant magnetic field B_z is applied perpendicular to the direction of incoming radiation (the y-direction). From the irradiated surface a diffusion current of electron-hole pairs flows into the interior of the semiconductor. The magnetic field deflects the electrons and holes in opposite directions, so that a current is created which is proportional to the magnetic field and to the primary diffusion current:

$$I_{\text{PEM}} = \int_0^a \int_0^b e(\mu_n + \mu_p) B_z D \left(\frac{\partial}{\partial y}\, \delta n\right) dy\, dz \quad (4.36)$$

If the light is mainly absorbed just below the surface and a is large compared to the diffusion length L, then δn drops off exponentially ($\delta n \sim e^{-y/L}$), and

$$I_{\text{PEM}} = e(\mu_n + \mu_p) B_z \frac{D}{L}\, \Delta n = e(\mu_n + \mu_p) B_z \sqrt{\frac{D}{\tau}}\, \Delta n \quad (4.37)$$

The quantity Δn in (4.35) and (4.37) can be replaced by $I_0\tau$, where I_0

is the effective photon flux (number of electron-hole pairs created per centimeter length of the semiconductor and per second if a quantum yield of unity is assumed).

These equations contain a number of restricting assumptions.

1. The lifetime τ is the average lifetime of an electron or hole in the steady-state condition. Here it is assumed that the neutrality condition in the form $\delta n = \delta p$ is approximately fulfilled everywhere. Even if neutrality exists it is possible that $\delta n \neq \delta p$, because of trapping. So we must define two different lifetimes for electrons and holes by the relationship $G = \delta n/\tau_n = \delta p/\tau_p$. The lifetimes entering (4.35) and (4.37) are then also different. One obtains:

$$I_{\mathrm{PC}} \sim \tau_{\mathrm{PC}}, \qquad \tau_{\mathrm{PC}} = \frac{\mu_n \tau_n + \mu_p \tau_p}{\mu_n + \mu_p} \tag{4.38}$$

$$I_{\mathrm{PEM}} \sim \sqrt{\tau_{\mathrm{PEM}}}, \qquad \tau_{\mathrm{PEM}} = \frac{p_{\mathrm{eq}} \tau_n + n_{\mathrm{eq}} \tau_p}{p_{\mathrm{eq}} + n_{\mathrm{eq}}} \tag{4.39}$$

with otherwise unchanged form of eqs. (4.35) and (4.37) (58Z3).

2. Equations (4.35)–(4.39) apply only in the limits of small magnetic fields. They can be extended to arbitrary B if all mobilities entering the lifetimes (4.38) and (4.39) and the ambipolar diffusion coefficient are replaced by $\mu(1 + \mu^2 B^2)^{-\frac{1}{2}}$. This factor takes on a still different form if the energy dependence in the relaxation time is taken into account.

3. Inclusion of the surface recombination adds an additional factor $(1 + \tau_s/L)^{-1} = (1 + L_s/L)^{-1}$ to (4.35) and (4.37). This factor can be neglected for $s \ll L/\tau = \sqrt{D/\tau}$, but for $s \gg L/\tau$ the term $\sqrt{\tau}$ is eliminated from (4.37) and I_{PEM} is entirely determined by s.

4. Further corrections of (4.35) and (4.37) are necessary if the light absorption takes place in the volume, namely, when the reciprocal absorption constant $1/K$ becomes comparable to or larger than L. As long as the two characteristic lengths are small compared to the sample thickness a, only (4.37) is changed by the simple factor $KL/(1 + KL)$. If only $L \ll a$, then both (4.35) and (4.37) contain correction factors of more complicated form (61L1), which depend on K, a, the diffusion length $L = \sqrt{\tau D}$, and the surface recombination velocity s.

After all these corrections the following restrictions remain: small extension of the sample in the y-direction compared to extensions in the x- and z-directions; small density deviations ($\delta n \ll n_0$, etc.); quantum yield equal to 1; diffusion length small compared to the sample thickness a. This last restriction is necessary, since otherwise the PEM effect is limited not only by the volume lifetime but also by the surface recombination of the rear surface. A more accurate discussion of all the restrictions and of the possibilities for extending this theory was given by Laff and Fan (61L1) and by Amith (59A5).

Indium Antimonide. The charge carriers in InSb have a short lifetime compared to those in germanium and silicon. Direct methods for determining the diffusion length are therefore difficult to apply. The first measurements of Avery and Jenkins (55A2) gave diffusion lengths of the order of 40 μ with a strong scatter about this average. Later investigations led to better results, consistent with the theory. Between 100 and 200°K, Galavanov, Kartuzova, and Nasledov (61G1) found diffusion lengths of 50–350 μ and good agreement of the calculated lifetimes with the Shockley-Read theory. According to Zolotarev and Nasledov (62Z3), the magnetic-field dependence of the ambipolar diffusion lengths agrees with theory under the assumption of polar scattering.

It has been found to be easier to determine lifetimes from measurements of photoconductivity and of the PEM effect. Early measurements have been improved repeatedly. The photoconductivity of InSb was first measured by Tauc, Šmirous, and Abraham (54T2), (54T3) and by Goodwin (57G6), simultaneous photoconduction and PEM effect by Kurnick, Strauss, and Zitter (54K3), (56K5), (56K6), and by Hilsum, Oliver, and Rickayzen (55H3). Extensions of the theory were first given by Moss (55M4) and Kurnick and Zitter (54K3).

We will not consider these papers in detail; rather we will discuss the later paper of Laff and Fan (61L1). Figure 4.54 shows typical results of the spectral dependence of the photocurrent and the PEM-short-circuit current. From the shape of the curves the diffusion length L can be determined, as well as the correction factors in (4.35) and (4.37), for the case where the approximation $1/K \ll L$ no longer applies. There are two ways to determine the lifetimes τ_n and τ_p: (1) from I_{PC} and I_{PEM}, which both depend on these parameters, or (2) from $L(\tau_n, \tau_p)$ and the ratio $I_{\mathrm{PC}}/I_{\mathrm{PEM}}$. In the second case I_0 need not be known.

The temperature dependence of the lifetimes determined in this way for a p-type sample is plotted in Fig. 4.55. One notices that at low temperatures the capture of minority carriers at traps is important. For example, at 77°K only 0.1% of electrons is not captured in traps ($\tau_n/\tau_p = \delta n/\delta p$). The theory which includes all the major

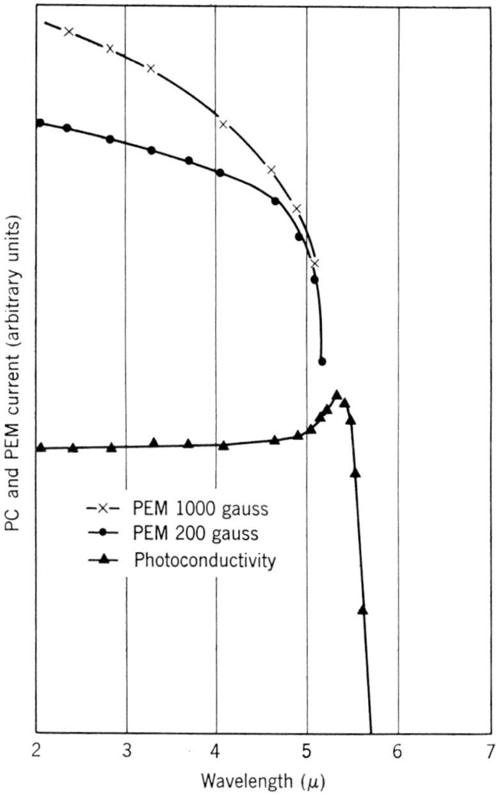

Fig. 4.54 Wavelength dependence of the PC and PEM current for InSb at 77°K [after Laff and Fan (61L1)].

corrections is shown by the dashed line. Agreement is good at low temperatures, but there are deviations at high temperatures where the influence of the trap centers decreases. This discrepancy can have a number of different origins. For example, there may be another competing recombination mechanism [see (59Z1)]. A detailed discussion, however, shows that neither radiation nor Auger recombination is sufficiently large in this case. Equally unlikely is the existence of a temperature dependence of the capture probability of electrons and holes in traps, as was inferred from an analysis of a number of different *n*- and *p*-type samples. Rather, Laff and Fan assumed that the center responsible for the recombination forms two states in the forbidden gap, whose contribution to the recombination is determined

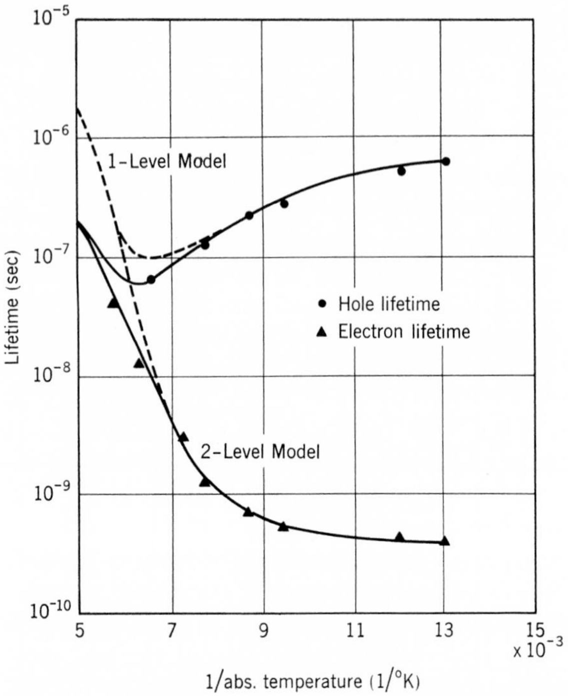

Fig. 4.55 Temperature dependence of the lifetimes of electrons and holes in a *p*-type InSb sample. The broken and solid curves apply to theoretical calculations with one and two recombination center levels, respectively [after Laff and Fan (61L1)].

by the location of the Fermi level and is consequently temperature dependent. An extension of the theory of the PC and PEM effect to this case gave excellent agreement with experiment (solid curve in Fig. 4.55).

The nature of this recombination center has not yet been determined unambiguously. It is probably associated with a lattice defect rather than an impurity, since, according to Laff and Fan, the number of these centers can be strongly increased by bombardment with 4.5-MeV electrons. It is remarkable that measurements on different samples and by different authors (56W5), (59Z1), (61L1), (62N1), (62Z4) almost always lead to the same type of recombination center. This supports the suggestion that it is a characteristic lattice defect in InSb which determines the recombination mechanism independently of the preparation or the doping of the sample.

The recombination in p-InSb in the temperature region covered by Fig. 4.55 can consequently be summarized as follows. At very low temperatures most of the minority carriers (electrons) are captured in the traps. The lifetimes τ_n and τ_p are very different from each other. With increasing temperature the Fermi level rises and therefore the number of electrons. The traps are filled with electrons, and fewer are available for capturing excess electrons (τ_n increases with increasing temperature). Simultaneously traps can now capture more holes (τ_p drops with increasing temperature). With further increase in temperature the two lifetimes approach each other and increase together according to the Shockley-Read theory. At the highest temperature other recombination mechanisms come into play. Measurements of Zitter, Strauss, and Attard (59Z1) and Wertheim (56W5) are shown in Fig. 4.56, together with theoretical curves for radiative recombination and Auger recombination. According to this figure, Auger recombination appears to be dominating the lifetime at high temperatures [see also (60B5)].

Numerous authors have calculated the lifetime for radiative recombination τ_{rad} from optical data and compared it with experiment. The curve shown in Fig. 4.56 is taken from an estimate of Wertheim (56W5). The room-temperature value of τ_{rad} was estimated to be 0.6–0.9 μsec by Mackintosh and Allen (55M1), (55A1), Landsberg and Moss (56L1), and Moss, Hawkins, and Smith (56M5), (57M4). A more accurate calculation by Goodwin and McLean (56G2) gave 0.36 μsec. These values apply to intrinsic InSb. With increasing difference between electron and hole concentration τ_{rad} drops very fast and is only about 20% of its maximum value for $n/p = 100$ or 0.01 (56L1).

Even though Auger recombination dominates at high temperatures, there will also be radiative transitions. The resulting recombination radiation was first observed by Moss and Hawkins (56M6) and was studied in more detail by Moss, Smith, and Hawkins (57M2) and later by Benoit à la Guillaume and Lavallard (62B8). Because of the high internal absorption of InSb 12-μ-thick samples were used. The early estimates gave 80% for the contribution of the radiative transitions to the total recombination, but Moss (57M3) and Landsberg (57L1) showed by more exact theoretical considerations that the contribution could be at most 20%.

According to eq. (4.37), there is a linear relation between the short-circuit current of the PEM effect and the number of photons falling on the sample per unit time ($I_{\text{PEM}} \sim I_0$). There is also a linear relationship between $(I_0 B_z / I_{\text{PEM}})^2$ and $B_z{}^2$, independent of the photon flux I_0.

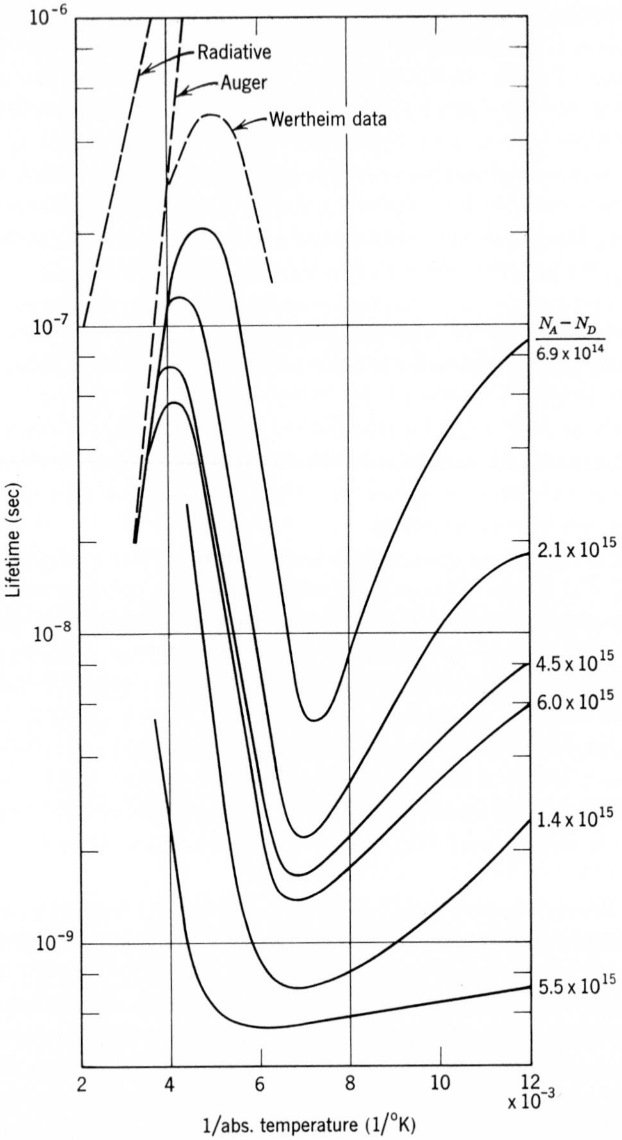

Fig. 4.56 Lifetime in InSb as determined from photoconductivity measurements [after Zitter, Strauss, and Attard (59Z1)]. Dashed curves: theoretical calculations for radiative and Auger recombination and measurements of Wertheim (56W5).

Both statements have been confirmed experimentally in numerous cases. Some discrepancies have, however, been observed at low temperatures. Beattie and Cunningham (62B3) found neither relationship to be satisfied at 80°K in p-InSb. The reason is that at this temperature the intrinsic concentration, n_i, and therefore the minority-carrier concentration, $n_{eq} = n_i^2/p_{eq}$, is very small, so that the condition $\delta n \ll n_{eq}$, which has been assumed so far, is no longer fulfilled. The hole density of the sample studied by Beattie and Cunningham was 10^{14} cm^{-3}, from which a minority concentration of $n_{eq} \approx 10^5$ cm^{-3} follows.

An extension of this theory to large density deviations leads to the following results. The lifetime of the minority carriers (defined as the ratio of excess electrons δn to the recombination rate R) increases with increasing δn. Simultaneously the previously neglected recombination at the irradiated surface can become influential. Finally, the dependence of the PEM current on the scattering mechanism becomes significant at large δn. An analysis of the experimental results by this theory furnishes an electron lifetime of 1.6×10^{-10} sec for small δn; it starts to increase above $\delta n = 10^9$ cm^{-3} up to a value 20 times larger at $\delta n = 5 \times 10^{10}$ cm^{-3}. The surface recombination, which is immeasurably small at small δn, increases to a value of 3.5×10^4 cm/sec at $\delta n = 3.8 \times 10^9$ cm^{-3}, and then drops again slightly. A satisfactory agreement between theory and experiment was possible only under the assumptions of impurity scattering.

Among other studies of the lifetime of InSb by measurements of the photoconduction and the PEM effect, we mention only the investigations of Goodwin (60G11), Hilsum (59H4), and Nasledov and coworkers (59N1), (61Z1), (62Z5), (63N2).

Aside from the volume lifetime τ these effects, of course, also give the surface recombination velocity s. Kurnick and Zitter (56K5), (56K6) find values between 10^4 and 10^6 cm/sec, depending on the surface treatment; Davis (61D1), values as low as 200 cm/sec.

All measurements discussed so far assume a quantum yield of 1. Measurements of Tauc (59T1), (59T2) justified this assumption near the absorption edge. Above a certain threshold the quantum yield increases with increasing energy of the photons. These observations were discussed in Section 415 and were found to be due to impact ionization (see Fig. 4.47).

From the spectral dependence of the photoconduction one can also determine the width of the forbidden gap. Characteristic results are E_G (0°K) ≈ 0.23 eV with a temperature coefficient of -2.4×10^{-4}

eV/°K between 5°K and room temperature (56F4), (60N2), in approximate agreement with the optical results.

Photoconduction due to photoionization of impurities has also been observed in InSb. We saw in Section 413 that the donors form an impurity band in InSb even at very small concentrations and that this band overlaps with the conduction band. Only in very pure samples can a finite separation of conduction band and donor levels be created by the application of a magnetic field (freeze-out effect). Pure photoconduction in n-InSb is therefore possible only in a magnetic field. This picture was generally confirmed by measurements of Putley (60P3), (61S9). The photoconductivity of an n-InSb sample with 4×10^{13} donors/cm^3 increased strongly at helium temperature with increasing magnetic field; the effective ionization energy was 2.7×10^{-4} eV at 4000 gauss and 7.5×10^{-4} eV at 8000 gauss. A small remaining photoconduction was also observed after removal of the magnetic field (61P10). This cannot be interpreted as photoionization of electrons bound at impurity levels into the conduction band, because of the overlapping of the impurity band with conduction band. A possible interpretation is the following. Electrons are lifted into higher states in the band by light absorption, and the effective temperature of the electrons is therefore increased. Since under the experimental conditions impurity scattering dominates, the mobility of the electrons increases with growing electron temperature, and therefore also the conductivity.

In contrast to the donors, the acceptors in InSb have a real ionization energy. Impurity photoconduction is to be expected in p-InSb and has been found experimentally. Of particular interest is the investigation of samples doped with gold, silver, or copper. These three elements form acceptors in InSb with two deep-lying levels in the forbidden gap. Photoconduction can be caused by transitions from the valence band into the conduction band or into one of the two acceptor levels, or by transitions from one of the acceptor levels into the conduction band. A selection between these processes can be made by additional doping with donors, i.e., by varying the number of electrons in the acceptor levels. Such investigations have been made by Blunt (58B2) and by Engeler, Levinstein, and Stannard (61E10). The question under investigation here is not so much the mechanism of photoconduction, but rather the determination of the location of the energy levels from the spectral response of the photoconduction. The ionization energies of the lower levels (0.023 eV for Cu and Ag, 0.032 eV for Au) known from Hall measurements were confirmed, and the values for the higher levels determined as 0.056 eV (Cu), 0.039 eV (Ag), and 0.066 eV (Au). When the lower levels are only partly filled, the wavelength dependence of the photoconductivity has an oscillatory character at helium temperature. For all three acceptors the energy separation of the individual oscillation minima from each other and the separation of the first minimum from the long wavelength edge is 0.0244 eV. This value corresponds exactly to the energy of the longitudinal optical phonon in InSb. Engeler, Levinstein, and Stannard (61E9) interpret these oscillations as a superposition of individual spectral curves which must be assigned to transitions of electrons from the valence band into the lower acceptor level with simultaneous emission of 0, 1, 2, 3, . . . longitudinal optical phonons.

Similar oscillations have been found for band-to-band transitions with simultaneous emission of LO phonons in *p*-InSb (64S5) and *p*-GaSb (64H1).

Photoconduction and the photoelectromagnetic effect in InSb find technical application in infrared detectors [see, e.g., (57G5), (57H2), (59K3)].

Indium Arsenide. For InAs only measurements of the PEM effect and photoconduction at room temperature are so far available (57D1). Figures 4.57a and b show the dependence of the short-circuit current I_{PEM} on the magnetic field for *n*-type and *p*-type InAs. Since no trapping is expected at room temperature, I_{PEM} for extrinsic conduction ($n_{\text{maj}} \gg n_{\text{min}}$) is given, according to (4.37), by

$$I_{\text{PEM}} = eI_0(\mu_n + \mu_p)B \frac{L}{1 + \tau s/L} \tag{4.40}$$

with

$$L = \sqrt{D\tau}, \quad D = \frac{kT}{e} \mu_{\text{min}}(1 + \mu_{\text{min}}{}^2 B^2)^{-1}$$

The factor $\mu_{\text{min}}B$, which contains the magnetic field, is smaller than 0.03 for the magnetic fields employed for *n*-type InAs, because $\mu_{\text{min}} = \mu_p$. In this region I_{PEM} increases approximately linearly with B. In *p*-type InAs, $\mu_{\text{min}} = \mu_n$ and $\mu_n/\mu_p \approx 100$, and the linear region is exceeded (Fig. 4.57b).

From these results and from measurements of the photocurrent the lifetime and the surface-recombination velocity were determined. Here τ is the same in I_{PC} and I_{PEM}, and the lifetime is given by the ratio of the two currents if B, $\mathcal{E}$, and D are known. Then s is determined from (4.40). Dixon finds in this way for *n*-InAs $\tau = 6 \times 10^{-8}$ sec and $s < 10^3$ cm/sec for etched surfaces, $\approx 10^5$ cm/sec for

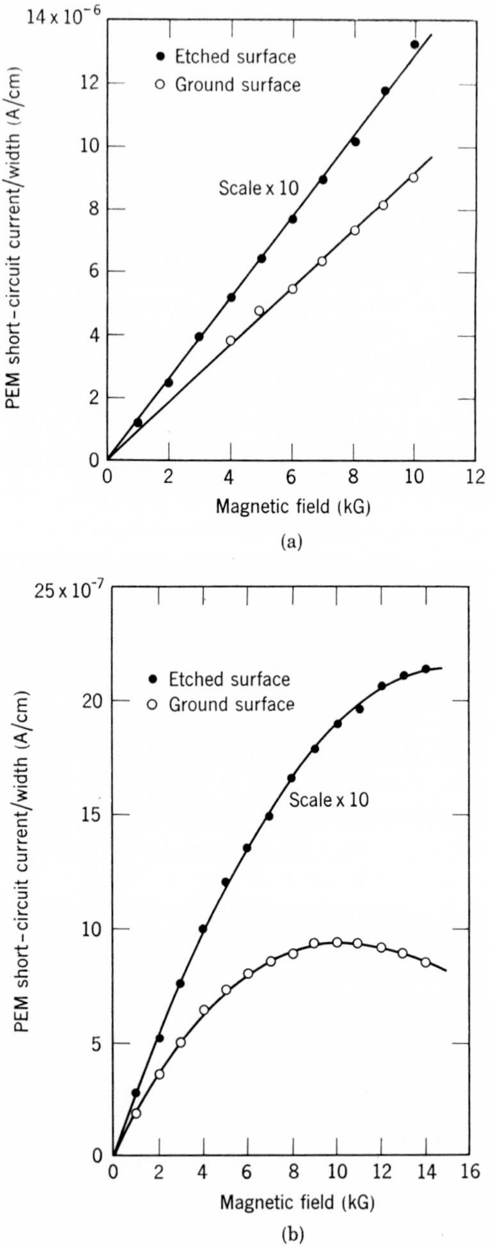

Fig. 4.57 Dependence of the PEM current on magnetic field at room temperature for (a) n-InAs and (b) p-InAs [after Dixon (57D1)].

ground surfaces. In p-InAs the photocurrent was too small to determine unambiguous values, and an estimate gave $\tau \approx 5 \times 10^{-10}$ sec.

For an n-type sample with donor concentration equal to that of Dixon ($n_D = 3 \times 10^{16}$ cm^{-3}) Hilsum (57H3) found a lifetime of 2×10^{-7} sec. The lifetime for radiative transitions in intrinsic material calculated from optical data [Dixon and Ellis (61D3)] is 1.3×10^{-5} sec. For n-type material with $n = 10^{16}$ cm^{-3} it drops to about 4×10^{-6} sec. These values are not upper limits for the lifetime because of the strong reabsorption of the recombination radiation in InAs.

Indium Phosphide. The PC and PEM effects were measured by Mikhailova, Nasledov, and Slobotchikov (62M6). Strong trapping was observed; the lifetime of holes τ_p lay between 2×10^{-6} and 2.5×10^{-7} sec, that of electrons between 1.7×10^{-3} and 2.2×10^{-3} sec at room temperature.

Gallium Antimonide. Only a few measurements are available on GaSb. Frederikse and Blunt (56F4) found at room temperature a width of the forbidden gap of 0.65 eV from the spectral response of the photoconduction, in good agreement with the optical value of Table 3.1. Lukeš (56L5) found a quadratic temperature dependence for E_G with a limiting value $E_G(0)$ of 0.773 eV.

Nothing is known about lifetimes in GaSb. Recombination radiation with a maximum at 0.625 eV was observed by Braunstein (55B3) after injection of charge carriers at contacts. This phenomenon is probably not due to radiative band-to-band transitions, which have been observed by Filinski, Johnson, and Fan (62F2), (62J2) with a peak at 0.72 eV (300°K) and 0.798 eV (72°K). They also found additional radiative transitions at 0.67 eV (and 0.778 eV at 72°K) and indications for radiative exciton recombination.

Gallium Arsenide. The forbidden gap of GaAs is much wider than that of InSb, InAs, and GaSb. Consequently trapping effects are still important at room temperature, and a determination of lifetimes from the I_{PC}/I_{PEM} ratio leads to wrong results. Hilsum and Holeman (61H11) found an effective lifetime of 31 sec in an n-type sample with $n = 2 \times 10^{16}$ cm^{-3} from the PC/PEM ratio, while an analysis of the measurement according to the theory given at the beginning of this section gave $\tau_n = 5.6 \times 10^{-5}$ sec and $\tau_p = 10^{-10}$ sec. The ratio of lifetimes, and therefore the ratio of added electrons in the conduction band to added holes in the valence band $\delta n/\delta p$, are in this case larger than 10^5. Separate evaluations of PEM and PC measurements

[Hilsum and Holeman (61H11), (61H4), Amith (59A5), Hurd (62H16)] gave the following upper limits for the lifetimes: electrons in n-type material, 6×10^{-5} sec, holes 5×10^{-8} sec; electrons in p-type material, 10^{-10} sec, holes 1.5×10^{-4} sec.

The values were measured in normal semiconducting GaAs. As we mentioned in Section 41, GaAs can also be prepared in a high-resistivity form, which contains only 10^6–10^7 electrons/cm^3 in the conduction band. Measurements of lifetime on such material gave, according to Hilsum and Holeman (61H14), for the majority carriers 0.5×10^{-8} sec $< \tau_n < 20 \times 10^{-8}$ sec, and for the minority carriers 0.2×10^{-8} sec $< \tau_p < 80 \times 10^{-8}$ sec for various samples. The ratio of lifetimes in these materials lies between 1 and 10, an indication of only weak trapping. The lifetimes herefrom expected for trap-free GaAs lie between 3×10^{-9} and 5×10^{-7} sec.

The spectral response of the photoconduction leads, according to Bube (60B9), to a width of the forbidden gap of 1.39–1.42 eV at room temperature and a temperature coefficient $\partial E_G/\partial T = -4 \times 10^{-4}$ eV/°K. From the spectral maximum of the recombination radiation of carriers injected at point contacts Braunstein (55B3) found a much smaller value, namely, $(1.22 - 4 \times 10^{-4}T)$ eV, i.e., 1.10 eV at room temperature. According to Nasledov, Rogachev, Ryvkin, and Tsarenkov (62N3), this maximum therefore cannot be due to direct band-to-band transitions. They observed the latter with a maximum at 1.47 eV at 77°K.

The investigation of photoconduction in GaAs also provides information about the position of impurity levels in the forbidden gap, as in other III-V compounds. We will consider these questions in Chapter 5.

Gallium Phosphide. Photoconduction in GaP has been observed by Nasledov and Slobotchikov (62N4).

Radiative transitions lie in the visible region in GaP and play an important role in connection with the electroluminescence of this semiconductor. This subject will be considered in Section 532.

5

Impurities and Defects

50 Introduction

In semiconductors of the fourth group of the periodic table foreign atoms from group III are built into the lattice substitutionally as acceptors, and foreign atoms from group V as donors. It is the number of valence electrons of the impurity relative to the number of valence electrons of the atoms of the lattice which determines the behavior of the impurities in the diamond lattice. The ionization energies of these donors and acceptors in germanium and silicon are small compared to the width of the forbidden gap. Other elements can also be incorporated into the lattice substitutionally or interstitially and can act as acceptors and donors, but this property plays only a minor role since the energy levels are far removed from the valence- and conduction-band edges. Such foreign atoms play a more important role as traps for electrons and holes and as recombination centers.

If this picture is extended to the III-V compounds, one suspects that the most important acceptors will be foreign atoms from group II of the periodic system which are located substitutionally in the sublattice of the trivalent lattice atoms. Similarly the main donors will be atoms of group VI in the sublattice of the pentavalent lattice atoms. These impurities will be the subject of the first section of this chapter. Atoms of group IV may be donors, if they are built into the III-sublattice, or acceptors, if they are in the V-sublattice. Which of these two possibilities applies in any given case will be discussed in Section 511.

Incorporating foreign atoms of group III or V of the periodic table will not change the concentration of carriers, since such atoms replace lattice atoms of the same valence. There will, however, be an effect on the physical properties of the host lattice. These and other problems related to the formation of mixed crystals between III-V compounds will be considered in Chapter 6.

A lattice atom built into the wrong sublattice, for example the replacement of an antimony atom in InSb by an indium atom, will cause a *deviation from stoichiometry*. Such deviations are well known in many semiconducting compounds. In contrast, no clear-cut evidence for nonstoichiometric behavior has yet been observed in III-V compounds, although there appears to be a certain amount of circumstantial evidence for it. In GaSb a residual concentration of about 10^{17} acceptors cm^{-3} cannot be reduced by any known purification technique. Many authors have here suspected a deviation from stoichiometry (see also Section 520). Since, however, other compounds, such as InSb, InAs, and GaAs, can be purified to a much higher level, and InP can be made at least as pure, it would be surprising if only GaSb were not stoichiometric. In GaP a dependence of the conductivity type on the phosphorus pressure during crystal growth has been observed (60G17). At low pressures the final substance was n-type with a donor ionization energy of 0.07 eV; at high pressures, p-type with an acceptor ionization energy of 0.19 eV. This behavior is consistent with nonstoichiometry, but it does not prove it. It may also be due to amphoteric impurities (see Section 511). Earlier Russian papers showed crystals to have different properties, depending on the growth technique employed, and suggested that this difference was due to nonstoichiometries. However, it is now well established that the crystals of the most important III-V compounds have the same physical properties whether they are produced from a stoichiometric or a nonstoichiometric melt. We therefore need not consider group III and V atoms as impurities.

The apparent complete stoichiometry does not exclude the possibility of lattice defects, such as vacancies, existing in III-V compounds. We will, in later sections, see strong evidence for the existence of lattice defects in GaAs.

The properties of all other impurities will be discussed in Section 512. This will be followed by a section containing those impurity data in the III-V compounds which have not yet been assigned to any known defect.

Knowledge of the properties of impurities after they are incorporated into the lattice is generally sufficient for the interpretation of experimental data. For the production of semiconducting crystals with well-defined properties it is, in addition, important to be able to produce predetermined impurity distributions. In Sections 520–523 we will discuss the more important methods of producing pure substances and of doping crystals, as well as the diffusion of impurities, the effect of annealing at elevated temperature on the impurity distribution, and the effect of radiation damage. We will not discuss the technological problems involved but rather will occupy ourselves with the question of what information about the properties of impurities can be obtained by these techniques.

51 Properties of Impurities in III-V Compounds

In Section 51 we will treat the influence of *impurities* on the electrical properties of the III-V compounds. Not much is yet known about the effect of the *lattice defects* on the electrical properties. Evidence for their existence will be considered in Section 522. Most of the knowledge about the influence of vacancies and interstitial atoms comes from investigations of the electrical properties of III-V compounds after particle bombardment. These will be discussed in Section 523. There is almost no literature about the influence of other kinds of lattice defects, such as dislocations and grain boundaries, on the electrical properties. We merely know that impurities like to cluster at dislocations, be it as donors or acceptors, or in electrically inactive form. Information about this will be found at a number of different points in this chapter. Other properties of dislocations (etch pits, etc.) and of similar lattice defects will be considered in the sections on the mechanical properties and on the surface properties (Chapter 8).

510 Acceptors and donors from groups II and VI of the periodic table. The most important acceptors in III-V compounds are *zinc* and *cadmium*. Both elements substitute for trivalent lattice atoms, and lack one of the electrons needed to form the tetrahedral bonds. In no III-V compound have any anomalies in the substitutional acceptor character of these elements been observed, except that at very high concentration a small fraction can be built in interstitially and then have donor character (62L5), (63W5). If one considers as a model for these impurities a hydrogen atom with an electron or hole of mass m^* in a medium of the dielectric constant of the host lattice, then the ionization energy of the acceptors in III-V compounds will be of the order of $\Delta E_A = 0.05$ eV. In contrast, the ionization energies which have unambiguously been assigned to zinc and cadmium are in InSb 0.0075 eV [Putley (59P5)] and in GaAs, for Zn 0.014 eV and for Cd 0.021 eV according to Meyerhofer (61M10). Fluorescence measurements by Nathan and Burns (62N10) suggest that ΔE_A (Zn) may be as high as 0.03 eV. In InP ΔE_A (Cd) = 0.05 eV (59G4), in GaSb ΔE_A (Zn) = 0.037 eV (54W2), in better agreement with the simple model.

Zinc and cadmium are highly soluble in III-V compounds. Quantitative values are so far available only for GaAs, where solubilities of $\geqslant 10^{19}$ cm^{-3} are obtained for Cd and $\geqslant 10^{20}$ cm^{-3} for Zn at the melting point [Goldstein (59G7)]. The highest value of cadmium concentration that has been measured is 2.5×10^{21} cm^{-3} at 400°C (63B11).

Magnesium is an acceptor in InSb, InAs, and GaSb (59E1), (56S2), (56S4). There are contradicting statements about its behavior in GaAs. According to Edmond (59E1), magnesium is a donor when GaAs is doped with 5.7×10^{19} Mg atoms/cm^3, whereas Weisberg, Rosi, and Herkart (60W2) report that the donor character appears only at low magnesium concentration and GaAs doped with 4.4×10^{18} Mg atoms/cm^3 becomes p-type. This would indicate that magnesium is then an acceptor. As a possible explanation, an interstitial position at low concentration and a substitutional position at high concentration are discussed. According to Knight (61K4), it is more likely that during doping of the GaAs melt in SiO_2 crucibles magnesium is bound by the reaction $2Mg + SiO_2 \rightarrow 2MgO + Si$, and the donor silicon is freed. Magnesium would then be an acceptor, and the donor character is simulated by the silicon. This assumption was confirmed by Bennett (62B7), who also reported the ionization energy of the magnesium in GaAs as $\Delta E_A = (0.0125 \pm 0.0001)$ eV.

Among the elements of group VI of the periodic system *selenium* and *tellurium* have been shown to be donors in all III-V compounds [(56H1), (56S2), (56S3), (56S4), (59N3), (60W2), and others]. *Sulfur* was determined to be a donor in InSb (56H1), InAs (56S2), and GaAs (60W2). About *oxygen* one knows only that it forms deep levels. Its trap behavior in GaAs will be discussed in Section 53.

We have seen in Chapter 4 that donors in InSb and InAs do not have a finite ionization energy. This is understandable when one considers the small effective mass of the electrons in these two compounds, with the consequently very large "orbit" of the electron in the hydrogen-like model of an impurity. The model gives an ionization energy of a donor of about one thousandth of an electron volt. Because of the large Bohr radius of the impurity an impurity band forms at small donor concentrations and overlaps with the bottom of the conduction band. The consequences of this impurity band for the transport properties in InSb and InAs at low temperatures were discussed in Section 413.

In the compounds InP and GaAs the ionization energy of shallow donors is still small, but somewhat larger than in InSb and InAs. Impurity bands no longer overlap with the conduction band at low donor concentrations. Only in AlSb have large ionization energies been observed. According to Nasledov and Slobotchikov (59N3), the value for selenium in AlSb is 0.27 eV, that for tellurium 0.13 eV. The latter value is in good agreement with one of the two ionization energies, 0.14 and 0.31 eV, that Blunt, Frederikse, Becker, and Hosler (54B3) found in Te-doped AlSb.

The solubility of selenium in GaSb at the melting point is 1.5×10^{18} cm^{-3}, according to Hall and Racette (61H4), and that of tellurium, 4×10^{18} cm^{-3}. Above these concentrations, compounds form between selenium or tellurium and gallium. We will return to this topic in Chapter 6 in the discussion of GaAs-Ga_2Se_3 mixed crystals.

Bate (62B2) was the first to point out that in III-V compounds with more than one subband of the conduction band the donor states below the bottom of the higher-lying subbands must also be taken into account. For example, in GaSb the donor-states below the (000)-minimum fuse into the conduction band; the ones lying below the (111)-minima, however, keep a finite ionization energy because of the larger effective mass of the electrons in these minima. These discrete impurity levels lie a few hundredths of an electron volt below the (111)-minima, but still *above* the (000)-minimum. Electrons in these states can then pass into the (000)-conduction band at constant energy. Thus the separation of the impurity levels from the (111)-conduction band is not a true ionization energy that must be overcome to make the donor electrons electrically active. The only property of these states is that they are empty at low electron concentration and filled at high concentration. In the first case they act as charged impurities, in the second at neutral ones. This can cause anomalies in the dependence of the electron mobility on the electron concentration. Bate believes that this model can explain the differences between the electrical properties of Se- and Te-doped GaSb that were reported in Section 411.

511 Impurities from group IV of the periodic system. Whereas impurities of groups II and VI of the periodic system are substitutionally built into the sublattices of the III and V atoms, respectively, the question of how atoms of group IV behave in the III-V compounds does not have as obvious an answer. Since here also there is one valence electron too few or too many when the atoms are built into one of the two sublattices, it may be assumed that they are also located substitutionally. Three possibilities can then be distinguished.

1. The group IV atoms occupy only one sublattice. They then act exclusively as donors (when they occupy the III-sublattice) or as acceptors (when they occupy the V-sublattice) (52W1).
2. The impurity atoms are located on two neighboring lattice sites as pairs and thereby remain electrically neutral. This possibility appears to be energetically favorable, according to (57K6).
3. The impurity atoms are distributed statistically onto the two sublattices, and the question of which sublattice is more heavily occupied depends on the nature and concentration of the impurities and on external conditions.

In Table 5.1 we present the behavior of carbon, silicon, germanium, tin, and lead in the most important III-V compounds, as determined by electrical measurements. The table shows that generally group IV impurities are preferentially built into one of the two sublattices. The simplest assumption to explain these results is that the impurity atoms prefer to occupy the sublattice whose atoms have the larger radius, whose vacancies therefore offer more space for the foreign atom. If the covalent radii (cf. Table 2.1) of the elements of group IV are compared with those of the elements of the III-sublattice and of the V-sublattice, the observed results can be explained by the fore-

Table 5.1 Electrical Behavior of Group IV Elements in III-V Compounds at Low Concentrations

A—acceptor, *D*—donor, *O*—no effect on the carrier concentration. For details, particularly for deviations from the indicated behavior at high impurity concentrations, see the discussion in the text.

Element	InSb	InAs	InP	GaSb	GaAs	AlSb
C					A^g	A^f
Si	A^b	D^c		A^b	D^b	A^f
Ge	A^a	D^a	D^a	A^a	D^d	A^f
Sn	D^a	D^a	D^a	A^a	D^b	$A + D^f$
Pb	O^a, D^b (?)	O^a	O^a	O^a	D^e	A^f, D^h (?)

[a] (57F2). [b] (59E1). [c] (56S2). [d] (58J2). [e] (60W2). [f] (62S5). [g] (61F3). [h] (55R1).

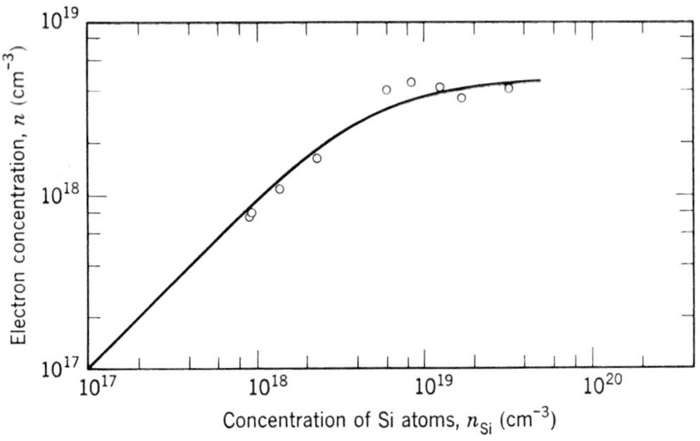

Fig. 5.1 Dependence of the electron concentration n in GaAs on the concentration of the silicon atoms, n_{Si}, built into the lattice [after Whelan, Struthers, and Ditzenberger (61W4)].

going assumptions with a few exceptions. An example of the latter is InSb, where silicon and germanium substitute for the lattice atoms with the smaller covalent radii. In some cases impurities have even a larger covalent radius than the atom for which they substitute. Particularly noteworthy is the location of tin (1.40 Å) on gallium sites (1.26 Å) in GaAs. Lead, with a still larger radius, is not built in at all.

To explain the anomalies in InSb, Folberth and Schillman (57F2) assume that there is a general tendency for the impurity atom to locate on the V-sublattice, even if the covalent radius is such that it should be occupying the III-lattice. This hypothesis is, however, partly contradicted by the results to be discussed next.

In the preceding cases the foreign atoms do not locate exclusively on one of the sublattices; they only prefer one over the other. This is shown by experiments on the position of silicon in GaAs (60W2), (61W4). By incorporating radioactive silicon atoms, Whelan, Struthers, and Ditzenberger were able to determine the relationship between the increased electron concentration due to the Si-doping and the amount of dissolved silicon. The result is shown in Fig. 5.1. For concentrations of the order of 10^{17} cm^{-3} almost every silicon atom acts as donor, while at higher concentrations the ratio n/n_{Si} decreases; not all additional silicon atoms are donors. This cannot be explained by the assumption that the atoms form donors but are not ionized, since at high concentrations the shallow impurity states form an impurity band which overlaps with the conduction band. Complete ionization of the impurities must be assumed. The silicon atoms must therefore partly substitute for arsenic atoms as their concentration increases. Then these acceptors partly compensate the donors on the gallium sites. With this assumption the measured curve could be interpreted quantitatively by the theory of amphoteric impurities by Longini and Greene. Nuclear-resonance measurements of Rhoderick (59R5) also confirmed that silicon locates on two possible sites in the GaAs-lattice.

The situation is similar for germanium in GaAs. According to (60W4), the ratio $n/n_{Ge} = 0.2$ for a doping of 1.5×10^{18} Ge atoms/cm^3. Above 2×10^{20} impurities/cm^3 further doping does not increase the carrier concentrations, according to (57K6) [see also (62V2)].

The statistical distribution of impurities onto the two sublattices is further supported by the experimental observation that the conductivity type of Ge-doped GaAs can be changed by annealing at different arsenic pressures (60M2). We will see in Section 521 that the vacancy equilibrium is closely connected with the distribution of amphoteric impurities between the two sublattices. If one changes the vacancy equilibrium in the arsenic sublattices by changing the arsenic pressure in the adjacent gas phase, one forces a transition of the impurity between the two sublattices and influences the conductivity type.

We therefore conclude that at small impurity concentration the atoms of group IV locate on one of the sublattices (according to the Folberth-Schillmann hypothesis) and that at higher concentration a distribution between both sublattices (perhaps with formation of pairs of nearest neighbors) becomes likely. According to Shaw (62S5), tin in AlSb locates equally on both sublattices, so that donors and acceptors form simultaneously.

The elements of group IV are soluble only up to 0.5–0.6 atomic % in GaAs (57K6). In this range the lattice constant decreases from 5.656 to 5.653 Å. A small increase of the forbidden gap has been observed under Si-, Sn-, and Pb-doping, and a small decrease under Ge-doping.

512 Other foreign atoms. Among the elements of the first group of the periodic table there exist some data on lithium, sodium, copper, silver, and gold. *Lithium* is known as a donor in germanium and silicon, which diffuses rapidly and is interstitially located in the lattice. In GaAs lithium has been investigated by Fuller and Wolfstirn (58H5), (62F3), (62F4), (62F5), (63F6). When lithium is diffused in, the electrical resistivity of GaAs increases to about 10 Ωcm independent of the initial doping. Annealing at elevated temperatures after removing the lithium source reduces the resistivity to 0.2 Ωcm, and originally n-type crystals become p-type. According to Fuller and Wolfstirn, lithium diffuses interstitially and can be built into both interstitial and substitutional positions. Interstitially lithium is a donor which is ionized at room temperature (Li^+). Substitutionally it is an atom of group I located in the III-sublattice and is a doubly charged acceptor (Li^{2-}_{subst}). Under saturation conditions one Li^+ associates with each such acceptor to form a ($Li^+Li^{2-}_{subst}$) complex which acts as a single acceptor. The remaining mobile lithium donors compensate all negatively charged acceptors; the crystal has a high resistance. During annealing in the absence of lithium the interstitially located Li^+ diffuses to the surface, grain boundaries, or dislocations and precipitates out to become electrically inactive. The remaining ($Li^+Li^{2-}_{subst}$) complexes reduce the resistance and make the crystal p-type.

The solubility of lithium in GaAs below 900°C is

$$n_{\mathrm{Li}} = 7.0 \times 10^{21} e^{-E/kT} \text{ cm}^{-3}$$

with $E = 0.57$ eV. At about 1050°C the solubility reaches a maximum and then decreases with increasing temperature up to the melting point.

In GaSb the residual acceptors can be made electrically ineffective by ion-pairing with lithium. According to Bate, Baxter, and Reid (63B4), the hole density decreases from 10^{17} to $(2 - 3) \times 10^{15}$ cm^{-3} when lithium is diffused into GaSb.

Kover (57K7) finds a similar increase of resistivity in AlSb under doping with lithium.

The only information about *sodium* is that it acts as an acceptor in GaAs (60W2).

Copper is an acceptor in GaSb (56S4), GaAs [(58A1), (60C8), and other references cited below], and GaP (62A1). In contrast, copper is a donor in InAs; this fact will be discussed more extensively in Section 522.

Activation energies on copper impurities have been determined only in GaAs and GaP. The behavior of copper in GaAs appears to be similar to that in germanium and silicon, except that the solubility is larger. Fuller and Whelan (58F6) found the solubility to be $3.7 \times 10^{23} e^{-E/kT}$ cm^{-3} with $E = 1.3$ eV (Fig. 5.2). Copper is located substitutionally as well as interstitially. The substitutional location is probably in the gallium lattice. In Cu-doped GaAs a large number of impurity states have been found. An acceptor level at (0.145 ±

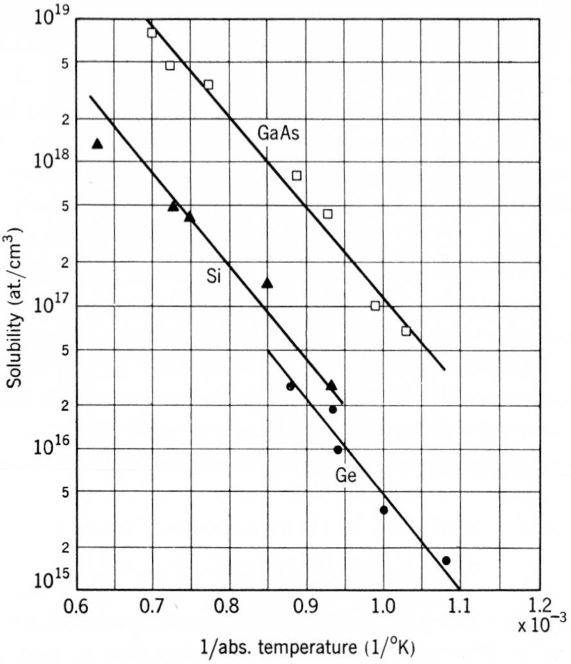

Fig. 5.2 Solubility of copper in GaAs, silicon, and germanium as a function of temperature [after Fuller and Whelan (58F6)].

0.005) eV is well established (60R5), (60W3), (61M10), (64B3). A second level at 0.023 eV (60R5), (60W2), (60W3), (61E8) has also been assigned to copper by some authors, while others ascribe it to vacancies in the gallium sublattice or to vacancy-impurity complexes (60W3); more recent work disagrees with the latter assumption (64F1). Other impurity states found in Cu-doped GaAs under various experimental conditions are a donor level (0.55 $\pm$ 0.02) eV below the conduction band and an acceptor level (0.24 $\pm$ 0.04) eV above the valence band (62B15), acceptor levels at 0.063 and 0.11 eV (58F6) and 0.05, 0.2, and 0.4 eV (61B15) above the valence band.

Hall and Racette (62H3), (64H3) investigated the solubility, diffusion, and location of copper in GaAs with radioactive tracers. The diffusion will be discussed in Section 521. The ratio of substitutional to interstitial copper atoms in intrinsic material at 600°C was found to be 30. Furthermore, there were indications that copper is a simple donor interstitially, and a double acceptor substitutionally. The two acceptor levels can be observed clearly in Si- and Sn-doped GaAs, but not in S- and Se-doped material. In the latter case there seems to be ion-pairing of the copper with sulfur or selenium. A complex formation of copper with donors has also been found by Blanc, Bube, and Rosi (61B15). Other properties of copper in GaAs will be discussed in Sections 522 and 531.

In p-GaP, doping with copper has no effect, while n-GaP is made semi-insulating ($\rho \approx 10^{10}$ Ωcm) by this process. The properties of this high-resistivity GaP were studied by Allen and Cherry (62A1), (62C7), who found an acceptor center 0.68 eV above the valence band. They also showed that copper can occupy different positions in GaP just as in GaAs.

Only a few data are available for *gold* and *silver*. Photoconductivity measurements (cf. Section 43) in InSb indicate that these elements are acceptors with two levels above the valence band (58B2), (61E10). Ionization energies are as follows: for Au, 0.032 and 0.066 eV; for Ag, 0.023 and 0.039 eV. Similar values for the smaller ionization energy were obtained by Engeler and Levinstein (61E8).

Iodine is only weakly soluble in GaP, according to (60A14) (about 10^{15} I atoms/cm^3 at the melting point). The location is interstitial. The small solubility is due to the covalent radius of iodine (1.33 Å) being larger than the interstitial position in GaP (1.26 Å). *Chlorine* is more highly soluble in InAs ($>10^{19}$ cm^{-3} at the melting point), according to the same author, as the covalent radius of chlorine (0.99 Å) is much smaller than the interstitial position (1.44 Å). Nothing is known about the properties of these two elements in III-V compounds.

Finally, *cobalt* and *nickel* form deep traps in GaAs, probably with acceptor character (60C8), (60W2). *Manganese* is also a deep acceptor with $\Delta E_A = 0.12$ eV (62V1), (64T2), *iron* an acceptor with $\Delta E_A = 0.37$ eV (64B2), and *chromium* an acceptor with $\Delta E_A = 0.70$ eV (64T5).

513 Unidentified impurity levels. Here we will just list some ionization energies which have been determined in undoped crystals by galvanomagnetic and photoelectric measurements.

In InSb Broom and Rose-Innes (56B2) found an ionization energy of $(0.010 - 2 \times 10^{-8}\, n_A{}^{1/3})$ eV for the dominant acceptor, where n_A is the acceptor concentration (in cm^{-3}) determined from the Hall effect. Other acceptor levels lie at 0.003 and 0.03 eV, according to (59L5).

A large number of photoelectrically determined levels in GaAs

(59A5), (60B9), (60W2), (63M9), (64B2) lie 0.30, 0.47, 0.55, 0.62, 0.70 and 0.76 eV below the conduction band and 0.09, 0.22, and 0.34 eV above the valence band. The 0.55 eV level seems to be identical with the donor found in high-resistivity GaAs by Whelan and Wheatley (58W6), which had $\Delta E_D = (0.54 \pm 0.05)$ eV.

Finally, the following acceptor levels have been observed in AlSb: $\Delta E_A = 0.018$ eV (60A9), 0.08 eV, 0.53 eV (53J1), 0.75 eV (54B2), and 0.77 eV (58N2).

52 Introduction and Removal of Impurities and Defects in III-V Compounds

520 Growth of pure crystals; doping. The creation of a predetermined impurity distribution in a semiconductor consists of two steps: unwanted contamination must be removed from the sample and then the desired foreign atoms must be incorporated in the required concentration and distribution. In the following sections we will discuss the physical aspects of these procedures, without attempting to treat all the relevant material or cite all the pertinent literature.

A large number of chemical procedures are available for the purification of the compound or of its components. These procedures, as well as the usual methods for the formation of the III-V compound out of its components, are part of the technology of the III-V compounds, and so fall outside the realm of this book. A number of thermodynamic data which are important for the technology, such as enthalpy of formation, free energy of formation, and entropy, have been collected by Renner (60R1). We also refer to his work for the vapor-pressure curves and for a list of references. Physicochemical data, such as phase diagrams, and technological questions, have been summarized in an article by Folberth (60F8). Here we merely list in Table 5.2 the melting points of the main III-V compounds.

We will restrict ourselves in this section to questions related to the removal of the last traces of foreign atoms and to the growth of single crystals. A crystal can be called free of imperfections only if all the foreign atoms are removed, and also all kinds of lattice defects, dislocations, and grain boundaries are absent. Of course, a completely imperfection-free crystal can never be produced, not only because of technological difficulties but also for fundamental reasons. Just as, at a given temperature, there is a well-defined electron and hole concentration in equilibrium, so a definite concentration of vacancies and interstitials is required by the equilibrium conditions.

The most important procedures for the production of ultra-pure

Table 5.2 Melting Points of Some of the III-V Compounds

Compound	Melting Point (°C)
InSb	530
InAs	942
InP	1058
InN	≈1200
GaSb	706
GaAs	1238
GaP	1467
GaN	≈1500
AlSb	1065
AlAs	>1600
AlP	>2000
AlN	>2400
BN	≈3000

single crystals are zone refining, normal freezing, and crystal pulling. In *zone refining* a semiconductor rod is melted in a small region by local heating, and this molten zone is passed through the rod by moving the heater. In *normal freezing* a molten ingot is moved in a temperature gradient, so that crystallization begins at one end and then progresses along the melt (horizontal Bridgman method). In *crystal pulling* a (single-crystal) seed is immersed in a crucible of molten material and then slowly withdrawn to form a single crystal (Czochralski method).

In all these procedures the purification depends on the fact that on solidification of the melt foreign atoms are built into the lattice with a different probability from that of the lattice atoms themselves. If the lattice atoms are preferred, then purification takes place during solidification; if the reverse is true, the foreign substance contained in the melt is enriched in the crystal. If one completely melts a rod of length L and then lets it freeze again directionally, so that the liquid-solid interface passes through the rod from $x = 0$ to $x = L$ (normal freezing), the concentration profile in the solidified rod is given by

$$C_s(x) = k_c C_{l0} \left(1 - \frac{x}{L}\right)^{k_c - 1} \tag{5.1}$$

The initial impurity concentration in the melt is C_{l0}. If, however, only a zone of length l is molten and if this zone is passed once through the rod, the impurity profile is given by

$$C_s(x) = C_{l0}[1 + (k_c - 1)e^{-k_c x/l}] \tag{5.2}$$

This purification or enriching process can be improved by repeated passage of the zone.

The parameter k_c in (5.1) and (5.2) is defined as the ratio of impurity concentration in the solid at the interface to the concentration in the melt: $k_c = C_s/C_l$ (distribution coefficient, segregation coefficient). The two equations apply only under idealized conditions, namely, a complete mixture of the melt, no diffusion of impurity atoms in the solid phase, no exchange of impurity atoms between the solid or liquid phase and the adjacent gas phase, and constant k_c. We will return to this topic in the discussion of the segregation coefficients in the individual III-V compounds.

The *doping* of a semiconductor with a desired amount of impurity atoms does not create any new physical problems. If the dopant is added into the pure melt, the impurity distribution in the solid is not homogeneous, unless the segregation coefficient of the impurity accidentally has the value 1. The distribution can be made homogeneous by repeated zone passing forward and backward (zone leveling). All these doping questions are no different for the III-V compounds from what they are for other semiconductors.

Indium Antimonide. Three properties of a material can cause technological difficulties in zone refining and in single-crystal growth: a high melting point, a high vapor pressure of the compound at the melting point, and the possibility of one component reacting with the crucible material. None of these occur in InSb. A small loss of antimony from the melt is possible under prolonged heating (60F8) but can easily be prevented. The melting point is at 530°C, and there is no reaction between indium or antimony and the usual crucible materials. The preparation of very-high-purity material is therefore technologically no more difficult than for germanium. Impurity concentrations of less than 10^{14} cm^{-3} have been obtained [see, e.g., Hulme (59H6) or Vinogradova *et al.* (59V2)]. Single crystals can be produced easily (53G1). In Table 5.3 the distribution coefficients for a number of elements in InSb are listed. Some of these values fluctuate widely, and a more detailed discussion is necessary.

For the distribution coefficient of zinc, values in the literature vary from 2.3 (58M5) to 10 (56H1). Systematic investigations of Strauss

Table 5.3 Distribution Coefficients $k_c = C_s/C_l$ for Some of the Elements in III-V Compounds

The scatter among some of the values is due to the fact that k_c depends strongly on the experimental conditions. This is discussed in more detail in the text.

Doping Element	Distribution Coefficient	Literature
Indium antimonide		
Zn	10	(56H1)
	4.13	(59S13)
	3.38	(58S6)
	3.0	(62M5)
	2.3	(58M5)
Cd	0.26	(58M5), (59S13)
Ga	2.4	(58M5)
Ge	0.045	(57F2)
Sn	0.057	(58M5)
P	0.16	"
As	5.4	"
S	0.1	(56H1)
Se	0.5	"
	0.35	(58M5)
	0.17	(59S13), (58S6)
Te	3.5	(60M5)
	≈ 1	(58M5)
	0.54	(59S13), (58S6)
Fe	0.04	(58M12)
Cu	6.6×10^{-4}	"
Ag	4.9×10^{-5}	"
Au	1.9×10^{-6}	"
Te	5.2×10^{-4}	"
Ni	6.0×10^{-5}	"
Indium arsenide		
Mg	0.7	(56S2)
Zn	0.77	"
Cd	0.13	"
Si	0.40	"
Ge	0.07	(57F2)
Sn	0.09	"
S	1.0	(56S2)
Se	0.93	"
Te	0.44	"
Indium phosphide		
Ge	0.05	(57F2)

Table 5.3 Distribution Coefficients $k_c = C_s/C_l$ for Some of the Elements in III-V Compounds (*Continued*)

Doping Element	Distribution Coefficient	Literature
Sn	0.03	(57F2)
S	≈0.8	(60F8)
Se	≈0.6	"
Gallium antimonide		
Zn	0.3	(61H4)
	0.16	(62W4)
Cd	0.02	(61H4)
In	≈1	(62W4)
Si	≈1	(61H4)
Ge	0.32	(57F2)
	0.2	(61H4)
	0.08	(62W4)
Sn	≈0.01	(57F2)
As	2–4	(62W4)
S	0.06	"
Se	0.18	"
	0.4	(61H4)
Te	0.4	(61H4), (62W4)
Gallium arsenide		
Ag	0.1	(60W2)
Mg	0.3	"
Ca	<0.02	"
Zn	0.1	"
	0.27–0.9	(60W4)
Cd	<0.02	(60W2)
Al	3	"
In	0.1	"
C	0.8	(60G9)
Si	0.1	(60W2)
	0.14	(60W4)
Ge	0.03	(60W2)
	0.018	(60W4)
Sn	0.03	(60W2)
Pb	<0.02	"
P	2	"
Sb	<0.02	"
S	0.3	"
	0.5–1.0	(60W4)
Se	0.44–0.55	(60W4)
Te	0.3	(60W2)
	0.054–0.16	(60W4)

Table 5.3 Distribution Coefficients $k_c = C_s/C_l$ for Some of the Elements in III-V Compounds (*Continued*)

Doping Element	Distribution Coefficient	Literature
Mn	0.05	(62V1)
Fe	0.003	(60W4)
Ni	<0.02	(60W2)
Cu	<0.002	(60W4)
Aluminum antimonide		
Mg	0.1	(60H6)
C	0.6	"
Si	0.045	(62S5)
Ge	0.026	"
Sn	$(2\text{–}8) \times 10^{-4}$	"
Fe	0.02	(60H6)
Cu	0.01	"
Mn	0.01	"
Co	0.002	"
Zn	0.02	"
Cd	0.002	"
S	0.003	"
Se	0.003	"
Te	0.01	"
B	0.01–0.02	(58A4)
Pb, V, Ni, Ti	0.01	"

(59S13) and Merten and Hatcher (62M5) showed that at least two parameters influence the distribution coefficient; the velocity with which the plane of solidification moves, and the zinc concentration in the melt. Strauss determined k_c on single crystals which were produced by the Czochralski method with different pulling speeds and different rates of rotation of the growing single crystal. For a pulling speed of 3.8 cm/hr and a rotation of 113 rpm, k_{Zn} was 2.71; at 39 rpm, it was only 2.44. For slower pulling speeds k_{Zn} rose to 3.52 at 1.5 cm/hr. From these measurements the value of 4.13, listed in the table, is obtained by extrapolating to zero pulling speed. Merten and Hatcher investigated k_{Zn} as a function of the zinc-concentration in the melt and found, below 10^{19} Zn atoms/cm^3, $k_{Zn} = 3$, and above this value a rapid decrease of k_{Zn} down to 0.2 at 3×10^{20} Zn atoms/cm^3. Since k_{Zn} is of the order of 1, zinc is difficult to remove from InSb by the procedures described. Hulme and Mullin (57H5) have therefore studied the possibility of zone pulling under vacuum, which causes vaporization of volatile impurities, such as zinc.

For selenium and tellurium Mullin and Hulme (60M5) and Allred and Bate (61A3) found a strong dependence of the distribution coefficient on the orientation of the plane of solidification relative to the crystal axes. The distribution coefficient is largest for both elements if the growth direction coincides with the [111]-direction. Crystals pulled in the [111]-direction by the Czochralski method have a core enriched with selenium or tellurium, since the solid-liquid interface is generally curved toward the edge of the crystal. According to Mullin and Hulme, k_{Te} in other growth directions can be as much as a factor of 6 smaller. This explains the scatter of the values of k_{Te} given in Table 5.3. The distribution coefficient of sulfur is also strongly direction dependent in InSb (62B1).

Hulme and Mullin (62H15) give an extensive discussion of the technology of InSb.

Indium Arsenide. Among all the III-V compounds only the antimonides have a negligible vapor pressure at the melting point (10^{-3} to 10^{-1} Torr). In contrast the vapor pressure of the arsenides lies between 0.1 and 1 atm and that of the phosphides between 50 and 60 atm. Zone refining and crystal pulling can take place only in closed ampules under special precautions, to prevent the vaporization of one of the components (56G5). The high vapor pressure can often be reduced by the use of a nonstoichiometric melt. For the technological procedures we refer to (60F8), for example.

In these procedures the melt strongly interacts with the gas phase, thus increasing the interchange of impurities with the gas phase. Distribution coefficients determined from the application of eq. (5.1) or (5.2) to measured impurity profiles no longer have any direct physical meaning, although they may still be of interest as a measure of the purification possible. The values will, however, depend on the experimental conditions.

The difficulties created by the vapor pressure at the melting point are still relatively small for InAs. The melting point lies below 1000°C and the vapor pressure is 0.3 atm.

The known distribution coefficients are listed in Table 5.3. Sulfur has a distribution coefficient of 1 and cannot be removed from InAs by zone refining. Selenium has a similarly unfortunate distribution coefficient. Nothing is known so far about the dependence of the distribution coefficient on the direction of growth, on the speed of growth, and on similar parameters.

The purest InAs produced so far had an electron concentration of about 10^{16} cm^{-3}. Intrinsic conductivity has not yet been reached at room temperature ($n_i \approx 2 \times 10^{15}$ cm^{-3}). For procedures for the preparation of very pure InAs Effer (61E2), for example, may be consulted.

Indium Phosphide. In InP the vapor pressure of the compound at the melting point (1058°C) is about 21 atm (63R2), and the vapor pressure of a melt of 55% In and 45% P is still 15–20 atm (58F2). For the technology of InP we refer, for example, to (60W2). Purities of 10^{16} impurity atoms/cm^3 have so far been obtained.

Not much is known about the distribution coefficients in InP. Some quantities are listed in Table 5.3.

Gallium Antimonide. Technologically GaSb is similar to InSb. However, under zone refining the impurity concentration cannot be reduced below 1.5×10^{17} acceptors/cm^3. This value is independent of the crucible material used, of the atmosphere, and of the procedures chosen for the chemical purification of the components. As we have mentioned elsewhere, this fact may be an indication of a true nonstoichiometry.

Distribution coefficients (Table 5.3) have been reported by Folberth and Schillmann (57F2), Hall and Racette (61H4), and Willardson (62W4). The values of Willardson's refer to growth in the [111]-direction. For other growth directions this author, in some cases, found different values.

Just as in InSb, Merten and Hatcher (63M6) also observed a strong dependence of the zinc distribution coefficient on the zinc concentration in the melt in GaSb. With increasing zinc concentration (as well as with increasing gallium content) k_{Zn} decreases.

Gallium Arsenide. The technology of GaAs is similar to that of InAs, except that the higher vapor pressure [1.0 atm (63R2)] at the melting point (1240°C) creates additional difficulties. There has, however, been a considerable interest in GaAs because of the many applications that this material is being used for, and its technology is particularly well developed [see, e.g., (60W2)]. It can be produced with extremely high resistance. This question will be considered in Section 531 in the discussion of "semi-insulating" GaAs and GaP.

The known distribution coefficients are given in Table 5.3. Some of the values are still uncertain. In particular, k_{Cu} is probably considerably smaller, since copper diffuses rapidly in the solid phase, smoothing out the copper distribution during zone-pulling.

Gallium Phosphide. The technology of GaP (61G10) is again similar to that of InP but is complicated by the higher melting point (1467°C) and vapor pressure (35 atm) (63R2). Like GaAs, it can be produced with very high resistivity. This topic will be considered in Section 531.

Aluminum Antimonide. This compound has a high melting point (1065°C) but a low vapor pressure above the melt (10^{-1} Torr). The technological difficulties of this material are due to the intense reaction of aluminum with crucible materials and to the fact that AlSb corrodes easily. Samples with hole concentration of 3×10^{15} cm^{-3} have been prepared. There are, however, no measurements of the amount of compensation of such samples, and so the purity achieved is not yet known.

Table 5.3 again contains values of distribution coefficients.

We will not present any technological details of the remaining arsenides, phosphides, and nitrides. For BN we refer to (57W2), (61B9), (62W3), for BP to (57P3), for AlN and GaN to (57K3), (59R4), (59W5), (60T2), (61A1), (62L6), and to literature cited in Section 532.

No distribution coefficients are known for any of these substances.

521 Diffusion. The methods discussed in Section 520 are not very suitable for producing predetermined inhomogeneous impurity distributions. It is possible to form adjacent zones of different doping in a single crystal by changing the doping in the melt during the growth of the crystals by the Czochralski method. Inhomogeneities can also be built into the crystal by partial melting, doping of the melt, and subsequent regrowth. However, this does not allow one to obtain a well-defined impurity gradient in the inside of the crystal. A more suitable method for this purpose is diffusion of a foreign impurity from the surface to the interior.

The diffusion of both impurities and lattice atoms in a semiconductor is also of interest for other reasons. All changes of the impurity distribution in a semiconductor take place through diffusion. The aging of rectifiers and other devices, and the evaporation of impurity atoms out of the semiconductor at elevated temperatures, are examples of processes to which diffusion contributes significantly.

The most important method for the determination of the diffusion of foreign atoms and lattice atoms in a semiconductor is the measurement of the penetration profile of the foreign substance, which was previously located on the surface or in an adjacent phase, and subsequently diffused into the crystal during annealing at elevated temperature. For the details of this method compare for example, (57G2) and (61G14). The penetration profile is determined most accurately by using radioactive tracer atoms. The surface is then removed, layer by layer, through grinding, and the specific activity in each removed layer is measured. In this way the concentration profile of the diffusing atoms is obtained as a function of the depth below the original surface. If the diffusion mechanism can be described by a single diffusion coefficient D, independent of the concentration of the diffusing atoms (Fick's law), then for a semi-infinite wafer the concentration profile $C(x)$ (x = the depth below the surface) is given by

$$C(x) = C(0)\left(1 - \operatorname{erf}\frac{x}{2\sqrt{Dt}}\right) = C(0)\operatorname{erfc}\frac{x}{2\sqrt{Dt}} \tag{5.3}$$

if the diffusion takes place from a neighboring phase of constant concentration, and by

$$C(x) = \frac{Q}{\sqrt{\pi Dt}} e^{-x^2/4Dt} \tag{5.4}$$

if the diffusion comes from a surface layer of thickness l and concentration $C = Q/l$.

Examples of the concentration profiles defined by (5.3) and (5.4) are given in Figs. 5.3 and 5.4.

The use of radioactive tracers is the only method that measures the concentration profile and not just a penetration depth. It thereby makes it possible to determine the diffusion mechanism unambiguously. Some of the other experiments that give information about the diffusion in semiconductors are potential measurements along a surface parallel to the diffusion direction and the determination of the location of the *p-n* junction after diffusing acceptors into a homogeneous *n*-type semiconductor.

The temperature dependence of the diffusion coefficient is generally given by $D = D_0 e^{-\Delta E/kT}$.

Indium Antimonide. The *self-diffusion* of indium and antimony in InSb was investigated by Eisen and Birchenall (57E3) and Boltaks and Kulinov (57B3). The results are summarized in Table 5.4, as are all the other experimental data to be presented in this section. The large discrepancy in the order of magnitudes of D_0 and ΔE between the two authors is striking. Since experimental details are not given in (57B3), one cannot unambiguously decide which of the two sets of values is correct. However, there is strong indirect evidence in favor of one set. We will see that the activation energies ΔE for the diffusion of zinc and cadmium lie somewhat below the value 1.81 eV, but well above the value 0.28 eV. It can safely be assumed that the diffusion mechanism for zinc, cadmium, and indium is the same in InSb, and, furthermore, that an indium atom is bound more strongly to the lattice than a zinc or cadmium, so that $\Delta E_{\mathrm{In}} \gtrsim \Delta E_{\mathrm{Zn}}, \Delta E_{\mathrm{Cd}}$. This implies that the values given by Eisen and Birchenall must be the correct ones. According to Goldstein (60G10), the much smaller values of Boltaks and Kulinov can perhaps be explained by the fact that the

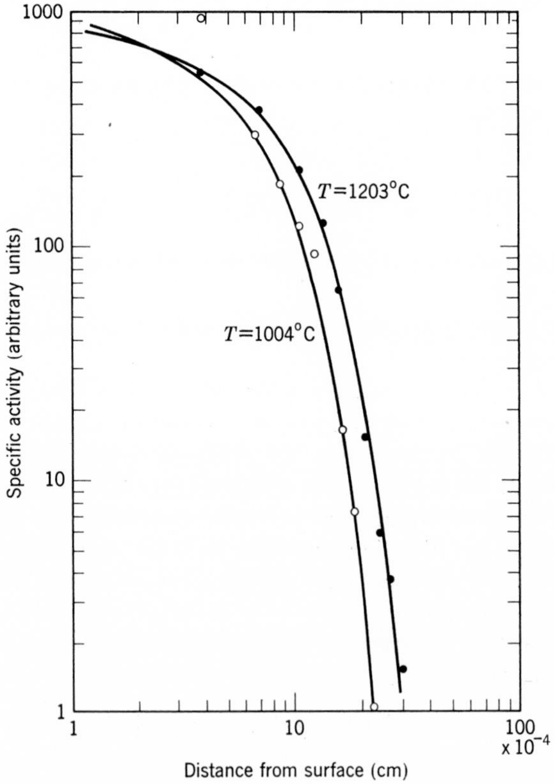

Fig. 5.3 Diffusion profile of sulphur in GaAs under diffusion from a neighboring gas phase [after Goldstein (61G14)].

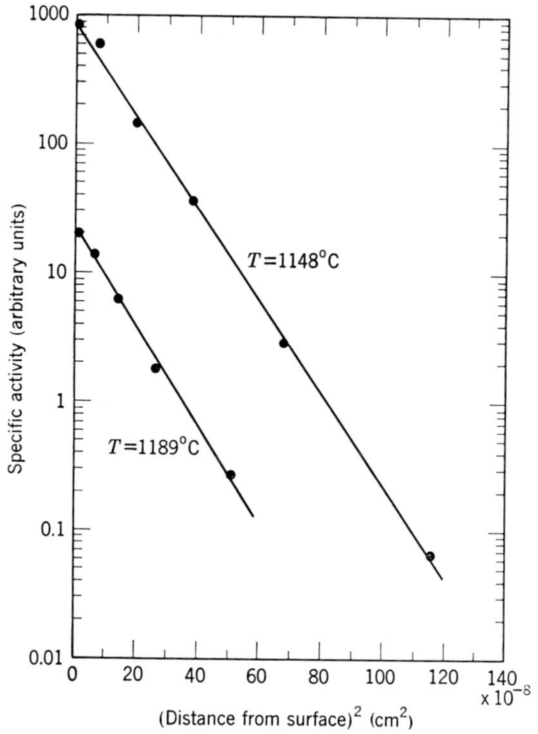

Fig. 5.4 Diffusion profile of gallium in GaAs under diffusion from a gallium layer on the surface [after Goldstein (61G14)].

samples investigated had a high dislocation density and that therefore a preferred diffusion took place along these dislocations. Another possibility is that at the elevated temperature antimony diffused out of the sample simultaneously with the indium indiffusion. This would simulate an increased indiffusion.

Even if this discrepancy between the experimental values is ignored, it is clear that the self-diffusion of indium and of antimony is different. Such a difference in the diffusion coefficients of the two components will also be found in the other III-V compounds. Eisen and Birchenall conclude therefrom that the two components diffuse separately in their respective sublattices. Substitutional diffusion takes place, in which the individual process is a jump of an atom into a vacancy located at the second-nearest-neighbor position. All the nearest neighbors of any given atom belong to the other sublattice in the

Table 5.4 Diffusion Coefficient $D = D_0 e^{-\Delta E/kT}$ for Self-Diffusion and for Diffusion of Foreign Atoms in III-V Compounds

Diffusing Element	D_0 (cm²/sec)	ΔE (eV)	Temp. (°C)	Method	Literature
Indium antimonide					
In	0.05	1.81	450–500	Tracer	(57E3)
"	1.8×10^{-9}	0.28		"	(57B3)
Sb	0.05	1.94	450–500	"	(57E3)
"	1.4×10^{-6}	0.75		"	(57B3)
Zn	0.5	1.35	360–500	"	(60G10)
"	1.6×10^{6}	2.3 ± 0.3	"	*p-n*	(59H7)
"	5.5	1.6	"	"	(62W5)
(single crystal)	1.4×10^{-7}	0.86	390–512	Tracer	(61S19)
(polycrystal)	1.7×10^{-7}	0.85	"	"	"
Cd	1.3×10^{-4}	1.2	360–500	*p-n*	(62W5)
	1.23×10^{-9}	0.52	442–519	Tracer	(63W1)
	1.0×10^{-5}	1.1	250–500	"	(63B11)
Sn	5.5×10^{-8}	0.75	390–512	"	(61S19)
Te	1.7×10^{-7}	0.57	300–500	"	(57B3)
Au	7×10^{-4}	0.32	140–510	"	(64B4)
Fe, Co, Ni	10^{-7}	0.25	440–510	"	(62W1)
Indium arsenide					
Mg	1.98×10^{-6}	1.17	600–900	*p-n*	(56S1)
Zn	3.11×10^{-3}	1.17	"	"	"
Cd	4.35×10^{-4}	1.17	"	"	"
Ge	3.74×10^{-6}	1.17	"	"	"
Sn	1.49×10^{-6}	1.17	"	"	"
S	6.78	2.20	"	"	"
Se	12.55	2.20	600–900	*p-n*	(56S1)
Te	3.43×10^{-5}	1.28	"	"	"
Indium phosphide					
In	1×10^{5}	3.85 ± 0.05	850–1000	Tracer	(61G14)
P	7×10^{10}	5.65 ± 0.06	"	"	"
Gallium antimonide					
Ga	3.2×10^{3}	3.15	650–700	"	(57E3)
Sb	3.4×10^{4}	3.44	"	"	"
	8.7×10^{-3}	1.13	470–570	"	(59B9)
In	1.2×10^{-7}	0.53	400–650	"	"
Sn	2.4×10^{-5}	0.80	320–570	"	"
Te	3.8×10^{-4}	1.2	400–650	"	"

Table 5.4 Diffusion Coefficient $D = D_0 e^{-\Delta E/kT}$ for Self-Diffusion and for Diffusion of Foreign Atoms in III-V Compounds (*Continued*)

Diffusing Element	D_0 (cm^2/sec)	ΔE (eV)	Temp. (°C)	Method	Literature
Gallium arsenide					
Ga	1×10^7	5.60 ± 0.32	1125–1250	Tracer	(61G14)
As	4×10^{21}	10.2 ± 1.2	1200–1250	"	"
Li	0.53	1.0	250–400	"	(62F4)
Cd	0.05 ± 0.04	2.43 ± 0.06	868–1149	"	(60G8)
Zn	15 ± 7	2.49 ± 0.05	800	"	"
S	4×10^3	4.04 ± 0.15	1000–1200	"	(61G14)
Se	3×10^3	4.16 ± 0.16	"	"	"
Sn	6×10^{-4}	2.5	1069–1215	"	(61G15)
Cu	0.03	0.52	100–600	"	(62H3)
Ag	4×10^{-4}	0.8 ± 0.05	500–1160	"	(63B10)
Au	10^{-3}	1.0 ± 0.2	740–1024	"	(64S3)
Aluminum antimonide					
Al		≈ 1.8			(59P4)
Sb		≈ 1.5			"
Zn	0.33 ± 0.15	1.93 ± 0.04	660–860	"	(62S4)
Cu	3.5×10^{-3}	0.36	150–500	"	(60W5)

zinc-blende structure. A diffusion through jumps to nearest-neighbor vacancies would mean equal diffusion coefficients for indium and antimony in InSb.

The experimental investigations of diffusion of foreign atoms in InSb and other III-V compounds confirm the mechanism of sublattice diffusion in these binary compounds. The diffusion of *zinc* in InSb was investigated by Goldstein (60G10), Hulme and Kemp (59H7), Wilson and Heasell (62W5), Sze and Wei (61S19), and Pumper and Prostoserdova (64P2). Whereas Goldstein used radioactive tracers (Zn^{65}), the other studies determined the penetration depth from the position of the *p-n* junction formed in Se-doped material. Two such measurements make it possible to determine D from eq. (5.3) *if* the diffusion front is given by (5.3). The latter requirement makes this method uncertain. Since the data of Hulme and Kemp agree only poorly with the values of Goldstein, Wilson and Heasell determined the penetration depth more thoroughly on a larger number of differently doped samples. They found that the diffusion profile cannot be described accurately by (5.3). Their discussion showed that two factors may impair the concentration profile, a simultaneous out-diffusion of selenium and a limited supply of zinc from the gas phase to the surface. Taking account of these two processes and using plausible parameters leads to the diffusion coefficients given in Table 5.4, which agree well with the values of Goldstein.

Sze and Wei found still different values for zinc diffusion in InSb, in particular, an activation energy which is only half as large as that found by the others. They point out that, especially in InSb, other lattice defects can influence the diffusion. Measurements on a polycrystal sample resulted in a diffusion coefficient about an order of magnitude larger than that on a single crystal, with about the same activation energy. They observed that the diffusion of *tin* in single-crystal InSb could be described by (5.3) with an activation energy smaller than that for zinc. In contrast, the diffusion profiles in polycrystalline matter had an entirely different appearance and suggested that grain-boundary diffusion was taking place. In interpreting this behavior, Sze and Wei assumed that tin, as an element of group IV, diffuses in both sublattices, but zinc as a group II element, only in the indium sublattice. This would explain the smaller activation energy in tin. If one assumes furthermore that the grain boundaries in InSb are rich in vacancies in the antimony sublattice, then the grain boundaries facilitate only the diffusion of tin, not that of zinc.

The size of the activation energy for zinc diffusion confirms the assumption of a substitutional diffusion, if one compares it with values obtained for germanium. In the latter $\Delta E = 3.0$ eV for self-diffusion, and $\Delta E \approx 2.5$ eV for substitutional diffusion, whereas for interstitial diffusion much smaller activation energies are observed (for lithium, e.g., 0.5 eV).

Table 5.4 also contains data for the diffusion of *gold, cadmium, tellurium, iron, cobalt,* and *nickel.* For the last three the diffusion profiles had a form proportional to $e^{-x/L}$. This behavior, which has also been observed in germanium, can be ascribed to simultaneous substitutional and interstitial diffusion with interaction between these two mechanisms, according to Watt and Chen (62W1).

The diffusion of *copper* in InSb is complicated because different diffusion mechanisms exist side by side at the same time. Aside from a rapid interstitial diffusion ($D \approx 10^{-5}$ cm^2/sec) various other mechanisms are possible, according to Stocker (63S8), in which there are interactions between copper atoms and lattice defects.

Indium Arsenide. Only measurements of Schillmann (56S1) are available for diffusion of foreign atoms in InAs. The values given in

Table 5.4 were obtained by a *p-n* method with the (unproved) assumption of a diffusion profile according to (5.3). Leaving out the uncertain value for tellurium, one finds that the impurity atoms of group II have a uniform activation energy, and that the same is true for the group VI atoms. This confirms the assumption of a sublattice diffusion in the III- and V-sublattices. Since germanium and tin have the same activation energy as the elements of group II, one can assume that these elements diffuse in the III-sublattice. This assumption is supported also by the donor character of germanium and tin in InAs (Table 5.1).

Indium Phosphide. Values of the diffusion coefficient for self-diffusion in InP are contained in Table 5.4. The difference in the activation energies again points to sublattice diffusion. If diffusion took place via the same lattice sites, the phosphorus atoms would have to have a smaller activation energy than the indium atoms, because of their much smaller radius. This is in contrast to the experimental findings.

Gallium Antimonide. The self-diffusion of gallium in GaSb was measured by Eisen and Birchenall (57E3), and for antimony in GaSb also by Boltaks and Gutorov (59B9). As in InSb, there is a strong discrepancy in the two reported values of the diffusion coefficient of antimony. Boltaks and Gutorov also determined the diffusion coefficients of some foreign atoms in GaSb. The values are contained in Table 5.4.

Gallium Arsenide. Among all the III-V compounds, the diffusion has been most thoroughly investigated in GaAs. On the one hand, this is due to the importance of GaAs for technical applications which require the production of *p-n* junctions with given impurity gradients, and, on the other hand, to the appearance of a number of peculiarities in the diffusion which are of interest from the physical standpoint.

The coefficients of *self-diffusion* of gallium and arsenic in GaAs differ strongly from one another. The values given in Table 5.4 show that the activation energy for diffusion in the V-sublattice is much larger than that for diffusion in the III-sublattice. Below 1200°C the diffusion coefficient of arsenic is temperature independent, and a diffusion along dislocation is the probable process, according to (61G14).

The diffusion coefficient of *phosphorus* in GaAs is about 5×10^{-14} cm^2/sec between 725°K and 1125°K, according to Goldstein and Dobin (62G8). Because of the formation of GaP the diffusion profiles cannot be described by eq. (5.3) or (5.4).

The diffusion of *zinc* below 800°C can be described by eq. (5.3) or (5.4), depending on the experimental conditions. The values determined in this temperature region by Goldstein (60G8) are contained in Table 5.4. The diffusion of *cadmium* takes place with the same activation energy as that of zinc, and the same is true of *tin*, which is built into GaAs as a donor in the III-sublattice and diffuses substitutionally in it.

Above 800°C the diffusion profile for the indiffusion of *zinc* in GaAs can no longer be represented by eq. (5.3). Figure 5.5 shows a typical measurement [Cunnell and Gooch (60C7)]. An interpretation of this profile was first attempted by Allen (60A8). He used a model which assumed an equilibrium between Zn^0 and Zn^- ions. The neutral zinc atoms were supposed to diffuse faster than the negatively charged ones. At high concentrations neutral atoms predominate, and diffusion should therefore be more rapid than at low concentrations. There are, however, experimental facts which disagree with this explanation. In particular, the assumption of a large concentration of neutral zinc atoms is not tenable (60G8). In addition, the dependence of the diffusion profile on the arsenic pressure in the neighboring gas phase (58A3), (60C7) cannot be reconciled with this model.

Longini (62L5) suggested that zinc could also diffuse interstitially

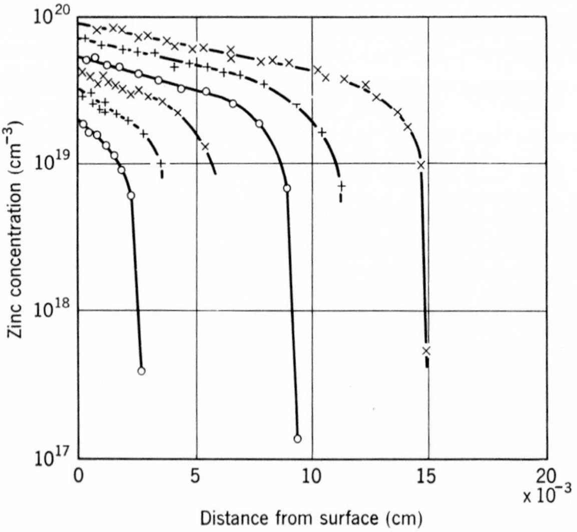

Fig. 5.5 Diffusion profiles of zinc in GaAs at 1000°C ($t = 10^4$ sec), for various surface concentrations [according to Cunnell and Gooch (60C7)].

in GaAs. The diffusion process would then consist of an interstitial diffusion with very large diffusion coefficient combined with a slower diffusion in the gallium sublattice. The two processes are coupled to one another by the equilibrium between interstitially and substitutionally located zinc atoms. Weisberg and Blanc (63W4) have made a quantitative calculation of this situation and have obtained complete agreement with the experimental results. Even though the concentration of interstitial zinc is a few orders of magnitude smaller than that of substitutional zinc, the former controls the diffusion process because of its larger diffusion coefficient.

For the diffusion of *cadmium* in GaAs Cunnell and Gooch (60C9) found a steep decrease of the cadmium concentration down to 30 μ below the surface, followed by an increase to a depth of about 400 μ and from there on a renewed slow decrease. The first steep decrease gave diffusion coefficients which agreed well with the values of Goldstein (60G8) given in Table 5.4. There are no indications how the subsequent maximum should be interpreted. For further work cf. (63B7), (64K1).

Copper diffuses very rapidly in GaAs (58F6), as in germanium and silicon. Since copper may be built into substitutional as well as interstitial sites, it is likely that the copper atom diffuses interstitially. The diffusion activation energy is correspondingly small (0.52 eV). Further information is contained in (64H3).

Fane and Gross (63F1) have shown that both *tin* and *selenium* also diffuse substitutionally and interstitially. Hence, by interaction of these two mechanisms the diffusion profiles often show an anomalous shape.

Lithium also diffuses very fast in the GaAs lattice (62F4). The diffusion does not follow Fick's law. This is connected with the formation of lithium complexes, which was discussed in Section 512.

The diffusion of *manganese* has been studied by Seltzer (64S2). It seems to occur in jumps involving pairs of lattice defects.

The generally observed sublattice diffusion of the substitutional impurities is controlled by the vacancy concentration in the relevant sublattice. The latter depends on the arsenic pressure in the neighboring gas phase. Vieland (61V1) therefore investigated the diffusion of different impurities in GaAs as a function of the arsenic-vapor pressure. The position of a *p-n* junction formed by the diffusing impurities after a fixed annealing time was taken as a measure of the diffusion. The results are shown in Fig. 5.6. Although large effects are observed, it would be premature to attempt to interpret these curves.

In vacancy diffusion the transition of a vacancy from one sublattice to the other is very unlikely, since a jump of an atom into the sublattice of the other component of the compound would take place at the same time. Only when impurities are contained in the lattice which can occupy both sublattices is such a vacancy transition possible. In this case the diffusion of vacancies will obey different laws from those prevailing when this transition is not possible. A qualitative proof of these considerations was provided by McCaldin (61M8) in investigating vacancy diffusion in GaAs with varying *germanium* content.

Gallium Phosphide. For GaP data are available only about the diffusion of zinc [Chang and Pearson (64C1)]. Below 900°C the diffusion can be described by $D = 7.5 \times 10^{-8} C^{0.45} e^{-2.5/kT}$ cm^2/sec, where $C = 2.6 \times 10^{23} e^{-0.85/kT}$ cm^{-3} is the solubility of zinc in GaP. The diffusion mechanism seems to be a superposition of interstitial and substitutional diffusion.

Aluminum Antimonide. The diffusion of zinc in AlSb can be described by eq. (5.3). For not too high doping, the diffusion constant is independent of other impurities contained in the crystal. For

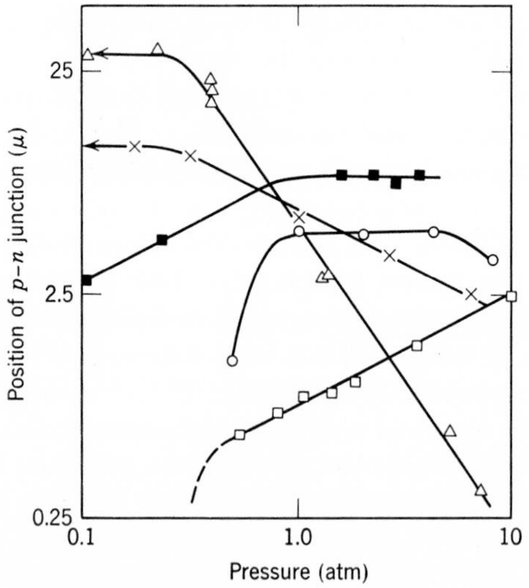

Fig. 5.6 Diffusion of various foreign atoms in GaAs as a function of the arsenic vapor pressure. Ordinate: position of the *p-n* junction below the surface after a controlled diffusion process [according to Vieland (61V1)]. ○, Sulfur: 1000°C, $t = 45$ min; △, manganese: 900°C, $t = 30$ min; ×, zinc: 800°C, $t = 45$ min; □, tin: 1000°C, $t = 60$ min; ■, silicon: 1150°C, $t = 90$ min.

acceptor densities larger than 5×10^{18} acceptors/cm^3 such a dependence is found, however. A similar dependence was observed when the donor concentration was larger than 3×10^{17} donors/cm^3. The latter phenomenon cannot be reconciled with a restriction of zinc diffusion to the aluminum sublattice, since the donors (tellurium) occupy the antimony sublattice.

Shaw, Jones, and Hazelby (62S4) therefore discuss the possibility that the diffusion of foreign atoms in this case does not take place in one sublattice alone. Rather, an impurity located substitutionally in one sublattice forms a complex with an impurity in the other sublattice, and the complex then diffuses as a whole. This model can qualitatively explain all anomalies of the zinc diffusion in AlSb and furthermore could furnish an explanation for the fact that in all compounds the activation energy for self-diffusion is higher than that for diffusion of impurity atoms.

Finally, Table 5.4 contains information about the diffusion of copper, and preliminary values of the self-diffusion coefficients of AlSb.

522 Heat treatment and lattice defects. The electrical properties of a semiconductor can often be changed if it is held at elevated temperature for a prolonged period of time and then quenched to room temperature. This change in electrical properties is caused by a change in impurity distribution. A number of different processes may play a role here:

1. At high temperatures the diffusion of impurities is facilitated. They may therefore diffuse into a semiconductor from a near-by phase.
2. Deviations from stoichiometry may be produced by the out-diffusion of atoms of one component of a semiconducting compound.
3. The solubility of foreign atoms in a semiconductor is temperature dependent. An excess of impurities may be frozen in by quenching from a high temperature. This process may be reversed by annealing and slow cooling to room temperature.
4. The higher concentration of lattice defects that is present in equilibrium at higher temperatures may be frozen in by quenching. This process is also reversible.

Extensive studies of the behavior of III-V compounds under prolonged heating are available for InAs and GaAs.

In **InAs** Dixon and Enright (59D1), (59D2) found an increase of donor density, independent of the original doping, after heat treatment above 450°C and subsequent rapid cooling of the sample. Changes in the carrier concentration of more than 10^{17} cm^{-3} were obtained. An example is shown in Fig. 5.7. The concentration change could be reversed by annealing below 300°C. The number of donors created by heating was a smooth function of the heating time for a given sample, but varied strongly from sample to sample. The smaller the mobility of the sample, the larger were the changes of its electrical properties. This fact suggests that the donors are electrically inactive scattering centers before annealing and are made electrically active by the heat treatment. It can be explained if one assumes, following Dixon and Enright, that the donors are foreign atoms which locate preferentially at dislocations where they only influence the mobility as scattering centers. During the heat treatment they diffuse away from the dislocations and then are locally frozen in by the quenching. They return to the dislocation during annealing at slightly elevated temperature.

Dixon and Enright first assumed the impurities to be sulfur or

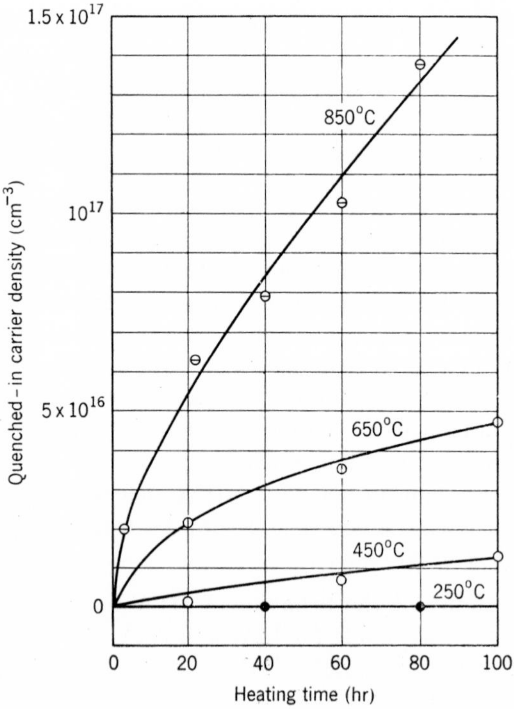

Fig. 5.7 Donor formation in n-InAs by heat treatment at elevated temperature and subsequent quenching [after Dixon and Enright (59D2)].

copper and excluded the possibility that they might be lattice defects. Later Hilsum (59H3) showed that the changes caused by heat treatment decrease by the same amount during annealing as changes in the electrical properties of InAs caused by doping with copper. Edmond and Hilsum (60E2) even found that effects caused by heat treatment slowly disappeared during prolonged storage at room temperature. A small remaining irreversible change (decrease below the original donor concentration) could not be interpreted.

These experiments suggest that the reversible changes of the electrical properties of InAs during heat treatment can be ascribed to the diffusion of copper and to its preferential location at dislocations.

In **InSb** an increase in the number of acceptors has been observed during heat treatment by Iljin and Gorbacheva (61I2). This result could be explained by the diffusion of copper, since this element is an acceptor in InSb. In **InP** a small decrease of the electron concentration in *n*-type material during heat treatment at 600°C has been observed, but a conversion from *n*- to *p*-type conduction has not been obtained (60W2). Attempts to create such a conversion by the indiffusion of copper were not successful, probably because of the formation of CuP on the surface of the sample.

Extensive measurements are available for **GaAs.** Even short-time heating to 800–1000°C converts *n*-GaAs to *p*-GaAs [cf., e.g., (63F5)]. Investigations of Wysocki (60W11) and Edmond (60E1) indicated that here also copper can be made responsible. Weisberg, Rosi, and Herkart (60W2) showed in more detail that most effects due to heat treatment in GaAs must be connected with copper. These authors annealed numerous GaAs samples for long times at temperatures up to 1000°C. The temperature at which conversion from *n*- to *p*-type conduction took place was independent of the initial concentration of electrons but was at least 600°C. The following observations confirmed the influence of copper. A vacancy indiffusion through evaporation of arsenic could be ruled out, since conversion did not depend on the composition of the gas phase or on the arsenic pressure. Rather it was determined that the indiffusion of an acceptor took place. The activation energy for the diffusion of this acceptor was 0.6–0.8 eV, and the diffusion coefficient was about 10^{-18} cm^2 sec^{-1} at 700°C. The solubility of the acceptor was about 10^{16} cm^{-3} at 700°C and 10^{17} cm^{-3} at 850°C. All these data were found in Section 521 to be characteristic of the diffusion and solubility of copper. Finally the ionization energy of the acceptors in heat-treated and in Cu-doped samples was the same.

Copper cannot be made electrically inactive in GaAs by annealing at low temperature, as is the case in InAs. For this the diffusion coefficient of the substitutional copper is too small. During heating in molten KCN, copper is segregated out because of formation of cyanide complexes. This procedure, as well as careful removal of all traces of copper in the starting materials, in the crucibles, and in the etching solutions, produces samples which no longer show conversion during heat treatment.

Investigations of Blanc, Bube, and Weisberg (62B10), (64B2) showed that annealing between 450 and 800°C can produce large numbers of traps in GaAs ($>10^{19}$ cm^{-3}). The annealing experiments can be interpreted by postulating the existence of one kind each of donors and acceptors which, during growth, are built into the lattice in the inactive state. Annealing then makes the defects electrically active. The active donors and acceptors appear as pairs, with ionization energies of 0.2 eV each, or separate, with ionization energies of 0.5 eV each. Extensive annealing experiments were performed on crystals grown by different methods, with and without the presence of copper. All observations point to the conclusion that the donors and acceptors are lattice defects and that copper acts only as a reaction center for the activation of the defects. Possible donor-acceptor pairs, according to Blanc, Bube, and Weisberg, are $Ga_{interstitial}$-$As_{vacancy}$ pairs or $As_{interstitial}$-$Ga_{vacancy}$ pairs, which can be built into the crystal as microprecipitates, or $Ga_{vacancy}$-$As_{vacancy}$ pairs, which are built in as microvoids.

We have seen in Section 512 that some authors ascribe levels found in Cu-doped GaAs to defects produced by copper. This question has been investigated by Fuller, Wolfstirn, and Allison (64F1). They assume two donor levels at 0.15 and 0.45 eV below the conduction band to be formed by copper at Ga-sites and one acceptor level at (0.10 ± 0.005) eV above the valence band to belong to a Ga-vacancy produced by the copper.

Large quantities of lattice defects in GaAs have also been observed by Goldstein and Almeleh (63G8) in paramagnetic resonance experiments. However, these are different kinds of defects from the ones we have discussed.

523 Bombardment with particles. The electrical properties of a semiconductor can be changed by bombardment with particles (neutrons, electrons, etc.). The change can be reversible (creation of lattice defects, which can act as acceptors, donors, or traps) or irreversible (nuclear reactions which transform a lattice atom into an impurity atom).

In elements such as germanium and silicon there are two possible different one-dimensional lattice defects: vacancies and interstitial atoms. In contrast, the number of possible lattice defects in binary compounds is considerably larger. Aside from vacancies in one of the sublattices, atoms of one sublattice can be located in the other sublattice. Both kinds of atoms can be built in interstitially, and there are two such locations in the zinc-blende lattice, one that is surrounded by four trivalent neighbors, and one that is surrounded by four pentavalent neighbors. All in all, there are eight kinds of lattice defects.

We have emphasized in Section 50 that the substitution of one lattice atom by another from the other sublattice is very unlikely. If we leave such replacements out of consideration, the remaining six defects can combine into four different vacancy-interstitial pairs (Frenkel defects). All can be created by particle bombardment. Because of this variety of lattice defects the number of possible states in the forbidden gap of a III-V compound is larger than in the case of a semiconducting element.

One method for investigating the defects produced and their energy levels is the measurement of the change of conductivity during the bombardment. Such a change will be due mainly to a decrease or an increase in the number of free carriers, and only to a small extent to a change in mobility caused by increased scattering at lattice defects. The measurement then gives the number of acceptors or donors created per absorbed particle.

The energy levels of the lattice defects generally lie deeper in the forbidden gap than the levels of the normal donors and acceptors which determine the conductivity. Particle bombardment will therefore first lead to the creation of traps for the free carriers and an increase in the resistance. If the number of lattice defects exceeds the number of impurities that were originally present in the crystal, the conductivity type is determined by the lattice defects and the resistance approaches a saturation value independent of its original value (location of the Fermi level at the energy level of the created lattice defects). An example is seen in Fig. 5.8, where the changes in conductivity of an n- and a p-type InSb sample during *neutron* bombardment are shown. The saturation value lies in the region of n-type conduction; the minimum in the curve of the p-type sample indicates the point of conversion to n-conductivity.

That the bombarding neutrons primarily create lattice defects is shown by the possibility of annealing out, at elevated temperatures, the changes in electrical conductivity created by the bombardment. An example is presented in Fig. 5.9.

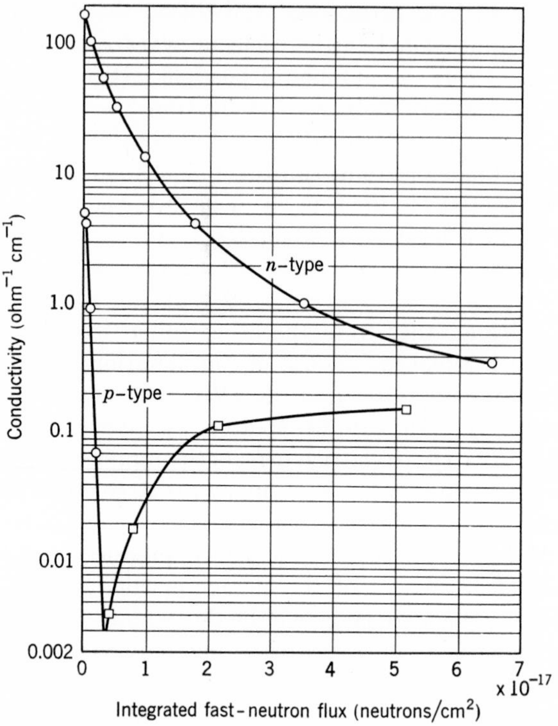

Fig. 5.8 Conductivity of InSb at $-196°C$ after bombardment in a reactor [after Cleland and Crawford (54C1)].

The behavior of the conductivity in Fig. 5.8 means that the final location of the Fermi level is in the upper half of the forbidden gap. Cleland and Crawford (54C1) interpret this under the assumption that vacancies and interstitial atoms are created in both sublattices. One suspects that indium and antimony atoms at interstitial positions act as donors, whose outermost electron can easily be split off. The donor levels are therefore close to the conduction band. An equal number of indium and antimony vacancies will be created. They act as acceptors, and it is likely that an antimony vacancy will more easily capture an electron than an indium vacancy. The acceptor levels of the antimony vacancy then lie deeper than those of the indium vacancy. When equal numbers of donors and acceptors are introduced, the electrons will immediately transfer from one to the other. The interstitial atoms leave their outermost electrons in the vacancy and act as

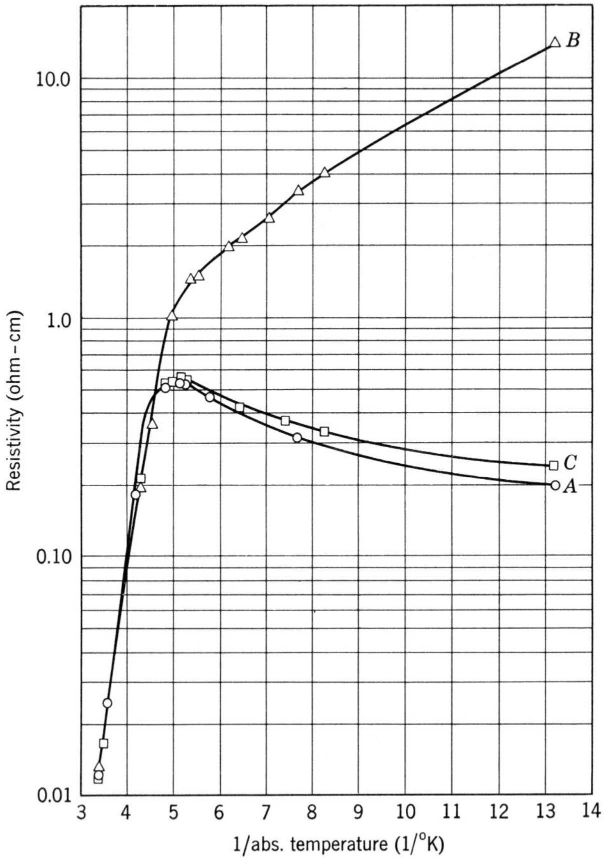

Fig. 5.9 Temperature dependence of the resistance of *p*-InSb before bombardment (*A*), after bombardment with 2×10^{16} neutrons/cm^2 (*B*), and after vacuum annealing for 40 hr at 350°C (*C*) [after Cleland and Crawford (54C1)].

electron traps; the vacancies in contrast will act as hole traps. If the number of defect pairs created exceeds that of the primary impurities, the Fermi level will come to lie between the levels of the interstitial atoms and those of the vacancies in the upper half of the forbidden gap.

Aside from these reversible lattice defects, irreversible changes take place in InSb, particularly under irradiation by thermal neutrons, for which In^{115} has a very large cross section (54C2).

Lattice defects are also created in InSb by bombardment with energetic *electrons*. Aukerman (59A6), (59A7) showed that the energy levels of Frenkel defects produced by 4.5-MeV electrons change with the temperature at which the bombardment takes place, or if the sample is annealed for a short time at an elevated temperature. The reason is that the defects are not stable, but anneal out. The annealing time for a given defect depends on the temperature. A short heat treatment may not lead to the complete elimination of the defects, but only to transformation into a different kind of defect, which has a different level spectrum. Thus 4.5-MeV electrons create a level 0.03 eV above the valence band at 80°K (other levels have not been identified), while at 200°K the levels are 0.048 and 0.081 eV above the valence band and there is an additional group of levels between 0.03 and 0.10 eV below the conduction band.

The number of Frenkel defects created per incoming particle generally lies between 1 and 3. Eisen and Bickel (59E7) were the first to measure this number as a function of energy of the incoming electrons. They observed a slow growth of this number up to about 0.28 MeV and then a steep increase, suggesting that there are two different radiation defects with different threshold energies for creation.

Such competing processes can be studied more easily by measuring *annealing* properties of the radiation defects. Two techniques are of particular interest here. In one, the sample irradiated at low temperature is annealed at various temperatures and the disappearance of the defects is measured as a function of time (isothermal annealing). In the other, the sample is heated in steps, remaining the same fixed time at each temperature. After each step the properties are measured at low temperature (isochronal annealing). As an example, the isochronal annealing of radiation defects in n-InSb is shown in Fig. 5.10. The defects were created by bombardment with 1-MeV electrons at 80°K (61E5). Below the bombardment temperature all the defects are stable; that is, no new defects appear under bombardment at still lower temperatures and anneal out below 80°K. Between liquid-nitrogen temperature and room temperature all radiation defects anneal out. Five steps (I–V on Fig. 5.10) which correspond to threshold energies for various defects can clearly be recognized. They lie at 90, 150, 175, 210, and 275°K, corresponding to threshold energies of 0.34, 0.60, 0.70, 0.79, and 0.96 eV. Of these five steps only the two lowest have been identified as due to recombinations of two close-lying partners of a Frenkel defect. The lower step then probably corresponds to a Frenkel defect in the indium sublattice, the higher one to a defect in the antimony sublattice. For a detailed discussion of these phenomena see (61E5), (63E1), (64E1).

The isochronal annealing in p-InSb is characterized by six steps at 87, 103, 157, 235, 305, and 385°K, according to Eisen (62E5), (63E2).

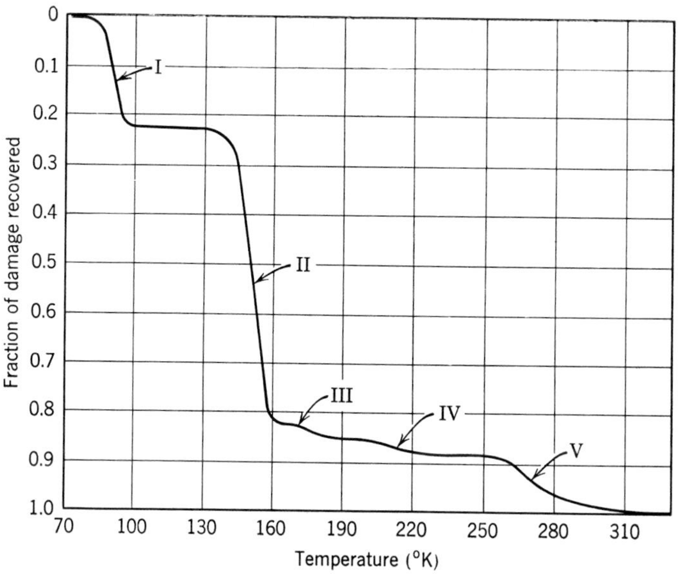

Fig. 5.10 Isochronal healing of radiation defects in *n*-InSb [after Eisen (61E5)].

The two lowest steps seem to correspond to the lowest steps in *n*-InSb. No correlation of the higher steps with those in *n*-InSb was possible.

A comparison of these results with the measurements of Aukerman suggests that perhaps the steps should not be assigned to the annealing out of different defects, but rather that one or more steps may represent threshold energies for the rearrangement of defects into more stable formations. Aukerman (59A7) himself found steps I, II, and V in the same temperature region as Eisen (61E5).

Investigations similar to the ones discussed for InSb have also been made on other III-V compounds.

Measurements on InAs by Aukerman and others (58C3), (59A6), (59A8) showed an *increase* in the conductivity of *n*-type samples under bombardment with neutrons and electrons. This discovery is in contrast to the decrease in conductivity found in InSb and all the other III-V compounds. In InAs radiation either must only create donors, or, if donors and acceptors are created in pairs, the donors must be doubly ionized, the acceptors singly. Only the second possibility agrees with the assumption that radiation defects are always vacancy-interstitial pairs, but this question is not yet completely decided. Bäuerlein (61B6) investigated the radiation damage in InAs from

400-keV electrons at 63°K and found steps at 85, 120, 300°K from isochronal annealing curves, corresponding to threshold energies of 0.23, 0.33, and 0.8 eV. Finally, under bombardment of *p*-type InAs samples Aukerman observed a double sign change in the temperature dependence of the Hall coefficient, as was discussed in Section 411.

A decrease in the conductivity under bombardment by neutrons was also found in GaSb (55C1), InP, GaAs, and AlSb (59A6).

Results of bombardment of GaAs by neutrons and electrons (59W4), (61A10), (64A9), (63V2) showed some anomalies. We will restrict ourselves here to the annealing processes. Figure 5.11 shows isochronal annealing curves for neutron-irradiated GaAs (curve *A*) and electron-irradiated GaAs (curve *B*). The annealing process is not completed in the temperature range under consideration. The radiation damage in electron-irradiated GaAs disappears completely in a single step at about 220°C. In neutron-irradiated GaAs the annealing takes place in a number of steps, of which the first one also lies at 220°C, with another one at about 450°C. A possible explanation (61A10) is that under neutron irradiation the crystal structure in regions along the trajectory of the neutron is badly disturbed, in addition to the individual Frenkel defects formed. The disturbed regions anneal in the second step, while the first step is due to the annealing of the Frenkel defects (which can also be created by electrons). An anomalous temperature dependence of the electron mobility, which was found by Willardson (59W4) in neutron-irradiated *n*-GaAs, can

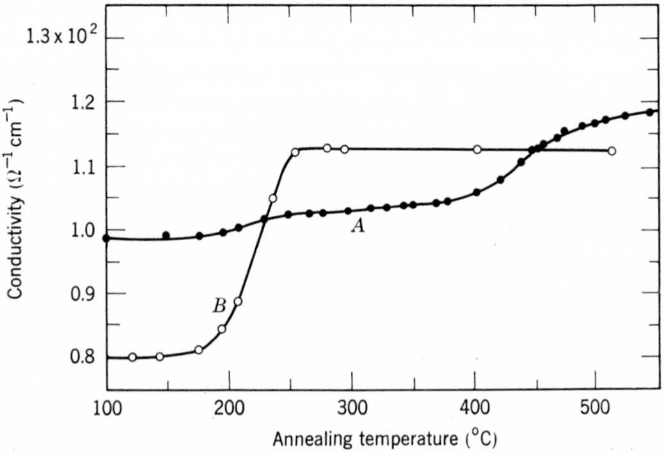

Fig. 5.11 Isochronal healing of radiation damage in GaAs after irradiation with neutrons (*A*) and electrons (*B*) [after Auckerman (61A10)].

also be explained by the appearance of microscopic inhomogeneities. For other details see, in particular, (62A6).

The appearance of strongly disturbed regions along the trajectories of *heavy particles* in III-V compounds was first suggested by Gonser and Okkerse and demonstrated in InSb and GaSb (57G3), (58G6). They assume a strong local heating along the track, a consequent melting of the lattice, and a subsequent solidification in a "liquid-like" structure under large stress (*thermal spikes*). They measured x-ray reflection spectra after irradiation with 12-MeV neutrons at low temperature. The interpretation of these spectra and the demonstration of a change in lattice constant confirmed this assumption in its main points. During warming this type of lattice defect anneals out at −110°C in GaSb. This appears to be the reason why Cleland and Crawford (55C1) were able to explain their radiation defects created at −125°C in GaSb without introducing thermal spikes. The behavior of the conductivity under bombardment was as expected, decreasing in both *n*- and *p*-type samples; in some *n*-type samples conversion was observed. The "final" position of the Fermi level must lie in the lower half of the forbidden gap. The annealing of these defects is complex. A single pairwise recombination of donors and acceptors was not sufficient to explain the results.

A *dilation of the lattice* after bombardment was observed by Kleitman and Yearian (57K5) in InSb and GaSb and by Vook (61V2) in InSb.

Finally, we want to consider some of the *threshold energies* for the creation of Frenkel defects by electrons. Such values follow from the isochronal annealing curves, and also from the dependence on electron energy of the number of defects created per incoming electron. According to Bäuerlein (59B4) [cf. also (63B5)], the following minimum energies are required for the creation of Frenkel defects: in the arsenic sublattice of InAs, 256 keV; in the phosphorus sublattice of InP, 118 keV; in the gallium sublattice of GaAs, 236 keV; and in the arsenic sublattice of the same compound, 267 keV. To these are added the values for InSb given by Eisen and Bickel (59E7): 250 keV (indium sublattice) and 300 keV (antimony sublattice). Just as the activation energies for diffusion are larger in the V-sublattices than in the III-sublattices, so is the threshold energy for the creation of a Frenkel defect larger in the V-sublattice than in the III-sublattice.

53 Special Cases

530 Anomalies in the mobility of charge carriers caused by impurities. In Chapter 4 we discussed at a number of places the influence of an inhomogeneous impurity distribution on the galvanomagnetic effects in III-V compounds. We saw in Section 411 that an inhomogeneous impurity distribution near the surface can explain the twofold sign reversal in the temperature dependence of the Hall coefficient of InAs. In Section 412 anomalies in the magnetoresistance were attributed to inhomogeneities in the impurity distribution. Similarly the appearance of a negative magnetoresistance can be related to the same effect, according to Section 413.

We will supplement these discussions in this section by considering some anomalies in the mobility of the charge carriers, which can be explained by fluctuations in the impurity distribution, by the formation of impurity aggregates, and by the appearance of statistically distributed microscopic inhomogeneities. Microscopic inhomogeneities appear because of anisotropic segregation coefficients (Section 520), because of complex formation of lattice atoms with foreign atoms, and because of the formation of clusters, dislocations, and similar lattice disturbances. Such inhomogeneities either can create regions of different carrier concentration (or the opposite conduction type) or can form, as a second phase, regions with a different width of the forbidden gap. For example, Eckhardt (62E2) found a colloidal phase of α-Ga_2O_3 in GaAs samples.

In all cases the concentration of free carriers in such inhomogeneities will deviate from the concentration in the surrounding medium, and space-charge regions will be formed surrounding the inhomogeneities. Such microscopically distributed space-charge regions, which act as scattering centers for charge carriers, make it possible to explain a number of anomalies in the mobility. The scattering by statistically distributed space-charge regions cannot be treated theoretically without a detailed model. If one assumes that the space-charge centers are solid spheres, which cannot be penetrated by the free carriers, then the mobility due to this scattering mechanism is proportional to $T^{-1/2}$. Such a temperature dependence was indeed found by Willardson in neutron-irradiated GaAs and interpreted by microscopic inhomogeneities produced by the irradiation. We have already mentioned these observations.

Anomalies in the mobility of free carriers in n-GaAs, InAs, and InP were found by Weisberg and Blanc (61W1). At 78°K the mobility in these semiconductors can be explained by known scattering mechanisms, but at 300°K large fluctuations about the theoretical mobility value were observed. There was no correlation between the carrier concentration and the mobility at room temperature, and an improvement in the mobility due to more extensive purification of the starting materials was observed only at 78°K and not at 300°K. These phenomena can be explained only under the assumption of a special type of impurity in the crystal, which does not influence the carrier concentration because of its low density but does reduce the mobility strongly because of a very large scattering cross section. The difference between the measurements at room temperature and at liquid nitrogen shows further that the mobility limited by scattering at such impurities must decrease with increasing temperature. All these points can be explained if these "mobility killers" are statistically distributed space-charge centers.

Other anomalies in the mobility appear in high-resistivity GaAs, which is discussed in the following section.

An anomalous temperature dependence of mobility has also been found in other III-V compounds. A comprehensive discussion of all the questions considered in this section was given by Weisberg (62W2), and we refer to this work for more details.

531 Semi-insulating GaAs and GaP. We have previously mentioned that GaAs can be prepared with particularly high electrical resistivity. The normal growth methods generally furnish n-type GaAs with an electron concentration of more than 10^{16} cm^{-3}, but the same methods sometimes lead to crystals with carrier concentrations of 10^{9} cm^{-3} or less. Such semi-insulating material is also obtained by floating zone refining and by growing crystals in a gas phase containing oxygen.

Semi-insulating GaAs is therefore not particularly pure, but rather contains a large number of impurities with deep levels, which compensate the normally present donors and acceptors with shallow levels. The main impurity is suspected to be oxygen. The fact that n-type high-resistivity GaAs is frequently obtained during growth indicates that the amount of oxygen built in is not critical for the compensation. This excludes the possibility that this element has only a single acceptor level in the forbidden gap associated with it because p-type high-resistivity GaAs would then generally be produced. Only if, accidentally, the donor and acceptor concentrations were almost equal would n-type high-resistivity material be created.

Two models have been proposed for the energy-level scheme of semi-insulating GaAs.

Allen (60A7) assumes that high-resistivity GaAs contains deep acceptors, which compensate the originally present shallow donors. The impurities which form the acceptors are, however, said to have two possible locations in the lattice, one electrically inactive, the other with acceptor character. When these impurities are neutral, the energetically favored location is the electrically inactive one; when they are charged negatively as acceptors, the electrically active location is favored. When the concentration of these centers is larger than that of the originally present donors, as many of the centers will go into the electrically active position as is necessary for the exact compensation of the donors.

This model therefore predicts self-compensation.

Another more probable model has been suggested by Blanc and Weisberg (61B16). This model does not require any self-compensation mechanism but suggests that the deep impurity is a donor. One need only assume that aside from this deep donor (concentration n_T), shallow donors (n_D) and shallow acceptors (n_A) are also present. If $n_A > n_D$, all shallow donors are compensated. When furthermore $n_T > n_A - n_D$, the remaining acceptors are also compensated and the Fermi level moves close to the location of the deep donor levels. High-resistivity GaAs results, independent of the exact concentration of the deep donors.

Both models make use of deep-lying impurity levels in the forbidden gap. Investigations of the temperature dependence of the Hall coefficient determined the distance of this level from the conduction band as 0.75 eV [Gooch, Hilsum, and Holeman (61G16), Haisty, Mehal, and Stratton (62H2); these papers also contain more extensive discussions of the properties of high-resistivity GaAs]. This value appears to be more reliable than earlier reported values (58W6), (60W2). The value of 0.75 eV corresponds to approximately half the width of the forbidden gap, so that high resistivity GaAs is essentially intrinsic. Figure 5.12 shows a comparison of the theoretically calculated intrinsic concentration as a function of temperature with measurements of Gooch, Hilsum, and Holeman (61G16), Whelan and Wheatley (58W6), and Bube (60B9). The temperature dependence of the Hall mobility fluctuates strongly from sample to sample. In some cases the mobility was temperature independent over a wide range.

Turner, Pettit, and Ainslie (63T4) found three levels 0.65, 1.0, and 1.34 eV below the conduction band in GaAs grown in an oxygen atmosphere.

High-resistivity n-type GaAs can also be produced by diffusing copper into low-resistivity n-type material [Blanc, Bube, McDonald, and Rosi (60B9), (61B14), (61B15)]. This is done by annealing GaAs at elevated temperatures in contact with a copper reservoir. The temperature required for the transition into high-resistivity GaAs depends on the primary-donor concentration. The solubility of copper at a given temperature therefore depends on the donor concentration. If one assumes Allen's model to apply to the undoped semi-insulating GaAs, one is forced to consider the latter and the Cu-doped variety, which does not require any self-compensation mechanism, as two different kinds of material. No such distinction is necessary under the Blanc-Weisberg model.

The properties of Cu-doped GaAs have also been investigated photoelectrically by Blanc *et al.* They discovered several states in the forbidden region: three donor states, 0.5, 0.6, and 0.7 eV below the conduction band, and five acceptor states, 0.04, 0.13, 0.22, 0.34, and 0.42 eV above the valence band. Some of these can be assigned to known impurities, but the origin of the others has not yet been explained.

Allen and Cherry (62A1) were able to produce GaP material with a resistivity of 10^{10} Ωcm by diffusing-in copper, and Gershenzon and

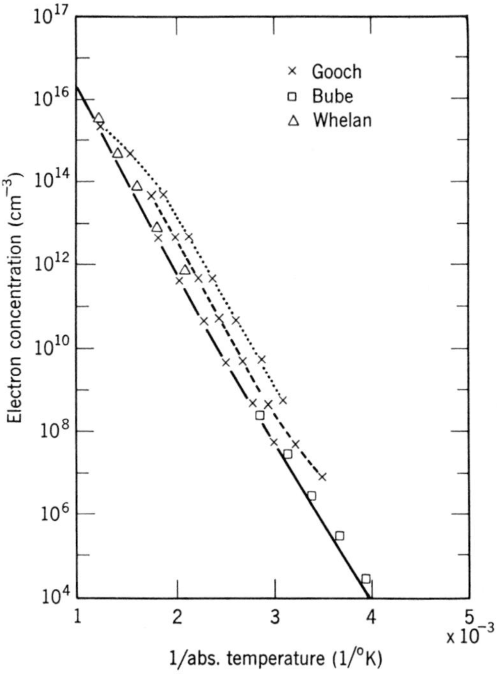

Fig. 5.12 Temperature dependence of the carrier concentration in high-resistivity GaAs [according to Gooch, Hilsum, and Holeman (61G16), Whelan and Wheatley (58W6), and Bube (60B9)]. The solid line is the theoretical curve for the intrinsic carrier concentration n_i (61G16).

Mikulyak (61G10) material of 10^{11}-10^{14} carriers/cm^3 by a special procedure, as mentioned in Section 512. The possibility of forming high-resistivity material is therefore not restricted to GaAs. In their high-resistivity forms these III-V compounds resemble strongly some II-VI compounds, such as CdSe. They have the advantage over the II-VI compounds that they can be produced in both *p*- and *n*-type form. Also, by counterdoping the same crystal can be made of low resistivity with properties similar to those of the semiconductors of column IV.

532 Electroluminescence. Polycrystalline GaP frequently shows strong luminescence when current is passed through it. This effect was first observed by Wolff, Hebert, and Broder (55W2) and is limited to small regions within a crystal. Depending on the experimental conditions and the doping, the color of the emitted light is orange, red, or green. This emission was shown to originate at grain boundaries and at contacts, suggesting that electroluminescence can be interpreted as radiative recombination of charge carriers at contacts or *p-n* junctions.

The appearance of luminescence in III-V compounds is expected because of their structural similarity to the luminescing II-VI compounds, such as ZnS. This effect is limited to GaP and a few other III-V compounds, because only these substances have a sufficiently wide forbidden gap to produce visible light from radiative transitions. As in the II-VI compounds, we can expect the radiation to be due to transitions to or from impurity states, rather than due to band-to-band transitions, which are inefficient in these indirect materials.

Electroluminescence in *p-n* junctions can be caused by two different mechanisms. Under forward bias the regions near the junction are flooded with injected minority carriers which recombine radiatively there. Under reverse bias, breakdown takes place above a certain threshold voltage with the creation of "hot" carriers by impact ionization. These hot carriers can also recombine with emission of radiation.

Systematic investigations of the electroluminescence of injected carriers at *p-n* junctions of GaP were performed by Grimmeiss and Koelmans (60G17), (61G19), (61G20), Allen *et al.* (59A4), (62S11), Loebner and Poor (59L4), Holt, Alfrey and Wiggins (58H4), (60A5), Vink and van Doorn (62V3), Ullman (61U1), and Gershenzon and co-workers (61G9), (62G4), (62G5), (64G2). Electroluminescence at point contacts of GaP was observed by Kikuchi *et al.* (60K3), (61I1), and by Gorton, Swartz, and Peet (60G12).

On GaP *p-n* junctions emission bands were observed at 0.565, 0.625, 0.71, and 0.945 μ under forward bias. The band at 0.565 μ

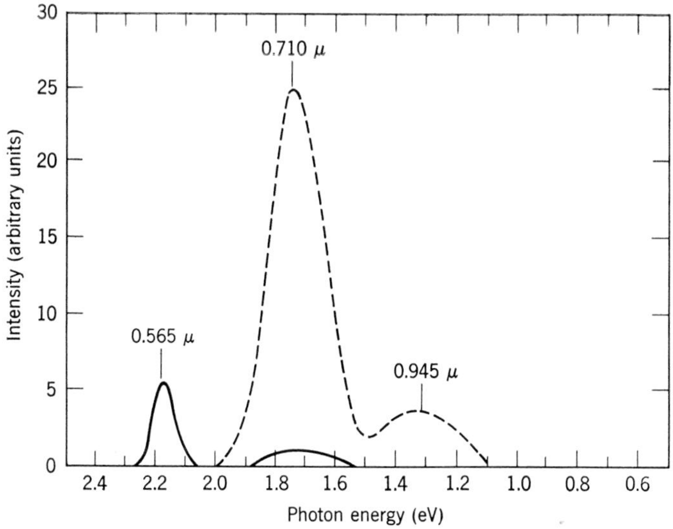

Fig. 5.13 Electroluminescent spectrum of GaP grown from a melt containing 0.05% zinc and either 0.025% (———) or 0.075% (– – –) oxygen [after Starkiewicz and Allen (62S11)].

(green luminescence) appears only for Zn-doping, according to Starkiewicz and Allen (62S11). Careful elimination of all traces of zinc made the band disappear. Its transition energy of 2.2 eV lies close to the band gap. It must therefore be due to a transition from the conduction band into a zinc level lying just above the valence band. The dependence of the band on the zinc concentration precludes the assumption of Loebner and Poor (59L4) that the emission is due to a bimolecular direct band-to-band transition. Similarly the assignment to a transition out of a phosphorus vacancy just below the conduction band into the valence band (60G17) is not tenable.

The red band at 0.7 μ has also been ascribed to zinc by many authors (energy level 0.4 eV above the valence band). Starkiewicz and Allen were able to show that it appears only if both zinc and oxygen are simultaneously present. This is demonstrated in Fig. 5.13. Whether this effect is connected with the formation of a Zn-O complex, or whether the presence of zinc increases the solubility of oxygen in GaP, and the transition takes place from an oxygen state, has not yet been decided.

Gershenzon and Mikulyak (62G4), in a different interpretation, assign the 0.7 μ transition to the radiative recombination into a donor

($\Delta E_D = 0.4$ eV). The donor is supposed to be formed by substitutional oxygen. The authors suggest that other imperfections affect this center by changing the equilibrium between substitutional and interstitial oxygen. Other transitions were assigned to interstitial oxygen and various impurities.

The 0.945 μ band which appears simultaneously with the red luminescence has not yet been identified. The emission at 0.625 μ was assigned to transitions from the conduction band into a gallium vacancy, by Grimmeiss and Koelmans (60G17), (61G20). Their papers also contain an extensive reaction-kinetic analysis of the *p-n* luminescence in GaP.

The electroluminescence of GaP *p-n* junctions under reverse bias (orange) has been investigated mainly by Logan and Chynoweth (62L4). They confirmed the suspicion that it is due to band-to-band recombination of "hot" carriers. All the experimental results on the mechanism of impact ionization in GaP show strong similarity to the conditions in silicon.

Grimmeiss *et al.* observed radiative recombination on GaN (59G12), (60G16) and on AlP (60G15). Wolff, Adams, and Mellichamp (59W5) report luminescence effects in AlN, Larach and Shrader (56L2) in BN, and Wolff, Hebert, and Broder (58W7) in III-V mixed crystals. All these results give a picture of the luminescence behavior but do not allow any deduction about other properties of these III-V compounds or about the impurities contained in them.

Electroluminescence has also been studied in other III-V compounds. We refer to (62V5) for InSb, (63C1) for GaSb, (63W7) and (63T3) for InP, (64A1) and (64F2) for $GaAs_{1-x}P_x$. The most extensive investigations have been made on the *p-n* junction luminescence of GaAs [references in Section 74, as well as (62N5), (62P3), (63A10), (63B9), (63B14), (63C6), (63D2), (63S1), (63N6), (63P3), (63L5), (63L7), (64D1), (64L1), and others]. Many of these papers are concerned with the connection between electroluminescence in III-V compounds and laser action. We will return to this topic in Section 74.

6

Mixed Crystals and Related Ternary Compounds

60 Introduction

In the other chapters of this book we discuss the III-V compounds only. The subject matter is divided up according to the various physical properties. In this chapter we will instead concern ourselves with a group of mixed crystals and ternary compounds related to the III-V compounds. This group is treated separately since so far little information is available about its main semiconductor parameters.

In the first part of this chapter we will consider *mixed crystals* between III-V compounds. We will be less concerned with the physical properties of a given mixed crystal than with the more general differences between mixed crystals and pure III-V compounds.

In addition to the III-V compounds there are a number of other semiconductors that crystallize with the zinc-blende structure. The treatment of their physical properties lies outside the framework of this book, but we will consider the formation of mixed crystals between them and III-V compounds. This makes it possible to study the transition from the doping of a semiconductor with individual impurities to the formation of mixed crystals.

Finally we will concern ourselves in this chapter with semiconductors which can be considered to be *derived* from the III-V compounds in the same sense in which the III-V compounds are derived from the semiconducting elements of group IV. We will limit this subject matter rather arbitrarily. Almost all semiconductors with zinc-blende structure can be derived from others by substituting for every pair of lattice atoms a pair of corresponding atoms located to the left and the right of the first pair in the periodic table. Thus the II-VI compounds can be formed from the III-V compounds in the same way as the latter from the semiconductors of group IV. However, we will consider only those ternary compounds as "derivatives" of the III-V compounds which are more closely related to the III-V compounds than to the II-VI or IV-IV compounds.

61 Mixed Crystals between III-V Compounds

610 Preliminary comments. The semiconducting elements of group IV of the periodic system only partially form mixed crystals: germanium and gray tin are only weakly soluble in one another; between germanium and silicon there does exist a continuous range of mixed crystals, in which the properties of germanium continuously change into those of silicon; a mixed crystal between silicon and carbon is formed only for the one composition SiC. One of the reasons for this variation in behavior is that the differing atomic sizes of carbon and of silicon (covalent radii 0.77 and 1.17 Å, respectively) as well as of germanium and tin (1.22 and 1.40 Å) discourage mixed-crystal formation. There are other requirements that influence this property in these elements, but we will not consider them here.

One requirement for the existence of mixed-crystal systems between III-V compounds would seem to be that the lattice constants of the two partners do not differ too much, since the lattice constant is determined by the atomic sizes of the two components. There will be another requirement which does not come into play for the elements. We have seen in Chapter 2 that the electron bonds in the III-V compounds are polarized, and that the binding therefore has a substantial ionic contribution. This ionic contribution to the chemical bond varies strongly from one III-V compound to another, and presumably the two partners of a mixed-crystal system will be required to have similar ionicities to prevent a strong distortion of the lattice.

The two requirements, that the atomic size and the polarization must not be *too* different, are only qualitative criteria and will not give well-defined limits for the mixed-crystal formation. It is only possible to postulate that a mixed crystal is more likely to occur in one case than in another.

Let us consider these requirements a little more closely. We will see in Chapter 9 that, according to Folberth, the relative polarization increases in this order: AlSb, GaSb, GaP, GaAs, InSb, InP, InAs. The three gallium compounds lie relatively closely together, while between InSb and the pair InP, InAs there is a larger separation. This means that the formation of mixed crystals is more likely in the system InAs-InP than in the system InSb-InAs. In InSb-InP there is the additional difficulty of the differences in size of antimony and phosphorus, so that the existence of such mixed crystal is very unlikely. The formation of mixed crystals among the gallium compounds is more likely. Aluminum antimonide will mix easily only with GaSb, and not with InSb. Finally, InSb is not likely to mix with GaSb. We will see these rough predictions confirmed in the following sections.

Other mixed-crystal systems can be imagined between III-V compounds which have both different trivalent and different pentavalent atoms. Such quaternary systems will be more difficult to handle technologically than ternary systems. Not much is known about their existence.

Mixed-crystal formation has been demonstrated in all systems studied so far, but the ease of formation of the various systems is determined by the foregoing considerations. For some systems the preparation procedures are very complicated and lengthy. We will discuss such technological questions only briefly in the following sections and will completely pass over the phase diagrams of the ternary systems and the quasi-binary systems. For the latter we refer to the literature to be cited, in particular to the works of Goryunova and Fedorova (55G2), Köster (58K4), and Peretti (53L1), (53S1), (58P1).

611 The system InSb-GaSb. Indium antimonide and GaSb are continuously miscible, but there are technological difficulties in producing homogeneous $In_{1-x}Ga_xSb$ crystals with a given mixing ratio x by procedures which rely on diffusion processes. If one mixes the powdered starting substances and sinters them at high temperatures, it takes weeks for equilibrium to be reached. These long diffusion times are the reason why some authors assumed that InSb and GaSb do not mix [Köster and Thoma (55K4) and Kolm, Kulin, and Averbach (57K6)]. The first crystals were produced by Goryunova and Fedorova (55G2), while the first reliable growth procedures were reported by Woolley and Smith (56W6), (58W9) and Ivanov-Omskii and Kolomiets (59I2).

According to Ivanov-Omskii and Kolomiets, homogeneous crystals can be obtained by very slow zone refining ($v < 1$ mm/h), alternating in the forward and the reverse direction. Woolley, Evans, and Gillett (59W7) report that the most reliable procedure is a single solidification of a melt with a crystallizing velocity of 4 mm/day. When the velocity is increased to 1 cm/day, inhomogeneities of ± 4 mole % appear perpendicular to the crystallization direction. A

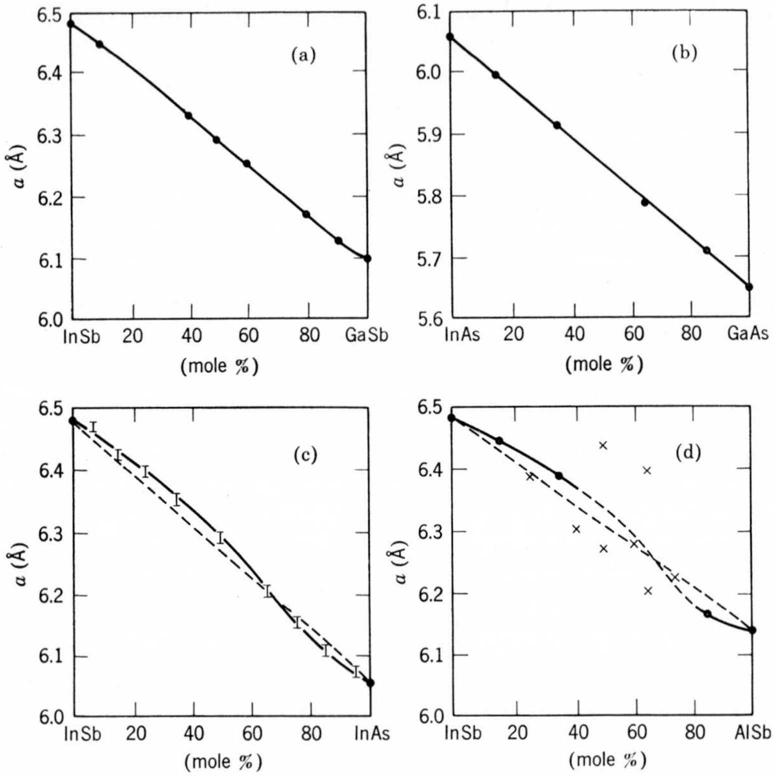

Fig. 6.1 Change of lattice constant with composition in the systems (a) InSb-GaSb, (b) InAs-GaAs, (c) InSb-InAs, (d) InSb-AlSb [after Woolley, Smith, and Evans (60W9)].

rod obtained by this procedure of course varies in composition along its length. From a melt of 50 mole % InSb and GaSb the composition varies between about 85% GaSb/15% InSb and 6% GaSb/94% InSb. If the rod is sufficiently long, single, approximately homogeneous crystals of every desired mixing ratio can be cut out of it.

The lattice constant changes linearly with composition (Vegard's law), as shown in Fig. 6.1, where measurements of the lattice constants of various mixed-crystal systems are plotted, after Woolley and Smith (58W9), (60W9).

The electrical and optical properties of $In_{0.5}Ga_{0.5}Sb$ were investigated in a number of studies by Ivanov-Omskii and Kolomiets (59I2), (59I3), (60I1), (61I3), (62I1). There is also a paper by Blakemore

(57B2), which, however, disagrees in some respects with later results. Woolley and co-workers studied the electrical (60W8), (61W5) and optical properties (59W7), (61W8) of the entire mixed-crystal system.

Optical measurements for the determination of the width of the forbidden gap as a function of the composition of the mixed crystal by Ivanov-Omskii and Kolomiets (59I1) and Woolley and Evans (59W7), (61W8) are collected in Fig. 6.2. The data refer to room temperature. The temperature coefficient of $E_{G,\mathrm{opt}}$ lies between 2.5 and 4.5×10^{-4} eV/°K for all mixed crystals. It can be seen that E_G increases monotonically from InSb to GaSb. A knee in the curves, such as appears in the corresponding curve for the mixed-crystal system $Ge_{1-x}Si_x$, has not been found. This confirms that, as in InSb and GaSb, the (000)-minimum forms the bottom of the conduction band in all the mixed crystals.

Figure 6.3 shows the width of the forbidden gap $E_G(0)$ determined from an analysis of conductivity and Hall-effect measurements (60W8). $E_G(0)$ agrees well with the values of the optical measurements extrapolated to $T = 0$ up to a mixing ratio of 65 mole % GaSb. Above 65% GaSb the curve of $\ln(n_i^2/T^3)$ vs. $(1/T)$, determined from

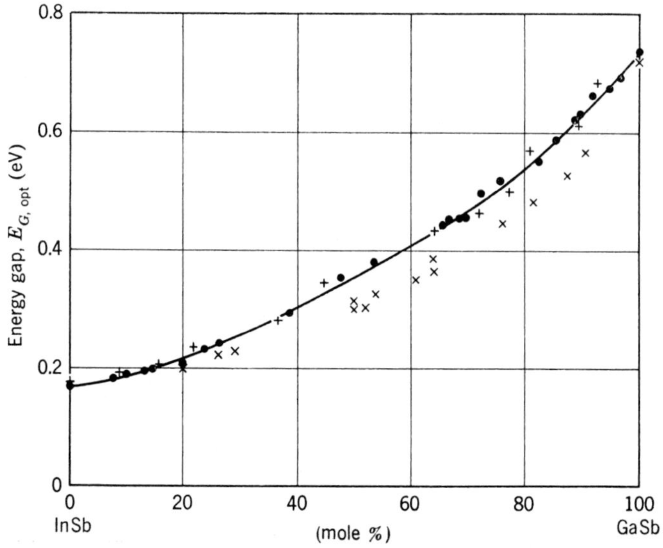

Fig. 6.2 Optically determined forbidden gap $E_{G,\mathrm{opt}}$ for the mixed-crystal system InSb-GaSb. Results of: (×), Ivanov-Omskii and Kolomiets (59I1); (●), Woolley, Evans, and Gillett (59W7); and (+), Woolley and Evans (61W8).

conductivity and Hall measurements, is no longer a straight line as required by the theory for nondegenerate semiconductors [cf. eq. (4.7)]. Rather it consists of two straight lines of different slopes. The apparent values of E_G determined from the two lines are both included in Fig. 6.3. The temperature at which the knee in the curve appears is also indicated. With increasing GaSb content the optical $E_G(0)$ values first coincide with the upper curve but finally transfer to the lower curve at 100% GaSb. We have seen in Chapters 3 and 4 that in GaSb two subbands contain electrons at room temperature. The energy difference between the edge of the lower-lying (000)-subband and that of the (111)-subband is about 0.08 eV. When both subbands are occupied, the n_i^2-curve is no longer expected to be a straight line. Also, one should not directly identify the two line sections of Fig. 6.3 with the separation of the valence band from the two subbands. A more exact analysis, which takes account of the distribution of elec-

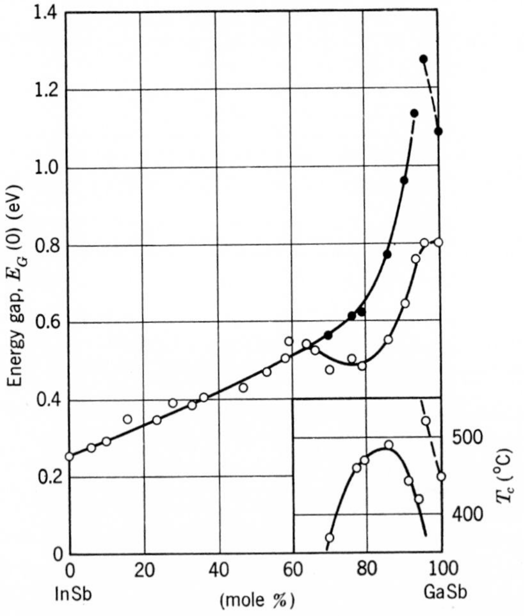

Fig. 6.3 Electrically determined forbidden gap $E_G(0)$ in the mixed-crystal system InSb-GaSb [after Woolley and Gillett (60W8)]. For crystals with more than 65 mole % GaSb the calculations gave two different E_G values, depending on whether the measurement temperature was above or below a critical temperature T_c (insert in lower right-hand corner).

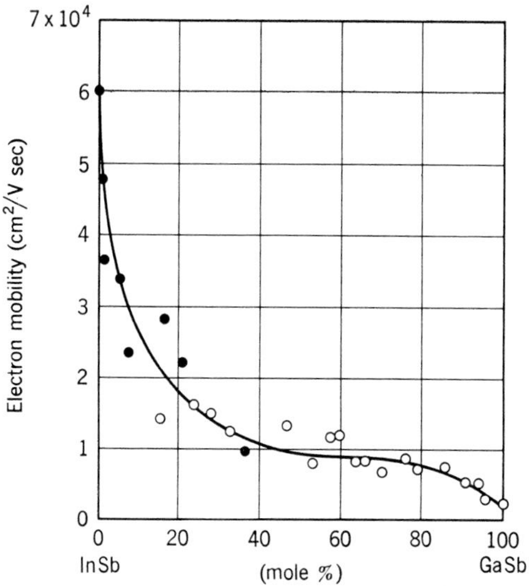

Fig. 6.4 Electron Hall mobility at room temperature in the system InSb-GaSb (○ from measurements on p-type samples, ● from measurements on n-type samples) [after Woolley and Gillett (60W8)].

trons between the two bands as a function of the temperature and of the dependence of the band edges on the mixing ratio and the temperature, is not available, since the values of the necessary parameters are not known. Other interpretations, such as a rearrangement of the lattice at the temperature of the knee and a resulting change of the band structure, can, however, be shown not to be tenable.

The Hall mobility of the electrons as a function of the composition of the mixed crystals (60W8) is shown in Fig. 6.4. The mobility decreases rapidly from InSb with increasing gallium content, reaches a plateau, and then drops only slightly in going to GaSb. Since mixed crystals with a given impurity concentration cannot yet be produced, the measurements were performed on undoped samples. Now, $In_{1-x}Ga_xSb$ crystals are found to be n-type only if the melt is In-rich; they grow p-type from a Ga-rich melt. Consequently, only in the left third of the figure are the data points directly measured Hall mobilities. The other points were determined indirectly. First the hole mobility was determined, and then the mobility ratio calculated from the quotient of the Hall coefficient value at its maximum (in the region of mixed conduction) to its value in the region of pure p-conduction. The theoretical value of this quotient is $(b - 1)^2/4b$. The mobility ratio drops from 90 for InSb to 25 for only 10 mole % GaSb; then it remains constant to 70% GaSb and finally decreases steadily to 5. Multiplication of b and μ_p gives the remaining electron mobilities plotted in Fig. 6.4. The reliability of these points is not very high because of the indirect method of determination. Figure 6.4 indicates an electron mobility of 10,000 cm^2/V sec for $In_{0.5}Ga_{0.5}Sb$, compared to the value of 30,000 cm^2/V sec reported by Ivanov-Omskii and Kolomiets (60I1). A similar discrepancy is found for $In_{0.75}Ga_{0.25}Sb$.

Of particular interest is the question of whether the mobility of the charge carriers is reduced in the mixed crystals by the statistical distribution of the atoms of the components (alloy scattering). The curve of Fig. 6.4 does show a reduction below the straight line connecting the mobility values of the two components InSb and GaSb. However, the parameters determining the mobility are mostly still unknown, and no conclusion can be drawn as to the scattering mechanism. The only point of reference is given by measurements of the temperature dependence of the mobility of various mixed crystals by Woolley and Gillett (60W8). In all samples μ_n follows a $T^{-\alpha}$ law, where, however, α takes on different values above and below a critical temperature, similarly to the E_G measurements. (This critical temperature has no connection to the corresponding temperature in Fig. 6.3, nor is the knee in the ln μ_n vs. T curve restricted to the region above 65 mole % GaSb.) If the measured α values below the corresponding critical temperatures are plotted as a function of the composition of the mixed crystal, then the curve shows a well-defined minimum, which Woolley and Gillett interpret as a sign of alloy scattering. The hypothesis is supported by the fact that α decreases to 0.5, a value given by the theory of alloy scattering. In contrast to these results Ivanov-Omskii and Kolomiets were not able to observe any influence of alloy scattering on the mobility.

612 The system InSb-AlSb. Indium antimonide and AlSb were for a long time also believed to be immiscible (55K4). The first mixed crystals were produced by Köster and Ulrich (58K4) and Woolley and Smith (58W9), (60W9). Woolley and Smith observed mixed-crystal formation only below 40 mole% AlSb and above 85% AlSb, but later Baranov and Goryunova (60B2) were able to demonstrate the existence of a continuous mixed-crystal system. The change of lattice constant with composition is shown in Fig. 6.1. Again an approximately linear behavior is observed. Long annealing times are again necessary for the production of the mixed crystals.

The electrical properties of these mixed crystals have not been studied to any extent. Ageev and Nasledov (60A4) give measured values for three crystals with the compositions $In_{0.9}Al_{0.1}Sb$, $In_{0.75}Al_{0.25}Sb$, and $In_{0.5}Al_{0.5}Sb$. The width of the forbidden gap $E_G(0)$, determined from the temperature dependence of the conductivity and of the Hall coefficient, increases with growing AlSb content. The data [$E_G(0) = 0.34$, 0.43, and 0.82 eV for the three crystals] are not sufficient for a discussion of the variation of E_G with composition. A linear dependence is not expected, since InSb and AlSb have conduction-band minima at different points in the Brillouin zone. The hole mobilities of the three p-type crystals were 600, 400, and 80 cm^2/V sec, respectively, at room temperature; the coefficients α of the temperature dependence $\mu_p \sim T^{-\alpha}$ were 1.67, 1.3, and 1.1, respectively. More values would be needed for a discussion of the scattering mechanism. Ageev, Emel'yanenko, and Nasledov (61A2) attempted to obtain information about this scattering mechanism from the sign of the Nernst coefficient. We have reported corresponding measurements on III-V compounds in Chapter 4 and observed that the interpretation of such measurements encounters difficulties, if the band is not parabolic. Except for the pure compounds InSb and AlSb the Nernst coefficient was always positive (according to the sign convention of the Russian authors, negative). This suggests ionized-impurity scattering or polar scattering. The theory of alloy scattering predicts a negative sign of the Nernst coefficient, so that it appears that alloy scattering has no influence on the mobility in this case.

613 The system GaSb-AlSb. The mixed crystals of the form $Ga_{1-x}Al_xSb$ have properties similar to those of the $In_{1-x}Al_xSb$ crystals. They can be produced by zone refining (58B6), (58G10). It is recommended first to homogenize the material by rapid forward and reverse movement and then to purify it by slow zone pulling (59B15). The dependence of the lattice constant on the composition has not been investigated, since the two starting substances have very similar lattice constants (6.10 Å for GaSb and 6.15 Å for AlSb).

Figure 6.5 shows the dependence of the width of the forbidden gap on the composition from measurements of the electrical and galvanomagnetic properties of the system by Burdiyan and Kolomiets (59B15). The dependence is not linear, since the conduction-band minima of GaSb and AlSb do not lie at the same point in the Brillouin zone. The composition at which the (000)- and (100)-minima have the same separation from the valence band can be only roughly estimated from Fig. 6.5. In contrast to these measurements, Miller, Goering, and Himes (60M3) did not find a knee in the E_G-composition curve.

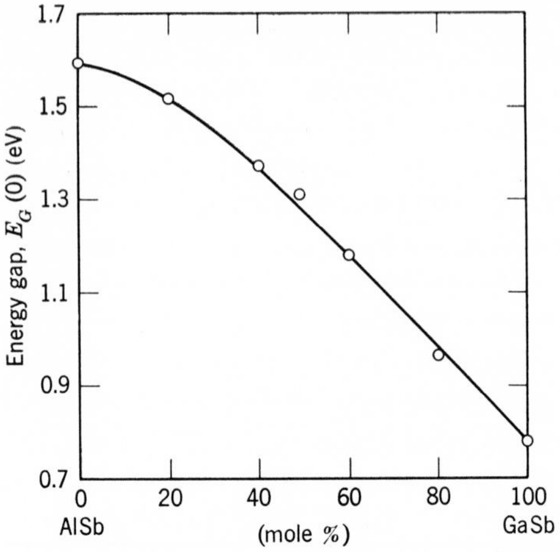

Fig. 6.5 Electrically determined forbidden gap $E_G(0)$ of the mixed-crystal system GaSb-AlSb [according to Burdiyan and Kolomiets (59B15)].

The optical gap $E_{G,\mathrm{opt}}$, determined from the position of the absorption edge (59B16), agrees well with Fig. 6.5 if the temperature dependence of E_G is taken into account.

The thermoelectric power increases in the mixed-crystal system with increasing AlSb content, according to Burdiyan, Rosneritsa, and Stepanov (61B19). The maximum lies in all cases between 350 and 500°K. The hole effective mass, determined from the thermoelectric power of p-type samples, is supposed to have higher values for the mixed crystals than for the two components, according to the same authors.

614 The system InAs-GaAs. The complete mixed-crystal system $In_{1-x}Ga_xAs$ can be produced by the same procedure as the system $In_{1-x}Ga_xSb$ (Section 611). The high vapor pressure of arsenic at the melting point of the compounds makes it necessary to take the same precautions as were discussed in Chapter 5 for production of the arsenides among the III-V compounds (57W3), (58W9), (60W9). The dependence of lattice constant on composition is included in Fig. 6.1.

The electrical properties of these compounds were investigated by Woolley, Gillett, and Evans (61W7) and by Abrahams, Braunstein, and Rosi (59A1), (60A2).

The optical forbidden gap is plotted in Fig. 6.6. The lower curve was obtained by Abrahams, Braunstein, and Rosi on samples that were not completely homogeneous. If one therefore assumes the upper curve to be more reliable, a linear increase of E_G with growing GaAs content is observed up to about 90 mole % GaAs. The remaining curve is characterized by a more rapid increase. It is not yet clear whether this is an anomaly similar to that found in the Ga-rich $In_{1-x}Ga_xSb$ mixed crystals.

The electron Hall mobility decreases rapidly with increasing GaAs content and passes through a minimum at about 85 mole % GaAs, according to Abrahams, Braunstein, and Rosi. Whether this result points to alloy scattering is questionable, according to Woolley, Gillett, and Evans. As prepared, GaAs-rich mixed crystals are generally found to be weakly *n*- or *p*-conducting, so that mixed conduction must be assumed. Then the product of conductivity and Hall coefficient is no longer a measure of the mobility of the carriers.

We have seen in the preceding sections that alloy scattering does not appear to be of importance as a scattering mechanism for the charge carriers in III-V mixed crystals. The mobility of electrons and holes is not influenced by the statistical distribution of the dissimilar atoms in one of the sublattices. The situation is different for the movement of

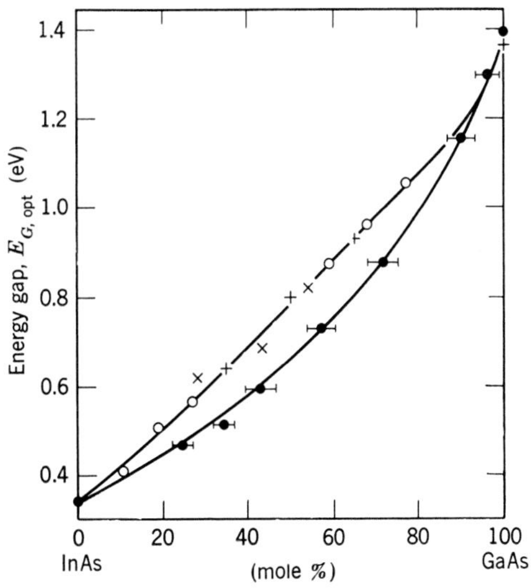

Fig. 6.6 Optically determined forbidden gap $E_{G,\mathrm{opt}}$ of the mixed-crystal system InAs-GaAs [upper curve by Woolley, Gillett, and Evans (61W7)]; lower curve by Abrahams, Braunstein, and Rosi (60A2).

phonons, namely, for the energy transport through the lattice itself. The alloying of two substances to a mixed crystal is accompanied by internal stresses in the crystal, which reinforce the anharmonicity of the lattice vibrations. In the description of the normal modes of the lattice vibrations as phonons this means stronger scattering of the phonons by the lattice and thus a decrease of their mean free path.

Consequently the thermal conductivity is smaller in the mixed crystals than in the components. This fact is of great importance for the application of semiconductors as thermoelectric generators and for the utilization of the Peltier effect. At the end of Section 421 we defined

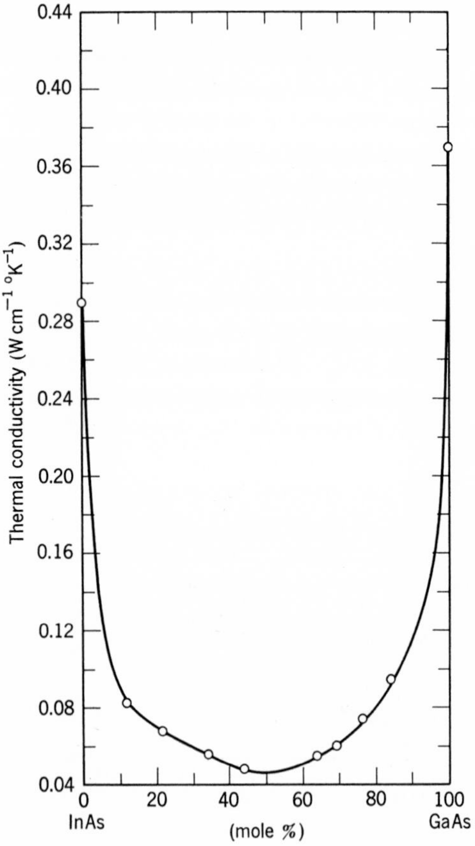

Fig. 6.7 Thermal conductivity in the system InAs-GaAs at room temperature [after Abrahams, Braunstein, and Rosi (60A2)].

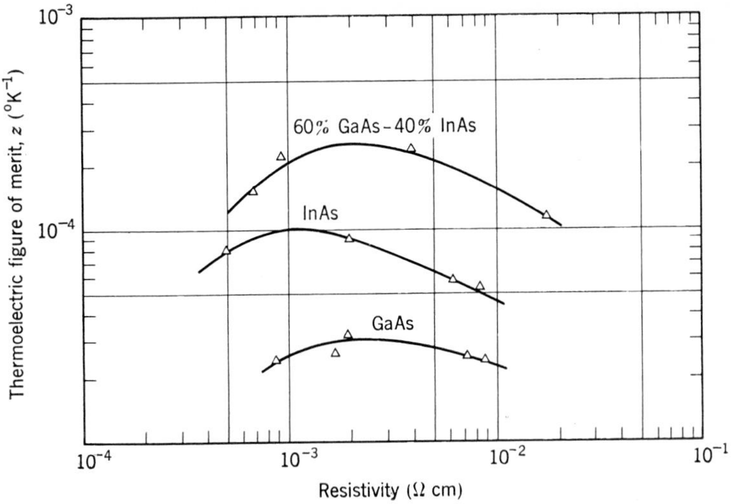

Fig. 6.8 Thermoelectric figure of merit as a function of the conductivity for InAs, GaAs, and $In_{0.4}Ga_{0.6}As$ at room temperature [after Rosi, Hockings, and Lindenblad (61R3)].

a "thermoelectric figure of merit," $z = \phi^2\sigma/\kappa'$, as an indication of the usefulness of a semiconductor and gave values of this number for InSb and InAs in Fig. 4.51. A decrease of thermal conductivity in the presence of otherwise unchanged parameters increases z. This is the reason for the peculiar interest in the thermoelectric properties of the mixed crystals.

Figure 6.7 shows the thermal conductivity of $In_{1-x}Ga_xAs$ mixed crystals as a function of composition according to Abrahams, Braunstein, and Rosi (59A1), (60A2). The free-carrier contribution to the thermal conductivity was calculated from Eq. (4.32). In all cases it was found to be only a negligible part of the entire value, so that the data of Fig. 6.7 can be identified with the lattice thermal conductivity. Figure 6.8 gives the thermoelectric figure of merit for a mixed crystal with the composition $In_{0.4}Ga_{0.6}As$, compared with that of the components InAs and GaAs (61R3).

615 The systems InSb-InAs and GaSb-GaAs. Only very limited information is so far available about the system InSb-InAs. The annealing times to produce homogeneous samples are even longer than those for the mixed crystals discussed so far, and no completely homogeneous samples have yet been reported. The dependence of the lattice constant on the composition is again shown in Fig. 6.1. As in the system InSb-AlSb, Vegard's law is not fulfilled. Further investigations are required to determine whether these deviations are also due to insufficient homogeneity of the samples or if there is a real breakdown of Vegard's law.

Nothing is known about the electrical properties of these mixed crystals.

For the system GaSb-GaAs the only information available is that its properties are similar to those of the $InSb_{1-x}As_x$ system (58W9).

616 The system InAs-InP. In contrast to the other mixed-crystal systems discussed in this chapter, $InAs_{1-x}P_x$ samples can be prepared by the same procedure that is used to prepare the two components, InAs and InP. No time-consuming homogenizing procedures are necessary. The electrical and optical properties of these mixed crystals are therefore much better known than those of the other III-V mixed-crystal systems. The first demonstration of the existence of the complete system, as well as of the system GaAs-GaP, was given by Folberth (55F2).

For the composition dependence of the lattice constant Vegard's law applies (60F4).

The optical width of the forbidden gap was measured by Oswald (59O1). In both components the bottom of the conduction band lies at the center of the Brillouin zone. The expected linear variation of the forbidden gap from InAs to InP was confirmed quantitatively. The dependence on mixing ratio x and on temperature was found to be

$$E_G = [0.44 + 0.98x - (3.5 + 1.1x)10^{-4}T] \text{ eV}$$

The forbidden gap was determined from electrical measurements by Weiss (56W2). The conductivity and Hall coefficient show the same behavior as the pure III-V compounds, in their dependence on temperature and doping. The transport parameters can be analyzed in the same fashion as in Section 411. In Fig. 6.9 the temperature dependence of the quotient n_i^2/T^3 is plotted, as determined from Hall-coefficient measurements. A straight line for ln n_i^2/T^3 vs. $1/T$ is observed, as expected for nondegenerate semiconductors from eq. (4.7). The $E_G(0)$ values, obtained from the slope of the measured line, are a linear function of x with parameter values similar to the results of the optical measurements.

The product of the two effective masses m_n and m_p can be determined from the ratio n_i^2/T^3, according to (4.7), if E_G and $\partial E_G/\partial T$ are known. Figure 6.9 shows that this product increases continuously

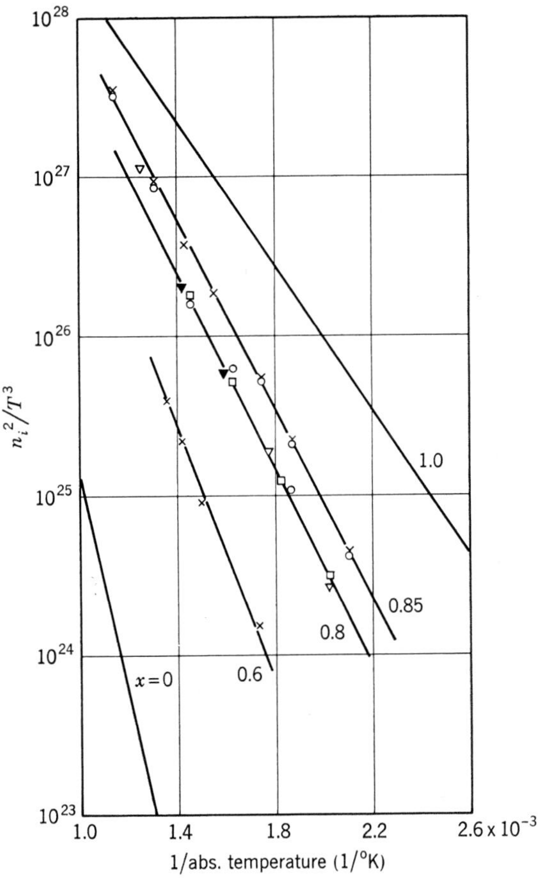

Fig. 6.9 n_i^2/T^3 vs. $1/T$ for mixed crystals of the composition $InAs_{1-x}P_x$ with various values of x [after Weiss (56W2)].

from InAs to InP. Oswald determined the electron mass alone from the free-carrier absorption, using the Drude theory. The application of this theory is rather limited in the III-V compounds, as we have seen in Section 320, since it requires the absorption constant to be proportional to the square of the wavelength. Such a proportionality has been found experimentally only for InSb. For the mixed-crystal system under discussion Oswald observed an increase of the exponent of the wavelength dependence from 1.85 for InAs to 2.3 for InP. For mixed crystals with mixing ratio $x = 0$ (InAs), 0.2, 0.4, 0.6, and

1 (InP), the electron-effective masses 0.02, 0.045, 0.06, 0.08, and 0.10 m were derived from the absorption constant. The two extreme values agree approximately with the known values for InAs and InP, thus providing some justification for this analysis.

The optical measurements of Oswald (59O1) also permit the determination of the longitudinal optical frequency ω_l and of the effective ion charge e_s^*. Both quantities increase continuously from InAs to InP, but the experimental accuracy was not sufficient to give the exact behavior of these parameters with composition.

Whereas the width of the forbidden gap decreases linearly with increasing InP content, the electron mobility first decreases very rapidly from its high value for InAs and reaches half its value for 20 mole % InP. Subsequently it decreases more slowly down to the InP value. The hole mobility also decreases from InAs to InP. The high mobility ratio of InAs and InP is conserved in the mixed-crystal system (56W2).

In Section 411 the dominating scattering mechanism for InAs and InP was found to be polar scattering (perhaps combined with ionized-impurity scattering), according to Ehrenreich (59E6). The same analysis was performed by Ehrenreich on the mixed-crystal system. In calculating the mobility of a mixed crystal he first assumed the same scattering mechanism to apply, as for the two components. The parameters entering the mobility formulas (4.2) and (4.3) were partly taken from experiment and partly estimated by interpolating from the values of the two components. The calculated theoretical mobility is compared with the experimental data of Weiss (56W2) in Fig. 4.6. The agreement is as good for the mixed crystals as for the two components. It should be noted that no adjustable parameters entered the theoretical curve of Fig. 4.6.

Ehrenreich also made an estimate of the alloy-scattering contribution. First the theoretical curve of Fig. 4.6 was made to agree with the experimental values at the end points, by choosing a new value of the effective ionic charge e_c^* in the theory. This quantity is not known accurately, anyhow. The mobilities of the mixed crystals were then calculated in the same way, neglecting alloy scattering. They were found to be larger than the experimental data. If the difference is assigned to alloy scattering one finds a mobility, limited by this scattering mechanism alone, which has a minimum of 15,000–45,000 cm^2/V sec for the composition In $As_{0.5}P_{0.5}$ and increases sharply with growing InAs or InP content. According to this analysis, the contribution of alloy scattering to the total scattering of electrons is at

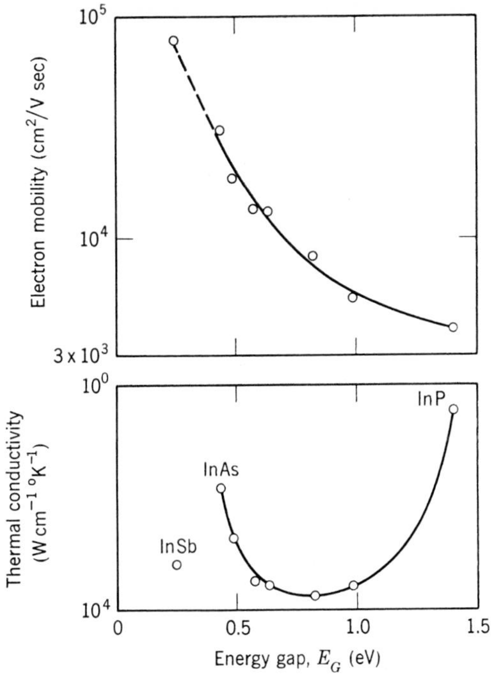

Fig. 6.10 Electron mobility μ_n and lattice thermal conductivity κ_l' as functions of E_G for InSb and the mixed-crystal system InAs-InP [after Weiss (59W2)].

most 10–40% in this mixed-crystal system at room temperature. The uncertainty in these values lies in the inaccurately known parameters which go into the theory.

Thermoelectric investigations of the mixed-crystal system $InAs_{1-x}P_x$ were performed by Weiss (59W2) and Bowers, Bauerle, and Cornish (59B10), (60U1). As in $In_{1-x}Ga_xAs$, one also finds a definite minimum in the thermal conductivity of $InAs_{1-x}P_x$ at approximately $x = 0.5$. The thermal conductivity as well as the electron mobility is plotted in Fig. 6.10 as a function of the energy gap E_G of the mixed crystal (59W2). The thermoelectric figure of merit z is calculated from these results and from measurements of the thermoelectric power and is plotted in Fig. 6.11 as a function of temperature for a number of mixed crystals (59B10). The electron concentrations of the four samples investigated were not the same, and a quantitative comparison is not possible. It can be observed, however, that z can be increased by a small admixture of InP to InAs, but that, at $x = 0.2$, z already drops below the value of InAs.

617 The system GaAs-GaP. Producing mixed crystals of the system GaAs-GaP is no more difficult than the production of GaAs and GaP crystals. Folberth (55F2) early demonstrated the existence of the complete mixed-crystal system. The entire system can also be produced by diffusing phosphorus into GaAs (62S12).

In GaAs the lowest minimum of the conduction band lies at $\mathbf{k} = (000)$, while in GaP it lies on the [100]-axes of the Brillouin zone. A change of band structure is therefore expected in the mixed-crystal series $GaAs_{1-x}P_x$. This change is observed as a kink in the $E_G(x)$-curve at the composition at which the two minima are located at the same energy. Figure 6.12 shows this for the optically determined energy gap (55F2). From this figure the exact mixing ratio for the crossover of the two bands cannot be determined. Allen and Hobdy (63A2) report the crossover point to be at $x = 0.53$.

In contrast to this the spin-orbit energy Δ is a linear function of composition, according to Hobdy (63H4).

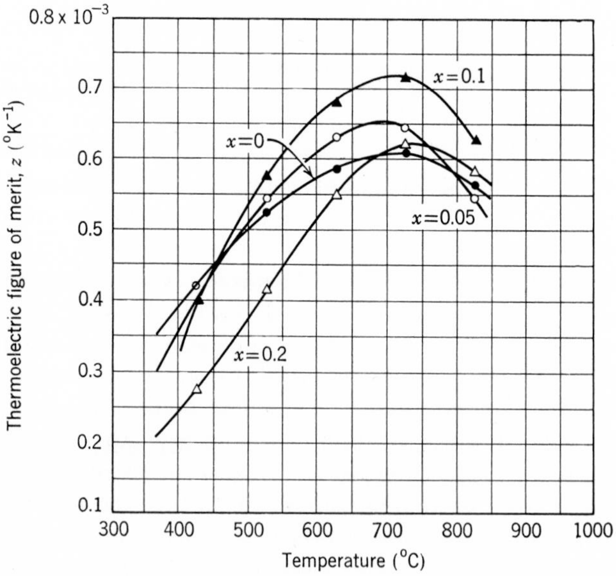

Fig. 6.11 Thermoelectric figure of merit for $InAs_{1-x}P_x$ mixed crystals as a function of temperature. The mixed crystals had carrier concentrations between 6×10^{16} cm^{-3} and 5×10^{17} cm^{-3} [after Bowers, Bauerle, and Cornish (59B10)].

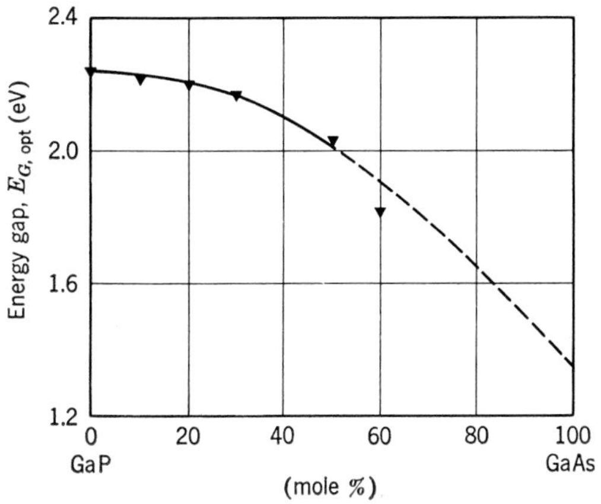

Fig. 6.12 Optically determined forbidden gap $E_{G,\mathrm{opt}}$ for the mixed crystal system GaAs-GaP [after Folberth (55F2)].

Measurements of the electrical properties of this system are not yet available; for optical properties compare (63A2) and (63H4).

62 Mixed Crystals between III-V Compounds and Other Semiconductors

620 Mixtures of III-V and III-VI compounds. The elements of group III and VI of the periodic table form semiconducting compounds of the type $A_2^{III}B_3^{VI}$. These compounds crystallize in a tetrahedral lattice, whose one sublattice is formed by the hexavalent atoms and whose other sublattice contains the trivalent atoms and additional empty lattice points. The number of these vacancies must be exactly half as large as the number of trivalent atoms. Two trivalent and three hexavalent atoms are therefore located on six lattice points, and the crystal contains four valence electrons for each lattice point, as is required for the formation of a tetrahedral lattice.

The vacancies are in general randomly distributed in the III-sublattice. In a few cases it is possible to order the vacancies by a special procedure. Then an ordered crystal of the same symmetry as the zinc-blende lattice but with a lattice constant three times as large is obtained. The unit cell contains 216 lattice sites, i.e. 3^3 times the number of atoms in the unit cell of the zinc-blende lattice (8). One of the two sublattices is completely occupied by hexavalent atoms. In the other sublattice the vacancies are distributed according to Fig.

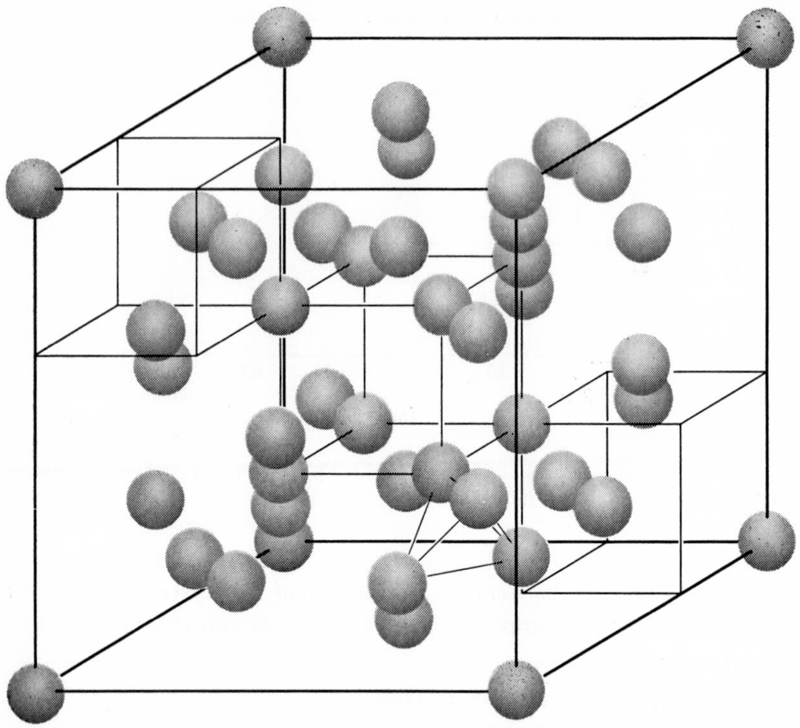

Fig. 6.13 Distribution of the vacancies in the III-sublattice of an ordered $A_2^{III}B_3^{VI}$ compound. The unit cell of the III-sublattice is shown. The spheres represent the vacancies. The trivalent atoms are located at all remaining corners and centers of faces of the twenty-seven cubes contained in the unit cell (only three are shown in the figure). The unit cell is a cubic face-centered lattice containing eight tetrahedrons formed by the vacancies along the body diagonals (one tetrahedron is drawn in the lower right-hand corner). Because of this arrangement of the vacancies an ordered $A_2^{III}B_3^{VI}$ compound has the same symmetry as the III–V compounds (space group T_d^2).

6.13. Such ordered structures have been obtained in In_2Te_3, Ga_2Se_3, and Ga_2Te_3. Ordered In_2Se_3 crystals have not yet been produced. In the following discussion we will concern ourselves with mixed crystals between these four III-VI compounds and some of the III-V compounds.

The electrical properties of the III-VI compounds have scarcely been investigated. The forbidden gaps are larger than the ones of the comparable III-V compounds. The mobilities lie lower, the resistivities higher. We will, however, restrict ourselves in the following discussion to one end of the mixed-crystal systems, so that an exact knowledge of the III-VI compounds is not required. For the physics of the III-V compounds the region up to a few mole % $A_2^{III}B_3^{VI}$ content is particularly interesting, for the following reason. For mixed crystals between III-V compounds the transition of the properties from one component to the other takes place continuously, commencing at arbitrarily small admixtures. Consider, in contrast, the system InSb-In_2Se_3. Starting from the pure InSb compound, the introduction of the first selenium atoms only produces a doping with donors. For larger selenium concentrations, however, additional selenium atoms do not act as donors. Rather, they incorporate into the lattice together with an appropriate number of vacancies and thereby change the crystal lattice itself.

Goryunova and Grigor'eva (56G3) were the first to show mixed-crystal formation in these systems, as well as in the system AlSb-Al_2Te_3 [cf. (59G8)], but no physical measurements have so far been made on the latter system.

The production of homogeneous mixed crystals is again characterized by long diffusion times. One of the procedures described in Section 611, such as zone homogenizing or slow directional freezing, must be used. Annealing just below the melting point requires very long annealing times. The time can be shortened by annealing under pressure (59G9). The dependence of lattice constant on composition was measured by Woolley and Smith (58W10), (60W9) for some of the mixed-crystal systems under discussion. Small deviations from Vegard's law are observed.

621 The systems InSb-In_2Se_3 and InSb-In_2Te_3. The compound In_2Se_3 is soluble in InSb up to 2.5 mole %, so that mixed-crystal formation is restricted to a small region (61W9). The electrical properties of this system show the same anomalies as those of the InSb-In_2Te_3 mixed crystals. The latter are more interesting to study because of a wider range of solubility.

Mixed crystals of InSb-In_2Te_3 were produced by Woolley, Gillett, and Evans (60W7). Figure 6.14 shows the change of lattice constant with mixing ratio. The mole % indication refers to the formula $A_3^{III}B_3^{V}$-$A_2^{III}B_3^{VI}$. The lattice constant decreases linearly up to 15 mole % III-VI content. Subsequently it remains constant, and a second phase with NaCl structure can be demonstrated. What new compound this represents is not yet known. In another context Goryunova, Radautsan, and Kjosse (59G8) assigned this NaCl phase to a so-far-unknown compound of the composition In_4SbTe_3.

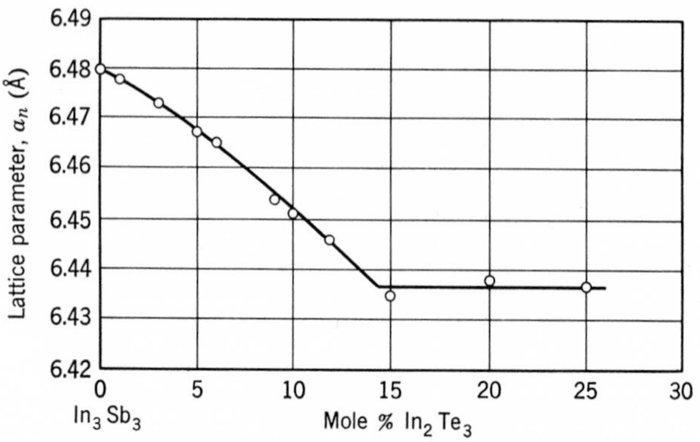

Fig. 6.14 Change of lattice constant with composition in the system InSb-In_2Te_3 [after Woolley, Gillett, and Evans (60W7)].

The solubility range is therefore restricted to 15 mole %. Within this region the conductivity and Hall coefficient were measured. The reciprocal Hall coefficient, representing the electron density, is shown in Fig. 6.15. Figure 6.16 shows the Hall mobility determined from the same measurements. The electron density changes in the expected

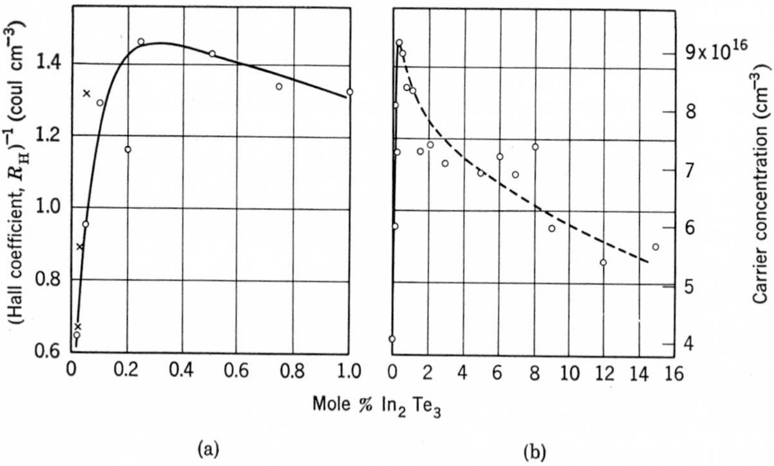

Fig. 6.15 Reciprocal Hall coefficient, as a measure of the electron density, in the system InSb-In_2Te_3: (a) 0–1 mole % In_2Te_3, (b) 0–15 mole % In_2Te_3 [after Woolley, Gillett, and Evans (60W7)].

way. First n increases rapidly, indicating that the tellurium atoms are built into the V-sublattice as donors, without a vacancy appearing in the III-sublattice for every three tellurium atoms. The additional indium in the InSb-In_2Te_3 melt is not built into the lattice, in agreement with the results of Chapter 5, namely, that stoichiometric III-V compounds are produced even from nonstoichiometric melts. Mixed-crystal formation starts only at a larger tellurium concentration which presumably corresponds to the solubility of tellurium in InSb. From there on, vacancies are also built in. Because of the binding requirements of the lattice they act as acceptors (electron traps). They cause the electron density to drop slowly. The large scatter of the values beyond the maximum is understandable, since a minute tellurium excess or vacancy excess immediately makes its presence felt, either as donors or as acceptors. The rapid decrease of the mobility can also be explained: first, the increase of donor concentration up to 0.3 mole % In_2Te_3 causes an increase of ionized-impurity scattering; subsequently, alloy scattering decreases the mobility further, and at the same time the transition starts to the considerably smaller mobility of In_2Te_3.

The thermal conductivity also decreases rapidly by alloying 0.1–5 mole % In_2Te_3 to InSb, according to Aliev and Dzhangirov (63A1).

Gasson, Jennings, Parrott, and Penn (62G3) have developed a reaction-kinetic model for the interaction of possible lattice defects

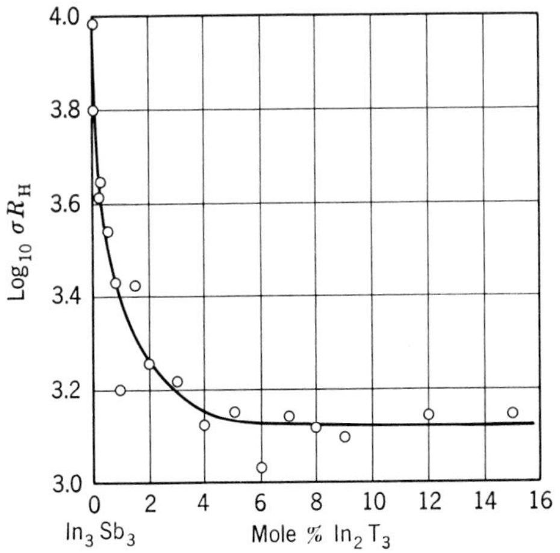

Fig. 6.16 Hall mobility of the electrons in the system InSb-In_2Te_3 up to 15 mole % In_2Te_3 [by Woolley, Gillett, and Evans (60W7)].

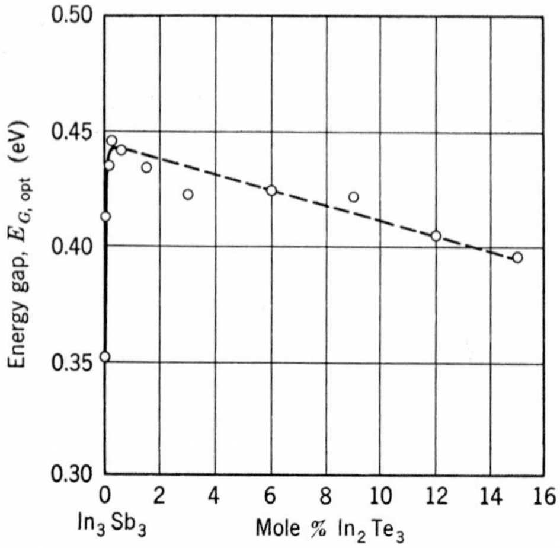

Fig. 6.17 Position of the absorption edge at room temperature in the system $InSb$-In_2Te_3 up to 15 mole % In_2Te_3 [after Woolley, Gillett, and Evans (60W7)].

and impurities with one another and with it have qualitatively described the change of electron concentration in the mixed-crystal system.

The measured position of the absorption edge is reproduced in Fig. 6.17. The results cannot be identified with a change of the forbidden gap by mixed-crystal formation. The increase of $E_{G,\mathrm{opt}}$ and the subsequent decrease rather are caused by a change of electron concentration and the accompanying filling of the conduction band (Burstein effect, Section 312).

Greenaway and Cardona (62G11) performed reflection measurements on mixed crystals up to 15 mole % In_2Te_3. The transitions at points X and L, which were discussed in Section 313, were also observed here. Their position changes with mixing ratio. This change is not always smooth, suggesting crossings of subbands.

Goryunova, Radautsan, and Kjosse (59G8) report that, in addition to the system $InSb$-In_2Te_3, the mixed-crystal system InSb-InTe also exists. The structure of InTe is unknown. The system also terminates in the appearance of a second NaCl-like phase, which is probably In_4SbTe_3.

622 The systems $InAs$-In_2Se_3 and $InAs$-In_2Te_3. The compound In_2Se_3 is soluble in InAs, up to at least 80 mole % (59G9), (61W9), while In_2Te_3 in InAs is completely soluble (61W6). The lattice constant increases approximately linearly with the mixing ratio. The first work on these mixed crystals was reported by Goryunova and Radautsan (58G8), (58G9).

The electrical and optical properties of the system $InAs$-In_2Se_3 were investigated by Nasledov, Pronina, and Radautsan (60N1), Radautsan and Malkovich (61R1), (62R1), and Woolley and Keating (61W9). The results agree in all points with those on the systems discussed in Section 621. The mobility of the electrons drops rapidly with the mixing ratio. The electron density increases rapidly and reaches a maximum value of 7×10^{19} cm^{-3} at 5 mole % In_2Se_3. The same maximum value is found in $InAs$-In_2Te_3 (5×10^{19} cm^{-3}), while in the systems $InSb$-In_2Se_3 and $InSb$-In_2Te_3 $n_{max} = 9 \times 10^{18}$ cm^{-3} was measured. The fact that the maximum electron concentration is independent of the III-VI compound caused Woolley and Keating to propose that these numbers do not represent the solubility of selenium or tellurium in InSb and InAs, but that they are given by a higher subband in the two III-V compounds. If the carriers in this higher subband have a considerably larger mass, they contribute only little to the Hall coefficient. The electron concentration calculated from the Hall coefficient then represents only the contribution of the lower-lying band. Even if some of the results of the measurements of Woolley and Keating are better explained by the second hypothesis, sufficient evidence is not available to confirm it definitely.

Figure 6.18 contains the width of the forbidden gap for $InAs$-In_2Se_3, determined from electrical and optical measurements. The large discrepancy between the two curves is caused by the fact that the Burstein effect simulates too-large optical E_G values. The crossing of the two curves can probably be assigned to measurement uncertainties. The "electric curve" consists of two linear sections, which could be explained by a change of the band structure at a few mole % In_2Se_3. If this hypothesis applies and the right part of the curves is to be assigned to a ($k \neq 000$)-minimum as the lowest minimum of the conduction band, then an extrapolation to the left would lead to an estimate of 0.2 eV for the separation of this minimum from the (000)-minimum in InAs. On one hand, this would support the hypothesis of Woolley and Keating; on the other hand, it cannot be reconciled with the experimental material on InAs reported in Chapter 4. Further experimental results must be awaited.

Optical, galvanomagnetic, and thermoelectric measurements on mixed crystals of $InAs$-In_2Te_3, by Woolley, Pamplin, and Evans (61W6), show strong similarities of this system to the systems $InAs$-In_2Se_3 and $InSb$-In_2Te_3, so that we need not treat these results in

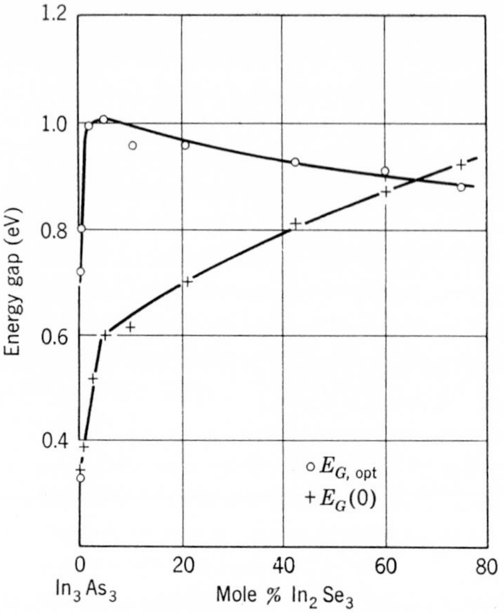

Fig. 6.18 Electrically and optically determined forbidden gap in the mixed-crystal system InAs-In_2Se_3 [after Woolley and Keating (61W9)].

detail. Again, InAs-rich mixed crystals are strongly degenerate. Only above 70 mole % In_2Te_3 do $E_{G,\text{opt}}$ and $E_{G,\text{electr}}$ agree. The electron mobility decreases continuously from InAs to In_2Te_3; the thermal conductivity shows a minimum (61G4). The reflection peaks assigned to X- and L-transitions change their position with the mixing ratio in such a fashion that band crossing must be assumed, according to Greenaway and Cardona (62G11). A definite statement about the change of the band model in this mixed-crystal system is therefore not yet possible.

623 The systems GaAs-Ga_2Se_3 and GaAs-Ga_2Te_3. The only thing known about the system GaSb-Ga_2Se_3 is that *no* mixed crystals are formed for 50 mole % of the two compounds (59W10).

The system GaAs-Ga_2Se_3 forms a continuous mixed-crystal system over the entire range (56G3), (58W10). In the system GaAs-Ga_2Te_3 mixed-crystal formation was observed only above 30 mole % Ga_2Te_3 (58W10). Deviations from Vegard's law were observed.

The electrical properties of GaAs-Ga_2Se_3 mixed crystals were investigated by Feltin'sh and Nasledov (59F1), (59N2), (60F2), (60N3), (61F1). The maximum in electron concentration at a few mole % Ga_2Se_3 again appeared. The width of the forbidden gap increased continuously from 1.40 to 1.98 eV for Ga_2Se_3. Since only four mixed crystals were studied, the exact change of E_G with mixing ratio is uncertain.

The transition region between Se-doped GaAs and GaAs-Ga_2Se_3 mixed crystals has been investigated by Vieland and Kudman (63V1).

624 Other mixed-crystal systems. The only other mixed crystals between III-V compounds and III-VI compounds that have been reported are in the system InP-In_2Se_3, up to 50% InP (62R1).

Mixed crystals between III-V compounds and elements of group IV were searched for by a number of authors. Under equilibrium conditions the elements of group IV are only weakly soluble in III-V compounds. According to Zitter, for example, less than 0.5% tin can be dissolved in InSb (58Z2). Germanium is soluble up to about 2% in GaAs (58J2). At the same time the width of the forbidden gap sinks by about 0.1 eV. We have discussed the donor character of the dissolved germanium in Chapter 5. In GaSb also only 2% germanium can be dissolved in equilibrium. Duwez, Willens, and Klement (60D2) were, however, able to obtain single-phase mixed crystals by rapid quenching of Ge-GaSb melts. In such a mixed-crystal system the lattice constant decreases linearly with composition.

No results of electrical measurements have been reported.

The weak solubility of the elements of group IV in the III-V compounds, despite similar atomic sizes, can, according to Section 610, be understood by the polarization of the electron bridges in the III-V compounds, which is absent for the elements.

Goryunova and co-workers considered the existence of *quaternary* mixed-crystal systems. They produced approximately homogeneous mixed crystals in the system GaAs-ZnSe (59G10). We will return to mixed crystals between III-V and II-IV-V compounds at the end of Section 631.

63 Related Ternary Compounds

630 General viewpoints. Tetrahedral phases, i.e., crystal lattices in which each atom has four equivalent nearest neighbors around it, are preferred, when the average number of valence electrons per atom that are available for the binding is equal to 4. The *elements* of group IV of the periodic system which crystallize in the tetrahedral diamond lattice have exactly four valence electrons for each atom. Among the *binary* tetrahedral compounds which crystallize in the zinc-blende or wurtzite lattices, we can distinguish three groups, the III-V, the II-VI, and the I-VII compounds. Here the sum of the valence electrons of two nearest neighbors is always equal to 8; the average number per atom again equal to 4. These binary phases can therefore be considered as derived from the group IV elements (cf. Chapter 1). In the same way *ternary* semiconductors can be derived from binary compounds by replacing one half of the atoms in one of the sublattices by lower-valent atoms, the other half by higher-valent atoms, at the same time *maintaining the average number of valence electrons per atom.*

The following two groups of ternary compounds can be derived from the III-V compounds:

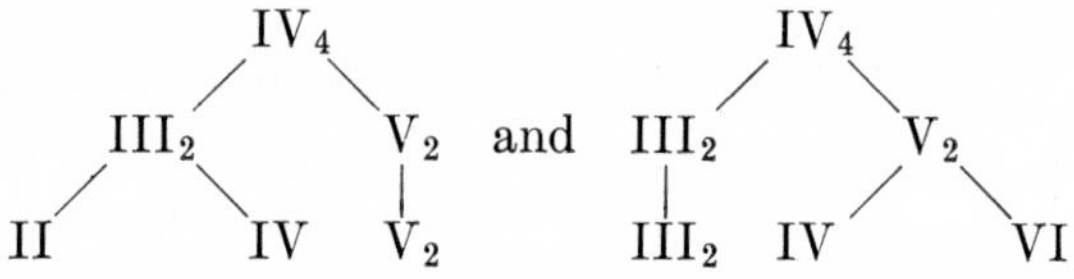

Here the atoms in one sublattice were replaced by the neighbors to right and left in the periodic system. More complicated "derivatives" can also be imagined, such as:

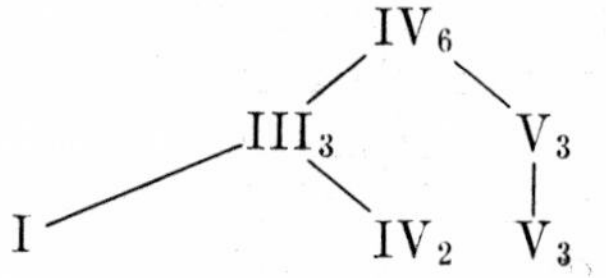

Ternary derivatives with substitution in both sublattices are also possible. In that case the new lattices tend to differ too much from the original compounds to still be considered as related to them. In this way the compounds $A_2^{III}B_3^{VI}$, which were treated in Section 620, can be derived from the III-V compounds by replacing the pentavalent atoms of one sublattice by hexavalent ones, and simultaneously substituting "zero-valent" vacancies for one third of the trivalent atoms in the other sublattice. The same compounds can, however, be derived from the II-VI compounds by substituting in only one of the sublattices:

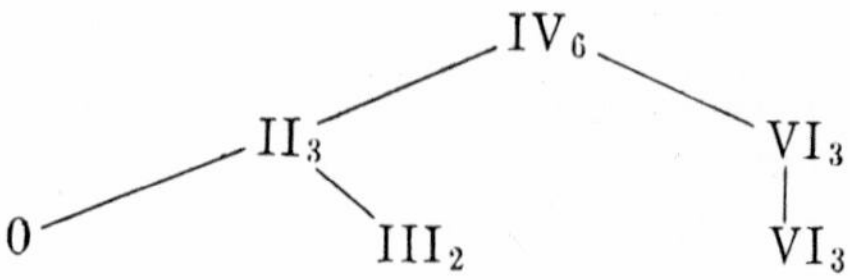

Quaternary compounds can similarly be imagined as derived from ternary ones. So far there are, however, no references to this case in the literature.

Of course, not all imaginable derivatives of the III-V compounds will exist. As for the mixed-crystal formation there will be the requirement that the substitutions do not distort the lattice too much. The sizes of the different atoms in the substituting sublattice must not be very different, and the polarization of the electron bridges from the two kinds of atoms to the atoms of the nonsubstituting sublattice must be approximately equal.

General criteria for the existence of ternary semiconducting compounds were first discussed by Folberth (58F3), (58F4), (59F2) and Goodman (57G4), (58G7). [See also Busch and Hulliger (60B10).] Following Folberth (59F2), let us consider the first two derivations diagrammed above, $A^{II}B^{IV}C_2^{V}$ and $A_2^{III}B^{IV}C^{VI}$. In the former it will be required that the polarizations of the II-V and of the IV-V bridges be not too different. Because of the greater charge difference the II-V bridge is undoubtedly polarized more strongly. The two bridges will be similar to each other only if the bivalent atoms can take up two electrons relatively easily, so that they can form a bond similar to that of the tetravalent atoms. This means, that the ternary compound will be more likely to form, the more electronegative the bivalent atoms are as compared with the tetravalent ones. Since the electronegativities are known, this criterion can be checked. The result is that many $A^{II}B^{IV}C_2^{V}$ compounds fulfill the condition, and indeed the existence of a large number of such compounds has been established. In contrast, *none* of the $A_2^{III}B^{IV}C^{VI}$ compounds fulfills the corresponding condition, and no stable compounds have yet been found. Goodman (58G7) was able to produce the compounds Al_2SnTe, Al_2SnSe, Al_2GeTe, and Al_2GeSe, but they decayed very rapidly with formation of H_2Te or H_2Se.

We will consider the $A^{II}B^{IV}C_2^{V}$ compounds in the following section. At this point we want only to mention the formation of the compounds $CuGe_2P_3$ and $CuSi_2P_3$ by Pfister and Folberth (61P8). These compounds belong to the third type of derivative pictured above. The measured lattice constants of these compounds agree within 2% with values calculated from the covalent radii of the partner under the assumption of a disordered zinc-blende lattice.

Mixed crystals can also be formed between the III-V compounds and their derivatives. This opens up a wide field for further semiconducting compounds. The following mixed crystals have been shown to exist: $Cd_{x/2}In_{1-x}Sn_{x/2}As$, $Zn_{x/2}In_{1-x}Sn_{x/2}As$, $Zn_{x/2}In_{1-x}Ge_{x/2}As$, and

$Zn_{x/2}Ga_{1-x}Ge_{x/2}As$, all belonging to the system $A^{III}D^{V}$-$B^{II}C^{IV}D_2^{V}$, and another mixed crystal of this type, in whose V-sublattice two different pentavalent atoms are found, namely $Zn_{0.25}In_{0.5}Sn_{0.25}As_{0.8}P_{0.2}$ (59F2).

631 $A^{II}B^{IV}C_2^{V}$ compounds. We have seen in Section 630 that $A^{II}B^{IV}C_2^{V}$ compounds can exist as derivatives of III-V compounds if the polarizations of the II-V and IV-V electron bridges are not too different from one another. For approximately equal polarization the bonds are equivalent and the crystal will have the zinc-blende lattice, with the bivalent and tetravalent atoms distributed randomly in the III-sublattice. For larger polarization differences the atoms will distribute themselves in the III-sublattice in such a way that each pentavalent atom is surrounded by two bivalent and two tetravalent nearest neighbors.

We have seen in Section 620 that when one *third* of the atoms in one of the sublattices of the zinc-blende lattice is replaced by vacancies, the full symmetry of the zinc-blende lattice remains intact (Fig. 6.13). This is no longer possible when one *half* of all the atoms of one sublattice is replaced by other atoms. The symmetry is then considerably reduced. The unit cell of this type of lattice is only twice as large as that of the zinc-blende lattice (*chalcopyrite* lattice). Frequently it is tetragonally distorted in addition. Figure 6.19 shows the comparison

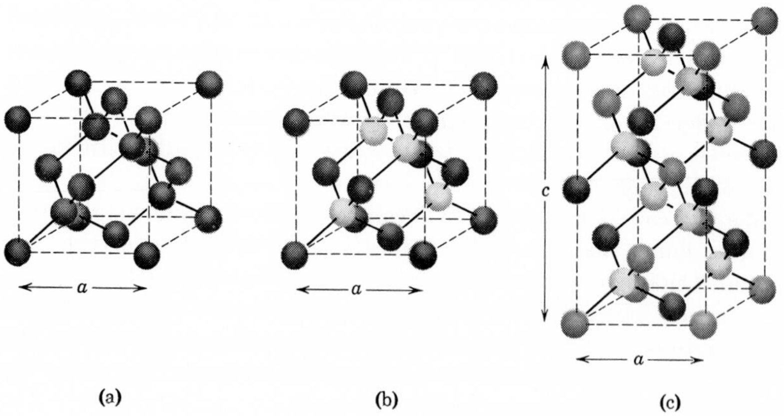

Fig. 6.19 (a) Diamond lattice, (b) zinc-blende lattice, (c) chalcopyrite lattice. The diamond and zinc-blende lattices differ only in the kinds of atoms they contain, but the chalcopyrite lattice is, in addition, slightly deformed, i.e., c is not equal to $2a$ (cf. Table 6.1).

Table 6.1 Lattice Constant *a* and Tetragonal Distortion $(2 - c/a)$ of Some $A^{II}B^{IV}C_2^{V}$ Compounds

The quantity in the last column is a measure of the difference of the polarization of the II-V and IV-V bonds after Pfister and Folberth (61P8).

Compound	a (Å)	$(2 - c/a)$	$(r^A/r^B)_{cov} - (r^A/r^B)_{ion}$
$ZnSnAs_2$	5.85_1	0.00	0.10
$MgGeP_2$	5.65_2	0.00	0.08
$ZnGeP_2$	5.46	0.03	0.33
$ZnGeAs_2$	5.67	0.03_3	0.33
$CdSnAs_2$	6.09_2	0.04_3	0.31
$ZnSiAs_2$	5.60_8	0.05_8	0.69
$ZnSiP_2$	5.39_8	0.06_6	0.69
$CdGeAs_2$	5.94_2	0.11_1	0.62
$CdGeP_2$	5.73_8	0.12_2	0.62

between the unit cells of the diamond, zinc-blende, and chalcopyrite lattices (58F3). Note that the unit cell of the chalcopyrite lattice is twice as large as that of the zinc-blende lattice. An undistorted chalcopyrite lattice has $c/a = 2$, and $(2 - c/a)$ is a measure of the tetragonal distortion.

The lattice constants of some $A^{II}B^{IV}C_2^{V}$ compounds were measured by Folberth and Pfister (58F3), (58P3), (60F7), (61P8) and by Goodman (57G4), (58G7). The results are contained in Table 6.1. In addition to these nine compounds $ZnSnP_2$ and $CdSnP_2$ also exist, according to Goodman (57G4), but their structure has not yet been determined. The compounds $CdSiP_2$ and $CdSiAs_2$ could not be produced, nor any of the antimonides and bismuthides. From Table 6.1 it can be seen that $ZnSnAs_2$ and $MgGeP_2$ have the disordered ZnS structure, while the other seven compounds crystallize in the chalcopyrite lattice. According to Pfister and Folberth (61P8), this can be explained by the above considerations. The ratio of the covalent radii of the two components $(r^A/r^B)_{cov}$ will agree most closely with the corresponding ratio of the ionic radii $(r^A/r^B)_{ion}$ when the polarizations of the two bonds are similar to each other. The difference between these two ratios is listed in Table 6.1. It clearly shows the distinction between the two compounds crystallizing in the ZnS structure and the chalcopyrite-like compounds.

Gasson and co-workers (62G2) have shown that $ZnSnAs_2$ can also have an ordered chalcopyrite phase in addition to the disordered ZnS phase. We will return to this topic later.

Table 6.2 Width of the Forbidden Gap of Some $A^{II}B^{IV}C_2^V$ Compounds [from optical measurements of Goodman (57G4), (58G7), Strauss and Rosenberg (68S15) and Goryunova *et al.* (63G9)]

Compound	$E_{G,opt}$ (eV)
$ZnGeP_2$	2.2 ± 0.2
$ZnSiAs_2$	2.1
$ZnSnP_2$	2.1
$CdGeP_2$	1.8
$CdSnP_2$	1.5
$ZnGeAs_2$	<1.1 >0.6
$CdGeAs_2$	0.53
$CdSnAs_2$	0.23

Table 6.2 contains a number of optically determined E_G values. Among these compounds only $CdSnAs_2$ has been investigated more closely. Folberth and Pfister (58F3) reported that in this compound the electron mobility exceeds the value 3000 cm^2/V sec. Strauss and Rosenberg (61S15) found for a sample with an electron concentration of 5.5×10^{17} cm^{-3} an electron mobility of 12,000 cm^2/V sec at room temperature. This value has been surpassed only by the binary semiconductors InSb, InAs, HgSe, and HgTe and lies well above the mobility values of germanium and silicon! It is evident that despite their seemingly complicated structure the ternary semiconductors can have properties which make them appear to be superior to simpler semiconductors for technical applications.

The compound $CdSnAs_2$ can be produced by melting the components together. Long annealing times are not necessary. According to Strauss and Rosenberg, the melting point lies at 590–600°C. One can describe $CdSnAs_2$ as a derivative of InAs, and indeed it resembles the latter in some of its other properties. The width of the forbidden gap is of the same order of magnitude (0.23 eV), and the Burstein effect is clearly apparent in the absorption spectrum. The shift of the absorption edge with doping points to a small effective electron mass, related to the high mobility. This mass was determined by Matyáš and Höschl (62M3), from measurements of the magnetic susceptibility, as $m_n = 0.02\ m$. From optical measurements Spitzer, Wernick, and Wolfe (61S11) obtained a value between 0.04 and 0.06 m.

The electron mobility measured by Matyáš and Höschl increased up to 25,000 cm^2/V sec at 500°K and then decreased with a $T^{-1.67}$ law. If this behavior is extrapolated to room temperature, an electron mobility of the same order of magnitude as that for InSb is found for $CdSnAs_2$. This material therefore has strong similarities to InSb and InAs and in addition, as a ternary compound, a thermal conductivity which is only about one quarter that of InAs (61S11), (62G9).

These properties of $CdSnAs_2$ lead one to suspect interesting properties in the mixed-crystal system InAs-$CdSnAs_2$. The first measurements by Mamaev, Nasledov, and Galavanov (61M2) [cf. also (63N1)] show a complete miscibility of the two components in one another and a monotonic change of properties between them. Only the width of the forbidden gap decreases linearly from InAs to a value below the energy gap of $CdSnAs_2$ and increases again after this minimum (Fig. 6.20).

The mixed-crystal systems InSb-$CdSnAs_2$ and InSb-$CdSnSb_2$ were investigated by Goryunova and Prochukhan (60G13). The zinc-blende structure remains for small additions of the ternary compound. Then a transition takes place to the chalcopyrite structure. Indium antimonide is completely miscible with $ZnSnAs_2$, but only partially soluble in $ZnGeAs_2$ and $CdGeAs_2$ (63B13).

The compound $ZnSnAs_2$ crystallizes in a disordered zinc-blende structure above 635°C (63B8), (63P4). Its melting point lies at

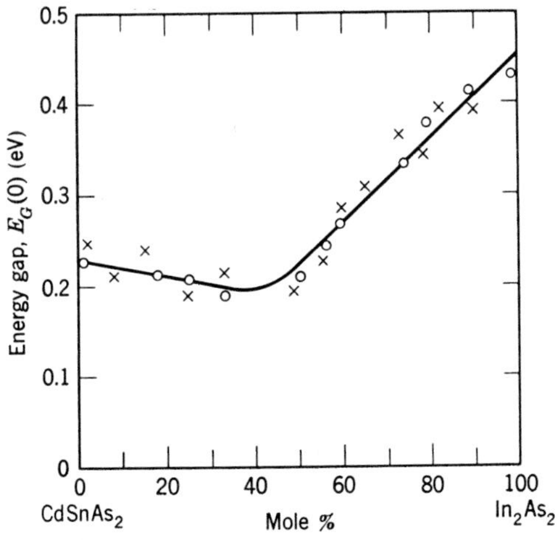

Fig. 6.20 Electrically determined width of the forbidden gap $E_G(0)$ in the mixed-crystal system InAs-$CdSnAs_2$ [after Mamaev, Nasledov, and Galavanov (61M2)].

775°C. Below 635°C crystallization is also possible in the chalcopyrite structure. Gasson, Holmes, Jennings, Marathe, and Parrott (62G2) [cf. also (64G3)] found that the two structures have the same c/a ratio (2.000 ± 0.012). A distinct difference exists, as expected, in the thermal conductivity, which is 0.115 W cm^{-1} deg^{-1} at room temperature for the ordered phase, and 0.070 W cm^{-1} deg^{-1} for the disordered phase. Other preliminary parameter values for this compound are a hole mobility of 22 cm^2/V sec for impure p-type samples, an effective hole mass of 0.5 m, and an optical width of the forbidden gap of about 0.6 eV.

The compound $CdGeAs_2$ has been investigated by Goryunova *et al.* (63G9). The energy gap has been found to be $E_G = 0.53$ eV and the electron effective mass $m_n = 0.27\ m$.

The thermal conductivity of a number of II-IV-V_2 compounds was measured by Leroux-Hugon (63L1).

It was seen in Chapter 2 that group-theoretical methods can furnish a qualitative picture of the band structure of a semiconductor. This picture may be improved quantitatively by the $k \cdot p$ theory. Sandrock and Treusch (64S7) and Lietz and Rössler (64L2) [cf. also (62C10), (63C7), (63G13)] have performed such calculations on the chalcopyrite lattice. The band structure is similar to that of the zinc-blende lattice. The splitting-off of the V_3-band at $\mathbf{k} = 0$, which appeared in Kane's theory when the spin was included, is present in the chalcopyrite lattice even without spin, because of the establishment of a unique c-axis. Since sufficient experimental data are not yet available, we will not discuss the theory in any more detail.

7

p-n Junctions

70 Introduction

No difficulties are encountered in forming *p-n* junctions in the III-V compounds. The methods used for germanium and silicon, such as alloying, diffusing, and counterdoping during the crystal pulling, can be taken over almost without change [(58S2), (58W4), (59H2), (62M7) and other literature referred to below]. Again, the same methods as those for germanium and silicon can be used to disclose the presence of *p-n* junctions [see, e.g. (62S7)].

Both diodes and transistors can be produced from III-V compounds. They will be considered in Sections 710 and 711. However, only in a few special cases do the III-V diodes and transistors have notable advantages for technical application as compared to the germanium and silicon devices.

The *p-n* junctions of III-V compounds are of greater interest as photodiodes and particle detectors and as tunnel diodes. These we will discuss in Sections 72 and 73.

Aside from *p-n* junctions, point-contact diodes have some importance because of their lower temperature sensitivity, their usually higher frequency cut-off, and the absence of hole-storage effects. Point contacts on GaAs, particularly, have been investigated in some detail (59S2), (60N4), (60N5). Their current-voltage characteristics show the usual behavior for semiconductor point contacts, but the absolute magnitude of the reverse-saturation current and its temperature dependence have not yet been explained quantitatively. Measurements on point contacts have also been made on other III-V compounds, such as AlSb (58H2), (58I1) and GaP (59M2), (60D1), (63W9).

A different kind of metal semiconductor diode is the "surface barrier rectifier." Mead and Spitzer (63M2), (64S4) have studied the photoresponse of such rectifiers and have therefrom deduced information about the band structure of the semiconductor. In the case of AlAs (63M2) they found indications of indirect transitions above 2.1 eV and of direct transitions above 2.9 eV. These are the only experiments so far that have furnished information about the nature of the conduction band of AlAs, aside from the pressure measurements of Paul (61P6), which predict a Δ minimum at the bottom of the conduction band. In $GaAs_{1-x}P_x$ Mead and Spitzer (64S4) found threshold energies for direct transitions between 1.37 eV for GaAs and 2.64 eV for GaP. Indirect transitions varied from 1.62 eV for GaAs to 2.2 eV for GaP. The band crossover occurred at $x = 0.38$.

The *p-n* junctions in III-V compounds with direct energy gaps show strong electroluminescence. This property has become of considerable importance due to the discovery of a new class of solid-state lasers made of these materials. We will discuss it in Section 74.

The ready miscibility of many III-V compounds permits the creation of *p-n* junctions where the adjacent bulk regions consist of two different semiconductors ("heterojunctions"). Then, not only the conduction type changes in the transition region, but also the width of the forbidden gap. The transition takes place continuously with a single-crystal structure, as contrasted to a *contact* between two different semiconductors. The current through such heterojunctions is characterized by most of the injection taking place in one direction, namely, from the semiconductor with the large E_G value into the other one. These junctions are therefore particularly suited for emitters of transistors.

Even if two semiconductors are not miscible, *p-n* (or *n-n*) junctions can be formed between them as long as they have approximately the same lattice constant. The transition from the E_G value of the one side to that of the other then takes place discontinuously in the space-charge region. The properties of such heterojunctions made of germanium and GaAs have been investigated experimentally by Anderson and compared with theory (60A13), (61A8), (62A4).

71 Diodes and Transistors

710 Diodes. The current-voltage characteristic of a *p-n* diode can be described by Shockley's theory of an ideal *p-n* junction:

$$I = I_s(e^{eV/kT} - 1) \tag{7.1}$$

Here I is the current, V the voltage difference across the p-n junction, and I_s the saturation current in the reverse direction.

In actual junctions deviations from (7.1) are usually observed. The most common ones are a voltage dependence of I_s in the reverse direction and a too-shallow exponential increase in the forward direction: $I \propto e^{eV/\alpha kT}$ $(\alpha > 1)$.

The derivation of eq. (7.1) neglects any recombination and generation of electron-hole pairs in the space-charge region of the junction. If this recombination is included (diffusion length of the charge carriers $\leq$ width of the transition region), the theory of Shockley, Sah, and Noyce leads to an exponential current in the forward direction with $\alpha = 2$, which only at higher voltages gradually goes over into the form given by (7.1).

Numerous investigations of InSb p-n junctions have been performed (59L3), (60L3), (60M1), (61G17), (61M5), (61S14), (62M4), (62M7), (62M8), (63G3). Figure 7.1 shows the I-V characteristic of a p-n junction-

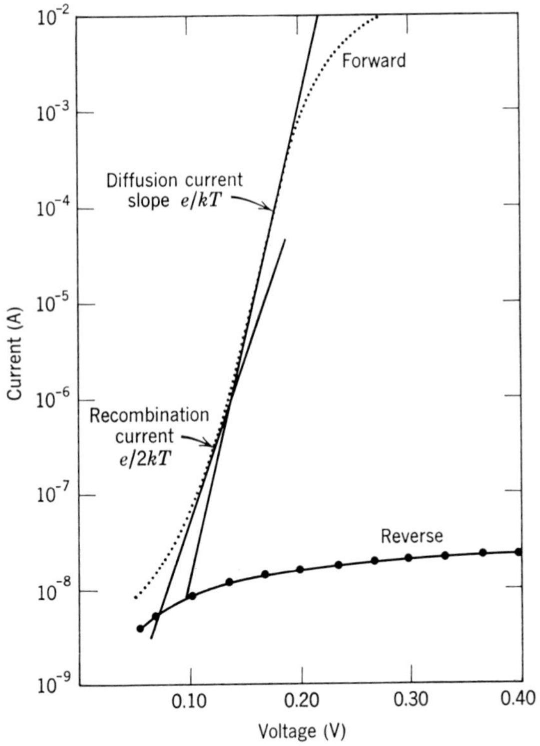

Fig. 7.1 I-V characteristic of an InSb diode at 78°K [after Stocker (61S14)].

tion formed in InSb by alloying, measured by Stocker (61S14). The characteristics can be interpreted quantitatively by the theory of Shockley, Sah, and Noyce. In the forward direction the two regions in which the exponential increase follows $e/2kT$ and e/kT are clearly separated. For diffused *p-n* junctions Stocker finds, in contrast, a current proportional to $e^{eV/2kT}$ up to voltages of the order of the built-in potential of the diode. According to Marfaing (60M1), the reverse current in InSb diodes does not show any saturation.

Melngailis and Rediker (62M4) discovered a negative-resistance region in the forward direction of InSb *p-n* diodes with heavily doped *n*-type sides. This has been ascribed to modulation of the conductivity in the *p*-region by injected minority carriers. The negative resistance can be removed by a transverse magnetic field. The sensitivity of the characteristic to weak magnetic fields is shown in Fig. 7.2. A change of the field by only 5 gauss can cause the forward current to change by up to 50 mA.

Investigations of *p-n* junctions in InAs have been published by Lucovsky (61L7), and in GaAs by Allen (59A3), Burdukov *et al.* (61B20), Lowen and Rediker (60L4), and others (62L2), (63K3), (63N3), (63R1), (63W3). Figure 7.3 shows, as an example, the characteristic of a GaAs diode (60L4).

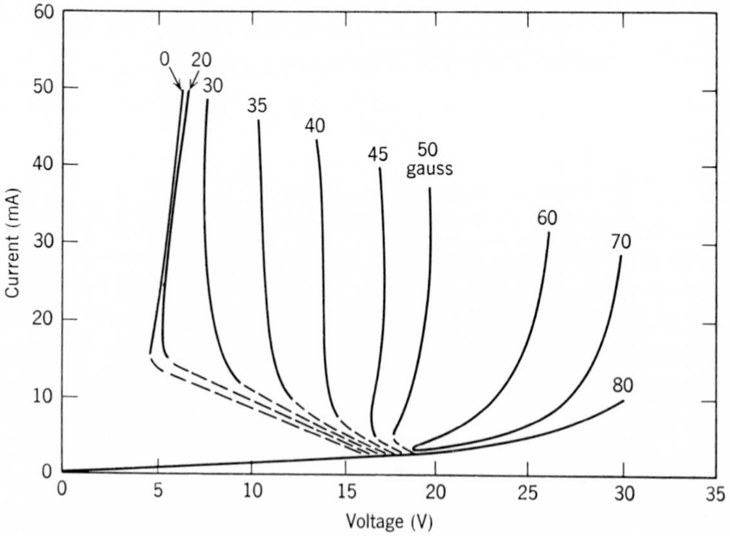

Fig. 7.2 Effect of a transverse magnetic field on the negative resistance region of an n^+p-InSb diode [after Melngailis and Rediker (62M4)].

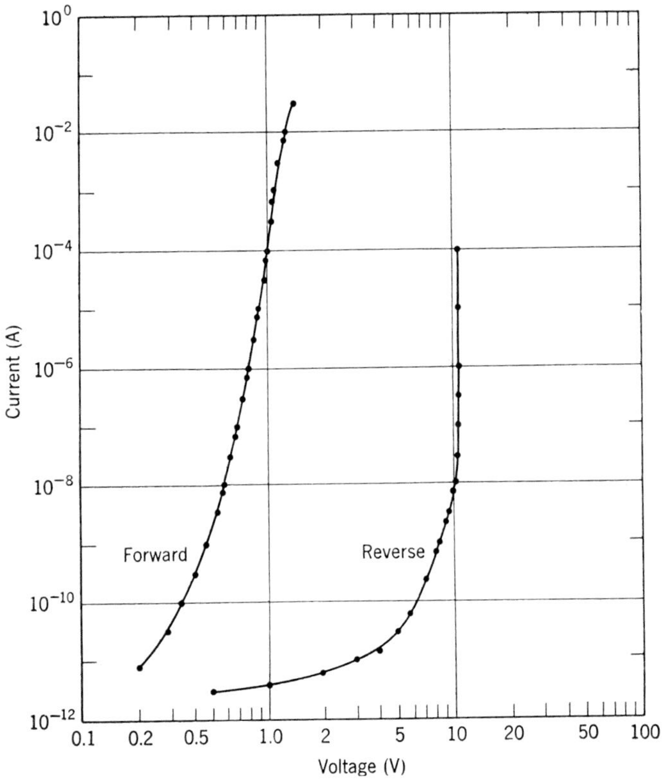

Fig. 7.3 Characteristic of a diffused GaAs diode [after Lowen and Rediker (60L4)].

711 Transistors. The possibility of using III-V compounds for transistors was critically discussed by Jenny (58J1). Two of the most important transistor parameters are the maximum operating temperature and the high-frequency cut-off. They can easily be estimated from the bulk properties of the semiconductor to be used. The maximum operating temperature is determined by the width of the forbidden gap, and, according to Jenny, is given in rough approximation by $T_{\max} = 533E_G - 273$ (T in °C, E_G in eV). The frequency cut-off for bipolar transistors is proportional to the square root of the product of electron and hole mobilities and inversely proportional to the fourth root of the dielectric constant of the semiconductors.

From these considerations it is evident that transistors made of GaAs, InP, and AlSb will operate at higher temperatures than germanium and silicon transistors, and that of these only GaAs transistors have a higher high-frequency cut-off than germanium transistors. The compounds InSb and InAs would make transistors of still higher frequencies, but they could not be used at room temperature.

All these estimates apply for bipolar transistors, but the conditions are similar for unipolar transistors.

A transistor effect, i.e., a power gain in *n-p-n* or point-contact structures, has so far been observed only for InSb, InP, and GaAs. At 77°K *n-p-n* transistors made of InSb operate with a high-frequency cut-off of about 300 Mc. Henneke (61H10) compared the properties of such InSb transistors with those of germanium transistors. An InP transistor was described by Jenny (58J1). A diffused *p-n* junction was used as a collector and a point contact as an emitter. The maximum power gain was 36 db. The transistor effect in InP was also described by Reynolds, Lilburne, and Dell (58R4). A GaAs transistor with a GaP-GaAs emitter (cf. Section 70) showed a power gain of 4 db (58J1).

72 Photoeffects at *p-n* Junctions

720 Photodiodes. The current-voltage characteristics of a *p-n* junction is modified by irradiation with light. The electron-hole pairs created by the light in the *p-n* junction are separated by the electric field of the transition region. This causes additional current to flow or—in the open-circuit case—a photovoltage to appear.

If the current-voltage characteristic has the Shockley form $[I = I_s(e^{eV/kT} - 1)]$, the photocurrent is given by

$$I = I_{\max} - I_s(e^{eV/kT} - 1) \tag{7.2}$$

where V is the voltage applied at the *p-n* junction. It has a maximum value for zero total current (open-circuit condition):

$$V_{\max} = \frac{kT}{e} \ln\left(\frac{I_{\max}}{I_s} + 1\right) \tag{7.3}$$

The maximum photocurrent $I_{\max}$ flows at $V = 0$ according to (7.2) (short-circuit condition).

The simplest case we can consider is one in which hole pairs are created homogeneously throughout the region around the junction with a rate G. The short-circuit electron current is then given by $I_{\max} = AeG(L_n + L_p)$, where A is the area of the junction and $L_{n,p}$ are the diffusion lengths in the *n*- and *p*-regions.

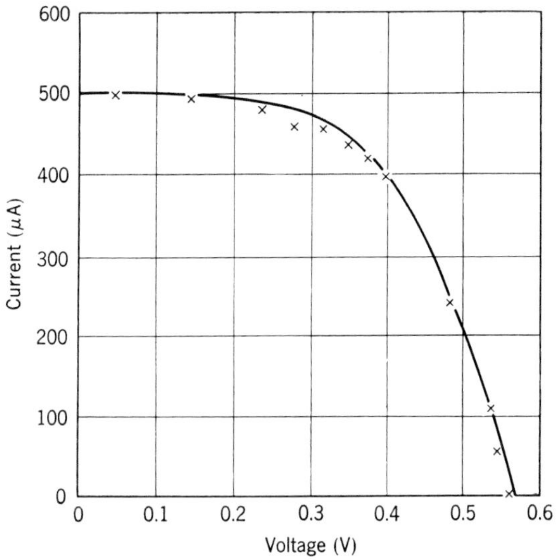

Fig. 7.4 Comparison of the theoretical current-voltage characteristic with experimental results on a GaAs photodiode [after Jenny, Loferski, and Rappaport (56J1)].

The experimental current-voltage characteristic of a GaAs photodiode is compared with eq. (7.2) in Fig. 7.4 (56J1).

One of the most important applications for photodiodes is the direct conversion of sunlight into electric energy (solar batteries). For this purpose the spectral sensitivity of the photodiodes in the visible range is of interest. Two factors influence the maximum attainable efficiency, the number of electron-hole pairs created by the photons and the voltage of the photodiode at the point of maximum power output. Both quantities depend on the size of the energy gap, E_G. With growing E_G, the part of the solar spectrum that contains photons of sufficient energy for the creation of electron-hole pairs becomes smaller. In contrast, the photovoltage grows with increasing E_G. This means that the efficiency must have a maximum at a certain E_G value. This maximum lies at 1.5–1.6 eV, according to Rittner (54R1). Therefore AlSb would be particularly suited for this application.

Subsequently, Loferski (56L3) discussed this question more thoroughly [see also Rappaport (59R1) and Moss (61M16)]. Atmospheric conditions must be taken into account in the choice of the most suitable semiconducting material. Only outside the atmosphere can a maximum efficiency be expected at $E_G = 1.6$ eV. The maximum moves to smaller E_G values with increasing optical path length of the light and with increasing water-vapor content of the air. Figure 7.5 shows some curves for the dependence of the efficiency η on E_G, calculated by Loferski. The parameter m represents the reciprocal cosine of the angle that the sun makes with the zenith, and it is therefore a measure of the optical path length. The absorption by water vapor was neglected. Loferski finds that semiconductors with energy gaps between 1.1 and 1.6 eV may be suitable for photodiodes, depending on

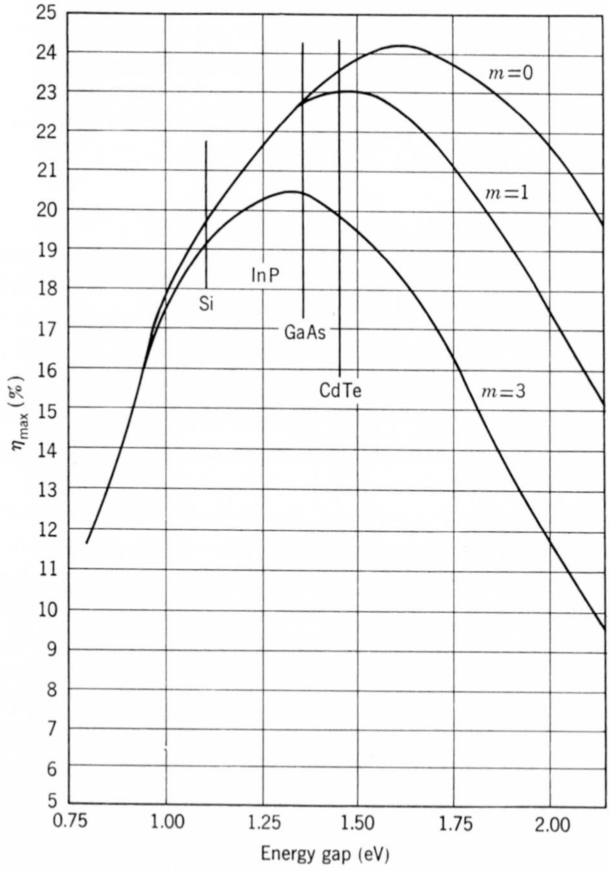

Fig. 7.5 Calculated efficiencies of solar batteries as functions of the energy gap E_G of the semiconductor. The absorption of the sunlight in the atmosphere is taken into account ($m = 1/\cos\theta$, where θ is the angle the sun makes with the zenith) [after Loferski (56L3)].

the atmospheric conditions. This means that InP and GaAs should have advantages over silicon which is now generally used for solar cells. The compound AlSb is excluded because of the technological difficulties it presents and because its E_G value lies at the maximum of the η-E_G curve only outside the atmosphere. All these results are true only in the Shockley limit of a photodiode (no recombination in the transition region). Deviations from this ideal case tend to flatten out the maxima of Fig. 7.5 and thereby diminish the differences between photodiodes made from semiconductors of different E_G values.

These theoretical predictions have not yet been confirmed experimentally. Photodiodes have been produced from the three III-V compounds mentioned, but promising results have been obtained only on GaAs photodiodes [Gremmelmaier (55G3), Jenny, Loferski, and Rappaport (56J1), and Gobat, Lamorte, and McIver (62G15)]. Gobat *et al.* obtained on a photodiode of 2 cm^2 area an efficiency of 12% for sunlight. The highest efficiency obtained on InP diodes was 2% (59R1).

The values of open-circuit voltage and short-circuit current of the photodiode shown in Fig. 7.4 are not the highest values obtained so far. Later investigations (60B11), (60W10), (62G15) gave open-circuit voltages of up to 0.90 V. Here GaAs photodiodes outperform silicon photodiodes (up to 0.58 eV) under visible light. The GaAs photodiodes have the added advantage that the saturation current I_s is a factor of 10^3 smaller than that for silicon diodes. However, the maximum efficiency of silicon photodiodes, which lies at 15%, has not yet been equaled.

Other measurements on GaAs photodiodes have been concerned mainly with the spectral response. According to Lucovsky and Cholet (60L5), the maximum sensitivity lies at 8500 Å. The half-power points lie at 5600 and at 9100 Å. These values were also confirmed by Nasledov and Tsarenkov (59N5), (62G14).

Investigations of the photoresponse of GaAs *p-n* junctions by Loh (63L4), (63L5), (63L6) in a broad spectral range showed the same interband transitions at various points in the Brillouin zone that have been observed in the reflectance (cf. Section 313).

Photodiodes of InSb and InAs are suitable for infrared detectors, since their maximum sensitivity lies at long wavelengths. Figure 7.6 shows the spectral sensitivity of an InAs photodiode according to the measurements of Talley and Enright (54T1). Photodiodes of InSb have been investigated by Mitchell, Goldberg and Kurnick (55M3), Avery, Goodwin, and Rennie (57A4), Lasser, Cholet, and Wurst (58L1), Galavanov and Erokhina (59G1), and Marfaing and Courrier

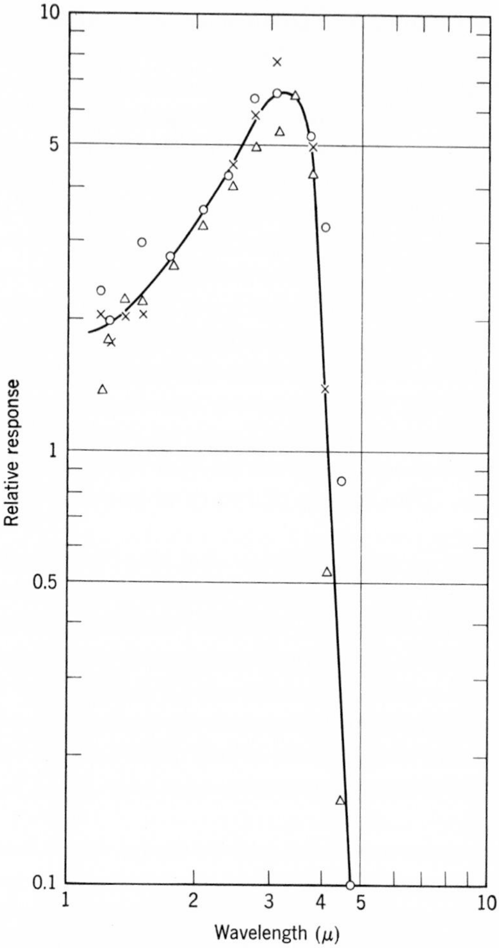

Fig. 7.6 Spectral response of an InAs photodiode at liquid-nitrogen temperature [after Talley and Enright (54T1)].

(61M4). Their response ranges out to 7 μ. They are, however, in many respects inferior to the PEM and PC detectors discussed in Section 43.

The photoeffect of GaP diodes was investigated by Grimmeiss, Kischio, and Koelmans (62G12).

721 Detection of x-rays, γ-rays, and energetic particles by *p-n* junctions. High-energy radiation and energetic particles can also be detected by the photodiodes described in Section 720. Certain peculiar effects caused by the different kinds of irradiation must be taken into account here.

Absorbed *x-rays* transfer their energy to electrons of the inner shells of the atoms. In a sequence of succeeding processes this energy is applied to the creation of a number of electron-hole pairs. Depending on the energy of the x-rays, Compton electrons may also be freed. This x-ray photoeffect on GaAs photodiodes and its possible applications are considered by Pfister (56P1), (59P2).

For very energetic radiation (e.g., *γ-radiation*) the electron-hole pairs are produced mainly by Compton electrons. The penetration depth of the radiation is usually large compared to the extension of the *p-n* junction, and the short-circuit current, according to Section 720, is proportional to the sum of the diffusion lengths and to the generation rate. This can be visualized by saying that all electron-hole pairs produced within one diffusion length from the junction contribute to the current. If one knows the diffusion lengths, one can determine the absorption of the radiation near the junction from the short-circuit current.

Often the opposite situation applies. For example, the absorption of γ-rays in GaAs is known quantitatively, but it is difficult to measure diffusion lengths near a *p-n* junction. Gremmelmaier (56G4) therefore used the γ-ray photoeffect to determine the very short diffusion lengths in InP and GaAs. In InP diffusion lengths of about 130 μ were measured, corresponding to a lifetime of 2×10^{-6} sec. In GaAs $L = 8\ \mu$ was found, and consequently $\tau = 9 \times 10^{-9}$ sec.

These photodiodes are not suited to be particle counters for individual γ-rays, since the range of the radiation exceeds the diffusion lengths by many orders of magnitude, and only a very small fraction of the absorbed energy is registered. Particle counters with a larger "effective volume" are better suited for this purpose. Such counters can, for example, be produced from high-resistivity GaAs (60H4).

Similar considerations apply also for the penetration of *ionizing radiation* into a photodiode. Pfister (57P2) investigated the effect of short-range electrons (7–26 μ) on a GaAs *p-n* junction. Photovoltage and short-circuit current increased linearly with intensity of the electron radiation. Therefore GaAs photodiodes are suited for intensity measurements in electron diffraction, for example.

In all these cases one must take into consideration that energetic radiation produces lattice defects (Section 523) and that therefore the properties of a photodiode may change with time. The damage from electron radiation appears only above a threshold energy, which, in GaAs, is about twice as large as in silicon.

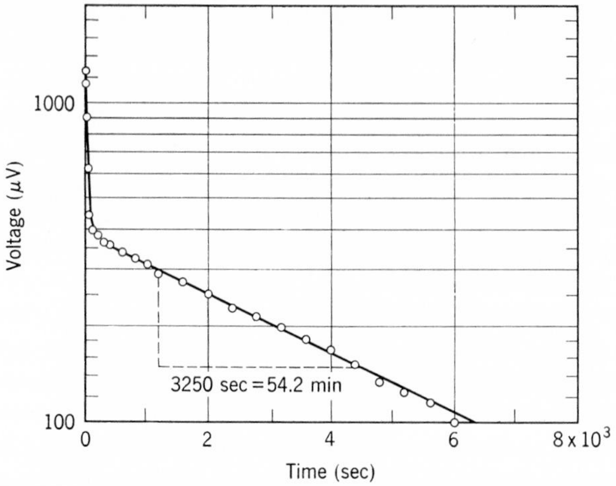

Fig. 7.7 Photovoltage of an InP particle counter after 30 min of neutron irradiation [after Gremmelmaier and Welker (56G4)].

Nuclear transmutations can be produced by irradiation of a semiconductor with nucleons, and this gives a possibility of detecting non-ionizing-particle radiation, such as *thermal neutrons.* Because of the large cross section of indium for thermal neutrons, InP photodiodes are particularly interesting in this connection. Gremmelmaier (56G4), (60G14) observed on an InP diode, after half an hour of neutron irradiation, the photovoltage shown in Fig. 7.7. The interpretation of this curve is as follows. Natural indium contains mainly the isotope In^{115}, which is transmuted into In^{116} by an (n, γ)-process. The γ-radiation can be detected by measuring the photovoltage during irradiation. *After* irradiation the photovoltage continues as long as the radioactive In^{116} atoms decay into Sn^{116} atoms by emission of electrons. This β-decay is characterized by two half-lives of 13 sec and 54.3 min. The photovoltage is proportional to the number of decaying In^{116} atoms per unit time. Hence it drops off proportionally to the radioactivity of the indium. The straight-line portions of the time dependence of the photovoltage in Fig. 7.7 have slopes which correspond exactly to these two half-life times.

73 Tunneling in *p-n* Junctions

In Chapter 3 we were able to obtain important details about the band structure of III-V compounds from investigations of optical transitions between the valence and the conduction band. Additional information can be obtained from phenomena connected with the quantum-mechanical *tunneling process.* Whereas the optical transitions are caused by the absorption of photons, band-to-band transitions by the tunneling effect are caused by an electric field.

The tunneling process can be observed only for sufficiently high field strengths. Such high-field regions are found in *p-n* junctions. The *I-V* characteristic of a *p-n* junction can be changed by the tunneling process in two different ways. On the one hand, electrons may tunnel from the valence band into the conduction band if a reverse bias is applied to the junction. This causes rapid creation of electron-hole pairs in the space-charge region of the junction and consequently a sharp increase of the reverse current. On the other hand, electrons can pass from the conduction band into the valence band under forward bias, if the bottom of the conduction band in the *n*-type region of the junction ($E_{c,n}$) lies lower in energy than the top of the valence band in the *p*-region ($E_{v,p}$). In this case most of the *I-V* characteristic will be determined by the tunneling process (*tunnel diode*). In the reverse direction the current will not saturate but will increase rapidly with voltage. In the forward direction the characteristic also starts off with a rapid current increase. Subsequently the current reaches a maximum and then drops off, since with increasing forward bias the difference $E_{v,p} - E_{c,n}$ becomes smaller. For $E_{v,p} = E_{c,n}$, tunneling is no longer possible. The current then increases again with increasing voltage according to the usual theory of a *p-n* junction [eq. (7.1)]. This behavior is depicted in Fig. 7.8 by the characteristics of three GaAs tunnel diodes (59G11).

The tunneling probability is calculated to be

$$W \sim \mathcal{E} e^{-A m_r^{1/2} E_G^{3/2} \mathcal{E}^{-1}} = \mathcal{E} e^{-\lambda} \tag{7.4}$$

where $\mathcal{E}$ is the electric field strength, E_G the width of the forbidden gap, m_r a reduced effective mass ($m_r^{-1} = m_n^{-1} + m_p^{-1}$), and A a constant of the order of $1/e\hbar$. Tunneling is therefore facilitated by small effective masses of electrons and holes and by a small energy gap.

These considerations give a qualitative picture of the current-voltage characteristic of tunnel diodes. For a more accurate discussion one must take into account that a variety of different band-to-band transitions can take place in semiconductors. Such transitions can be *direct*, with conservation of electron energy and momentum. Direct transitions can also be combined with the emission of a phonon or a photon. Then the electron momentum remains unchanged, but not its energy. *Indirect* transitions are also possible with emission

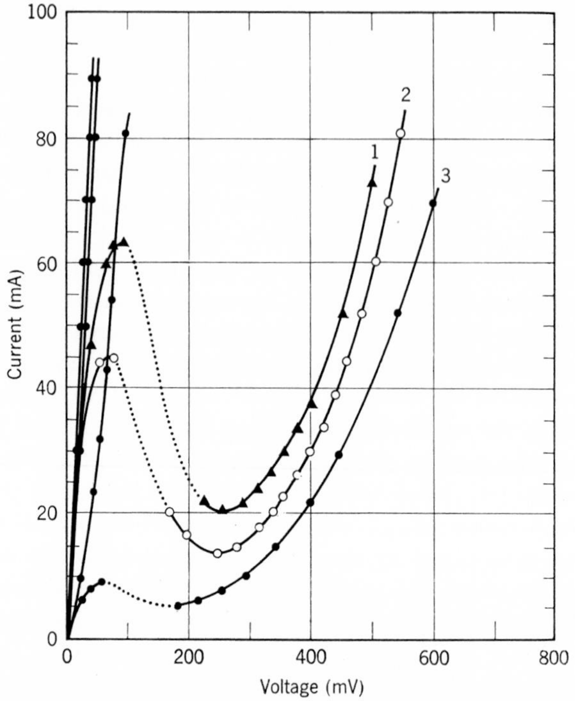

Fig. 7.8 Room-temperature characteristics of three GaAs tunnel diodes (forward and reverse bias) [after Gremmelmaier and Henkel (59G11)].

or absorption of a phonon. Then neither energy nor momentum of the electron is conserved. These three processes require different threshold energies and therefore can produce a fine structure in the characteristic of a tunnel diode at low temperatures. Finally, tunneling transitions can take place from one band into *impurity states*. For such transitions the condition that $E_{c,n}$ lie below $E_{v,p}$ need not be fulfilled. They can therefore cause anomalies in the characteristic even above the minimum of Fig. 7.8 ("excess currents").

Just as the magnetic field changes the absorption spectrum by rearranging the states of a band, so it changes the current of a tunnel diode.

The first *tunnel diodes* of a III-V compound (GaAs) were fabricated by Gremmelmaier and Henkel (59G11). For this purpose GaAs is particularly suited, as compared to other semiconductors. Although a small forbidden gap is desirable for the tunneling process, as we have seen from eq. (7.4), one has to consider that for small E_G the normal diode current is large and may swamp the tunnel current. It will be necessary to compromise to achieve a large ratio of tunnel current to normal current. Thus, the large band gap, combined with its small effective masses of electrons and light holes, makes GaAs seem especially promising. We will not consider the technical applications of GaAs tunnel diodes here. Numerous references to this topic are available [see, e.g. (60H2), (60H10), (61B21), and others we have mentioned].

The first InSb tunnel diodes were produced by Batdorf, Dacey, Wallace, and Welsh (60B3). At room temperature the ratio of tunnel current to normal forward current is too small for practical use (Fig. 7.9), but at low temperatures device applications are feasible (61H17).

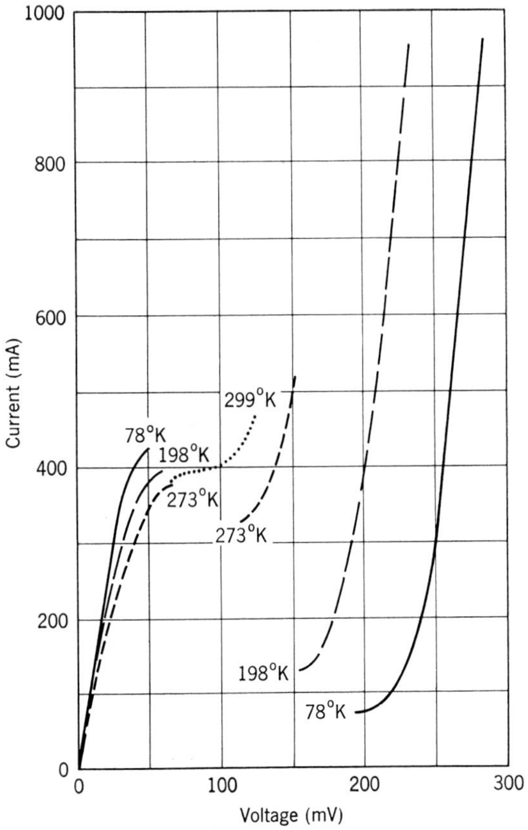

Fig. 7.9 Temperature dependence of the forward characteristic of an InSb tunnel diode [after Batdorf, Dacey, Wallace, and Welsh (60B3)].

However, InSb tunnel diodes are also of particular theoretical interest because the requirements of (7.4) are optimally fulfilled at low temperatures. The field and temperature dependence of the InSb tunnel currents agree quantitatively with the theory of direct tunnel transitions without participation of phonons [eq. (7.4)], according to Chynoweth and Logan (60C3). Furthermore, InSb is ideally suited for investigating the anomalies in high magnetic fields because of the very small effective masses of electrons and light holes. This topic we will consider in more detail later.

Hall, Racette, and Ehrenreich (60H1), (61H3), (61H5) studied the *fine structure* of the tunnel-diode characteristics at helium temperature. This fine structure is difficult to observe in the I-V characteristic itself but appears much more clearly in the voltage dependence of the differential conductivity (dI/dV). Figure 7.10 shows dI/dV-V characteristics of tunnel diodes made of InSb, InAs, InP, GaSb, GaAs, and GaP. The compound AlSb could not be doped sufficiently heavily to obtain tunnel currents large enough for observation of the fine structure.

All characteristics have in common the appearance of a minimum near the origin and of at least one other minimum at larger voltage. Hall, Racette, and Ehrenreich interpret the first minimum from the polar character of the III-V compounds. The tunnel process takes place rapidly compared to the relaxation time of the lattice, and the lattice polarization energy which is necessary for the transition of an electron from one polar state into another must be supplied by the applied field. There will therefore be a threshold energy (formation energy of a polaron) for the transition. This energy is determined by the polar coupling constants of electrons and holes in the phonon field, α_n and α_p (cf. Chapter 9), and by the energy of the longitudinal optical phonons, $\hbar\omega_l$, as $E = \frac{1}{2}(\alpha_n + \alpha_p)\hbar\omega_l$. Since α_n and α_p differ only in the effective masses and the transitions take place primarily between the conduction band and the V_2-band ($m_{p2} \approx m_n$), this relation simplifies to $E \approx \alpha_n\hbar\omega_l$.

The second set of minima in the curves of Fig. 7.10 is assigned to direct transitions with participation of an optical phonon of energy $\hbar\omega_l$. The InAs curve shows yet a third minimum in Fig. 7.10, whose separation from the second minimum is the same as the interval between the first and the second minimum. This would suggest a transition with two optical phonons participating. These hypotheses can be tested by comparing the threshold energies obtained from Fig. 7.10 with the equation $E = (\alpha_n + q)\hbar\omega_l$ ($q = 0, 1, 2$), where α_n is calculated from eq. (9.6) and $\hbar\omega_l$ is known from other experiments (see

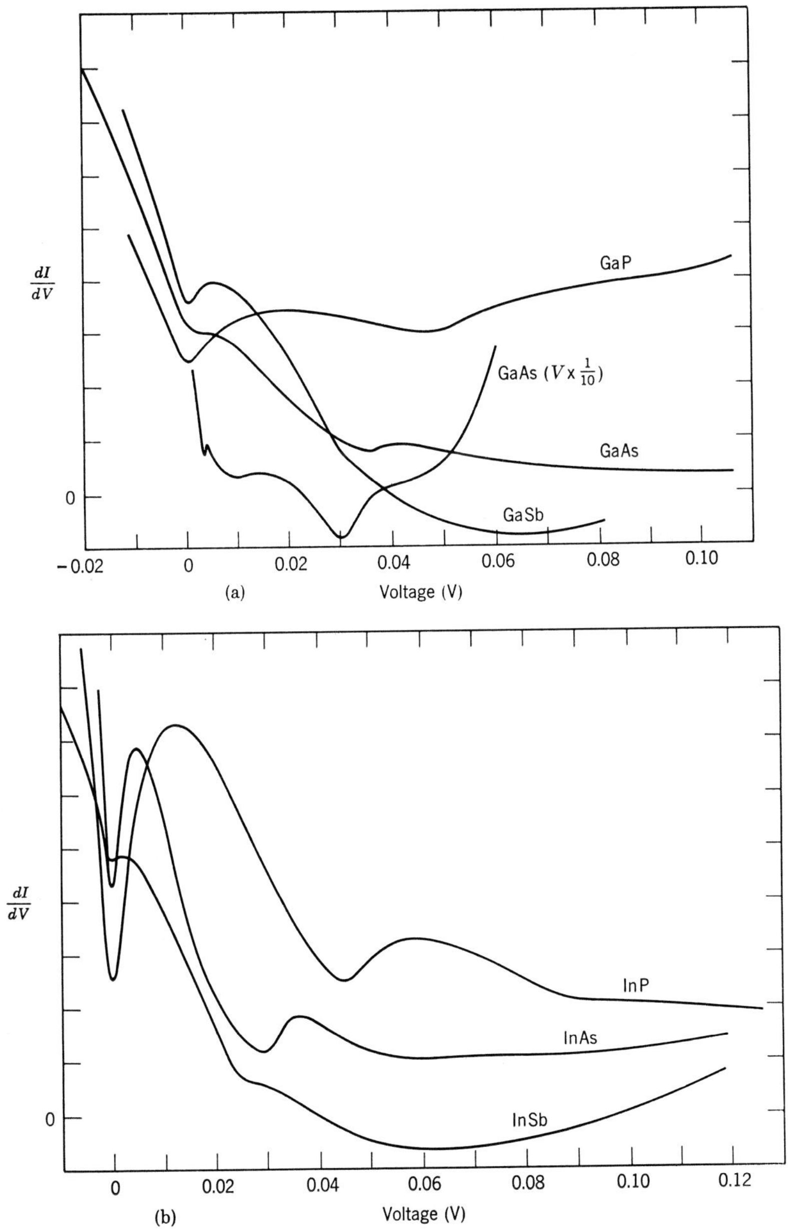

Fig. 7.10 Differential conductivity (dI/dV) as a function of bias for tunnel diodes of InSb, InAs, GaSb, GaAs, and GaP at 4.2°K [after Hall (61H3)].

Table 7.1 Energies of the Long-Wavelength Longitudinal Optical Phonons in III-V Compounds as Determined from Measurements of the dI/dV vs. V Characteristics of Tunnel Diodes [according to Hall and Racette (61H5)]

Compound	$\hbar\omega_l$ (10^{-3} eV)
InSb	23.8 ± 0.4
InAs	30.1 ± 0.3
InP	45.0 ± 1.5
GaSb	29.2 ± 0.4
GaAs	34.9 ± 0.5
GaP	51.0 ± 1.5

Chapter 3). With few exceptions this comparison shows excellent agreement between theory and experiment. Table 7.1 lists the values of $\hbar\omega_l$ calculated from the measurements on tunnel diodes. A comparison with Table 3.6 shows complete agreement with the optical values for the gallium compounds, while for the indium compounds the "tunnel values" are slightly higher than the optical values. The value 23.8 meV given for InSb in Table 7.1 lies between the optical value of 22.8 meV and the value of 24.4 meV derived from the oscillations of the photoconductivity (cf. Section 43).

Polaron minima do not appear, as expected, in the characteristics of germanium and silicon tunnel diodes. These diodes do show a fine structure which is characteristic for *indirect* transitions under phonon participations. Such a structure would be expected only in AlSb and GaP among the III-V compounds. The GaP curve of Fig. 7.10 does not show this Ge-like behavior, possibly because the tunnel current passes from the valence band into an impurity band adjacent to the conduction band. Indirect transitions into the conduction band would then require that the conduction band in the *n*-region be further lowered relative to the valence band in the *p*-region; in other words, higher doping is necessary. This has not yet been obtained because of the limited solubility of donors in GaP.

A theory of the direct tunneling under participation of polar phonons was developed by Dumke, Miller, and Haering (62D3). This theory concludes that 0.3% of the direct transitions are accompanied by phonons. This ratio can be determined experimentally from the ratio of the differential conductivity at a voltage $\hbar\omega_l/e$ to that at zero volts.

A ratio thirty times larger than predicted is obtained from the data. The discrepancy has not yet been explained.

Anomalies of the tunnel-diode current at *biases above the minimum* cannot be due to band-to-band transitions, since the bottom of the conduction band in the *n*-region now lies above the top of the valence band in the *p*-region. Phonon- or photon-assisted transitions are still possible, but not the usually dominating direct transitions with conservation of electron energy and momentum. Transitions from the conduction band into impurity states above the valence band (with subsequent "vertical" transition into the valence band) or transitions from impurity states below the conduction band into the valence band can also still take place.

Such anomalies have been observed in GaAs and InP tunnel diodes. Holonyak (61H15) found the characteristic shown in Fig. 7.11 on an InP diode. The tunnel current does not commence at the origin, but only at a finite threshold energy. From the known doping of the *p*- and *n*-regions of this diode it follows that already, at $V = 0$, $E_{c,n}$ lies above $E_{v,p}$. No normal tunnel current can therefore flow. The kink in the characteristic can be explained only by transitions into impurity states or into an impurity band above the valence band in the heavily doped *p*-region of the diode.

Two maxima have been observed in the current of one GaAs diode by Holonyak, at 0.2 V (43 mA) and at 1.1 V (14 mA). The former is

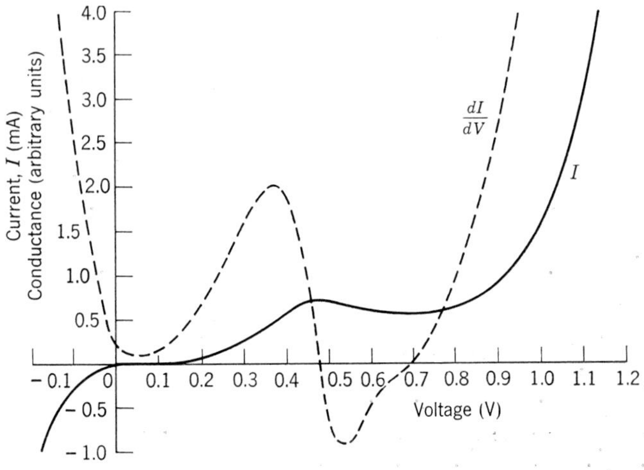

Fig. 7.11 Abnormal characteristic of an InP tunnel diode at 78°K [after Holonyak (61H15)].

the normal tunnel maximum; the latter must be ascribed to transitions from the conduction band into an impurity band 0.1–0.3 eV in width, lying 1 eV above the valence band.

Excess currents in GaAs tunnel diodes have also been observed by Winstel, Tropper, and Colani (62W6), Claassen (60C6), and Shibata (61S4), (62S6). Shibata found that they depended on the type of impurities present. Bumps in the I-V characteristic of a GaAs tunnel diode at 0.4 and at 0.9 V were created artificially by Pierce, Sander, and Kantz (62P8) through bombardment of the junction with 2-MeV electrons, i.e., through the creation of lattice defects.

In a *magnetic field* the tunneling transition probability for band-to-band transitions is altered because of the redistribution of the band states into magnetic subbands (cf. Section 315). Calawa, Rediker, Lax, and McWhorter (60C1) first investigated the behavior of InSb tunnel diodes in a magnetic field. According to them, eq. (7.4) must be changed just as eq. (3.4) was, when it was transformed into (3.9).

Figure 7.12 shows experimental results on InSb diodes. The tunnel current drops with increasing magnetic field for both longitudinal and transverse fields (field direction normal to the junction and in the plane of the junction, respectively). In addition, the tunnel maximum moves to higher voltages in a transverse magnetic field.

Haering and Adams (61H2) pointed out that transitions in a longitudinal and in a transverse magnetic field differ fundamentally from one another. In a longitudinal field the tunnel energy of an electron (i.e., the energy corresponding to the electron momentum perpendicular to the junction plane) is equal to its total energy minus the quantized part $(n' + \frac{1}{2})\hbar\omega_c$ (the energy in the junction plane). The tunnel energy and therefore the transition probability is a maximum for $n' = 0$. In the transverse field the tunnel energy is equal to $(n' + \frac{1}{2})\hbar\omega_c$ and is largest at large quantum numbers. We will not go into the theoretical consequences of this fact. We refer instead to the work of Haering and Adams and also to a calculation of Argyres (62A5).

The theoretical results were compared with experiments on InSb tunnel diodes by Butcher, Hulbert, and Hulme (61B23) and by Esaki and Haering (62E7). The theory of Haering and Adams permits the calculation of the tunnel exponent λ in (7.4) from the ratio of the tunnel current in the longitudinal magnetic field to that in the transverse field. This gives the possibility of determining the electric field in the interior of a *p-n* junction. From the theory of the *p-n* junction, λ also depends on the applied voltage, according to the law $\lambda = \lambda_0(1 - V/V_0)^{-1/\gamma}$. Esaki and Haering found the parameter values

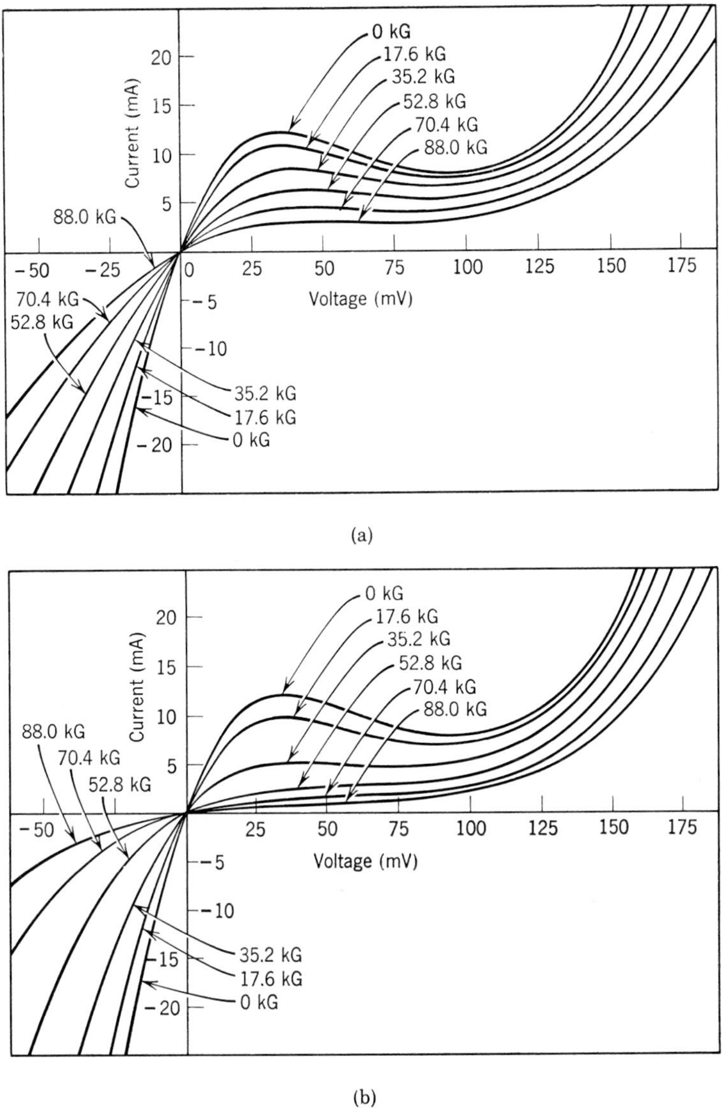

Fig. 7.12 Current-voltage characteristics at 77°K of an InSb tunnel diode in various longitudinal (a) and transverse (b) magnetic fields [after Calawa, Rediker, Lax, and McWhorter (60C1)].

$\lambda_0 = 10.7 \pm 0.02$, $V_0 = 0.2$ V, and $\gamma = 2.2$. The electrical field of the *p-n* junction was then calculated to be 5.7×10^4 V/cm in good agreement with the value determined from the known doping of the *n*- and *p*-regions under the assumption of an abrupt junction.

In addition to the behavior shown in Fig. 7.12 one finds oscillations in the magnetic-field dependence of the tunnel current in a longitudinal field at low temperatures. According to Chynoweth, Logan, and Wolff (60C5) these oscillations are caused by a periodic change in the density of states at the Fermi level with increasing magnetic field, similar to the de Haas-Shubnikov oscillations in the magnetoresistance (Section 413). This interpretation has been questioned by Haering and Miller (61H1) on the basis that longitudinal tunneling is an effect of small quantum numbers to which the conditions near the Fermi level do not contribute much. On the other hand, periodic fluctuations of the Fermi level about its average value in the growing magnetic field could lead to a periodic change of the electrical field in the transition region and thereby cause the oscillations.

Among the remaining studies on tunnel diodes in III-V compounds, (60C4), (61K3), (61M12), (61N3), (61S10), (62B13), (62C4), (62H5), (62H10), (62N2), (62N5), (62P3), we select only a few results for discussion.

In an InSb tunnel diode at helium temperature Chynoweth, Wannier, Logan, and Thomas (60C4) observed weak oscillations in the voltage dependence of the conductivity. They can perhaps be explained by the splitting of a band in the electric field into a succession of "Stark ladders," as Wannier predicted theoretically.

Kleinknecht (61K3) found a fine structure in InAs diodes at 4°K, which in some cases can be ascribed to phonon-assisted transitions, but in others must clearly be interpreted as a surface effect.

Nathan and Paul (61N3) investigated the pressure dependence of the *I-V* characteristic of GaAs and GaSb tunnel diodes. Such a pressure effect is expected because of the change of E_G with P (Section 311) and was observed. The results were not sufficiently detailed for a quantitative discussion.

According to eq. (7.4), tunnel currents depend sensitively on the electric field in the transition region, and so also on the width of this region. Small changes of the impurity gradient at the junction (aging and "current degradation" of diodes) cause large changes in the properties of a tunnel diode (61G13), (62H10), (63P8).

Tunnel currents are expected not only in heavily doped *p-n* junctions of a single semiconductor, but also at the contact between two such semiconductors. In Section 70 we mentioned the possibility of producing single-crystal *p-n* junctions, whose one bulk region consists of germanium and the other of GaAs. Tunnel currents in such junctions were observed by Nathan and Marinace (62N7), (62N9). They are of particular interest because of the difference in the band structure of the two semiconductors, which can cause new kinds of anomalies in the characteristics. The measurements demonstrated the existence of "phonon-assisted transitions," typical of germanium, in the same *I-V* curve with polaron minima. Additional structure was also observed, which is characteristic of neither germanium nor GaAs.

74 Spontaneous and Stimulated Light Emission from *p-n* Junctions

During studies of electroluminescence from GaAs *p-n* junctions (compare Section 532) Pankove and Massoulié (62P2), (62P3) and Keyes and Quist (62K2) observed a very high quantum efficiency in the process. According to Keyes and Quist, more than 85% of the carriers traversing the junction recombine radiatively. Later studies even suggest the possibility of a 100% efficiency. This value is orders of magnitude higher than had previously been observed in other materials. The main reason for the high efficiency is that the band-to-band transitions are direct and therefore the radiative recombination cross section is very large. This is of course related to the very steep absorption edge that is observed (cf. Section 313).

The line width of the strongest emission line of a GaAs *p-n* junction ($0.84\ \mu = 1.47$ eV, at low temperatures) decreases, as the current flowing through the junction is increased, to values of a few kT. This suggests the possibility of obtaining coherent emission, as was discussed theoretically by Bernard and Duraffourg (61B11) and Dumke (62D4). True laser action in GaAs *p-n* junctions was demonstrated by Hall, Fenner, Kingsley, Soltys, and Carlson (62H4), by Nathan, Dumke, Burns, Dill, and Lasher (62N8), and by Quist, Rediker, Keyes, Krag, Lax, McWhorter, and Zeiger (62Q1). This solid-state device is called an "injection laser" because its excitation mechanism consists of electrically injecting excess free carriers into a region of the crystal.

Laser action has also been observed in InP at $0.91\ \mu$ [Weiser and Levitt (63W6)], in InAs at $3.1\ \mu$ [Melngailis (63M3)], and in the mixed-crystal systems GaAs-GaP [Holonyak and Bevacqua (62H13)], InAs-GaAs [Melngailis *et al.* (63M5)], and InP-InAs [Alexander *et al.* (64A2)]. All these materials have direct transitions, and it is to be expected that the remaining III-V compounds with direct band gaps, as well as other direct compounds and alloys, can also be made to oscillate coherently. Indeed, superradiance was observed in InSb by Bernard *et al.* (63B8) and spontaneous emission by Phelan *et al.* (63P5), but the latter only after the transition probability had been increased by applying a large magnetic field parallel to the current.

The injection laser cavity is formed by the boundaries of the crystal at right angles to the plane of the junction. A sizable fraction of the light is reflected at these boundaries because of the large index-of-refraction change, so that standing waves are set up in the cavity. The condition for the frequency of these standing-wave modes is

$$q\frac{c}{\nu} = 2n_r l \tag{7.5}$$

where q is an integer, l the length between the reflecting boundaries, and n_r the index of refraction. Consequently the separation between adjacent modes is

$$\Delta\nu = \frac{c}{2l\left(n_r + \nu\dfrac{\partial n_r}{\partial \nu}\right)} \tag{7.6}$$

and the change of index of refraction with frequency can be determined accurately from a measurement of the mode separation (63B15). Similarly, measurements of the mode frequency as function of temperature (63E1) and hydrostatic pressure (63S7), (63F2), (63F3) permit the determination of the corresponding variations of the index of refraction.

Many more studies of the interesting physical phenomenon of the injection-laser action have been published in the short time since its discovery. However, they do not provide us with any substantial information about fundamental properties of the III-V compounds and therefore do not fall within the realm of this book. For further information the review articles of Hall (63H1), Nathan (63N4), and McWhorter (63M1) should be consulted.

So far we have not considered the exact nature of the transition which causes the light emission from these *p-n* junctions. The peak of the emission does not lie exactly at the band gap but at a slightly lower energy. Furthermore, the energy changes with doping and with the current flowing through the junction. Numerous investigations have attempted to explain these observations, but no clear-cut answer is available at present. The situation is considerably more complicated than in the case of the bulk measurements of optical absorption and fluorescence, both because a *p-n* junction is a complicated structure with an unknown distribution of imperfections, and because electroluminescence can be observed only at fairly high dopings where the band edges and impurity states are perturbed from the ideal band structure.

Pankove and Massoulié (62P2), (62P3) assume that the radiation is due to band-to-band transitions, possibly accompanied by some tunneling. The lowering of the energy is caused by the width of the forbidden gap being reduced by the heavy doping. These suggestions are supported by Nelson *et al.* (63N7) and Archer *et al.* (63A10) in measurements of the radiation frequency as a function of current.

Keyes and Quist (62K2) suggest that the radiative transitions take place via an impurity state. Whether this is an acceptor center (62N10), a donor center (63G4), or an impurity band (63N7) is not yet clear. The dependence of the energy of the emission maximum on the square of the applied magnetic field was interpreted by Galeener *et al.* (63G4) as due to a displacement of the ground state of a hydrogen-like donor in a magnetic field. On the other hand, Phelan *et al.* (63P5) find that the effect of a magnetic field on the radiation energy from an InSb *p-n* junction suggests that the transition is taking place directly from the conduction to the valence band.

Further detailed experiments will have to be awaited before the question of the nature of the transition can be answered. Measurements of the doping dependence of the emission (cf. 63D2) and of the effects of various external parameters [e.g., uniaxial stress (63M8)] can eventually be expected to provide new information about the physical properties of III-V compounds.

8

Miscellaneous Physical Properties

80 Magnetic Susceptibility

Measurement of the magnetic susceptibility is another way to get information about the band structure of semiconductors. The magnetic susceptibility χ can be divided into three parts:

1. That of the free carriers (electrons and holes), χ_c.
2. That of the electrons in the valence band and in the atomic cores, χ_l.
3. That of the charge carriers bound to impurities, χ_{imp}.

The contribution of the *free carriers* to the magnetic susceptibility in an isotropic parabolic band is given by

$$\chi_c = \frac{\mu_B{}^2}{3\rho}\left\{\frac{\partial n}{\partial \zeta}\left[3 - \left(\frac{m}{m_n}\right)^2\right] + \frac{\partial p}{\partial \zeta}\left[3 - \left(\frac{m}{m_p}\right)^2\right]\right\} \tag{8.1}$$

where μ_B is the Bohr magneton. The two terms in the sum represent the contributions of the electron and holes. For nondegenerate statistics, the ζ-derivatives of the carrier concentrations are equal to the concentrations themselves divided by kT. For complete degeneracy they are proportional to the third root of the carrier concentration.

When the g-factor of the carriers deviates from the value 2, then the first terms in the two differences in (8.1) must be multiplied by $g^2/4$.

For anisotropic bands, the factors $(m/m^*)^2$ in (8.1) are replaced by sums of terms containing second derivatives of the energy with respect to the different wave-vector components. The same is true for nonparabolic bands. Here $(m/m^*)^2$ is to be replaced by

$$\frac{1}{3}\frac{m}{m_2}\left(\frac{2m}{m_3}+\frac{m}{m_2}\right) \tag{8.2}$$

according to Geist (58G1), (59G2), where m_2 and m_3 are the effective masses given in Table 2.3.

The *free-carrier* susceptibility of *n*-InAs was measured by Geist. It is compared in Fig. 8.1 with the theoretical behavior for Boltzmann statistics (light doping) and Fermi statistics (heavy doping) calculated for a parabolic band. The change expected when the nonparabolicity of the conduction band is taken into account is also shown. Quantitative agreement is poor, but Fig. 8.1 does show the strong dependence of the susceptibility on the details of the band structure and the possibility of determining such details on degenerate samples.

One of the reasons for the poor agreement is that eq. (8.2) does not take all the peculiarities of Kane's band model into account. Bowers and Yafet (59B11), (59B12) calculated the susceptibility of InSb on the basis of the complete model. They found that the influence of higher-lying bands, which gives only a small correction to the energy-wave-number dependence, contributes markedly to the susceptibility at higher doping. Figure 8.2 shows, just like Fig. 8.1, a comparison between the theory of Bowers and Yafet and their experimental results on InSb. There is complete agreement within experimental accuracy.

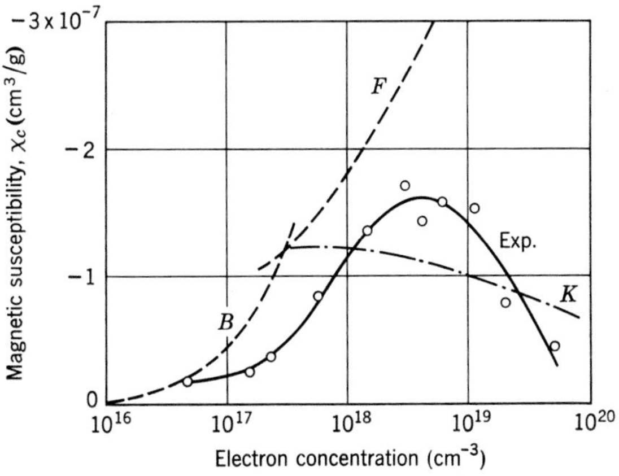

Fig. 8.1 Magnetic susceptibility of electrons in InAs. Theoretical curves (– – –): *B*, constant effective mass, Boltzmann statistics; *F*, constant effective mass, Fermi statistics; *K*, Kane's theory (simplified version) [after Geist (58G1)].

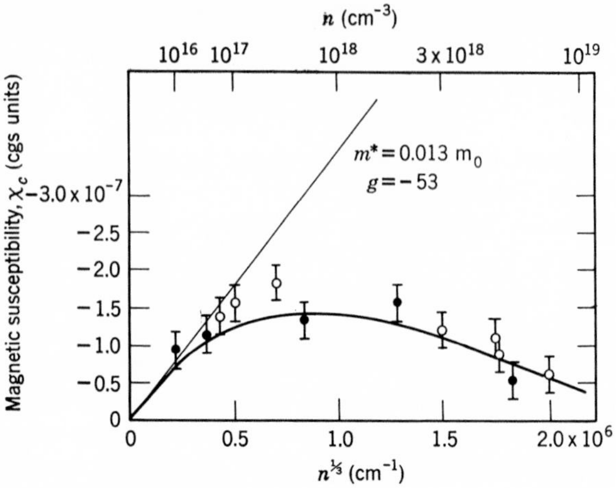

Fig. 8.2 Comparison of the carrier magnetic susceptibility calculated from Kane's theory with experimental results on InSb [after Bowers and Yafet (59B11)].

The theory of Bowers and Yafet was applied to measurements on InAs and GaAs by Römelt and Geist (62R2), but the influence of the higher-lying bands was not taken into account. Consequently, the agreement between theory and experiment is good only for small electron concentrations.

Other studies on the contribution of the free carriers to the magnetic susceptibility in InSb, InAs, and other III-V compounds [Busch and Kern (59B18), Busch, Menth, and Natterer (62B14), Stevens and Crawford (55S3), Matyáš (58M4), Römelt, Geist, and Schlabitz (59R8), and Busch and Yuan (59B19)] are concerned with the temperature dependence of the susceptibility, which makes it possible to separate the lattice and free-carrier contributions, and with the determination of the effective masses. Figure 8.3 gives the temperature dependence of the susceptibility of a number of III-V compounds compared with those of germanium, silicon, and α-tin (59B18). The temperature dependence of the susceptibility of InSb is also shown in Fig. 8.4 for a number of differently doped samples.

We will not list the effective masses that were obtained from the studies referred to above. We have seen that eq. (8.1) is incomplete for InSb and InAs, and for other III-V compounds the experimental numbers are too rough to deduce useful m^* values. For want of other, more accurate values of the effective electron mass the value of 0.02 m, which was determined from susceptibility measurements, was listed for $CdSnAs_2$ (62M3) (Chapter 6).

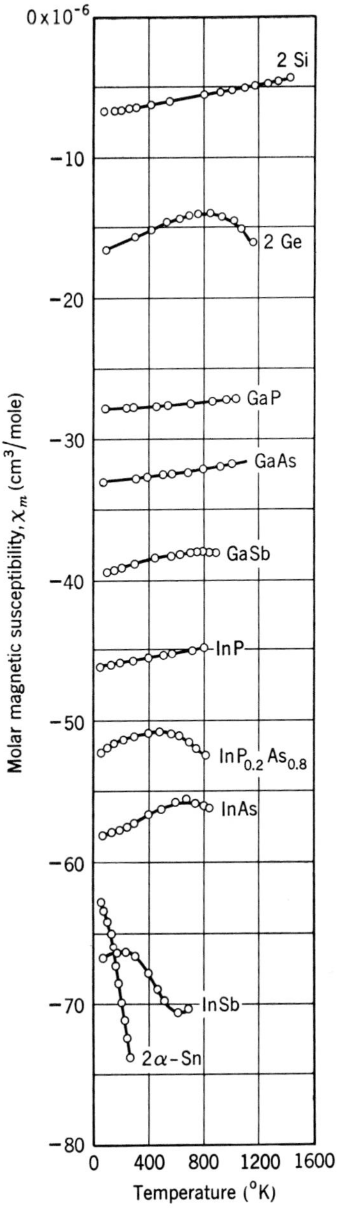

Fig. 8.3 Molar susceptibility as a function of temperature for a number of III-V compounds and group IV elements [after Busch and Kern (59B18)].

The *lattice* contribution to the susceptibility is very small in the degenerate samples and can be neglected. It becomes more important in less heavily doped samples. There it can be separated out by making measurements on samples of different doping.

The lattice susceptibility is practically temperature independent. For a discussion of the factors that contribute to it, we refer to the

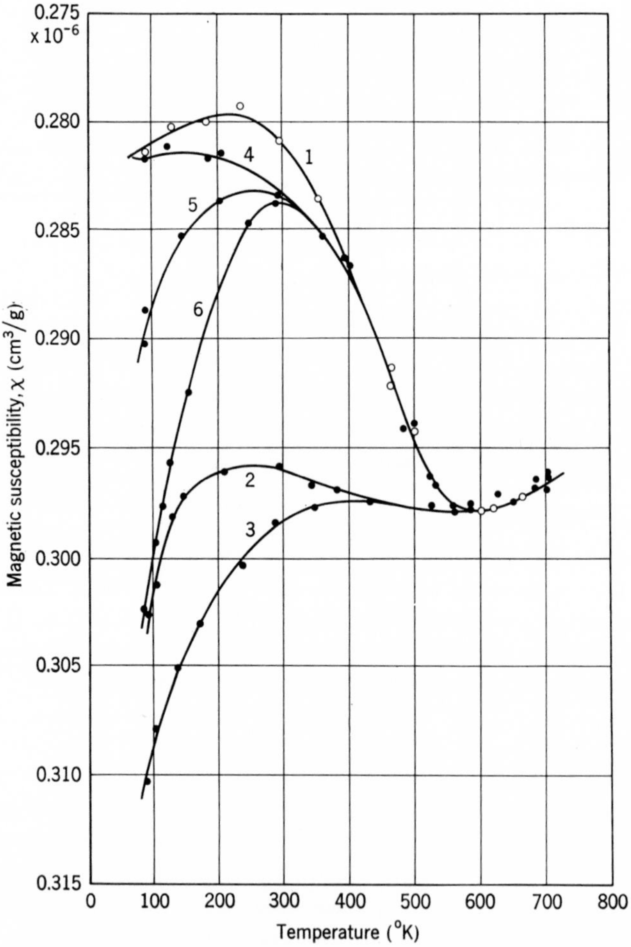

Fig. 8.4 Temperature dependence of the magnetic susceptibility of InSb samples of various doping [after Busch and Kern (59B18)]: 1, $n = 6.2 \times 10^{15}$ cm^{-3}; 2, $n = 5.5 \times 10^{17}$ cm^{-3}; 3, $n = 8.0 \times 10^{18}$ cm^{-3}; 4, $p = 1.4 \times 10^{16}$ cm^{-3}; 5, $p = 3.6 \times 10^{16}$ cm^{-3}; 6, $p = 2.2 \times 10^{17}$ cm^{-3}.

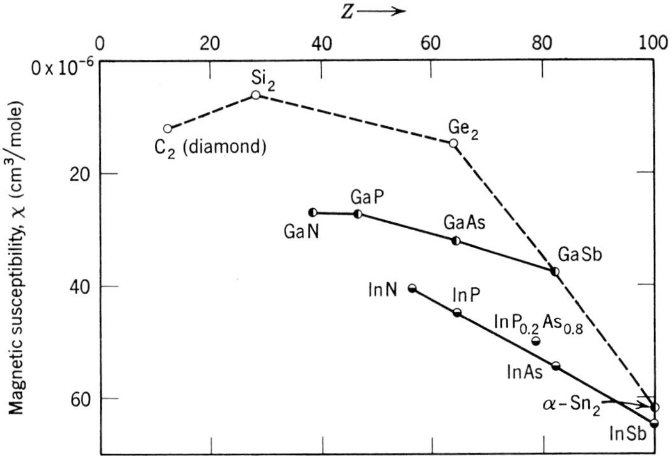

Fig. 8.5 Molar lattice susceptibility of some III-V compounds and group IV elements vs. total atomic number per unit cell [after Busch and Kern (59B18)].

work of Busch and Kern (59B18). Figure 8.5 shows the molar lattice susceptibility of many III-V compounds as a function of the total number of electrons per unit cell ($Z_{\mathrm{III}} + Z_{\mathrm{V}}$). This relationship can be represented by the empirical formula

$$\chi_{\mathrm{mol}} = -[Z_{\mathrm{III}}(Z_{\mathrm{III}} + Z_{\mathrm{V}})/100 + 13] \times 10^{-6} \tag{8.3}$$

according to Matyáš (59M4). The relationship applies not only to pure III-V compounds but also to their mixed crystals (61M7). In this connection we mention the paper of Matyáš (62M2) on the interrelation between magnetic susceptibility and chemical binding in semiconducting compounds with zinc-blende structure.

81 Thin Films

There are a number of reasons why one would like to be able to produce thin films of III-V compounds. For one thing, optical measurements in the region of high absorption can be performed only on very thin samples. Also, thin films would be useful for a number of technical applications (Hall generators, photocells, etc.).

One of the main techniques for producing thin films is the evaporation onto a substrate. If the two components are evaporated simultaneously, inhomogeneous films with continuously varying composition are usually obtained. Such films were first deposited by Presnov and Synorov (57P6) in the systems In-Sb, Ga-Sb, and Al-Sb. They showed that for a 1:1 composition ratio these films had semiconductor character. These investigations were continued by other Russian authors [Kurov and Pinsker (58K6), (58K7), Kot and Sorokin (58K5), Kurov (59K6), and others]. It was found that InSb films can have wurtzite structure as well as zinc-blende structure (59K6) and that, in addition to AlSb, the compound Al_9Sb can also have semiconducting properties (58K5). The mobilities of the carriers in these evaporated layers were very small compared to the values in normal material (of the order of 20 cm^2/V sec).

Similar investigations were performed by deLaunay, Colombani, and Paparoditis (57C3), (57L2), (57L3), (60P1) and Dale and Senecal (62D1) on InSb and by Martinuzzi (61M6), (62M1) on GaAs. These authors did achieve higher mobilities, but the electrical properties of the films, in many respects, still did not come up to the volume properties. The optical properties of thin InSb films were studied by Potter and Kretschmar (61P9).

Günther (58G12), (58G13), (61G22) was able to obtain a considerable improvement by revising the usual evaporation procedure. He evaporated the two components from crucibles held at different temperatures, and he heated the substrate. For an appropriate choice of the three temperatures, it is possible to achieve the condition where only molecules of the compound which form in the vapor phase condense on the substrate, while atoms of the more volatile components are reemitted from the condensation surface. A small range of substrate temperatures will satisfy this condition. Films of InSb and InAs produced by the three-temperature technique have the same properties as bulk semiconductors, in all the main points. Films of InSb 0.5–5 μ thick had electron mobilities up to 20,000 cm^2/V sec; InAs films, up to 13,000 cm^2/V sec. A comparison of typical measurements of conductivity and Hall coefficient made on InAs films and crystals is shown in Fig. 8.6. The Hall mobilities in the films are smaller than those in the bulk material, since they have been reduced by grain-boundary scattering. The grain size of the film grew with increasing temperature of the substrate during evaporation, within the temperature region in which condensation was possible. The Hall mobility also increased with crystallite size.

In connection with this, Reimer (58R3) investigated the structure of InSb films as a function of substrate temperature, by electron diffraction and electron microscopy.

A completely different procedure for the preparation of thin InSb films was described by Bate and Taylor (60B4). They squeezed a drop

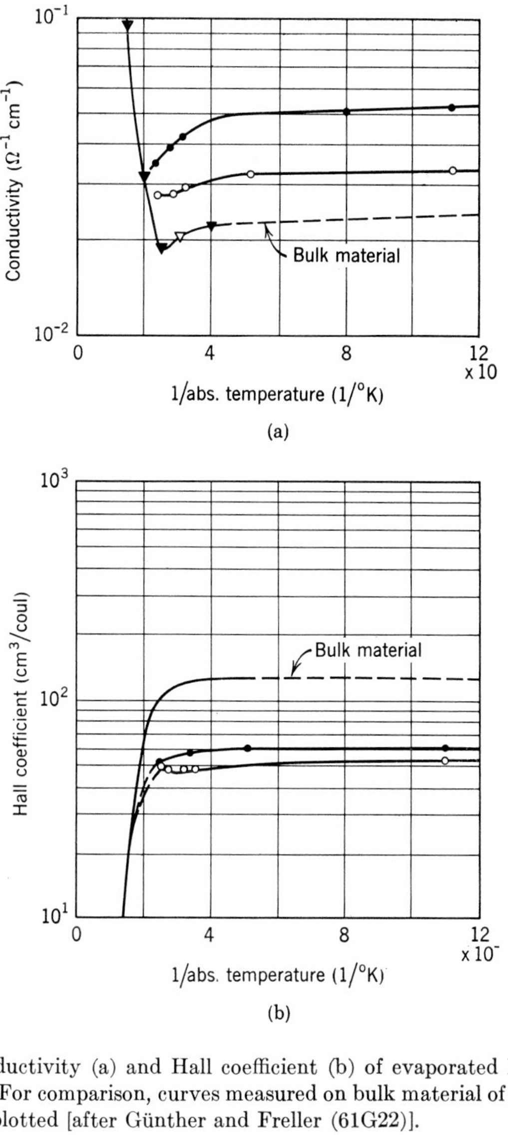

Fig. 8.6 Conductivity (a) and Hall coefficient (b) of evaporated InSb films vs. temperature. For comparison, curves measured on bulk material of $n = 7 \times 10^{16}$ cm^{-3} are also plotted [after Günther and Freller (61G22)].

of InSb between two optically flat and parallel slides and let it freeze. The resulting self-supporting films had a thickness of about 10 μ and areas up to 1 cm^2. At an electron concentration of 3×10^{16} cm^{-3} the electron mobility at room temperature was 23,800 cm^2/V sec, and the hole mobility 595 cm^2/V sec.

82 Surface Conduction and Field Effect

Since the volume properties of the III-V compounds are very similar to those of germanium and silicon, it seems reasonable to expect a corresponding similarity in surface properties (accumulation and depletion regions, "slow" and "fast" surface states, and others). We have already found experimental indications of the changes of volume properties in the regions near the surfaces from the anomalies in the Hall effect of InAs (Section 411) and from the dependence of the surface recombination on the surface treatment.

Quantitative measurements of the surface conduction and its dependence on electric field and irradiation with light have so far been performed only on InSb [Eaton, King, Morten, Partridge, and Smith (62E1)]. For such measurements n-type InSb is not suitable, since the large volume conductivity obscures any surface conduction. The measurements were therefore restricted to p-type material at 77°K. Figure 8.7 shows the dependence of the conduction of various samples on their thickness. The existence of a surface contribution can easily be recognized from the fact that the line drawn through the experimental points does not go through zero. The two higher-resistance

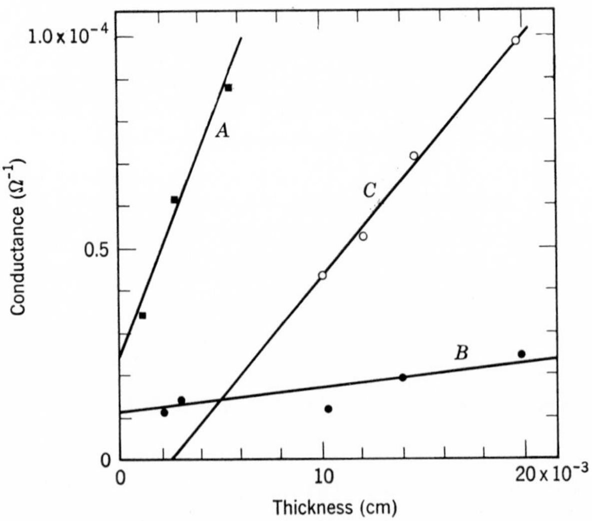

Fig. 8.7 Change of conductivity of InSb samples with sample thickness. *A*, sample resistivity, 14 Ω cm; *B*, 200 Ω cm; *C*, 0.3 Ω cm [after Eaton, King, Morten, Partridge, and Smith (62E1)].

samples show a positive contribution to the conductivity for zero thickness; the low-resistance sample, a negative one. Apparently a depletion region exists in the first case, and an accumulation region in the second. These conclusions were confirmed by showing that the surface conduction could be modulated by an electric field applied transverse to the surface (field effect). The fact that the time constant of the field effect was a few microseconds, well below that of germanium, demonstrates the existence of "fast" surface states.

"Slow" surface states with time constants of many hours were observed in irradiation experiments. Under white-light irradiation at 77°K, the conductivity of *p*-type InSb samples increased and remained constant for many hours after turning off the light source. Brief heating and renewed cooling re-established the original conductivity. The responsible "slow" states appear to be connected with the oxide layers on the surface.

Surface conduction in anodically oxidized InSb has been studied by Jacobson and Mueller (63J1). The field effect on GaAs surfaces has been discussed by Pilkuhn (63P9) and by Flinn and Emmony (63F4).

Evidence of surface states has been found in GaSb by Habegger and Fan (64H2) and Rupprecht and Gilbert (64R2).

83 Surface Properties and the Polarity of the Zinc-Blende Lattice

If it is assumed that the crystal lattice remains unchanged right up to the surface, then the three major crystalline surfaces of the zinc-blende lattice can be pictured as follows.

The (100)-surfaces of an $A^{III}B^{V}$ compound are formed by cubically arranged A or B atoms (Fig. 8.8a). Every atom is bound by two of its sp^3-bonds to atoms of the layer lying just below. The other two bonds are free (dangling bonds). The structure is independent of whether the topmost layer is formed by A atoms or B atoms.

The (110)-surfaces contain equal numbers of A atoms and B atoms. Every atom is connected by one bond with the next lower-lying layer. Two bonds extend in the surface plane to the two next-nearest neighbors, and the fourth bond is dangling (Fig. 8.8b).

For (111)-surfaces, two cases must be distinguished. In each, the topmost atomic plane contains only A atoms or only B atoms (A and B surfaces). Either these can be connected by three bonds with three atoms of the next lower-lying layer (Fig. 8.8c), with one dangling bond remaining, or they are bound by only one bond and have three dangling bonds. The two cases alternate as the (111)-surface is built up layer

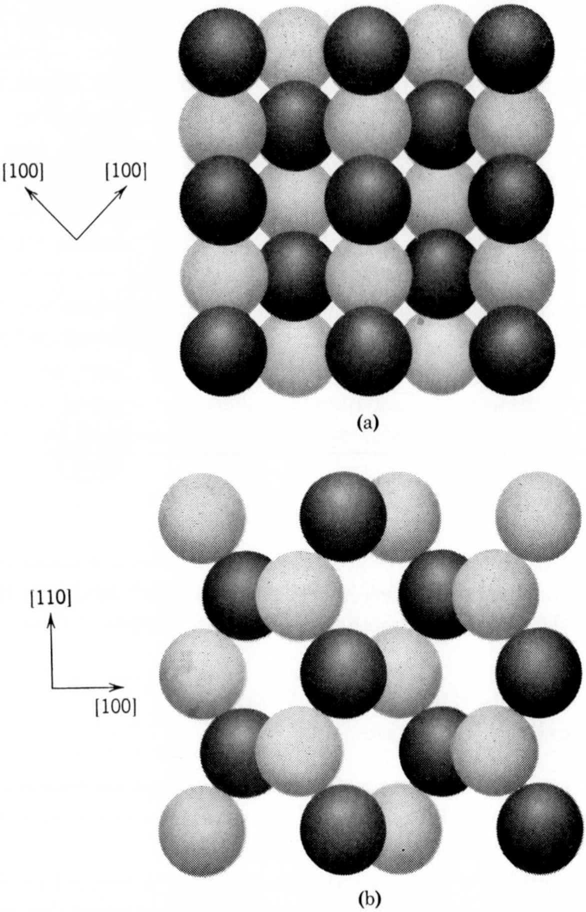

Fig. 8.8 Top views of the three main crystal surfaces of the zinc-blende lattice: (a) (100)-, (b) (110)-, (c) (111)-surface. In (a) alternating layers of identical atoms succeed one another. The top four layers are visible. The fifth layer lies below the first, the sixth below the second, etc. In (b) only two layers are visible. Each one contains equal numbers of the two kinds of atoms. In (c) the first, second, and fourth layers are visible. The third layer lies under the second one, the fifth under the fourth. The distance between the first and second and between the third and fourth layers, etc., is smaller than between the other adjacent layers.

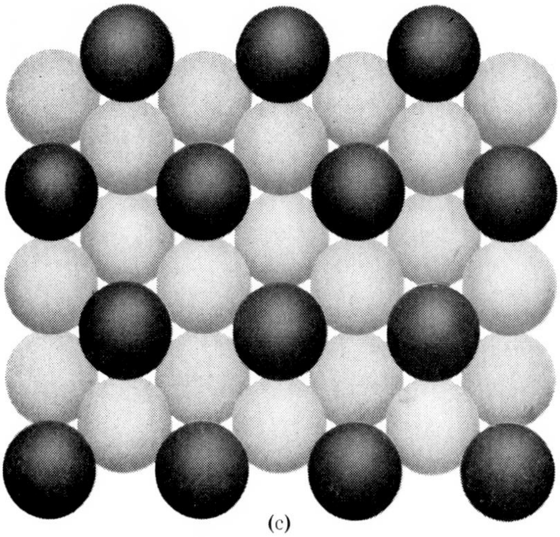

(c)

by layer. It is easily seen that the first of the possibilities will be more stable. Indeed, the second possibility does not appear to exist at all, and crystal growth and etching always seem to take place in double layers.

We have seen in Chapter 1 that the zinc-blende structure has a polar axis in the [111]-direction. The reason for this is that the layers formed from A atoms and B atoms do not follow each other with equal separations. Rather, the layers connected by three bonds per atom have a smaller separation than the ones connected by only one bond per atom. Consequently, the [111]-direction and the opposite $[\bar{1}\,\bar{1}\,\bar{1}]$-direction are not equivalent. If one assumes that the (111)-surfaces in the zinc-blende lattices always consist of threefold bound atoms with one dangling bond, then one of the two surfaces has to be formed by A atoms, the other by B atoms. We will see that all experimental results support this assumption. Generally the [111]-direction is defined as that pointing to an A surface; the $[\bar{1}\,\bar{1}\,\bar{1}]$-direction, as that pointing to a B surface.

Up to now, we have assumed that the crystal structure at the surface is the same as that in the interior. This cannot be rigorously correct, since only one-sided binding forces act on the surface atoms. The tetrahedral symmetry will probably be disturbed. Haneman (60H3), (61H7), (61H8) has obtained information about the distortion of the tetrahedral symmetry from electron-diffraction measurements on pure surfaces of semiconductors with diamond and zinc-blende structures. The interpretation of the diffraction patterns shows the top atomic

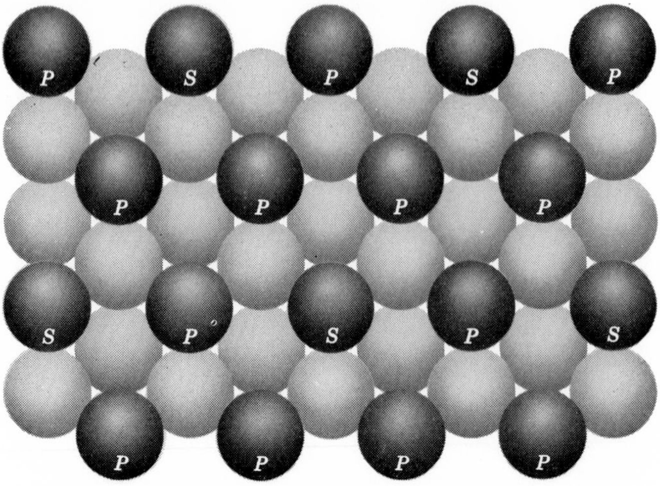

Fig. 8.9 Model of a (111)-surface of the zinc-blende lattice [after Haneman (61H8)]. *S*: atoms with one *s*-bond and three *p*-bonds; *P*: atoms with one *p*-bond and three sp^2-bonds.

layer of the (111)-surfaces to have a "lattice constant" twice as large as an undistorted atomic layer. This can, for example, be obtained by distorting the individual rows of atoms of the top layer such that every second atom in every other row protrudes out of the crystal relative to its normal location (Fig. 8.9). The remaining surface atoms lie closer to the next lower layer.

The existence of such a configuration can readily be made plausible. The four equivalent sp^3-bonds of the interior of the crystal are split at the surface into three equal bonds and one dangling bond. This can happen in two ways; in one, three *p*-bonds (with smaller angles between each other than those in sp^3-bonds) and one *s*-bond are formed; in the other, three sp^2-bonds (which lie undistorted in one plane) and one *p*-bond are formed. In the first case, the separation of one surface atom from the next lower layer would be larger, and in the second case, smaller, than that in a tetrahedrally bound layer. If only one of these possibilities took place, it would create excessive stresses at the surface. An orderly array, as described above, therefore appears more probable.

This picture of the (111)-surface of crystals with diamond or zinc-blende structure is undoubtedly still incomplete for the zinc-blende structure (III-V compounds). The A and B surfaces differ from each other in that the first is formed by trivalent atoms, the second by pentavalent atoms. This means that on B surfaces the sp^3-bonds are practically unchanged, since aside from the three electron pairs in the bonds to the nearest neighbors, a fourth electron pair is directed outward. The A surfaces will be much more strongly distorted, since all valence electrons of the trivalent surface atoms are used up in the bonds pointing inward.

This difference in the structure of the A and B surfaces of the III-V compounds makes it possible to interpret a large number of experimental results on the differing behavior of these two surfaces.

It was observed early that upon etching (111)-surfaces etch pits appeared only on the A surfaces, never on the B surfaces. [For the etching of surfaces of III-V compounds and the appearance of etch pits compare, e.g., (57S1), (58A6), (58L2), (58M1), (58N1), (58V1), (59W3), (60F1), (60G1), (60G3), (60R2).] Later it was found that some etches behaved in the opposite way, causing etch pits only on B surfaces, while still others created them on both surfaces (60R2). Furthermore, etches which usually formed etch pits only on A surfaces could be made to form etch pits on the B surfaces as well (60G1), (60G3), by adding an inhibitor such as stearic acid. These differences can be explained as follows. Etch pits form if the removal of surface atoms takes place preferentially at the positions of the crystal surfaces at which dislocations terminate. Because B surfaces have two free electrons per surface atom, they react much more easily with oxidizing etches than A surfaces, which have no dangling electrons. They are therefore very strongly attacked by many etches, and no etch pits form. Inhibitors similarly locate on the B surfaces, where they bind the free electrons and so eliminate the difference in the reactivities of the two surface types.

Gatos and co-workers, who have furnished the main contribution to explaining the different behaviors of the A and B surfaces, were able to show that a doping of III-V compounds with amphoteric atoms of group IV reduces the differences between the reactions of the two surfaces to etching (60G3).

The different etching behavior of opposite surfaces is not restricted to (111)-surfaces. Other surfaces also show different numbers and shapes of etch pits, depending on their relative orientations to the polar axes (60G4), (60G5).

According to Warekois, Gatos, and Lavine (60W1), (61G5), (61G8), B surfaces are attacked more strongly than A surfaces not only by etching solutions, but also by mechanical procedures, such as sand blasting and grinding.

Corresponding considerations apply to the *growth* of (111)-surfaces (59E8), (60G2), (60L2), (62B11), (62F1). The crystallization velocity for freely growing (111)-surfaces is different for the A and B surfaces. Crystals growing in the $[\bar{1}\,\bar{1}\,\bar{1}]$-direction tend to show less twinning and grain-boundary formation than those growing in the [111]-direction. This difference can be related to the larger stresses in the A surfaces.

Differences in oxidation (60R4), (61M11) and absorption [see, e.g., (60G1), (61H8)] have also been observed on A and B surfaces.

The surface model of Gatos discussed above, which assumes no dangling bonds on the A surfaces and two per atom on the B surfaces, does not agree completely with Haneman's model of Fig. 8.9. For further discussion of the two models, we refer to Gatos (61G6), Haneman (62H7), and Holt (60H11).

Whether a given surface is of the A or B type can be determined from x-ray reflection measurements [Warekois and Metzger (59W1), Pfister (61P7)]. The geometrical structure factors are different for the two surfaces, leading to different integrated intensities of certain x-ray reflections. The direction of the polar axes in III-V compounds can, however, be determined much more easily by the experimental differences in the behaviors of the two surface types (now that the surfaces have been identified by x-ray measurements).

The distortion of (100)-surfaces of III-V compounds is such that the neighboring atom rows form atomic pairs in agreement with experimental observations.

84 Plastic Deformation; Dislocations

We saw in Section 413 that the density of dislocations in InSb could be increased considerably by plastic deformation and that a change of sign of the magnetoresistance was connected therewith. In addition, a number of other effects of dislocations on the properties of III-V compounds can be demonstrated.

Generally, the density of dislocations in a III-V compound is determined by etching the surfaces and counting the etch pits. We mentioned in Section 83 that etch pits appear mainly at those locations on the surface where dislocations terminate. Dislocations can also be made visible by decoration with the Dash procedure. This method, which was originally developed for silicon, can be applied to GaAs, according to Huffman and Taylor (59H5). Copper, silver, gold, and nickel atoms are suitable for decoration. Twin and grain boundaries can also be decorated in GaAs in contrast to silicon.

One of the most important dislocations formed in the III-V compounds is the "60° dislocation," which extends along a [111]-axis. It is depicted in Fig. 8.10. A number of identical atoms, each of which is bound only to three neighbor atoms, are located along this dislocation. In germanium and silicon these atoms have a free valence electron. They can act as acceptors by giving up this electron, or as donors by taking on a second electron and forming a saturated electron pair. Haasen (57H1) was the first to show that this dislocation type has different properties in III-V compounds, depending on whether the row of unsaturated atoms consists of trivalent or of pentavalent atoms. In the first case, no excess valence electrons are present in the dislocation, which therefore acts as a row of acceptors. In the second case, each atom has a saturated electron pair, and the dislocation has donor character. Such α- and β-dislocations were observed in InSb by Gatos, Finn, and Lavine (61G7). They were also discussed by Venables and Broudy (58V1), (59V1). Other dislocation types in the zinc-blende lattice were treated by Holt (62H14).

Duga (62D2), in extensive studies of dislocations in InSb, always observed acceptor action. The electron concentration decreased with increasing dislocation density through trapping. The electron mobility was decreased by the dislocations if the electrons moved per-

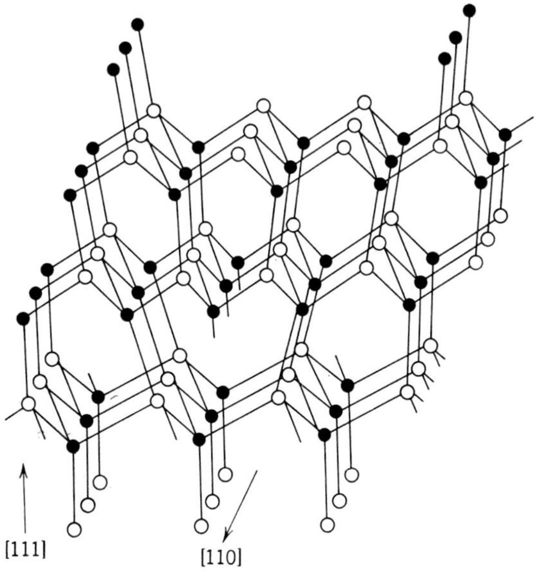

Fig. 8.10 Model of a 60° dislocation in the zinc-blende lattice [after Venables and Broudy (58V1)].

pendicular to the bending axis of the plastic deformation. For current parallel to this axis the electron mobility was essentially unchanged. This suggests that the drop in mobility is due to scattering on dislocations extended parallel to the bending axis. A sufficiently high dislocation density was found only in crystals deformed by plastic bending. In contrast, a plastic deformation by compression alone has, according to Duga, Willardson, and Beer (59D4), an effect on the electrical properties of InSb which can be explained by the creation of vacancies and interstitial atoms alone.

Mackintosh (56M1) observed that grain boundaries act as donors in InSb, since they had no effect on current passage through *n*-type InSb but created large potential jumps in *p*-type InSb.

Other studies concerning the plastic deformation of III-V compounds (mainly InSb) were made by Kolm, Warekois, and Kulin (58K3), Allen (57A2), (58A2), Haasen (62H1), (62P4), and Mueller and Jacobson (62M14).

Elementary semiconductors of group IV cleave primarily in the (111)-planes. In the III-V compounds, however, the (110)-planes are the preferred cleavage planes. Pfister (55P2) explained this fact by the ionic contribution to the bonds in the III-V compounds. The (111)-planes in the zinc-blende lattice are formed by layers of identical atoms. Two successive atomic layers contain different atoms and therefore attract each other more strongly than two atomic layers of a (110)-plane, which are built up equally out of the two different kinds of atoms. In this connection, Wolff and co-workers (58W8) derived the relative ionic contributions of some III-V compounds from cleavage experiments. These results do not agree, however, with the heteropolar binding contributions that will be discussed in Chapter 9. The consideration is questionable also for the reason that the polarization of the electron bonds essentially balances out the differences in ionic charges of neighboring (111)-atomic planes. Abrahams and Ekstrom (60A1), therefore, interpret the preferred (110)-cleavage planes in III-V compounds by conglomerates of "Lomer" dislocations, which lead to microfractures in the (110)-planes and facilitate the splitting in these planes. In lattices without a polar axis the structure of these dislocations is different. Microfractures then do not appear in the (110)-planes.

85 Elastic Constants; Expansion Coefficients

The elastic properties of a cubic crystal can be described by three coefficients, C_{11}, C_{12}, and C_{44} (similar to the piezoresistance; cf. Section

Table 8.1 Elastic Constants of Some III-V Compounds

Substance	Temp. (°K)	C_{11} (10^{11} dyn/cm^2)	C_{12} (10^{11} dyn/cm^2)	C_{44} (10^{11} dyn/cm^2)	Literature
InSb	298	6.717 ± 3%	3.665 ± 0.5%	3.018 ± 0.3%	(56M3)
	300	6.6 ± 0.3	3.8 ± 0.2	3.0 ± 0.1	(56D1)
	300	6.699	3.645	3.020	(59S4)
	0	6.66	3.35	3.14	(56P2)
	300	6.472	3.265	3.071	(56P2)
	600	5.906	2.888	2.958	(56P2)
InAs	300	8.329	4.526	3.959	(63G5)
GaSb	298	8.849 ± 3%	4.037 ± 0.5%	4.325 ± 0.3%	(56M3)
GaAs	0	12.26 ±0.7%	5.71 ±2.5%	6.00 ±6.7	(61G2)
	77.4	12.21 ±0.7%	5.66 ±2.5%	5.99 ±6.7	(61G2)
	300	11.81 ±0.7%	5.32 ±2.5%	5.94 ±6.7	(61G2)
	298	11.88	5.38	5.94	(59B3)
AlSb	300	8.939 ± 0.02	4.425 ± 0.02	4.155 ± 0.008	(60B7)

414). These coefficients are determined experimentally from three independent measurements, e.g., of the propagation velocity of longitudinal and transverse acoustic waves.

Numerical values of the elastic constants are available for InSb, InAs, GaSb, GaAs, and AlSb (Table 8.1). In addition, Potter (56P2) has made such measurements on InSb for the entire temperature region of 100–600°K. The 0°K value in the table was extrapolated from these measurements. The study by Slutsky and Garland (59S4) also contains data for a number of temperatures below 300°K.

The observation that the ratio C_{11}/C_{12} takes on the value 2.65 for germanium and silicon and decreases with increasing heteropolarity to a value of 1.49 for InSb was interpreted by Potter (57P5) by means of Born's theory of the diamond lattice. According to this, it is possible to estimate the ionic contribution to the binding from the value of C_{11}/C_{12}. For InSb and GaSb Potter finds good agreement with data obtained in other ways.

The measurement of the elastic constants also allows the determination of the Debye temperature. Potter (56P2) finds a Debye temperature of 208°K (referred to 0°K) for InSb, while Slutsky and Garland (59S4) report $\theta_D = 205°K \pm 2°K$, and Beers, Cody, and Abeles (62B5) 202.5°K. Values for other materials (also referred to 0°K) are as follows: GaAs, 345°K ± 3°K [Garland and Park (62G1)]; GaSb, 266.1°K, and AlSb, 295.4°K [Beers, Cody, and Abeles (62B5)].

The Debye temperature can also be determined from specific heat measurements. In particular, this makes it possible to determine the values of θ_D at finite temperatures. The most extensive study of this kind was made by Piesbergen (63P5) on InSb, InAs, InP, GaSb, GaAs, and AlSb over the range 12°K < T < 275°K. His results are reproduced in Fig. 8.11. Other measurements have been made by Gul'tyaev and Petrov (59G15), according to whom θ_D (InSb) has a value of 228°K at 80°K, reaches a maximum of 254°K at 130°K, and

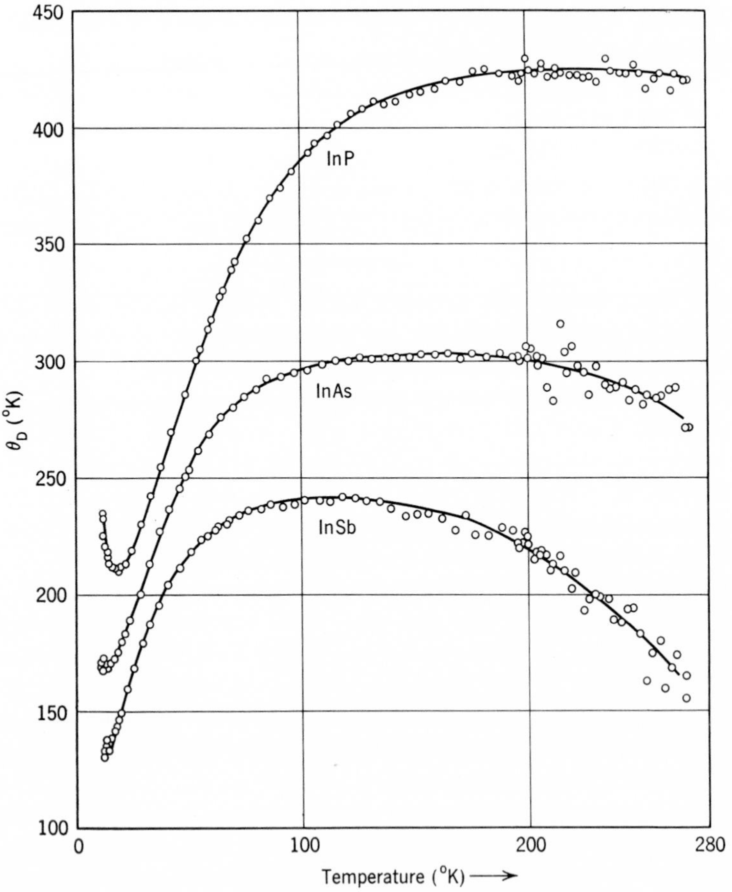

Fig. 8.11 Debye temperature for several III-V compounds

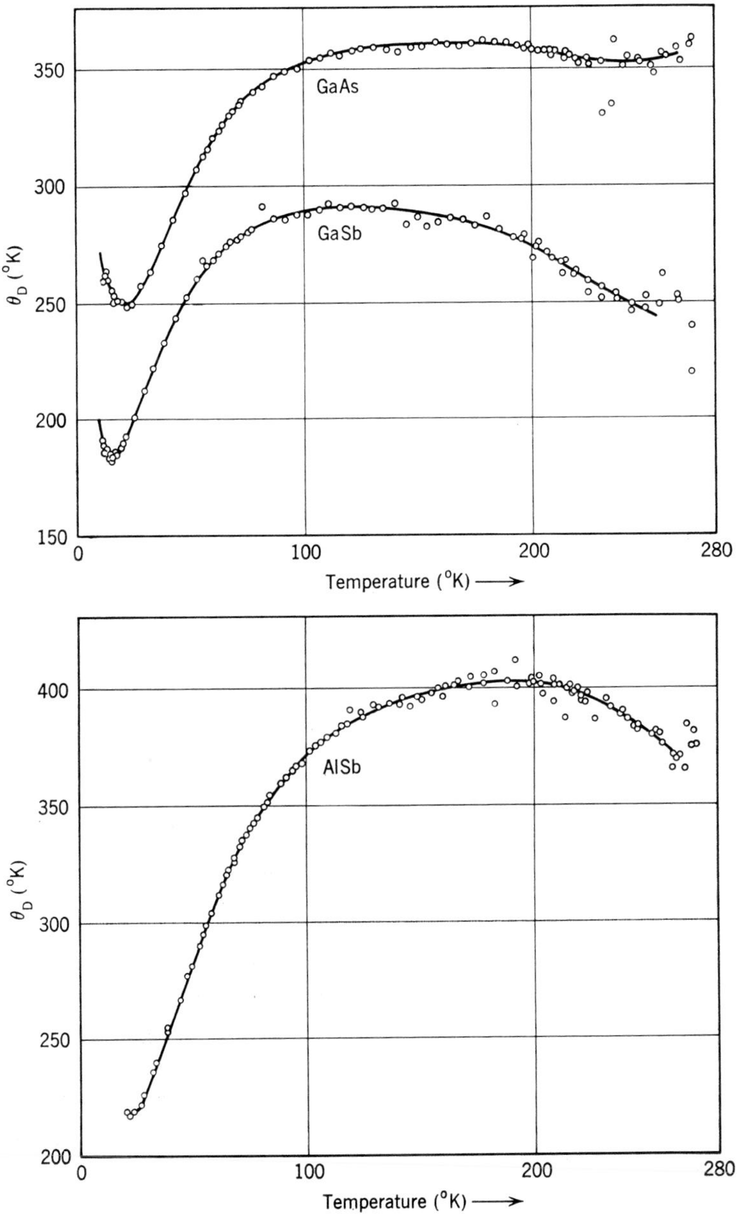

as a function of temperature [according to Piesbergen (63P5)].

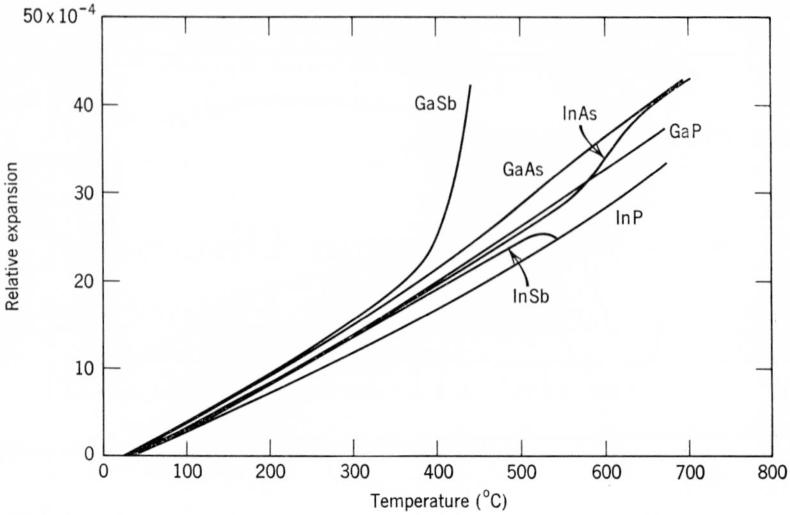

Fig. 8.12 Thermal expansion coefficients of six III-V compounds vs. temperature [after Bernstein and Beals (61B12)].

drops off to 204°K at 250°K. For GaSb and AlSb at 80°K these authors report values of 270°K and 350°K, respectively.

Keyes (62K3) has observed phenomenologically that the product of the elastic constants and the fourth power of the interatomic distance is approximately constant within each of three groups of semiconductors, the group IV atoms, the III-V compounds, and the II-VI compounds. This fact enabled Steigmeier (63S5) to calculate C_{11} and θ_D for twelve III-V compounds.

The thermal expansion of the III-V compounds was measured by Welker and Weiss (56W3) and Gibbons (58G2) at room temperature, and by Bernstein and Beals (61B12) and Novikova (60N6), (61N4), (63N8) over a wide temperature range. Just as in the semiconductors of group IV, the thermal expansion coefficients of the III-V compounds are negative at low temperatures, then go through zero [in InSb at 57.5°K (60N6) and in GaAs at 55°K (61N4)], and remain positive above this temperature. Figure 8.12 shows the thermal expansion of the most important III-V compounds as a function of temperature after Bernstein and Beals.

9

Summarizing Discussion of the Main Properties of the III-V Compounds

90 Preliminary Remarks

In this final chapter we will summarize some of the more important properties of III-V compounds discussed previously. This summary is particularly valuable for those parameters which are involved in more than one experimental measurement and therefore appear in a number of chapters.

For example, we deduced the main features of the band structure of the III-V compounds from the experimental results in Chapter 3. However, the transport properties considered in Chapter 4 and other factors added in later chapters supplement these experimental results, so that an all-inclusive discussion of the band structure is only now feasible. This will be the subject of Section 91. We will find that we have a quite complete picture of the band structure of the main III-V compounds. Of course, it is not possible to collect all parameters discussed previously; only the most important ones will be listed in this chapter. For more detailed information the reader is referred to the extensive subject index at the end of this book. There the pages are indicated on which the values of a given parameter are discussed for each of the most important III-V compounds.

After the band structure parameters we will once again briefly consider the scattering mechanisms which determine the transport properties of the III-V compounds (Section 92). Finally, in Section 93, we will again take up the discussion about the chemical binding that was started in Section 20. We will attempt to understand the physical properties of the III-V compounds on the basis of the chemical binding, or at least try to make a plausible connection between the two.

91 The Band Structure

The experimental material obtained from the optical measurements (Chapter 3), supplemented by results of the electrical measurements, makes it possible to quantitatively describe the band structure of the most important III-V compounds. This information is summarized in Tables 9.1 and 9.2, where representative values of the band-structure parameters of InSb, InAs, InP, GaSb, GaAs, GaP, and AlSb are listed.

Let us first consider the *forbidden gap* E_G.

Table 9.1 contains three kinds of E_G values. Two of these are obtained from optical measurements, either at room temperature or near absolute zero, and the other from electrical measurements. The optical values for InSb, for InAs at 300°K, and for GaSb at 4°K were taken from measurements of magnetoabsorption; the other optical values, from measurements of the position of the absorption edge. The value in parentheses is obtained by linearly extrapolating higher-temperature data to 0°K (cf. Table 3.1). The measured linear temperature dependence applies only over a region near room temperature, and extrapolation to 0°K generally leads to values which are somewhat too large. The "electrical" width of the forbidden gap, obtained from the intrinsic carrier concentration, is approximately equal to E_G (0°K). It also depends on a linear extrapolation from high temperatures.

In the three indium compounds, GaSb, and GaAs, the transitions for which E_G is the threshold energy are direct transitions from the valence band into the lowest (000)-minimum of the conduction band. In GaP and AlSb the transitions are indirect into a (100)-minimum of the conduction band.

Measurements of the pressure dependence of the absorption edge and of the electrical resistance, as well as measurements of the magnetoresistance and of other transport properties, have shown us that in InSb and InAs the *conduction band* can be described by a single approximately isotropic band with the minimum in the center of the Brillouin zone. Pressure measurements in InAs did seem to indicate the existence of a second subband [(111) ?]. However, the magnitude of the pressure coefficient would predict this second subband to start 0.1 eV above the (000)-minimum, at normal pressure. In that case, the influence of this band would have made itself felt in other experimental results in contradiction to all the available data.

In InP a second subband with minima along the (100)-axes is indicated by the pressure dependence of the absorption edge.

In GaSb three subbands lie so close to each other that they must all be taken into consideration in interpreting the experimental material.

It has been shown that in GaAs also more than one subband of the conduction band plays a role. All experimental facts—except those of Kravchenko and Fan, which were discussed in Section 412—indicate that (100)-minima lie about 0.36 eV above the lowest (000)-minimum. These results are supported by a careful interpretation of Fig. 6.12, where the energy gap of the mixed-crystal system $Ga(P_xAs_{1-x})$ is plotted. With increasing x, E_G increases approximately linearly up to $x = 0.55$. There the curve changes into another linear portion with a smaller slope. If one interprets the kink as the cross-over point of the (000)- and (100)-subbands, one can extrapolate to the position of the (100)-subband in GaAs, and one finds for the separation $E_{100} - E_{000}$ about 0.4 eV. Other values (crossover at $x = 0.38$, $E_{100} - E_{000} = 0.25$ eV in GaAs) have been found by Spitzer and Mead (cf. Section 70) and by Allen and Hobdy (63A2) ($x = 0.53$, $E_{100} - E_{000} = 0.27$ eV).

In GaP and AlSb the lowest minimum of the conduction band has been shown to be a (100)-minimum. Transitions to a higher subband, which probably lies in the center of the Brillouin zone, were observed in both semiconductors. That this high band indeed is a (000)-subband can be shown for AlSb from the pressure dependence of the absorption edge, and for both semiconductors from an extrapolation of the linear regions in the $E_G(x)$-dependence of the $Ga(P_xAs_{1-x})$ and $(Al_xGa_{1-x})Sb$ mixed crystals. The latter arguments follow the same line of reasoning that we have just used in the discussion of GaAs. In AlAs also, a Γ-minimum lies above the lowest Δ-minimum ($\Delta E \approx 0.8$ eV), as mentioned in Section 70.

The energy separations between the (000)-minimum and other minima of the conduction band of III-V compounds ($\Delta E_{\Gamma\Delta}$, $\Delta E_{\Gamma\Lambda}$), as far as they are known, are listed in rows 4 and 5 of Table 9.1.

The (000)-subbands of the conduction bands of the III-V compounds are not parabolic, according to Kane's theory. This has been supported experimentally in InSb and InAs, the two III-V compounds in which other subbands do not play any role. In other compounds, such as GaAs, Kane's theory also gives excellent agreement with experiment as long as the doping is low enough so that only the (000)-subband is occupied with electrons.

In Table 9.2 the effective masses of the electrons at the bottom of the conduction band are listed. So far, a change of effective electron

Tables 9.1–9.2 Summary of the Most Important Band-Structure Parameters of the III-V Compounds InSb, InAs, InP, GaSb, GaAs, GaP, and AlSb

For an explanation of the values we refer to the detailed discussion in the text. The figures in brackets have been obtained by calculation. The others are the best experimental data or have been derived from them.

Table 9.1 Energy Parameters

Parameter (eV)	Compound						
	InSb	InAs	InP	GaSb	GaAs	GaP	AlSb
Lowest conduction band minimum at	(000)	(000)	(000)	(000)	(000)	(100)	(100)
Higher subband minima at			(100)?	(111) (100)	(100)	(000)	(000)
Band gap							
$E_{G,\text{opt}}$ (300°K)	0.180	0.36	1.26	0.67–0.725	1.430	2.24	1.6
$E_{G,\text{opt}}$ (4°K)	0.2357	0.425	1.416	0.813	1.517	2.325	(1.7)
$E_{G,\text{el}}$ (0°K)	0.27	0.47	1.34	0.77–0.82	1.4		1.65
Separation of subbands of the conduction band							
$\Delta E_{\Gamma\Delta}$	...	...	0.7	0.4	0.25–0.40	−0.35	−0.29
$\Delta E_{\Gamma\Lambda}$	...	...	...	0.074	...	...	...
Higher-energy transitions							
E_{L1}	1.87	2.50	3.15	2.08	2.99	3.71	3.23
E_{L2}	2.45	2.85	3.29	2.55	3.23		3.18
E_{L3}	5.3	6.4	6.9	5.7	6.6	7.0	6.5
E_{L4}	6.0	7.0			6.9		

E_{X1}	4.20	4.83	5.0	4.33	5.12	5.3	4.5
E_{X2}	4.70	5.30		4.70	5.55		
$E_{\Gamma 2}$	3.45	4.63	4.1	3.74	4.52	3.76	4.3
Spin-orbit splittings							
Δ	0.98	0.43			0.33	0.127	0.75
	(0.98)	(0.41)	(0.18)	(0.81)		(0.10)	(0.76)
$\frac{3}{2}\Delta_L$	(0.87)	(0.52)	(0.21)	(0.71)	(0.32)	(0.15)	(0.6)
Δ_L	0.58	0.35	0.14	0.47	0.24	0.1	0.4

Table 9.2 Effective Masses

Mass (units of the electron mass)	Compound						
	InSb	InAs	InP	GaSb	GaAs	GaP	AlSb
$m_{n,\text{opt}}$	0.0116 (300°K) 0.0155 (4°K)	0.023–0.027	0.077	0.047	0.043–0.071	0.34	0.39
$m_{n,\text{el}}$	0.01–0.02	0.02	0.05	$m_{111} = 0.9$	$m_{100} = 1.2$		
$m_{n,\text{th}}$	(0.0152)	(0.026)	(0.072)	(0.046)	(0.084)	(0.13)	(0.11)
$m_{p1,\text{opt}}$	0.40–0.50 (0.18?)	0.4		0.23	0.68		
$m_{p1,\text{el}}$	~0.5	0.3	0.2	0.39	0.5	0.5	0.4–0.9
$m_{p1,\text{th}}$	(0.53)	(0.82)	(1.0)	(0.71)	(1.0)	(0.56)	(1.1)
$m_{p2,\text{exp}}$	0.0149	0.025			0.12		
$m_{p2,\text{th}}$	(0.016)	(0.031)	(0.086)	(0.053)	(0.10)	(0.13)	(0.12)
$m_{p3,\text{exp}}$		0.083			0.20		
$m_{p3,\text{th}}$	(0.12)	(0.11)	(0.18)	(0.16)	(0.21)	(0.22)	(0.27)

mass with temperature has been measured only in InSb. In that case, the values at room temperature and at helium temperature are given. Both values were derived from cyclotron-resonance measurements. Electrical measurements gave an electron mass of the same order of magnitude. The values reported in the literature scatter considerably, however.

For InAs two "optical" values are listed. They were obtained from cyclotron resonance and from the Faraday effect. For InP the effective mass was obtained from cyclotron resonance; for GaSb, from magnetoabsorption. For GaAs the smaller value comes from plasma reflection, and the larger one from cyclotron resonance. Finally, the AlSb and GaP values were derived from the Faraday effect.

The second row of Table 9.2 contains the electrically determined values of the effective electron mass. For GaSb and GaAs the density-of-states masses of the higher subband are listed, as determined from magnetoresistance measurements. The "theoretical" effective electron mass entered in the third row of Table 9.2 will be discussed in more detail below. It is derived from Kane's theory for the (000)-minimum of the conduction band.

The *valence band* in InSb and InAs has the structure predicted by Kane. This follows from a large number of independent experimental results. No indications of deviation from this structure were ever found in any of the more thoroughly investigated III-V compounds. We are therefore justified in extending Kane's theory to the valence bands of all the other III-V compounds.

Tables 9.1 and 9.2 again contain the most important parameter values of the valence bands. Consider first the experimentally determined parameter values of the valence bands.

The nonparabolicity of the V_2-band, as required by Kane's theory, has been confirmed experimentally in InSb, as has the anisotropic structure of the V_1-band. The effective mass in the V_1-band is 0.4–0.5 m from most optical and electrical measurements, whereas a few measurements suggest a value of 0.18 m. We have discussed this discrepancy in Chapters 3 and 4. The effective mass of the light holes (V_2-band) is much smaller. From magnetoabsorption a value is determined which coincides approximately with the effective *electron* mass. We will come back to this point later.

In InAs the effective masses of all three valence bands are known from comparison of the inter-valence-band transitions with Kane's theory. The electrically determined heavy-hole mass agrees with these results. So far, InAs is the only material in which the linear terms in k, in the V_1-band near the center of the Brillouin zone, (predicted by Kane's theory) have been observed. This deviation from the parabolic first approximation of Kane's theory is small, however. The maxima of the valence band on the [111]-axes lie only a few thousandths of an electron volt above the energy value at point Γ and are separated by only a very small distance from this point (Section 314).

Nothing is known about the valence band of InP from optical measurements. We therefore list only the electrically determined mass of the heavy holes. Information is just as scant for GaP and AlSb.

A little more is known about GaSb. The optically determined hole mass m_{p1} is considerably smaller than the one derived from electrical measurements.

The more extensive information about the valence band of GaAs was again obtained from measurements of the inter-valence-band transitions. With Kane's theory the parameters of the valence band can be determined accurately.

The spin-orbit splitting of the valence band (Δ), i.e., the separation of the maximum of the V_3-band from the maximum of the V_1-band, has been calculated from the measured inter-valence-band transitions in InSb, InAs, and AlSb. The values of this energy parameter are listed in Table 9.1.

In Section 313 we extensively discussed the band structure at *higher energies* as it can be derived from reflection measurements. The experimentally determined energy separations between the band extrema at these points were tabulated in Table 3.3. The most important of these data are reproduced in Table 9.1. The four possible transitions at point L are numbered consecutively E_{L1} through E_{L4}, and the two possible transitions at X, E_{X1} and E_{X2}. $E_{\Gamma 2}$ is a transition at Γ into a higher subband of the conduction band.

With the aid of *Kane's theory* we will now combine all these experimental results into one coherent picture. We will try to predict from this theory the parameter values of the band structure of III-V compounds which are not yet known. We will see that this prediction is possible for the effective masses as well as for the energy separation of the V_1- and V_3-bands, Δ. The values obtained in this way are entered in Tables 9.1 and 9.2, where they are set in parentheses.

The first approximation of Kane's theory (neglecting the influence of all bands except that of the lowest conduction band and of three valence bands) requires the parameters E_G, Δ, and P for the calculation of the effective masses m_n, m_{p2}, and m_{p3}, at the various band extrema. In the following discussion we will formulate the calculations in terms of the energy parameter $E_P = (2m/\hbar^2)P^2$ rather than of the matrix element P. The heavy-hole effective mass cannot be determined from these three parameters alone; it even has the wrong sign in this approximation: $(m_{p1} = -m)$(!).

Of the three parameters E_G, Δ, and E_P, only E_G can be measured readily. The spin-orbit splitting Δ has been determined experimentally in some of the compounds under discussion, using the theory itself to interpret the data. To estimate Δ for the other III-V compounds we employ a method of Kane's [(57K2); see also (62B12)]. The parameter Δ is determined primarily by the charge distribution within the atomic cores of the lattice and is only weakly influenced by the valence electrons which are responsible for the binding. It would therefore seem permissible to make use of the known spin-orbit splitting of the atomic one-electron wave functions. Kane averages over all possible configurations and finds the following atomic spin-orbit splitting energies Δ_{at}:

Al	0.016 eV	Si	0.028 eV	P	0.046 eV
Ga	0.12 eV	Ge	0.20 eV	As	0.29 eV
In	0.27 eV	Sn	0.60 eV	Sb	0.80 eV

In germanium the spin-orbit splitting Δ is 0.29 eV, in silicon about 0.04 eV. In both cases Δ is about 1.45 times the atomic splitting, Δ_{at}. Kane therefore assumes the spin-orbit splitting of a compound to be given by the formula:

$$\Delta = 1.45(t^{\text{III}}\,\Delta_{at}^{\text{III}} + t^{\text{V}}\,\Delta_{at}^{\text{V}}) \tag{9.1}$$

Here t^{III} is the (relative) time that a valence electron spends at an atom of group III, and $t^{\text{V}} = 1 - t^{\text{III}}$ the time it spends at an atom of group V. To calculate Δ from the atomic values, the factor 1.45 applying to germanium and silicon was used unchanged.

For the relative occupation time Kane and other authors originally used the effective ion charges e_s^*/e and $(1 - e_s^*/e)$, respectively. We will find, however, in Section 93 that the experimentally determined ion charges have very little relationship to the theoretical effective charges that were introduced in Section 21. In (62B12) Kane assumes t^{III} and t^{V} to be the same for all III-V compounds and to be such that for GaAs the experimentally determined spin-orbit splitting results. This requires that the electron spend 35% of the time at the III atom and 65% at the V atom. These values are somewhat smaller than the theoretical values given in Table 2.2, but they are of the right order of magnitude. In Table 9.1 the Δ values in parentheses were calculated by this procedure.

The experimentally determined spin-orbit splittings of the valence band at point L provide another indication of how justified the procedure is. These splittings can be calculated as the difference of the energies E_{L2} and E_{L1} in Table 9.1. They are listed as Δ_L in that same table. In germanium Δ_L has about two thirds the value of Δ. If this ratio is assumed to be the same in the III-V compounds, then the values of Δ and of $\frac{3}{2}\Delta_L$ in Table 9.1 must agree with each other. This can indeed be seen to be the case.

The parameter E_P is most accurately determined from the experimental effective mass value of the electrons at the edge of the conduction band. Kane's theory gives for this

$$E_P = 3\left(\frac{m}{m_n} - 1\right)\left(\frac{2}{E_G} + \frac{1}{E_G + \Delta}\right)^{-1} \tag{9.2}$$

If the values of Table 9.1 are inserted in (9.2), it is found that all III-V compounds describable by Kane's theory have, within less than 20%, the same value: $E_P = 20$ eV (61E4).

This agreement makes it possible to write down simple formulas for estimating the effective electron masses and the hole masses m_{p2} and m_{p3}:

$$m_n \approx m\left[1 + \frac{20}{3}\left(\frac{2}{E_G} + \frac{1}{E_G + \Delta}\right)\right]^{-1} \tag{9.3}$$

$$\approx \frac{m}{20} E_G \quad \text{for } \Delta \ll E_G \ll 20 \text{ eV}$$

$$m_{p2} \approx m\left[\frac{40}{3E_G} - 1\right]^{-1} \approx \frac{3m}{40} E_G \tag{9.4}$$

$$m_{p3} \approx m\left[\frac{20}{3(E_G + \Delta)} - 1\right]^{-1} \approx \frac{3m}{20}(E_G + \Delta) \tag{9.5}$$

The theoretical values of the effective masses that we have listed in Table 9.2 are somewhat different from these approximate values. They are ones calculated by Cardona according to the improved Kane theory that was mentioned in Section 213. The numbers are set in parentheses in Table 9.2.

The quantities in Tables 9.1 and 9.2 may now be used to calculate other structure parameters of the band model, in the framework of Kane's theory. The g-factor of the electrons for $\mathbf{k} = 0$ follows from eq. (3.11). If the parameter values of Tables 9.1 and 9.2 are inserted in eq. (3.11), good agreement is obtained, for InSb and GaAs, with the g-values, determined from spin resonance, that were mentioned in connection with eq. (3.11).

Herman *et al.* (63H3) have shown that in many cases "relativistic" corrections may further change the value of Δ. In these corrections the unrelativistic Schrödinger equation with the spin-orbit coupling term is replaced by the Dirac equation. Preliminary estimates suggested that the corrected theoretical Δ-values will agree still more closely with the experimental ones.

This discussion sets down quantitatively the band structure of the III-V compounds, although the details are not yet known as well as for germanium and silicon.

Lately a number of additional correlations have been discovered, which relate the band structures of the various semiconductors, such as the ones we have used for determining Δ and for interrelating Δ and Δ_L. For example, Cardona and Greenaway (62C1) have shown that the energy separation of the points Γ and L in the V_1-band takes on the value of (1.35 ± 0.15) eV for almost all the semiconductors with diamond and zinc-blende structure. Such empirical laws, which can also be made theoretically plausible, can be used to shed more light on the band structure of many semiconductors. We will not go into this subject further and will only refer to (62P7).

92 The Transport Properties

In germanium and silicon the movement of the charge carriers under the influence of external forces is characterized by the (longitudinal and transverse) effective masses of the electrons in the (111)- and (100)-minima, respectively, and by the isotropic effective masses of the holes in the V_1- and V_2-bands. The other important variables are the scattering mechanisms. Acoustic deformation-potential scattering and ionized-impurity scattering are the ones that generally limit the mobility. The existence of a number of equivalent minima in the conduction band furthermore forces one to consider the intervalley scattering in addition to the intravalley scattering.

In many respects the situation is more complicated in the III-V compounds; in some ways it is simpler. The valence bands of these compounds are essentially equivalent to those of the group IV semiconductors. The conduction bands of most of the III-V compounds under discussion are isotropic, and we need only assume a single scalar electron mass. This mass is, however, doping dependent. When a number of subbands are occupied with electrons, as in heavily doped GaSb and GaAs, additional electrons with different (tensor) effective masses must be taken into consideration.

The formal theory of the transport phenomena therefore becomes somewhat more complex, as there are not only two kinds of holes to be included but also different electrons and electrons of varying mass.

The main complication of the theory is caused not by the band structure, but by the scattering. We saw in Chapter 4 that in most III-V compounds it is polar scattering that limits the mobility over a large temperature range. It is not possible to define a relaxation time for polar scattering, so that the transport parameters cannot be represented in closed form as a function of the effective masses, of the exponent r of the energy dependence of the relaxation time, of the doping, temperature, etc., as can be done for acoustic scattering. One is restricted to numerical calculations which require considerable effort. This is why we defined a "substitute parameter" r for polar scattering, in Fig. 4.1. It is temperature dependent and takes on different values for different transport parameters.

The dominance of polar optical scattering over deformation potential scattering in the III-V compounds is due to a number of facts. For one, the coupling constant describing the interaction of the charge carriers with the polar lattice vibrations

$$\alpha = \frac{e^2}{\hbar}\left(\frac{m^*}{2\hbar\omega_l}\right)^{1/2}\left[\frac{1}{\kappa(\infty)} - \frac{1}{\kappa(0)}\right] \tag{9.6}$$

is generally larger than that for the deformation potential scattering. Also, the small electron mass in many III-V compounds causes polar scattering to be preferred, since the mobility for acoustic scattering is proportional to $m^{*-5/2}$, that for polar optical scattering proportional to $m^{*-3/2}$. This is not true at all temperatures. At high temperatures μ_{acoustic} drops more rapidly with increasing temperature ($\sim T^{-1.5}$) than μ_{polar} ($\sim T^{-0.5}$), and at very high temperatures acoustic scattering may become noticeable.

These arguments apply only to a comparison of acoustic and polar scattering for electrons which can be characterized by a scalar effective mass. The situation is different in the anisotropic minima of the conduction band of GaP and AlSb, and in the high-lying minima of GaSb and GaAs. Not enough experimental data are yet available to determine unambiguously the scattering mechanism in these cases.

In Table 9.3 we have summarized the most important data about the mobilities of electrons and holes in III-V compounds. We have listed the best available values of electron and hole mobility at room tem-

Table 9.3 Carrier Mobilities
Calculated values in brackets.

Mobility (cm^2/V sec)	Compound						
	InSb	InAs	InP	GaSb	GaAs	GaP	AlSb
μ_n (300°K)	77,000	27,000	4,500	2,500 $\mu_{000} = 4000$ $\mu_{111} < 700$	8,500	>100	>60
μ_n (78°K)	620,000		23,400		22,000		
μ_p (300°K)	700	450	150	1,420	435	150	400
$\mu_{n,\mathrm{polar}}$ (300°K)	(200,000)	(21,000–40,000)	(4,700–6,800)	(14,000–44,000)	(9,300–11,000)		
$\mu_{p,\mathrm{polar}}$ (300°K)	(600)	(500)	(160–500)	(1,200)	(600)	(250)	(800)

perature and of electron mobility at 78°K. The table also lists the theoretical mobility for polar scattering, for which different authors obtain strongly varying values because some of the parameters in the theory are not known with sufficient accuracy. For a discussion of these data, we refer to Section 411.

93 The Relationship between Chemical Bond and Semiconductor Properties

In Chapter 2 we started the discussion of the chemical bond in compounds with zinc-blende structure. We will now continue this discussion and try to explain some of the physical properties of the III-V compounds.

The chemical bond can be characterized by a number of parameters. One parameter (λ) was introduced in Chapter 2. It is a measure of the contribution of the sp^3-hybrid wave functions of two nearest neighbors to the bond. From it the probability of occupation of the two neighbors by an electron can be derived, and therefrom an effective ionic charge e^* calculated for the trivalent and pentavalent lattice atoms.

Another approach is to build up the wave function of a bond out of the wave functions for the two extreme cases of pure covalent binding and ionic binding:

$$\chi = A\chi_{\text{cov}} + B\chi_{\text{ion}} \tag{9.7}$$

The ratio B/A represents the ionic part of the bond. Since the wave functions have to be normalized, A in (9.7) can be expressed in terms of B. The most useful form is

$$\chi = (1 - \lambda')^{1/2}\chi_{\text{cov}} + \lambda'^{1/2}\chi_{\text{ion}} \tag{9.8}$$

Here λ' is equal to 0 for pure homopolar binding and equal to 1 for pure heteropolar binding. The parameter λ of Chapter 2 is related to λ' by $\lambda' = (1 - \lambda^2)/(1 + \lambda^2)$. The neutral bond is realized for $\lambda' = \lambda_0' = \frac{1}{4}$. The "effective" ion charge is $e^* = (4\lambda' - 1)e = 4(\lambda' - \lambda_0')e$.

One frequently calls λ' (or even B/A) the *ionicity* and e^* the *polarity* of a bond. This notation is not completely consistent, since the neutral bond has the ionicity $\frac{1}{4}$. Some authors, therefore, also distinguish between the formal ionicity λ' and the effective ionicity $\lambda_{\text{eff}} = (4\lambda' - 1)/3 = e^*/3$. The effective ionicity is 0 for neutral binding and 1 for pure ionic binding.

The theoretical determination of this parameter was discussed in

Chapter 2. Accordingly, the seven most important III-V compounds (we will restrict the following discussion to these seven) can be arranged into a sequence of increasing ionicity: GaSb, AlSb, GaP, GaAs and InSb, InAs, and InP. The effective ionic charge increases in this sequence from $+0.43e$ to $+0.49e$.

Suchet (61S17), (61S18) suggested the formula

$$e^* = 3(1 - s(Z^A/r^B + Z^B/r^A))e \tag{9.9}$$

for the effective ionic charge. Z^A and Z^B are the number of electrons of the A^{3+} and B^{3-} ions, and r^A and r^B are the associated ionic radii. The constant s is determined so that e^* disappears (in the average) for the semiconductors of group IV of the periodic system. With this formula Suchet finds the sequence AlSb, GaSb, InSb, GaAs, InAs, InP, GaP, which differs from the sequence given above in that GaSb and GaP have different positions. The corresponding ionic charges lie between $-0.98e$ and $+1.50e$, where InSb has almost exactly $e^* = 0$.

An even different sequence has been derived by Folberth (58F4) from the following arguments. The polarization of electron bonds must be larger, the larger the ionic part E_{ion} of the bond energy $E_B = E_{ion} + E_{cov}$ is, compared to the covalent part E_{cov}. The polarization will also depend on the degree by which the electrons of the inner shells of the atoms can be displaced. From this argument, a "relative polarization"

$$J = \frac{E_{ion}}{E_{cov}} (Z^{III} + Z^{V})^{3/2} \tag{9.10}$$

follows. For E_{cov} the binding energy of the isoelectronic semiconductor of group IV can be used in first approximation. The energy E_{ion} is proportional to the square of the electronegativities, according to Pauling. This calculation does not result in any absolute numbers. For the relative polarization the following sequence is determined: AlSb, GaSb, GaP, GaAs, InSb, InP, InAs.

The electronegativities of the lattice atoms are often used in connection with the bonding properties of the III-V compounds to obtain statements about the ionicity or the polarization. This technique is reliable as long as one compares the semiconductors of an isoelectronic sequence, in which the difference of the electronegativities of the two components of a compound varies strongly among the different compounds of the sequence [(54G2), (59P1), and others]. Within the III-V compounds this difference, however, always lies between 0.3 and 0.6, where the average error can be ± 0.1 because of the inaccurately known values of the electronegativities. Therefore any separation of the III-V compounds according to the "differences in electronegativities" must be very inaccurate. This topic will not be considered any further here.

The binding cannot be characterized unambiguously by the concept of polarization. We saw in Chapter 2 that polarization can be defined to be either polarization of electron bonds (increasing ionicity) or polarization of lattice ions (decreasing ionicity). Even if the latter point of view is taken, the relationship between polarization and ionicity (or effective ionic charge) is not clear cut. The ratio of the ionic radii of the two binding partners determines how much the effective charge of the two partners is changed by a given deformation of the electron cloud. For these reasons the concepts "absolute polarization" and "relative polarization" (referred to the size of the ions) were introduced.

So far we have made no reference to the experimental "effective ionic charges" that were discussed in previous chapters. Most of those values were obtained from optical measurements. According to eq. (3.41), the effective ionic charge can be determined from the difference of the dielectric constants at frequencies 0 and ∞, or from the frequency ratio of the longitudinal and transverse optical lattice vibrations, ω_l/ω_t. Then e^* is a parameter which describes the dynamic behavior of the lattice. It appeared in the formulas for polar scattering of the charge carriers and, in addition, determines a number of dynamic quantities, such as the piezoelectric coefficients, the coefficients of the piezoresistance, and the elastic constants. The "dynamic" charge is, however, completely unsuited to be a measure of the ionicity of a bond, as was particularly emphasized by Matossi (59M3) and Cochran (61C10). Indeed the effects mentioned above lead to effective charges that differ completely from one another. Effective charges for III-V compounds have been determined from the piezoelectric effect by Zerbst and Bornofka (63Z2) and from electron-resonance experiments by Kimmel (63K1).

Other methods of determining the effective charge, such as x-ray diffraction, assume that the lattice ions are clearly separated from each other by regions of very small charge density. Because of the existence of the electron bonds this is not the case here (see also Fig. 2.1). This difficulty completely precludes a quantitative definition of a uniform "effective charge."

Finally, cleavage experiments were employed for an experimental determination of the ionicity of the lattice (55P2), (58W8), (59W6). This again makes it possible to arrange the III-V compounds in a sequence of increasing ionicity which differs from the sequences given above. We have seen in Section 85 that these cleavage experiments can also be interpreted in a different fashion.

All these considerations force one to conclude that it is not possible at this time to describe the binding in III-V compounds quantitatively and to form a solid foundation for the interpretation of their semiconductor properties. All comparisons between chemical binding and the physical properties can therefore be based only on plausibility arguments.

Consider first the width of the forbidden gap. When we compare the E_G values within the III-V compounds and the group IV semiconductors, we must consider that the bottom of the conduction band is not formed by the same subband in all these semiconductors. The question of which subband of the conduction band forms the bottom of the band cannot be definitely answered from our knowledge of the chemical binding. Two arguments do exist which can perhaps give us rough indication. In the group IV semiconductors the electron bonds are not polarized. A conduction electron moves in a periodic potential with the symmetry of the diamond lattice. In the III-V compounds the polarization of the electron bridges causes the valence electrons to concentrate around the anions. The valence electrons therefore tend to shield the atoms of the B-sublattice, and the probability of finding a conduction electron near an atom of the A-sublattice is larger than that near the B-sublattice. The conduction electrons consequently only "see" a cubic face-centered lattice of simpler structure than the diamond lattice. Theoretical estimates show this lattice to have a conduction-band minimum at the center of the Brillouin zone. According to the consideration of Folberth, cited above, the weakest polarization is found in AlSb, GaSb, and GaP, namely, in the III-V compounds in which the (111)- or (100)-minima of the conduction band play a role. In addition to this argument of Folberth we should mention a consideration of Edwards, Slykhouse, and Drickamer (59E3), which is based on the results of the one-dimensional model of Seraphin-Adawi (Section 215). According to this model, E_G increases in the transition from a one-dimensional array of equal potential wells to an array of unequal wells. In the zinc-blende lattice one finds different atoms alternating as one proceeds in the (111)- or in the (100)-direction. For the (111)- and (100)-minima an increase of E_G would therefore be expected in the transition from the diamond structure to the zinc-blende structure. This does not apply to the (000)-minima in the diamond and zinc-blende lattices, since these are built up out of s-wave functions, and no direction of the wave vector is preferred.

We encounter similar uncertainties in comparing the mobilities of the various III-V compounds with those of the group IV semiconductors. Chapter 4 showed us that the scattering mechanism which limits the mobility of electrons in most of the III-V compounds is not the same as that in the semiconducting elements. Furthermore, the maximum values of the mobilities are not definitely known in all the substances. Finally, the effective masses which enter into the mobilities are parameters of different subbands of the conduction band. This difficulty does not appear for the effective masses of the valence band, since the valence bands of all the interesting semiconductors are similar in their main outlines.

If we assign the isoelectronic III-V compounds to their group IV semiconductors, we obtain the following diagram:

Diamond				BN			
SiC			BP		AlN		
Si		BAs		AlP		GaN	
$Si_{0.5}Ge_{0.5}$	BSb		AlAs		GaP		InN
Ge		AlSb		GaAs		InP	
—			GaSb		InAs		
Sn				InSb			

Two systematic regularities are immediately apparent within this diagram: (1) The binding energy decreases as one goes down in the vertical direction. It is largest for diamond (and for BN), smallest for α-tin (InSb). As the binding energy drops, the forbidden gap becomes smaller, and the mobility of the electrons grows. (2) In the horizontal transition from the group IV semiconductor to the isoelectronic III-V compound the binding energy grows and with it the width of the forbidden gap and the electron mobility. These two statements are generally called "Welker's rule."

Consider the first statement. The drop in binding energy downward can easily be explained. With increasing atomic number the valence electrons which form the bonds are more and more loosely bound. Even the simplest band theory predicts that with decreasing binding the individual bands become wider, and the forbidden gaps therefore narrower. Also narrow bands are associated with large effective masses at the band edge (and therefore small mobilities of the free carriers), wide bands with small effective masses (high mobilities). These statements have a real meaning only if one assumes that all the other properties of the semiconductors that are being compared do not change.

The increase of the binding energy in the transition from IV to III-V can be explained by similar arguments. The increased electron mobility arises, as we know, from the fact that in the main III-V compounds the (000)-minimum forms the bottom of the conduction band. A more detailed comparison does not appear to be useful for the reasons stated above.

The decrease of the hole mobility from IV to III-V can be understood, on one hand, by the increasing binding energy, and, on the other hand, by the fact that with increasing polarization of the electron bonds the valence electrons (and therefore the "holes") concentrate more and more around the anions. This concentration makes it more difficult for a valence electron to transfer from one anion to another and thereby decreases the hole mobility.

The preceding discussion has explained some of the differences between the semiconductors under consideration, or at least has made them plausible. We have not yet considered differences among isoelectronic III-V compounds, such as among AlSb, GaAs, and InP or between GaSb and InAs (see the diagram on p. 365). Here we must make use of arguments which take the differing ionicity or polarization of the binding into account. We know from considerations at the beginning of this section that the ionic contribution to the binding increases along the sequence AlSb, GaAs, InP. This change should be accompanied by an increase of the forbidden gap. Experimentally, the opposite is found. Folberth (60F6) has given an explanation for this phenomenon. It proceeds from the fact that a displacement of the center of gravity of the electron bridge changes the effective charge of the ions by an amount depending on the ionic radii. Therefore the "absolute" polarization can increase in a sequence of otherwise equal compounds, while simultaneously the "relative" polarization (referred to the ionic radius of the anion) decreases. In this case, according to Folberth, the compound with the smallest cation and the largest anion has the largest energy gap, in agreement with the experimental facts of the sequence InP, GaAs, AlSb.

A detailed discussion of the polarization allows Folberth (58F4), (59F3), (60F5), (60F6) also to interpret other properties of the III-V compounds, such as differing inclinations to form mixed crystals between different III-V compounds and the solubility of atoms of group IV in III-V compounds. We have considered some of these topics in Chapter 6.

Since our present knowledge of the chemical binding of the III-V compounds allows only rough quantitative conclusions as to the physical properties of these semiconductors, it is not surprising that a number of empirical formulas have been proposed to interrelate the parameters of the various III-V compounds. They can then be used to predict as yet unknown properties of other III-V compounds.

Such formulas have been constructed mainly for the width of the energy gap. Hrivnák (61H16) gives a relationship between E_G and the modulus of elasticity C_{11}: $E_G = A\sqrt{C_{11}} - B$, where A and B are constants. The formulas agree with experiment for InSb, GaSb, and GaAs and (with a different set of constants) for tin, germanium, silicon, and diamond.

Miyauchi (57M1) finds a linear relationship $E_G = A(a_1/a_2) - B$, where a_1 is half the separation of two nearest neighbors, and a_2 the average radius of the positive ions. This formula describes experimental experiences on III-V compounds relatively well, as well as (with different constants) those on II-VI compounds, while, among the elements, silicon falls way outside this equation.

Goodman (55G1) finds a linear relationship between $(E_G)^{1/2}$ and $1/a'^2$, where a' is the interatomic separation, for the group IV elements only. Goodman interpretes deviations from this formula, in the case of the III-V compounds, as an ionic contribution to E_G. He uses the latter value to determine the ionic contribution to the binding.

Manca (61M3) extends the considerations of Goodman and calculates the binding energy of a single bond E_s, which is proportional to $1/a'^2$ for pure homopolar binding. According to Manca, the empirical formula $E_G = AE_s - B$ then also applies to the III-V and II-VI compounds. The constants A and B are chosen differently for the elements, the III-V compounds, and the II-VI compounds.

Suchet (60S11) also separates E_G into a homopolar and a heteropolar part. He determines E_{hom} from a formula similar to that of Goodman, and E_{het} from an empirical formula which contains atomic numbers and electronegativities. He finds agreement with experiment.

Sclar (62S1) connects the width of the forbidden gap with the ionic radius of the A atoms and the covalent radius of the B atoms and tests this formula on the known III-V compounds and on some rare earth nitrides. He then predicts a large number of E_G values.

In this connection we mention also a systematic discussion by Pearson (59P1) of the width of the forbidden gaps on the basis of electronegativity differences of ionic radii and of the position of the components in the periodic system.

Finally, Suchet (61S18) finds a relationship between the electron mobilities of the III-V compounds and the parameter λ, which was introduced at the beginning of this section.

In connection with all these studies we once more point out the difficulties which we have discussed that impede a comparison of the properties of semiconductors of different band structures and with different scattering mechanisms.

References

1913

H 1 Honda, K., T. Soné, *Sci. Rept. Tôhoku* I. **2,** 8.

1925

F 1 Friedrich, E., *Z. Physik* **31,** 813.

1926

G 1 Goldschmidt, V. M., *Vid. Akad. Skr. M.-N. Kl.* **8,** 22.

1941

I 1 Iandelli, A., *Gazz. Chim. Ital.* **71,** 58.

1951

B 1 Blum, A. I., N. P. Mokrovski, A. R. Regel, *Zhur. Tekh. Fiz.* **21,** 237.

G 1 Goryunova, N. A., A. P. Obuchov, *Zhur. Tekh. Fiz.* **21,** 237.

1952

W 1 Welker, H., *Z. Naturforsch.* **7a,** 744.

1953

B 1 Breckenridge, R. G., *Phys. Rev.* **90,** 488.

C 1 Cunnell, F. A., E. W. Saker, J. T. Edmond, *Proc. Phys. Soc.* **66B,** 1115.

F 1 Folberth, O. G., R. Grimm, H. Weiss, *Z. Naturforsch.* **8a,** 826.

F 2 Folberth, O. G., O. Madelung, *Z. Naturforsch.* **8a,** 673.

G 1 Gremmelmaier, R., O. Madelung, *Z. Naturforsch.* **8a,** 333.

J 1 Justi, E., G. Lautz, *Abhandl. Braunschweig. Wiss. Ges.* **5,** 36.

L 1 Liu, T. S., E. A. Peretti, *Trans. ASM* **45,** 677.

M 1 Madelung, O., *Z. Naturforsch.* **8a,** 791.

P 1 Pearson, G. L., M. Tanenbaum, *Phys. Rev.* **90,** 153.

S 1 Shih, L., E. A. Peretti, *J. Am. Chem. Soc.* **75,** 608.

T 1 Tanenbaum, M., J. P. Maita, *Phys. Rev.* **91,** 1009.

T 2 Tanenbaum, M., H. B. Briggs, *Phys. Rev.* **91,** 1561.

W 1 Weiss, H., *Z. Naturforsch.* **8a,** 463.

W 2 Welker, H., *Z. Naturforsch.* **8a,** 248.

1954

A 1 Adams, E. N., *Phys. Rev.* **96,** 803.
A 2 Austin, I. G., D. R. McClymont, *Physica* **20,** 1077.
A 3 Avery, D. G., D. W. Goodwin, W. D. Lawson, T. S. Moss, *Proc. Phys. Soc.* **67B,** 761.
B 1 Barrie, R., F. A. Cunnell, J. T. Edmond, J. M. Ross, *Physica* **20,** 1087.
B 2 Blunt, R. F., W. R. Hosler, H. P. R. Frederikse, *Phys. Rev.* **96,** 576.
B 3 Blunt, R. F., H. P. R. Frederikse, J. H. Becker, W. R. Hosler, *Phys. Rev.* **96,** 578.
B 4 Born, M., K. Huang, *Dynamical Theory of Crystal Lattices,* Oxford Press.
B 5 Breckenridge, R. G., R. F. Blunt, W. R. Hosler, H. P. R. Frederikse, J. H. Becker, W. Oshinsky, *Phys. Rev.* **96,** 571.
B 6 Breckenridge, R. G., *et al., Physica* **20,** 1073.
B 7 Bruns, H., G. Lautz, *Abhandl. Braunschweig. Wiss. Ges.* **6,** 47.
B 8 Burstein, E., *Phys. Rev.* **93,** 632.
B 9 Busch, G., O. Vogt, *Helv. Phys. Acta* **27,** 241.
B 10 Busch, G., M. Schneider, *Helv. Phys. Acta* **27,** 196.
B 11 Busch, G., M. Schneider, *Helv. Phys. Acta* **27,** 1084.
C 1 Cleland, J. W., J. H. Crawford, *Phys. Rev.* **95,** 1177.
C 2 Cleland, J. W., J. H. Crawford, *Phys. Rev.* **93,** 894.
F 1 Folberth, O. G., F. Oswald, *Z. Naturforsch.* **9a,** 1050.
F 2 Folberth, O. G., O. Madelung, H. Weiss, *Z. Naturforsch.* **9a,** 954.
G 1 Goldsmid, H. J., *Proc. Phys. Soc.* **67B,** 360.
G 2 Goodman, C. H. L., *Proc. Phys. Soc.* **67B,** 258.
H 1 Harman, T. C., R. K. Willardson, A. C. Beer, *Phys. Rev.* **95,** 699.
H 2 Hartel, W., *Siemens-Z.* **28,** 376.
H 3 Hatton, J., B. V. Rollin, *Proc. Phys. Soc.* **67A,** 385.
H 4 Hrostowski, H. J., G. H. Wheatley, W. F. Flood, *Phys. Rev.* **95,** 1683.
H 5 Hrostowski, H. J., M. Tanenbaum, *Physica* **20,** 1065.
K 1 Kuhrt, F., *Siemens-Z.* **28,** 370.
K 2 Kuhrt, F., E. Braunersreuther, *Siemens-Z.* **28,** 299.
K 3 Kurnick, S. W., A. J. Strauss, R. N. Zitter, *Phys. Rev.* **94,** 1791.
L 1 Leifer, H. N., W. C. Dunlap, *Phys. Rev.* **95,** 51.
M 1 Madelung, O., H. Weiss, *Z. Naturforsch.* **9a,** 527.
M 2 Moss, T. S., *Proc. Phys. Soc.* **67B,** 775.
O 1 Oswald, F., *Z. Naturforsch.* **9a,** 181.
O 2 Oswald, F., R. Schade, *Z. Naturforsch.* **9a,** 611.
R 1 Rittner, E. S., *Phys. Rev.* **96,** 1708.
R 2 Roosbroeck, W. van, W. Shockley, *Phys. Rev.* **94,** 1558.
S 1 Sasaki, W., N. Sakamoto, M. Kuno, *J. Phys. Soc. Japan* **9,** 650.
S 2 Seraphin, B., *Z. Naturforsch.* **9a,** 450.
S 3 Slater, J. C., F. Koster, *Phys. Rev.* **94,** 1498.
T 1 Talley, R. M., D. P. Enright, *Phys. Rev.* **95,** 1092.
T 2 Tauc, J., A. Abrahám, *Czechoslov. J. Phys.* **4,** 478.
T 3 Tauc, J., K. Šmirous, A. Abrahám, *Czechoslov. J. Phys.* **4,** 255.
W 1 Weiss, H., H. Welker, *Z. Phys.* **138,** 322.
W 2 Welker, H., *Physica* **20,** 893.
W 3 Willardson, R. K., A. C. Beer, A. E. Middleton, *J. Electrochem. Soc.* **101,** 354.
Z 1 Zhuze, V. P., *Doklady Akad. Nauk. S.S.S.R.* **98,** 711.

1955

A 1 Allen, J. W., I. M. Mackintosh, *J. Electronics* **1,** 138.
A 2 Avery, D. G., D. P. Jenkins, *J. Electronics* **1,** 145.
B 1 Barrie, R., J. T. Edmond, *J. Electronics* **1,** 161.
B 2 Binnie, W. P., *Phys. Rev.* **98,** 228.
B 3 Braunstein, R., *Phys. Rev.* **99,** 1892.
C 1 Cleland, J. W., J. H. Crawford, *Phys. Rev.* **100,** 1614.
D 1 Detwiler, D. P., *Phys. Rev.* **97,** 1575.
D 2 Dresselhaus, G., A. F. Kip, C. Kittel, *Phys. Rev.* **100,** 618.
D 3 Dresselhaus, G., A. F. Kip, C. Kittel, C. Wagoner, *Phys. Rev.* **98,** 556.
D 4 Dresselhaus, G., *Phys. Rev.* **100,** 580.
F 1 Folberth, O. G., H. Weiss, *Z. Naturforsch.* **10a,** 615.
F 2 Folberth, O. G., *Z. Naturforsch.* **10a,** 502.
F 3 Frederikse, H. P. R., E. V. Mielczarek, *Phys. Rev.* **99,** 1889.
F 4 Fritzsche, H., K. Lark-Horovitz, *Phys. Rev.* **99,** 400.
G 1 Goodman, C. H. L., *J. Electronics* **1,** 115.
G 2 Goryunova, N. A., N. N. Fedorova, *Zhur. Tekh. Fiz.* **25,** 1339.
G 3 Gremmelmaier, R., *Z. Naturforsch.* **10a,** 501.
H 1 Herman, F., *J. Electronics* **1,** 103.
H 2 Herring, C., *Bell. System Tech. J.* **34,** 237.
H 3 Hilsum, C., D. J. Oliver, G. Rickayzen, *J. Electronics* **1,** 134.
H 4 Hrostowski, H. J., F. J. Morin, T. H. Geballe, G. H. Wheatley, *Phys. Rev.* **100,** 1672.
K 1 Kaiser, W., H. Y. Fan, *Phys. Rev.* **98,** 966.
K 2 Kanai, Y., *J. Phys. Soc. Japan* **10,** 718.
K 3 Keyes, R. W., *Phys. Rev.* **99,** 490.
K 4 Köster, W., B. Thoma, *Z. Metallk.* **46,** 293.
L 1 Lax, M., E. Burstein, *Phys. Rev.* **97,** 39.
L 2 Long, D., *Phys. Rev.* **99,** 388.
M 1 Mackintosh, I. M., J. W. Allen, *Proc. Phys. Soc.* **68B,** 985.
M 2 Mansfield, R., *J. Electronics* **1,** 175.
M 3 Mitchell, G. R., A. E. Goldberg, S. W. Kurnick, *Phys. Rev.* **97,** 239.
M 4 Moss, T. S., *J. Electronics* **1,** 126.
O 1 Oswald, F., *Z. Naturforsch.* **10a,** 927.
P 1 Parmenter, R. H., *Phys. Rev.* **100,** 573.
P 2 Pfister, H., *Z. Naturforsch.* **10a,** 79.
P 3 Price, P. J., *Phil. Mag.* **46,** 1252.
R 1 Regel, R., M. S. Sominskii, *Zhur. Tekh. Fiz.* **25,** 768.
R 2 Roberts, V., J. E. Quarrington, *J. Electronics* **1,** 152.
R 3 Rollin, B. V., A. D. Petford, *J. Electronics* **1,** 171.
R 4 Ross, I. M., E. W. Saker, *J. Electronics* **1,** 223.
S 1 Spitzer, W. G., H. Y. Fan, *Phys. Rev.* **99,** 1893.
S 2 Stern, F., R. M. Talley, *Phys. Rev.* **100,** 1638.
S 3 Stevens, D. K., J. H. Crawford, *Phys. Rev.* **99,** 487.
T 1 Talley, R. M., F. Stern, *J. Electronics* **1,** 186.
T 2 Tauc, J., M. Matyáš, Czech. *J. Phys.* **5,** 369.
T 3 Taylor, J. H., *Phys. Rev.* **100,** 1593.
T 4 Thullier, J. M., *Compt. Rend.* **241,** 1121.
W 1 Welker, H., *J. Electronics* **1,** 181.
W 2 Wolff, G. A., R. A. Hebert, I. D. Broder, *Phys. Rev.* **100,** 1144.

1956

A 1 Aigrain, P., C. Rigeaux, J. M. Thullier, *Compt. Rend.* **242,** 1145.

B 1 Blount, E., J. Callaway, M. Cohen, W. Dumke, J. C. Phillips, *Phys. Rev.* **101,** 563.

B 2 Broom, R. F., A. C. Rose-Innes, *Proc. Phys. Soc.* **69B,** 1269.

B 3 Burstein, E., G. S. Picus, H. A. Gebbie, F. Blatt, *Phys. Rev.* **103,** 826.

B 4 Burstein, E., G. S. Picus, H. A. Gebbie, *Phys. Rev.* **103,** 825.

C 1 Chasmar, R. P., R. Stratton, *Phys. Rev.* **102,** 1686.

D 1 De Vaux, L. H., F. A. Pizzarello, *Phys. Rev.* **102,** 85.

F 1 Fan, H. Y., *Repts. Progr. Phys.* **19,** 107.

F 2 Folberth, O. G., H. Weiss, *Z. Naturforsch.* **11a,** 510.

F 3 Frederikse, H. P. R., W. R. Hosler, *Can. J. Phys.* **34,** 1377.

F 4 Frederikse, H. P. R., R. F. Blunt, *Photoconductivity Conference at Atlantic City,* John Wiley and Sons, New York, p. 414.

G 1 Gielessen, J., K. H. v. Klitzing, *Z. Physik* **145,** 151.

G 2 Goodwin, D. W., T. P. McLean, *Proc. Phys. Soc.* **69B,** 689.

G 3 Goryunova, N. A., V. S. Grigor'eva, *Zhur. Tekh. Fiz.* **26,** 2157.

G 4 Gremmelmaier, R., H. Welker, *Z. Naturforsch.* **11a,** 420.

G 5 Gremmelmaier, R., *Z. Naturforsch* **11a,** 511.

G 6 Gubanov, A. I., *Zhur. Tekh. Fiz.* **26,** 2170.

H 1 Harman, T. C., *J. Electrochem. Soc.* **103,** 128.

H 2 Harman, T. C., H. L. Goering, A. C. Beer, *Phys. Rev.* **104,** 1562.

H 3 Harrison, W. A., *Phys. Rev.* **101,** 903.

H 4 Heywang, W., B. Seraphin, *Z. Naturforsch.* **11a,** 425.

J 1 Jenny, D. A., J. J. Loferski, P. Rappaport, *Phys. Rev.* **101,** 1208.

K 1 Kanai, Y., W. Sasaki, *J. Phys. Soc. Japan* **11,** 1017.

K 2 Keyes, R. W., R. J. Sladek, *Phys. Chem. Solids* **1,** 143.

K 3 Keyes, R. J., S. Zwerdling, S. Foner, H. H. Kolm, B. Lax, *Phys. Rev.* **104,** 1804.

K 4 Kover, F., *Compt. Rend.* **243,** 648.

K 5 Kurnick, S. W., R. N. Zitter, *J. Appl. Phys.* **27,** 278.

K 6 Kurnick, S. W., R. N. Zitter, *Photoconductivity Conference at Atlantic City,* John Wiley and Sons, New York, p. 531.

L 1 Landsberg, P. T., T. S. Moss, *Proc. Phys. Soc.* **69B,** 661.

L 2 Larach, S., R. E. Shrader, *Phys. Rev.* **102,** 582, **104,** 68.

L 3 Loferski, J. J., *J. Appl. Phys.* **27,** 777.

L 4 Long, D., *Phys. Rev.* **101,** 1256.

L 5 Lukeš, F., Czech. *J. Phys.* **6,** 359.

M 1 Mackintosh, I. M., *J. Electronics* **1,** 554.

M 2 Mackintosh, I. M., *Proc. Phys. Soc.* **69B,** 403.

M 3 McSkimin, H. J., W. L. Bond, G. L. Pearson, H. J. Hrostowski, *Bull. Am. Phys. Soc.* **1,** 111.

M 4 Moss, T. S., *Photoconductivity Conference at Atlantic City,* John Wiley and Sons, New York, p. 427.

M 5 Moss, T. S., T. H. Hawkins, *Phys. Rev.* **101,** 1609.

M 6 Moss, T. S., T. H. Hawkins, *J. Phys. Radium* **17,** 712.

N 1 Nasledov, D. N., A. Yu. Khalilov, *Zhur. Tekh. Fiz.* **26,** 6.

N 2 Nasledov, D. N., A. Yu. Khalilov, *Zhur. Tekh. Fiz.* **26,** 251.

P 1 Pfister, H., *Z. Naturforsch.* **11a,** 434.

P 2 Potter, R. F., *Phys. Rev.* **103,** 47.

1956 (Continued)
P 3 Potter, R. F., *Phys. Rev.* **103,** 861.
P 4 Price, P. J., *Proc. Phys. Soc.* **69B,** 851.
R 1 Rigeaux, C., J. M. Thullier, *Compt. Rend.* **242,** 2710.
R 2 Rodot, M., *Compt. Rend.* **243,** 129.
S 1 Schillmann, E., *Z. Naturforsch.* **11a,** 472.
S 2 Schillmann, E., *Z. Naturforsch.* **11a,** 463.
S 3 Šmirous, K., *Czechoslov. J. Phys.* **6,** 299.
S 4 Šmirous, K., *Czechoslov. J. Phys.* **6,** 39.
W 1 Weiss, H., *Z. Naturforsch.* **11a,** 131.
W 2 Weiss, H., *Z. Naturforsch.* **11a,** 430.
W 3 Welker, H., H. Weiss, *Solid State Physics,* Vol. 3, Academic Press, New York.
W 4 Welker, H., *Ergeb. exakt. Naturw.* **29,** 276.
W 5 Wertheim, G. K., *Phys. Rev.* **104,** 662.
W 6 Woolley, J. C., B. A. Smith, D. G. Lees, *Proc. Phys. Soc.* **69B,** 1339.
Y 1 Yafet, Y., R. W. Keyes, E. N. Adams, *Phys. Chem. Solids* **1,** 137.
Y 2 Yoshinaga, H., R. A. Oetjen, *Phys. Rev.* **101,** 526.
Z 1 Zwerdling, S., R. J. Keyes, S. Foner, H. H. Kolm, B. Lax, *Phys. Rev.* **104,** 1805.

1957
A 1 Adawi, I., *Phys. Rev.* **105,** 789.
A 2 Allen, J. W., *Phil. Mag.* **2,** 1475.
A 3 Antell, G. R., R. P. Chasmar, C. H. Champness, E. Cohen, *Proceedings of the Rugby Conference,* The Physical Society, London, p. 99.
A 4 Avery, D. G., D. W. Goodwin, A. E. Rennie, *J. Sci. Instr.* **34,** 394.
B 1 Berman, L. S., *Zhur. Tekh. Fiz.* **27,** 1192.
B 2 Blakemore, J. S., *Can. J. Phys.* **35,** 91.
B 3 Boltaks, B. I., G. S. Kulinov, *Zhur. Tekh. Fiz.* **27,** 82.
B 4 Boyle, W. S., A. D. Brailsford, *Phys. Rev.* **107,** 903.
B 5 Burns, F. P., A. A. Fleischer, *Phys. Rev.* **107,** 1281.
B 6 Burstein, E., G. S. Picus, *Phys. Rev.* **105,** 1123.
B 7 Busch, G., R. Kern, B. Lüthi, *Helv. Phys. Acta* **30,** 470.
C 1 Callaway, J., *J. Electronics* **2,** 330.
C 2 Champness, C. H., R. P. Chasmar, *J. Electronics* **3,** 494.
C 3 Colombani, A., J. de Launay, *Compt. Rend.* **245,** 1607.
D 1 Dixon, J. R., *Phys. Rev.* **107,** 374.
D 2 Drabble, J. R., R. Wolfe, *J. Electronics* **2,** 259.
D 3 Dumke, W. P., *Phys. Rev.* **105,** 139.
E 1 Edmond, J. T., R. F. Broom, F. A. Cunnell, *Proceedings of the Rugby Conference,* The Physical Society, London, p. 109.
E 2 Ehrenreich, H., *J. Phys. Chem. Solids* **2,** 131.
E 3 Eisen, F. H., C. E. Birchenall, *Acta Met.* **5,** 265.
F 1 Fischer, G., G. K. C. MacDonald, *Phil. Mag.* **2,** 1393.
F 2 Folberth, O. G., E. Schillmann, *Z. Naturforsch.* **12a,** 943.
F 3 Frederikse, H. P. R., W. R. Hosler, *Phys. Rev.* **108,** 1136.
F 4 Frederikse, H. P. R., W. R. Hosler, *Phys. Rev.* **108,** 1146.
G 1 Geballe, T. H., *Bull. Am. Phys. Soc.* **2,** 56.
G 2 Goldstein, B., *Rev. Sci. Instr.* **28,** 289.
G 3 Gonser, U., B. Okkerse, *Phys. Rev.* **105,** 757.

1957 (**Continued**)
G 4 Goodman, C. H. L., *Nature* **179,** 828.
G 5 Goodwin, D. W., *J. Sci. Instr.* **34,** 367.
G 6 Goodwin, D. W., *Proceedings of the Rugby Conference,* The Physical Society, London, p. 137.
H 1 Haasen, P., *Acta Met.* **5,** 598.
H 2 Hilsum, C., I. M. Ross, *Nature* **179,** 146.
H 3 Hilsum, C., *Proc. Phys. Soc.* **70B,** 1011.
H 4 Howarth, D. J., R. H. Jones, E. H. Putley, *Proc. Phys. Soc.* **70B,** 124.
H 5 Hulme, K. F., J. B. Mullin, *J. Electronics* **2,** 160.
K 1 Kanai, Y., W. Sasaki, *J. Phys. Soc. Japan* **12,** 1169.
K 2 Kane, E. O., *J. Phys. Chem. Solids* **1,** 249.
K 3 Kauer, E., A. Rabenau, *Z. Naturforsch.* **12a,** 942.
K 4 Kimmel, H., *Z. Naturforsch.* **12a,** 1016.
K 5 Kleitman, D., H. J. Yearian, *Phys. Rev.* **108,** 901.
K 6 Kolm, C., S. A. Kulin, B. L. Averbach, *Phys. Rev.* **108,** 965.
K 7 Kover, F., A. Quilliet, *Compt. Rend.* **244,** 1739.
L 1 Landsberg, P. T., *Proc. Phys. Soc.* **70B,** 1175.
L 2 de Launay, J., A. Colombani, *Compt. Rend.* **245,** 1809.
L 3 de Launay, J., *Compt. Rend.* **245,** 1122.
M 1 Miyauchi, T., *J. Phys. Soc. Japan* **12,** 308.
M 2 Moss, T. S., S. D. Smith, T. D. F. Hawkins, *Proc. Phys. Soc.* **70B,** 776.
M 3 Moss, T. S., *Proc. Phys. Soc.* **70B,** 247.
M 4 Moss, T. S., T. Hawkins, S. D. Smith, *Proceedings of the Rugby Conference,* The Physical Society, London, p. 133.
P 1 Perlmutter, A., *Bull. Am. Phys. Soc.* **2,** 66.
P 2 Pfister, H., *Z. Naturforsch.* **12a,** 217.
P 3 Popper, P., T. A. Ingles, *Nature* **179,** 1075.
P 4 Potter, R. F., *Phys. Rev.* **108,** 652.
P 5 Potter, R. F., *J. Phys. Chem. Solids* **3,** 223.
P 6 Presnov, V. A., V. F. Synorov, *Zhur. Tekh. Fiz.* **27,** 123.
R 1 Rodot, M., *Compt. Rend.* **245,** 1051.
R 2 Ross, I. M., E. W. Saker, N. A. C. Thomson, *J. Sci. Instr.* **34,** 479.
S 1 Schell, H. A., *Z. Metallk.* **48,** 158.
S 2 Sladek, R. J., *Phys. Rev.* **105,** 460.
S 3 Spitzer, W. G., H. Y. Fan, *Phys. Rev.* **106,** 882.
S 4 Stern, F., R. M. Talley, *Phys. Rev.* **108,** 158.
S 5 Stern, F., *Bull. Am. Phys. Soc.* **2,** 347.
S 6 Stuckes, A. D., *Phys. Rev.* **107,** 427.
S 7 Stuckes, A. D., R. P. Chasmar, *Proceedings of the Rugby Conference,* The Physical Society, London, p. 119.
T 1 Tuzzolino, A. J., *Phys. Rev.* **105,** 1411.
V 1 Vinogradova, K. I., V. V. Galavanov, D. N. Nasledov, *Zhur. Tekh. Fiz.* **27,** 1976.
W 1 Weiss, H., *Z. Naturforsch.* **12a,** 80.
W 2 Wentorf, R. H., *J. Chem. Phys.* **27,** 956.
W 3 Woolley, J. C., B. A. Smith, *Proc. Phys. Soc.* **70B,** 153.
Z 1 Zwerdling, S., B. Lax, L. M. Roth, *Phys. Rev.* **108,** 1402.

1958
A 1 Averkieva, G. K., O. V. Emel'yanenko, *Zhur. Tekh. Fiz.* **28,** 1945.
A 2 Allen, J. W., *Phil. Mag.* **3,** 1297.

1958 (Continued)

A 3 Allen J. W., F. A. Cunnell, *Nature* **182,** 1158.
A 4 Allred, W. P., B. Paris, M. Genser, *J. Electrochem. Soc.* **105,** 93.
A 5 Angello, S. J., *Proc. IRE* **46,** 568.
A 6 Auleytner, J., B. Kolakowski, *Acta Phys. Polon.* **17,** 93.
B 1 Barcus, L. C., A. Perlmutter, J. Callaway, *Phys. Rev.* **111,** 167.
B 2 Blunt, R. F., *Bull. Am. Phys. Soc.* **3,** 115.
B 3 Braunstein, R., L. Magid, *Phys. Rev.* **111,** 480.
B 4 Broom, R. F., *Proc. Phys. Soc.* **71,** 470.
B 5 Broom, R., R. Barrie, I. M. Ross, *Semiconductors and Phosphors,* Vieweg and Son, Braunschweig, p. 453.
B 6 Burdiyan, I. I., A. S. Borshchevskii, *Zhur. Tekh. Fiz.* **28,** 2684.
C 1 Champness, C. H., *J. Electronics and Control* **4,** 201.
C 2 Champness, C. H., *Phys. Rev. Letters* **1,** 439.
C 3 Cleland, J. W., J. H. Crawford, *Bull. Am. Phys. Soc.* **3,** 142.
D 1 Dixon, J. R., D. P. Enright, *Bull. Am. Phys. Soc.* **3,** 255.
D 2 Dumke, W. P., *Phys. Rev.* **108,** 1419.
E 1 Elpatyevskaya, O. D., I. A. Matus, V. A. Perchuk, *Zhur. Tekh. Fiz.* **28,** 2029.
E 2 Emel'yanenko, O. V., D. N. Nasledov, *Zhur. Tekh. Fiz.* **28,** 1177.
F 1 Fischer, G., D. K. C. McDonald, *Can. J. Phys.* **36,** 527.
F 2 Folberth, O. G., *J. Phys. Chem. Solids* **7,** 295.
F 3 Folberth, O. G., H. Pfister, *Semiconductors and Phosphors,* Vieweg and Son, Braunschweig, p. 474.
F 4 Folberth, O. G., *Z. Naturforsch.* **13a,** 856.
F 5 Frederikse, H. P. R., W. R. Hosler, *Phys. Rev.* **110,** 880.
F 6 Fuller, C. S., J. M. Whelan, *J. Phys. Chem. Solids* **6,** 173.
G 1 Geist, D., *Z. Naturforsch.* **13a,** 699.
G 2 Gibbons, D. F., *Phys. Rev.* **112,** 136.
G 3 Giesecke, G., H. Pister, *Acta Cryst.* **11,** 369.
G 4 Glicksman, M., K. Weiser, *J. Electrochem. Soc.* **105,** 728.
G 5 Glicksman, M., M. C. Steele, *Phys. Rev.* **110,** 1204.
G 6 Gonser, U., B. Okkerse, *Phys. Rev.* **109,** 663.
G 7 Goodman, C. H. L., *J. Phys. Chem. Solids* **6,** 305.
G 8 Goryunova, N. A., S. I. Radautsan, *Zhur. Tekh. Fiz.* **28,** 1917.
G 9 Goryunova, N. A., S. I. Radautsan, *Doklady Akad. Nauk S.S.S.R.* **121,** 848.
G 10 Goryunova, N. A., I. I. Burdiyan, *Doklady Akad. Nauk S.S.S.R.* **120,** 1031.
G 11 Gremmelmaier, R., *Proc. IRE* **46,** 1045.
G 12 Günther, K. G., *Z. Naturforsch.* **13a,** 1081.
G 13 Günther, K. G., *Naturwissenschaften* **45,** 415.
H 1 Herman, F., *Revs. Modern Phys.* **30,** 102.
H 2 Herzog, A., R. R. Haberecht, A. E. Middleton, *J. Electrochem. Soc.* **105,** 533.
H 3 Hilsum, C., R. Barrie, *Proc. Phys. Soc.* **71,** 676.
H 4 Holt, D. A., G. F. Alfrey, C. S. Wiggins, *Nature* **181,** 109.
H 5 Hrostowski, H. J., C. S. Fuller, *J. Phys. Chem. Solids* **4,** 155.
I 1 Ilisavskii, Yu. V., *Zhur. Tekh. Fiz.* **28,** 965.
J 1 Jenny, D. A., *Proc. IRE* **46,** 959.
J 2 Jenny, D. A., R. Braunstein, *J. Appl. Phys.* **29,** 596.

1958 (Continued)

K 1 Kanai, Y., *J. Phys. Soc. Japan* **13,** 1065.
K 2 Kanai, Y., *J. Phys. Soc. Japan* **13,** 967.
K 3 Kolm, C., E. P. Warekois, S. A. Kulin, *Trans. AIME* **212,** 827.
K 4 Köster, W., W. Ulrich, *Z. Metallk.* **49,** 365.
K 5 Kot, M. W., G. T. Sorokin, *Zhur. Tekh. Fiz.* **28,** 1657.
K 6 Kurov, G. A., S. G. Pinsker, *Zhur. Tekh. Fiz.* **28,** 2130.
K 7 Kurov, G. A., S. G. Pinsker, *Zhur. Tekh. Fiz.* **28,** 299.
L 1 Lasser, M. E., P. Cholet, E. C. Wurst, *J. Opt. Soc.* **48,** 468.
L 2 Lavine, M. C., A. J. Rosenberg, H. C. Gatos, *J. Appl. Phys.* **29,** 1131.
L 3 Lippmann, H. J., F. Kuhrt, *Naturwissenschaften* **45,** 156.
L 4 Lippmann, H. J., F. Kuhrt, *Z. Naturforsch.* **13a,** 462.
L 5 Lippmann, H. J., F. Kuhrt, *Z. Naturforsch.* **13a,** 474.
M 1 Maringer, R. E., *J. Appl. Phys.* **29,** 1261.
M 2 Matossi, F., F. Stern, *Phys. Rev.* **111,** 472.
M 3 Matossi, F., *Z. Naturforsch.* **13a,** 767.
M 4 Matyáš, M., *Czechoslov. J. Phys.* **8,** 544.
M 5 Mullin, J. B., *J. Electronics and Control* **4,** 358.
N 1 Nasledov, D. N., A. Ya. Patrakova, B. V. Tsarenkov, *Zhur. Tekh. Fiz.* **28,** 779.
N 2 Nasledov, D. N., S. V. Slobotchikov, *Zhur. Tekh. Fiz.* **28,** 4.
N 3 Newman, R., *Phys. Rev.* **111,** 1518.
P 1 Peretti, E. A., *Transact. AIME* **212,** 79.
P 2 Perri, J. A., S. LaPlaca, B. Post, *Acta Cryst.* **11,** 310.
P 3 Pfister, H., *Acta Cryst.* **11,** 221.
P 4 Prior, A. C., *J. Electronics and Control* **4,** 165.
R 1 Ramdas, A. K., H. Y. Fan, *Bull. Am. Phys. Soc.* **3,** 121.
R 2 Reid, F. J., R. K. Willardson, *J. Electronics and Control* **5,** 54.
R 3 Reimer, L., *Z. Naturforsch.* **13a,** 148.
R 4 Reynolds, W. N., M. T. Lilburne, R. M. Dell, *Proc. Phys. Soc.* **71,** 416.
R 5 Rupprecht, H., *Z. Naturforsch.* **13a,** 1094.
S 1 Sagar, A., *Phys. Rev.* **112,** 1533.
S 2 Schell, H. A., *Z. Metallk.* **49,** 140.
S 3 Sladek, R. J., *Phys. Rev.* **110,** 817.
S 4 Sladek, R. J., *J. Phys. Chem. Solids* **5,** 157.
S 5 Steele, M. C., M. Glicksman, *Bull. Am. Phys. Soc.* **3,** 377.
S 6 Strauss, A. J., *Bull. Am. Phys. Soc.* **3,** 119.
T 1 Taylor, J. H., *Bull. Am. Phys. Soc.* **3,** 121.
T 2 Tuzzolino, A. J., *Phys. Rev.* **112,** 30.
T 3 Tuzzolino, A. J., *Phys. Rev.* **109,** 1980.
V 1 Venables, J. D., R. M. Broudy, *J. Appl. Phys.* **29,** 1025.
W 1 Wallis, R. F., *J. Phys. Chem. Solids* **4,** 102.
W 2 Wasilik, J. H., R. B. Flippen, *Phys. Rev. Letters* **1,** 233.
W 3 Weisberg, L. R., J. R. Woolston, M. Glicksman, *J. Appl. Phys.* **29,** 1514.
W 4 Weiser, K., *J. Appl. Phys.* **29,** 229.
W 5 Weiss, H., *Semiconductors and Phosphors,* Vieweg and Son, Braunschweig, p. 497.
W 6 Whelan, J. M., G. H. Wheatley, *J. Phys. Chem. Solids* **6,** 169.
W 7 Wolff, G. A., R. A. Hebert, J. D. Broder, *Semiconductors and Phosphors,* Vieweg and Son, Braunschweig, p. 547.

1958 (Continued)

W 8 Wolff, G. A., L. Toman, N. J. Field, J. C. Clark, *Semiconductors and Phosphors*, Vieweg and Son, Braunschweig, p. 463.

W 9 Woolley, J. C., B. A. Smith, *Proc. Phys. Soc.* **72,** 214.

W 10 Woolley, J. C., B. A. Smith, *Proc. Phys. Soc.* **72,** 867.

Z 1 Zhuze, V. P., I. M. Tsidil'kovskii, *Zhur. Tekh. Fiz.* **28,** 2372.

Z 2 Zitter, R. N., *Transact. AIME* **212,** 31.

Z 3 Zitter, R. N., *Phys. Rev.* **112,** 852.

1959

A 1 Abrahams, M. S., R. Braunstein, F. D. Rosi, *J. Phys. Chem. Solids* **10,** 204.

A 2 Adams, E. N., T. D. Holstein, *J. Phys. Chem. Solids* **10,** 254.

A 3 Allen, J. W., *J. Electronics and Control* **7,** 254.

A 4 Allen, J. W., P. E. Gibbons, *J. Electronics and Control* **7,** 518.

A 5 Amith, A., *Phys. Rev.* **116,** 793.

A 6 Aukerman, L. W., *J. Appl. Phys.* **30,** 1239.

A 7 Aukerman, L. W., *Phys. Rev.* **115,** 1125.

A 8 Aukerman, L. W., *Phys. Rev.* **115,** 1133.

B 1 Bate, R. T., R. K. Willardson, A. C. Beer, *J. Phys. Chem. Solids* **9,** 119.

B 2 Barrie, R., *Can. J. Phys.* **37,** 893.

B 3 Bateman, T. B., H. J. McSkimmin, J. M. Whelan, *J. Appl. Phys.* **30,** 544.

B 4 Bäuerlein, R., *Z. Naturforsch.* **14a,** 1069.

B 5 Beattie, A. R., P. T. Landsberg, *Proc. Roy. Soc. (London)* **245,** 16.

B 6 Beer, A. C., *J. Phys. Chem. Solids* **8,** 507.

B 7 Blum, A. I., G. P. Ryabtsova, *Fiz. Tv. Tela* **1,** 761.

B 8 Blum, A. I., *Fiz. Tv. Tela* **1,** 766.

B 9 Boltaks, B. I., Yu. A. Gutorov, *Fiz. Tv. Tela* **1,** 1015.

B 10 Bowers, R., J. E. Bauerle, A. J. Cornish, *J. Appl. Phys.* **30,** 1050.

B 11 Bowers, R., Y. Yafet, *Phys. Rev.* **115,** 1165.

B 12 Bowers, R., *J. Phys. Chem. Solids* **8,** 206.

B 13 Bowers, R., R. W. Ure, J. E. Bauerle, A. J. Cornish, *J. Appl. Phys.* **30,** 930.

B 14 Braunstein, R., *J. Phys. Chem. Solids* **8,** 280.

B 15 Burdiyan, I. I., S. I. Kolomiets, *Fiz. Tv. Tela* **1,** 1165.

B 16 Burdiyan, I. I., *Fiz. Tv. Tela* **1,** 1360.

B 17 Burstein, E., G. S. Picus, R. F. Wallis, F. Blatt, *Phys. Rev.* **113,** 15.

B 18 Busch, G., R. Kern, *Helv. Phys. Acta* **32,** 24.

B 19 Busch, G., S. Yuan, *Helv. Phys. Acta* **32,** 465.

D 1 Dixon, J. R., D. P. Enright, *J. Appl. Phys.* **30,** 1462.

D 2 Dixon, J. R., D. P. Enright, *J. Appl. Phys.* **30,** 753.

D 3 Dixon, J. R., *J. Appl. Phys.* **30,** 1412.

D 4 Duga, J. J., R. K. Willardson, A. C. Beer, *J. Appl. Phys.* **30,** 1798.

E 1 Edmond, J. T., *Proc. Phys. Soc.* **73,** 622.

E 2 Edwards, D. F., G. S. Hayne, *J. Opt. Soc.* **49,** 414.

E 3 Edwards, D. F., T. E. Slykhouse, H. G. Drickamer, *J. Phys. Chem. Solids* **11,** 140.

E 4 Ehrenreich, H., *J. Phys. Chem. Solids* **8,** 130.

E 5 Ehrenreich, H., *J. Phys. Chem. Solids* **9,** 129.

E 6 Ehrenreich, H., *J. Phys. Chem. Solids* **12,** 97.

E 7 Eisen, F. H., P. W. Bickel, *Phys. Rev.* **115,** 345.

1959 (**Continued**)

E 8 Ellis, S. G., *J. Appl. Phys.* **30,** 947.
E 9 Emel'yanenko, O. V., N. V. Zotova, D. N. Nasledov, *Fiz. Tv. Tela* **1,** 1868.
E 10 Emel'yanenko, O. V., D. N. Nasledov, *Fiz. Tv. Tela* **1,** 985.
F 1 Feltin'sh, I. A., *Latvijas PSR Zinātnu Akad. Vēstis* **12,** 61.
F 2 Folberth, O. G., *Z. Naturforsch.* **14a,** 94.
F 3 Folberth, O. G., H. Welker, *J. Phys. Chem. Solids* **8,** 14.
G 1 Galavanov, V. V., N. R. Erokhina, *Fiz. Tv. Tela* **1,** 1198.
G 2 Geist, D., *Z. Physik* **157,** 335.
G 3 Glasser, M. L., *J. Phys. Chem. Solids* **10,** 229.
G 4 Glicksman, M., K. Weiser, *J. Phys. Chem. Solids* **10,** 337.
G 5 Glicksman, M., M. C. Steele, *Phys. Rev. Letters* **2,** 461.
G 6 Glicksman, M., *J. Phys. Chem. Solids* **8,** 511.
G 7 Goldstein, B., *Bull. Am. Phys. Soc.* **4,** 408.
G 8 Goryunova, N. A., S. I. Radautsan, G. A. Kiosse, *Fiz. Tv. Tela* **1,** 1858.
G 9 Goryunova, N. A., S. I. Radautsan, V. I. Deryabina, *Fiz. Tv. Tela* **1,** 512.
G 10 Goryunova, N. A., N. N. Fedorova, *Fiz. Tv. Tela* **1,** 344.
G 11 Gremmelmaier, H., H. J. Henkel, *Z. Naturforsch.* **14a,** 1072.
G 12 Grimmeiss, H. G., H. Koelmans, *Z. Naturforsch.* **14a,** 264.
G 13 Grubbs, W. J., *Bell System Tech. J.* **38,** 853.
G 14 Gubanov, A. I., A. A. Nran'yan, *Fiz. Tv. Tela* **1,** 1044.
G 15 Gul'yaev, P. V., A. V. Petrov, *Fiz. Tv. Tela* **1,** 368.
H 1 Haslett, J. C., W. F. Love, *J. Phys. Chem. Solids* **8,** 518.
H 2 Henkel, H. J., *Z. Metallk.* **50,** 53.
H 3 Hilsum, C., *Proc. Phys. Soc.* **73,** 685.
H 4 Hilsum, C., *Proc. Phys. Soc.* **74,** 81.
H 5 Huffman, D. R., H. L. Taylor, *Bull. Am. Phys. Soc.* **4,** 84.
H 6 Hulme, K. F., *J. Electronics and Control* **6,** 397.
H 7 Hulme, K. F., J. E. Kemp, *J. Phys. Chem. Solids* **10,** 335.
I 1 Ivanov-Omskii, V. I., B. T. Kolomiets, *Doklady Akad. Nauk S.S.S.R.* **127,** 135.
I 2 Ivanov-Omskii, V. I., B. T. Kolomiets, *Fiz. Tv. Tela* **1,** 913.
I 3 Ivanov-Omskii, V. I., B. T. Kolomiets, *Fiz. Tv. Tela* **1,** 568.
K 1 Kanai, Y., R. Nii, *J. Phys. Chem. Solids* **8,** 338.
K 2 Kanai, Y., *J. Phys. Soc. Japan* **14,** 1302.
K 3 Kruse, P. W., *J. Appl. Phys.* **30,** 770.
K 4 Kuhrt, F., H. S. Lippmann, K. Wiehl, *Naturwissenschaften* **46,** 351.
K 5 Kurnick, S. W., J. M. Powell, *Phys. Rev.* **116,** 597.
K 6 Kurov, G. A., *Fiz. Tv. Tela* **1,** 172.
L 1 Landsberg, P. T., A. R. Beattie, *J. Phys. Chem. Solids* **8,** 73.
L 2 Lax, B., L. M. Roth, S. Zwerdling, *J. Phys. Chem. Solids* **8,** 311.
L 3 Lee, C. A., G. Kaminski, *J. Appl. Phys.* **30,** 2021.
L 4 Loebner, E. E., E. W. Poor, *Phys. Rev. Letters* **3,** 23.
L 5 Lien Chih-ch'ao, D. Nasledov, *Fiz. Tv. Tela* **1,** 570.
M 1 Madelung, O., *Z. Naturforsch.* **14a,** 951.
M 2 Mandelkorn, J., *Proc. IRE,* **47,** 2012.
M 3 Matossi, F., *Z. Naturforsch.* **14a,** 791.
M 4 Matyáš, M., *Czechoslov. J. Phys.* **9,** 257.
M 5 Mielczarek, E. V., H. P. R. Frederikse, *Phys. Rev.* **115,** 888.
M 6 Moss, T. S., S. D. Smith, K. W. Taylor, *J. Phys. Chem. Solids* **8,** 323.

1959 (Continued)

M 7 Moss, T. S., A. K. Walton, *Physica* **25,** 1142.
M 8 Moss, T. S., A. K. Walton, *Proc. Phys. Soc.* **74,** 131.
N 1 Nasledov, D. N., Yu. S. Smetannikova, *Fiz. Tv. Tela* **1,** 556.
N 2 Nasledov, D. N., I. A. Feltin'sh, *Fiz. Tv. Tela* **1,** 565.
N 3 Nasledov, D. N., S. V. Slobotchikov, *Fiz. Tv. Tela* **1,** 748.
N 4 Nasledov, D. N., N. N. Smirnova, B. V. Tsarenkov, *Fiz. Tv. Tela,* Suppl. **II,** 96.
N 5 Nasledov, D. N., B. V. Tsarenkov, *Fiz. Tv. Tela* **1,** 1467.
O 1 Oswald, F., *Z. Naturforsch.* **14a,** 374.
P 1 Pearson, W. B., *Can. J. Phys.* **37,** 1191.
P 2 Pfister, H., *Z. angew. Physik* **11,** 290.
P 3 Picus, G., E. Burstein, B. W. Henvis, M. Hass, *J. Phys. Chem. Solids* **8,** 282.
P 4 Pines, B. Ya., E. F. Chaikovskii, *Fiz. Tv. Tela* **1,** 946.
P 5 Putley, E. H., *Proc. Phys. Soc.* **73,** 128.
P 6 Putley, E. H., *Proc. Phys. Soc.* **73,** 131.
P 7 Putley, E. H., *Proc. Phys. Soc.* **73,** 280.
R 1 Rappaport, P., *RCA Rev.* **20,** 373.
R 2 Rashba, E. I., *Fiz. Tv. Tela* **1,** 407, **2** (Sbornik), 162.
R 3 Raychaudhuri, A., *Proc. Nat. Inst. Sci. India* **25A,** 201.
R 4 Renner, T., *Z. anorg. u. allgem. Chem.* **298,** 22.
R 5 Rhoderick, E. H., *J. Phys. Chem. Solids* **8,** 498.
R 6 Richmond, I. R., *Research* **12,** 374.
R 7 Rodot, M., *J. Phys. Chem. Solids* **8,** 358.
R 8 Römelt, G., D. Geist, W. Schlabitz, *Z. Naturforsch.* **14a,** 923.
R 9 Roth, L. M., B. Lax, S. Zwerdling, *Phys. Rev.* **114,** 90.
R 10 Rupprecht, H., H. Weiss, *Z. Naturforsch.* **14a,** 531.
S 1 Sasaki, W., C. Yamanouchi, *J. Phys. Soc. Japan* **14,** 849.
S 2 Sharpless, W. M., *Bell System Tech. J.* **38,** 259.
S 3 Sladek, R. J., *J. Phys. Chem. Solids* **8,** 515.
S 4 Slutsky, L. J., C. W. Garland, *Phys. Rev.* **113,** 167.
S 5 Smith, S. D., T. S. Moss, K. W. Taylor, *J. Phys. Chem. Solids* **11,** 131.
S 6 Spitzer, W. G., J. M. Whelan, *Phys. Rev.* **114,** 59.
S 7 Spitzer, W. G., M. Gershenzon, C. J. Frosch, D. F. Gibbs, *J. Phys. Chem. Solids* **11,** 339.
S 8 Steele, M. C., M. Glicksman, *J. Phys. Chem. Solids* **8,** 242.
S 9 Steele, M. C., *Bull. Am. Phys. Soc.* **4,** 28.
S 10 Steele, M. C., *J. Phys. Chem. Solids* **9,** 93.
S 11 Stern, F., *J. Phys. Chem. Solids* **8,** 277.
S 12 Stern, F., J. R. Dixon, *J. Appl. Phys.* **30,** 268.
S 13 Strauss, A. J., *J. Appl. Phys.* **30,** 559.
T 1 Tauc, J., *J. Phys. Chem. Solids* **8,** 219.
T 2 Tauc, J., A. Abraham, *Czechoslov. J. Phys.* **9,** 95.
V 1 Venables, D. J., R. M. Broudy, *J. Appl. Phys.* **30,** 122.
V 2 Vinogradova, K. I., V. V. Galavanov, D. N. Nasledov, L. I. Solov'eva, *Fiz. Tv. Tela* **1,** 403.
V 3 Volokobinskaya, N. I., V. V. Galavanov, *Fiz. Tv. Tela,* Suppl. **I,** 122.
V 4 Volokobinskaya, N. I., V. V. Galavanov, D. N., Nasledov, *Fiz. Tv. Tela* **1,** 755.
W 1 Warekois, E. P., P. H. Metzger, *J. Appl. Phys.* **30,** 960.

1959 (Continued)

W 2 Weiss, H., *Ann. Phys.* **4,** 121.

W 3 White, I. G., W. C. Roth, *J. Appl. Phys.* **30,** 946.

W 4 Willardson, R. K., *J. Appl. Phys.* **30,** 1158.

W 5 Wolff, G. A., I. Adams, J. W. Mellichamp, *Phys. Rev.* **114,** 1262.

W 6 Wolff, G. A., J. D. Broder, *Acta Cryst.* **12,** 313.

W 7 Woolley, J. C., S. A. Evans, C. M. Gillett, *Proc. Phys. Soc.* **74,** 244.

Z 1 Zitter, R. N., A. S. Strauss, A. E. Attard, *Phys. Rev.* **115,** 266.

Z 2 Zotova, N. V., D. N. Nasledov, *Fiz. Tv. Tela* **1,** 1690.

Z 3 Zwerdling, S., B. Lax, K. J. Button, L. M. Roth, *J. Phys. Chem. Solids* **9,** 320.

1960

A 1 Abrahams, M. S., L. Ekstrom, *Acta Met.* **8,** 654.

A 2 Abrahams, M. S., R. Braunstein, F. D. Rosi, Metallurgical Society Conferences, Vol. 5, *Properties of Elemental and Compound Semiconductors,* Interscience Publishers, New York, p. 275.

A 3 Abrahams, M. S., L. Ekstrom, Metallurgical Society Conferences, Vol. 5, *Properties of Elemental and Compound Semiconductors,* Interscience Publishers, New York, p. 239.

A 4 Agaev, Ya., D. N. Nasledov, *Fiz. Tv. Tela* **2,** 826.

A 5 Alfrey, G. F., C. S. Wiggins, *Solid State Physics in Electronics and Telecommunications,* Vol. 2, Academic Press, p. 747.

A 6 Alfrey, G. F., C. S. Wiggins, *Z. Naturforsch.* **15a,** 267.

A 7 Allen, J. W., *Nature* **187,** 403.

A 8 Allen, J. W., *J. Phys. Chem. Solids* **15,** 134.

A 9 Allred, W. P., W. L. Meffert, R. K. Willardson, *J. Electrochem. Soc.* **107,** 117.

A 10 Amirkhanov, Kh. I., R. I. Bashirov, Yu. E. Zakiev, *Doklady Akad. Nauk S.S.S.R.* **132,** 793.

A 11 Amirkhanova, D. Kh., *Fiz. Tv. Tela* **2,** 1125.

A 12 Amirkhanova, D. Kh., R. I. Bashirov, *Fiz. Tv. Tela* **2,** 1597.

A 13 Anderson, R. L., *IBM J.* **4,** 283.

A 14 Antell, G. R., *J. Appl. Phys.* **31,** 1686.

A 15 Aukerman, L. W., R. K. Willardson, *J. Appl. Phys.* **31,** 293.

A 16 Austin, I. G., *J. Electronics and Control* **8,** 167.

B 1 Balkanski, M., J. des Cloizeaux, *J. Phys. Radium* **21,** 859.

B 2 Baranov, B. V., N. A. Goryunova, *Fiz. Tv. Tela* **2,** 284.

B 3 Batdorf, R. L., G. C. Dacey, R. L. Wallace, and D. J. Walsh, *J. Appl. Phys.* **31,** 613.

B 4 Bate, G., K. N. R. Taylor, *J. Appl. Phys.* **31,** 991.

B 5 Beattie, A. R., P. T. Landsberg, *Proc. Roy. Soc.* (*London*) **258,** 486.

B 6 Bemski, G., *Phys. Rev. Letters* **4,** 62.

B 7 Bolef, D. I., M. Menes, *J. Appl. Phys.* **31,** 1426.

B 8 Braunersreuther, E., F. Kuhrt, H. J. Lippmann, *Z. Naturforsch.* **15a,** 795.

B 9 Bube, R. H., *J. Appl. Phys.* **31,** 315.

B 10 Busch, G., F. Hulliger, *Helv. Phys. Acta* **33,** 657.

B 11 Bylander, E. G., A. J. Hodges, J. A. Roberts, *J. Opt. Soc. Am.* **50,** 983.

C 1 Calawa, A. R., R. H. Rediker, B. Lax, A. L. McWhorter, *Phys. Rev. Letters* **5,** 55.

C 2 Cardona, M., *Z. Physik.* **161,** 99.

C 3 Chynoweth, A. G., R. A. Logan, *Phys. Rev.* **118,** 1470.

1960 (Continued)

C 4 Chynoweth, A. G., G. H. Wannier, R. A. Logan, D. E. Thomas, *Phys. Rev. Letters* **5,** 57.

C 5 Chynoweth, A. G., R. A. Logan, P. A. Wolff, *Phys. Rev. Letters* **5,** 548.

C 6 Claassen, R. S., *Bull. Am. Phys. Soc.* **5,** 406.

C 7 Cunnell, F. A., C. A. Gooch, *J. Phys. Chem. Solids* **15,** 127.

C 8 Cunnell, F. A., J. T. Edmond, W. A. Harding, *Solid-State Electronics* **1,** 97.

C 9 Cunnell, F. A., C. H. Gooch, *Nature* **188,** 1096.

D 1 Davies, R. E., Metallurgical Society Conferences, Vol. 5, *Properties of Elemental and Compound Semiconductors,* Interscience Publishers, New York, p. 295.

D 2 Duwez, P., R. H. Willens, W. Klement, *J. Appl. Phys.* **31,** 1500.

E 1 Edmond, J. T., *J. Appl. Phys.* **31,** 1428.

E 2 Edmond, J. T., C. Hilsum, *J. Appl. Phys.* **31,** 1300.

E 3 Ehrenreich, H., *Phys. Rev.* **120,** 1951.

E 4 Emel'yanenko, O. V., D. N. Nasledov, R. V. Petrov, *Fiz. Tv. Tela* **2,** 2455.

F 1 Faust, J. W., A. Sagar, *J. Appl. Phys.* **31,** 331.

F 2 Feltin'sh, I. A., *Latvijas PSR Zinātnu Akad. Vēstis* **9,** 73.

F 3 Fischer, G., *Helv. Phys. Acta* **33,** 463.

F 4 Flicker, H., P. G. Harkart, *Bull. Am. Phys. Soc.* **5,** 407.

F 5 Folberth, O. G., *Z. Naturforsch.* **15a,** 425.

F 6 Folberth, O. G., *Z. Naturforsch.* **15a,** 432.

F 7 Folberth, O. G., H. Pfister, *Acta Cryst.* **13,** 199.

F 8 Folberth, O. G., *Halbleiterprobleme*, Vol. 5, Vieweg and Son, Braunschweig, p. 40.

F 9 Fray, S. J., F. A. Johnson, R. H. Jones, *Proc. Phys. Soc.* **76,** 939.

F 10 Frederikse, H. P. R., W. R. Hosler, *Solid State Physics in Electronics and Telecommunications,* Vol. 2, Academic Press, p. 651.

G 1 Gatos, H. C., M. C. Lavine, *J. Phys. Chem. Soc.* **14,** 169.

G 2 Gatos, H. C., P. L. Moody, M. C. Lavine, *J. Appl. Phys.* **31,** 212.

G 3 Gatos, H. C., M. C. Lavine, *J. Appl. Phys.* **31,** 743.

G 4 Gatos, H. C., M. C. Lavine, *J. Electrochem. Soc.* **107,** 433.

G 5 Gatos, H. C., M. C. Lavine, *J. Electrochem. Soc.* **107,** 427.

G 6 Gebbie, H. A., P. L. Smith, I. G. Austin, J. H. King, *Nature* **188,** 1095.

G 7 Gobeli, G. W., H. Y. Fan, *Phys. Rev.* **119,** 613.

G 8 Goldstein, B., *Phys. Rev.* **118,** 1024.

G 9 Goldstein, B., L. R. Weisberg, *Bull. Am. Phys. Soc.* **5,** 407.

G 10 Goldstein, B., Metallurgical Society Conferences, Vol. 5, *Properties of Elemental and Compound Semiconductors,* Interscience Publishers, New York, p. 155.

G 11 Goodwin, D. W., *Solid State Physics in Electronics and Telecommunications,* Vol. 2, Academic Press, New York, p. 759.

G 12 Gorton, H. C., J. M. Swartz, C. S. Peet, *Nature* **188,** 303.

G 13 Goryunova, N. A., V. D. Prochukhan, *Fiz. Tv. Tela* **2,** 176.

G 14 Gremmelmaier, R., *Solid State Physics in Electronics and Telecommunications,* Vol. 2, Academic Press, New York, p. 741.

G 15 Grimmeiss, H. G., W. Kischio, A. Rabenau, *J. Phys. Chem. Solids* **16,** 302.

G 16 Grimmeiss, H. G., R. Groth, J. Maak, *Z. Naturforsch.* **15a,** 799.

G 17 Grimmeiss, H. G., H. Koelmans, *Philips Research Repts.* **15,** 290.

H 1 Hall, R. N., J. H. Racette, H. Ehrenreich, *Phys. Rev. Letters* **4,** 456.

1960 (**Continued**)

H 2 Hambleton, K. G., J. J. Low, R. J. Sherwell, *Nature* **185,** 676.

H 3 Haneman, D., *J. Phys. Chem. Solids* **14,** 162.

H 4 Harding, W. R., C. Hilsum, M. E. Moncaster, D. C. Northrop, O. Simpson, *Nature* **187,** 405.

H 5 Hartel, W., *Solid State Physics in Electronics and Telecommunications,* Vol. 2, Academic Press, New York, p. 723.

H 6 Hazelbee, D., J. L. Parmee, *J. Electrochem. Soc.* **107,** 144.

H 7 Herring, C., *J. Appl. Phys.* **31,** 1939.

H 8 Hilsum, C., *Solid State Physics in Electronics and Telecommunications,* Vol. 2, Academic Press, New York, p. 733.

H 9 Hilsum, C., *Proc. Phys. Soc.* **76,** 414.

H 10 Holonyak, N., I. A. Lesk, *Proc. IRE,* **48,** 1405.

H 11 Holt, D. B., *J. Appl. Phys.* **31,** 2231.

I 1 Ivanov-Omskii, V. I., B. T. Kolomiets, *Fiz. Tv. Tela* **2,** 388.

K 1 Kanai, Y., *J. Phys. Soc. Japan* **15,** 830.

K 2 Keyes, R. W., M. Pollak, *Phys. Rev.* **118,** 1001.

K 3 Kikuchi, M., T. Iizuka, *J. Phys. Soc. Japan* **15,** 935.

K 4 Kleinman, L., J. C. Phillips, *Phys. Rev.* **117,** 460.

K 5 Kleinman, D. A., W. G. Spitzer, *Phys. Rev.* **118,** 110.

K 6 Kleinman, D. A., *Phys. Rev.* **118,** 118.

K 7 Kopeć, Z., *Bull. Acad. Polon. Sci.* **8,** 111.

K 8 Kopeć, Z., *Bull. Acad. Polon. Sci.* **8,** 105.

K 9 Kopeć, Z., *Acta Phys. Polon.* **19,** 295.

K 10 Kover, F., *Solid State Physics in Electronics and Telecommunications,* Vol. 2, Academic Press, New York, p. 768.

L 1 Lax, B., G. B. Wright, *Phys. Rev. Letters* **4,** 16.

L 2 Lax, B., S. Zwerdling, *Progress in Semiconductors,* Vol. 5, Heywood and Co., London, p. 221.

L 3 Lee, C. A., G. Kaminsky, *J. Appl. Phys.* **31,** 1717.

L 4 Lowen, L., R. H. Rediker, *J. Electrochem. Soc.* **107,** 26.

L 5 Lucovsky, G., P. H. Cholet, *J. Opt. Soc. Am.* **50,** 979.

L 6 Lien Chih-ch'ao, D. N., Nasledov, *Fiz. Tv. Tela* **2,** 793.

M 1 Marfaing, Y., *Compt. Rend.* **250,** 3608.

M 2 McCaldin, J. O., R. Harada, *J. Appl. Phys.* **31,** 2065 (Erratum, **32,** 557).

M 3 Miller, J. F., H. L. Goering, R. C. Himes, *J. Electrochem. Soc.* **107,** 527.

M 4 Moody, P. L., H. C. Gatos, M. C. Lavine, *J. Appl. Phys.* **31,** 1696.

M 5 Mullin, J. B., K. F. Hulme, *J. Phys. Chem. Solids* **17,** 1 (Erratum, **17,** 352).

N 1 Nasledov, D. N., M. P. Pronina, S. I. Radautsan, *Fiz. Tv. Tela* **2,** 50.

N 2 Nasledov, D. N., M. P. Pronina, Yu. A. Smetannikova, *Fiz. Tv. Tela* **2,** 239.

N 3 Nasledov, D. N., I. A. Feltin'sh, *Fiz. Tv. Tela* **2,** 823.

N 4 Nasledov, D. N., *J. Chim. Phys.* **57,** 479.

N 5 Nasledov, D. N., N. N. Smirnova, B. V. Tsarenkov, *Fiz. Tv. Tela* **2,** 2762.

N 6 Novikova, S. I., *Fiz. Tv. Tela* **2,** 2341.

N 7 Nran'yan, A. A., *Fiz. Tv. Tela* **2,** 474.

P 1 Paparoditis, C., *Solid State Physics in Electronics and Telecommunications,* Vol. 2, Academic Press, New York, p. 639.

P 2 Putley, E. H., *Solid State Physics in Electronics and Telecommunications,* Vol. 2, Academic Press, New York, p. 751.

1960 (Continued)

P 3 Putley, E. H., *Proc. Phys. Soc.* **76,** 802.

R 1 Renner, T., *Solid State Electronics* **1,** 39.

R 2 Richards, J. L., A. J. Crocker, *J. Appl. Phys.* **31,** 611.

R 3 Rodot, M., *Solid State Physics in Electronics and Telecommunications,* Vol. 2, Academic Press, New York, p. 680.

R 4 Rosenberg, A. J., *J. Phys. Chem. Solids* **14,** 175.

R 5 Rosi, F. D., D. Meyerhofer, R. V. Jensen, *J. Appl. Phys.* **31,** 1105.

R 6 Rupprecht, H., R. Weber, H. Weiss, *Z. Naturforsch.* **15a,** 783.

S 1 Sagar, A., *Phys. Rev.* **117,** 93.

S 2 Sagar, A., *Phys. Rev.* **117,** 101.

S 3 Sheard, F. W., *Phil. Mag.* **5,** 887.

S 4 Sladek, R. J., *J. Phys. Chem. Solids* **16,** 1.

S 5 Sladek, R. J., *Phys. Rev.* **120,** 1589.

S 6 Smith, S. D., T. S. Moss, *Solid State Physics in Electronics and Telecommunications,* Vol. 2, Academic Press, New York, p. 671.

S 7 Steele, M. C., M. Glicksman, *Phys. Rev.* **118,** 474.

S 8 Stone, B., D. Hill, *Phys. Rev. Letters* **4,** 282.

S 9 Strutt, M. J. O., *Solid State Physics in Electronics and Telecommunications,* Vol. 2, Academic Press, New York, p. 706.

S 10 Stuckes, A. D., *Phil. Mag.* **5,** 84.

S 11 Suchet, J. P., *J. Phys. Chem. Solids* **16,** 265.

T 1 Tauc, J., E. Antončik, *Phys. Rev. Letters* **5,** 253.

T 2 Taylor, K. M., C. Lenie, *J. Electrochem. Soc.* **107,** 308.

T 3 Teitler, S., E. D. Palik, *Phys. Rev. Letters* **5,** 546.

T 4 Turner, W. J., W. E. Reese, *Phys. Rev.* **117,** 1003.

U 1 Ure, R. W., R. Bowers, R. C. Miller, Metallurgical Society Conferences, Vol. 5, *Properties of Elemental and Compound Semiconductors,* Interscience Publishers, New York, p. 245.

V 1 Visvanathan, S., *Phys. Rev.* **120,** 376.

W 1 Warekois, E. P., M. C. Lavine, H. C. Gatos, *J. Appl. Phys.* **31,** 1302.

W 2 Weisberg, L. R., F. D. Rosi, P. G. Herkart, Metallurgical Society Conferences, Vol. 5, *Properties of Elemental and Compound Semiconductors,* Interscience Publishers, New York, p. 25.

W 3 Whelan, J. M., C. S. Fuller, *J. Appl. Phys.* **31,** 1507.

W 4 Whelan, J. M., J. D. Struthers, J. A. Ditzenberger, Metallurgical Society Conferences, Vol. 5, *Properties of Elemental and Compound Semiconductors,* Interscience Publishers, New York, p. 275.

W 5 Wieber, R. H., H. C. Gorton, C. S. Peet, *J. Appl. Phys.* **31,** 608.

W 6 Willardson, R. K., J. J. Duga, *Proc. Phys. Soc.* **75,** 280.

W 7 Woolley, J. C., C. M. Gillett, J. A. Evans, *J. Phys. Chem. Solids* **16,** 138.

W 8 Woolley, J. C., C. M. Gillett, *J. Phys. Chem. Solids* **17,** 34.

W 9 Woolley, J. C., B. A. Smith, J. A. Evans, *Solid State Physics in Electronics and Telecommunications,* Vol. 2, Academic Press, New York, p. 802.

W 10 Wysocki, J. J., P. Rappaport, *J. Appl. Phys.* **31,** 571.

W 11 Wysocki, J. J., *J. Appl. Phys.* **31,** 1686.

1961

A 1 Addamiano, A., *J. Electrochem. Soc.* **108,** 1072.

A 2 Agaev, Ya., O. V. Emel'yanenko, D. N. Nasledov, *Fiz. Tv. Tela* **3,** 194.

A 3 Allred, W. P., R. F. Bate, *J. Electrochem. Soc.* **108,** 258.

1961 (Continued)

A 4 Amirkhanova, D. Kh., R. I. Bashirov, *Fiz. Tv. Tela* **3,** 819.

A 5 Amirkhanov, Kh. I., R. I. Bashirov, Yu. E. Zakiev, *Zhur. Eksp. i Teoret. Fiz.* **41,** 1699.

A 6 Amirkhanov, Kh. I., R. I. Bashirov, M. M. Gadzhialiev, *Fiz. Tv. Tela* **3,** 3743.

A 7 Ancker-Johnson, B., R. W. Cohen, M. Glicksman, *Phys. Rev.* **124,** 1745.

A 8 Anderson, R. L., *Proceedings of the International Conference on Semiconductors,* Prague, Publishing House of the Czechoslovakian Academy of Science, p. 563.

A 9 Ansel'm, A. I., B. M. Askerov, *Fiz. Tv. Tela* **3,** 3668.

A 10 Aukerman, L. W., *Proceedings of the International Conference on Semiconductors,* Prague, Publishing House of the Czechoslovakian Academy of Science, p. 946.

B 1 Basov, N. G., B. D. Osipov, A. N. Khvoshchev, *Zhur. Eksp. i Teoret. Fiz.* **40,** 1882.

B 2 Bassani, F., V. Celli, *J. Phys. Chem. Solids* **20,** 64.

B 3 Bate, R. T., A. C. Beer, *Proceedings of the International Conference on Semiconductors,* Prague, Publishing House of the Czechoslovakian Academy of Science, p. 177.

B 4 Bate, R. T., J. C. Bell, A. C. Beer, *J. Appl. Phys.* **32,** 806.

B 5 Bate, R. T., A. C. Beer, *J. Appl. Phys.* **32,** 800.

B 6 Bäuerlein, R., *Z. Naturforsch.,* **16a,** 1002.

B 7 Becker, W. M., A. K. Ramdas, H. Y. Fan, *J. Appl. Phys.* **32,** 2094.

B 8 Beer, A. C., *J. Appl. Phys.* **32,** 2107.

B 9 Belforti, D., S. Blum, B. Bovarnick, *Nature* **190,** 901.

B 10 Bemski, G., B. Szymanski, *J. Phys. Chem. Solids* **17,** 335.

B 11 Bernard, M. G., G. Duraffourg, *Phys. Status Solidi,* **1,** 699.

B 12 Bernstein, L., R. J. Beals, *J. Appl. Phys.* **32,** 122.

B 13 Bir, G. L., G. E. Picus, *Fiz. Tv. Tela* **3,** 3050.

B 14 Blanc, J., R. H. Bube, H. E. McDonald, *J. Appl. Phys.* **32,** 1666.

B 15 Blanc, J., R. H. Bube, F. D. Rosi, *Proceedings of the International Conference on Semiconductors,* Prague, Publishing House of the Czechoslovakian Academy of Science, p. 936.

B 16 Blanc, J., L. R. Weisberg, *Nature* **192,** 155.

B 17 Bogner, G., H. Rupprecht, *Z. Naturforsch.* **16a,** 1152.

B 18 Bok, J., R. Veilex, *Proceedings of the International Conference on Semiconductors,* Prague, Publishing House of the Czechoslovakian Academy of Science, p. 173.

B 19 Burdiyan, I. I., Ya. A. Rosneritsa, G. I. Stepanov, *Fiz. Tv. Tela* **3,** 1879.

B 20 Burdukov, Yu. M., A. N. Imenkov, D. N. Nasledov, B. V. Tsarenkov, *Fiz. Tv. Tela* **3,** 991.

B 21 Burrus, C. A., *J. Appl. Phys.* **32,** 1031.

B 22 Busch, G., E. Steigmeier, *Helv. Phys. Acta* **34,** 1.

B 23 Butcher, P. N., J. A. Hulbert, K. F. Hulme, *J. Phys. Chem. Solids* **21,** 320.

C 1 Cardona, M., *Proceedings of the International Conference on Semiconductors,* Prague, Publishing House of the Czechoslovakian Academy of Science, p. 388.

C 2 Cardona, M., *J. Phys. Chem. Solids* **17,** 336.

C 3 Cardona, M., *Phys. Rev.* **121,** 756.

1961 (Continued)

C 4 Cardona, M., *J. Appl. Phys.* **32,** 958.
C 5 Cardona, M., *J. Appl. Phys.* **32,** 2151.
C 6 Champness, C. H., *Can. J. Phys.* **39,** 452.
C 7 Chasmar, R. P., *J. Phys. Chem. Solids* **20,** 164.
C 8 Chynoweth, A. G., A. A. Murray, *Phys. Rev.* **123,** 515.
C 9 Cochran, W., S. J. Fray, F. A. Johnson, J. E. Quarrington, N. Williams, *J. Appl. Phys.* **32,** 1202.
C 10 Cochran, W., *Nature* **191,** 60.
D 1 Davis, J. L., *Bull. Am. Phys. Soc.* **6,** 18.
D 2 Dixon, J. R., *Proceedings of the International Conference on Semiconductors,* Prague, Publishing House of the Czechoslovakian Academy of Science, p. 366.
D 3 Dixon, J. R., J. M. Ellis, *Phys. Rev.* **123,** 1560.
E 1 Edwards, A. J., H. G. Drickamer, *Phys. Rev.* **122,** 1149.
E 2 Effer, D., *J. Electrochem. Soc.* **108,** 357.
E 3 Ehrenreich, H., *Proceedings of the International Conference on Semiconductors,* Prague, Publishing House of the Czechoslovakian Academy of Science, p. 67.
E 4 Ehrenreich, H., *J. Appl. Phys.* **32,** 2155.
E 5 Eisen, F. H., *Phys. Rev.* **123,** 736.
E 6 Emel'yanenko, O. V., T. S. Lagunova, D. N. Nasledov, *Fiz. Tv. Tela* **3,** 198.
E 7 Emel'yanenko, O. V., F. P. Kesamanly, D. N. Nasledov, *Fiz. Tv. Tela* **3,** 1161.
E 8 Engeler, W., H. Levinstein, *Bull. Am. Phys. Soc.* **6,** 156.
E 9 Engeler, W., H. Levinstein, C. Stannard, *Phys. Rev. Letters* **7,** 62.
E 10 Engeler, W., H. Levinstein, C. Stannard, *J. Phys. Chem. Solids* **22,** 249.
F 1 Feltin'sh, I. A., *Trudy Inst. Energ. Akad. Nauk Latv. S.S.R.* **11,** 5.
F 2 Fray, S. A., F. A. Johnson, J. E. Quarrington, N. Williams, *Proc. Phys. Soc.* **77,** 215.
F 3 Frosch, C. F., M. Gershenzon, L. Derick, *J. Appl. Phys.* **32,** 2060.
G 1 Galavanov, V. V., I. A. Kartuzova, D. N. Nasledov, *Fiz. Tv. Tela* **3,** 2973.
G 2 Gashimzade, F. M., V. E. Khartsiev, *Fiz. Tv. Tela* **3,** 1453.
G 3 Gashimzade, F. M., F. P. Kesamanly, *Fiz. Tv. Tela* **3,** 1255.
G 4 Gasson, D. B., P. J. Homes, I. C. Jennings, J. E. Parrott, A. W. Penn, *Proceedings of the International Conference on Semiconductors,* Prague, Publishing House of the Czechoslovakian Academy of Science, p. 1032.
G 5 Gatos, H. C., M. C. Lavine, E. P. Warekois, *Proceedings of the International Conference on Semiconductors,* Prague, Publishing House of the Czechoslovakian Academy of Science, p. 519.
G 6 Gatos, H. C., *J. Appl. Phys.* **32,** 1232.
G 7 Gatos, H. C., M. C. Finn, M. C. Lavine, *J. Appl. Phys.* **32,** 1174.
G 8 Gatos, H. C., M. C. Lavine, E. P. Warekois, *J. Electrochem. Soc.* **108,** 645.
G 9 Gershenzon, M., R. M. Mikulyak, *J. Appl. Phys.* **32,** 1338.
G 10 Gershenzon, M., R. M. Mikulyak, *J. Electrochem. Soc.* **108,** 548.
G 11 Glazov, V. M., S. N. Chizhevskaya, *Fiz. Tv. Tela* **3,** 2694.
G 12 Glicksman, M., R. A. Powlus, *Phys. Rev.* **121,** 1659.
G 13 Gold, R. D., B. Goldstein, L. R. Weisberg, R. M. Williams, *Bull. Am. Phys. Soc.* **6,** 312.

1961 (**Continued**)

G 14 Goldstein, B., *Phys. Rev.* **121,** 1305.

G 15 Goldstein, B., H. Keller, *J. Appl. Phys.* **32,** 1180.

G 16 Gooch, C. H., C. Hilsum and B. R. Holeman, *J. Appl. Phys.* **32,** 2069.

G 17 Gorton, H. C., A. R. Zacaroli, F. J. Reid, C. S. Peet, *J. Electrochem. Soc.* **108,** 354.

G 18 Green, M., *J. Appl. Phys.* **32,** 1286, 2047.

G 19 Grimmeiss, H. G., A. Rabenau, H. Koelmans, *J. Appl. Phys.* **32,** 2123.

G 20 Grimmeiss, H. G., H. Koelmans, *Phys. Rev.* **123,** 1939.

G 21 Gross, E. F., G. K. Kalyuzhnaya, D. S. Nedzvetskii, *Fiz. Tv. Tela* **3,** 3543.

G 22 Günther, K. G., H. Freller, *Z. Naturforsch.* **16a,** 279.

H 1 Haering, R. R., P. B. Miller, *Phys. Rev. Letters* **6,** 269.

H 2 Haering, R. R., E. N. Adams, *J. Phys. Chem. Solids* **19,** 8.

H 3 Hall, R. N., *Proceedings of the International Conference on Semiconductors,* Prague, Publishing House of the Czechoslovakian Academy of Science, p. 193.

H 4 Hall, R. N., J. H. Racette, *J. Appl. Phys.* **32,** 856.

H 5 Hall, R. N., und J. H. Racette, *J. Appl. Phys.* **32,** 2078.

H 6 Hambleton, K. G., C. Hilsum, B. R. Holeman, *Proc. Phys. Soc.* **77,** 1147.

H 7 Haneman, D., *Proceedings of the International Conference on Semiconductors,* Prague, Publishing House of the Czechoslovakian Academy of Science, p. 540.

H 8 Haneman, D., *Phys. Rev.* **121,** 1093.

H 9 Harper, H. T., H. Roth, W. B. Teutsch, *Bull. Am. Phys. Soc.* **6,** 502.

H 10 Henneke, H. L., *Solid State Electronics* **3,** 159.

H 11 Hilsum, C., B. Holeman, *Proceedings of the International Conference on Semiconductors,* Prague, Publishing House of the Czechoslovakian Academy of Science, p. 962.

H 12 Hilsum, C., A. C. Rose-Innes, *Semiconducting III-V Compounds,* Pergamon Press, New York.

H 13 Hobden, M. V., M. D. Sturge, *Proc. Phys. Soc.* **78,** 615.

H 14 Holeman, B. R., C. Hilsum, *J. Phys. Chem. Solids* **22,** 19.

H 15 Holonyak, N., *J. Appl. Phys.* **32,** 130.

H 16 Hrivnák, L., *Czechoslov. J. Phys.* **11,** 808.

H 17 Hulme, K. F., *Brit. J. Appl. Phys.* **12,** 651.

I 1 Iizima, S., M. Kikuchi, *J. Phys. Soc. Japan* **16,** 1784.

I 2 Iljin, V. E., E. E. Gorbacheva, *Fiz. Tv. Tela* **3,** 535.

I 3 Ivanov-Omskii, V. I., B. T. Kolomiets, *Fiz. Tv. Tela* **3,** 3553.

J 1 Jayaraman, A., R. C. Newton, G. C. Kennedy, *Nature* **191,** 1288.

J 2 Johnson, F. A., S. J. Fray, R. H. Jones, *Proceedings of the International Conference on Semiconductors,* Prague, Publishing House of the Czechoslovakian Academy of Science, p. 349.

K 1 Kessler, F. R., E. Sutter, *Z. Naturforsch.* **16a,** 1173.

K 2 King, R. E. J., B. E. Bartlett, *Phil. Tech. Rev.* **22,** 217.

K 3 Kleinknecht, H., *Solid State Electronics* **2,** 133.

K 4 Knight, J. R., *Nature* **190,** 999.

K 5 Kołodziejczak, J., *Proceedings of the International Conference on Semiconductors,* Prague, Publishing House of the Czechoslovakian Academy of Science, p. 950.

K 6 Kołodziejczak, J., *Acta Phys. Polon.* **20,** 289.

1961 (Continued)

K 7 Kopeć, Z, *Proceedings of the International Conference on Semiconductors*, Prague, Publishing House of the Czechoslovakian Academy of Science, p. 953.

K 8 Kudman, I., T. Seidel, *Bull. Am. Phys. Soc.* **6,** 312.

L 1 Laff, R. A., H. Y. Fan, *Phys. Rev.* **121,** 53.

L 2 Lavine, M. C., H. C. Gatos, M. C. Finn, *J. Electrochem. Soc.* **108,** 974.

L 3 Lax, B., *Proceedings of the International Conference on Semiconductors*, Prague, Publishing House of the Czechoslovakian Academy of Science, p. 321.

L 4 Lax, B., J. G. Mavroides, H. J. Zeiger, R. J. Keyes, *Phys. Rev.* **122,** 31.

L 5 Lax, B., Y. Nishina, *J. Appl. Phys.* **32,** 2128.

L 6 Love, W. F., J. C. Haslett, *Bull. Am. Phys. Soc.* **6,** 129.

L 7 Lucovsky, G., *Brit. J. Appl. Phys.* **12,** 311.

L 8 Lien Chih-ch'ao, D. N. Nasledov, *Fiz. Tv. Tela* **3,** 1458.

L 9 Lien Chih-ch'ao, D. N. Nasledov, *Fiz. Tv. Tela* **3,** 1185.

M 1 Maker, P. D., J. Baker, D. F. Edwards, *Bull. Am. Phys. Soc.* **6,** 116.

M 2 Mamaev, S., D. N. Nasledov, V. V. Galavanov, *Fiz. Tv. Tela* **3,** 3405.

M 3 Manca, P., *J. Phys. Chem. Solids* **20,** 268.

M 4 Marfaing, Y., G. Courrier, *Proceedings of the International Conference on Semiconductors*, Prague, Publishing House of the Czechoslovakian Academy of Science, p. 970.

M 5 Marfaing, Y., *Compt. Rend.* **253,** 809.

M 6 Martinuzzi, S., *Compt. Rend.* **253,** 1157.

M 7 Matyáš, M., *Czechoslov. J. Phys.* **11,** 461.

M 8 McCaldin, J. O., *Bull. Am. Phys. Soc.* **6,** 172.

M 9 McLean, T. P., E. G. S. Paige, *Proceedings of the International Conference on Semiconductors*, Prague, Publishing House of the Czechoslovakian Academy of Science, p. 71.

M 10 Meyerhofer, D., *Proceedings of the International Conference on Semiconductors*, Prague, Publishing House of the Czechoslovakian Academy of Science, p. 958.

M 11 Miller, D. P., J. G. Garper, T. R. Perry, *J. Electrochem. Soc.* **108,** 1123.

M 12 Montgomery, M. D., *J. Appl. Phys.* **32,** 2408.

M 13 Morrison, R. E., *Phys. Rev.* **124,** 1314.

M 14 Moss, T. S., A. K. Walton, *Proceedings of the International Conference on Semiconductors*, Prague, Publishing House of the Czechoslovakian Academy of Science, p. 338.

M 15 Moss, T. S., *J. Appl. Phys.* **32,** 2136.

M 16 Moss, T. S., *Solid State Electronics* **2,** 222.

N 1 Nasledov, D. N., *Proceedings of the International Conference on Semiconductors*, Prague, Publishing House of the Czechoslovakian Academy of Science, p. 974.

N 2 Nasledov, D. N., *J. Appl. Phys.* **32,** 2140.

N 3 Nathan, M. I., W. Paul, *Proceedings of the International Conference on Semiconductors*, Prague, Publishing House of the Czechoslovakian Academy of Science, p. 209.

N 4 Novikova, S. I., *Fiz. Tv. Tela* **3,** 178.

P 1 Palik, E. D., G. S. Picus, S. Teitler, R. F. Wallis, *Proceedings of the International Conference on Semiconductors*, Prague, Publishing House of the Czechoslovakian Academy of Science, p. 587.

1961 (**Continued**)

P 2 Palik, E. D., R. F. Wallis, *Phys. Rev.* **123,** 131.

P 3 Palik, E. D., G. S. Picus, S. Teitler, R. F. Wallis, *Phys. Rev.* **122,** 475.

P 4 Palik, E. D., S. Teitler, R. F. Wallis, *J. Appl. Phys.* **32,** 2132.

P 5 Palik, E. D., J. R. Stevenson, R. F. Wallis, *Phys. Rev.* **124,** 701.

P 6 Paul, W., *J. Appl. Phys.* **32,** 2082.

P 7 Pfister, H., *Z. Naturforsch.* **16a,** 427.

P 8 Pfister, H., O. G. Folberth, *Acta Cryst.* **14,** 325.

P 9 Potter, R. F., G. G. Kretschmar, *J. Opt. Soc. Am.* **51,** 693.

P 10 Putley, E. H., *J. Phys. Chem. Solids* **22,** 241.

R 1 Radautsan, S. I., B. E. Malkovich, *Fiz. Tv. Tela* **3,** 3324.

R 2 Rodot, M., *Compt. Rend.* **252,** 2526.

R 3 Rosi, F. D., E. F. Hockings, N. E. Lindenblad, *RCA Rev.* **22,** 82.

R 4 Rupprecht, H., *Z. Naturforsch.* **16a,** 395.

S 1 Sagar, A., R. C. Miller, *J. Appl. Phys.* **32,** 2073.

S 2 Sasaki, W., C. Yamagouchi, *Proceedings of the International Conference on Semiconductors,* Prague, Publishing House of the Czechoslovakian Academy of Science, p. 159.

S 3 Shalyt, S. S., *Fiz. Tv. Tela* **3,** 2887.

S 4 Shibata, A., *J. Phys. Soc. Japan* **16,** 1261.

S 5 Simmons, C. A., *J. Appl. Physics* **32,** 1970.

S 6 Sirota, N. N., N. M. Olekhnovich, *Doklady Akad. Nauk S.S.S.R.* **136,** 660.

S 7 Sirota, N. N., N. M. Olekhnovich, *Doklady Akad. Nauk S.S.S.R.* **136,** 879.

S 8 Sirota, N. N., E. M. Gololobov, *Doklady Akad. Nauk S.S.S.R.* **138,** 162.

S 9 Smith, R. A., *Proceedings of the International Conference on Semiconductors,* Prague, Publishing House of the Czechoslovakian Academy of Science, p. 452.

S 10 Solomon, R., R. Neuman, N. R. Kyle, *J. Electrochem. Soc.* **108,** 716.

S 11 Spitzer, W. G., J. H. Wernick, R. Wolfe, *Solid State Electronics* **2,** 96.

S 12 Stern, F., *Proceedings of the International Conference on Semiconductors,* Prague, Publishing House of the Czechoslovakian Academy of Science, p. 363.

S 13 Stern, F., *J. Appl. Phys.* **32,** 2166.

S 14 Stocker, H. J., *J. Appl. Phys.* **32,** 322.

S 15 Strauss, A. J., A. J. Rosenberg, *J. Phys. Chem. Solids* **17,** 278.

S 16 Strauss, A. J., *Phys. Rev.* **121,** 1087.

S 17 Suchet, J. P., *Proceedings of the International Conference on Semiconductors,* Prague, Publishing House of the Czechoslovakian Academy of Science, p. 904.

S 18 Suchet, J. P., *J. Phys. Chem. Solids* **21,** 156.

S 19 Sze, S. M., L. Y. Wei, *Phys. Rev.* **124,** 84.

T 1 Tauc, J., A. Abrahám, *Proceedings of the International Conference on Semiconductors,* Prague, Publishing House of the Czechoslovakian Academy of Science, p. 375.

T 2 Teitler, S., E. D. Palik, R. F. Wallis, *Phys. Rev.* **123,** 1631.

T 3 Toyozawa, Y., *Proceedings of the International Conference on Semiconductors,* Prague, Publishing House of the Czechoslovakian Academy of Science, p. 215.

1961 (Continued)

U 1 Ullman, F. G., *Nature* **190,** 161.

V 1 Vieland, L. J., *J. Phys. Chem. Solids* **21,** 318.

V 2 Vook, F. L., *Bull. Am. Phys. Soc.* **6,** 420.

W 1 Weisberg, L. R., J. Blanc, *Proceedings of the International Conference on Semiconductors,* Prague, Publishing House of the Czechoslovakian Academy of Science, p. 940.

W 2 Weiss, H., *J. Appl. Phys.* **32,** 2064.

W 3 Welker, H., *Proceedings of the International Conference on Semiconductors,* Prague, Publishing House of the Czechoslovakian Academy of Science, p. 889.

W 4 Whelan, J. M., J. D. Struthers, J. A. Ditzenberger, *Proceedings of the International Conference on Semiconductors,* Prague, Publishing House of the Czechoslovakian Academy of Science, p. 943.

W 5 Woolley, J. C., *Proceedings of the International Conference on Semiconductors,* Prague, Publishing House of the Czechoslovakian Academy of Science, p. 966.

W 6 Woolley, J. C., B. R. Pamplin, J. A. Evans, *J. Phys. Chem. Solids* **19,** 147.

W 7 Woolley, J. C., C. M. Gillett, J. A. Evans, *Proc. Phys. Soc.* **77,** 700.

W 8 Woolley, J. C., J. A. Evans, *Proc. Phys. Soc.* **78,** 354.

W 9 Woolley, J. C., P. N. Keating, *Proc. Phys. Soc.* **78,** 1009.

W 10 Wright, B., B. Lax, *J. Appl. Phys.* **32,** 2113.

Z 1 Zolotarev, V. F., D. N. Nasledov, *Fiz. Tv. Tela* **3,** 3306.

Z 2 Zwerdling, S., W. H. Kleiner, J. P. Theriault, *J. Appl. Phys.* **22,** 2118.

1962

A 1 Allen, J. W., R. J. Cherry, *J. Phys. Chem. Solids* **23,** 509.

A 2 Ancker-Johnson, B., *Phys. Rev. Letters* **9,** 485.

A 3 Ancker-Johnson, B., *Proceedings of the International Conference on Semiconductor Physics,* Exeter, The Institute of Physics and the Physical Society, p. 141.

A 4 Anderson, R. L., *Solid State Electronics* **5,** 342.

A 5 Argyres, P. N., *Phys. Rev.* **126,** 1386.

A 6 Aukerman, L. W., R. D. Graft, *Phys. Rev.* **127,** 1576.

B 1 Banus, M. D., H. C. Gatos, *J. Electrochem. Soc.* **109,** 829.

B 2 Bate, R. T., *J. Appl. Phys.* **33,** 26.

B 3 Beattie, A. R., R. W. Cunningham, *Phys. Rev.* **125,** 533.

B 4 Beattie, A. R., *J. Phys. Chem. Solids* **23,** 1049.

B 5 Beers, D. S., G. D. Cody, B. Abeles, *Proceedings of the International Conference on Semiconductor Physics,* Exeter, The Institute of Physics and the Physical Society, p. 41.

B 6 Bemski, G., *J. Phys. Chem. Solids* **23,** 1433.

B 7 Bennett, R. J., *J. Phys. Chem. Solids* **23,** 1679.

B 8 Benoit à la Guillaume, C., P. Lavallard, *Proceedings of the International Conference on Semiconductor Physics,* Exeter, The Institute of Physics and the Physical Society, p. 875.

B 9 Blanc, J., R. H. Bube, L. R. Weisberg, *Bull. Am. Phys. Soc.* **7,** 89.

B 10 Blanc, J., R. H. Bube, L. R. Weisberg, *Phys. Rev. Letters* **9,** 252.

B 11 Booker, G. R., *J. Appl. Phys.* **33,** 750.

B 12 Braunstein, R., E. O. Kane, *J. Phys. Chem. Solids* **23,** 1423.

B 13 Burrus, C. A., *Solid State Electronics* **5,** 357.

1962 (Continued)

B 14 Busch, G., A. Menth, B. Natterer, *Helv. Phys. Acta* **35,** 499.

C 1 Cardona, M., D. L. Greenaway, *Phys. Rev.* **125,** 1291.

C 2 Cardona, M., G. Harbeke, *Phys. Rev. Letters* **8,** 90.

C 3 Carlson, R. O., S. J. Silverman, H. Ehrenreich, *J. Phys. Chem. Solids* **23,** 422.

C 4 Carr, W. N., *Solid State Electronics* **5,** 261.

C 5 Challis, L. J., J. D. N. Cheeke, J. B. Harness, *Phil. Mag.* **7,** 1941.

C 6 Cherry, R. J., J. W. Allen, *J. Phys. Chem. Solids* **23,** 163.

C 7 Cherry, R. J., J. W. Allen, *Proceedings of the International Conference on Semiconductor Physics,* Exeter, The Institute of Physics and the Physical Society, p. 384.

C 8 Coulson, C. A., L. B. Redei, D. Stocker, *Proc. Roy. Soc.* **270,** 357, 373, 383, 397.

C 9 Cunningham, R. W., E. E. Harp, W. M. Bullis, *Proceedings of the International Conference on Semiconductor Physics,* Exeter, The Institute of Physics and the Physical Society, p. 732.

C 10 Chaldychev, V. A., G. F. Karavaer, *Isv. vysshikh uchebnykh zavedenii, Fizika* **2,** 98.

D 1 Dale, E. B., G. Senecal, *J. Appl. Phys.* **33,** 2526.

D 2 Duga, J. J., *J. Appl. Phys.* **33,** 169.

D 3 Dumke, W. P., P. B. Miller, R. R. Haering, *J. Phys. Chem. Solids* **23,** 501.

D 4 Dumke, W. P., *Phys. Rev.* **127,** 1559.

E 1 Eaton, G. K., R. E. J. King, F. D. Morten, A. T. Partridge, J. G. Smith, *J. Phys. Chem. Solids* **23,** 1473.

E 2 Eckhardt, G., *J. Appl. Phys.* **33,** 1016.

E 3 Edwards, D. F., P. D. Maker, *J. Appl. Phys.* **33,** 2466.

E 4 Ehrenreich, H., H. R. Philipp, J. C. Phillips, *Phys. Rev. Letters* **8,** 59.

E 5 Eisen, F. H., *Bull. Am. Phys. Soc.* **7,** 187.

E 6 Emel'yanenko, O. V., F. P. Kesamanly, D. N. Nasledov, *Fiz. Tv. Tela* **4,** 546.

E 7 Esaki, L., R. R. Haering, *J. Appl. Phys.* **33,** 2106.

F 1 Faust, J. W., H. F. John, *J. Phys. Chem. Solids* **23,** 1119.

F 2 Filinski, I., H. Y. Fan, *Bull. Am. Phys. Soc.* **7,** 185.

F 3 Fuller, C. S., K. B. Wolfstirn, *J. Appl. Phys.* **33,** 745.

F 4 Fuller, C. S., K. B. Wolfstirn, *J. Appl. Phys.* **33,** 2507.

F 5 Fuller, C. S., K. B. Wolfstirn, *Proceedings of the International Conference on Semiconductor Physics,* Exeter, The Institute of Physics and the Physical Society, p. 745.

G 1 Garland, C. W., K. C. Park, *J. Appl. Phys.* **33,** 759.

G 2 Gasson, D. B., P. J. Holmes, I. C. Jennings, B. R. Marathe, J. E. Parrott, *J. Phys. Chem. Solids* **23,** 1291.

G 3 Gasson, D. B., P. J. Holmes, I. C. Jennings, J. E. Parrott, A. W. Penn, *Proceedings of the International Conference on Semiconductor Physics,* Exeter, The Institute of Physics and the Physical Society, p. 681.

G 4 Gershenzon, M., R. M. Mikulyak, *Solid State Electronics* **5,** 313.

G 5 Gershenzon, M., D. G. Thomas, R. E. Dietz, *Proceedings of the International Conference on Semiconductor Physics,* Exeter, The Institute of Physics and the Physical Society, p. 752.

G 6 Giterman, M. Sh., L. A. Krol', V. A. Medvedev, M. P. Orlova, G. S. Pado, *Fiz. Tv. Tela* **4,** 1383.

G 7 Glazov, V. M., S. N. Chizhevskaya, *Fiz. Tv. Tela* **4,** 1841.

1962 (Continued)

G 8 Goldstein, B., C. Dobin, *Solid State Electronics* **5,** 411.

G 9 Goryunova, N. A., S. Mamaev, V. D. Prochukhan, *Doklady Akad. Nauk S.S.S.R.* **142,** 623.

G 10 Greenaway, D. L., *Phys. Rev. Letters* **9,** 97.

G 11 Greenaway, D. L., M. Cardona, *Proceedings of the International Conference on Semiconductor Physics,* Exeter, The Institute of Physics and the Physical Society, p. 666.

G 12 Grimmeiss, H. G., W. Kischio, H. Koelmans, *Solid State Electronics* **5,** 155.

G 13 Guseva, G. I., I. M. Tsidilkovskii, *Fiz. Tv. Tela* **4,** 2490.

G 14 Gutkin, A. A., D. N. Nasledov, V. E. Sedov, B. V. Tsarenkov, *Fiz. Tv. Tela* **4,** 2338.

G 15 Gobat, A. R., M. F. Lamorte, G. W. McIver, *IRE Trans. Military Electronics* **MIL-6,** 20.

H 1 Haasen, P., *Z. Physik* **167,** 461.

H 2 Haisty, R. W., E. W. Mehal, R. Stratton, *J. Phys. Chem. Solids* **23,** 829.

H 3 Hall, R. N., J. H. Racette, *Bull. Am. Phys. Soc.* **7,** 234.

H 4 Hall, R. N., G. E. Fenner, J. D. Kingsley, T. J. Soltys, R. O. Carlson, *Phys. Rev. Letters* **9,** 366.

H 5 Hamaker, R. W., H. F. Quinn, *J. Appl. Phys.* **33,** 2396.

H 6 Haneman, R. E., M. C. Finn, H. C. Gatos, *J. Phys. Chem. Solids* **23,** 1553.

H 7 Haneman, D., *Proceedings of the International Conference on Semiconductor Physics,* Exeter, The Institute of Physics and the Physical Society, p. 842.

H 8 Hass, M., B. W. Henvis, *Bull. Am. Phys. Soc.* **7,** 78.

H 9 Hass, M., B. W. Henvis, *J. Phys. Chem. Solids* **23,** 1099.

H 10 Henkel, H. J., *Z. Naturforsch.* **17a,** 358.

H 11 Hieronymus, H., H. Weiss, *Solid State Electronics* **5,** 71.

H 12 Hollander, L. E., P. L. Castro, *Bull. Am. Phys. Soc.* **7,** 174.

H 13 Holonyak, N., S. F. Bevacqua, *Appl. Phys. Letters* **1,** 82.

H 14 Holt, D. B., *J. Phys. Chem. Solids* **23,** 1353.

H 15 Hulme, K. F., J. B. Mullin, *Solid State Electronics* **5,** 211.

H 16 Hurd, C. M., *Proc. Phys. Soc.* **79,** 42.

I 1 Ivanov-Omskii, V. I., B. T. Kolomiets, *Fiz. Tv. Tela* **4,** 299.

I 2 Ivanov-Omskii, V. I., B. T. Kolomiets, Chou-Huang, *Fiz. Tv. Tela* **4,** 383.

J 1 Johnson, E. J., H. Y. Fan, *Bull. Am. Phys. Soc.* **7,** 185.

J 2 Johnson, E. J., I. Filinski, H. Y. Fan, *Proceedings of the International Conference on Semiconductor Physics,* Exeter, The Institute of Physics and the Physical Society, p. 375.

K 1 Keyes, R. W., *J. Chem. Phys.* **37,** 72.

K 2 Keyes, R. J., T. M. Quist, *Proc. IRE* **50,** 1822.

K 3 Keyes, R. W., *J. Appl. Phys.* **33,** 3371.

K 4 Kołodziejczak, J., L. Sosnowski, *Acta Phys. Polon.* **21,** 399.

K 5 Kołodziejczak, J., R. Kowalczyk, *Acta Phys. Polon.* **21,** 389.

K 6 Kołodziejczak, J., *Acta Phys. Polon.* **21,** 637.

K 7 Kołodziejczak, J., L. Sosnowski, W. Zawadzki, *Proceedings of the International Conference on Semiconductor Physics,* Exeter, The Institute of Physics and the Physical Society, p. 94.

K 8 Kravchenko, A. F., and H. Y. Fan, *Proceedings of the International Conference on Semiconductor Physics,* Exeter, The Institute of Physics and the Physical Society, p. 737.

1962 (Continued)

K 9 Kudman, I., T. Seidel, *J. Appl. Phys.* **33,** 771.

L 1 Lax, B., J. G. Mavroides, J. Kołodziejczak, *Proceedings of the International Conference on Semiconductor Physics,* Exeter, The Institute of Physics and the Physical Society, p. 353.

L 2 Logan, R. A., A. G. Chynoweth, B. G. Cohen, *Phys. Rev.* **128,** 2518.

L 3 Lifshits, T. M., Sh. M. Kogan, A. N. Vystavkin, P. G. Mel'nik, *Zhur. Eksp. i Teoret. Fiz.* **42,** 959.

L 4 Logan, R. A., A. G. Chynoweth, *J. Appl. Phys.* **33,** 1649.

L 5 Longini, R. L., *Solid State Electronics* **5,** 127.

L 6 Lorenz, M. R., B. B. Binkowski, *J. Electrochem. Soc.* **109,** 24.

L 7 Lukeš, F., E. Schmidt, *Physics Letters* **2,** 288.

L 8 Lukeš, F., E. Schmidt, *Proceedings of the International Conference on Semiconductor Physics,* Exeter, The Institute of Physics and the Physical Society, p. 389.

M 1 Martinuzzi, S., *Compt. Rend.* **255,** 110.

M 2 Matyáš, M., *Czechoslov. J. Phys.* **12,** 838.

M 3 Matyáš, M., P. Höschl, *Czechoslov. J. Phys.* **12,** 788.

M 4 Melngailis, I., R. H. Rediker, *J. Appl. Phys.* **33,** 1892.

M 5 Merten, U., A. P. Hatcher, *J. Phys. Chem. Solids* **23,** 533.

M 6 Mikhailova, M. P., D. N. Nasledov, S. V. Slobodchikov, *Fiz. Tv. Tela* **4,** 1227.

M 7 Minamoto, M. T., *J. Appl. Phys.* **33,** 1826.

M 8 Minamoto, M. T., C. M. Allen, *Solid State Electronics* **5,** 263.

M 9 Minomura, S., H. G. Drickamer, *J. Phys. Chem. Solids* **23,** 451.

M 10 Minomura, S., G. A. Samara, H. G. Drickamer, *J. Appl. Phys.* **33,** 3196.

M 11 Mochan, I. V., Yu. N. Obrastsov, T. V. Smirnova, *Fiz. Tv. Tela* **4,** 1021.

M 12 Moss, T. S., T. D. F. Hawkins, *Infrared Phys.* **1,** 111.

M 13 Moss, T. S., A. K. Walton, B. Ellis, *Proceedings of the International Conference on Semiconductor Physics,* Exeter, The Institute of Physics and the Physical Society, p. 295.

M 14 Mueller, R. K., R. L. Jacobson, *J. Appl. Phys.* **33,** 2341.

N 1 Nasledov, D. N., Yu. S. Smetannikova, *Fiz. Tv. Tela* **4,** 110.

N 2 Nasledov, D. N., S. V. Slobotchikov, *Fiz. Tv. Tela* **4,** 2755.

N 3 Nasledov, D. N., A. A. Rogachev, S. M. Ryvkin, B. V. Tsarenkov, *Fiz. Tv. Tela* **4,** 1062.

N 4 Nasledov, D. N., S. V. Slobotchikov, *Fiz. Tv. Tela* **4,** 3161.

N 5 Nasledov, D. N., A. A. Rogachev, S. M. Ryvkin, V. E. Khartsiev, B. V. Tsarenkov, *Fiz. Tv. Tela* **4,** 3346.

N 6 Nasledov, D. N., O. V. Emel'yanenko, *Proceedings of the International Conference on Semiconductor Physics,* Exeter, The Institute of Physics and the Physical Society, p. 163.

N 7 Nathan, M. I., J. C. Marinace, *Bull. Am. Phys. Soc.* **7,** 232.

N 8 Nathan, M. I., W. P. Dumke, G. Burns, F. H. Dill, G. Lasher, *Appl. Phys. Letters* **1,** 62.

N 9 Nathan, M. I., J. C. Marinace, *Phys. Rev.* **128,** 2149.

N 10 Nathan, M. I., G. Burns, *Appl. Phys. Letters* **1,** 89.

O 1 Oliver, D. J., *Phys. Rev.* **127,** 1045.

O 2 Oliver, D. J., *Proceedings of the International Conference on Semiconductor Physics,* Exeter, The Institute of Physics and the Physical Society, p. 133.

1962 (Continued)

O 3 Omura, Y., M. Wakatsuki, *J. Phys. Soc. Japan* **17,** 1207.

O 4 Osipov, B. D., A. N. Khvoshchev, *Zhur. Eksp. i Teoret. Fiz.* **43,** 1179.

P 1 Palik, E. D., S. Teitler, B. W. Henvis, R. F. Wallis, *Proceedings of the International Conference on Semiconductor Physics,* Exeter, The Institute of Physics and the Physical Society, p. 288.

P 2 Pankove, J. I., M. J. Massoulié, *Bull. Am. Phys. Soc.* **7,** 88.

P 3 Pankove, J. I., *Phys. Rev. Letters* **9,** 283.

P 4 Peissker, E., P. Haasen, H. Alexander, *Phil. Mag.* **7,** 1279.

P 5 Philipp, H. R., H. Ehrenreich, *Phys. Rev. Letters* **8,** 92.

P 6 Phillips, J. C., L. Liu, *Phys. Rev. Letters* **8,** 94.

P 7 Phillips, J. C., *Phys. Rev.* **125,** 1931.

P 8 Pierce, C. B., H. H. Sander, A. D. Kantz, *J. Appl. Phys.* **33,** 3108.

P 9 Pleskov, Yu. V., *Doklady Akad. Nauk S.S.S.R.* **143,** 1399.

P 10 Presnov, V. A., *Fiz. Tv. Tela* **4,** 548.

Q 1 Quist, T. M., R. H. Rediker, R. J. Keyes, W. E. Krag, B. Lax, A. L. McWhorter, H. J. Zeiger, *Appl. Phys. Letters* **1,** 91.

R 1 Radautsan, S. I., *Czechoslov. J. Phys.* **12,** 382.

R 2 Römelt, G., D. Geist, *Z. angew. Physik* **14,** 99.

R 3 Rose, K., *J. Appl. Phys.* **33,** 761.

S 1 Sclar, N., *J. Appl. Phys.* **33,** 2999.

S 2 Shalyt, S. S., A. L. Éfros, *Fiz. Tv. Tela* **4,** 1233.

S 3 Shalyt, S. S., *Fiz. Tv. Tela* **4,** 1915.

S 4 Shaw, D., P. Jones, D. Hazelby, *Proc. Phys. Soc.* **80,** 167.

S 5 Shaw, D., *Proc. Phys. Soc.* **80,** 161.

S 6 Shibata, A., *J. Phys. Soc. Japan* **17,** 770.

S 7 Silverman, S. J., *J. Electrochem. Soc.* **109,** 166.

S 8 Sirota, N. N., E. M. Gololobov, *Doklady Akad. Nauk S.S.S.R.* **143,** 156.

S 9 Smith, P. L., J. E. Martin, *Nature* **196,** 762.

S 10 Smith, S. D., C. R. Pidgeon, V. Prosser, *Proceedings of the International Conference on Semiconductor Physics,* Exeter, The Institute of Physics and the Physical Society, p. 301.

S 11 Starkiewicz, J., J. W. Allen, *J. Phys. Chem. Solids* **23,** 881.

S 12 Stone, L. E., *J. Appl. Phys.* **33,** 2795.

S 13 Sturge, M. D., *Phys. Rev.* **127,** 768.

T 1 Tauc, J., *Proceedings of the International Conference on Semiconductor Physics,* Exeter, The Institute of Physics and the Physical Society, p. 333.

T 2 Tsidil'kovskii, I. M., *Fiz. Tv. Tela* **4,** 2539.

T 3 Tsidil'kovskii, I. M., G. I. Guseva, *Proceedings of the International Conference Semiconductor Physics,* Exeter, The Institute of Physics and the Physical Society, p. 23.

T 4 Turner, W. J., W. E. Reese, *Phys. Rev.* **127,** 126.

U 1 Ukhanov, Yu. I., Yu. V. Maltsev, *Fiz. Tv. Tela* **4,** 3215.

V 1 Vieland, L. J., *J. Appl. Phys.* **33,** 2007.

V 2 Vieland, L. J., T. Seidel, *J. Appl. Phys.* **33,** 2414.

V 3 Vink, A. T., C. I. van Doorn, *Phys. Letters* **1,** 332.

V 4 Vinogradova, K. I., V. V. Galavanov, D. N. Nasledov, *Fiz. Tv. Tela* **4,** 1673.

V 5 Vul, B. M., A. P. Shotov, V. S. Bagaev, *Fiz. Tv. Tela* **4,** 3676.

W 1 Watt, L. A., W. S. Chen, *Bull. Am. Phys. Soc.* **7,** 89.

1962 (**Continued**)

W 2 Weisberg, L. R., *J. Appl. Phys.* **33,** 1817.
W 3 Wentorf, R. H., *J. Chem. Phys.* **36,** 1990.
W 4 Willardson, R. K., *Ultrapurification of Materials, Conference Report, Boston, 1961,* The Macmillan Company, New York.
W 5 Wilson, R. B., E. L. Heasell, *Proc. Phys. Soc.* **79,** 403.
W 6 Winstel, G., H. Tropper, K. Colani, *Z. Naturforsch.* **17a,** 700.
Z 1 Zallen, R., W. Paul, J. Tauc, *Bull. Am. Phys. Soc.* **7,** 185.
Z 2 Zerbst, M., *Z. Naturforsch.* **17a,** 649.
Z 3 Zolotarev, V. F., D. N. Nasledov, *Fiz. Tv. Tela* **4,** 977.
Z 4 Zolotarev, V. F., D. N. Nasledov, *Fiz. Tv. Tela* **4,** 1952.
Z 5 Zolotarev, V. F., D. N. Nasledov, *Fiz. Tv. Tela* **4,** 2567.
Z 6 Zotova, N. V., D. N. Nasledov, *Fiz. Tv. Tela* **4,** 681.
Z 7 Zwerdling, S., W. H. Kleiner, J. P. Theriault, *Proceedings of the International Conference on Semiconductor Physics,* Exeter, The Institute of Physics and the Physical Society, p. 455.

1963

A 1 Aliev, M. M., A. Yu. Dzhangirov, *Fiz. Tv. Tela* **5,** 3338.
A 2 Allen, J. W., J. W. Hobdy, *Proc. Phys. Soc.* **82,** 315.
A 3 Allen, J. W., M. E. Moncaster, *Phys. Letters* **4,** 27.
A 4 Amirkhanov, Kh. I., R. I. Bashirov, Z. A. Ismailov, *Fiz. Tv. Tela* **5,** 2832.
A 5 Amirkhanov, Kh. I., R. I. Bashirov, Yu. E. Zakiev, *Doklady Akad. Nauk S.S.S.R.* **148,** 1279.
A 6 Amirkhanov, Kh. I., R. I. Bashirov, Yu. E. Zakiev, *Fiz. Tv. Tela* **5,** 469.
A 7 Ancker-Johnson, B., *Appl. Phys. Letters* **3,** 104.
A 8 Attard, A. E., L. V. Azároff, *J. Appl. Phys.* **34,** 774.
A 9 Aukerman, L. W., P. W. Davis, R. D. Graft, T. S. Shilliday, *J. Appl. Phys.* **34,** 3590.
A 10 Archer, R. J., R. C. C. Leiter, A. Yariv, S. P. S. Porto, J. M. Whelan, *Phy. Rev. Letters* **10,** 483.
B 1 Bagguley, D. M. S., M. L. A. Robinson, R. A. Stradling, *Phys. Letters,* **6,** 143.
B 2 Banus, M. D., R. E. Haneman, A. N. Mariano, E. P. Warekois, H. C. Gatos, J. A. Kafalas, *Appl. Phys. Letters* **2,** 35.
B 3 Bassani, F., M. Yoshimine, *Phys. Rev.* **130,** 20.
B 4 Bate, R. T., R. D. Baxter, F. J. Reid, *Bull. Am. Phys. Soc.* **8,** 471.
B 5 Bäuerlein, R., *Z. Physik* **176,** 498.
B 6 Becker, W. M., H. Y. Fan, *Bull. Am. Phys. Soc.* **8,** 246.
B 7 Bendik, M. A., R. L. Petrusevich, E. S. Sollertinskaya, *Fiz. Tv. Tela* **5,** 3247.
B 8 Bernard, M., C. Chipaux, G. Duraffourg, M. Jean-Louis, J. Loudette, J.-P. Noblanc, *Compt. Rend.* **257,** 2984.
B 9 Black, J., H. Lockwood, S. Mayburg, *J. Appl. Phys.* **34,** 178.
B 10 Boltaks, B. I., F. S. Shishijanu, *Fiz. Tv. Tela* **5,** 2310.
B 11 Boltaks, B. I., V. I. Skolov, *Fiz. Tv. Tela* **5,** 1077.
B 12 Borchers, H., R. G. Maier, *Metall* **17,** 775.
B 13 Borchers, H., R. G. Maier, *Metall* **17,** 1006.
B 14 Braunstein, R., J. I. Pankove, H. Nelson, *Appl. Phys. Letters* **3,** 31.
B 15 Burns, G., F. H. Dill, M. I. Nathan, *Proc. IEEE,* **51,** 947.
B 16 Byszawski, P., J. Kołodziejczak, S. Žukotyński, *Phys. Status Solidi* **3,** 1880.

1963 (Continued)

C 1 Calawa, A. R., *J. Appl. Phys.* **34,** 1660.

C 2 Calawa, A. R., I. Melngailis, *Bull. Am. Phys. Soc.* **8,** 29.

C 3 Cardona, M., *J. Phys. Chem. Solids* **24,** 1543.

C 4 Cardona, M., G. Harbeke, *J. Appl. Phys.* **34,** 813.

C 5 Champness, C. H., *Can. J. Phys.* **41,** 890.

C 6 Cheroff, G., F. Stern, S. Triebwasser, *Appl. Phys. Letters* **2,** 173.

C 7 Chaldychev, V. A., G. F. Karavaev, *Isv. vysshikh uchebnykh zavedenii, Fizika* **5,** 103.

D 1 Deslattes, R. D., *Phys. Rev.* **129,** 1511.

D 2 Dousmanis, G. C., C. W. Mueller, H. Nelson, *Appl. Phys. Letters* **3,** 133.

D 3 Duncan, W., E. E. Schneider, *Phys. Letters* **7,** 23.

E 1 Engeler, W. E., M. Garfinkel, *J. Appl. Phys.* **34,** 2746.

E 2 Eisen, F. H., *Bull. Am. Phys. Soc.* **8,** 235.

F 1 Fane, R. W., A. J. Gross, *Solid State Electronics* **6,** 383.

F 2 Feinleib, J., S. Groves, W. Paul, R. Zallen, *Phys. Rev.* **131,** 2070.

F 3 Fenner, G. E., *J. Appl. Phys.* **34,** 2955.

F 4 Flinn, I., D. C. Emmony, *Phys. Letters* **6,** 133.

F 5 Fuller, C. S., K. B. Wolfstirn, *J. Appl. Phys.* **34,** 2287.

F 6 Fuller, C. S., K. B. Wolfstirn, *Appl. Phys. Letters* **2,** 45.

G 1 Galavanov, V. V., N. L. Karaseva, *Fiz. Tv. Tela* **5,** 36.

G 2 Galavanov, V. V., O. V. Emel'yanenko, F. P. Kesamanly, *Fiz. Tv. Tela* **5,** 616.

G 3 Galavanov, V. V., U. Zijakhanov, D. N. Nasledov, *Fiz. Tv. Tela* **5,** 3048.

G 4 Galeener, G., G. B. Wright, W. E. Krag, T. M. Quist, H. J. Zeiger, *Phys. Rev. Letters* **10,** 472.

G 5 Gerlich, D., *J. Appl. Phys.* **34,** 2915.

G 6 Gershenzon, M., R. M. Mikulyak, *Solid State Electronics* **5,** 313.

G 7 Glicksman, M., W. A. Hicinbothem, *Phys. Rev.* **129,** 1572.

G 8 Goldstein, B., N. Almeleh, *Appl. Phys. Letters* **2,** 130.

G 9 Goryunova, N. A., F. P. Kesamanly, É. O. Osmanov, *Fiz. Tv. Tela* **5,** 2031.

G 10 Green, M., *Solid State Electronics* **6,** 63.

G 11 Groos, E. F., N. S. Kochneva, D. S. Nedzvetskii, *Doklady Akad. Nauk S.S.S.R.* **153,** 574.

G 12 Guseva, G. I., I. M. Tsidil'kovskii, *Fiz. Tv. Tela* **5,** 253.

G 13 Gashimzade, F. M., *Fiz. Tv. Tela* **5,** 1199.

H 1 Hall, R. N., *Solid State Electronics* **6,** 405.

H 2 Harman, T. C., J. M. Honig, B. M. Tarmy, *J. Phys. Chem. Solids* **24,** 835.

H 3 Herman, F., C. D. Kuglin, K. F. Cuff, R. L. Kortum, *Phys. Rev. Letters* **11,** 541.

H 4 Hobdy, J. W., *Proc. Phys. Soc.* **82,** 324.

H 5 Holonyak, N., S. F. Bevaqua, C. V. Bielan, S. J. Lubowski, *Appl. Phys. Letters* **3,** 47.

H 6 Hopfield, J. J., D. G. Thomas, M. Gershenzon, *Phys. Rev. Letters* **10,** 162.

J 1 Jacobson, R. L., R. K. Mueller, *Bull. Am. Phys. Soc.* **8,** 310.

J 2 Jayaraman, A., W. Klement, G. C. Kennedy, *Phys. Rev.* **130,** 540.

K 1 Kimmel, H., *Z. Naturforschung* **18a,** 650.

K 2 Kravtchenko, A. F., H. Y. Fan, *Fiz. Tv. Tela* **5,** 660.

K 3 Kressel, H., A. Blicker, *J. Appl. Phys.* **34,** 2495.

1963 (Continued)

K 4 Kudman, I., L. Vieland, *J. Phys. Chem. Solids* **24,** 967.
K 5 Kuriani, N. I., *Fiz. Tv. Tela* **5,** 2022.
L 1 Larsen, T. L., *Appl. Phys. Letters* **3,** 113.
L 2 Leroux-Hugon, P., *Compt. Rend.* **256,** 3991.
L 3 Lockwood, H. F., *J. Appl. Phys.* **34,** 2110.
L 4 Loh, E., *J. Appl. Phys.* **34,** 416.
L 5 Loh, E., *J. Phys. Chem. Solids* **24,** 493.
L 6 Loh, E., J. C. Phillips, *J. Phys. Chem. Solids* **24,** 495.
L 7 Lucovsky, G., C. J. Repper, *Appl. Phys. Letters* **3,** 71.
M 1 McWhorter, A. L., *Solid State Electronics* **6,** 417.
M 2 Mead, C. A., W. C. Spitzer, *Phys. Rev. Letters* **11,** 358.
M 3 Melngailis, I., *Appl. Phys. Letters* **2,** 176.
M 4 Melngailis, I., R. H. Rediker, *Appl. Phys. Letters* **2,** 202.
M 5 Melngailis, I., A. J. Strauss, R. H. Rediker, *Proc. IEEE* **51,** 1154.
M 6 Merten, U., A. P. Hatcher, *J. Phys. Chem. Solids* **24,** 1064.
M 7 Mette, H., *Z. Phys.* **176,** 329.
M 8 Meyerhofer, D., R. Braunstein, *Appl. Phys. Letters* **3,** 171.
M 9 Michel, A. E., W. J. Turner, W. E. Reese, *Bull. Am. Phys. Soc.* **8,** 215.
M 10 Mitra, S. S., *Phys. Rev.* **132,** 986.
N 1 Nasledov, D. N., S. Mamaev, O. V. Emel'yanenko, *Fiz. Tv. Tela* **5,** 147.
N 2 Nasledov, D. N., Yu. G. Popov, *Fiz. Tv. Tela* **5,** 3031.
N 3 Nasledov, D. N., B. V. Tsarenkov, *Fiz. Tv. Tela* **5,** 1181.
N 4 Nathan, M. I., *Solid State Electronics* **6,** 425.
N 5 Nathan, M. I., G. Burns, *Phys. Rev.* **129,** 125.
N 6 Nathan, M. I., G. Burns, S. E. Blum, J. C. Marinace, *Phys. Rev.* **132,** 1482.
N 7 Nelson, D. F., M. Gershenzon, A. Ashkin, L. A. D'Asaro, J. C. Sarace, *Appl. Phys. Letters* **2,** 182.
N 8 Novikova, S. I., N. Kh. Abriskosov, *Fiz. Tv. Tela* **5,** 2138.
P 1 Palik, E. D., J. R. Stevenson, *Phys. Rev.* **130,** 1344.
P 2 Palik, E. D., R. F. Wallis, *Phys. Rev.* **130,** 41.
P 3 Petree, M. C., *Appl. Phys. Letters* **3,** 67.
P 4 Pfister, H., *Acta Cryst.* **16,** 153.
P 5 Phelan, R. J., A. R. Calawa, R. H. Rediker, R. J. Keyes, B. Lax, *Appl. Phys. Letters* **3,** 143.
P 6 Philipp, H. R., H. Ehrenreich, *Phys. Rev.* **129,** 1550.
P 7 Piesbergen, U., *Z. Naturforschung* **18a,** 141.
P 8 Pikor, A., G. Elie, R. Glicksman, *J. Electrochem. Soc.* **110,** 178.
P 9 Pilkuhn, M. H., *Bull. Am. Phys. Soc.* **8,** 310.
P 10 Piller, H., *J. Phys. Chem. Solids* **24,** 425.
P 11 Piller, H., V. A. Patton, *Phys. Rev.* **129,** 1169.
P 12 Piller, H., G. Zaeschmar, *Bull. Am. Phys. Soc.* **8,** 245.
P 13 Porowski, S., A. Duracz, S. Žukotyński, *Phys. Status Solidi* **3,** 1555.
P 14 Puri, S. M., *Bull. Am. Phys. Soc.* **8,** 219.
P 15 Puri, S. M., T. H. Geballe, *Bull. Am. Phys. Soc.* **8,** 309.
R 1 Rediker, R. H., T. M. Quist, *Solid State Electronics* **6,** 657.
R 2 Richman, D., *J. Phys. Chem. Solids* **24,** 1131.
R 3 Rooymans, C. J. M., *Phys. Letters* **4,** 186.
R 4 Ryan, F. M., R. C. Miller, *Appl. Phys. Letters* **3,** 162.

1963 (Continued)

S 1 Schaufele, R. F., H. Statz, J. M. Lavine, A. A. Iannini, *Appl. Phys. Letters* **3,** 40.
S 2 Silverman, S. J., R. O. Carlson, H. Ehrenreich, *J. Appl. Phys.* **34,** 456.
S 3 Sladek, R. J., *Bull. Am. Phys. Soc.* **8,** 223.
S 4 Spitzer, W. G., *J. Appl. Phys.* **34,** 792.
S 5 Steigmeier, E. F., *Appl. Phys. Letters* **3,** 6.
S 6 Steigmeier, E. F., I. Kudman, *Phys. Rev.* **132,** 508.
S 7 Stevenson, M. J., J. D. Axe, J. R. Lankard, *IBM J.* **7,** 155.
S 8 Stocker, H. J., *Phys. Rev.* **130,** 2160.
T 1 Thomas, D. G., M. Gershenzon, J. J. Hopfield, *Phys. Rev.* **131,** 2397.
T 2 Tric, C., C. Benôit à la Guillaume, J. M. Debever, *Compt. Rend.* **255,** 3152.
T 3 Turner, W. J., G. D. Pettit, *Appl. Phys. Letters* **3,** 102.
T 4 Turner, W. J., G. D. Pettit, N. G. Ainslie, *J. Appl. Phys.* **34,** 3274.
U 1 Ukhanov, Yu. I., *Fiz. Tv. Tela* **5,** 108.
U 2 Ukhanov, Yu. I., Yu. V. Mal'tsev, *Fiz. Tv. Tela* **5,** 2926.
V 1 Vieland, L. J., I. Kudman, *J. Phys. Chem. Solids* **24,** 437.
V 2 Vitovsky, N. A., T. V. Mashovets, S. M. Ryvkin, R. Yu. Khansevarov, *Fiz. Tv. Tela* **5,** 3510.
V 3 Voronkova, N. M., D. N. Nasledov, S. V. Slobodtchikov, *Fiz. Tv. Tela* **5,** 3259.
W 1 Watt, L. A. K., R. W. Orth, *Bull. Am. Phys. Soc.* **8,** 472.
W 2 Waugh, J. L., G. Dolling, *Phys. Rev.* **132,** 2410.
W 3 Weinstein, M., A. I. Mlavsky, *Appl. Phys. Letters* **2,** 97.
W 4 Weisberg, L., J. Blanc, unpublished work.
W 5 Weiser, K., *J. Appl. Phys.* **34,** 3387.
W 6 Weiser, K., R. L. Levitt, *Appl. Phys. Letters* **2,** 178.
W 7 Weiser, K., R. L. Levitt, *Bull. Am. Phys. Soc.* **8,** 29.
W 8 Weiss, H., M. Wilhelm, *Z. Physik* **176,** 399.
W 9 White, H. G., R. A. Logan, *J. Appl. Phys.* **34,** 1990.
Y 1 Yafet, Y., D. G. Thomas, *Phys. Rev.* **131,** 2405.
Z 1 Zawadzki, W., *Phys. Letters* **4,** 190.
Z 2 Zerbst, M., H. Bornofka, *Z. Naturforschung* **18a,** 642.
Z 3 Zotova, N. V., T. S. Lagunova, D. N. Nasledov, *Fiz. Tv. Tela* **5,** 3329.

1964

A 1 Ainslie, N., M. Pilkuhn, H. Rupprecht, *J. Appl. Phys.* **35,** 105.
A 2 Alexander, F. B., V. R. Bird, D. R. Carpenter, G. W. Manley, P. S. McDermott, J. R. Peloke, H. F. Quinn, R. J. Riley, L. R. Yetter, *Appl. Phys. Letters* **4,** 13.
B 1 Becker, W. M., H. Y. Fan, *Bull. Am. Phys. Soc.* **9,** 258.
B 2 Blanc, J., R. H. Bube, L. Weisberg, *J. Phys. Chem. Solids* **25,** 221.
B 3 Blanc, J., L. Weisberg, *J. Phys. Chem. Solids* **25,** 225.
B 4 Boltaks, B. I., V. J. Sokolov, *Fiz. Tv. Tela* **6,** 771.
C 1 Chang, L. L., G. L. Pearson, *J. Appl. Phys.* **35,** 374.
D 1 Dousmanis, G. C., C. W. Mueller, H. Nelson, K. G. Petzinger, *Phys. Rev.* **133,** A316.
E 1 Eisen, F. H., *Bull. Am. Phys. Soc.* **9,** 290.
F 1 Fuller, C. S., K. B. Wolfstirn, H. W. Allison, *Appl. Phys. Letters* **4,** 48.
F 2 Fulton, T. A., D. B. Fitchen, G. E. Fenner, *Appl. Phys. Letters* **4,** 9.

1964 (Continued)

G 1 Galavanov, V. V., *Fiz. Tv. Tela* **6,** 625.
G 2 Gershenzon, M., R. A. Logan, D. G. Thomas, *Bull. Am. Phys. Soc.* **9,** 236.
G 3 Goryunova, N. A., F. P. Kesamanly, D. N. Nasledov, Yu. V. Rud', *Fiz. Tv. Tela* **6,** 113.
H 1 Habegger, M. A., H. Y. Fan, *Phys. Rev. Letters* **12,** 99.
H 2 Habegger, M. A., H. Y. Fan, *Bull. Am. Phys. Soc.* **9,** 237.
H 3 Hall, R. N., J. H. Racette, *J. Appl. Phys.* **35,** 379.
H 4 Haneman, R. E., M. D. Banus, H. C. Gatos, *J. Phys. Chem. Solids* **25,** 293.
H 5 Hill, D. E., *Phys. Rev.* **133,** A866.
K 1 Kendall, D. L., *Appl. Phys. Letters* **4,** 67.
K 2 Kesamanly, F. P., E. E. Klotyn'sh, Yu. Mal'tsev, D. N. Nasledov, Yu. I. Ukhanov, *Fiz. Tv. Tela* **6,** 134.
K 3 Kesamanly, F. P., E. E. Klotyn'sh, T. S. Lagunova, D. N. Nasledov, *Fiz. Tv. Tela* **6,** 958.
K 4 Korenblit, L. L., D. V. Mashovets, S. S. Shalyt, *Fiz. Tv. Tela* **6,** 559.
K 5 Kudman, I., E. F. Steigmeier, *Phys. Rev.* **133,** A1665.
L 1 Leite, R. C. C., J. C. Sarace, A. Yariv, *Appl. Phys. Letters* **4,** 69.
L 2 Lietz, M., U. Rössler, *Z. Naturforschung* (to be published).
M 1 Miller, S. C., *Phys. Rev.* **133,** A1138.
M 2 Mooradian, A., H. Y. Fan, *Bull. Am. Phys. Soc.* **9,** 237.
M 3 Moss, T. S., B. Ellis, *Proc. Phys. Soc.* **83,** 217.
N 1 Nelson, D. F., L. F. Johnson, M. Gershenzon, *Bull. Am. Phys. Soc.* **9,** 236.
P 1 Phelan, R. J., Jr., W. F. Love, *Phys. Rev.* **133,** A1134.
P 2 Pumper, E. Ya., J. V. Prostoserdova, *Fiz. Tv. Tela* **6,** 899.
R 1 Roth, L. M., *Phys. Rev.* **133,** A542.
R 2 Rupprecht, G., J. F. Gilbert, *Bull. Am. Phys. Soc.,* **9,** 258.
S 1 Schönwald, H., *Z. Naturforschung* (to be published).
S 2 Seltzer, M. S., *Bull. Am. Phys. Soc.* **9,** 49.
S 3 Sokolov, V. I., F. S. Shishijanu, *Fiz. Tv. Tela* **6,** 328.
S 4 Spitzer, W. G., C. A. Mead, *Phys. Rev.* **133,** A872.
S 5 Stocker, H. J., C. R. Stannard, Jr., H. Kaplan, H. Levinstein, *Phys. Rev. Letters* **12,** 163.
S 6 Sun, S. F., *J. Appl. Phys.* **35,** 211.
S 7 Sandrock, R., J. Treusch, *Z. Naturforschung* (to be published).
T 1 Thomas, D. G., M. Gershenzon, F. A. Trumbore, *Phys. Rev.* **133,** A269.
T 2 Tsidil'kovskii, I. M., *Fiz. Tv. Tela* **6,** 627.
T 3 Tufte, O. N., E. L. Stelzer, *Phys. Rev.* **133,** A1450.
T 4 Turner, W. J., W. E. Reese, *J. Appl. Phys.* **35,** 350.
T 5 Turner, W. J., G. D. Pettit, *Bull. Am. Phys. Soc.* **9,** 269.
V 1 Vook, F. L., *Bull. Am. Phys. Soc.* **9,** 289.
W 1 Wagini, H., *Z. Naturforschung* (to be published).
Z 1 Zallen, R., W. Paul, *Bull. Am. Phys. Soc.* **9,** 61.

Subject Index

Key words which refer directly to the properties of one of the compounds are not listed here. Instead they are collected in the following Substance Index.

Substance Index